Cassell
English-Japanese
Business Dictionary

This dictionary was made possible
by grants from the Parker Initiative
and Mitsubishi Electric UK Limited.

Special thanks to Sir Peter Parker,
Steve Cook at Cassell, Kevin O'Neill,
Mr and Mrs J. H. Ferber, and
Dr and Mrs J. F. Robinson
for their support and encouragement.

Cassell
English-Japanese
Business Dictionary

Gene Ferber

CASSELL

Cassell
Villiers House, 41/47 Strand
London WC2N 5JE
387 Park Avenue South
New York, NY 10016-8810

© Gene Ferber 1993

First published 1993

British Library Cataloguing-in-Publication Data
A catalogue entry for this book is available from the British
Library.

Library of Congress Cataloging-in-Publication Data is
available from the Library of Congress.

ISBN 0-304-32552-X

Typeset by Book Creation Services Limited, London
in Helvetica, Times and Honmincho.

Printed and bound in Malta by Interprint Ltd.

Contents

Foreword

There is a double lustre to this illuminating book. First, it is a shining example of a revolutionary change in Western attitudes. Among the many revolutions of recent years, there is one less spectacular than most but still possibly among the most lasting in its influence: amazingly the West has now taken seriously the learning of the Japanese language. The idea that Japanese is too difficult ('and anyway the Japanese are speaking English/American so much better these days') – that idea is collapsing. More quietly than the Berlin Wall, and more slowly, but just as surely it is collapsing. I find the enthusiasm for the study of things Japanese, culture and business, to be one of the most heartening signs of East meeting West. It has been my good fortune to have shared in the promotion of Japanese, and this has involved the enhancement of all types of teaching resources, both people and publications.

But I have been conscious of a real gap in the mounting range of manuals: a comprehensive language dictionary which is organized around special interests. Gene Ferber has answered this felt need meticulously. I particularly admire the flexibility of the book; it provides a reference by subject, as a teaching aid, and a romanized index.

This is the second lustrous distinction of the Dictionary: its originality. No other specialist dictionary of this size has been designed with the Western customer in mind. Its topical order makes it accessible to Western students and business practitioners. There is no better way to learn a language than rooting the learning process in one's special area of interest.

This book represents a mammoth effort by one individual. It comprehends over 15,000 terms with additional notes on etymology, usage, register, synonyms and on etiquette and psychology in Japanese business. When Dr Johnson illustrated 'dull' in his famous work, he said, 'To make dictionaries is dull work.' Actually, that cannot have been true of the inspiration that kept him at his lexicograph, nor can it possibly be true about Gene Ferber who must have sensed all the excitement that doing something new can give.

This brave and thorough publication should prove invaluable to the West in its entry into the decisive trade arena of the Pacific Century.

I am delighted to welcome it as a real contribution to the improving understanding of Japanese in the West. Here is an enlightened revolutionary handbook.

Sir Peter Parker, London 1993

Preface

Increasing trade and communication between Western countries and Japan is encouraging a great number of English speakers to learn the Japanese language. The 1990s are seeing an acceleration of this trend, which is reflected in the current abundance of Japanese language teaching manuals. While varying in style and presentation, all of these manuals aim to introduce Japanese grammar together with basic items of general and business vocabulary.

Despite so much grammatical material there is a paradoxical lack of comprehensive Japanese business-language dictionaries for those Western learners who need to acquire a specific Japanese terminology in its spoken form. Specialized dictionaries produced in Japan for native use do not include the roman transcription of the Japanese characters and the romanized dictionaries available to Westerners are unspecialized, tending to concentrate on basic words.

This dictionary is designed to provide students and business people with a comprehensive list of Japanese terms pertaining specifically to the fields of economics, trade and industry, finance, insurance, business, company law, employment and personnel, both in the native script for users who are familiar with Japanese characters and in romanized form for those only concerned with spoken Japanese.

Gene Ferber, London 1993

How to use this book

This book can and should be used in several ways.

The first and most conventional method is to use it as a reference work. Check the Table of Contents for the chapter and section relating to the term required, then look up the term in the appropriate alphabetical list. For example, 'economic summit' will be found under letter E of the section on 'General terms' in Chapter 1, Economics; Trade and Industry; 'bill of exchange' will be found under letter B of the section on 'Banking' in Chapter 2, Finance. Where a word is common to several topics, it is repeated in the appropriate chapters and sections. For example, 'credit' appears first in the section on 'General terms' in Chapter 1, Economics; Trade and industry, and again in the section on 'Credit; Investment; Speculation' in Chapter 2, Finance.

The second method allows the book to be used as a teaching aid rather than as a reference work. As it is organized by topic, the book enables the user to study the terminology of the specific subject required. For instance, someone interested in a particular aspect of finance such as currency speculation can concentrate on the words pertaining to this subject in the section on 'Currency; Foreign exchange; Gold; Silver' in Chapter 2, Finance. This topical organization facilitates the assimilation of Japanese ideograms representing similar concepts or objects which are often repeated within a given subject. At the same time, the roman transcriptions of these ideograms enable users to concentrate on memorizing the sound of the Japanese words in question, thereby eliminating the time-consuming process of looking up the readings of characters in character dictionaries. Notes and additional expressions have been included at the end of appropriate sections to clarify the more difficult and complex terms.

The third way of using this book is to access Japanese terms by referring to the Japanese-English index included at the end. These terms have been listed in strict A-Z alphabetical order according to their romanized readings rather than by topic as has been done in Chapters 1-5; the English equivalent has been given next, followed by the romanized form. Encountering a Japanese word for the first time, a Western reader or speaker of Japanese may not necessarily be able to place it within a particular topic. The page reference or references given in the index will easily enable the user to find out which topic or topics a term applies to.

The following illustrations show the most important elements of the book's arrangement and portray the way in which this arrangement permits maximum flexibility of use.

A section title (i.e topic).

B English words listed alphabetically within each topic.

C synonyms or explanations appear in parentheses and clarify the meaning of the basic words.

D register appears in square brackets and indicates whether a word is formal, less formal or informal.

E romanized Japanese equivalents for easy reference to Japanese words in their spoken form.

F Japanese characters.

G notes, which are indicated in the alphabetical lists by a superscript number or 'see note 00', appear at the end of certain sections. The explanatory texts clarify the more complex Japanese terms.

H additional expressions, which appear at the end of certain sections, give explanations for Japanese idioms with no ready English equivalents. These expressions provide a more human dimension to what is essentially a list of conventional business terms.

I romanized words listed alphabetically in one sequence.

J English equivalents.

K verbal expressions related to the main term.

L page references.

English-Japanese Business Dictionary

A — Work description; Titles and departments; Personnel affairs

B — **worker**
rōdōsha
労働者

D — **working environment**
[formal]
sagyō kankyō
作業環境

[less formal]
shigoto no kankyō
仕事の環境

workplace
(office, place of — **C**
employment)
kinmusaki
勤務先

(office, working place)
shigotoba — **E**
仕事場

(post)
shokuba
職場 — **F**

G — **Notes**

28. corporate anthem (shaka 社歌): the company anthem is sung by the employees of large Japanese corporations before starting the day's work or on certain occasions, such as the anniversary of the founding of the company, to promote company spirit and a feeling of corporate identity among the workforce.

29. demotion (sasen 左遷): 'sasen' can also be the transfer of an employee to a regional office without his rank actually being lowered.

H — **Additional expressions**

dōki 同期 ('same class') is a term applied to employees recruited at the same time by the company they are working for.

dokushin kizoku 独身貴族 ('the unmarried aristocracy') is the name given by married company employees to young single colleagues who do not have the responsibility of a family and can enjoy their salaries and leisure time freely.

Japanese-English index

Chapter 1

Economics; Trade and industry

abatement
haijo
排除

abatement cost
haijo hiyō
排除費用

ability to compete
kyōsōryoku
競争力

ability to pay
shiharai nōryoku
支払能力

able-bodied poor
kyōsōtai hinkonsha
競争体貧困者

abolition
haishi
廃止

above-the-line
kakusenjō
画線上

above-the-line items
kakusenjō no kōmoku
画線上の項目

absolute advantage
zettai yūi
絶対優位

absolute cost advantage
zettaiteki hiyō no rieki
絶対的費用の利益

absolute income hypothesis
zettai shotoku kasetsu
絶対所得仮設

absolute monopoly
zettai dokusen
絶対独占

absolute poverty
zettaiteki hinkon
絶対的貧困

absolute prices
zettai kakaku
絶対価格

absolute scarcity
zettaiteki kishō
絶対的希少

absolute value
zettaichi
絶対値

absorption approach
ābusōpushon-apurōchi
アーブソープション・
アプローチ

abstinence (interest theory of)
seiyokusetsu
制欲説

abundance
hōfu
豊富

accelerated depreciation
kasoku shōkyaku
加速償却

accelerating inflation
infurēshon no kasoku
インフレーションの
加速

acceleration
kasoku(do)
加速(度)
sokushin
促進

accelerator
kasokudo inshi
加速度因子
sokushinzai
促進剤

accelerator coefficient
kasokudo keisū
加速度係数

accelerator principle
kasokudo genri
加速度原理

accelerator theory (of investment)
kasokudo riron
加速度理論

accession (to the EC)
kanyū
加入

accession rate
nyūshokuritsu
入職率

accommodating transactions
chōseiteki torihiki
調整的取引

acreage allotment
sakuzuke wariate
作付け割当て

across-the-board tariff changes
kanzei no ikkatsu hikisage
関税一括引下げ

action lag
jisshijō no okure
実施上の遅れ

active
(dynamic)
kappatsu na
活発な

(lively, brisk)
katsudōteki
活動的

active balance
katsudō zandaka
活動残高

active balance of payments
kokusai shūshi no kuroji
国際収支の黒字

active balance of trade
bōeki shūshi no kurojijiri
貿易収支の黒字尻

activity
(boom, prosperity)
kakkyō
活況

(liveliness)
katsudō
活動

(good economic times)
kōkeiki
好景気

activity analysis
katsudō bunseki
活動分析

activity rate
rōdōryokukaritsu
労働力化率

actual cost
jissai genka
実際原価
jitsuhi
実費

actual demand
jitsuju
実需

actual goods
genpin
現品

actual income
genjitsu shotoku
現実所得

actual rate of growth
genjitsu seichōritsu
現実成長率

ad-valorem tax
jūkazei
従価税

adaptive expectations
tekigō kitai
適合期待

addition rule
kahō teiri
加法定理

additional budget
tsuika yosan
追加予算

additional worker hypo-thesis
genkai rōdōsha kasetsu
限界労働者仮設

adjust
chōsei suru
調整する

adjusted income
chōsei shotoku
調整所得

adjustment
chōsei
調整

adjustment mechanism
chōsei kikō
調整機構

adjustment period
chōsei kikan
調整期間

adjustment process
chōsei katei
調整過程

administered prices
kanri kakaku
管理価格

administration
gyōsei
行政

administrative action
gyōsei shobun
行政処分

administrative authorities
gyōsei kanchō
行政官庁

administrative expenses
gyōsei kyōtsūhi
行政共通費

administrative guidance
gyōsei shidō
行政指導

administrative lag (policy)
seisaku no ragu
政策のラグ

(financial policy)
kin'yū seisaku no ragu
金融政策のラグ

(monetary policy)
tsūka seisaku no ragu
通貨政策のラグ

administrative measures
gyōsei sochi
行政措置

administrative organ
gyōsei kikan
行政機関

administrative power
gyōseiken
行政権

administrative reform
gyōsei kaikaku
行政改革

administrative reorganization
gyōsei seiri
行政整理

administrators
gyōseikan
行政官

advanced countries
senshinkoku
先進国

advanced technologies
sentan gijutsu
先端技術

adversarial trade
tekitai bōeki
敵対貿易

adverse balance of trade
gyakuchō
逆調

(in deficit)
kokusai shūshi no akaji
国際収支の赤字

(excessive imports)
yunyū chōka
輸入超過

adverse factors
akka yōin
悪化要因

AEA (American Economic Association)
beikeizai gakkai
米経済学会

affluent society
yutaka na shakai
豊かな社会

after-effects
kōishō
後遺症

age composition of population
jinkō nenrei kōsei
人口年齢構成

age distribution
nenrei bunpu
年齢分布

age group
nenrei kaisō
年齢階層
nenreisō
年齢層

Agency for International
Development (AID) [US]
kokusai kaihatsukyoku
国際開発局

aggregate
shūkeiryō
集計量
sōkei
総計

aggregate demand
sōjuyō
総需要

aggregate demand curve
sōjuyō kyokusen
総需要曲線

aggregate economic activity
sōtaiteki keizai katsudō
総体的経済活動

aggregate economic analysis
sōtaiteki keizai bunseki
総体的経済分析

aggregate expenditure
sōshishutsu
総支出

aggregate income
sōshotoku
総所得

aggregate output
sōseisanryō
総生産量

aggregate production function
sōtai seisan kansū
総体生産関数

aggregate supply
sōkyōkyū
総供給

aggregate supply curve
sōkyōkyū kyokusen
総供給曲線

aging population
rōjin jinkō
老人人口

aging workforce
rōreika suru rōdōryoku
老齢化する労働力

Agrarian Revolution
nōgyō kakumei
農業革命

agreement
kyōtei
協定

agribusiness
nōgyō kanren sangyō
農業関連産業

agricultural census
nōgyō dōtai chōsa
農業動態調査
nōgyō sensasu
農業センサス

agricultural commodities
nōgyō seihin
農業製品

agricultural co-operatives
nōgyō kyōdō kumiai
農業協同組合

agricultural country
nōgyōkoku
農業国

agricultural credit
nōgyō kin'yū
農業金融

agricultural crisis
nōgyō kyōkō
農業恐慌

agricultural disaster
nōgyō saigai
農業災害

agricultural disaster indemnity
nōgyō saigai hoshō
農業災害補償

agricultural earnings
nōgyō shotoku
農業所得

agricultural economy
nōgyō keizai
農業経済

agricultural exports
nōsanbutsu yushutsu
農産物輸出

agricultural financing
nōgyō kin'yū
農業金融

agricultural goods
nōsanbutsu
農産物

agricultural imports
nōsanbutsu yunyū
農産物輸入

agricultural income
nōgyō shotoku
農業所得

agricultural labour
nōgyō rōdō
農業労働

agricultural lag
nōgyō seisaku no ragu
農業政策のラグ

agricultural land
nōchi
農地

agricultural land reform
nōchi kaikaku
農地改革

agricultural levies
nōgyō fukakin
農業賦課金

agricultural mechanization
nōgyō kikaika
農業機械化

agricultural modernization
nōgyō kindaika
農業近代化

agricultural output
nōgyō seisan
農業生産

agricultural parity index
nōgyō pariti shisū
農業パリティ指数

agricultural policy
nōgyō seisaku
農業政策

agricultural pollution
nōgyō osen
農業汚染

agricultural population
nōgyō jinkō
農業人口

agricultural price support
policy
nōsanbutsu kakaku shiji
seisaku
農産物価格支持政策

agricultural prices
nōsanbutsu kakaku
農産物価格

agricultural problems
nōgyō mondai
農業問題

agricultural produce
nōsanbutsu
農産物

agricultural production
nōgyō seisan
農業生産

agricultural productivity
nōgyō seisanryoku
農業生産力

agricultural products
nōsanbutsu
農産物

agricultural reform
nōgyō kaikaku
農業改革

agricultural resources
nōgyō shigen
農業資源

agricultural sector
nōgyō bumon
農業部門

agricultural society
nōgyō shakai
農業社会

agricultural statistics
nōgyō tōkei
農業統計

agricultural structure
nōgyō kōzō
農業構造

agricultural subsidies
nōgyō hojokin
農業補助金

agricultural technology
nōgyō gijutsu
農業技術

agricultural wages
nōgyō chingin
農業賃金

Agricultural Wages Board
[UK]
nōgyō chingin i'inkai
農業賃金委員会

agricultural waste
nōgyō haikibutsu
農業廃棄物

agricultural workers
nōgyō rōdōsha
農業労働者

agriculture
nōgyō
農業

agronomics
nōgyō kei'ei(gaku)
農業経営(学)

agronomy
(study)
nōgaku
農学

(economics)
nōgyō keizai
農業経済

aid
enjo
援助

AID (Agency for International
Development) [US]
kokusai kaihatsukyoku
国際開発局

aid-giving country
enjokoku
援助国

aid-receiving country
hienjokoku
被援助国

ailing economy
yameru keizai
病める経済

ailing industry
yameru sangyō
病める産業

air pollution
taiki osen
大気汚染

alienation
sogai
疎外
sokaku
疎隔

alignment
chōsei
調整

all-time high
saikō kiroku
最高記録

all-time low
saitei kiroku
最低記録

allocation
(distribution)
haibun
配分

(assignment)
wariate
割当て

allocation of costs
hiyō haibun
費用配分
keihi wariate
経費割当て

allocation of resources
shigen haibun
資源配分

allocative efficiency
haibun kōritsu
配分効率

alternative technology
daitai gijutsu
代替技術

American Economic
Association (AEA)
  beikeizai gakkai
  米経済学会

American Statistical
Association (ASA)
  beikoku tōkei kyōkai
  米国統計協会

amount of money
  kaheiryō
  貨幣量

amplitude of cycle
  shinpuku
  振幅

analysis
  bunseki
  分析

analysis of variance (ANOVA)
  bunsan bunseki
  分散分析

analyst
  anarisuto
  アナリスト
  bunsekika
  分析家

annual economic growth rate
  nenkan keizai seichōritsu
  年間経済成長率

annual economic report
  nenji keizai hōkokusho
  年次経済報告書

annual expenditure
  saishutsu
  歳出

annual improvement factor
  nenjō shōyōin
  年上昇要因

annual rate
  nenritsu
  年率

annual rate of inflation
  infure nenritsu
  インフレ年率

annual revenue
  sainyū
  歳入

annual survey
  nenji chōsa
  年次調査

ANOVA (analysis of variance)
  bunsan bunseki
  分散分析

anticipated inflation rate
  yosoku infureritsu
  予測インフレ率

anticipation
  mikoshi
  見越し

anticipation survey
  mitōshi chōsa
  見通し調査

anti-cyclical measures
  keiki taisaku
  景気対策

anti-cyclical policy
  keiki seisaku
  景気政策

anti-dumping duties
  danpingu bōshi kanzei
  ダンピング防止関税

anti-dumping policy
  danpingu bōshi seisaku
  ダンピング防止政策

anti-inflation measures
  infure taisaku
  インフレ対策

anti-inflation policy
  infure taisaku
  インフレ対策

anti-recession policy
  fukyō taisaku
  不況対策

anti-trust laws
  dokusen kinshihō
  独占禁止法

APC (average propensity to
consume)
  heikin shōhi seikō
  平均消費性向

applied economics
  ōyō keizaigaku
  応用経済学

applied research
  ōyō kenkyū
  応用研究

applied technology
  ōyō gijutsu
  応用技術

appreciation
  zōka
  増価

(currency)
  tōki
  騰貴

appropriate products
  tekitō seisanbutsu
  適当生産物

appropriate technology
  tekitō gijutsu
  適当技術

appropriation
(earmarking)
  jūtō
  充当

(earmarked money)
  jūtōkin
  充当金

appropriation committee
  yosan i'inkai
  予算委員会

areas
  chi'iki
  地域

aristocracy of labour
  rōdō kizoku
  労働貴族

arithmetic mean
  sanjutsu heikin
  算術平均

artificial prosperity
  kara keiki
  空景気

ASA (American Statistical
Association)
  beikoku tōkei kyōkai
  米国統計協会

ASEAN (Association of South-East Asian Nations)
tōnan ajia shokoku rengō
東南アジア諸国連合

asset(s)
shisan
資産

assistance
enjo
援助
fujo
扶助

assisted areas
hienjo chi'iki
被援助地域

Association of South-East Asian Nations (ASEAN)
tōnan ajia shokoku rengō
東南アジア諸国連合

associations
kumiai
組合

**assumption
(supposition)**
kasetsu
仮説

(hypothesis)
katei
仮定

atomistic competition
genshiteki kyōsō
原子的競争

attribute
seihin tokushitsu
製品特質

**austerity
(contraction)**
kinshuku
緊縮

(retrenchment)
taibō
耐乏

austerity budget
kinshuku yosan
緊縮予算
taibō yosan
耐乏予算

austerity measures
kinshuku seisaku sochi
緊縮政策措置
taibō seisaku sochi
耐乏政策措置

austerity policy
kinshuku seisaku
緊縮政策
taibō seisaku
耐乏政策

austerity programme
taibō seikatsu keikaku
耐乏生活計画

autarchy (autarky)
jikyūjisoku
自給自足
keizaiteki jikyūjisoku
経済的自給自足

automatic stabilizers
jidō antei sōchi
自動安定装置

automobile tax
jidōshazei
自動車税

autonomous capital movements
jihatsuteki shihon idō
自発的資本移動

autonomous expenditures
dokuritsu shishutsu
独立支出

autonomous investment
dokuritsu tōshi
独立投資

autonomous tariff
kokuteizeiritsu
国定税率

autonomous variable(s)
dokuritsu hensū
独立変数

available resources
riyōkanō shigen
利用可能資源

average
heikin
平均

average annual output
nenkan heikin sanshutsu-ryō
年間平均産出量

average annual rate of growth
nenkan heikin seichōritsu
年間平均成長率

average consumption
heikin shōhi
平均消費

average cost
heikin genka
平均原価
heikin hiyō
平均費用

average cost pricing
heikin hiyō kakaku keisei
平均費用価格形成

average crop
heikinsaku
平均作

average demand
heikin juyō
平均需要

average earnings
heikin shūnyū
平均収入

average error
heikin gosa
平均誤差

average fixed cost(s)
heikin kotei hiyō
平均固定費用

average income
heikin shotoku
平均所得

average labour rate
heikin chinritsu
平均賃率

average life expectancy
heikin yomei
平均余命

average life span
heikin jumyō
平均寿命

average per capita
hitori atari heikin
一人当たり平均

average price
heikin kakaku
平均価格

average product
heikin seisanbutsu
平均生産物

**average productivity
(production capacity)**
heikin seisanryoku
平均生産力

(people's)
heikin seisansei
平均生産性

**average propensity to
consume (APC)**
heikin shōhi seikō
平均消費性向

average propensity to save
heikin chochiku seikō
平均貯蓄性向

average revenue
heikin shūnyū
平均収入

average total cost(s)
heikin sōhiyō
平均総費用

average unit cost
ittan'i atari no heikin genka
一単位当たりの平均
原価

average variable cost(s)
heikin kahen hiyō
平均可変費用

average velocity of circulation
heikin kahei ryūtsū sokudo
平均貨幣流通速度

average wage
heikin chingin
平均賃金

baby boom
bebii-būmu
ベビー・ブーム

baby boomers
bebii-būmu sedai
ベビー・ブーム世代

backward integration
kōhō tōgō
後方統合

backwash effects
gyakuryū kōka
逆流効果

bad crop
kyōsaku
凶作

bad inflation
akusei infure
悪性インフレ

**bad times
(hard times, recession)**
fukeiki
不景気

(depression, slump)
fukyōji
不況時

bad year
kyōnen
凶年

**balance of current account
(nation's)**
keijō shūshijiri
経常収支尻

balance of payments
kokusai shūshi
国際収支

balance of trade
bōeki shūshi
貿易収支

balanced budget
kinkō yosan
均衡予算

balanced-budget multiplier
kinkō yosan jōsū
均衡予算乗数

**balanced economic
development**
kinsei keizai hatten
均整経済発展

balanced growth
kinkō seichō
均衡成長

balancing item
chōsei kōmoku
調整項目

ban (noun)
kinshi
禁止

ban (verb)
kinshi suru
禁止する

ban on exports
yushutsu kinshi
輸出禁止

ban on imports
yunyū kinshi
輸入禁止

bandwagon effect
bandowagon kōka
バンドワゴン効果

bank accounts
ginkō kanjō
銀行勘定

bank crash
ginkō hatan
銀行破綻

**bank credit
(credit)**
ginkō shin'yō
銀行信用

(finance)
ginkō yūshi
銀行融資

(loans)
ginkō kashidashi
銀行貸出し

bank deposits
ginkō yokin
銀行預金

**Bank for International
Settlements (BIS)**
kokusai kessai ginkō
国際決済銀行

bank loans
ginkō kashidashi
銀行貸出し
ginkō kashitsuke
銀行貸付け

bank loans and discounts
ginkō kashidashi
銀行貸出し

bank money
yokin tsūka
預金通貨

bank note issues
ginkōken hakkōdaka
銀行券発行高

Bank Rate
chūō ginkō waribiki buai
中央銀行割引歩合
kōtei buai
公定歩合

banks
ginkō
銀行

bargaining tariff
kakehiki kanzei
掛引関税

bargaining theory of wages
chingin kōshō ketteisetsu
賃金交渉決定説

barrier
(obstacle)
shōgai
障害

(wall)
shōheki
障壁

barriers to entry
sannyū shōheki
参入障壁

barriers to imports
yunyū shōheki
輸入障壁

barriers to trade
bōeki shōgai
貿易障害

barter
bātā
バーター
butsubutsu kōkan
物々交換

barter agreements
bātā kyōtei
バーター協定

barter economy
bātā keizai
バーター経済
butsubutsu kōkan keizai
物々交換経済

barter trade
bātā bōeki
バーター貿易

base-period
kijun kikan
基準期間

base rate
kijun kinri
基準金利

base year
kijunnen
基準年

basic activities
kisoteki akutibitii
基礎的アクティビティー

basic balance of payments
kisoteki shūshi
基礎的収支

basic exports
kisoteki yushutsu
基礎的輸出

basic industries
(key industries)
kikan sangyō
基幹産業

(fundamental industries)
kiso sangyō
基礎産業

basic-needs philosophy
kihonteki yōkyū shisō
基本的要求思想

basic-point system
kiten kakaku seido
基点価格制度

basic technology
kiso gijutsu
基礎技術

basic unit
gentan'i
原単位

basic wage
kihon chingin
基本賃金

battle against inflation
infure to no tatakai
インフレとの闘い

beating inflation
infure kokufuku
インフレ克服

before tax
zeikomi
税込み

beggar-my-neighbour policy
kinrin kyūbōka seisaku
近隣窮乏化政策

behaviour
kōdō
行動

behavioural equation
kōdō hōteishiki
行動方程式

behavioural expectations
kōdō kitai
行動期待

behavioural theories of the firm
kigyō kōdō no riron
企業行動の理論

behind-the-scenes consensus
butaiura de no gōi
舞台裏での合意

below-the-line
kakusenka
画線下

below-the-line items
kakusenka no kōmoku
画線下の項目

benchmark
benchi-māku
ベンチ・マーク

(criterion, standard)
kijunten
基準点

(measurement criterion)
sokutei kijun
測定基準

benefit principle
rieki gensoku
利益原則

benefit theory of taxation
sozei no juekisha futan
gensoku
租税の受益者負担
原則

benign neglect
zen'i no mushi
善意の無視

bilateral agreement
nikokukan kyōtei
二国間協定

bilateral assistance
nikokukan enjo
二国間援助

bilateral monopoly
sōhō dokusen
双方独占

bilateral trade
sōmu bōeki
双務貿易

bilateral trade agreement
sōmu bōeki kyōtei
双務貿易協定

bilateral treaty
sōmu jōyaku
双務条約

bilateralism
sōmu bōeki shugi
双務貿易主義

birth rate
shussanritsu
出産率
shusshōritsu
出生率

BIS (Bank for International Settlements)
kokusai kessai ginkō
国際決済銀行

black market
yami shijō
闇市場

black-market prices
yamine
闇値

black-marketeers
yami shōnin
闇商人

block economy
burokku keizai
ブロック経済

blockade
fūsa
封鎖

blockade policy
fūsa seisaku
封鎖政策

blockade zone
fūsa ku'iki
封鎖区域

Blue Book [UK]
seisho
青書

blue-collar workers
nikutai rōdōsha
肉体労働者

Board of Trade [UK]
shōmushō
商務省

boom
būmu
ブーム

(business upswing)
keiki jōshō
景気上昇

(period of prosperity)
kōkyō
好況

boom period
kōkyōki
好況期

borrower countries
kariirekoku
借入国
shakkinkoku
借金国

borrowers (countries)
kariirekoku
借入国
shakkinkoku
借金国

borrowing
kariire
借入れ

bottle-neck industry
airo sangyō
あい路産業

**bounties [UK]
(subsidies)**
hojokin
補助金

(incentives)
shōreikin
奨励金

bounty system
hōshō seido
報奨制度

boycott (noun)
boikotto
ボイコット

(not buying)
fubai dōmei
不買同盟

(rejection)
haiseki
排斥

boycott (verb)
boikotto suru
ボイコットする

boycott movement
fubai undō
不買運動

boycott of foreign goods
gaika haiseki
外貨排斥

bracket
kaisō
階層

brain drain
zunō ryūshutsu
頭脳流出

break (noun)
bōraku
暴落

break-even level of income
saisan suijun
採算水準

Bretton Woods agreement
buretton-uzzu kyōtei
ブレットン・ウッズ
協定

**British Overseas Trade Board
[UK]**
eikoku kaigai bōeki i'inkai
英国海外貿易委員会

**British Technology Group
[UK]**
eikoku gijutsu gurūpu
英国技術グループ

broad money
kōgi no manē-sapurai
広義のマネー・
サプライ

Brussels Tariff Nomenclature
burasseru kanzei jōkyohyō
ブラッセル関税
譲許表

bubble
hōmatsu
泡沫

bubble companies
hōmatsu gaisha
泡沫会社

budget
yosan
予算

budget allocations
yosan wariategaku
予算割当額

budget committee
yosan i'inkai
予算委員会

budget compilation
yosan hensei
予算編成

budget constraint
yosan seiyaku
予算制約

budget cutters
yosan sakugen ronsha
予算削減論者

budget deficit
yosan akaji
予算赤字
zaisei akaji
財政赤字

budget drafting
yosan sakusei
予算作成

budget forecast
yosan yosoku
予算予測

(estimation)
yosan mitsumori(sho)
予算見積り(書)

budget implementation
yosan no shikkō
予算の執行

budget items
yosan kōmoku
予算項目

budget line
yosansen
予算線

budget outline
yosan taikō
予算大綱

budget overrun
yosan chōka
予算超過

budget policy
yosan seisaku
予算政策

budget proposal
yosan'an
予算案

budget provisions
yosan sōsoku
予算総則

budget reform
yosan kaikaku
予算改革

budget surplus
yosan jōyo
予算剰余
zaisei kuroji
財政黒字

budgetary control
yosan tōsei
予算統制

built-in stabilizers
jidō antei sōchi
自動安定装置

bumper crop
hōsaku
豊作

bumper year
hōnen
豊年

**buoyancy
(buoyant force)**
furyoku
浮力

(prosperity)
kakkyō
活況

buoyant
kakkyō no
活況の

bureaucracy
kanryō(sei)
官僚(制)

burden rate (production)
seizō kansetsuhi haifuritsu
製造間接費配布率

**business
(operation, trade)**
eigyō
営業

(industry)
jitsugyō
実業

(commerce, trade)
shōbai
商売

business activity
keiki
景気
keizai katsudō
経済活動

business barometer
keiki shihyō
景気指標

business climate
keiki
景気

business community
(business world)
gyōkai
業界

(industrial world)
jitsugyōkai
実業界

business conditions
keikyō
景況

(present conditions)
keiki genjō
景気現状

business confidence
kigyōka no kakushin
企業家の確信

business cycle
keiki junkan
景気循環

business diagnosis
gyōkyō shindan
業況診断

business economics
kei'ei keizaigaku
経営経済学

business failure rate
tōsanritsu
倒産率

business fluctuations
keiki hendō
景気変動

business forecast
keiki yosoku
景気予測

business indicators
keiki shihyō
景気指標

business motive
eigyō dōki
営業動機

business observation
keiki kansoku
景気観測

business observers
gyōkai
業界

business outlook
keiki genjō
景気現状

business people
jitsugyōka
実業家

business performance
kigyō gyōseki
企業業績

business recession
keiki gentai
景気減退

business recovery
keiki kaifuku
景気回復

business report (economic experts')
gyōkai no hōkoku
業界の報告

business research
gyōkyō chōsa
業況調査

business slump
keiki fushin
景気不振

business statistics
kigyō tōkei
企業統計

business survey
keiki dōkō chōsa
景気動向調査

business trend
keiki dōkō
景気動向

business warning indicators
keiki keikoku shihyō
景気警告指標

business world
gyōkai
業界

(industry, trade)
jitsugyōkai
実業界

(finance)
zaikai
財界

businesses
(enterprises, undertakings)
kigyō
企業

(commercial companies)
shōji gaisha
商事会社

(trading companies)
shōsha
商社

businessmen
jitsugyōka
実業家

buy-outs
(take-overs)
baishū
買収

(acquisitions)
kaitori
買取り

buying power
kōbairyoku
購買力

by-products
fukusanbutsu
副産物

cache
intoku
隠匿

calculations
keisan
計算

campaign
undō
運動

canon of taxation
sozei gensoku
租税原則

CAP (Common Agricultural Policy) [EC]
kyōtsū nōgyō seisaku
共通農業政策

capacity
nōryoku
能力

capacity utilization rate (production)
seisan nōryoku riyōritsu
生産能力利用率

(equipment)
setsubi kadōritsu
設備稼働率

capital
shihon
資本

capital account
shihon kanjō
資本勘定

capital budget
kotei shishutsu yosan
固定支出予算
shihon shishutsu yosan
資本支出予算

capital budgeting
shihon no yosan hensei
資本の予算編成

capital coefficients
shihon keisū
資本係数

capital consumption
shihon shōhi
資本消費

capital consumption allowance [US]
shihon genmō hikiate
資本減耗引当て

capital cost
shihonhi(yō)
資本費(用)

capital deepening
shihon no shinka
資本の深化

capital demand
shihon juyō
資本需要

capital equipment
shihon setsubi
資本設備

capital/equipment ratio
shihon sōbiritsu
資本装備率

capital expenditure
shihon shishutsu
資本支出

capital export
shihon yushutsu
資本輸出

capital-exporting country
shihon yushutsukoku
資本輸出国

capital flight
shihon tōhi
資本逃避

capital flow
shihon no nagare
資本の流れ

capital formation
shihon keisei
資本形成

capital gains
shihon ritoku
資本利得

capital goods
shihonzai
資本財

capital grants
tōshi hojokin
投資補助金

capital import
shihon yunyū
資本輸入

capital-importing country
shihon yunyūkoku
資本輸入国

capital/income ratio
shihon-shotoku hiritsu
資本・所得比率

capital inflow
shihon ryūnyū
資本流入

capital intensity
shihon shūyakudo
資本集約度

capital-intensive
shihon shūyakuteki
資本集約的

capital-intensive economy
shihon shūyakuteki keizai
資本集約的経済

capital-intensive industries
shihon shūyakuteki sangyō
資本集約的産業

capital-intensive sector
shihon shūyakuteki bumon
資本集約的部門

capital-intensive techniques
shihon shūyakuteki gijutsu
資本集約的技術

capital/labour ratio
shihon-rōdō hiritsu
資本・労働比率

capital-labour substitution
shihon-rōdō no daitai
資本・労働の代替

capital loss
shihon sonshitsu
資本損失

capital outflow
shihon ryūshutsu
資本流出

capital/output ratio
shihon-sanshutsudaka hiritsu
資本・産出高比率

capital market
shihon shijō
資本市場

capital movements
shihon idō
資本移動

capital/profit ratio
shihon-riekiritsu
資本・利益率

capital rationing (limits)
shihon seigen
資本制限

(allocation)
shihon wariate
資本割当て

capital requirements
shihon juyō
資本需要

capital reserves
shihon junbikin
資本準備金

capital stock
shihon sutokku
資本ストック

capital stock adjustment principle
shihon sutokku chōsei genri
資本ストック調整
原理

capital surplus
shihon jōyo
資本剰余

capital turnover
shihon kaiten
資本回転

capital widening
shihon kakuchō
資本拡張

capitalism
shihon shugi
資本主義

capitalist
shihon shugisha
資本主義者

capitalist country
shihon shugishakoku
資本主義者国

capitalist economy
shihon shugi keizai
資本主義経済

capitalist society
shihon shugi shakai
資本主義社会

capitalist system
shihon shugi taisei
資本主義体制

cardinal utility
kisūteki kōyō
基数的効用

cartel
karuteru
カルテル
kigyō rengō
企業連合

cartelization
karuteruka
カルテル化

cartelized industries
karuteruka sangyō
カルテル化産業

case-by-case examination
kobetsu shinsa
個別審査

case study
jirei kenkyū
事例研究

cash-balance approach
genkin zandaka sekkinhō
現金残高接近法

cash-balance effect
genkin zandaka kōka
現金残高効果

cash budget
genkin shūshi yosan
現金収支予算

cash limit
genkin seigen
現金制限

cashflow
kasshu-furō
キャッシュ・フロー

casino economy
kajino keizai
カジノ経済

casino society
kajino shakai
カジノ社会

casual employment
rinji koyō
臨時雇用

cautious monetary policy
keikaigata kin'yū seisaku
警戒型金融政策

cautious optimism
keikaiteki rakkan
警戒的楽観

CBI (Confederation of British Industry)
eikoku sangyō renmei
英国産業連盟

CEA (Council of Economic Advisors) [US]
daitōryō keizai shimon i'inkai
大統領経済諮問
委員会

ceiling
saikō gendo
最高限度

ceiling on imports
yunyū gendo
輸入限度

ceiling price
saikō kakaku
最高価格

census
sensasu
センサス

(national)
kokusei chōsa
国勢調査

census form
kokusei chōsa hōkokusho
国勢調査報告書

central bank
chūō ginkō
中央銀行

central bank credit
chūō ginkō shin'yō
中央銀行信用

central bank intervention
chūō ginkō kainyū
中央銀行介入

central government borrowing requirements (CGBR) [UK]
chūō seifu kariire juyō
中央政府借入需要

central government finance
chūō zaisei
中央財政

central planning
chūō keikaku
中央計画

Central Statistical Office (CSO) [UK]
chūō tōkeitōkyoku
中央統計当局

centrally planned economies
chūō keikaku keizai
中央計画経済

CGBR (central government borrowing requirements) [UK]
chūō seifu kariire juyō
中央政府借入需要

Chamber of Commerce
shōgyō kaigisho
商業会議所

Chamber of Commerce and Industry
shōkō kaigisho
商工会議所

Chancellor of the Exchequer [UK]
ōkura daijin
大蔵大臣

changes in technology
gijutsu henka
技術変化

characteristics theory
tokusei riron
特性理論

cheap labour
teichingin rōdō
低賃金労働

cheap-labour policy
teichingin rōdō seisaku
低賃金労働政策

cheap land
yasui yōchi
安い用地

cheap money
teikinri shikin
低金利資金

cheap-money policy
teikinri seisaku
低金利政策

child labour
yōji rōdō
幼児労働

choice of technology
gijutsu sentaku
技術選択

choice variable
sentaku hensū
選択変数

chronic depression
manseiteki fukyō
慢性的不況

chronic inflation
manseiteki infurēshon
慢性的インフレーション

chronic unemployment
manseiteki shitsugyō
慢性的失業

circulating capital
ryūdō shihon
流動資本

(floating)
ryūtsū shihon
流通資本

City, the [UK]
rondon no shitii (kin'yū machi)
ロンドンのシティー
(金融町)

classical economics
kotenha keizaigaku
古典派経済学

classification
bunrui
分類

clearing banks
tegata kōkan kumiai ginkō
手形交換組合銀行

closed economy
fūsa keizai
封鎖経済

closures
kōjō heisa
工場閉鎖

coefficient
keisū
係数

coefficient of concentration
shūchū keisū
集中係数

coefficients of production
seisan keisū
生産係数

COLA (cost-of-living adjustment)
seikeihi chōsetsu
生計費調節

collapse
gakai
瓦解

collective agreement
dantai kyōyaku
団体協約
shūdan kyōyaku
集団協約

collective bargaining
dantai kōshō
団体交渉

collective choice
shūdanteki sentaku
集団的選択

collective goods
kyōdōzai
共同財
shūgōzai
集合財

collectivism
shūsan shugi
集産主義

collusion
kyōbō
共謀

COMECON (Council for Mutual Economic Aid)
komekon
コメコン
tōō keizai sōgo enjo kaigi
東欧経済相互援助会議

command economy
shirei keizai
指令経済

commerce
(export and import, international trade)
bōeki
貿易

(business, trade)
shōgyō
商業

(trade)
tsushō
通商

Commerce Department [US]
shōmushō
商務省

commercial activity
shōgyō katsudō
商業活動

commercial banks
shōgyō ginkō
商業銀行

commercial offensives
shōgyō kōsei
商業攻勢

commercial policies
tsūshō seisaku
通商政策

commercial sector
shōgyō bumon
商業部門

commercial transaction
shōtorihiki
商取引

commercial treaty
tsūshō jōyaku
通商条約

commercialism
shōgyō shugi
商業主義

commodities
shōhin
商品

commodity market
shōhin shijō
商品市場

commodity money
shōhin kahei
商品貨幣

commodity prices
bukka
物価

commodity terms of trade
shōhin kōeki jōken
商品交易条件

Common Agricultural Policy (CAP) [EC]
kyōtsū nōgyō seisaku
共通農業政策

Common Customs Tariff [EC]
kyōtsu kanzeiritsu
共通関税率

Common External Tariff
ikigai kyōtsū kanzei
域外共通関税

Common Market, the
kyōdō shijō
共同市場

communism
kyōsan shugi
共産主義

communist economy
kyōsan shugi keizai
共産主義経済

communist society
kyōsan shugi shakai
共産主義社会

communist system
kyōsan shugi taisei
共産主義体制

community
kyōdōtai
共同体

community indifference curve
shakaiteki musabetsu kyokusen
社会的無差別曲線

companies
kaisha
会社

comparability
hikaku kanōsei
比較可能性

comparative advantage
hikaku yūi
比較優位

comparative analysis
hikaku bunseki
比較分析

comparative cost
hikaku genka
比較原価

comparative dynamics
hikaku dōgaku
比較動学

comparative statics
hikaku seigaku
比較静学

comparison
hikaku
比較

compensation imports
daishō yunyū
代償輸入

compensation principle
hoshō genri
補償原理

compensation trade
kyūshō bōeki
求償貿易

compensatory finance
hoshō yūshi
補償融資

competition
kyōsō
競争

competitive
kyōsōteki
競争的

competitive commodities
kyōsōhin
競争品
kyōsōteki shōhin
競争的商品

competitive demand
kyōsōteki juyō
競争的需要

competitive goods
kyōsōzai
競争財

competitive industry
kyōsōteki sangyō
競争的産業

competitive market place
kyōsō shijō
競争市場

competitive markets
kyōsō shijō
競争市場

competitive power
kyōsōryoku
競争力

competitive strength
kyōsōryoku
競争力

competitive supply
kyōsōteki kyōkyū
競争的供給

competitive trade
kyōsōteki bōeki
競争的貿易

competitiveness
kyōsōryoku
競争力

competitors (countries)
kyōsōkoku
競争国

complementary demand
sōhoteki juyō
相補的需要

complementary goods
hokanzai
補完財

complementary trade
hokanteki bōeki
補完的貿易

complements
hokanzai
補完財

composite demand
fukugō juyō
複合需要

composite supply
fukugō kyōkyū
複合供給

compulsory education
gimu kyōiku
義務教育

compulsory national health system
kyōsei kokumin kenkō hoken seido
強制国民健康保険制度

compulsory saving
kyōsei chochiku
強制貯蓄

concealed dumping
inpei danpingu
隠蔽ダンピング

concentration
shūchū
集中

concentration ratio
shūchūdo
集中度

concertation
kyōchō
協調

concerted action
kyōchō kōdō
協調行動

concessions
jōho
譲歩

Confederation of British Industry (CBI)
eikoku sangyō renmei
英国産業連盟

confidence
kakushin
確信

confrontation
taiketsu
対決

confrontation policy
taiketsu seisaku
対決政策

conglomerates
fukugō kigyō
複合企業

conservation (protection, safeguard)
hogo
保護

(preservation)
hozon
保存

(saving, economizing)
setsuyaku
節約

conservation of resources
shigen setsuyaku
資源節約

conservation policy
hogo seisaku
保護政策

conservationist
hogo shugisha
保護主義者

conserve
setsuyaku suru
節約する

consistency
itchi
一致

consolidated fund [UK]
seiri kōsai kikin
整理公債基金

consortium of creditor nations
saikenkoku kaigi
債権国会議

conspicuous consumption
kojiteki shōhi
誇示的消費

constant capital
fuhen shihon
不変資本

constant cost(s)
fuhen hiyō
不変費用

constant-cost supply
hiyō fuhen kyōkyū
費用不変供給

constant prices
fuhen kakaku
不変価格

constant returns to scale
kibo ni taisuru shūeki fuhen
規模に対する収益
不変

constraint
(coercion, compulsory-making)
kyōsei
強制

(limitations, restrictions)
seiyaku
制約

consumable goods
shōhizai
消費財
shōmōhin
消耗品

consume
shōhi suru
消費する

consumer
shōhisha
消費者

consumer behaviour
shōhisha kōdō
消費者行動

consumer buying
shōhisha kōbai
消費者購買

consumer credit
shōhisha shin'yō
消費者信用

consumer credit control
shōhisha shin'yō tōsei
消費者信用統制

consumer demand
shōhisha juyō
消費者需要

consumer demand theory
shōhisha juyō riron
消費者需要理論

consumer durables
taikyū shōhizai
耐久消費財

consumer equilibrium
shōhisha kinkō
消費者均衡

consumer expenditure
shōhisha shishutsu
消費者支出

consumer finance
shōhisha kin'yū
消費者金融

consumer goods
shōhizai
消費財
shōmōhin
消耗品

consumer groups
shōhi dantai
消費団体

consumer habits
shōhisha shūkan
消費者習慣

consumer instalment credit
shōhisha fubarai shin'yō
消費者賦払信用

consumer lending
shōhisha kin'yū
消費者金融

consumer loans
shōhisha kin'yū
消費者金融

**consumer price index (CPI)
[US]**
shōhisha bukka shisū
消費者物価指数

consumer price survey
shōhisha bukka chōsa
消費者物価調査

consumer prices
shōhisha bukka
消費者物価
shōhisha kakaku
消費者価格

consumer product
shōhizai seisanbutsu
消費財生産物

consumer resistance
kaishiburi
買いしぶり

consumer sector
shōhisha bumon
消費者部門

consumer sovereignty
shōhisha shuken
消費者主権

consumer spending
shōhisha shishutsu
消費者支出

consumer survey
shōhisha chōsa
消費者調査

consumer's preference
shōhisha senkō
消費者選好

consumer's surplus
shōhisha yojō
消費者余剰

consumers' association
shōhisha kumiai
消費者組合

consumers' debt
shōhisha fusai
消費者負債

consumerism
shōhisha shugi
消費者主義

consumption
shōhi
消費

consumption capital
shōhi shihon
消費資本

consumption curve
shōhi kyokusen
消費曲線

consumption expenditure
shōhi shishutsu
消費支出

consumption expenditure
levels
shōhi suijun
消費水準

consumption function
shōhi kansū
消費関数

consumption/income ratio
shōhi-shotoku hiritsu
消費・所得比率

consumption inflation
shōhi infure
消費インフレ

consumption lag
shōhi no ragu
消費のラグ

consumption level
shōhi suijun
消費水準

consumption product
shōhizai seisanbutsu
消費財生産物

consumption tax
shōhizei
消費税

contingency
gūhatsu jiken
偶発事件

continuous variable
renzokugata hensū
連続型変数

contraband goods
kinseihin
禁制品

contraband trade
mitsuyu bōeki
密輸貿易

contract curve
keiyaku kyokusen
契約曲線

contract immigrant labour
keiyaku imin rōdō
契約移民労働

contraction
(cutbacks)
shukushō
縮小

(process)
shukushō katei
縮小過程

(shrinkage)
shūshuku
収縮

contractionary phase
shūshuku kyokumen
収縮局面

contractual wages
kyōtei chingin
協定賃金

contributions (paid to
government)
kyoshutsukin
拠出金

control
tōsei
統制

control of inflation
infure yokusei
インフレ抑制

controlled economy
tōsei keizai
統制経済

controlled trade
tōsei bōeki
統制貿易

convergence
shūsoku
収束

convertibility
(conversion)
dakansei
兌換性

(exchangeability)
kōkansei
交換性

co-operation
kyōdō
協同
kyōryoku
協力

co-operative
kyōdō kumiai
協同組合

co-operative world trade
kyōryokuteki sekai bōeki
協力的世界貿易

co-ordination
chōwa
調和

corporate capitalism
kigyō shihon shugi
企業資本主義

corporate growth
kigyō seichō
企業成長

corporate income tax
hōjin shotokuzei
法人所得税

corporate saving
hōjin chochiku
法人貯蓄

corporate state
kigyō kokka
企業国家

corporate tax
hōjinzei
法人税

corporations
kigyō
企業

correlation
sōkan
相関

cost
kosuto
コスト

(prime cost)
genka
原価

(expenses)
hiyō
費用

cost analysis
genka bunseki
原価分析

cost behaviour
genka kōdō
原価行動

cost/benefit analysis
hiyō-ben'eki bunseki
費用・便益分析

cost/benefit ratio
hiyō-ben'eki hiritsu
費用・便益比率

cost-consciousness
genka ishiki
原価意識

cost control
genka kanri
原価管理

cost curve
hiyō kyokusen
費用曲線

cost-effectiveness
hiyō yūkōdo
費用有効度

cost-effectiveness analysis
hiyō yūkōdo bunseki
費用有効度分析

cost factor
genka yōso
原価要素

cost function
hiyō kansū
費用関数

cost-inflation
kosuto-infurēshon
コスト・インフレーション

cost minimization
hiyō kyokushōka
費用極小化

cost of capital
shihon kosuto
資本コスト

cost of import
yunyū genka
輸入原価

cost of living
seikatsuhi
生活費
seikeihi
生計費

cost-of-living adjustment (COLA)
seikeihi chōsetsu
生計費調節

cost-of-living index
seikeihi shisū
生計費指数

cost-plus pricing
baika keisei
売価形成

cost-price squeeze
genka hikishime
原価引締め

cost/productivity ratio
hiyō-seisanryoku hiritsu
費用・生産力比率

cost-push inflation
kosuto-pusshu-infurēshon
コスト・プッシュ・インフレーション

cost-push theory
kosuto-pusshu riron
コスト・プッシュ理論

cost reduction
genka kirisage
原価切下げ

costs of protection
hogo hiyō
保護費用

Council for Mutual Economic Aid (COMECON)
komekon
コメコン
tōō keizai sōgo enjo kaigi
東欧経済相互援助会議

Council of Economic Advisors (CEA) [US]
daitōryō keizai shimon i'inkai
大統領経済諮問委員会

countercyclical
hanjunkanteki
反循環的

counter-measure
taisaku
対策

countervailing power
taikōryoku
対抗力

country
kuni
国

covering of deficit
akaji hoten
赤字補填

CPI (consumer price index) [US]
shōhisha bukka shisū
消費者物価指数

crash
hōkai
崩壊

crawling inflation
shinobiyoru infurēshon
しのびよるインフレーション

creation of credit
shin'yō sōzō
信用創造

credit
shin'yō
信用

(finance, financing)
kin'yū
金融

(accommodation of funds, financing)
yūshi
融資

credit ceiling
yūshi gendo
融資限度

credit control
shin'yō chōsetsu
信用調節
shin'yō tōsei
信用統制

credit creation
shin'yō sōzō
信用創造

credit crisis
shin'yō kyōkō
信用恐慌

credit demand
jushi
需資
shikin juyō
資金需要

credit inflation
shin'yō infure
信用インフレ

credit markets
kin'yū shijō
金融市場

credit policy
kin'yū seisaku
金融政策

**credit rationing
(limits)**
shin'yō seigen
信用制限

(allocation)
shin'yō wariate
信用割当て

credit relaxation
kin'yū kanwa
金融緩和

credit restraint
shin'yō hikishime
信用引締め

**credit restrictions
(regulations)**
shin'yō kisei
信用規制

(limits)
shin'yō seigen
信用制限

credit squeeze
kin'yū hikishime
金融引締め

creditor nations
saikenkoku
債権国

creeping inflation
shinobiyoru infurēshon
しのびよるインフレーション

**crisis
(critical point)**
kiki
危機

(panic, scare, alarm)
kyōkō
恐慌

criterion
kijun
基準

**crop
(farm products)**
sakumotsu
作物

(harvest)
shūkaku
収穫

crop yield
shūkakudaka
収穫高

cross elasticity of demand
juyō no kōsa kakaku
danryokusei
需要の交差価格
弾力性

cross-section
ōdanmen
横断面

cross-section analysis
ōdanmen bunseki
横断面分析

**cross-section consumption
function**
ōdanmen shōhi kansū
横断面消費関数

cross-subsidy
naibu hojo
内部補助

crowding-out
kuraudingu-auto
クラウディング・
アウト

**CSO (Central Statistical
Office) [UK]**
chūō tōkeitōkyoku
中央統計当局

cultivated land
kōchi
耕地

cultivation
kōsaku
耕作

currency
tsūka
通貨

currency flow
tsūka ryūryō
通貨流量

**current account (national
accounts)**
keijō shūshi kanjō
経常収支勘定

current account balance
keijō shūshi
経常収支

current balance
keijō shūshi
経常収支

current deposits
tōza yokin
当座預金

current economic conditions
genzai no keizai jōsei
現在の経済情勢

current expenditure
keijō shishutsu
経常支出

curve
kyokusen
曲線

custom barrier
kanzei shōheki
関税障壁

customs union
kanzei dōmei
関税同盟

cutbacks
sakugen
削減
shukushō
縮小

cuts
sakugen
削減
shukushō
縮小

cycle
junkan
循環

cyclical
junkanteki
循環的

cyclical fluctuations
keiki hendō
景気変動

cyclical growth
junkanteki seichō
循環的成長

cyclical unemployment
junkanteki shitsugyō
循環的失業

daily necessities
nichiyōhin
日用品

damage cost
songai hiyō
損害費用

data
dēta
データ
shiryō
資料

DCE (domestic credit expansion)
kokunai shin'yō zōkagaku
国内信用増加額

dear money
kōkinri shikin
高金利資金

dear-money policy
kōkinri seisaku
高金利政策

death rate
shibōritsu
死亡率

debt bomb
saimu bakudan
債務爆弾

debt crisis
saimu kiki
債務危機

debt management
kokusai kanri
国債管理

debt-management policy
kokusai kanri seisaku
国債管理政策

debtor nations
saimukoku
債務国
shakkinkoku
借金国

deceleration
donka
鈍化
gensoku
減速

decentralization
bunkenka
分権化

decentralization of power
chihō bunken
地方分権

decentralized decision-taking
bunkenteki seisaku kettei
分権的政策決定

decision
kettei
決定

decision function
kettei kansū
決定関数

decision lag
kettei no ragu
決定のラグ

decision-making
ishi kettei
意思決定

decision-making organ
ishi kettei kikan
意思決定機関

decision rule
kettei gensoku
決定原則

decision theory
ishi ketteiron
意思決定論

decline
(bad business, recession)
fukyō
不況

(drop, fall, slump)
geraku
下落

(downturn)
kakō
下降

(regression, recession)
kōtai
後退

decline in exports
yushutsu no gentai
輸出の減退

decline in prices
bukka geraku
物価下落

decline in production
seisan no genshō
生産の減少

declining industries
shayō sangyō
斜陽産業

decontrol
tōsei teppai
統制撤廃

decrease
genshō
減少

decreasing cost
hiyō teigen
費用逓減

decreasing-cost industry
hiyō teigen sangyō
費用逓減産業

decreasing returns
shūkaku teigen
収穫逓減

decreasing returns to scale
kibo ni kansuru shūkaku teigen
規模に関する収穫逓減

deductions (from salaries)
kōjo
控除

defence-related expenses
bōei kankeihi
防衛関係費

defence spending
bōei shishutsu
防衛支出

deferred rebate system
unchin nobemodoshisei
運賃延戻し制

deficiency payments
fusokubarai
不足払い

deficit
(red figures)
akaji
赤字

(shortage)
fusoku
不足

deficit balance
akaji zandaka
赤字残高

deficit budget
akaji yosan
赤字予算

deficit country
(in the red)
akajikoku
赤字国

(with excess of imports)
nyūchōkoku
入超国

deficit financing
akaji zaisei
赤字財政

deficit on current account
keijō kanjō no akaji
経常勘定の赤字

deficit units
akaji tan'i
赤字単位

deflation
defure
デフレ
defurēshon
デフレーション
tsūka shūshuku
通貨収縮

deflationary gap
defure-gyappu
デフレ・ギャップ

deflationary policy
defure seisaku
デフレ政策

deflationary trend
defure keikō
デフレ傾向

deflationist
defure ronsha
デフレ論者

deflator
defurētā
デフレーター

degradation of the environment
kankyō teika
環境低下

degree of homogeneity (of a function)
dōjiseido
同次性度

degrees of freedom
jiyūdo
自由度

degressive tax
ruigenzei
累減税

deindustrialization
sangyō kūdōka
産業空洞化

demand
juyō
需要

demand backlog
mijūsoku juyō
未充足需要

demand curve
juyō kyokusen
需要曲線

demand-deficient unemployment
juyōfusoku no shitsugyō
需要不足の失業

demand factor
juyō yōin
需要要因

demand for labour
rōdō juyō
労働需要

demand for leisure
yoka juyō
余暇需要

demand for money
kahei juyō
貨幣需要

demand forecast
juyō yosoku
需要予測

demand function
juyō kansū
需要関数

demand increase
juyō zōka
需要増加

demand inflation
juyō infurēshon
需要インフレーション

demand management
juyō kanri
需要管理

demand pressure
juyō atsuryoku
需要圧力

demand-pull inflation
demando-puru-infurēshon
ディマンド・プル・
インフレーション

demand restraint
juyō yokusei
需要抑制

demand schedule
juyōhyō
需要表

demand-shift inflation
demando-shifuto-infurēshon
ディマンド・
シフト・インフレー
ション

demography
jinkō tōkei
人口統計

densely populated areas
jinkō kamitsu chi'iki
人口過密地域
jinkō misshū chi'iki
人口密集地域

density
jinkō no mitsudo
人口の密度

dependence
izon
依存

dependence on exports
yushutsu izon
輸出依存

dependence on foreign trade
gaikoku bōeki izon
外国貿易依存

dependence on imports
yunyū izon
輸入依存

dependence on oil
sekiyu izon
石油依存

dependence rate
izonritsu
依存率

dependent economy
jūzoku keizai
従属経済

dependent variable
jūzoku hensū
従属変数

depopulation
jinkō genshō
人口減少

deposit/loan ratio
yokin-kashitsuke hiritsu
預金・貸付比率
yotaihiritsu
預貸比率

depreciation
genka
減価

(currency)
tsūka kachi geraku
通貨価値下落

depressed areas
fukyō chi'iki
不況地域

**depressed businesses and
industries**
fukyō gyōshu
不況業種

depressed industries
fukyō sangyō
不況産業

depressed market
fushin shikyō
不振市況

depressed regions
fukyō chi'iki
不況地域

depressed times
fukeiki na toki
不景気な時

depression
(hard times)
fukeiki
不景気

(recession, slump)
fukyō
不況

(regression, recession)
keiki kōtai
景気後退

deregulate
kisei o teppai suru
規制を撤廃する

deregulation
kisei teppai
規制撤廃

deregulation policy
kisei teppai seisaku
規制撤廃政策

derivative (noun)
dōkansū
導関数

derived demand
hasei juyō
派生需要

destabilization
fuanteika
不安定化

destabilizing effect
fuantei kōka
不安定効果

destabilizing factor
fuantei yōin
不安定要因

destruction of the environment
kankyō hakai
環境破壊

destructive competition
hakaiteki kyōsō
破壊的競争

deterioration
akka
悪化

**deterioration of the
environment**
kankyō akka
環境悪化

determinant
kettei yōin
決定要因

devaluation
heika kirisage
平価切下げ

develop
kaihatsu suru
開発する

developed countries
senshinkoku
先進国

developing countries
hatten tojōkoku
発展途上国
kaihatsu tojōkoku
開発途上国

developing regions
hatten tojō chi'iki
発展途上地域

**development
(expansion, growth)**
hatten
発展

(exploitation)
kaihatsu
開発

(progress, evolution)
shinten
進展

development aid
kaihatsu enjo
開発援助

development areas
kaihatsu chi'iki
開発地域

development finance
kaihatsu kin'yū
開発金融

development gap
kaihatsu kakusa
開発格差

development planning
kaihatsu keikaku
開発計画

development programme
kaihatsu keikaku
開発計画

development strategy
kaihatsu senryaku
開発戦略

deviation
hensa
偏差

**difference between domestic
and foreign interest rates**
naigai kinrisa
内外金利差

difference equation
sabun hōteishiki
差分方程式

difference principle
sabun genri
差分原理

differentials
chingin kakusa
賃金格差

**differentiation
(function)**
bibun
微分

(production)
sabetsuka
差別化

difficult times
konnan na jiki
困難な時期

diffusion
fukyū
普及

diminishing marginal utility
genkai kōyō teigen
限界効用逓減

direct costs
chokusetsuhi
直接費

direct expenses
chokusetsu keihi
直接経費

direct export
chokuyushutsu
直輸出

direct exporters
chokuyushutsushō
直輸出商

direct exports
chokuyushutsuhin
直輸出品

direct import
chokuyunyū
直輸入

direct importers
chokuyunyūshō
直輸入商

direct imports
chokuyunyūhin
直輸入品

direct investment
chokusetsu tōshi
直接投資

direct taxation
chokusetsuzei
直接税

direct taxes
chokusetsuzei
直接税

directive
shirei
指令

disagreement on policy
seisakujō no iken no sōi
政策上の意見の相違

disaster indemnity
saigai hoshō
災害補償

**disaster reconstruction
expenses**
saigai fukkyū tōjigyōhi
災害復旧等事業費

disaster relief
saigai fukkyū
災害復旧

disbursement
shishutsu
支出

discharges (employment)
kaikoritsu
解雇率

discount rate policy
waribiki buai seisaku
割引歩合政策

discounting
waribiki
割引

discriminating monopoly
sabetsu dokusen
差別独占

discrimination
sabetsu
差別

discriminatory pricing
sabetsuteki kakaku keisei
差別的価格形成

diseconomies of growth
seichō no fukeizai
成長の不経済

diseconomies of scale
kibo no fukeizai
規模の不経済

diseconomy
fukeizai
不経済

disequilibrium
fukinkō
不均衡

disguised unemployment
gisō shitsugyō
偽装失業

disincentive
hiyūin
非誘因
kujiku mono
くじくもの

disinflation
disinfurēshon
ディスインフレーション

disinvestment
shihonzai no genshō
資本財の減少

displacement effect
ten'i kōka
転位効果

disposable income
kashobun shotoku
可処分所得

dissaving
fu no chochiku
負の貯蓄

distortions
hizumi
歪み

distributed lags
bunpu no ragu
分布のラグ

distribution
bunpai
分配

(theory of)
bunpai no riron
分配の理論
bunpairon
分配論

distribution function
bunpai kinō
分配機能

distribution market
ryūtsū shijō
流通市場

distribution sector
ryūtsū bumon
流通部門

disutility
fukōyō
不効用

(negative utility)
fu no kōyō
負の効用

diversification
tayōka
多様化

division of labour
bungyō
分業

dole (to be on the)
shitsugyō teate (o ukeru)
失業手当(を受ける)

domestic and foreign demand
naigaiju
内外需

domestic business picture
kokunai keikyō
国内景況

domestic capital formation
kokunai shihon keisei
国内資本形成

domestic competition
kokunai kyōsō
国内競争

domestic consumption
kokunai shōhi
国内消費

domestic credit expansion (DCE)
kokunai shin'yō zōkagaku
国内信用増加額

domestic demand
kokunai juyō
国内需要
naiju
内需

domestic economy
kokunai keizai
内需経済

domestic industry
kokunai sangyō
国内産業

domestic investment
kokunai tōshi
国内投資

domestic market
kokunai shijō
国内市場

domestic policy
kokunai seisaku
国内政策

domestic production
kokunai seisan
国内生産

domestic products
kokusanpin
国産品

domestic trade
naikoku bōeki
内国貿易

double counting
nijū keisan
二重計算

double-digit
futaketa no
二桁の

double-digit inflation
futaketa no infurēshon
二桁のインフレー
ション

double-digit unemployment
futaketa no shitsugyō
二桁の失業

double-income families
tomokasegi katei
共稼ぎ家庭

double switching
saitenkan
再転換

double taxation
nijū kazei
二重課税

downswing
kakō
下降

downtrend
kakō keikō
下降傾向

downturn
kakō
下降

downward phase
kakō kyokumen
下降局面

draft budget
yosan gen'an
予算原案

driving force
kudōryoku
駆動力

drop in prices
nesage
値下げ

drop in private investment
minkan tōshi no genshō
民間投資の減少

drought
kanbatsu
旱魃

dual economy
nijū keizai
二重経済

dual-labour-market hypothesis
nijū rōdō shijō kasetsu
二重労働市場仮説

dualism (theory of)
nijū keizairon
二重経済論

duality
nijūsei
二重性

dumping
danpingu
ダンピング

duopoly
fukusen
複占

duopsony
juyō fukusen
需要複占

durable consumer goods
taikyū shōhizai
耐久消費財
taikyūzai
耐久財

durables
taikyū shōhizai
耐久消費財
taikyūzai
耐久財

duration of unemployment
shitsugyō kikan
失業期間

dutiable goods
yūzeihin
有税品

duties (tariffs)
kanzei
関税

duty-free goods
menzeihin
免税品

duty-free imports
menzei yunyūhin
免税輸入品

dying industries
shayō sangyō
斜陽産業

dynamic economics
dōtaiteki keizaigaku
動態的経済学

dynamic economy
dōtaiteki keizai
動態的経済

dynamic growth
dōtaiteki seichō
動態的成長

dynamic model
dōgaku moderu
動学モデル

dynamics
dōgaku
動学

earmarking
shitei
指定

earned income
kinrō shotoku
勤労所得

earning lag
shūnyū no ragu
収入のラグ

earnings (= income)
shotoku
所得

earnings drift
shotoku dorifuto
所得ドリフト

earnings function
shotoku kansū
所得関数

earnings-related benefits
chingin hirei kyūfu
賃金比例給付

easing of restrictions
kisei kanwa
規制緩和

easy money
kanwa na kin'yū
緩和な金融
teikinri shikin
低金利資金

easy-money policy
(financial relaxation)
kin'yū kanwa seisaku
金融緩和政策

(low interests)
teikinri seisaku
低金利政策

easy-money times
kin'yū kanwaki
金融緩和期

EC (European Community)
ōshū kyōdōtai
欧州共同体

ECAFE (Economic
Commission for Asia and
the Far East)
ajia kyokutō keizai i'inkai
アジア極東経済
委員会

ECE (Economic Commission
for Europe) (= United Nations
Economic Commission for
Europe)
ōshū keizai i'inkai
欧州経済委員会

ecologist
seitaigakusha
生態学者

ecology
seitaigaku
生態学

econometric model
keiryō keizai moderu
計量経済モデル

econometric model analysis
keiryō keizai moderu
bunseki
計量経済モデル分析

econometrics
keiryō keizaigaku
計量経済学

economic activity
keizai katsudō
経済活動

economic adviser
keizai komon
経済顧問

economic affairs
keizai jijō
経済事情

economic ailments
keizai no manbyō
経済の万病

economic analysis
keizai dōkō bunseki
経済動向分析

Economic and Monetary
Union
(ōshū) keizai tsūka dōmei
(欧州) 経済通貨同盟

Economic and Social Council
(ECOSOC)
keizai shakai rijikai
経済社会理事会

economic barometer
keizai kansoku shihyō
経済観測指標
keizai shihyō
経済指標

economic base
keizai kiban
経済基盤

economic base multiplier
keizai kiban jōsū
経済基盤乗数

economic block
keizai burokku
経済ブロック

economic blockade
keizai fūsa
経済封鎖

economic centre
keizai katsudō no chūshin
経済活動の中心

economic climate
keizai jōsei
経済情勢

Economic Commission for
Asia and the Far East (ECAFE)
ajia kyokutō keizai i'inkai
アジア極東経済
委員会

Economic Commission for
Europe (ECE) (= United
Nations Economic
Commission for Europe)
ōshū keizai i'inkai
欧州経済委員会

economic community
keizaikai
経済界

economic competition
keizai kyōsō
経済競争

economic conditions
keizai jōkyō
経済状況
keizai jōsei
経済情勢

economic co-operation
keizai kyōryoku
経済協力

economic crisis
(critical moment)
keizai kiki
経済危機

(panic, scare)
keizai kyōkō
経済恐慌

economic cycle
keizai junkan
経済循環

economic development
(expansion)
keizai hatten
経済発展

(exploitation)
keizai kaihatsu
経済開発

Economic Development
Committee [UK]
kokumin keizai hatten
shingikai
国民経済発展審議会

economic dynamics
keizai dōgaku
経済動学

economic efficiency
keizai kōritsu
経済効率

economic expansion
keizai kakuchō
経済拡張

economic fluctuations
keizai hendō
経済変動

economic force
keizai katsuryoku
経済活力

economic forecast
(observation)
keizai kansoku
経済観測

(prediction)
keizai yosoku
経済予測

economic freedom
keizaiteki jiyū
経済的自由

economic frontiers
keizaiteki shinkaichi
経済的新開地

economic good
keizaizai
経済財

economic growth
keizai seichō
経済成長

economic growth rate
keizai seichōritsu
経済成長率

economic hardship
keizaiteki kunan
経済的苦難

economic history
keizaishi
経済史

economic imperialism
keizaiteki teikoku shugi
経済的帝国主義

economic improvements
keizai kaikaku
経済改革

economic indicators
keizai shihyō
経済指標

economic infrastructure
keizai kiso kiban
経済基礎基盤

economic injustices
keizaiteki fukōsei
経済的不公正

economic instability
keizaiteki fuanteisei
経済的不安定性

economic integration
keizai tōgō
経済統合

economic internationalism
keizaiteki kokusai shugi
経済的国際主義

economic liberalism
keizaiteki jiyū shugi
経済的自由主義

economic magazine
keizai zasshi
経済雑誌

economic man
keizaijin
経済人

economic management
keizai un'ei
経済運営

economic measures
keizai sochi
経済措置

economic mission
keizai shisetsudan
経済使節団

economic model
keizai moderu
経済モデル

economic nationalism
keizaiteki kokumin shugi
経済的国民主義

economic order
keizai chitsujo
経済秩序

economic organization
keizai soshiki
経済組織

economic outlook
keizai mitōshi
経済見通し

economic parasites
keizaiteki kiseichū
経済的寄生虫

economic penetration
keizaiteki shinshutsu
経済的進出

economic planning
keizai keikaku
経済計画

economic policy
keizai seisaku
経済政策

economic policy co-ordination
keizai seisaku chōsei
経済政策調整

economic power
keizairyoku
経済力

economic pressure
keizaiteki atsuryoku
経済的圧力

economic principle
keizai gensoku
経済原則

economic problems
keizai mondai
経済問題

economic progress
keizai shinpo
経済進歩

economic prospects
keizai mitōshi
経済見通し

economic question
keizai mondai
経済問題

economic realities
keizai no jittai
経済の実態

economic reality
keizaiteki genjitsu
経済的現実

economic recovery
keizai kaifuku
経済回復

economic reform
keizai kaikaku
経済改革

economic rent
keizai chidai
経済地代

economic report
keizai hōkokusho
経済報告書

economic research
keizai kenkyū
経済研究

economic research institute
keizai kenkyūjo
経済研究所

economic sanctions
keizaiteki seisai
経済的制裁

economic scene
keizai jōsei
経済情勢

economic sector
keizai bumon
経済部門

economic stabilization
keizai antei
経済安定

economic statistics
keizai tōkei
経済統計

economic strength
keizairyoku
経済力

economic summit
keizai shunō kaigi
経済首脳会議

economic superpower
keizai taikoku
経済大国

economic support
keizai enjo
経済援助

economic survey
keizai chōsa
経済調査

economic system
keizai taisei
経済体制

economic tasks
keizai no kadai
経済の課題

economic theory
keizai riron
経済理論

economic theory of politics
seiji no keizai riron
政治の経済理論

economic thought
keizai shisō
経済思想

economic trend
keizai dōkō
経済動向

economic union
keizai dōmei
経済同盟

economic unit
keizai tan'i
経済単位

economic unity
keizai tōitsu
経済統一

economic value
keizai kachi
経済価値

economic volatility
keizai hendō
経済変動

economic warfare
keizai sensō
経済戦争

economic welfare
(economic well-being)
keizai fukushi
経済福祉

(social welfare)
keizai kōsei
経済厚生

economic white paper
keizai hakusho
経済白書

economic world
keizaikai
経済界

economically viable
jiritsu kei'ei no
自立経営の

economics
keizaigaku
経済学

economics of consumption
shōhi keizaigaku
消費経済学

economics of growth
seichō no keizaigaku
成長の経済学

economics of high wages
kōchingin no keizaigaku
高賃金の経済学

economies of scale
kibo no keizai
規模の経済

economies of scope
han'i no keizai
範囲の経済

economist
ekonomisuto
エコノミスト
keizaigakusha
経済学者

economy
keizai
経済

ECOSOC (Economic and Social Council)
keizai shakai rijikai
経済社会理事会

ECSC (European Coal and Steel Community)
ōshū sekitan tekkō kyōdōtai
欧州石炭鉄鋼共同体

education
kyōiku
教育

education expenditure
kyōikuhi
教育費

EEC (European Economic Community)
ōshū keizai kyōdōtai
欧州経済共同体

effect
(influence)
eikyō
影響

(result)
kekka
結果

(effectiveness)
kōka
効果

effective competition
yūkō kyōsō
有効競争

effective demand
yūkō juyō
有効需要

effective price
jikkō kakaku
実効価格

effective rate of production
yūkō seisanritsu
有効生産率

efficiency
nōritsu
能率

efficiency earnings
nōritsu shotoku
能率所得

efficiency units
nōritsu tan'i
能率単位

efficiency wages
nōritsu chingin
能率賃金

EFTA (European Free Trade Association)
ōshū jiyū bōeki rengō
欧州自由貿易連合

EIB (European Investment Bank) [EC]
ōshū tōshi ginkō
欧州投資銀行

elastic currency [US]
danryokuteki tsūka
弾力的通貨

elastic demand
danryokuteki juyō
弾力的需要

elastic supply
danryokuteki kyōkyū
弾力的供給

elasticity
danryokusei
弾力性

elasticity of demand
juyō no danryokusei
需要の弾力性

elasticity of substitution
daitai no danryokusei
代替の弾力性

elasticity of supply
kyōkyū no danryokusei
供給の弾力性

EMA (European Monetary Agreement)
ōshū tsūka kyōtei
欧州通貨協定

embargo
(trade)
tsūshō kinshi
通商禁止

(exports)
yushutsu kinshi
輸出禁止

embargo goods
kin'yu shōhin
禁輸商品
kin'yuhin
禁輸品

embodied technical progress
taika sareta gijutsu shinpo
体化された技術進歩

emergency
kinkyū
緊急

emergency imports
kinkyū yunyū
緊急輸入

emergency measures
kinkyū sochi
緊急措置

emigrant
imin
移民

emigration
ijū
移住

empire
teikoku
帝国

employed, the
hikoyōsha
被雇用者

employers
koyōsha
雇用者

employers' associations [UK]
kei'eisha no renmei
経営者の連盟

employers' federations
kei'eisha no renmei
経営者の連盟

employment
koyō
雇用

Employment Act
koyōhō
雇用法

employment adjustment
koyō chōsei
雇用調整

employment exchange statistics
shokugyō shōkai tōkei
職業紹介統計

employment figures
shūgyō tōkei
就業統計

employment-generating measures
koyō sokushinsaku
雇用促進策

employment index
koyō shisū
雇用指数

employment migration
koyō imin
雇用移民

employment multiplier
koyō jōsū
雇用乗数

employment opportunities
koyō kikai
雇用機会

employment policy
koyō seisaku
雇用政策

employment practices
koyō kankō
雇用慣行

employment rate
koyōritsu
雇用率

employment situation
koyō jōsei
雇用情勢

employment statistics
koyō tōkei
雇用統計

employment subsidies
koyō hojokin
雇用補助金

EMS (European Monetary System)
ōshū tsūka seido
欧州通貨制度

EMU (European Monetary Union)
ōshū tsūka dōmei
欧州通貨同盟

energy
enerugii
エネルギー

energy conservation
enerugii hogo
エネルギー保護

energy consumption
enerugii shōhi
エネルギー消費

engagements (= new hires)
nyūshokuritsu
入職率

enlarged EC
kakudai kyōdō shijō
拡大共同市場

enquiry
ankēto chōsa
アンケート調査

**enterprise
(undertaking, project)**
jigyō
事業

(business, company)
kigyō
企業

enterprise culture
kigyō bunka
企業文化

entitlement principle
fukushi jukyū tokuten gensoku
福祉受給特典原則

**entrepreneur
(business person)**
jigyōka
事業家

(person of enterprise)
kigyōka
企業家

entrepreneur spirit
kigyōka seishin
企業家精神
kigyōshin
企業心

entrepreneurship
kigyōka seishin
企業家精神
kigyōshin
企業心

environment
kankyō
環境

environmental abuse
kankyō ran'yō
環境濫用

environmental clean-up
kankyō jōka
環境浄化

environmental conditions
kankyō jōken
環境条件

environmental crisis
kankyō kiki
環境危機

environmental determinism
kankyō ketteiron
環境決定論

environmental disaster
kankyō saigai
環境災害

environmental impact analysis
kankyō hyōka
環境評価

environmental issues
kankyō mondai
環境問題

environmental policy
kankyō seisaku
環境政策

environmental pollution
kankyō osen
環境汚染

environmental pollution cost
kankyō kosuto
環境コスト

environmental reform
kankyō kaikaku
環境改革

environmental research
kankyō chōsa
環境調査

environmentalist
kankyō shugisha
環境主義者

equal advantage
rieki kintō
利益均等

equal employment law
danjo koyō byōdōhō
男女雇用平等法

equal employment opportunity
koyō kikai kintō
雇用機会均等

Equal Employment
Opportunity Act [US]
koyō kikai kintōhō
雇用機会均等法

Equal Employment
Opportunity Commission
[US]
koyō kikai kintō i'inkai
雇用機会均等委員会

equal opportunity
kikai kintō
機会均等

equal-opportunity employer
[UK]
kikai kintō koyōsha
機会均等雇用者

equal pay
dōitsu chingin
同一賃金

equal pay for equal work
dōitsu rōdō dōitsu chingin
同一労働同一賃金

equalization grants
heikō kōfukin
平衡交付金

equilibrium
kinkō
均衡

equilibrium level of national
income
kinkō kokumin shotoku
均衡国民所得

equilibrium price
kinkō kakaku
均衡価格

equilibrium quantity
kinkōryō
均衡量

equilibrium rate of inflation
kinkō infureritsu
均衡インフレ率

equitable world trade
kōsei sekai bōeki
公正世界貿易

equity (concept of justice)
kōhei
公平

equivalence scale
tōka kibo
等価規模

ERDF (European Regional
Development Fund)
ōshū chi'iki kaihatsu kikin
欧州地域開発基金

ergonomics
āgonomikkusu
アーゴノミックス
ningen kōgaku
人間工学

error
gosa
誤差

escalators
esukarētā jōkō
エスカレーター条項

escape clause
menseki jōkō
免責条項

essential goods
hitsujuhin
必需品

essential industries
jūyō sangyō
重要産業

estimates
suiteiryō
推定量

estimation (assumption)
suitei
推定

estimator
suiteishi
推定子

European Coal and Steel
Community (ECSC)
ōshū sekitan tekkō kyōdōtai
欧州石炭鉄鋼共同体

European Commission
ōshū i'inkai
欧州委員会

European Community (EC)
ōshū kyōdōtai
欧州共同体

European Development Fund
ōshū kaihatsu kikin
欧州開発基金

European Economic
Community (EEC)
ōshū keizai kyōdōtai
欧州経済共同体

European Economic
Community Budget
ōshū keizai kyōdōtai yosan
欧州経済共同体予算

European Free Trade Area
ōshū jiyū bōeki chi'iki
欧州自由貿易地域

European Free Trade
Association (EFTA)
ōshū jiyū bōeki rengō
欧州自由貿易連合

European Fund
ōshū kikin
欧州基金

European Investment Bank
(EIB) [EC]
ōshū tōshi ginkō
欧州投資銀行

European Monetary
Agreement (EMA)
ōshū tsūka kyōtei
欧州通貨協定

European Monetary System
(EMS)
ōshū tsūka seido
欧州通貨制度

European Monetary Union
(EMU)
ōshū tsūka dōmei
欧州通貨同盟

European Regional
Development Fund (ERDF)
ōshū chi'iki kaihatsu kikin
欧州地域開発基金

ex ante
jizenteki
事前的

ex post
jigoteki
事後的

excess
(surplus)
chōka
超過

(overabundance)
kajō
過剰

excess capacity
kajō nōryoku
過剰能力

(plant and equipment)
kajō setsubi
過剰設備

excess demand
chōka juyō
超過需要
kajō juyō
過剰需要

excess of exports
yushutsu chōka
輸出超過

excess of imports
yunyū chōka
輸入超過

excess supply
kyōkyū kajō
供給過剰

excess supply capacity
kyōkyū yoryoku
供給余力

excessive competition
katō kyōsō
過当競争

excessive exports
kajō yushutsu
過剰輸出

excessive imports
nyūchō
入超
yunyū chōka
輸入超過

exchange
(foreign exchange)
kawase (gaikoku kawase)
為替 (外国為替)

(place of trading)
torihikijo
取引所

Exchequer, the [UK]
kokko
国庫

exclusion
haijo
排除
haita
排他

exclusion principle
haita gensoku
排他原則

exclusive dealing
haitateki torihiki
排他的取引

exhaustion of resources
shigen no kokatsu
資源の枯渇

expand
kakudai suru
拡大する

expanding industry
kakkyō sangyō
活況産業

expansion
(enlargement, extension)
kakuchō
拡張

(augmentation, magnification)
kakudai
拡大

expansion path
kakuchō keiro
拡張経路

expansionary
kakuchōteki
拡張的
kakudaiteki
拡大的

expansionary phase
kakuchō kyokumen
拡張局面

expansionist policy
kakudai seisaku
拡大政策

expatriates
(employees posted abroad)
kaigai chūzaiin
海外駐在員

(residents abroad)
kokugai zaijūsha
国外在住者

expectations
kitai
期待

expectations lag
kitai no ragu
期待のラグ

expected inflation
yosō infureritsu
予想インフレ率

expected rate of economic growth
yosō keizai seichōritsu
予想経済成長率

expected value
kitaichi
期待値

expedience (expediency)
bengi
便宜

expedient
rinji no sochi
臨時の措置

expenditure
shishutsu
支出

(in Treasury's accounts)
saishutsu
歳出

expenditure lag
shishutsu no ragu
支出のラグ

expenditure-switching policies
shishutsu tenkan seisaku
支出転換政策

expenditure tax
shishutsuzei
支出税

explanatory variable
setsumei hensū
説明変数

explicit function
yōkansū
陽関数

exploitation
(development)
kaihatsu
開発

(of people)
sakushu
搾取

exploitation theory
sakushusetsu
搾取説

exponential function
shisū kansū
指数関数

export (noun)
yushutsu
輸出

export (verb)
yushutsu suru
輸出する

export and import price indexes
yushutsunyū bukka shisū
輸出入物価指数

export ban
yushutsu kinshi
輸出禁止

export boom
yushutsu būmu
輸出ブーム

export bounties
yushutsu joseikin
輸出助成金
yushutsu shōreikin
輸出奨励金

export businesses
yushutsugyō
輸出業

export capacity
yushutsu yoryoku
輸出余力

export-centred enterprises
yushutsu shudō kigyō
輸出主導企業

export-centred industries
yushutsu shudō sangyō
輸出主導産業

export credit
yushutsu shin'yō
輸出信用

Export Credits Guarantee Department [UK]
yushutsu shin'yō hoshō-kyoku
輸出信用保証局

export data
yushutsu shiryō
輸出資料

export demand
yushutsu juyō
輸出需要

export drive
yushutsu shinkōsaku
輸出振興策

export duties
yushutsu kanzei
輸出関税
yushutsuzei
輸出税

export earnings
yushutsu shotoku
輸出所得

export finance
yushutsu kin'yū
輸出金融

export firms
yushutsu gyōsha
輸出業者

export goods
yushutsuhin
輸出品

export incentives
yushutsu shōrei
輸出奨励

export-intensive industries
yushutsu shūyakuteki sangyō
輸出集約的産業

export-led growth
yushutsu senkōgata seichō
輸出先行型成長

export market
yushutsu shijō
輸出市場

export of technology
gijutsu yushutsu
技術輸出

export-oriented industry
yushutsu shikō sangyō
輸出指向産業

export price index
yushutsu bukka shisū
輸出物価指数

export promotion
yushutsu sokushin
輸出促進

export quota
yushutsu wariate
輸出割当て

export rebates
yushutsu waribiki
輸出割引

export restrictions
yushutsu seigen
輸出制限

export subsidies
yushutsu hojokin
輸出補助金

export surplus
shutchō
出超

export trade
yushutsu bōeki
輸出貿易

export volume
yushutsuryō
輸出量

export without foreign exchange
mugawase yushutsu
無為替輸出

exporters
(individual firms)
yushutsu gyōsha
輸出業者

(countries)
yushutsukoku
輸出国

exporting country
yushutsukoku
輸出国

exports
yushutsuhin
輸出品

extensive development
gaienteki hatten
外延的発展

extensive margin
sohō genkai
粗放限界

external balance
kokusai kinkō
国際均衡
taigai kinkō
対外均衡

external convertibility
taigai kōkansei
対外交換性

external debt
taigai saimu
対外債務

external deficit
kokusai shūshi no akaji
国際収支の赤字

external diseconomies
gaibu fukeizai
外部不経済

external economies
gaibu keizai
外部経済

external economies and diseconomies of scale
gaibu keizai to kibo no fukeizai
外部経済と規模の不経済

external growth
gaibu seichō
外部成長

external imbalances
taigai fukinkō
対外不均衡

external labour market
gaibu rōdō shijō
外部労働市場

external reserve
gaika junbi
外貨準備

external surplus
kaigai yojō
海外余剰

external trade
taigai bōeki
対外貿易

externalities
gaibu kōka
外部効果

extraordinary budget
rinji yosan
臨時予算

factor
(cause, origin)
gen'in
原因

(primary factor)
yōin
要因

(essential element, requisite)
yōso
要素

factor analysis
yōin bunseki
要因分析

factor-augmenting technical progress
yōso zōdaiteki gijutsu kakushin
要素増大的技術革新

factor cost
yōso hiyō
要素費用

factor incomes
yōso shotoku
要素所得

factor payments
yōso shiharai
要素支払い

factor price
yōso kakaku
要素価格

factor-price differentials
yōso kakakusa
要素価格差

factor-price frontier
yōso kakaku henkyōsen
要素価格辺境線

factor reversal
yōso tenkan
要素転換

factor utilization
yōso riyō
要素利用

factors of production
seisan yōso
生産要素

fair competition
kōsei kyōsō
公正競争

fair price
kōsei kakaku
公正価格

fair trade
(international)
kōsei bōeki
公正貿易

(transaction)
kōsei torihiki
公正取引

fair trade agreement
kōsei torihiki kyōtei
公正取引協定

Fair Trade Commission (FTC)
kōsei torihiki i'inkai
公正取引委員会

Fair Trade Law [US]
kōsei torihikihō
公正取引法

fair trade policy
kōsei torihiki seisaku
公正取引政策

fair trade practices
kōsei torihiki kanshū
公正取引慣習

Fair Trading Act [UK]
kōsei torihikihō
公正取引法

fair wages
kōsei chingin
公正賃金

families living in poverty
hinkon kazoku
貧困家族

Family Expenditure Survey [UK]
kakei shishutsu chōsa
家計支出調査

family income
kakei shotoku
家計所得

family-unit agriculture
jika nōgyō
自家農業

FAO (United Nations Food and Agriculture Organization)
shokuryō nōgyō kikō
食料農業機構

farm aid programmes
nōgyō enjo keikaku
農業援助計画

farm economy
nōka keizai
農家経済

farm household economic survey
nōka keizai chōsa
農家経済調査

farm households
nōka
農家

farm mechanization
nōgyō kikaika
農業機械化

farm price support policy
nōsanbutsu kakaku shiji seisaku
農産物価格支持政策

farm prices
nōsanbutsu kakaku
農産物価格

farm subsidies
nōsanbutsu kakaku shiji hojokin
農産物価格支持補助金

farm workers
nōgyō rōdōsha
農業労働者

farmers
nōmin
農民

farmers' co-operatives
nōka kyōdō kumiai
農家協同組合

farming income
nōgyō shūnyū
農業収入

farming population
nōgyō jinkō
農業人口

favourable balance of payments
kokusai shūshi no kuroji
国際収支の黒字

favourable balance of trade (black figures)
bōeki shūshi no kuroji
貿易収支の黒字

(export surplus)
yushutsu chōka
輸出超過

favourable factors
kōten yōin
好転要因

feasibility study
kanōsei no kentō
可能性の検討

featherbedding
mizumashi koyō
水増し雇用

Federation of Economic Organizations [J]
keidanren (keizai dantai rengōkai)
経団連 (経済団体連合会)

female labour
joshi rōdōsha
女子労働者

female labour force
joshi rōdōryoku
女子労働力

female working population
josei rōdō jinkō
女性労働人口

figures
sūji
数字

final consumer
saishū shōhisha
最終消費者

final consumption
saishū shōhi
最終消費

final demand
saishū juyō
最終需要

final goods
saishū seihin
最終製品

final products
saishū seihin
最終製品
saishū seisanbutsu
最終生産物

final supply
saishū kyōkyū
最終供給

finance minister
zōsō
蔵相

financial activity
kin'yū katsudō
金融活動

financial adviser
zaisei komon
財政顧問

financial affairs
zaimu
財務

financial crisis
zaisei kiki
財政危機

financial deregulation
kin'yū kanwa
金融緩和

financial inducements
kin'yūjō no yūgū sochi
金融上の優遇措置

financial liberalization
kin'yū jiyūka
金融自由化

financial machinery
kin'yū kikō
金融機構

financial markets
kin'yū shijō
金融市場

financial model
kin'yū moderu
金融モデル

financial operations
kin'yū sōsa
金融操作

financial reconstruction
zaisei tatenaoshi
財政建直し

financial regulation
kin'yū kisei
金融規制

financial revolution
kin'yū kakumei
金融革命

financial structure
kin'yū kōzō
金融構造

financial system
kin'yū taikei
金融体系

financial year [UK]
kaikei nendo
会計年度

financing
  (procurement)
  chōtatsu
  調達

  (banking, finance)
  kin'yū
  金融

  (credit facility, loan)
  yūshi
  融資

financing operations
kin'yū chōtatsu sōsa
金融調達操作

findings
chōsa kekka
調査結果

finetuning
bichōsei
微調整

finished goods
seihin
製品

firms
  (companies)
  kaisha
  会社

  (businesses)
  kigyō
  企業

first half of the year
kamihanki
上半期

first quarter
dai'ichi shihanki
第一四半期

fiscal and monetary policy
zaisei-kin'yū seisaku
財政・金融政策

fiscal budget
zaisei yosan
財政予算

fiscal burden
zaisei futan
財政負担

fiscal drag
zaiseiteki hadome
財政的歯止め

fiscal expenditure
zaisei shishutsu
財政支出

fiscal funds
zaisei shikin
財政資金

fiscal investments and loans
zaisei tōyūshi
財政投融資

fiscal multiplier
zaisei jōsū
財政乗数

fiscal policy
zaisei seisaku
財政政策

fiscal revenue
zaisei shūnyū
財政収入

fiscal revenue and
expenditure
zaisei shūshi
財政収支

fiscal year [US] [UK government]
kaikei nendo
会計年度

fishermen
gyogyōsha
漁業者

fishery co-operatives
gyogyō rōdō kumiai
漁業労働組合

fishing
gyogyō
漁業

fishing rights
gyogyōken
漁業権

fixed capital
kotei shihon
固定資本

fixed costs
koteihi
固定費

fixed factors
kotei yōin
固定要因

fixed income
kotei shūnyū
固定収入

fixed labour costs
kotei rōdō kosuto
固定労働コスト

fixed proportions in production
seisan kotei hiritsu
生産固定比率

fixed targets
meikaku na mokuhyō
明確な目標

**floating debt
(floating liabilities)**
ryūdō fusai
流動負債

(short-term government debt)
tanki kōsai
短期公債

flood disaster
suigai
水害

flood disaster relief
suigai taisaku
水害対策

floor (trade cycle)
soko
底

flow
furō
フロー

flow analysis
furō bunseki
フロー分析

flow of funds
shikin junkan
資金循環

flow of funds accounts
shikin junkan kanjō
資金循環勘定

flow of funds analysis
shikin junkan bunseki
資金循環分析

**fluctuations
(ups and downs)**
agarisagari
上がり下がり

(changes)
hendō
変動

**Food and Agriculture
Organization (FAO)
(= United Nations Food and
Agriculture Organization)**
shokuryō nōgyō kikō
食料農業機構

food shortage
shokuryō fusoku
食料不足

footloose industries
ritchi jōken ni kōsoku
sarenai sangyō
立地条件に拘束
されない産業

forced labour
kyōsei rōdō
強制労働

forced saving
kyōsei chochiku
強制貯蓄

**forecast (noun)
(expectation)**
yosō
予想

(prediction)
yosoku
予測

forecast (verb)
yosō suru
予想する
yosoku suru
予測する

forecaster
yosokuka
予測家

forecasting
yosoku seido
予測制度

forecasting model
yosoku moderu
予測モデル

foreign aid
taigai enjo
対外援助

foreign-aid programme
taigai enjo keikaku
対外援助計画

foreign assets
gaikoku shisan
外国資産

foreign balance
taigai baransu
対外バランス

foreign borrowings
taigai kariire
対外借入れ

foreign capital
gaishi
外資

foreign-capital import
gaishi yunyū
外資輸入

foreign competition
gaikoku kara no kyōsō
外国からの競争

foreign corporations
gaikoku gaisha
外国会社
gaikoku kigyō
外国企業

foreign currency
gaika
外貨

foreign currency deposits
gaika yokin
外貨預金

foreign debt
(foreign bond)
gaisai
外債

(external debt)
taigai saimu
対外債務

foreign demand
gaiju
外需

foreign economic situation
kaigai keizai
海外経済

foreign exchange
gaikoku kawase
外国為替

foreign firms
gaikoku gaisha
外国会社
gaikoku kigyō
外国企業

foreign goods
gaikokuhin
外国品

foreign investment
(investment from abroad)
gaikoku kara no tōshi
外国からの投資

foreign manufactured goods
gaikoku seihin
外国製品

foreign market
kaigai shijō
海外市場

foreign market research
kaigai shijō chōsa
海外市場調査

foreign payments
taigai shiharai
対外支払い

foreign policy
gaikō seisaku
外交政策

foreign products
gaikoku seihin
外国製品

foreign trade
bōeki
貿易
gaikoku bōeki
外国貿易

foreign trade balance
bōeki shūshijiri
貿易収支尻

foreign trade barriers
gaikoku no bōeki shōheki
外国の貿易障壁

foreign trade control
bōeki kanri
貿易管理

foreign trade financing
bōeki kin'yū
貿易金融

foreign trade index
bōeki shisū
貿易指数

foreign trade multiplier
gaikoku bōeki jōsū
外国貿易乗数

foreign trade policy
gaikoku bōeki seisaku
外国貿易政策

foreign trade position
bōeki shūshijiri
貿易収支尻

foreign trade statistics
bōeki tōkei
貿易統計

form of business organization
gyōtai
業態

forward integration
zenpō tōgō
前方統合

fourth world
daiyon sekai
第四世界

free competition
jiyū kyōsō
自由競争

free economies
jiyū shokoku no keizai
自由諸国の経済

free economy
jiyū keizai
自由経済

free enterprise
jiyū kigyō
自由企業

free-enterprise economy
jiyū kigyō keizai
自由企業経済

free export
mugawase yushutsu
無為替輸出

free goods
jiyūzai
自由財

free import
mugawase yunyū
無為替輸入

free market
jiyū shijō
自由市場

free-market economy
jiyū shijō keizai
自由市場経済

free marketeers
jiyū shijō shugisha
自由市場主義者

free trade
jiyū bōeki
自由貿易

free-trade area
jiyū bōeki chi'iki
自由貿易地域

free-trade organization
jiyū bōekiha dantai
自由貿易派団体

free world
jiyū sekai
自由世界

free world trade
jiyū sekai bōeki
自由世界貿易

freedom of entry
shijō sannyū no jiyū
市場参入の自由

freeze (salaries)
(chingin o) tōketsu suru
(賃金を) 凍結する

frenzied buying
isogikai
急ぎ買い

frequency distribution
dosū bunpu
度数分布

frictional unemployment
masatsuteki shitsugyō
摩擦的失業

frugality
ken'yaku
倹約
setsuyaku
節約

FTC (Fair Trade Commission)
kōsei torihiki i'inkai
公正取引委員会

full capacity
kanzen nōryoku
完全能力

full cost
furu-kosuto
フル・コスト

full-cost pricing
furu-kosuto kakaku keisei
フル・コスト価格
形成

full-cost principle
furu-kosuto gensoku
フル・コスト原則

full employment
kanzen koyō
完全雇用

full-employment budget surplus
kanzen koyō yosan jōyo
完全雇用予算剰余

full-employment level
kanzen koyō suijun
完全雇用水準

full-employment national income
kanzen koyō kokumin shotoku
完全雇用国民所得

full equilibrium
kanzen kinkō
完全均衡

function (mathematics)
kansū
関数

(utility)
kinō
機能

functional analysis
kinō bunseki
機能分析

functional costing
kinōbetsu genka keisan
機能別原価計算

fund shortage
shikin fusoku
資金不足

fund supply
shikin kyōkyū
資金供給

fundamental changes
kihonteki henka
基本的変化

fundamental disequilibrium
kisoteki fukinkō
基礎的不均衡

funding
shikin chōtatsu
資金調達

funds
shikin
資金

future industries
shōrai sangyō
将来産業

gainfully occupied population
yūgyō jinkō
有業人口

gains from trade
bōeki rieki
貿易利益

galloping inflation
kyūshin infurēshon
急進インフレーション

game theory
gēmu no riron
ゲームの理論

gap
gyappu
ギャップ
kakusa
格差

gap analysis
gyappu bunseki
ギャップ分析

GATT (General Agreement on Tariffs and Trade)
kanzei oyobi bōeki ni kansuru ippan kyōtei
関税および貿易に
関する一般協定

GDE (gross domestic expenditure)
kokunai sōshishutsu
国内総支出

GDP (gross domestic product)
kokunai sōseisan
国内総生産

gearing
giaringu
ギアリング

gearing ratio
giaringu-rēshio
ギアリング・レーシオ
fusai-shihon hiritsu
負債・資本比率

general account
ippan kaikei
一般会計

General Agreement on Tariffs and Trade (GATT)
kanzei oyobi bōeki ni kansuru ippan kyōtei
関税および貿易に
関する一般協定

general budget
sōyosan
総予算

general economic conditions
ippan keizai jōsei
一般経済情勢

general economy
ippan keizai
一般経済

general equilibrium
ippan kinkō
一般均衡

general equilibrium analysis
ippan kinkō bunseki
一般均衡分析

general equilibrium theory
ippan kinkō riron
一般均衡理論

general funds (government's)
ippan zaisei shikin
一般財政資金

general liquidity effect
ippan ryūdōsei kōka
一般流動性効果

general price index
ippan bukka shisū
一般物価指数

general strike
sōhigyō
総罷業

general trend
taisei
大勢

gentlemen's agreement
shinshi kyōtei
紳士協定

geographic distribution
chi'iki bunpu
地域分布

geographic frontier
chiriteki henkyō
地理的辺境

geometric mean
kika heikin
幾何平均

geometric progression
tōhi kyūsū
等比級数

global trend
sekaiteki torendo
世界的トレンド

globalization
kokusaika
国際化

glut
kyōkyū kajō
供給過剰

GND (gross national demand)
kokumin sōjuyō
国民総需要

GNE (gross national expenditure)
kokumin sōshishutsu
国民総支出

GNI (gross national income)
kokumin sōshotoku
国民総所得

GNP (gross national product)
kokumin sōseisan
国民総生産

gold and foreign exchange reserves
kin-gaika junbidaka
金・外貨準備高

Gold Standard
kinhon'i
金本位

Gold Standard system
kinhon'isei
金本位制

golden rule
ōgonritsu
黄金律

golden rule of accumulation
chikuseki no ōgonritsu
蓄積の黄金律

goods
shōhin
商品

goods and services
zai-sābisu
財・サービス

governed economy
kanri keizai
管理経済

government accounts
seifu kaikei
政府会計

government bonds
kokusai
国債

government borrowing
seifu kariire
政府借入れ

government budget
seifu yosan
政府予算

government consumption
seifu shōhi
政府消費

government corporations
seifu kigyō
政府企業

government current deposits
seifu tōza yokin
政府当座預金

**government debt
(national)**
kokusai
国債

(public)
kōsai
公債

government deficit
seifu akaji
政府赤字

government demand
seifu juyō
政府需要

government deposits
seifu yokin
政府預金

government earnings
seifu shūnyū
政府収入

government expenditure
seifu shishutsu
政府支出

government expenditure policy
seifu shishutsu seisaku
政府支出政策

government finance
seifu zaisei
政府財政

government funds
seifu shikin
政府資金

government grants
seifu hojokin
政府補助金

government institutions
seifu kikan
政府機関

government lending
seifu kashidashi
政府貸出し

government monopoly
seifu dokusen
政府独占

government officials
seifu tōkyokusha
政府当局者

government ownership
kokuyū
国有

government policy
seifu no seisaku
政府の政策

government procurement
seifu chōtatsu
政府調達

government purchase of goods and services
seifu no zai-sābisu kōnyū
政府の財・サービス購入

government receipts
seifu shūnyū
政府収入

government revenue
seifu shūnyū
政府収入

government savings
seifu chochiku
政府貯蓄

government sector
seifu bumon
政府部門

government services
seifu yōeki
政府用役

government spending
seifu shishutsu
政府支出

(fiscal expenditure)
zaisei shishutsu
財政支出

government subsidies
seifu hojokin
政府補助金

(state aid)
kokko hojo
国庫補助

government-to-government trade
seifukan bōeki
政府間貿易

government trade
seifu bōeki
政府貿易

government transactions
seifu torihiki
政府取引

gradual decrease
teigen
逓減
zengen
漸減

gradual increase
teizō
逓増
zenzō
漸増

gradualism
zenshin shugi
漸進主義

grants
hojokin
補助金
kōfukin
交付金

Great Depression, the [US]
daikyōkō
大恐慌

green revolution
midori no kakumei
緑の革命

grey areas [UK]
fukyō no chūkan chi'iki
不況の中間地域

gross average hourly earnings
heikin jikan atari sōshūnyū
平均時間当たり総収入

gross average weekly earnings
heikin shūatari sōshūnyū
平均週当たり総収入

gross average yearly earnings
nenkan heikin sōshūnyū
年間平均総収入

gross barter terms of trade
sōkōeki jōken
総交易条件

gross domestic capital
kokunai sōshihon
国内総資本

gross domestic consumption
kokunai sōshōhi
国内総消費

gross domestic demand
kokunai sōjuyō
国内総需要

gross domestic expenditure (GDE)
kokunai sōshishutsu
国内総支出

gross domestic fixed capital formation
kokunai sōkotei shihon keisei
国内総固定資本形成

gross domestic output
kokunai sōseisandaka
国内総生産高

gross domestic product (GDP)
kokunai sōseisan
国内総生産

gross domestic savings
kokunai sōchochiku
国内総貯蓄

gross domestic supply
kokunai sōkyōkyū
国内総供給

gross earnings
sōshūnyū
総収入

gross expenditure
sōshishutsu
総支出

gross investment
sotōshi
総投資

gross national demand (GND)
kokumin sōjuyō
国民総需要

gross national expenditure (GNE)
kokumin sōshishutsu
国民総支出

gross national income (GNI)
kokumin sōshotoku
国民総所得

gross national output
kokumin sōseisanryō
国民総生産量

gross national product (GNP)
kokumin sōseisan
国民総生産

gross national product deflator
GNP defurētā
GNP デフレーター
kokumin sōseisan defurētā
国民総生産デフレーター

gross national supply
kokumin sōkyōkyū
国民総供給

gross national wealth
kokumin sōshisan
国民総資産

gross savings
sōchochiku
総貯蓄

Group of Five
gokakoku zōsō kaigi
5か国蔵相会議

Group of 77
hattentojō nanajūnana-kakoku gurūpu
発展途上77か国グループ

Group of Ten
senshin jūkakoku
先進10か国

growing economy
seichō keizai
成長経済

growing industry
seichō sangyō
成長産業

growth
seichō
成長

growth budget
seichō yosan
成長予算

growth curve
seichō kyokusen
成長曲線

growth forecast
seichō yosoku
成長予測

growth-gap unemployment
seichō kakusa shitsugyō
成長格差失業

growth index
seichō shisū
成長指数

growth industry
seichō sangyō
成長産業

growth path
seichō rosen
成長路線

growth phase
seichōki
成長期

growth potential
seichō senzairyoku
成長潜在力

growth-profitability function
seichō-shūekisei kansū
成長・収益性関数

growth rate
seichōritsu
成長率

growth retardant
seichō yokuseizai
成長抑制剤

growth sector
seichō bumon
成長部門

growth theories of the firm
kigyō seichō riron
企業成長理論

growth theory
seichō riron
成長理論

guaranteed income
hoshō shūnyū
保証収入

guaranteed wage
hoshō chingin
保証賃金

guidelines
gaidorain
ガイドライン
shidō kijun
指導基準

guideposts
gaidoposuto
ガイドポスト

guilds
dōgyōsha no dantai
同業者の団体
girudo
ギルド

habit hypothesis
kanshū kasetsu
慣習仮説

half-year
hanki
半期

hard-core unemployed
manseiteki shitsugyōsha
慢性的失業者

hard times
fukyōji
不況時

harmonization
heijunka
平準化

haves and have-nots
moteru mono to motazaru
mono
持てる者と持たざる
者

healthy economy
kenzen keizai
健全経済

healthy industries
kenzen sangyō
健全産業

heavy consumption
tairyō shōhi
大量消費

heavy demand
tairyō juyō
大量需要

heavy unemployment
tairyō shitsugyō
大量失業

hedging
kaketsunagi
掛けつなぎ

hefty investment
tagaku tōshi
多額の投資

hegemony
haken
覇権

heterogeneity
ishitsusei
異質性

hidden inflation
kakureta infurēshon
隠れたインフレー
ション

hidden unemployment
kakureta shitsugyō
隠れた失業

high employment
kōkoyō
高雇用

high income
kōshotoku
高所得

high-income bracket
kōshotokusō
高所得層

high-income earners
kōshotokusha
高所得者

high-income nations
kōshotokukoku
高所得国

high interest rates
kōkinri
高金利

high interest rates policy
kōkinri seisaku
高金利政策

high-powered money
hai-pawādo-manē
ハイ・パワード・
マネー

high-pressure economy
kōatsu keizai
高圧経済

high-quality labour
ryōshitsu no rōdōryoku
良質の労働力

high technology (high tech)
kōdo gijutsu (haiteku)
高度技術 (ハイテク)

high-technology industry
kōdo gijutsu sangyō
高度技術産業

high-technology-oriented firms
kōdo gijutsu shikō kigyō
高度技術指向企業

high unemployment rate
kōshitsugyōritsu
高失業率

high-wage economy
kōchingin keizai
高賃金経済

high-wage nations
kōchinginkoku
高賃金国

higher education
kōtō kyōiku
高等教育

highly industrialized countries
kōdo kōgyōkoku
高度工業国

hiring rate
koyōritsu
雇用率
nyūshokuritsu
入職率

hiring standards
koyō hyōjun
雇用標準

historical cost(s)
shutoku genka
取得原価

historical models
rekishiteki moderu
歴史的モデル

historicism
rekishi shugi
歴史主義

hoarded goods
taizō busshi
退蔵物資

hoarding
taizō
退蔵

home economics
kaseigaku
家政学

homogeneity
dōshitsusei
同質性

homogeneous functions
dōji kansū
同次関数

homogeneous nation
dōminzoku kokka
同民族国家

homogeneous product
dōshitsuteki seisanbutsu
同質的生産物

homogeneous society
dōshitsuteki shakai
同質的社会

horizontal division of labour
suiheiteki bungyō
水平的分業

horizontal integration
suiheiteki tōgō
水平的統合

horizontal merger
suiheiteki gappei
水平的合併

horizontal trade
suihei bōeki
水平貿易

host nation
ukeirekoku
受入国

hot-house economy
kahogo keizai
過保護経済

household consumption
kakei shōhi
家計消費

household economy
kakei
家計
katei keizai
家庭経済

household economy survey
kakei chōsa
家計調査

household expenses
kakeihi
家計費

households
katei
家庭
setai
世帯

housing
jūtaku
住宅

housing authorities
kōkyō jūtaku kikan
公共住宅機関

housing corporations
jūtaku kōdan
住宅公団

housing credit
jūtaku kin'yū
住宅金融

housing demand
jūtaku juyō
住宅需要

housing estates
danchi
団地

housing expenditure
jūtaku shishutsu
住宅支出

housing finance
jūtaku kin'yū
住宅金融

housing investment
jūtaku tōshi
住宅投資

housing market
jūtaku shijō
住宅市場

housing policy
jūtaku seisaku
住宅政策

housing problems
jūtaku mondai
住宅問題

housing programme
jūtaku keikaku
住宅計画

housing shortage
jūtaku fusoku
住宅不足
jūtakunan
住宅難

human capital
jinteki shihon
人的資本

human depreciation
ningen no genka
shōkyakuhi
人間の減価償却費

human investment
jinteki tōshi
人的投資

human labour
ningen rōdō
人間労働

human resources
jinteki shigen
人的資源

humanism
jinpon shugi
人本主義

hunger
kiga
飢餓

hunger export
kiga yushutsu
飢餓輸出

hunger march
kiga kōshin
飢餓行進

hyper-inflation
haipā-infurēshon
ハイパー・
インフレーション

hypothesis
kasetsu
仮説
katei
仮定

hypothesis testing
kasetsu kentei
仮説検定

IBRD (International Bank for Reconstruction and Development)
kokusai fukkō kaihatsu ginkō
国際復興開発銀行

ICC (International Chamber of Commerce)
kokusai shōgyō kaigisho
国際商業会議所

ICOR (incremental capital/ output ratio)
genkai shihon-sanshutsudaka hiritsu
限界資本・産出高比率

IDA (International Development Association)
kokusai kaihatsu kyōkai
国際開発協会

ideal
risō
理想

identification problem
dōtei mondai
同定問題

identity (equation)
kōtōshiki
恒等式

ideology
kannenron
観念論

idle balances
yūkyū zandaka
遊休残高

idle capacity (production)
yūkyū seisan nōryoku
遊休生産能力

(equipment)
yūkyū setsubi
遊休設備

idle capital
yūkyū shihon
遊休資本
yūshi
遊資

idle money
yūkin
遊金
yūkyū shikin
遊休資金

idle resources
yūkyū shigen
遊休資源

illegal trade
fuhō torihiki
不法取引

illiquidity
hiryūdōsei
非流動性

ILO (International Labour Organization)
kokusai rōdō kikō
国際労働機構

imbalance
fukinkō
不均衡

IMC (International Monetary Conference)
kokusai kin'yū kaigi
国際金融会議

IMF (International Monetary Fund)
kokusai tsūka kikin
国際通貨基金

immigrant labour
imin rōdōryoku
移民労働力

immigrant workers
imin rōdōsha
移民労働者

immigration
inyū
移入

immigration policy
imin seisaku
移民政策

immigration quotas
inyūmin wariatesei
移入民割当制

immiserizing growth
kyūbōkateki seichō
窮乏化的成長

impact
inpakuto
インパクト

(influence)
eikyōryoku
影響力

(shock)
shōgeki
衝撃

impact multiplier
sokujiteki jōsū
即時的乗数

impact of taxation
sozei futan
租税負担

imperfect competition
fukanzen kyōsō
不完全競争

imperfect information
fukanzen jōhō
不完全情報

imperfect market
fukanzen shijō
不完全市場

imperialism
teikoku shugi
帝国主義

imperialist
teikoku shugisha
帝国主義者

imperialistic economy
teikoku shugi keizai
帝国主義経済

impetus (motivating force)
gendōryoku
原動力

(stimulus)
shigeki
刺激

implementation
(enforcement)
jisshi
実施

(execution, performance)
rikō
履行

implementation lag
seisakujō no ragu
政策上のラグ

implicit contracts
mokuyaku
黙約

implicit cost
anmokuteki hiyō
暗黙的費用

implicit function
inkansū
陰関数

import (noun)
yunyū
輸入

import (verb)
yunyū suru
輸入する

import barriers
yunyū shōheki
輸入障壁

import bounties
yunyū shōreikin
輸入奨励金

import controls
yunyū kisei
輸入規制
yunyū tōsei
輸入統制

import deposits
yunyū yotakukin
輸入預託金

import duties
yunyū kanzei
輸入関税

import-financing credit
yunyū shikin kin'yū
輸入資金金融

import price index
yunyū bukka shisū
輸入物価指数

import priority
yunyū yūsen jun'i
輸入優先順位

import quota
yunyū wariate
輸入割当て

import quota restriction
yunyū wariate seigen
輸入割当制限

import quota system
yunyū wariate seido
輸入割当制度

import regulations
yunyū kisoku
輸入規則

import restrictions
yunyū seigen
輸入制限

import substitutes
yunyū daitaizai
輸入代替財

import substitution
yunyū daitai
輸入代替

import tariffs
yunyū zeiritsu
輸入税率

import trade
yunyū bōeki
輸入貿易

import volume
yunyūryō
輸入量

import without foreign
exchange
mugawase yunyū
無為替輸入

imported goods
yunyūhin
輸入品

imported inflation
yunyū infure
輸入インフレ

imported raw materials
yunyū genzairyō
輸入原材料

imported technology
yunyū gijutsu
輸入技術

importers
(individual firms)
yunyū gyōsha
輸入業者

(countries)
yunyūkoku
輸入国

imports
yunyūhin
輸入品

impoverishment
hinkonka
貧困化
kyūbōka
窮乏化

improvement
(betterment)
kairyō
改良

(reformation)
kaizen
改善

(turn for the better)
kōten
好転

improvement of living
conditions
seikatsu kaizen
生活改善

improvement of living
standards
seikatsu suijun kōjō
生活水準向上

improvement of the
environment
kankyō kaizen
環境改善

impure public good
junkōkyōzai
準公共財

imputed rent
kizoku chidai
帰属地代

inactive money
fukatsudō kahei
不活動貨幣

inactivity
fukappatsu
不活発

incentive
yūin
誘因

incentive payment system
shōrei chinginsei
奨励賃金制

incentive wage system
shōrei chinginsei
奨励賃金制

incentives
(bounties, subsidies)
shōreikin
奨励金

(favourable measures)
yūgū sochi
優遇措置

incidence of taxation
sozei futan
租税負担

income
(earnings)
shotoku
所得

(return, revenue, receipts)
shūnyū
収入

income analysis
shotoku bunseki
所得分析

income and expenditure
equation
shūshi hōteishiki
収支方程式

income bracket
shotoku kaisō
所得階層
shotokusō
所得層

income-consumption curve
shotoku-shōhi kyokusen
所得・消費曲線

income determination
shotoku kettei
所得決定

income differentials
chingin kakusa
賃金格差

income distribution
shotoku bunpu
所得分布

income earners
shotokusha
所得者

income effect
shotoku kōka
所得効果

income elasticity of demand
juyō no shotoku
danryokusei
需要の所得弾力性

income-expenditure model
shotoku-shishutsu moderu
所得・支出モデル

income from capital
shihon shotoku
資本所得

income from work
kinrō shotoku
勤労所得

income group
shotoku kaisō
所得階層
shotokusō
所得層

income index
shotoku shisū
所得指数

income level
shotoku suijun
所得水準

income maintenance
shotoku iji
所得維持

income structure
shotoku kōzō
所得構造

income tax
shotokuzei
所得税

income tax filing deadline
shotokuzei shinkoku
shimekiri kijitsu
所得税申告締切期日

income tax return
shotokuzei shinkoku
所得税申告

(form)
shotokuzei shinkokusho
所得税申告書

income tax schedule
shotokuzeihyō
所得税表

income tax withheld at source
gensen shotokuzei
源泉所得税

income terms of trade
shotoku kōeki jōken
所得交易条件

income velocity of money
kahei no shotoku sokudo
貨幣の所得速度

incomes policy
shotoku seisaku
所得政策

inconsistency
fuitchi
不一致

inconsistent statistics
ikkan no nai tōkeiryō
一貫のない統計量

inconvertibility
(non-conversion)
hidakansei
非兌換性
(non-exchangeability,
non-transferability)
hikōkansei
非交換性

increase

(expansion, inflation)
bōchō
膨張

(augmentation)
zōdai
増大

(addition, rise)
zōka
増加

increase in demand
juyō zōdai
需要増大

increase in exports
yushutsu zōka
輸出増加
yushutsu zōdai
輸出増大

(gradual)
yushutsu teizō
輸出逓増

increase in population
jinkō zōka
人口増加

increase in production
zōsan
増産

increase in subsidies
hojokin zōka
補助金増加

increasing cost(s)
hiyō teizō
費用逓増

increasing-cost supply
hiyō teizō kyōkyū
費用逓増供給

increasing returns
shūkaku teizō
収穫逓増

increasing returns to scale
kibo no rieki
規模の利益

incremental capital/output ratio (ICOR)
genkai shihon-sanshutsudaka hiritsu
限界資本・産出高比率

independent income
dokuritsu shotoku
独立所得
dokutoku
独得

independent variable
dokuritsu hensū
独立変数

index
shisū
指数

index-linked minimum wage
infuremiai no saitei chingin
インフレ見合いの
最低賃金

index numbers
shisū
指数

index of retail prices
kouri bukka shisū
小売物価指数

indexation [UK]
infure bōei sochi
インフレ防衛措置

indexing
bukka shisū suraidosei
物価指数スライド制

indication
chōkō
兆候

indicative planning
shijiteki keikaku
指示的計画

indicator
shihyō
指標

indifference
musabetsu
無差別

indifference analysis
musabetsu bunseki
無差別分析

indifference curve
musabetsu kyokusen
無差別曲線

indifference map
musabetsu zuhyō
無差別図表

indirect cost
kansetsuhi
間接費

indirect expenses
kansetsu keihi
間接経費

(general expenses)
ippan keihi
一般経費

indirect import
kansetsu yunyū
間接輸入

indirect investment
kansetsu tōshi
間接投資

indirect labour
kansetsu rōdō
間接労働

indirect production
kansetsu seisan
間接生産

indirect taxation
kansetsu sozei
間接租税

indirect taxes
kansetsuzei
間接税

indirect trade
kansetsu bōeki
間接貿易

indirect utility function
kansetsu kōyō kansū
間接効用関数

individual bargaining
kojin kōshō
個人交渉

individual consumption
kojin shōhi
個人消費

individual demand
kobetsu juyō
個別需要

individual expenditure
kojin shishutsu
個人支出

individual income tax
kojin shotokuzei
個人所得税

individual wealth
kojin shisan
個人資産

individuals
kojin
個人

indivisibility
fukabunsei
不可分性

induced capital movements
yūhatsuteki shihon idō
誘発的資本移動

induced consumption
yūhatsu shōhi
誘発消費

induced investment
yūhatsu tōshi
誘発投資

industrial activity
sangyō katsudō
産業活動

industrial adjustment
sangyō chōsei
産業調整

industrial areas
kōgyō chi'iki
工業地域

industrial associations
sangyō kumiai
産業組合

industrial banks
kōgyō ginkō
工業銀行

industrial boom
sangyō kōkeiki
産業好景気

industrial capital
sangyō shihon
産業資本

industrial centre
kōgyō chūshinchi
工業中心地

industrial circles
kōgyōkai
工業界

industrial classification
sangyōshubetsu bunrui
産業種別分類

industrial complex
kōgyō danchi
工業団地

industrial complex analysis
kōgyō danchi bunseki
工業団地分析

industrial concentration
sangyō shūchū
産業集中

industrial conflicts
rōshi tōsō
労使闘争

industrial conglomerates
zaibatsu
財閥

industrial conversion
sangyō tenkan
産業転換

industrial countries
kōgyōkoku
工業国

industrial credit
sangyō yūshi
産業融資

**industrial crisis
(manufacturing industry)**
kōgyō kyōkō
工業恐慌

(any industry)
sangyō kyōkō
産業恐慌

industrial demand
kōgyō seihin juyō
工業製品需要

industrial democracy
sangyō minshu shugi
産業民主主義

industrial development
sangyō kaihatsu
産業開発

**industrial development
agencies**
sangyō kaihatsu kikan
産業開発機関

industrial disputes
rōshi sōgi
労使争議

industrial economy
sangyō keizai
産業経済

industrial expansion
kōgyō seisan no kakudai
工業生産の拡大

industrial facilities
sangyō setsubi
産業設備

industrial finance
sangyō kin'yū
産業金融

industrial funds
sangyō shikin
産業資金

**industrial goods
(manufactured goods)**
kōgyō seihin
工業製品

(products)
seisanzai
生産財

industrial growth
kōgyō seisan no seichō
工業生産の成長

industrial independence
kōgyō jiritsu
工業自立

industrial inertia
sangyō no hi'idōsei
産業の非移動性

industrial infrastructure
sangyō kiban
産業基盤

industrial investment
sangyō tōshi
産業投資

industrial know-how
sangyō gijutsu
産業技術

industrial location
kōgyō ritchi
工業立地

industrial location policy
kōgyō ritchi seisaku
工業立地政策

industrial materials
kōgyō genryō
工業原料

industrial migration
sangyō idō
産業移動

industrial nations
kōgyōkoku
工業国

industrial organization
sangyō soshiki
産業組織

industrial output
kōgyō seisan
工業生産

industrial policy
kōgyō seisaku
工業政策

industrial polluter
kōgai sangyō
公害産業

industrial pollution
sangyō kōgai
産業公害

industrial prices
kōgyō seihin kakaku
工業製品価格

industrial production
kōgyō seisan
工業生産

industrial production index
kōkōgyō seisan shisū
鉱工業生産指数

industrial products
kōkōgyō seihin
鉱工業製品

industrial rationalization
sangyō gōrika
産業合理化

industrial relations
rōshi kankei
労使関係

industrial reorganization
sangyō saihensei
産業再編成

Industrial Revolution
sangyō kakumei
産業革命

industrial sector
sangyō bumon
産業部門

industrial site
sangyōyōchi
産業用地

industrial society
sangyō shakai
産業社会

industrial spy
sangyō supai
産業スパイ

industrial statistics
kōgyō tōkei
工業統計

industrial structure
sangyō kōzō
産業構造

industrial technology
kōgyō gijutsu
工業技術

industrial towns
kōgyō toshi
工業都市

industrial unions
sangyōbetsu rōdō kumiai
産業別労働組合

industrial wage differentials
sangyō chingin kakusa
産業賃金格差

industrial wage structure
sangyō chingin kōzō
産業賃金構造

industrial waste
sangyō haikibutsu
産業廃棄物

industrial waste water
sangyō haisui
産業廃水

industrial workers
sangyō rōdōsha
産業労働者

industrial world
sangyōkai
産業界

(manufacturing)
kōgyōkai
工業界

industrial zone
kōgyō chitai
工業地帯

industrialization
kōgyōka
工業化
sangyōka
産業化

industrialized countries
kōgyōkoku
工業国

industrialists
sangyōnin
産業人

(entrepreneurs)
jitsugyōka
実業家

industry
(any industry)
sangyō
産業

(manufacturing)
kōgyō
工業

industry-wide bargaining
sangyōbetsu dankō
産業別団交

industry-wide issues
sangyōkyōtsū mondai
産業共通問題

inefficiency
hinōritsu
非能率

inelastic demand
hidanryokuteki juyō
非弾力的需要

inelastic supply
hidanryokuteki kyōkyū
非弾力的供給

inelasticity
hidanryokusei
非弾力性

inequality
fubyōdō
不平等

inequality of incomes
shotoku no fubyōdō
所得の不平等

infant industry
yōchi sangyō
幼稚産業

infant industry argument for protection
yōchi sangyō hogoron
幼稚産業保護論

inference (statistical)
(tōkeiteki) suisoku
(統計的) 推測

inferior goods
kakyūzai
下級財

inflation
infure
インフレ
infurēshon
インフレーション

inflation accounting
infure shūsei kaikei
インフレ修正会計

inflation-adjusted
bukka hendō chōsei no
物価変動調整の

inflation-compensating pay rises
infuremiai no chin'age
インフレ見合いの
賃上げ

inflation control
infure no yokusei
インフレの抑制

inflation-free growth
infurenaki seichō
インフレなき成長

inflation-free recovery
infurenaki kaifuku
インフレなき回復

inflation policy
infure seisaku
インフレ政策

inflation problem
infure mondai
インフレ問題

inflation-proofing [US]
infure bōei sochi
インフレ防衛措置

inflation rate
infureritsu
インフレ率

inflation subsidy
infure hojokin
インフレ補助金

inflationary
infure no
インフレの
infurēshon no
インフレーションの
infure keikō no
インフレ傾向の
infureteki na
インフレ的な

inflationary gap
infure-gyappu
インフレ・ギャップ

inflationary pressure
infure atsuryoku
インフレ圧力

inflationary recession
infure fukyō
インフレ不況

inflationary spiral
akusei infure
悪性インフレ
infure akujunkan
インフレ悪循環

inflationary trend
infure keikō
インフレ傾向

inflationist
infure shugisha
インフレ主義者

influx of foreign capital
gaishi ryūnyū
外資流入

informal sector
infōmaru bumon
インフォーマル部門

information technology (IT)
jōhō gijutsu
情報技術

infrastructure
infurasutorakucha
インフラストラクチ
ュア

inheritance tax [UK]
sōzokuzei
相続税

initiative (plan)
kōsō
構想

injections
chūnyū
注入

Inland Revenue [UK]
naikoku shūzeikyoku
内国収税局

inland trade
naikoku bōeki
内国貿易

innovations
shinkijiku
新機軸

input
tōnyū
投入

input amount
tōnyūdaka
投入高

input-output analysis
tōnyū-sanshutsu bunseki
投入・産出分析

input/output ratio
tōnyū-sanshutsu hiritsu
投入・産出比率

inside lag
insaido-ragu
ンサイド・ラグ

inside money
naibu kahei
内部貨幣

insolvency
(bankruptcy)
hasan
破産

(inability to pay)
shiharaifunō
支払不能

instability
fuantei
不安定

institutional economics
seidoha keizaigaku
制度派経済学

institutional training
shisetsunai kunren
施設内訓練

instrument of monetary policy
kin'yū seisaku shudan
金融政策手段

instrumental variables
shudan hensū
手段変数

instruments
shudan
手段

insufficiency
fusoku
不足

insurance
hoken
保険

intangible assets
mukei shisan
無形資産

integrated economy
tōgō keizai
統合経済

integration
tōgō
統合

intended inventory investment
ito shita zaiko tōshi
意図した在庫投資

intensive margin
shūyakuteki genkai
集約的限界

intercept
yokodori suru
横取りする

interdependence
sōgo izon
相互依存

interest
(money rates)
kinri
金利

(profit, gains, return)
rieki
利益

(interest on loan or deposit)
rishi
利子

(interest on loan or deposit)
risoku
利息

interest-free loans
murishi yūshi
無利子融資

interest payments
kinri shiharai
金利支払い

interest-rate deregulation
kinri jiyūka
金利自由化

interest-rate mechanism
kinri kikō
金利機構

interest-rate structure
rishiritsu kōzō
利子率構造

interest rates (money rates)
kinri
金利

interest rates control
kinri no kontorōru
金利のコントロール

interest rates movements
kinri dōkō
金利動向

interest rates policy
kinri seisaku
金利政策

interest subsidies
rishi hokyū
利子補給

intergovernment agreements
seifukan kyōtei
政府間協定

intergovernmental grants
seifukan hojokin
政府間補助金

interim budget
zantei yosan
暫定予算

intermediate areas
fukyō no chūkan chi'iki
不況の中間地域

intermediate demand
chūkan juyō
中間需要

intermediate goods
chūkanzai
中間財

intermediate lag
chūkan ragu
中間ラグ

intermediate products
chūkan seisanbutsu
中間生産物

intermediate technology
chūkan gijutsu
中間技術

internal balance
kokunai kinkō
国内均衡

internal debt
naisai
内債

internal diseconomies
naibu fukeizai
内部不経済

internal economies
naibu keizai
内部経済

internal equilibrium
kokunai kinkō
国内均衡

**internal labour market
(intercompany)**
kigyōnai rōdō shijō
企業内労働市場

internal rate of return
naibu shūekiritsu
内部収益率

**Internal Revenue Service (IRS)
[US]**
naikoku sainyūchō
内国歳入庁

internal tax
naikokuzei
内国税

internal trade
kokunai bōeki
国内貿易

internal wage differentials
naibu chingin kakusa
内部賃金格差

international agreement
kokusai kyōtei
国際協定

international aid
kokusai enjo
国際援助

international alliance
kokusai dōmei
国際同盟

**international balance of
payments**
kokusai shūshi
国際収支

**International Bank for
Reconstruction and
Development (IBRD)**
kokusai fukkō kaihatsu
ginkō
国際復興開発銀行

international cartel
kokusai karuteru
国際カルテル

**International Chamber of
Commerce (ICC)**
kokusai shōgyō kaigisho
国際商業会議所

International Clearing Union
kokusai seisan dōmei
国際清算同盟

international commerce
kokusai tsūshō
国際通商

**international commodity
agreements**
kokusai shōhin kyōtei
国際商品協定

international competition
kokusai kyōsō
国際競争

international competitiveness
kokusai kyōsōryoku
国際競争力

**International Co-operation
Administration**
kokusai kyōryokukyoku
国際協力局

**International Development
Association (IDA)**
kokusai kaihatsu kyōkai
国際開発協会

international division of labour
kokusai bungyō
国際分業

**international economic
conference**
kokusai keizai kaigi
国際経済会議

**international economic
co-operation**
kokusai keizai kyōryoku
国際経済協力

international economics
kokusai keizaigaku
国際経済学

international economy
kokusai keizai
国際経済

international equilibrium
kokusai kinkō
国際均衡

international flow of capital
kokusai shihon idō
国際資本移動

international indebtedness
kokusai saimu
国際債務
kokusai taishaku
国際貸借

**international industrial
competitiveness**
sangyō kokusai kyōsōryoku
産業国際競争力

International Labour Office
kokusai rōdō jimukyoku
国際労働事務局

**International Labour
Organization (ILO)**
kokusai rōdō kikō
国際労働機構

international liquidity
kokusai ryūdōsei
国際流動性

international monetarism
kokusai tsūka shugi
国際通貨主義

**International Monetary
Conference (IMC)**
kokusai kin'yū kaigi
国際金融会議

**International Monetary Fund
(IMF)**
kokusai tsūka kikin
国際通貨基金

**international monetary
organization**
kokusai tsūka kikō
国際通貨機構

international monetary reform
kokusai tsūka seido
kaikaku
国際通貨制度改革

international monetary system
kokusai tsūka seido
国際通貨制度

international organization
kokusai kikō
国際機構

international payments
kokusai taishaku no kessai
国際貸借の決済

international payments imbalances
kokusai shūshi fukinkō
国際収支不均衡

international payments mechanism
kokusai kessai kikō
国際決済機構

international sanctions
kokusaiteki seisai
国際的制裁

international technology exchanges
kokusai gijutsu kōryū
国際技術交流

international trade
bōeki
貿易
kokusai bōeki
国際貿易
kokusai tsūshō
国際通商

International Trade Commission (ITC)
kokusai bōeki i'inkai
国際貿易委員会

International Trade Organization (ITO)
kokusai bōeki kikō
国際貿易機構

international waters
kōkai
公海

internationalization
kokusaika
国際化

interpersonal comparisons of utility
kōyō no kojinkan hikaku
効用の個人間比較

intra-industry division of labour
sangyōnai bungyō
産業内分業

intra-trade
ikinai bōeki
域内貿易

inventories
zaiko
在庫

inventory analysis
zaiko bunseki
在庫分析

inventory cycle
zaiko junkan
在庫循環
zaiko tōshi junkan
在庫投資循環

inventory index
zaiko shisū
在庫指数

inventory investment
zaiko tōshi
在庫投資

inventory investment cycle
zaiko tōshi junkan
在庫投資循環

investment
tōshi
投資

investment abroad
kaigai tōshi
海外投資
taigai tōshi
対外投資

investment boom
tōshi keiki
投資景気

investment credit
tōshi shin'yō
投資信用

investment criteria
tōshi kijun
投資基準

investment curve
tōshi kyokusen
投資曲線

investment demand
tōshi juyō
投資需要

investment demand schedule
tōshi juyōhyō
投資需要表

investment drive
tōshi iyoku
投資意欲

investment effort
tōshi doryoku
投資努力

investment expenditure
tōshi shishutsu
投資支出

investment function
tōshi kansū
投資関数

investment grants
tōshi hojokin
投資補助金

investment in plant and equipment
setsubi tōshi
設備投資

investment incentives
tōshi yūin
投資誘因

investment-led growth
tōshi shudōgata seichō
投資主導型成長

investment multiplier
tōshi jōsū
投資乗数

investment outlets
tōshi taishō
投資対象

investment outlook
tōshi mitōshi
投資見通し

investment policies
tōshi seisaku
投資政策

investment programmes
tōshi keikaku
投資計画

Investors in Industry [UK]
sangyō tōshika
産業投資家

invisible balance of trade
bōekigai shūshi
貿易外収支

invisible exports
mukei yushutsu
無形輸出

invisible hand, the
miezaru te
見えざる手

invisible imports
bōekigai yunyū
貿易外輸入

invisible poor, the
kakureta hinkonsha
隠れた貧困者

**invisible trade
(invisible balance of
trade)**
bōekigai shūshi
貿易外収支

(non-trade transaction)
bōekigai torihiki
貿易外取引

invisibles
bōekigai shiharai
貿易外支払

involuntary unemployment
hijihatsuteki shitsugyō
非自発的失業
kyōsei shitsugyō
強制失業

iron law of wages
chingin tessoku
賃金鉄則

irregularity
fukisoku
不規則

**IRS (Internal Revenue Service)
[US]**
naikoku sainyūchō
内国歳入庁

iso-cost curves
tōhi kyokusen
等費曲線

isolated economy
koritsu keizai
孤立経済

iso-outlay curve
tōhi kyokusen
等費曲線

iso-product curves
tōsanshutsuryō kyokusen
等産出量曲線

isoquants
tōryō kyokusen
等量曲線

iso-revenue curve
tōshūnyū kyokusen
等収入曲線

IT (information technology)
jōhō gijutsu
情報技術

**ITC (International Trade
Commission)**
kokusai bōeki i'inkai
国際貿易委員会

**ITO (International Trade
Organization)**
kokusai bōeki kikō
国際貿易機構

**Japan Chamber of Commerce
and Industry**
nihon shōkō kaigisho
日本商工会議所

**Japan External Trade
Organization (JETRO)**
jetoro
ジェトロ
nihon bōeki shinkōkai
日本貿易振興会

**Japanese Industrial Standards
(JIS)**
nihon kōgyō kikaku
日本工業規格

Japanese residing abroad
zaigai hōjin
在外邦人

**JETRO (Japan External Trade
Organization)**
jetoro
ジェトロ
nihon bōeki shinkōkai
日本貿易振興会

**JIS (Japanese Industrial
Standards)**
nihon kōgyō kikaku
日本工業規格

job analysis
shokumu bunseki
職務分析

**job-application/job-opening
ratio**
kyūshokubairitsu
求職倍率

job centres [UK]
shokugyō shōkaijo
職業紹介所

job classification
shokukaisei
職階制

job cluster
jobu-kurasuta
ジョブ・クラスタ

job competition theory
shigoto kyōsōron
仕事競争論

job creation
koyō sōshutsu
雇用創出
shokugyō sōshutsu
職業創出

job development
koyō sokushin
雇用促進

job evaluation
shokumu hyōka
職務評価

job factor
shokumu yōso
職務要素

job holders
teishokusha
定職者

job losses
shisshoku
失職

job market
kyūjin shijō
求人市場

job offers
kyūjin
求人

job-placement/job-opening ratio
kyūjin-jūsoku hiritsu
求人・充足比率

job search
kyūshoku
求職

job search channels
kyūshoku rūto
求職ルート

job security
koyō antei
雇用安定

job seekers
kyūshokusha
求職者

job shopping
jobu-shoppingu
ジョブ・ショッピング

job stability
shigoto anteisei
仕事安定性

job training
shokugyō kunren
職業訓練

jobless, the
shitsugyōsha
失業者

jobless figures
shitsugyō tōkei
失業統計

jobless rate
shitsugyōritsu
失業率

jobs
(work)
shigoto
仕事

(employment, work)
shoku
職

(occupation, profession)
shokugyō
職業

joint costs
ketsugō hiyō
結合費用

joint demand
ketsugō juyō
結合需要

joint production
ketsugō seisan
結合生産

joint products
ketsugō seisanbutsu
結合生産物

joint profit maximization
ketsugō rijun no kyokudaika
結合利潤の極大化

joint research
kyōdō kenkyū
共同研究

joint supply
ketsugō kyōkyū
結合供給

joint survey
kyōdō chōsa
共同調査

Joint US–Japan Committee on Trade and Economic Affairs
nibei bōeki keizai gōdō i'inkai
日米貿易経済合同委員会

joint venture (= joint project)
kyōdō jigyō
共同事業

just price
kōsei kakaku
公正価格

just wage(s)
kōsei chingin
公正賃金

just-wage principle
kōsei chingin no gensoku
公正賃金の原則

key bargaining
kijun kōshō
基準交渉

key exports
shuyō yushutsuhin
主要輸出品

key industries
kikan sangyō
基幹産業

Keynes plan, the
kinzuan
ケインズ案

Keynesian economics
kinzu keizaigaku
ケインズ経済学

Keynesian growth theory
kinzu no seichōron
ケインズの成長論

Keynesian monetary policy
kinzu no zaisei seisaku
ケインズの財政政策

Keynesian theory of interest
kinzu no rishiron
ケインズの利子論

kinked demand curve
kussetsu juyō kyokusen
屈折需要曲線

knife edge
naifu no ha
ナイフの刃

knockdown export
genchi kumitate yushutsu
現地組立輸出

knockdown import
genchi kumitate yunyū
現地組立輸入

know-how
nouhau
ノウハウ

knowledge
chishiki
知識

knowledge-intensive industries
chishiki shūyakuteki sangyō
知識集約的産業

labour
rōdō
労働

(labour force)
rōdōryoku
労働力

(labourers)
rōdōsha
労働者

labour agreements
rōdō kyōyaku
労働協約

labour-augmenting technical progress
rōdō zōdaiteki gijutsu shinpo
労働増大的技術進歩

labour availability
rōdō riyō kanōsei
労働利用可能性

labour capital
rōshi
労資

labour code
rōdō kiyaku
労働規約

labour control
rōmu kanri
労務管理

labour cost
rōdō kosuto
労働コスト
rōmuhi
労働費

labour cuts
rōdōryoku no setsugen
労働力の節減

labour demand
rōdō juyō
労働需要

labour demand/supply ratio
rōdō juyō-kyōkyū hiritsu
労働需要・供給比率

labour demands
rōdōsha no yōkyū
労働者の要求

labour disputes
rōdō sōgi
労働争議

labour economics
rōdō keizai
労働経済

(study)
rōdō keizaigaku
労働経済学

labour efficiency
rōdō nōritsu
労働能率

labour force
rōdōryoku
労働力

labour-force participation rate
rōdōryoku sankaritsu
労働力参加率

labour immigration
rōdōsha inyū
労働者移入

labour immobility
rōdō no hiidōsei
労働の非移動性

labour inputs
rōdō tōnyūryō
労働投入量

labour-intensive
rōdō shūyakuteki na
労働集約的な

labour-intensive industries
rōdō shūyakuteki sangyō
労働集約的産業

labour issues
rōdō mondai
労働問題

labour law(s)
rōdōhō
労働法

labour leaders
rōdō kumiai shidōsha
労働組合指導者

labour legislation
rōdō rippō
労働立法

labour market
rōdō shijō
労働市場

labour mobility
rōdō no idōsei
労働の移動性

labour movement
rōdō undō
労働運動

labour offensives
rōdō kōsei
労働攻勢

labour officials
rōdō kumiai kanbu
労働組合幹部

labour policy
rōdō seisaku
労働政策

labour power
rōdōryoku
労働力

labour practices
rōdō kōi
労働行為
rōdō kanshū
労働慣習

labour productivity
rōdō seisansei
労働生産性

labour productivity index
rōdō seisansei shisū
労働生産性指数

labour relations
rōdō kankei
労働関係

labour's share
rōdō bunpairitsu
労働分配率

labour-saving
rōdō setsuyaku
労働節約
shōryoku
省力

labour-saving technical progress
rōdō setsuyakuteki gijutsu shinpo
労働節約的技術進歩

labour-saving techniques
rōdō setsuyakuteki gijutsu
労働節約的技術

labour shortage
rōdōryoku fusoku
労働力不足

labour shortage areas
rōdōryoku fusoku chi'iki
労働力不足地域

labour standard
rōdō hon'i(sei)
労働本位(制)

Labour Standard Law [J]
rōdō kijunhō
労働基準法

labour statistics
rōdō tōkei
労働統計

labour supply
rōdō kyōkyū
労働供給

labour supply and demand
rōdō jukyū
労働需給

labour surplus
rōdō yojō
労働余剰

labour surplus economy
rōdō yojō keizai
労働余剰経済

labour survey
rōdōryoku chōsa
労働力調査

labour theory of value
rōdō kachisetsu
労働価値説

labour turnover
rōdō idō
労働異動
rōdōsha idō
労働者異動

labour union [US] (see trade union [UK])
rōdō kumiai
労働組合

labour unrest
rōdō fuan
労働不安

labourers
rōdōsha
労働者

lag
okure
遅れ
ragu
ラグ

lagging indicator
chikō shihyō
遅行指標

laissez-faire
jiyū kyōsō shugi
自由競争主義

land
tochi
土地

land classification
tochi kubun
土地区分

land-intensive
tochi shūyakuteki na
土地集約的な

land management
tochi kanri
土地管理

land reform
tochi kaikaku
土地改革

land tax
chiso
地租

land tenure
tochi hoyū
土地保有

last quarter
daiyon shihanki
第四四半期

latent demand
senzai juyō
潜在需要

latent inflation
senzai infurēshon
潜在インフレーション

latent supply
senzai kyōkyū
潜在供給

latent unemployment
senzai shitsugyō
潜在失業

lateral integration
sokumen tōgō
側面統合

law of comparative advantage
hikaku yūi no hōsoku
比較優位の法則

law of constant returns
shūkaku fuhen no hōsoku
収穫不変の法則

law of cost
seisanhi no hōsoku
生産費の法則

law of demand
juyō no hōsoku
需要の法則

law of diminishing marginal productivity
genkai seisanryoku teigen no hōsoku
限界生産力逓減の法則

law of diminishing marginal utility
genkai kōyō teigen no hōsoku
限界効用逓減の法則

law of diminishing returns
shūkaku teigen no hōsoku
収穫逓減の法則

law of diminishing utility
kōyō teigen no hōsoku
効用逓減の法則

law of increasing costs
seisanhi zenzō no hōsoku
生産費漸増の法則

law of increasing returns
shūkaku teizō no hōsoku
収穫逓増の法則

law of indifference
shijō musabetsu no hōsoku
市場無差別の法則

law of returns to scale
kibo ni kansuru shūkaku
hōsoku
規模に関する収穫
法則

law of supply and demand
juyō to kyōkyū no hōsoku
需要と供給の法則

law of variable proportions
kahen hiritsu no hōsoku
可変比率の法則

lay-offs
ichiji kaiko rōdōsha
一時解雇労働者
rinji shitsugyōsha
臨時失業者
reiofu
レイオフ

LDCs (less developed countries)
teikaihatsukoku
低開発国

leaders
shidōsha
指導者

leading business indicators
shuyō keiki shihyō
主要景気指標

leading indicators
senkō shihyō
先行指標

leading industrial countries
senshin kōgyōkoku
先進工業国

leading industry
sendō sangyō
先導産業

leading sector
sendō bumon
先導部門

leapfrogging
dashinuki
出し抜き

learning
gakushū riron
学習理論

learning by doing
gakushū riron
学習理論

leasing
riisu
リース

least-cost method of production
saishō hiyō seisan hōshiki
最小費用生産方式

least squares
saishō nijō
最小二乗

least squares method
saishō nijōhō
最小二乗法

leftward-shifting
sahō idō
左方移動

legal minimum wage
hōtei chingin
法定賃金

legal tender
hōka
法貨
hōtei tsūka
法定通貨

leisure
yoka
余暇

lender of last resort
saishū no kashite
最終の貸手

lenders
kashite
貸手

less developed countries (LDCs)
teikaihatsukoku
低開発国

level
suijun
水準

level of consumption
shōhi suijun
消費水準

level of significance
yūisei suijun
有意性水準

level out
yokobai suru
横這いする

levelling-out
yokobai
横這い

leverage [US]
teiritsu
挺率

levies
nōzei
納税

levies in kind
butsunōzei
物納税

levies in money
kinsen nōzei
金銭納税

liberal economic policy
jiyū shugiteki keizai seisaku
自由主義的経済政策

liberalism
jiyū shugi
自由主義

liberalization
jiyūka
自由化

liberalization measures
jiyūka sochi
自由化措置

liberalization of trade
bōeki no jiyūka
貿易の自由化

life-cycle hypothesis
raifu-saikuru kasetsu
ライフ・サイクル
仮説

life expectancy
heikin yomei
平均余命

lifestyle
seikatsu yōshiki
生活様式

lifting of embargo
kaikin
解禁

likelihood
yūdo
尤度

likelihood function
yūdo kansū
尤度関数

likelihood ratio
yūdohi
尤度比

likelihood ratio test
yūdohi kentei
尤度比検定

limit pricing
seigen kakaku keisei
制限価格形成

limitation on imports
yunyū seigen
輸入制限

limited competition
seigenteki kyōsō
制限的競争

limited industrialization
bubunteki kōgyōka
部分的工業化

limited information
seigen jōhō
制限情報

limited market
yūgenteki shijō
有限的市場

limited resources
yūgen shigen
有限資源

limited supply of labour
rōdō no yūgenteki kyōkyū
労働の有限的供給

liquid assets hypothesis
ryūdō shisan kasetsu
流動資産仮説

liquid capital goods
ryūdō shihonzai
流動資本財

liquidity
ryūdosei
流動性

liquidity basis
ryūdosei bēsu
流動性ベース

liquidity of money
kahei no ryūdōsei
貨幣の流動性

liquidity preference
ryūdōsei senkō
流動性選好

liquidity preference theory
ryūdōsei senkōsetsu
流動性選好説

liquidity theory
ryūdōseisetsu
流動性説

liquidity trap
ryūdosei torappu
流動性トラップ

livable environment
seikatsu tekisei kankyō
生活適性環境

livelihood
seikei
生計

living conditions
seikatsu jōtai
生活状態

living difficulties
seikatsunan
生活難

living environment
seikatsu kankyō
生活環境

living expenses
seikatsuhi
生活費

living standards
seikatsu suijun
生活水準

living wage
seikatsu chingin
生活賃金

loanable funds theory of interest
rishi no kashitsuke shikin jukyūsetsu
利子の貸付資金
需給説

lobby
robii
ロビー

lobbyist
robiisuto
ロビイスト

local authorities
chihō kanchō
地方官庁

local development
chihō kaihatsu
地方開発

local employment
chihō koyō
地方雇用

local expenditure
chihōhi
地方費

local finance
chihō zaisei
地方財政

local government finance
chihō zaisei
地方財政

local labour
(zone)
chihō rōdō
地方労働

(native)
dochaku rōdō
土着労働

local labour market
chihō rōdō shijō
地方労働市場

local monopoly
chihō dokusen
地方独占

local public enterprises
chihō kōei kigyō
地方公営企業

local public entities
chihō kōkyō dantai
地方公共団体

local public finance
chihō zaisei
地方財政

local tax
sozei
租税

(rates [UK])
chihōzei
地方税

local unions
chiku rōdō kumiai
地区労働組合

localization
chi'ikiteki shūchū
地域的集中

localization of industry
sangyō no chi'ikiteki
shūchū
産業の地域的集中

localization of labour
rōdō no chi'ikiteki shūchū
労働の地域的集中

location of industry
sangyō ritchi
産業立地

location theory
ritchiron
立地論

lock-outs
rokku-auto
ロック・アウト

(place of business)
jigyōsho heisa
事業所閉鎖

(factory)
kōjō heisa
工場閉鎖

long-run
chōki no
長期の

long-run average cost
chōki heikin hiyō
長期平均費用

**long-run consumption
function**
chōki shōhi kansū
長期消費関数

long-run cost curves
chōki hiyō kyokusen
長期費用曲線

long-run equilibrium
chōki kinkō
長期均衡

long-term
chōki no
長期の
chōkiteki na
長期的な

**long-term capital (balance of
payments)**
chōki shikin shūshi
長期資金収支

long-term development
chōki kaihatsu
長期開発

long-term economic forecast
chōki keizai yosoku
長期経済予測

long-term economic outlook
chōki keizai tenbō
長期経済展望

long-term effects
chōkiteki eikyō
長期的影響

long-term expectation
chōki kitai
長期期待

long-term financial strategy
chōki zaimu senryaku
長期財務戦略

long-term forecast
chōki yosoku
長期予測

long-term foreign trade credits
chōki bōeki shin'yō
長期貿易信用

long-term growth
chōki seichō
長期成長

long-term outlook
chōkiteki tenbō
長期的展望

long-term planning
chōki keikaku
長期計画

long-term trend
chōki keikō
長期傾向

loopholes
nukeana
抜け穴

loss function
sonshitsu kansū
損失関数

low income
teishotoku
低所得

low-income bracket
teishotokusō
低所得層

low-income earners
teishotokusha
低所得者

low-income nations
teishotokukoku
低所得国

low-interest loans
teiri yūshi
低利融資

low interest rates
teikinri
低金利

low interest rates policy
teikinri seisaku
低金利政策

low-pressure economy
teiatsu keizai
低圧経済

low-wage economy
teichingin keizai
低賃金経済

low-wage nation
teichinginkoku
低賃金国

low wages
teichingin
低賃金

lower and medium income groups
chūtei shotokusō
中低所得層

luxury
shashi
奢侈

luxury goods
shashihin
奢侈品
zeitakuhin
ぜい沢品

luxury taxes
shashizei
奢侈税

macro-dynamic theory
kyoshiteki dōtairon
巨視的動態論

macro-economic model
kyoshiteki keizai moderu
巨視的経済モデル
makuro keizai moderu
マクロ経済モデル

macro-economic policy
kyoshiteki keizai seisaku
巨視的経済政策
makuro keizai seisaku
マクロ経済政策

macro-economics
kyoshiteki keizaigaku
巨視的経済学
makuro keizaigaku
マクロ経済学

main industries
shuyō sangyō
主要産業

mainstream economists
shuryūha no keizaigakusha
主流派の経済学者

maintenance of services
sābisu no iji
サービスの維持

major countries
shuyōkoku
主要国

major disturbances
ōkii dōyō
大きい動揺

major employers
daikoyōnushi
大雇用主

major industrial nations
shuyō kōgyōkoku
主要工業国

major industries
shuyō sangyō
主要産業

majority rule
tasūketsu gensoku
多数決原則

male working population
danshi rōdō jinkō
男子労働人口

malleable capital
junnōsei shihon
順応性資本

Malthusian theory of population
marusasuteki jinkōron
マルサス的人口論

Malthusianism
marusasu jinkōron
マルサス人口論
marusasu shugi
マルサス主義

managed economy
kanri keizai
管理経済

management (control)
kanri
管理

(administration, operation)
kei'ei
経営

management science
kei'eigaku
経営学

managerial capitalism
kei'eisha shihon shugi
経営者資本主義

managerial discretion
kei'eisha no sairyōteki kōdō
経営者の裁量的行動

managerial economies
kei'ei no keizai
経営の経済

managerial power
kei'eiryoku
経営力

managerial revolution
kei'eisha kakumei
経営者革命

managerial theories of the firm
kei'ei no kigyōtai riron
経営の企業体理論

manpower (human resources)
jinteki shigen
人的資源

(labour force)
rōdōryoku
労働力

manpower policy
jinteki shigen seisaku
人的資源政策

manpower shortage
rōdōryoku fusoku
労働力不足

manual labour
kinniku rōdō
筋肉労働
nikutai rōdō
肉体労働

manual workers
kinniku rōdōsha
筋肉労働者
nikutai rōdōsha
肉体労働者

manufacture
seizō suru
製造する

manufactured goods
seihin
製品

manufactured imports
kōgyōhin yunyū
工業品輸入

manufacturers
seizōgyōsha
製造業者

manufacturers' associations
kōgyōkai
工業会

manufacturing
seizō
製造

manufacturing business
seizōgyō
製造業

manufacturing capacity
seizō nōryoku
製造能力

manufacturing cost
seizō genka
製造原価

manufacturing output
seizōgyō no seisan zentai
製造業の生産全体

manufacturing plants
seizō kōjō
製造工場

margin
genkai
限界

margin of error
gosa
誤差

marginal analysis
genkai bunseki
限界分析

marginal consumer
genkai shōhisha
限界消費者

marginal consumption
genkai shōhi
限界消費

marginal cost
genkai genka
限界原価

marginal cost of acquisition
genkai shutoku hiyō
限界取得費用

marginal cost of production
genkai seisanhi
限界生産費

marginal cost pricing
genkai hiyō kakaku keisei
限界費用価格形成

marginal disutility
genkai fukōyō
限界不効用

marginal efficiency of capital
shihon no genkai kōritsu
資本の限界効率

marginal efficiency of investment
tōshi no genkai kōritsu
投資の限界効率

marginal expenses
genkai hiyō
限界費用

marginal labour
genkai rōdō
限界労働

marginal physical product
butsuteki genkai seisanbutsu
物的限界生産物

marginal product
genkai seisanbutsu
限界生産物

marginal productivity doctrine
genkai seisanryokusetsu
限界生産力説

marginal productivity of capital
shihon no genkai seisansei
資本の限界生産性

marginal productivity of labour
rōdō no genkai seisansei
労働の限界生産性

marginal productivity theory of wages
chingin no genkai seisan-ryokusetsu
賃金の限界生産力説

marginal propensity to consume (MPC)
genkai shōhi seikō
限界消費性向

marginal propensity to import
genkai yunyū seikō
限界輸入性向

marginal propensity to save
genkai chochiku seikō
限界貯蓄性向

marginal propensity to tax
genkai sozei seikō
限界租税性向

marginal rate of substitution (MRS)
genkai daitairitsu
限界代替率

marginal rate of tax
genkai zeiritsu
限界税率

marginal rate of technical substitution
gijutsu genkai daitairitsu
技術限界代替率

marginal rate of transformation
genkai henkeiritsu
限界変形率

marginal revenue
genkai shūnyū
限界収入

marginal revenue product
genkai shūnyū seisanbutsu
限界収入生産物

marginal unit
genkai tan'i
限界単位

marginal utility
genkai kōyō
限界効用

marginal utility of income
shotoku no genkai kōyō
所得の限界効用

marginal utility of money
kahei no genkai kōyō
貨幣の限界効用

marginal workers
genkai rōdōsha
限界労働者

market (noun)
shijō
市場

market access
shijō akusesu
市場アクセス

market analysis
shijō bunseki
市場分析

market classification
shijō bunrui
市場分類

market demand curve
shijō juyō kyokusen
市場需要曲線

market demand curve for labour
rōdō shijō juyō kyokusen
労働市場需要曲線

market economy
shijō keizai
市場経済

market failure
shijō no shippai
市場の失敗

market forces
shijō yōin
市場要因

market forecast
shijō mitōshi
市場見通し

market imperfection
shijō fukanzen
市場不完全

market index
shijō shisū
市場指数

market mechanism
shijō mekanizumu
市場メカニズム

market orientation
shijō shikō
市場指向

market power
shijōryoku
市場力

market price fluctuations
shika hendō
市価変動

market prices
shika
市価

market researcher
shijō chōsaka
市場調査家

market socialism
shijō shakai shugi
市場社会主義

market structure
shijō kōzō
市場構造

market supply
shijō kyōkyū
市場供給

Marxian economics
marukusu keizaigaku
マルクス経済学

Marxian theory of distribution
marukusu bunpairon
マルクス分配論

mass consumption
tairyō shōhi
大量消費

mass market
taishū shōhi shijō
大衆消費市場

mass media
taishū baitai
大衆媒体

mass poverty
taishūteki hinkon
大衆的貧困

mass production
tairyō seisan
大量生産

mass unemployment
tairyō shitsugyō
大量失業

massive borrowing
tairyō kariire
大量借入れ

massive subsidies
tagaku no hojokin
多額の補助金

massive trade deficit
ōhaba bōeki akaji
大幅貿易赤字

master budget
sōkatsu yosan
総括予算

material resources
butsuteki shigen
物的資源

materialism
busshitsu shugi
物質主義
yuibutsu shugi
唯物主義

materialist
busshitsu shugisha
物質主義者
yuibutsu shugisha
唯物主義者

materials
(raw materials)
genryō
原料

(stuff, matter)
zairyō
材料

matrix
gyōretsu
行列
matorikkusu
マトリックス

maximization
kyokudaika
極大化

maximum (value of a function)
kyokudaichi
極大値

maximum wage
saikō chingin
最高賃金

mean (adjective)
heikin no
平均の

mean (noun)
heikin
平均

means of livelihood
seikatsu shudan
生活手段

means test
shisan chōsa
資産調査

**measure
(means, way)**
shudan
手段

(action, step)
sochi
措置

measurement error
sokutei gosa
測定誤差

median
chūisū
中位数

medium and long-term credit
chūchōki shin'yō
中長期信用

**medium and long-term
interest rates**
chūchōki kinri
中長期金利

**medium and small
manufacturers**
chūshō shōkōgyōsha
中小商工業者

medium of exchange
kōkan shudan
交換手段

medium-term
chūki no
中期の

**medium-term economic
forecast**
chūki keizai yosoku
中期経済予測

**medium-term economic
outlook**
chūki keizai tenbō
中期経済展望

**medium-term financial
strategy**
chūki zaimu senryaku
中期財務戦略

medium-term forecast
chūki yosoku
中期予測

**medium-term investment
cycle**
chūki tōshi junkan
中期投資循環

member states
kameikoku
加盟国

mercantilism
jūshō shugi
重商主義

mercantilist
jūshō shugisha
重商主義者

mercantilist economic policies
jūshō shugiteki seisaku
重商主義的政策

merchant banks
shōgyō ginkō
商業銀行

methodology
hōhōron
方法論

micro-economic model
bishiteki keizai moderu
微視的経済モデル

micro-economic policy
bishiteki keizai seisaku
微視的経済政策

micro-economics
bishiteki keizaigaku
微視的経済学

middle class
chūkan kaikyū
中間階級

middle-income bracket
chūkan shotoku kaisō
中間所得階層
chūshotokusō
中所得層

middle-income nations
chūshotokukoku
中所得国

migrant workers
ijū rōdōsha
移住労働者

mild recession
keibi na keiki kōtai
軽微な景気後退

military expenditure
gunjihi
軍事費

minimum (value of a function)
kyokushōchi
極小値

minimum lending rate (MLR)
saitei kashidashi buai
最低貸出歩合

minimum taxable income
kazei saitei shotoku
課税最低所得

minimum wage
saitei chingin
最低賃金

(legal)
hōtei chingin
法定賃金

minimum wage legislation
saitei chinginhō
最低賃金法

mini-recession
kogata no risesshon
小型のリセッション

Ministry of International Trade and Industry (MITI) [J]
tsūshō sangyōshō
通商産業省
tsūsanshō
通産省

Ministry of Trade and Industry [UK]
bōeki kōgyōshō
貿易工業省

minor business cycle
shōjunkan
小循環

minor industries
chūshō sangyō
中小産業

misalignment
fuchōsei
不調整

misallocation
futekisei haibun
不適正配分

misappropriation of funds
ryūyō
流用

miscalculations
gosan
誤算

miscellaneous receipts (government's)
zasshūnyū
雑収入

MITI (Ministry of International Trade and Industry) [J]
tsūshō sangyōshō
通商産業省
tsūsanshō
通産省

mixed economy
kongō keizai
混合経済

mixed goods
kongōzai
混合財

mixed-market economy
kongō keizai
混合経済

MLR (minimum lending rate)
saitei kashidashi buai
最低貸出歩合

mobility of labour
rōdōryoku no idōsei
労働力の移動性

mode (a variable)
saihinchi
最頻値

mode of production
seisan yōshiki
生産様式

model
moderu
モデル

moderate inflation
keido infurēshon
軽度インフレーション

modern industries
gendai sangyō
現代産業

modernization
kindaika
近代化

modus operandi
un'ei hōshin
運営方針

monetarism
tsūka shugi
通貨主義

monetarist
tsūka shugisha
通貨主義者

monetarist policy
tsūka shugisha no seisaku
通貨主義者の政策

monetary agreement
tsūka kyōtei
通貨協定

monetary analysis
kahei bunseki
貨幣分析

monetary authorities
tsūka tōkyoku
通貨当局

monetary base
kaheiteki bēsu
貨幣的ベース

monetary crisis
tsūka kiki
通貨危機

monetary discipline
kin'yū setsudo
金融節度

monetary economy
kin'yū keizai
金融経済

monetary equilibrium
kaheiteki kinkō
貨幣的均衡

monetary expansion
kin'yū kakudai
金融拡大

monetary flow
kahei no ryūtsū
貨幣の流通

monetary growth
tsūka kyōkyū nobiritsu
通貨供給伸び率

monetary instability
tsūka fuan
通貨不安

monetary management
tsūka kanri
通貨管理

monetary policy (finance)
kin'yū seisaku
金融政策

(currency)
tsūka seisaku
通貨政策

monetary reform
tsūka kaikaku
通貨改革

monetary relaxation
kin'yū kanwa
金融緩和

monetary reserves
tsūka junbi
通貨準備

monetary restraint
kin'yū hikishime
金融引締め

monetary situation
kin'yū jijō
金融事情

monetary stabilization
tsūka antei
通貨安定

monetary stability
tsūka anteisei
通貨安定性

monetary stringency
kin'yū hippaku
金融逼迫

monetary structure
tsūka taisei
通貨体制

monetary system
kahei seido
貨幣制度
tsūka seido
通貨制度

monetary theory
kahei shugi
貨幣主義

monetary union
kahei dōmei
貨幣同盟

monetary unit
kahei tan'i
貨幣単位
tsūka tan'i
通貨単位

monetary unrest
tsūka fuan
通貨不安

monetary upheaval
tsūkaryō no gekidō
通貨量の激動

monetary value
kahei kachi
貨幣価値

monetary war
tsūka sensō
通貨戦争

monetization
kaheika
貨幣化

monetization of debt
kōsai no kaheika
公債の貨幣化

money
(general)
kane
金

(cash, specie)
genkin
現金

(coinage, currency)
kahei
貨幣

(funds)
shikin
資金

money balances
kahei zandaka
貨幣残高

money capital
kahei shihon
貨幣資本

money flow
shikin junkan
資金循環

money flow analysis
shikin junkan bunseki
資金循環分析

money illusion
kahei sakkaku
貨幣錯覚

money income
genkin shūnyū
現金収入

money-losing companies
akaji no kigyō
赤字の企業

money market
kin'yū shijō
金融市場

money multiplier
kahei jōsū
貨幣乗数

money stock
kahei sutokku
貨幣ストック

money supply
manē-sapurai
マネー・サプライ
tsūka kyōkyūryō
通貨供給量

money supply analysis
manē-sapurai bunseki
マネー・サプライ分析

money terms
meimoku
名目

money wages
genkin chingin
現金賃金

**Monopolies and Mergers Act
[UK]**
dokusen to gappeihō
独占と合併法

**Monopolies and Mergers
Commission [UK]**
dokusen to gappei i'inkai
独占と合併委員会

monopolist
dokusen ronsha
独占論者

monopolistic competition
dokusenteki kyōsō
独占的競争

monopolistic market
dokusenteki shijō
独占的市場

monopoly
(exclusive possession)
dokusen
独占

(exclusive sale)
senbai
専売

monopoly capital
dokusen shihon
独占資本

monopoly capitalism
dokusen shihon shugi
独占資本主義

monopoly power
dokusenryoku
独占力

monopoly profit
dokusen rijun
独占利潤

monopsonist
juyō dokusensha
需要独占者

monopsony
juyō dokusen
需要独占

monthly average
tsuki heikin
月平均

monthly economic report
getsurei hōkoku
月例報告

monthly index
maigetsu no shisū
毎月の指数

moonlighting
fukugyō
副業

mortality rate
shibōritsu
死亡率

most favoured nation
saikeikoku
最恵国

most-favoured-nation clause
saikeikoku jōkō
最恵国条項

motive for holding money
kahei hoyū no dōki
貨幣保有の動機

moving average
idō heikin
移動平均

moving average method
idō heikinhō
移動平均法

MPC (marginal propensity to consume)
genkai shōhi seikō
限界消費性向

MRS (marginal rate of substitution)
genkai daitairitsu
限界代替率

multi-industrial unions
tasangyōkan rōdō kumiai
多産業間労働組合

multilateral agreement
takokukan kyōtei
多国間協定

multilateral aid
takaku enjo
多角援助
takokukan enjo
多国間援助

multilateral trade
takaku bōeki
多角貿易

multilateral trade negotiations
takokukan bōeki kōshō
多国間貿易交渉
takakuteki tsūshō kōshō
多角的通商交渉

multilateralism
takaku shugi
多角主義

multinational corporations (= multinationals)
takokuseki kigyō
多国籍企業

multiplier
jōsū
乗数

multiplier-accelerator model
jōsū-kasokudo moderu
乗数・加速度モデル

multiplier analysis
jōsū bunseki
乗数分析

multiplier effect
jōsū kōka
乗数効果

multi-product firms
tasū shōhin seizō gaisha
多数商品製造会社

multisector growth model
tabumon seichō moderu
多部門成長モデル

municipal tax
shichōsonzei
市町村税

mutual aid
sōgo enjo
相互援助

nation, the
kokumin
国民

national accounts
kokumin keizai keisan
国民経済計算

national assets
kokuyū zaisan
国有財産

national balance sheet
kokumin taishaku taishōhyō
国民貸借対照表

National Bureau for Economic Research (NBER) [US]
kokumin keizai kenkyūjo
国民経済研究所

national capital
kokumin shihon
国民資本

national capital account
kokumin shihon kanjō
国民資本勘定

national consensus
kokuminteki gōi
国民的合意

national debt
kokka saimu
国家債務
kokusai
国債

national debt expenses
kokusaihi
国債費

national debt interest
kokka saimu rishi
国家債務利子

national debt management
kokusai kanri
国債管理

national defence
kokubō
国防

national defence budget
kokubō yosan
国防予算

national defence expenses
kokubō shishutsu
国防支出

national dividend
kokumin bunpaibun
国民分配分

national economic activity
kokunai keiki
国内景気

National Economic
Development Council
(Neddy, NEDC) [UK]
kokumin keizai hatten
shingikai
国民経済発展審議会

National Economic Development Office (NEDO) [UK]
kokumin keizai hattenkyoku
国民経済発展局

national economy
kokumin keizai
国民経済

National Enterprise Board
(NEB) [UK]
kokka kigyō kōsha
国家企業公社

national expenditure
kokumin shishutsu
国民支出

national health insurance
kokumin kenkō hoken
国民健康保険

National Health Service (NHS)
[UK]
kokumin hoken sābisu
国民保険サービス

national income
kokumin shotoku
国民所得

national income accounting
kokumin shotoku keisan
国民所得計算

national income analysis
kokumin shotoku bunseki
国民所得分析

national income distributed
bunpai kokumin shotoku
分配国民所得

national income expended
shishutsu kokumin shotoku
支出国民所得

national income produced
seisan kokumin shotoku
生産国民所得

national income statistics
kokumin shotoku tōkei
国民所得統計

National Institute of
Economics and Social
Research (NIESR) [UK]
kokumin keizai shakai
kenkyūjo
国民経済社会研究所

National Insurance [UK]
kokumin hoken
国民保険

National Insurance
contributions [UK]
kokumin hoken futan
国民保険負担

National Insurance Fund [UK]
kokumin hoken kikin
国民保険基金

National Labour Relations Act
[US]
zenkoku rōdō kankeihō
全国労働関係法

national output
kokunai seisanryō
国内生産量

national planning
kokka keikaku
国家計画
kokumin keikaku
国民計画

national product
kokumin seisanbutsu
国民生産物

national resources
kokka shigen
国家資源

national savings
kokumin chochiku
国民貯蓄

national savings rate
kokumin chochikuritsu
国民貯蓄率

national wealth
kokufu
国富

nationalistic one-upmanship
aikokuteki na warekoso
愛国的なわれこそ

nationalization
kokuyūka
国有化

nationalized industry
kokuyū sangyō
国有産業

nationals (of a country)
dōkokujin
同国人

natural division of labour
shizenteki bungyō
自然的分業

natural economy
shizen keizai
自然経済

natural law
shizenhō
自然法

natural monopoly
shizen dokusen
自然独占

natural price
shizen kakaku
自然価格

natural rate of growth
shizen seichōritsu
自然成長率

natural rate of unemployment
shizen shitsugyōritsu
自然失業率

natural resources
tenzen shigen
天然資源

natural selection hypothesis
shizen tōta kasetsu
自然淘汰仮説

NBER (National Bureau for Economic Research) [US]
kokumin keizai kenkyūjo
国民経済研究所

near money
juntsūka
準通貨

NEB (National Enterprise Board) [UK]
kokka kigyō kōsha
国家企業公社

necessities of life
seikatsu hitsujuhin
生活必需品

necessity (a good)
hitsuyōhin
必要品

NEDC (National Economic Development Council) (Neddy) [UK]
kokumin keizai hatten shingikai
国民経済発展審議会

Neddy (see NEDC)

NEDO (National Economic Development Office) [UK]
kokumin keizai hattenkyoku
国民経済発展局

need
yōkyū
要求

negative balance of payments
gyakuchō kokusai shūshi
逆調国際収支

negative balance of trade
gyakuchō bōeki shūshi
逆調貿易収支

negative growth rate
mainasu no seichōritsu
マイナスの成長率

negative income tax
gyakushotokuzei
逆所得税

negotiations
kōshō
交渉

neo-classical economics
shinkotenha keizaigaku
新古典派経済学

neo-classical growth theory
shinkotenha seichō riron
新古典派成長理論

neo-imperialism
shinteikoku shugi
新帝国主義

neo-Malthusianism
shinmarusasu shugi
新マルサス主義

neo-orthodoxy
shinseitōha
新正統派

net barter terms of trade
junshōhin kōeki jōken
純商品交易条件

net budget
junkei yosan
純計予算

net consumption
junshōhi
純消費

net debtor countries
junsaimukoku
純債務国

net deficit
jun'akaji
純赤字

net demand
junjuyō
純需要

net domestic income
kokumin junshotoku
国民純所得

net exports
jun'yushutsu
純輸出

net exports of goods and services
zai-sābisu no jun'yushutsu
財・サービスの純輸出

net income
junshotoku
純所得

net investment
juntōshi
純投資

net national income
kokumin junshotoku
国民純所得

net national product (NNP)
kokumin junseisan
国民純生産

net output
junsanshutsuryō
純産出量

net present value (NPV)
jungenzai kachi
純現在価値

net production
junseisandaka
純生産高

net savings
junchochiku
純貯蓄

net surplus
junjōyokin
純剰余金

neutral budget
chūritsu yosan
中立予算

neutral monetary policy
chūritsugata kin'yū seisaku
中立型金融政策

neutral money
chūritsu kahei
中立貨幣

neutral rate of interest
chūritsuteki rishiritsu
中立的利子率

neutral technical progress
chūritsuteki gijutsu shinpo
中立的技術進歩

neutrality of money
kahei no chūritsusei
貨幣の中立性

new industrial materials
shinsozai
新素材

new industrial states
shinsangyō kokka
新産業国家

new industry
shinsangyō
新産業

new inflation
atarashii infurēshon
新しいインフレー
ション

new products
shinseihin
新製品

newly industrialized countries (NICs)
shinkō kōgyōkoku
新興工業国

NHS (National Health Service) [UK]
kokumin hoken sābisu
国民保険サービス

NICs (newly industrialized countries)
shinkō kōgyōkoku
新興工業国

NIESR (National Institute of Economics and Social Research) [UK]
kokumin keizai shakai kenkyūjo
国民経済社会研究所

NNP (net national product)
kokumin junseisan
国民純生産

noise pollution
sōon kōgai
騒音公害

nominal balances
meimoku genkin zandaka
名目現金残高

nominal GNP
meimoku kokumin sōseisan
名目国民総生産

nominal income
meimoku shotoku
名目所得

nominal terms
meimoku
名目

nominal wages
meimoku chingin
名目賃金

non-aligned nations
hidōmei shokoku
非同盟諸国

non-competing groups
mukyōsō shūdan
無競争集団

non-discriminatory trade
musabetsu bōeki
無差別貿易

non-durable consumer goods
hitaikyū shōhizai
非耐久消費材

non-durable goods
hitaikyūzai
非耐久材

non-excludability
haijo fukanōsei
排除不可能性

non-export agreement
yushutsu kinshi kyōtei
輸出禁止協定

non-farm households
hinōka
非農家

non-farming population
hinōgyō jinkō
非農業人口

non-labour income
furōshotoku
不労所得

non-manual labour
zunō rōdō
頭脳労働

non-manual workers
zunō rōdōsha
頭脳労働者

non-manufactured goods
hikōgyō seihin
非工業製品

non-oil-producing countries
hisan'yukoku
非産油国

non-pecuniary goals
hikinsenteki mokuhyō
非金銭的目標

non-permanent resources
hieikyūteki shigen
非永久的資源

non-price competition
kakakugai kyōsō
価格外競争

non-profit institutions
hi'eiri kikan
非営利機関

non-profit organizations
hi'eiri dantai
非営利団体

non-renewable resources
hisaisei shigen
非再生資源

non-restricted industries
hiseigen gyōshu
非制限業種

non-rival consumption
hikyōgōteki shōhi
非競合的消費

non-tariff barrier (NTB) [US]
hikanzei shōheki
非関税障壁

non-tariff trade distortions
hikanzei bōeki yugami
非関税貿易歪み

non-tax revenue
zeigai shūnyū
税外収入

non-taxable income
hikazei shotoku
非課税所得

non-wage labour costs
hichingin rōdōhi
非賃金労働費

norm
kijun
規準

normal cost pricing
seijō kosuto kakaku keisei
正常コスト価格形成

normal distribution
seiki bunpu
正規分布

normal good
seijōzai
正常財

normal profits
seijō rijun
正常利潤

normal unemployment rate
seijō shitsugyōritsu
正常失業率

normative economics
kihanteki keizaigaku
規範的経済学

notional demand
gainenteki juyō
概念的需要

nouveaux riches
narikin
成金

NPV (net present value)
jungenzai kachi
純現在価値

NTB (non-tariff barrier) [US]
hikanzei shōheki
非関税障壁

OAP (old-age pensioner) [UK]
rōrei nenkin jukyūsha
老齢年金受給者

objective
(target)
mokuhyō
目標

(aim)
mokuteki
目的

objective function
mokuteki kansū
目的関数

obsolescence
chinpuka
陳腐化

obsolete
chinpuka shita
陳腐化した

obstructionism
bōgai kōsaku
妨害工作

occupation
shokugyō
職業

occupation census
shokugyō tōkei chōsa
職業統計調査

occupational classification
shokumu bunrui
職務分類

occupational differentiation
shokugyō bunka
職業分化

occupational distribution
shokugyō bunpai
職業分配

occupational groups
shokugyō shūdan
職業集団
shokushu
職種

occupational wage differentials
shokugyō chingin kakusa
職業賃金格差

occupational wage structure
shokugyō kyūyo kōzō
職業給与構造

OECD (Organization for Economic Co-operation and Development)
keizai kyōryoku kaihatsu kikō
経済協力開発機構

OEEC (Organization for European Economic Co-operation)
ōshū keizai kyōryoku kikō
欧州経済協力機構

Office of Fair Trading [UK]
kōsei torihikikyoku
公正取引局

Office of Management and Budget [US]
gyōsei kanri yosankyoku
行政管理予算局

official discount rate
kōtei buai
公定歩合

official index
kōshiki no shisū
公式の指数

official price of goods
kōtei kakaku
公定価格

official settlement basis
kōteki kessai bēsu
公的決済ベース

offshore investment centres
zeikin hinanchi
税金避難地

oil-consuming countries
sekiyu shōhikoku
石油消費国

oil consumption
sekiyu shōhi
石油消費

oil crisis
sekiyu kiki
石油危機

oil embargo
sekiyu yushutsu kinshi
石油輸出禁止

oil-exporting countries
sekiyu yushutsukoku
石油輸出国

oil exports
sekiyu yushutsu
石油輸出

oil-importing countries
sekiyu yunyūkoku
石油輸入国

oil imports
sekiyu yunyū
石油輸入

oil-induced deficit
sekiyu akaji
石油赤字

oil prices
sekiyu kakaku
石油価格

oil producers
sekiyu seisan kigyō
石油生産企業

oil-producing cartel
san'yukoku karuteru
産油国カルテル

oil-producing countries
san'yukoku
産油国

oil-rich countries
sekiyu fuyūkoku
石油富裕国

oil shock
sekiyu shokku
産油ショック

oil spill
sekiyu rōshutsu
産油漏出

old-age benefits
rōrei nenkin kyūfukin
老齢年金給付金

old-age pension
yōrō nenkin
養老年金

old-age pensioner (OAP) [UK]
rōrei nenkin jukyūsha
老齢年金受給者

old industrial countries
oitaru kōgyōkoku
老いたる工業国

oligopolist
kasensha
寡占者

oligopolistic behaviour
kasenteki kōi
寡占的行為

oligopolistic competition
kasenteki kyōsō
寡占的競争

oligopolistic economy
kasen keizai
寡占経済

oligopoly
kasen
寡占

oligopsonist
shōsū kōbai dokusen
ronsha
少数購買独占論者

oligopsony
shōsū kōbai dokusen
少数購買独占

one-sector growth model
ichibumon seichō moderu
一部門成長モデル

one-sided foreign trade
katabōeki
片貿易

OPEC (Organization of Petroleum Exporting Countries)
opekku
オペック
sekiyu yushutsukoku kikō
石油輸出国機構

open competition
kōkai kyōsō
公開競争

open economy
kaihō keizai
開放経済

open inflation
kaihōgata infurēshon
開放型インフレー
ション

open market
kōkai shijō
公開市場

open-market operations
kōkai shijō sōsa
公開市場操作

open-market place
kaihō shijō
開放市場

open-market policy
kaihō shijō seisaku
開放市場政策

open-price system
kōkai kakaku seido
公開価格制度

open pricing
kōkai kakaku keisei
公開価格形成

open trade policy
kaihō bōeki seisaku
開放貿易政策

open unemployment
kaihō shitsugyō
開放失業

open world trade
kaihō sekai bōeki
開放世界貿易

opening of financial markets
kin'yū shijō no kaihō
金融市場の開放

operating rate
setsubi kadōritsu
設備稼働率

operational lag
sōsajō no ragu
操作上のラグ

opportunism
gotsugō shugi
御都合主義
hiyorimi shugi
日和見主義

opportunity
kikai
機会

opportunity cost
kikai hiyō
機会費用

optimal capacity
saiteki nōryoku
最適能力

optimal distribution
saiteki bunpai
最適分配

optimal growth
saiteki seichō
最適成長

optimal growth policy
saiteki seichō seisaku
最適成長政策

optimal level of pollution
kōgai no saiteki suijun
公害の最適水準

optimal rate of growth
saiteki seichōritsu
最適成長率

optimal resource allocation
shigen tekisei haibun
資源適正配分

optimism
rakkan
楽観

optimum
saiteki
最適

optimum allocation
saiteki haibun
最適配分

optimum capacity
saiteki nōryoku
最適能力

optimum density
saiteki mitsudo
最適密度

optimum population
tekisei jinkō
適正人口

optimum specialization
saiteki bungyōka
最適分業化

optimum tariff
saiteki kanzei
最適関税

optional consumption
sentakuteki shōhi
選択的消費

ordinal utility
josūteki kōyō
序数的効用

ordinate
jūzahyō
縦座標

organic composition of capital
shihon no yūkiteki kōsei
資本の有機的構成

organization
(group)
dantai
団体

(mechanism)
kikō
機構

(association)
kyōkai
協会

(construction, formation)
soshiki
組織

Organization for Economic Co-operation and Development (OECD)
keizai kyōryoku kaihatsu kikō
経済協力開発機構

Organization for European Economic Co-operation (OEEC)
ōshū keizai kyōryoku kikō
欧州経済協力機構

Organization of Petroleum Exporting Countries (OPEC)
opekku
オペック
sekiyu yushutsukoku kikō
石油輸出国機構

organized labour
soshiki rōdōsha
組織労働者

original budget
tōsho yosan
当初予算

ostentatious consumption
kojiteki shōhi
誇示的消費

outlook
mikomi
見込み
mitōshi
見通し

outposts
desaki
出先

output
(production, yield)
sanshutsu
産出

(volume of output)
sanshutsuryō
産出量

(yield)
seisandaka
生産高

output budgeting
seisandaka yosan seido
生産高予算制度

output lag
seisanryō no ragu
生産量のラグ

output maximization
sanshutsuryō no kyokudaika
産出量の極大化

outside lag
autosaido-ragu
アウトサイド・ラグ

outside money
gaibu kahei
外部貨幣

overall balance (of payments)
(kokusai shūshi) sōgō shūshi
(国際収支) 総合収支

overall budget
sōgō yosan
総合予算

overall demand
sōjuyō
総需要

overall economy
keizai zentai
経済全体

overall policy
sōgō seisaku
総合政策

overbuoyant period
ijō būmuki
異常ブーム期

overcapacity
chōka nōryoku
超過能力

overcrowding
kamitsu jōtai
過密状態

overemployed workers
kajō koyō rōdōsha
過剰雇用労働者

overemployment
kajō koyō
過剰雇用

overfull employment
chōkanzen koyō
超完全雇用

overheads
kansetsuhi
間接費

overidentification
kajō shikibetsu
過剰識別

overloaded economy
kafuka keizai
過負荷経済

overpopulated
jinkō kamitsu no
人口過密の

overpopulated cities
kamitsu toshi
過密都市

overpopulation
jinkō kajō
人口過剰

overproduction
kajō seisan
過剰生産

overprotected industry
kahogo sangyō
過保護産業

overseas assets (government)
zaigai shisan
在外資産

overseas business
kaigai jigyō
海外事業

overseas deployment
kaigai tenkai
海外展開

overseas sector
kaigai bumon
海外部門

overseas trade
kaigai bōeki
海外貿易
taigai bōeki
対外貿易

overstock
yojō zaiko
余剰在庫

oversupply
kyōkyū kajō
供給過剰

overtime
chōka kinmu
超過勤務
zangyō
残業

package of measures
sōgō taisaku
総合対策

pact
gōisho
合意書

panel data
paneru-dēta
パネル・データ

panel research
paneru chōsa
パネル調査

panic buying
kaiasari
買漁り

parabola
hōbutsusen
放物線

paradox of thrift
setsuyaku no gyakusetsu
節約の逆説

paradox of voting
tōhyō no gyakuri
投票の逆理

parallel imports
heikō yunyū
平行輸入

parameter
keisū
係数
paramētā
パラメーター

Pareto conditions
parētoteki saiteki jōken
パレート的最適条件

Pareto's law
parēto no hōsoku
パレートの法則

parsimony
kyokudo no ken'yaku
極度の倹約

partial adjustment
bubun chōsei
部分調整

partial equilibrium
bubun kinkō
部分均衡

partial equilibrium analysis
bubun kinkō bunseki
部分均衡分析

partial monopoly
bubun dokusen
部分独占

participation rate
yūgyōritsu
有業率

passive balance
kokusai shūshi no akaji
国際収支の赤字

past performance
kako no jisseki
過去の実績

pattern bargaining
hinagata kōshō
雛型交渉

pauper labour
hinmin rōdō
貧民労働

pay-as-you-earn (PAYE) [UK]
gensen kazei
源泉課税

pay-back method
shihon kaishū
資本回収

pay ceiling
chingin saikō gendo
賃金最高限度

pay cuts
chingin kirisage
賃金切下げ
genpō
減俸

pay freeze
chingin tōketsu
賃金凍結

pay increases
chin'age
賃上げ
shōkyū
昇給

pay level
kyūyo suijun
給与水準

pay pause [UK]
chingin tōketsu
賃金凍結

pay rises
chin'age
賃上げ
shōkyū
昇給

pay talks
chingin kōshō
賃金交渉

PAYE (pay-as-you-earn) [UK]
gensen kazei
源泉課税

payment by results
nōritsukyū
能率給

PDI (personal disposable income)
kojin kashobun shotoku
個人可処分所得

peace-time economy
heiji keizai
平時経済

peak period labour demand
saikōki no rōdō juyō
最高期の労働需要

penetration (capital)
shintō
浸透

pension fund
nenkin kikin
年金基金

(government employees)
onkyū kikin
恩給基金

pension scheme (government employees)
onkyū seido
恩給制度

pensioners
nenkin jukyūsha
年金受給者

(government employees)
onkyū juryōsha
恩給受領者

pensions
nenkin
年金

pensions-related expenses
onkyū kankeihi
恩給関係費

per capita
hitori atari no
一人当たりの

per capita consumption
hitori atari shōhi
一人当たり消費

per capita income
hitori atari shotoku
一人当たり所得

perfect competition
kanzen kyōsō
完全競争

perfect information
kanzen jōhō
完全情報

perfect market
kanzen shijō
完全市場

perfect monopoly
kanzen dokusen
完全独占

perfect oligopoly
kanzen kasen
完全寡占

performance (business results)
gyōseki
業績

(actual results, performance record)
jisseki
実績

period
kikan
期間

period analysis
kikan bunseki
期間分析

period of depressed activity
fushinki
不振期

period of prosperity
kōkeiki jidai
好景気時代

period of recession
fukyōji
不況時

period of restraint
hikishimeki
引締め期

periodic economic crisis
shūkiteki keizai kyōkō
周期的経済恐慌

permanent consumption
kōjō shōhi
恒常消費

permanent income
kōjō shotoku
恒常所得

permanent income hypothesis
kōjō shotoku kasetsu
恒常所得仮説

permanent resources
eikyūteki shigen
永久的資源

permissible error
kyoyō gosa
許容誤差

permissible level
kyoyō suijun
許容水準

personal consumption
kojin shōhi
個人消費

personal disposable income
(PDI)
kojin kashobun shotoku
個人可処分所得

personal income
kojin shotoku
個人所得

personal saving
kojin chochiku
個人貯蓄

personal taxation
taijin kazei
対人課税

perspective
(expectation)
mikomi
見込み

(outlook)
mitōshi
見通し
tenbō
展望

(forecast)
yosoku
予測

pessimism
hikan
悲観

petrodollars
sekiyu doru
石油ドル

petroleum (see oil)
sekiyu
石油

phase
kyokumen
局面

phenomenon
genshō
現象

Phillips curve
firippusu kyokusen
フィリップス曲線

physical controls
butsuryō kanri
物量管理

physical inputs
butsuteki tōnyū
物的投入

physical terms
sūryō
数量

physiocrats
jūnō shugisha
重農主義者

Pink Book [UK]
pinku-bukku
ピンク・ブック

plan
(course, line)
hōshin
方針

(project, scheme)
keikaku
計画

(idea, conception)
kōsō
構想

planned economy
keikaku keizai
計画経済

planned industry
keikaku sangyō
計画産業

planner
keikakusha
計画者

planning
keikakuka
計画化

plant and equipment
setsubi
設備

plant bargaining
kōjō kōshō
工場交渉

pleasure economy
kairaku keizai
快楽経済

point elasticity
tendanryokusei
点弾力性

policy
seisaku
政策

(line of policy)
hōshin
方針

policy administration
seisaku no kanri
政策の管理

policy implementation
seisaku no suikō
政策の遂行

policy indicator
seisaku shihyō
政策指標

policy instruments
seisaku shudan
政策手段

policy lag
seisaku no ragu
政策のラグ

policy makers
seisaku ketteisha
政策決定者

policy-making
seisaku kettei
政策決定

policy-making body
seisaku kettei kikan
政策決定機関

policy measures
seisaku sochi
政策措置

policy objective
seisaku mokuteki
政策目的

policy operation
seisaku un'ei
政策運営

policy package
sōgō seisaku
総合政策

policy priority
seisaku yūsen jun'i
政策優先順位

policy recommendation
seisaku kankoku
政策勧告

policy relaxation
seisaku kanwa
政策緩和

policy stance
seisaku taido
政策態度

policy targets
seisaku mokuhyō
政策目標

political economy
seiji keizaigaku
政治経済学

poll tax
jintōzei
人頭税

pollutants
osenbutsu
汚染物

polluted areas
osen chi'iki
汚染地域

polluter
kōgai hannin
公害犯人
kōgai hasseisha
公害発生者
osensha
汚染者

polluter-pays principle
osensha futan no gensoku
汚染者負担の原則

pollution
(environmental pollution)
kōgai
公害

(contamination)
osen
汚染

pollution control
osen kisei
汚染規制

(prevention)
kōgai bōshi
公害防止

pollution cost
kōgai kosuto
公害コスト

pollution export
kōgai yushutsu
公害輸出

pollution of the environment
kankyō osen
環境汚染

pollution rights
kōgaiken
公害権
osenken
汚染権

poor
binbō na
貧乏な

poor, the
hinkonsha
貧困者
hinmin
貧民

poor countries
binbōkoku
貧乏国
hinkonkoku
貧困国

population
jinkō
人口

population census
jinkō chōsa
人口調査
jinkō sensasu
人口センサス

population concentration
jinkō shūchūdo
人口集中度

population control
jinkō yokusei
人口抑制

population density
jinkō mitsudo
人口密度

population distribution
jinkō haibun
人口配分

population explosion
jinkō no bakuhatsu zōka
人口の爆発増加

population-food problem
jinkō-shokuryō mondai
人口・食料問題

population growth
jinkō zōka
人口増加

population policy
jinkō seisaku
人口政策

population pressure
jinkō atsuryoku
人口圧力

population problem
jinkō mondai
人口問題

population programme
jinkō keikaku
人口計画

population pyramid
jinkō bunpu piramiddo
人口分布ピラミッド

population redistribution
jinkō saibunpai
人口再分配

population statistics
jinkō tōkei
人口統計

population study
jinkō kenkyū
人口研究

population theory
jinkō riron
人口理論

population trap
jinkō no otoshiana
人口の落し穴

positive balance of trade
junchō bōeki sagaku
順調貿易差額

positive economics
jisshō(teki) keizaigaku
実証(的) 経済学

positivism
jisshō shugi
実証主義

post-industrial age
datsukōgyō jidai
脱工業時代

post-industrial economy
datsukōgyōka keizai
脱工業化経済

post-industrial society
datsukōgyō shakai
脱工業社会

post-Keynesian economics
gokikinzuha keizaigaku
後期ケインズ派
経済学

post-war period
sengoki
戦後期

potential (noun)
senzairyoku
潜在力

potential inflation
senzaiteki infurēshon
潜在的インフレー
ション

potential national income
senzaiteki kokumin shotoku
潜在的国民所得

potential output
senzaiteki seisanryō
潜在的生産量

potential unemployment
senzaiteki shitsugyō
潜在的失業

poverty
(destitution)
binbō
貧乏

(indigence)
hinkon
貧困

(want, privation)
kyūbō
窮乏

(financial distress)
kyūhaku
窮迫

poverty areas
hinkon chi'iki
貧困地域

poverty line
binbōsen
貧乏線
hinkonsen
貧困線

poverty trap
hinkon no otoshiana
貧困の落し穴

practical measures
jissaiteki shudan
実際的手段
jissaiteki sochi
実際的措置

precautionary motive
yobiteki dōki
予備的動機

precautionary unemployment
yobiteki shitsugyō
予備的失業

preference
(choice, screening)
senkō
選好

(choice, selection)
sentaku
選択

(priority)
yūsen
優先

preference revelation
senkō kenji
選好顕示

preferential hiring
kumiai'in yūsen koyō
組合員優先雇用

preferential tariffs
tokkei kanzei
特恵関税

preferential tax treatment for savings
chochiku yūgū sochi
貯蓄優遇措置

preliminary data
yobi dēta
予備データ

preliminary figures
zantei sūji
暫定数字

present conditions
genjō
現状

preservation of the environment
kankyō hozen
環境保全

pressure
atsuryoku
圧力

pressure groups
atsuryoku dantai
圧力団体

prevailing wages
ippan chingin
一般賃金

price(s)
(price of commodities)
bukka
物価

(cost, value)
kakaku
価格

(price figure)
nedan
値段

price adjustment
bukka chōsei
物価調整

price analysis
kakaku bunseki
価格分析

price cartel
kakaku karuteru
価格カルテル

price ceiling
kakaku saikō gendo
価格最高限度

Price Commission [UK]
bukka tōsei i'inkai
物価統制委員会

price competition
kakaku kyōsō
価格競争

price competitiveness
kakaku kyōsōryoku
価格競争力

price-consumption curve
kakaku-shōhi kyokusen
価格・消費曲線

price control
bukka tōsei
物価統制
kakaku tōsei
価格統制

price-cutting
kakaku kirisage
価格切下げ

price decontrol
bukka tōsei kaijo
物価統制解除
kakaku tōsei kaijo
価格統制解除

price-determined
kakaku ketteiteki
価格決定的

price-determining
kakaku kettei
価格決定

price discrimination
kakaku sabetsu
価格差別

price effect
kakaku kōka
価格効果

price elasticity
kakaku danryokusei
価格弾力性

price elasticity of demand
juyō no kakaku danryokusei
需要の価格弾力性

price explosion
bukka bakuhatsu
物価爆発
kakaku bakuhatsu
価格爆発

price-fixing
kakaku kotei
価格固定

price-fixing agreement
kakaku kyōtei
価格協定

price-fluctuation clause
kakaku hendō jōkō
価格変動条項

price fluctuations
bukka hendō
物価変動

price forecast
bukka mitōshi
物価見通し

price freeze
bukka tōketsu
物価凍結

price hikes
binjō neage
便乗値上げ

price increase
bukka jōshō
物価上昇
bukka tōki
物価騰貴

price index
bukka shisū
物価指数

price inflation
bukka infurēshon
物価インフレーション

price leadership
kakaku sendōsei
価格先導制

price level
bukka suijun
物価水準

price maintenance
kakaku iji
価格維持

price mechanism
kakaku kikō
価格機構

price movement
kakaku hendō
価格変動

price-pegging
bukka kugizuke
物価釘付け

price policy
bukka seisaku
物価政策

price pressures
bukka atsuryoku
物価圧力

price-push inflation
kakaku atsuryoku infurēshon
価格圧力インフレーション

price reduction
bukka hikisage
物価引下げ

price regulation
bukka chōsetsu
物価調節

price revolution
kakaku kakumei
価格革命

price rise
bukka jōshō
物価上昇
kakaku jōshō
価格上昇

price setter
kakaku setteisha
価格設定者

price-setting
kakaku settei
価格設定

price stability
bukka antei
物価安定

price stabilization
bukka anteika
物価安定化

price-stabilization policy
bukka anteika seisaku
物価安定化政策

price standardization
kakaku hyōjunka
価格標準化

price structure
kakaku kōzō
価格構造

price support
kakaku shiji
価格支持

price-support scheme
kakaku shijisaku
価格支持策

price system
kakaku taikei
価格体系

price taker
kakaku juyōsha
価格受容者

price theory
kakakuron
価格論

price trends
bukka dōkō
物価動向

price-wage spiral
bukka-chingin akujunkan
物価・賃金悪循環

prices and incomes policy
kakaku to shotoku seisaku
価格と所得政策

pricing
kakaku keisei
価格形成

primary commodities
dai'ichiji sanpin
第一次産品

primary employment
dai'ichiji koyō
第一次雇用

primary goods
dai'ichiji sanpin
第一次産品

primary industry
dai'ichiji sangyō
第一次産業

primary market
dai'ichiji shijō
第一次市場

(key, main)
shuyō shijō
主要市場

primary money
dai'ichiji kahei
第一次貨幣

primary products
dai'ichiji sanpin
第一次産品

primary workers
dai'ichiji rōdōsha
第一次労働者

prime cost
genka
原価

prime factor
shuyōso
主要素

prime geographical position
sairyō no chiriteki jōken
最良の地理的条件

prime rate [US]
puraimu-rēto
プライム・レート

primitive communism
genshi kyōsan shugi
原始共産主義

primitive country
mikaihatsukoku
未開発国

primitive economy
genshiteki keizai
原始的経済

primitive industry
genshiteki sangyō
原始的産業

primitive technology
genshiteki gijutsu
原始的技術

principle
(theory)
genri
原理

(guiding principle)
gensoku
原則

principle of profitability
eirisei gensoku
営利性原則

principle of substitution
daitai genri
代替原理

principle of taxation
sozei gensoku
租税原則

priority
(preference)
jūten
重点

(emphasis)
yūsen
優先

priority industries
jūten sangyō
重点産業

priority production
jūten seisan
重点生産

**private companies
(= closed corporations)
[US]**
kabushiki hikōkai gaisha
株式非公開会社

(non-governmental)
minkan kigyō
民間企業

(= limited) [UK]
shigaisha
私会社
yūgen gaisha
有限会社

private consumer sector
kojin shōhisha bumon
個人消費者部門

**private consumption
(individual)**
kojin shōhi
個人消費

(non-governmental)
minkan shōhi
民間消費

**private consumption
expenditure**
kojin shōhi shishutsu
個人消費支出

**private economic research
group**
minkan keizai chōsa
gurūpu
民間経済調査
グループ

private enterprise
shikigyō
私企業

private enterprise system
shikigyō seido
私企業制度

private expenditure
minkan shishutsu
民間支出

private foreign capital
minkangaishi
民間外資

private goods
shitekizai
私的財

private investment
minkan tōshi
民間投資

private ownership
shiyū
私有

private property
shiyū zaisan
私有財産

private savings
minkan chochiku
民間貯蓄

**private sector
(individual)**
kojin bumon
個人部門

(non-governmental)
minkan bumon
民間部門

privatization
min'eika
民営化

probability
kakuritsu
確率

probability density function
kakuritsu mitsudo kansū
確率密度関数

probability distribution
kakuritsu bunpu
確率分布

**process
(course, progress)**
katei
過程

(course, development)
keika
経過

(work process)
kōtei
工程

(production process)
seisan kōtei
生産工程

process innovation
seisan kōtei de no gijutsu
kakushin
生産工程での技術
革新

processed goods
kakōhin
加工品

**proclamation of a state of
emergency**
hijō jitai sengen
非常事態宣言

**producer price index for
manufactured goods**
kōgyō seihin seisansha
bukka shisū
工業製品生産者物価
指数

producer's surplus
seisansha yojō
生産者余剰

producers
seisansha
生産者

producers' associations
seisansha kumiai
生産者組合

producers' co-operatives
seisansha kyōdō kumiai
生産者協同組合

producers' planning
seisansha keikaku
生産者計画

producers' price index
seisansha bukka shisū
生産者物価指数

producers' prices
seisansha bukka
生産者物価

producers' shipments
seisansha shukka
生産者出荷

producing countries
sanshutsukoku
産出国
seisankoku
生産国

product
(general)
seisanbutsu
生産物

(produce)
sanbutsu
産物

(products)
sanpin
産品

(manufactured, finished)
seihin
製品
seizōhin
製造品

product cycle
seihin jumyō
製品寿命

product differentiation
seihin sabetsuka
製品差別化
seisanbutsu sabetsuka
生産物差別化

product function
seisan kansū
生産関数

product innovation
seisanbutsu no kakushin
生産物の革新

product of high-added value
kōdo no fuka kachi seihin
高度の付加価値製品

product proliferation
seisanbutsu no zōshoku
生産物の増殖

production
seisan
生産

(output, yield)
sanshutsu
産出

production activity
seisan katsudō
生産活動

production adjustment
seisan chōsei
生産調整

production amount
sanshutsuryō
産出量

production capacity
seisan nōryoku
生産能力

production capacity index
seisan nōryoku shisū
生産能力指数

production cost(s)
seisanhi
生産費

production cuts
gensan
減産

production differentiation
seisanbutsu sabetsuka
生産物差別化

production facilities
seisan setsubi
生産設備

production frontier
seisan furontia
生産フロンティア

production function
seisan kansū
生産関数

production gap
seisan gyappu
生産ギャップ

production index
seisan shisū
生産指数

production on a large scale
daikibo seisan
大規模生産

production on a small scale
shōkibo seisan
小規模生産

production plan
seisan keikaku
生産計画

production possibility curve
seisan kanōsei kyokusen
生産可能性曲線

production process
seisan kōtei
生産工程

production quota
seisan wariate
生産割当て

production rate
seisanritsu
生産率

production restraint
seisan seigen
生産制限

production technology
seisan gijutsu
生産技術

production workers
seisan rōdōsha
生産労働者

production yield
seisandaka
生産高

productive capital
seisan shihon
生産資本

productive consumption
seisanteki shōhi
生産的消費

productive efficiency
seisan kōritsu
生産効率

productive expenditure
seisanteki shishutsu
生産的支出

productive investment
seisanteki tōshi
生産的投資

productive labour
seisanteki rōdōryoku
生産的労働力

productive potential
seisan kanōsei
生産可能性

productive power
seisanryoku
生産力

productive resources
seisan shigen
生産資源

productivity
seisansei
生産性

productivity bargaining
purodakutibiti-bāgeningu
プロダクティビティ・
バーゲニング

productivity curve
seisansei kyokusen
生産性曲線

productivity deal
seisansei kyōyaku
生産性協約

productivity drive
seisansei kōjō undō
生産性向上運動

productivity effect
seisanryoku kōka
生産力効果

productivity function
seisansei kansū
生産性関数

productivity index
seisansei shisū
生産性指数

productivity measurement
seisan sokutei
生産測定

productivity of capital
shihon seisansei
資本生産性

productivity of investment
tōshi seisansei
投資生産性

productivity of labour
rōdō seisansei
労働生産性

productivity unemployment
seisansei shitsugyō
生産性失業

products for mass consumption
tairyō shōhizai
大量消費財

professions, the
senmonshoku
専門職

profit
rijun
利潤

profit function
rijun kansū
利潤関数

profit margin
jun'ekiritsu
純益率

profit maximization
rijun kyokudaika
利潤極大化

profit motive
rijun dōki
利潤動機

profit squeeze
rijun asshuku
利潤圧縮

profitability
shūekisei
収益性

(money-making)
eirisei
営利性

profitability principle
shūekisei genri
収益性原理

profiteer
('thief')
bōriya
暴利屋

(excessive profit maker)
futō ritokusha
不当利得者

profiteering
(usury)
bōri
暴利

(excessive profits)
futō ritoku kōi
不当利得行為

profits
rijun
利潤

(benefit, gain, return)
rieki
利益

(gain, return)
ritoku
利得

(earnings, return)
shūeki
収益

profits-push inflation
rijun atsuryoku infurēshon
利潤圧力インフレー
ション

programme
keikaku
計画

programme budgeting
keikaku yosan hensei
計画予算編成

progress
(march, progression)
shinkō
進行

(advancement, improvement)
shinpo
進歩

(development, evolution)
shinten
進展

progressive tax
ruishin kazei
累進課税
ruishinzei
累進税

prohibitive prices
kinshiteki kakaku
禁止的価格

project
keikaku
計画

project analysis
keikaku bunseki
計画分析

project appraisal
keikaku hyōka
計画評価

project evaluation
keikaku hyōka
計画評価

projection
mitōshi
見通し

proletariat
musan kaikyū
無産階級

proliferation
kakusan
拡散

promotion
suishin
推進

promotional bodies
suishin soshiki
推進組織

propensity
seikō
性向

propensity to consume
shōhi seikō
消費性向

propensity to export
yushutsu seikō
輸出性向

propensity to hoard
hozō seikō
保蔵性向

propensity to import
yunyū seikō
輸入性向

propensity to invest
tōshi seikō
投資性向

propensity to save
chochiku seikō
貯蓄性向

proportional tax
hirei kazei
比例課税
hireizei
比例税

proposal
teian
提案

**prospects
(hope, possibility,
outlook)**
mikomi
見込み

(perspective)
mitōshi
見通し

(forecast)
yosoku
予測

**prosperity
(affluence)**
han'ei
繁栄

(good times)
kōkeiki
好景気

**(boom, period of
prosperity)**
kōkyō
好況

**prosperous
(flourishing, thriving)**
sakan na
盛んな

(affluent)
han'ei no
繁栄の

protected industry
hogo sangyō
保護産業

protected trade
hogo bōeki
保護貿易

protection
hogo
保護

protection of the environment
kankyō hogo
環境保護

protectionism
hogo bōeki shugi
保護貿易主義

protectionist
hogo bōeki ronsha
保護貿易論者

protectionist legislation
hogo bōekihō
保護貿易法

protectionist measures
hogo bōeki seisaku sochi
保護貿易政策措置

protectionist policy
hogo bōeki seisaku
保護貿易政策

protective duties
hogo kanzei
保護関税

protective tariffs
hogo kanzei
保護関税

protective trade
hogo bōeki
保護貿易

protective trade policy
hogo bōeki seisaku
保護貿易政策

provisional budget
zantei yosan
暫定予算

provisional figures
zantei sūji
暫定数字

public, the
kokumin
国民
kōshū
公衆

public affairs
kōmu
公務

public assistance
kōteki fujo
公的扶助
seikatsu hogo
生活保護

public bonds
kōsai
公債

public companies
(public subscription)
kabushiki kōbo gaisha
株式公募会社

(public utility)
kōkyō kigyō
公共企業

(limited responsibility)
yūgen gaisha
有限会社

public consumption
kōkyō shōhi
公共消費

public credit
kōshin'yō
公信用

public debt
kōsai
公債

public deposits
kōkin yokin
公金預金

public economic policy
kōkyō keizai seisaku
公共経済政策

public education
gakkō kyō'iku
学校教育

public employment
programme
kōkyō koyō keikaku
公共雇用計画

public enterprises
kōei kigyō
公営企業

public entities
kōkyō dantai
公共団体

public expenditure
kōkyō shishutsu
公共支出

Public Expenditure Survey
Committee [UK]
kōkyō shishutsu chōsa
i'inkai
公共支出調査委員会

public finance
zaisei
財政

public funds
kōkin
公金
kōsai
公債

public goods
kōkyōzai
公共財

public groups
kōkyō dantai
公共団体

public health
hoken eisei
保健衛生

public health service
expenses
hoken eisei taisakuhi
保健衛生対策費

public information and
propaganda
kōhō senden
広報宣伝

public investment
kōkyō tōshi
公共投資

public money
kōkin
公金

public opinion poll
seron chōsa
世論調査

public organizations
kōkyō dantai
公共団体

public ownership
kōyū
公有

public policy
kōkyō seisaku
公共政策
kōteki seisaku
公的政策

public policy-making
kōteki seisaku kettei
公的政策決定

public pressure
shakaiteki atsuryoku
社会的圧力

public property
kōkyō zaisan
公共財産

public sector
kōkyō bumon
公共部門

public sector borrowing
requirements
kōkyō bumon kariire juyō
公共部門借入需要

public sector financial deficit
kōkyō bumon kanjō akaji
公共部門勘定赤字

public services
kōkyō yōeki
公共用役

(enterprises)
kōkyō jigyō
公共事業

public utilities
(works)
kōkyō jigyō
公共事業

(facilities)
kōkyō shisetsu
公共施設

public utility (common good)
kōeki
公益

public utility company
kōeki gaisha
公益会社
kōkyō kigyō
公共企業

public welfare
kōkyō fukushi
公共福祉
kōsei
厚生

public works
kōkyō jigyō
公共事業

public works expenses
kōkyō jigyō kankeihi
公共事業関係費

pump-priming
sasoimizu seisaku
誘い水政策
yobimizu seisaku
呼び水政策
yobimizushiki keizai
seisaku
呼び水式経済政策

pump-priming measures
keiki shinkōsaku
景気振興策

purchase tax
kōbaizei
購買税

purchasing power
kōbairyoku
購買力

purchasing power parity
kōbairyoku heika
購買力平価

pure competition
junsui kyōsō
純粋競争

pure interest
junsui rishi
純粋利子

pure monopoly
junsui dokusen
純粋独占

pure profit
junrieki
純利益
junrijun
純利潤

push-exports policy
yushutsu zōkyō seisaku
輸出増強政策

push-up wages
oshiage chingin
押上げ賃金

pushfulness
kumiai no atsuryoku
組合の圧力

pyramiding
piramiddogata kanri
ピラミッド型管理

quality of life
seikatsu no shitsu
生活の質

quality of the environment
kankyō no shitsu
環境の質

quantitative analysis of money
kahei sūryōteki bunseki
貨幣数量的分析

quantity equation
sūryō hōteishiki
数量方程式

quantity index of foreign trade
bōeki sūryō shisū
貿易数量指数

quantity of money
kahei sūryō
貨幣数量

quantity theory of money
kahei sūryōsetsu
貨幣数量説

quarter
shihanki
四半期

quarterly average
shihanki heikin
四半期平均

quarterly rate of growth
shihanki seichōritsu
四半期成長率

quasi-rent
junchidai
準地代

questionnaire
shitsumonsho
質問書

questionnaire survey
ankēto chōsa
アンケート調査

quit rate
rishokuritsu
離職率

quits
rishokusha
離職者

quota
(apportionment)
wariate
割当て

(allotment)
wariategaku
割当額

(human quota)
wariatesū
割当数

quota system
wariatesei
割当制

R & D (research and development)
kenkyū-kaihatsu
研究・開発
rando
ランド

radical economics
kyūshinteki keizaigaku
急進的経済学

radical measures
bapponteki sochi
抜本的措置

rampant inflation
kyōran infurēshon
狂乱インフレーション

random variable
kakuritsu hensū
確率変数

range (observations)
kansoku han'i
観測範囲

ranking of projects
keikaku no yūsen jun'i
計画の優先順位

rapid growth
kōdo seichō
高度成長

rate of commodity substitution
shōhin daitairitsu
商品代替率

rate of price increase
bukka jōshōritsu
物価上昇率

rate of return
riekiritsu
利益率

rate of surplus value
jōyo kachiritsu
剰余価値率

rate of technical substitution
gijutsuteki daitairitsu
技術的代替率

rate of time preference
jikan senkōritsu
時間選好率

rates [UK]
chihōzei
地方税

rates of interest (money rates)
kinri
金利

rates of investment
tōshi hiritsu
投資比率

ratio
hiritsu
比率

ration (<u>verb</u>)
haikyū suru
配給する

ration books
haikyū tsūchō
配給通帳

rational expectations
gōriteki kitai
合理的期待

rationalism
gōri shugi
合理主義

rationality
gōrisei
合理性

rationalization
gōrika
合理化

(personnel)
jin'in seiri
人員整理

rationalization cartel
gōrika karuteru
合理化カルテル

rationalization investment
gōrika tōshi
合理化投資

rationalization measures
gōrika sochi
合理化措置

rationalization of consumption
shōhi gōrika
消費合理化

rationalization of industry
sangyō gōrika
産業合理化

rationalization of production
seisan gōrika
生産合理化

rationalization of rationing
haikyū gōrika
配給合理化

rationalization policy
gōrika seisaku
合理化政策

rationed goods
haikyū busshi
配給物資

rationing
haikyū
配給

rationing coupons
haikyū kippu
配給キップ

raw materials
genzairyō
原材料

raw materials consumers
genzairyō shōhisha
原材料消費者

raw materials consumption index
genzairyō shōhi shisū
原材料消費指数

raw materials cost
genzairyō kosuto
原材料コスト

raw materials inventory index
genzairyō zaiko shisū
原材料在庫指数

raw materials producers
genzairyō seisansha
原材料生産者

re-adjustment
saichōsei
再調整

Reaganomics
rēganomikkusu
レーガノミックス

real analysis
jitsubutsu bunseki
実物分析

real balance effect
jisshitsu zandaka kōka
実質残高効果

real capital
jitsubutsu shihon
実物資本

real consumer spending
jisshitsu shōhi shishutsu
実質消費支出

real costs
jisshitsu hiyō
実質費用

real deposits
jisshitsu yokin
実質預金

real economy
jittai keizai
実体経済

real flow
jitsubutsu no nagare
実物の流れ

real GNP
jisshitsu kokumin sōseisan
実質国民総生産

real growth rate
jisshitsu seichōritsu
実質成長率

real income
jisshitsu shotoku
実質所得

real interest rates
jisshitsu kinri
実質金利

real money
jisshitsu kahei
実質貨幣

real money balances
jisshitsu genkin zandaka
実質現金残高

real phase (of the economy)
keizai no jittaimen
経済の実体面

real price
jisshitsu kakaku
実質価格

real terms
jisshitsu tāmu
実質ターム
jitsubutsu shōko
実物称呼

real wages
jisshitsu chingin
実質賃金

real wealth
jisshitsu zaisan
実質財産

re-allocation of resources
shigen saihaibun
資源再配分

receipts
uketori
受取り

receipts from disposal of government properties
seifu shisan seiri shūnyū
政府資産整理収入

receipts from government enterprises and properties
kangyō ekikin oyobi kangyō shūnyū
官業益金および官業収入

recession
risesshon
リセッション

(bad times)
fukeiki
不景気

(bad business)
fukyō
不況

(decline in business activity)
keiki kōtai
景気後退

(regression)
kōtai
後退

recession phase
kōtai kyokumen
後退局面

reciprocal demand
sōgo juyō
相互需要

reciprocal duties
gokei kanzei
互恵関税

reciprocal swap arrangements
gokei suwappu kyōtei
互恵スワップ協定

reciprocal tariffs
gokei kanzei
互恵関税

reciprocal trade
gokei bōeki
互恵貿易

(commercial exchange)
gokei tsūshō
互恵通商

reciprocal trade agreement
gokei bōeki kyōtei
互恵貿易協定

Reciprocal Trade Agreements Act [US]
gokei tsūshō kyōteihō
互恵通商協定法

reciprocal treaty
gokei jōyaku
互恵条約

reciprocity
gokei shugi
互恵主義

recognition lag
ninshiki no ragu
認識のラグ

recontract
saikeiyaku
再契約

record level
kirokuteki suijun
記録的水準

recovery
kaifuku
回復

recovery path
kaifuku keiro
回復経路

recovery period
kaifukuki
回復期

recovery phase
kaifuku kyokumen
回復局面

recovery process
kaifuku katei
回復過程

recycle (capital)
kanryū suru
還流する

recycle (waste)
saisei riyō suru
再生利用する

(re-use)
sairiyō suru
再利用する

recycling (capital)
kanryū
還流

recycling (waste)
saijunkan
再循環
saisei
再生

(re-using)
sairiyō
再利用

red tape
kanryōteki keishiki shugi
官僚的形式主義

redevelopment
saikaihatsu
再開発

rediscounting
saiwaribiki
再割引

redistribution
saibunpai
再分配

reduction
(decline, decrease)
genshō
減少

(cutbacks)
setsugen
節減

(curtailment)
shukushō
縮小
sakugen
削減

reduction in expenditure
shishutsu sakugen
支出削減

reduction in prices
bukka hikisage
物価引下げ

reduction in production
gensan
減産
seisan no genshō
生産の減少

reduction in tariffs
kanzei no hikisage
関税の引下げ

redundancies
yojō rōdōsha
余剰労働者

redundancy payments
yojō rōdōsha hoshōkin
余剰労働者補償金

redundant labour force
yojō rōdōryoku
余剰労働力

re-export (noun)
saiyushutsu
再輸出

re-export (verb)
saiyushutsu suru
再輸出する

re-exports
saiyushutsuhin
再輸出品

reflation
rifurēshon
リフレーション
tsūka saibōchō
通貨再膨張

reflationary policy
keiki shigekisaku
景気刺激策

reform
(reorganization)
kaikaku
改革

(amendment, revision)
kaisei
改正

region
chihō
地方
chi'iki
地域

regional development
chi'iki kaihatsu
地域開発

regional development grants
[UK]
chi'iki kaihatsu hojokin
地域開発補助金

regional development policy
chi'iki kaihatsu seisaku
地域開発政策

regional difference index
chi'ikisa shisū
地域差指数

regional disparity
chi'ikikan kakusa
地域間格差

regional economic planning
chi'iki keizai keikaku
地域経済計画

regional economics
chi'iki keizai
地域経済

regional economy
chi'iki keizai
地域経済

regional employment
chi'ikiteki koyō
地域的雇用

regional growth
chi'ikiteki seichō
地域的成長

regional integration
chi'iki tōgō
地域統合

regional policy
chi'iki seisaku
地域政策

regional structure
chi'iki kōzō
地域構造

regional wage differentials
chi'ikikan chingin kakusa
地域間賃金格差

regional wage structure
chi'ikikan chingin kōzō
地域間賃金構造

regionalism
chihō bunken shugi
地方分権主義

registered unemployed
tōroku sareta shitsugyōsha
登録された失業者

regression
kaiki
回帰

regression analysis
kaiki bunseki
回帰分析

regressive tax
gyakushinzei
逆進税

re-import (noun)
gyakuyunyū
逆輸入
saiyunyū
再輸入

re-import (verb)
gyakuyunyū suru
逆輸入する
saiyunyū suru
再輸入する

re-imports
saiyunyūhin
再輸入品

re-investment
saitōshi
再投資

rejection of budget proposal
yosan fuseiritsu
予算不成立

relation
kankei
関係
kanren
関連

relative deprivation
sōtaiteki kyūbōka
相対的窮乏化

relative income
sōtai shotoku
相対所得

relative income hypothesis
sōtai shotoku kasetsu
相対所得仮説

relative price
sōtai kakaku
相対価格

relative wages
sōtai chingin
相対賃金

relativities
hikaku chingin
比較賃金

relaxation
kanwa
緩和

relaxation of monetary restraint
hikishime seisaku kaijo
引締政策解除

relocation of industry
kōgyō saihaichi
工業再配置

relocation of labour
rōdō saihaichi
労働再配置

removal of restrictions
hikishime no kaijo
引締めの解除

remuneration
hōshū
報酬

renewability (of resources)
saisei kanōsei
再生可能性

renewable resources
saisei shigen
再生資源

rent
chidai
地代

rent of ability
nōryoku chidai
能力地代

rentiers
(non-work income)
furōshotoku seikatsusha
不労所得生活者

(income from interest)
kinri seikatsusha
金利生活者

reopening of trade
bōeki saikai
貿易再開

reparation
baishō
賠償

reparation treaty
baishō kyōtei
賠償協定

reparations in kind
genbutsu baishō
現物賠償

repercussion
hankyō
反響

replacement cost
torikae genka
取替原価

replacement investment (renewal)
kōshin tōshi
更新投資

(substitution)
okikae tōshi
置換投資

replacement price
saishutoku kakaku
再取得価格

replacement ratio
(rōdō) kōtai hojūritsu
(労働) 交替補充率

report
hōkoku(sho)
報告(書)

representative firm
daihyōteki kigyō
代表的企業

repressed inflation
yokuatsugata infurēshon
抑圧型インフレーション

resale-price maintenance (RPM)
saihanbai kakaku iji
再販売価格維持

research
kenkyū
研究

research and development (R & D)
kenkyū-kaihatsu
研究・開発
rando
ランド

research and development expenditure
kenkyū kaihatsuhi
研究開発費

research grants
kenkyū hojokin
研究補助金

reserve assets (Bank of England)
junbi shisan
準備資産

reserve assets ratio
junbi shisanritsu
準備資産率

reserve base
junbi bēsu
準備ベース

reserve currency
junbi tsūka
準備通貨

reserve ratio
junbiritsu
準備率

residual (noun)
zan'yo
残余

residual unemployment
zan'yo shitsugyō
残余失業

residual value
zan'yo kachi
残余価値

resource allocation
shigen haibun
資源配分

resource-intensive industries
shigen shūyakuteki sangyō
資源集約的産業

resource-intensive technology
shigen shūyakuteki gijutsu
資源集約的技術

resource-saving
shigen setsuyaku
資源節約
shōshigen
省資源

resource-saving technology
shigen setsuyakuteki gijutsu
資源節約的技術
shōshigenteki gijutsu
省資源的技術

resources
shigen
資源

restrained budget
kinshuku yosan
緊縮予算

restraint
hikishime
引締め

restraint measures
hikishime sochi
引締め措置

restricted industries
seigen sangyō
制限産業

restrictions
(restraint)
hikishime
引締め

(limits)
seigen
制限

(suppression, clamp)
yokusei
抑制

restrictions on export
yushutsu seigen
輸出制限

restrictions on import
yunyū seigen
輸入制限

restrictive labour practices
seigenteki rōdō kanshū
制限的労働慣習

restrictive measures
(limiting)
seigenteki shudan
制限的手段

(curbing)
yokusei sochi
抑制措置

Restrictive Practices Court [UK]
torihiki seigen saibansho
取引制限裁判所

restrictive trade practices
torihiki seigen kankō
取引制限慣行

Restrictive Trade Practices Act [UK]
torihiki seigen kankōhō
取引制限慣行法

reswitching
saitenkan
再転換

retail
kouri
小売り

retail goods
kouri shōhin
小売商品

retail market
kouri shijō
小売市場

retail price index (RPI) [UK]
kouri bukka shisū
小売物価指数

retail price survey
kouri kakaku chōsa
小売価格調査

retail prices
kouri kakaku
小売価格

retail trade
kourigyō
小売業

retailers
kourigyōsha
小売業者
kourishō
小売商

retained earnings
ryūho rieki
留保利益

retaliate
hōfuku suru
報復する

retaliation
hōfuku
報復

retaliatory tariffs
hōfuku kanzei
報復関税

retention ratio
ryūhoritsu
留保率

retentions
ryūho
留保

retirement
taishoku
退職

retirement benefits
taishokukin
退職金

retraining
saikunren
再訓練

retrenchment
kinshuku
緊縮

retrenchment budget
kinshuku zaisei yosan
緊縮財政予算

retrenchment policy
kinshuku seisaku
緊縮政策

return on capital employed
shihon shūeki
資本収益

returns to scale
kibo ni kansuru shūkaku
規模に関する収穫

revealed preference
kenji senkō
顕示選好

revenue
(government revenue)
sainyū
歳入

(profit, earnings, return)
shūeki
収益

(income, earnings, receipts)
shūnyū
収入

(tax revenue)
zeishū
税収

revenue and expenditure
shūshi
収支

revenue maximization
shūnyū kyokudaika
収入極大化

revenue shortfall
sainyū kekkan
歳入欠陥

reverse dumping
gyakudanpingu
逆ダンピング

revised budget
shūsei yosan
修正予算

revised figures
kaitei keisū
改定計数

revision
kaitei
改定

revival
fukkatsu
復活

revolution
kakumei
革命

rich, the
kanemochiren
金持連

rich countries
fuyūkoku
富裕国

right to strike
higyōken
罷業権
sutoken
スト権

right to work
rōdōken
労働権

right-to-work law [US]
rōdōkenhō
労働権法

rightward-shifting
migihō ikō
右方移行

rigidity
kōchokusei
硬直性

rise in unemployment
shitsugyō no zōka
失業の増加

rising prices
bukka jōshō
物価上昇
bukka tōki
物価騰貴
tōki
騰貴

risk
kiken
危険

risk aversion
kiken kaihi
危険回避

risk averters
kiken kaihisha
危険回避者

risk bearers
kiken futansha
危険負担者

risk-bearing
kiken futan
危険負担

risk capital
kiken futan shihon
危険負担資本

risk lovers
kiken aikōsha
危険愛好者

risk neutrals
kiken chūritsusha
危険中立者

rival goods
kyōsōzai
競争財

rivalness
kyōsō
競争

rollback
bukka hikisage seisaku
物価引下政策

roundabout methods of production
ukai seisan hōshiki
迂回生産方式

roundabout production
ukai seisan
迂回生産

roundabout trade
ukai bōeki
迂回貿易

roundaboutness
ukai seisan
迂回生産

royalties (from mineral resources)
kōzan shiyōryō
鉱山使用料

RPI (retail price index) [UK]
kouri bukka shisū
小売物価指数

RPM (resale-price maintenance)
saihanbai kakaku iji
再販売価格維持

rule of thumb
keikensoku
経験則

run-away inflation
chōinfurēshon
超インフレーション

rural community
nōson kyōdōtai
農村共同体

rural development
nōson kaihatsu
農村開発

rural economy
nōgyō keizai
農業経済

rural exodus
nōmin rison
農民離村

rural issues
nōmin mondai
農民問題

rural planning
nōson keikaku
農村計画

rural policy
nōson seisaku
農村政策

rural population
nōson jinkō
農村人口

rural society
nōson shakai
農村社会

sackings
kubikiri
首切り

salaried people
hōkyū seikatsusha
俸給生活者

salaries
(payroll)
hōkyū
俸給

(monthly pay)
kyūryō
給料

(remuneration)
kyūyo
給与

salary study
kyūyo no chōsa
給与の調査

sales
hanbaidaka
販売高

sales maximization hypothesis
hanbairyō kyokudaika kasetsu
販売量極大化仮説

sales tax
(commodity tax, excise tax)
buppinzei
物品税

(turnover tax)
uriagezei
売上税

salvage value
zanzon kakaku
残存価格

sample
hyōhon
標本

sampling
hyōhon chūshutsu
標本抽出
sanpuringu
サンプリング

sampling survey
hyōhon chōsa
標本調査

sanctions
seisai
制裁

saturation
hōwa
飽和
shinjun
浸潤

saving
chochiku
貯蓄

saving encouragement
chochiku shōrei
貯蓄奨励

saving-investment analysis
chochiku-tōshi bunseki
貯蓄・投資分析

saving-investment
controversy
chochiku-tōshi ronsō
貯蓄・投資論争

saving-investment theory of
income determination
chochiku-tōshi no shotoku
ketteiron
貯蓄・投資の所得
決定論

saving mentality
chochikushin
貯蓄心

saving motivation
chochiku keihatsu
貯蓄啓発

savings
chokin
貯金

savings and deposits
yochokin
預貯金

savings drive
chochiku suishin undō
貯蓄推進運動

savings function
chochiku kansū
貯蓄関数

savings/income ratio
chochiku-shotoku hiritsu
貯蓄・所得比率

savings promotion
chochiku shōrei
貯蓄奨励

savings promotion campaign
chochiku shōrei undō
貯蓄奨励運動

savings rate
chochikuritsu
貯蓄率

scarce goods
kishō zaika
希少財貨

scarce resources
kishō shigen
希少資源

scarcity
(shortage)
fusoku
不足

(rarity)
kishōsei
希少性

scarcity of labour
rōdōryoku fusoku
労働力不足

scarcity of resources
shigen fusoku
資源不足

schedule
hyō
表

schemes
keikaku
計画

school leavers (high-school
graduates)
gakusotsusha
学卒者

school of economics
keizai gakuha
経済学派

scientific tariff
kagakuteki kanzei
科学的関税

sea pollution
kaiyō osen
海洋汚染

search unemployment
(concept of)
shitsugyō no tansaku riron
失業の探索理論

seasonal adjustment
kisetsu chōsei
季節調整

seasonal commodities
kisetsu shōhin
季節商品

seasonal demand
kisetsu juyō
季節需要

seasonal distortions
kisetsuteki hensa
季節的偏差

seasonal employment
kisetsu koyō
季節雇用

seasonal fluctuations
kisetsu hendō
季節変動

seasonal goods
kisetsu shōhin
季節商品

seasonal growth
kisetsuteki seichō
季節的成長

seasonal index
kisetsu shisū
季節指数

seasonal industry
kisetsuteki sangyō
季節的産業

seasonal labour
kisetsu rōdōryoku
季節労働力

seasonal migrant labour
kisetsu ryūnyū rōdōryoku
季節流入労働力

seasonal supply
kisetsu kyōkyū
季節供給

seasonal unemployment
kisetsuteki shitsugyō
季節的失業

seasonal variations
kisetsu hendō
季節変動

seasonally adjusted
kisetsu chōseizumi
季節調整済み

seasonally adjusted figures
kisetsu chōseizumi sūji
季節調整済み数字

second best (theory of)
jizen no riron
次善の理論

second half of the year
shimohanki
下半期

second quarter
daini shihanki
第二四半期

secondary employment
dainiji koyō
第二次雇用

secondary industry
dainiji sangyō
第二次産業

secondary market
dainiji shijō
第二次市場

secondary products
dainiji seihin
第二次製品

secondary workers
dainiji rōdōsha
第二次労働者

sector
bumon
部門

secular trend
chōkiteki keikō
長期的傾向

self-employed, the
jieigyōsha
自営業者

self-employment
jieigyō
自営業
jiko koyō
自己雇用

self-governing industry
jichiteki sangyō
自治的産業

self-help
jijo doryoku
自助努力

self-regulating organizations
jiko kisei dantai
自己規制団体

self-reliance
jiriki kōsei
自力更正

self-sufficiency
jikyūjisoku
自給自足

self-sufficient countries
jikyūjisokukoku
自給自足国

self-sufficient economy
jikyūjisoku keizai
自給自足経済

self-supporting economy
jiritsu keizai
自立経済

semi-finished goods
hanseihin
半製品

semi-finished products
hanseihin
半製品

semi-skilled labour
hanjukuren rōdōsha
半熟練労働者
hanjukurenkō
半熟練工

semi-skilled workers
hanjukuren rōdōsha
半熟練労働者

semi-variable costs
hanhendō hiyō
半変動費用

seniority-based wage system
nenkōjoretsugata chingin
seido
年功序列型賃金制度

seniority practices
nenkōjoretsusei
年功序列制

sensitivity analysis
kannō bunseki
感応分析

separation of ownership from control
shoyū to kei'ei no bunri
所有と経営の分離

separation of taxation
bunri kazei
分離課税

SERPS (state earnings-related pension scheme) [UK]
kokumin hoken no taishoku
nenkin seido
国民保険の退職年金
制度

service economy
sābisu keizai
サービス経済

service-oriented
sābisu chūshingata
サービス中心型

service sector
sābisu bumon
サービス部門

service trade
sābisugyō
サービス業

services
sābisu
サービス
sābisu sangyō
サービス産業

shadow price
senzai kakaku
潜在価格

shadow wage
senzai chingin
潜在賃金

shadow wage rate
senzai chinginritsu
潜在賃金率

sharp rise
kōtō
高騰

sheltered employment
hogo koyō
保護雇用

sheltered industry
higo sangyō
庇護産業

(protected)
hogo sangyō
保護産業

sheltered trade
hogo bōeki
保護貿易

shift
shifuto
シフト

shifting
ikō
移行

shock
shokku
ショック

shock effect
shokku kōka
ショック効果

short-run
tanki no
短期の

short-run average cost
tanki heikin hiyō
短期平均費用

short-run consumption function
tanki shōhi kansū
短期消費関数

short-run cost curves
tanki hiyō kyokusen
短期費用曲線

short-run equilibrium
tanki kinkō
短期均衡

short supply
kyōkyūbusoku
供給不足
kyōkyūhaku
供給薄

short-term
tanki no
短期の

short-term economic policy
tanki keizai seisaku
短期経済政策

short-term expectation
tanki kitai
短期期待

short-term forecast
tanki yosoku
短期予測

short-term foreign trade credits
tanki bōeki shin'yō
短期貿易信用

short-term growth
tankiteki seichō
短期的成長

short-term marginal cost
tanki genkai hiyō
短期限界費用

short-term outlook
tankiteki tenbō
短期的展望

short-term planning
tanki keikaku
短期計画

short-time working
sōgyō tanshuku
操業短縮
sōtan
操短

shortage
fusoku
不足

shortage of financial resources
zaigennan
財源難

shortfall
fusokugaku
不足額

shrinkage
shukushō
縮小

shutdowns
kōjō heisa
工場閉鎖

SIC (standard industrial classification)
hyōjun sangyō bunrui
標準産業分類

siege economy
kinkyū keizai
緊急経済

signs
(symptoms)
chōkō
徴候

(symptoms, indications)
kizashi
兆し

simple correlation and regression
tanjun sōkan to kaiki
単純相関と回帰

simulation
shimurēshon
シミュレーション

single-digit
hitoketa no
一桁の

single-digit inflation
hitoketa no infurēshon
一桁のインフレーション

single-digit unemployment
hitoketa no shitsugyō
一桁の失業

single-person households
tanshin setai
単身世帯

single persons
dokushinsha
独身者

six-figure income
rokuketa no shūnyū
6桁の収入

size distribution of firms
kigyō no kibo bunpai
企業の規模分配

skill differentials
jukuren kakusa
熟練格差

skilled labour
jukuren rōdōsha
熟練労働者
jukurenkō
熟練工

skilled workers
jukuren rōdōsha
熟練労働者

slack
(slow moving)
kanman
緩慢

(stagnation)
teitai
停滞

slave labour
dorei rōdōsha
奴隷労働者

(forced labour)
kyōsei rōdō
強制労働

(forced and badly paid labour)
kyōsei teichingin rōdō
強制低賃金労働

sliding scale
suraidosei
スライド制

sliding-scale wages
suraidosei no chingin
スライド制の賃金

slow economic growth
teikeizai seichō
低経済成長

slowdown
donka
鈍化

(deceleration)
gensoku
減速

(decline)
gentai
減退

slump
keiki chintai
景気沈滞

(crash)
bōraku
暴落

(recession)
fukyō
不況

(dullness, inactivity)
fushin
不振

small firms
shōkigyō
小企業

social accounting
kokumin keizai keisan
国民経済計算

social assistance
shakai fujo
社会扶助

social benefits
shakaiteki ben'eki
社会的便益

social capital
shakai shihon
社会資本

social choice
shakaiteki sentaku
社会的選択

social climate
shakaiteki kankyō
社会的環境

social contract [UK]
shakai keiyaku
社会契約

social cost
shakai hiyō
社会費用

social decision rule
shakaiteki kettei gensoku
社会的決定原則

social economics
shakai keizaigaku
社会経済学

social expenditure
shakaiteki shishutsu
社会的支出

social indicator
shakai shihyō
社会指標

social inequality
shakaiteki fubyōdō
社会的不平等

social insurance
shakai hoken
社会保険

social insurance contributions
shakai hoken futan
社会保険負担

social insurance expenses
shakai hokenhi
社会保険費

social insurance system
shakai hoken hōshiki
社会保険方式

social issues
shakai mondai
社会問題

social optimum
shakaiteki saiteki
社会的最適

social organization
shakai soshiki
社会組織

social overhead capital
shakai kansetsu shihon
社会間接資本

social planning
shakai keikaku
社会計画

social policy
shakai seisaku
社会政策

social problems
shakai mondai
社会問題

social reforms
shakai kaikaku
社会改革

social responsibility
shakaiteki sekinin
社会的責任

social security
shakai hoshō
社会保障

social security benefits
shakai hoshō kyūfu
社会保障給付

social security contributions
shakai hoshō futan
社会保障負担

social security expenses
shakai hoshō kankeihi
社会保障関係費

social security system
shakai hoshō seido
社会保障制度

social spending
shakaiteki shishutsu
社会的支出

social statistics
shakai tōkei
社会統計

social time preference rate
shakaiteki jikan senkōritsu
社会的時間選好率

social welfare
shakai fukushi
社会福祉
shakai kōsei
社会厚生

social welfare expenses
shakai fukushihi
社会福祉費

social welfare function
shakai kōsei kansū
社会厚生関数

social work
shakai jigyō
社会事業

socialism
shakai shugi
社会主義

socialistic economy
shakai shugi keizai
社会主義経済

socially necessary labour
shakaiteki hitsuyō rōdō
社会的必要労働

society
shakai
社会

socio-economic policy
shakai keizai seisaku
社会経済政策

socio-economic problems
shakai keizai mondai
社会経済問題

socio-economics
shakai keizaigaku
社会経済学

soft goods
hitaikyūzai
非耐久財

soil contamination
dojō osen
土壌汚染

solidarity strike
dōjō sutoraiki
同情ストライキ

solution to inflation
infure shūsoku
インフレ収束

sophistication
kōdoka
高度化

source of fiscal revenue
zaigen
財源

source of income
shotokugen
所得源
shūnyūgen
収入源

special goods
senmon yōhin
専門用品

speciality goods [UK]
senmonhin
専門品

specialization
(persons)
senmonka
専門化

(goods)
tokka
特化

specialization coefficient
tokka keisū
特化係数

specialty goods [US]
senmonhin
専門品

specie flow mechanism
seika ryūshutsunyū kikō
正貨流出入機構

specific tax
jūryōzei
従量税

specification error
shitei gosa
指定誤差

speculative boom
tōkiteki būmu
投機的ブーム

speculative demand for money
tōkiteki kahei juyō
投機的貨幣需要

speculative motive
tōkiteki dōki
投機的動機

spending
shishutsu
支出

spending boom
shōhi būmu
消費ブーム

spillover
ryūshutsu
流出

sponsorship
kōen
後援
shien
支援

spread effects
hakyū kōka
波及効果

squeeze (noun)
asshuku
圧縮

stability
antei(sei)
安定(性)

stability of employment
koyō anteisei
雇用安定性

stabilization
anteika
安定化

stabilization function
anteika kinō
安定化機能

stabilization of employment
koyō antei
雇用安定

stabilization policy
anteika seisaku
安定化政策

stabilization programme
antei keikaku
安定計画

stabilize
antei suru
安定する

stabilizer
antei sōchi
安定装置

stabilizing effect
antei kōka
安定効果

stabilizing force
anteiseiryoku
安定性力

stable
antei shita
安定した

stable economic growth
antei keizai seichō
安定経済成長

stable economy
antei keizai
安定経済

stable equilibrium
antei kinkō
安定均衡

stable growth
antei seichō
安定成長

stable growth path
antei seichō rosen
安定成長路線

stable prices
antei kakaku
安定価格

stable wage system
antei chinginsei
安定賃金制

stable wages
antei chingin
安定賃金

stages of growth
seichō dankai
成長段階

stagflation
sutagufurēshon
スタグフレーション

stagnation
(dullness, inactivity)
fushin
不振

(slack)
teitai
停滞

stamp duty [UK]
inshizei
印紙税

standard(s)
hyōjun
標準

standard commodity
kachi shakudozai
価値尺度財

standard cost of living
hyōjun seikatsuhi
標準生活費

standard deviation
hyōjun hensa
標準偏差

standard error
hyōjun gosa
標準誤差

standard industrial
classification (SIC)
hyōjun sangyō bunrui
標準産業分類

standard of living
seikatsu suijun
生活水準

standard rate of pay
hyōjun chinginritsu
標準賃金率

standard wages
hyōjun chingin
標準賃金

standard weekly hours
hyōjun rōdōshū jikan
標準労働週時間

standard working hours
hyōjun rōdō jikan
標準労働時間

standard working week
hyōjun rōdōshū
標準労働週

standardization
hyōjunka
標準化

staple industries
shuyō sangyō
主要産業

starvation wages
kiga chingin
飢餓賃金

state aid
kokko hojo
国庫補助

state bankruptcy
kokka hasan
国家破産

state capitalism
kokka shihon shugi
国家資本主義

state earnings-related
pensions scheme (SERPS)
[UK]
kokumin hoken no taishoku
nenkin seido
国民保険の退職年金
制度

state finance
kokka zaisei
国家財政

state industry
kokuyū sangyō
国有産業

state intervention
seifu kainyū
政府介入

state of emergency
hijōjitai
非常事態

state-owned
kokuyū no
国有の

state-owned industry
kokuyū sangyō
国有産業

state-planned economy
kokka keikaku keizai
国家計画経済

state planning
kokka keikaku
国家計画

state-run
kokuei no
国営の

state-run businesses
kokuei kigyō
国営企業

state-run industries
kokuei sangyō
国営産業

state trading
kokuei bōeki
国営貿易

static economy
seitai keizai
静態経済

static expectations
seigakuteki kitai
静学的期待

stationary state
teijō jōtai
定常状態

statism
kokka tōsei
国家統制

statistical analysis
tōkei bunseki
統計分析

statistical cost analysis
tōkeiteki hiyō bunseki
統計的費用分析

statistical data
tōkei shiryō
統計資料

statistical figures
tōkei sūji
統計数字

statistical hypothesis
tōkei kasetsu
統計仮説

statistical indicator
tōkei shihyō
統計指標

statistical inference
tōkeiteki suiron
統計的推論

statistical observation
tōkei kansoku
統計観測

statistical report
tōkei hōkoku
統計報告

statistical research
tōkeiteki chōsa
統計的調査

statistical significance
tōkeiteki yūi
統計的有意

statistical survey
tōkei chōsa
統計調査

Statistical Yearbook [UK]
tōkei nenkan
統計年鑑

statistician
tōkeika
統計家

statistics
tōkei
統計

(study)
tōkeigaku
統計学

steady growth
kōjōteki seichō
恒常的成長

steady-state growth
kōjōteki seichō
恒常的成長

steady-state growth path
kōjōteki seichō keiro
恒常的成長経路

steady-state models
kōjō jōtai moderu
恒常状態モデル

stereotypes (set patterns)
monkirigata
紋切型

stimulation of business activity
keiki shigeki
景気刺激

stimulatory measures
shigekisaku
刺激策

stimulus
shigeki
刺激

stock
zaiko
在庫

stock appreciation
zaiko kachi tōki
在庫価値騰貴

stock building
zaiko tsumimashi
在庫積増し

stock control
zaiko kanri
在庫管理

stock cycle
zaiko junkan
在庫循環

stockpiling
zaiko chikuseki
在庫蓄積

(stocking for emergency)
bichiku
備蓄

stocks/sales ratio
zaikoritsu
在庫率

stop-go economy
sutoppu-ando-gō keizai
ストップ・アンド・
ゴー経済

store of value
kachi hozō
価値保蔵

strategic goods
senryaku busshi
戦略物資

strategic industries
senryaku sangyō
戦略産業

strategy
senryaku
戦略

strike insurance
higyō hoken
罷業保険

strike measures
higyō taisaku sochi
罷業対策措置

strikers
higyōsha
罷業者

strikes
higyō
罷業
suto
スト
sutoraiki
ストライキ

stringency
hippaku
逼迫

structural changes
kōzō henka
構造変化

structural employment
kōzōteki koyō
構造的雇用

structural unemployment
kōzōteki shitsugyō
構造的失業

structure
(construction, framework)
kōzō
構造

(organization, system)
taikei
体系

structure of interest rates
kinri kōzō
金利構造

structure of taxes
sozei kōzō
租税構造

struggle for existence
seizon kyōsō
生存競争

study
kenkyū
研究

sub-economy
bubun keizai
部分経済

subsidiary coin
hojo kahei
補助貨幣

subsidiary industry
hojo sangyō
補助産業

subsidies
hojokin
補助金
hokyūkin
補給金
kōfukin
交付金

subsidize
hojokin o ataeru
補助金を与える

subsidized companies
hojo gaisha
補助会社

subsidized industry
josei sangyō
助成産業

subsidized market
hojokintsuki shijō
補助金付市場

subsidizing policy
hojo seisaku
補助政策

subsistence
seizon
生存

subsistence expenditure
seizon shishutsu
生存支出

subsistence income
saitei seikatsu suijun
shotoku
最低生活水準所得
seizon suijun shotoku
生存水準所得

subsistence level
seikei iji suijun
生計維持水準
seizon suijun
生存水準

subsistence theory of wages
seizon chinginsetsu
生存賃金説

subsistence wage
seizon chingin
生存賃金

substitutes
daitaibutsu
代替物
daiyōhin
代用品

substitution
daitai
代替
daiyō
代用

substitution effect
daitai kōka
代替効果

summit conference
shunō kaigi
首脳会議

sunk costs
maibotsu genka
埋没原価

superior goods
yūryōzai
優良財

super-normal profits
chōka rijun
超過利潤

super-power
kyodaikoku
巨大国

supplementary budget
hosei yosan
補正予算

supplementary costs
hosokuteki hiyō
補足的費用

suppliers
kyōkyūsha
供給者

supply
kyōkyū
供給

supply and demand
jukyū
需給

supply capacity
kyōkyū nōryoku
供給能力

supply constraint
kyōkyūjō no seiyaku
供給上の制約

supply curve
kyōkyū kyokusen
供給曲線

supply-demand imbalance
jukyū fukinkō
需給不均衡

supply function
kyōkyū kansū
供給関数

supply of labour
rōdō kyōkyū
労働供給

supply price
kyōkyū kakaku
供給価格

supply services
kyōkyū sābisu
供給サービス

supply-side economics
kyōkyūgawa keizai
供給側経済

support (of currency)
shiji
支持

supported price
shiji kakaku
支持価格

surge in inflation
infure gekka
インフレ激化

surplus
(balance, residue)
jōyo
剰余

(excess, overabundance)
kajō
過剰

(excess, overhang)
yojō
余剰

surplus capacity
kajō setsubi
過剰設備

surplus commodities
kajō shōhin
過剰商品

surplus country
(in the black)
kurojikoku
黒字国

(with excess of exports)
shutchōkoku
出超国

surplus finance
chōkinkō zaisei
超均衡財政

surplus food
yojō shokuryō
余剰食料

surplus funds
yojō shikin
余剰資金

surplus goods
kajō shōhin
過剰商品

surplus labour
(overemployment)
kajō rōdō
過剰労働

(redundant labour force)
yojō rōdōryoku
余剰労働力

surplus on current account
keijō kaigai yojō
経常海外余剰

surplus production
jōyo seisan
剰余生産

surplus products
jōyo seisanbutsu
剰余生産物

surplus reserves
jōyo tsumitatekin
剰余積立金

surplus stocks
kajō zaiko
過剰在庫

surplus unit
kuroji tan'i
黒字単位

surplus value
jōyo kachi
剰余価値

survey
(ankēto) chōsa
(アンクート) 調査

survival
seizon
生存

sustainable growth
jizokuteki seichō
持続的成長

swap arrangements
suwappu kyōtei
スワップ協定

swaps
suwappu
スワップ

sweat-shop
sakushu kōjō
搾取工場

sweat-shop system
kukan seido
苦汗制度
rōdōsha sakushu seido
労働者搾取制度

sweated industry
kukan sangyō
苦汗産業

sweated labour
kukan rōdōsha
苦汗労働者
sakushu rōdōsha
搾取労働者

take-home pay
tedori chingin
手取り賃金

take-off (noun)
ririku
離陸

take-over bids
kabushiki kōkai kaitsuke
株式公開買付け

take-overs
(kigyō no) nottori
(企業の) 乗っ取り

target industries
mokuhyō sangyō
目標産業

targets
mokuhyō
目標

tariff autonomy
kanzei jishuken
関税自主権

tariff barriers
kanzei shōheki
関税障壁

tariff factory
kanzei kōjō
関税工場

tariff policy
kanzei seisaku
関税政策

tariff quota
kanzei wariate
関税割当て

tariff structure
kanzei kōzō
関税構造

tariff treaty
kanzei jōyaku
関税条約

tariff truce
kanzei kyūsen
関税休戦

tariff union
kanzei dōmei
関税同盟

tariff war
kanzei sensō
関税戦争

tariffs
kanzei
関税

tâtonnement
mosaku
模索
tesaguri
手探り

tax
sozei
租税
zei
税

tax administration
sozei kanri
租税管理

tax administrators
sozei kanrisha
租税管理者

tax and stamp receipts
sozei oyobi inshi shūnyū
租税および印紙収入

tax assessment
sozei satei
租税査定

tax assessor
kazei sateinin
租税査定人

tax authorities
sozei tōkyoku
租税当局

tax avoidance
datsuzei
脱税
nōzei kaihi
納税回避

tax base
kazei kijun
課税基準

tax bracket
zeiritsu tōkyū
税率等級

tax breaks
zeisei yūgū sochi
税制優遇措置

tax burden
sozei futan
租税負担

tax burden ratio
sozei futanritsu
租税負担率

tax changes
zeisei henkō
税制変更

tax collection
chōzei
徴税
shūzei
収税

tax collector
shūzeinin
収税人

tax credit
zeigaku kōjo
税額控除

tax credit schemes
zeigaku kōjo taikei
税額控除体系

tax cuts
genzei
減税
sozei hikisage
租税引下げ

tax deductions
kazei kōjo
課税控除
sozei kōjo
租税控除

tax delinquency
tainō
滞納

tax disincentive
sozei hiyūin
租税非誘因

tax dodge
datsuzei
脱税

tax evaders
datsuzeisha
脱税者

tax evasion
datsuzei
脱税
nōzei kaihi
納税回避

tax-exempt
hikazei no
非課税の
menzei no
免税の

tax exemption
menzei
免税
sozei menjo
租税免除

tax expenditure
sozei shishutsu
租税支出

tax-free
hikazei no
非課税の

tax-gathering season
nōzeiki
納税期

tax havens
sozei hinanchi
租税避難地
zeikin hinanchi
税金避難地

tax in kind
genbutsu nōzei
現物納税

tax incentives
sozei yūin
租税誘因

tax incidence
sozei futan
租税負担

tax increases
zōzei
増税

tax law
zeihō
税法

tax liability
nōzei gimu
納税義務

tax loophole
sozei no nukeana
租税の抜け穴

tax office
zeimusho
税務署

tax officer
zeimushoin
税務署員

tax offset
sozei kōjo
租税控除

tax payers
nōzeisha
納税者

tax payment
nōzei
納税

tax-push inflation
zeiritsu atsuryoku
infurēshon
税率圧力インフレー
ション

tax rate
kazeiritsu
課税率
zeiritsu
税率

tax rebate
sozei kanpu(kin)
租税還付(金)

tax receipts
sozei shūnyū
租税収入

tax reduction
genzei
減税

tax reform
zeisei kaikaku
税制改革

tax refund
modoshizei
戻し税
sozei kanpukin
租税還付金

tax relief
zeisei yūgū sochi
税制優遇措置

tax return
nōzei shinkokusho
納税申告書

tax revenue
sozei shūnyū
租税収入
zeishū
税収

tax revolt
hanzei undō
反税運動

tax schedule
zeiritsuhyō
税率表

tax shelters
zeikin hinan shudan
税金避難手段

tax structure
sozei kōzō
租税構造

tax system
zeisei
税制

tax treaty
sozei jōyaku
租税条約

tax yield
sozei shūnyū
租税収入

taxable goods
kazeihin
課税品

taxable income
kazei shotoku
課税所得

taxation
(imposition of taxes)
kazei
課税

(rates, taxes)
sozei
租税

taxation at source
gensen kazei
源泉課税

taxation system
sozei taikei
租税体系
zeisei
税制

taxes
zei
税

(rates)
sozei
租税

(dues)
zeikin
税金

technical adviser
gijutsu komon
技術顧問

technical aid
gijutsu enjo
技術援助

technical co-operation
gijutsu kyōryoku
技術協力

technical economies
gijutsu no keizai
技術の経済

technical factors
gijutsuteki yōin
技術的要因

technical guidance
gijutsu shidō
技術指導

technical know-how
gijutsu nouhau
技術ノウハウ

technical monopoly
gijutsuteki dokusen
技術的独占

technical progress
gijutsu shinpo
技術進歩

technical skills
gijutsuteki jukuren
技術的熟練
gikō
技巧

techniques
gijutsu
技術

technological assessment
gijutsu hyōka
技術評価

technological assistance
gijutsu enjo
技術援助

**technological assistance
contract**
gijutsu enjo keiyaku
技術援助契約

**technological assistance
financing**
gijutsu teikyō kin'yū
技術提供金融

technological change
gijutsuteki henka
技術的変化

technological dualism
gijutsuteki nijūsei
技術的二重性

technological gap
gijutsu kakusa
技術格差

technological innovation
gijutsu kakushin
技術革新

technological power
gijutsuryoku
技術力

technological progress
gijutsu shinpo
技術進歩

technological tie-up
gijutsu teikei
技術提携

technological unemployment
gijutsuteki shitsugyō
技術的失業

technology
gijutsu
技術
kōgyō gijutsu
工業技術

technology export(s)
gijutsu yushutsu
技術輸出

technology future
gijutsu no shōrai
技術の将来

technology import(s)
gijutsu yunyū
技術輸入

technology matrix
gijutsu gyōretsu
技術行列

technology protectionism
gijutsu hogo shugi
技術保護主義

technology transfer
gijutsu iten
技術移転

technostructure
gijutsusha shūdan
技術者集団

temporary boom
niwakageiki
いわか景気

temporary employment
ichiji koyō
一時雇用

temporary equilibrium
ichijiteki kinkō
一時的均衡

temporary lay-offs
ichiji kaiko rōdōsha
一時解雇労働者

temporary measure
ichijiteki shudan
一時的手段

temporary unemployment
ichijiteki shitsugyō
一時的失業

tendency
keikō
傾向

tension
kinchō
緊張

terms of trade
kōeki jōken
交易条件

terms-of-trade index
kōeki jōken shisū
交易条件指数

territorial waters
ryōkai
領海

tertiary employment
daisanji koyō
第三次雇用

tertiary industry
daisanji sangyō
第三次産業

tertiary products
daisanji seihin
第三次製品

tertiary sector
daisanji bumon
第三次部門

tertiary workers
daisanji rōdōsha
第三次労働者

test statistics
kentei tōkeiryō
検定統計量

theoretical cost of living
riron seikatsuhi
理論生活費

theory
riron
理論

theory of comparative costs
hikaku seisanhisetsu
比較生産費説

**theory of consumer's
behaviour**
shōhisha kōdō no riron
消費者行動の理論

theory of consumer's choice
shōhisha sentaku no riron
消費者選択の理論

theory of distribution
bunpai no riron
分配の理論

theory of employment
koyō riron
雇用理論

theory of games
gēmu no riron
ゲームの理論

**theory of income
determination**
shotoku kettei no riron
所得決定の理論

theory of production
seisan no riron
生産の理論

theory of second best
jizen no riron
次善の理論

theory of the firm
kigyō no riron
企業の理論

theory of unemployment
shitsugyō no riron
失業の理論

theory of value
kachiron
価値論

third quarter
daisan shihanki
第三四半期

third world
daisan sekai
第三世界

threat
(intimidation)
kyōhaku
脅迫

(danger, menace)
kyōi
脅威

threat effect
kyōhaku kōka
脅迫効果

threshold
iki
いき

threshold agreement [UK]
ikichi kyōtei
いき値協定

thrift
(saving)
chochiku
貯蓄

(frugality)
ken'yaku
倹約

thrift mentality
chochikushin
貯蓄心

tide of imports
yūnyū no chōryū
輸入の潮流

tied aid
himotsuki enjo
ひもつき援助

tied loan
himotsuki yūshi
ひもつき融資

tight economy
hippaku shita keizai
逼迫した経済

tight money
kin'yū hikishime
金融引締め

tight-money policy
kin'yū hikishime seisaku
金融引締政策

tightening of monetary restraint
kin'yū hikishime seisaku kyōka
金融引締政策強化

time allocation
jikan wariate
時間割当て

time preference
jikan senkō
時間選好

time series
jikeiretsu
時系列

token money (nominal)
meimoku kahei
名目貨幣

top priority
saiyūsen
最優先

total cost
zenbu hiyō
全部費用

total cost curve
sōhiyō kyokusen
総費用曲線

total demand
sōjuyō
総需要

total demand curve
sōjuyō kyokusen
総需要曲線

total expenditure
sōshishutsu
総支出

total goods
sōzaika
総財貨

total income
sōshotoku
総所得

total production
sōseisan
総生産

total revenue
sōshūnyū
総収入

total supply
sōkyōkyū
総供給

total utility
sōkōyō
総効用

trade (noun)
　(international trade)
　bōeki
　貿易

　(barter, interchange)
　kōeki
　交易

　(business, deal)
　shōbai
　商売

　(business, commerce)
　shōgyō
　商業

　(transaction)
　torihiki
　取引

　(commercial exchange)
　tsūshō
　通商

trade (verb)
　bōeki suru
　貿易する
　torihiki suru
　取引する

trade agreement
bōeki kyōtei
貿易協定
tsūshō kyōtei
通商協定

trade area
bōekiken
貿易圏
shōken
商圏

trade association
　(same business)
　dōgyō kumiai
　同業組合

　(industrial)
　sangyō dantai
　産業団体

　(business)
　shōgyō kumiai
　商業組合

trade balance
bōeki shūshi
貿易収支

trade barrier
bōeki shōgai
貿易障害
bōeki shōheki
貿易障壁

trade block
bōeki burokku
貿易ブロック

trade cartel
bōeki karuteru
貿易カルテル

trade commission
bōeki i'inkai
貿易委員会

trade conflict
bōeki masatsu
貿易摩擦

trade control
bōeki tōsei
貿易統制

trade creation
bōeki sōshutsu
貿易創出

trade credit
bōeki shin'yō
貿易信用

　(inter-business)
　kigyōkan shin'yō
　企業間信用

trade cycle
keiki junkan
景気循環

trade deficit
bōeki akaji
貿易赤字
bōeki shūshi no akaji
貿易収支の赤字

(excessive imports)
nyūchō
入超

trade deterioration
bōeki shūshi akka
貿易収支悪化

trade dispute
bōeki funsō
貿易紛争

trade diversion
bōeki tenkan
貿易転換

trade federation
bōeki rengō
貿易連合

trade friction
bōeki masatsu
貿易摩擦

trade gap
bōeki kesson
貿易欠損

trade liberalization
bōeki jiyūka
貿易自由化

trade-off
torēdo-ofu
トレード・オフ

trade performance
bōeki jisseki
貿易実績

trade policy
bōeki seisaku
貿易政策

trade practice
bōeki kanshū
貿易慣習

trade problems
bōeki mondai
貿易問題

trade restrictions
bōeki seigen
貿易制限

trade surplus
bōeki kuroji
貿易黒字

trade terms
bōeki jōken
貿易条件

trade turnovers
torihikidaka
取引高

trade union [UK]
(rōdō) kumiai
(労働) 組合

trade union activities [UK]
kumiai katsudō
組合活動
kumiai undō
組合運動

trade union leaders [UK]
kumiai shidōsha
組合指導者

**trade union membership
(number of members)**
kumiai'insū
組合員数

(affiliation)
kumiai kamei
組合加盟

trade union officials [UK]
kumiai kanbu
組合幹部
kumiai yakuin
組合役員

trade unionism [UK]
rōdō kumiai shugi
労働組合主義

trade unionist [UK]
rōdō kumiai'in
労働組合員

trade ups and downs
keiki no agarisagari
景気の上がり下がり

trade war
bōeki sensō
貿易戦争

traded goods
bōekizai
貿易財

trader
bōeki gyōsha
貿易業者
bōekishō
貿易商
shōnin
商人

trading companies
shōji gaisha
商事会社
shōsha
商社

trading countries
bōekikoku
貿易国

trading partners (countries)
bōeki aitekoku
貿易相手国

traditional sectors
dentōteki bumon
伝統的部門

training
kunren
訓練

training grants
kunren hojokin
訓練補助金

training programmes
kunren keikaku
訓練計画

training schemes
kunren keikaku
訓練計画

transaction theory of money
shotoku sūryōsetsu
所得数量説

transactions balances
torihiki zandaka
取引残高

transactions costs
torihiki hiyō
取引費用

**transactions demand for
money**
kahei no torihiki juyō
貨幣の取引需要

transactions motive
torihiki dōki
取引動機

transactions velocity of circulation
torihiki ryūdō sokudo
取引流動速度

transfer earnings
iten shotoku
移転所得

transfer incomes
furikae shotoku
振替所得
iten shotoku
移転所得

transfer of technology
gijutsu iten
技術移転

transfer payments
iten shishutsu
移転支出

transfer pricing
furikae kakaku keisei
振替価格形成

transfer problems
iten mondai
移転問題

transformation
henkei
変形

transformation curve
henkei kyokusen
変形曲線

transformation function
henkei kansū
変形関数

transformation of tax
zei no shōten
税の消転

transition
(transitory stage)
katoki
過渡期

(turning point)
tenkanki
転換期

transitional period
katoki
過渡期

transitory consumption
hendō shōhi
変動消費

transitory income
hendō shotoku
変動所得

Treasury, the
(national treasury,
state coffers)
kokko
国庫

(Finance Ministry,
Exchequer [UK],
Department of the
Treasury [US])
ōkurashō
大蔵省

[US]
zaimushō
財務省

Treasury accounts
kokko keisan
国庫計算

Treasury accounts items
kokko keisan kamoku
国庫計算科目

Treasury deposits
kokko yokin
国庫預金

Treasury funds
kokkokin
国庫金

Treasury payments
kokko shishutsu
国庫支出

Treasury receipts
kokko shūnyū
国庫収入

Treasury remittances
kokko sōkin
国庫送金

Treasury surplus
kokko yoyūkin
国庫余裕金

treaty
jōyaku
条約

trend
(movement)
dōkō
動向

(tendency)
keikō
傾向
sūsei
趨勢

trend analysis
sūsei bunseki
趨勢分析

triangular trade
sankaku bōeki
三角貿易

truck system
genbutsu kyūyo
現物給与

turning point
tenkanten
転換点

turnover [UK]
sōuriagedaka
総売上高

turnover tax
sōuriagezei
総売上税

two-digit inflation
futaketa no infurēshon
二桁のインフレー
ション

two-digit unemployment
futaketa no shitsugyō
二桁の失業

two-sector growth model
nibumon seichō moderu
二部門成長モデル

two-tier wage clause
nijū chingin jōkō
二重賃金条項

two-tier wage system
nijū chinginsei
二重賃金制

type of industry
gyōshu
業種

U-turn
tenkan
転換
U tān
U ターン

UN (United Nations)
kokuren
国連

UN Economic and Social Council (ECOSOC)
kokuren keizai shakai rijikai
国連経済社会理事会

UN Economic Commission for Asia and the Far East (ECAFE)
kokuren ajia kyokutō keizai i'inkai
国連アジア極東経済委員会

UN Food and Agriculture Organization (FAO)
kokuren shokuryō nōgyō kikō
国連食料農業機構

unanticipated inflation
fusoku no infurēshon
不測のインフレーション

unbalanced budget
fukinkō yosan
不均衡予算

unbalanced economic growth
fukinkō keizai seichō
不均衡経済成長

uncertainty
fukakujissei
不確実性

UNCTAD (United Nations Conference on Trade and Development)
ankutaddo
アンクタッド
kokuren bōeki kaihatsu kaigi
国連貿易開発会議

undercapacity
kashō setsubi
過少設備

underdeveloped
teikaihatsu no
低開発の

underdeveloped country
teikaihatsukoku
低開発国

underdeveloped region
teikaihatsu chi'iki
低開発地域

underdevelopment
teikaihatsu
低開発

underemployed workers
fukanzen shūgyōsha
不完全就業者

underemployment
fukanzen koyō
不完全雇用
kashō koyō
過少雇用

underemployment equilibrium
fukanzen koyō kinkō
不完全雇用均衡

underidentification
futei shikibetsu
不定識別

underinvestment
kashō tōshi
過少投資

underpopulated
jinkō kaso no
人口過疎の

underpopulated areas
kaso chi'iki
過疎地域

underpopulation
jinkō kaso
人口過疎

underproduction
kashō seisan
過少生産
seisanbusoku
生産不足

undeveloped
mikaihatsu no
未開発の

undeveloped area
mikaihatsu chi'iki
未開発地域

undeveloped country
mikaihatsukoku
未開発国

UNDP (United Nations Development Programme)
kokuren kaihatsu keikaku
国連開発計画

unearned income
furōshotoku
不労所得

uneconomic
fukeizaiteki na
不経済的な

uneconomic services
fukeizaiteki sābisu
不経済的サービス

unemployables, the
koyō futekikakusha
雇用不適格者
koyōfunōsha
雇用不能者

unemployed, the
shitsugyōsha
失業者

unemployed capital
yūkyū shihon
遊休資本

unemployment
shitsugyō
失業

unemployment benefits
shitsugyō kyūfu
失業給付
shitsugyō teate
失業手当

unemployment census
shitsugyō chōsa
失業調査

unemployment compensation
shitsugyō hoshō
失業補償

unemployment equilibrium
shitsugyō kinkō
失業均衡

unemployment expenses
shitsugyō taisakuhi
失業対策費

unemployment insurance
shitsugyō hoken
失業保険

unemployment measures
shitsugyō taisaku
失業対策

unemployment rate
shitsugyōritsu
失業率

unemployment roll
shitsugyōsha meibo
失業者名簿

unemployment statistics
shitsugyō tōkei
失業統計

unequal exchange
fukintō kōkan
不均等交換

unfair competition
fukōsei kyōsō
不公正競争

unfair foreign trade practices
gaikoku no fukōsei kankō
外国の不公正慣行

unfair labour practices
futō rōdō kōi
不当労働行為

unfair trade
fukōsei bōeki
不公正貿易

unfair trade practices
fukōsei bōeki kankō
不公正貿易慣行

unfair wage policy
fukōsei chingin seisaku
不公正賃金政策

unfair wages
fukōsei chingin
不公正賃金

unfavourable balance of payments
kokusai shūshi no akaji
国際収支の赤字

unfavourable balance of trade
bōeki gyakuchō
貿易逆調

(trade deficit)
bōeki shūshi no akaji
貿易収支の赤字

unfilled vacancies
mijūsoku kyūjin
未充足求人

UNIDO (United Nations Industrial Development Organization)
yunidō
ユニドー
kokuren kōgyō kaihatsu kikō
国連工業開発機構

UNIDO guidelines
yunidō no gaidorain
ユニドーのガイドライン

uniform tariff
tōitsu kanzei
統一関税

uniform wages
kin'itsu chingin
均一賃金

unilateral agreement
henmu keiyaku
片務契約

unilateral treaty
henmu jōyaku
片務条約

unilateralism
yuniraterarizumu
ユニラテラリズム

union (see trade union)
(rōdō) kumiai
(労働) 組合

union density
rōdō kumiai kamei rōdōsha no saiteki mitsudo
労働組合加盟労働者の最適密度

union/non-union differential
rōdō kumiai-hirōdō kumiai kakusa
労働組合・非労働組合格差

union shop
yunion-shoppu
ユニオン・ショップ

unionized labour
rōdō kumiai kamei rōdōsha
労働組合加盟労働者

uniqueness
ichi'isei
一意性

unit of account
keisan tan'i
計算単位

unit of output
gentan'i
原単位

United Nations (UN)
kokuren
国連

United Nations Conference on Trade and Development (UNCTAD)
ankutaddo
アンクタッド
kokuren bōeki kaihatsu kaigi
国連貿易開発会議

United Nations Development Programme (UNDP)
kokuren kaihatsu keikaku
国連開発計画

United Nations Industrial Development Organization (UNIDO)
yunidō
ユニドー
kokuren kōgyō kaihatsu kikō
国連工業開発機構

unorganized labour
misoshiki rōdōsha
未組織労働者

unorganized workers
misoshiki rōdōsha
未組織労働者

unproductive
fuseisanteki na
不生産的な
hiseisanteki na
非生産的な

unproductive consumption
hiseisanteki shōhi
非生産的消費

unproductive labour
fuseisanteki rōdōryoku
不生産的労働力

unrest
fuan
不安

unskilled labour
mijukuren rōdōsha
未熟連労働者
mijukurenkō
未熟連工

unskilled marginal workers
mijukuren genkai rōdōsha
未熟連限界労働者

unstable economic growth
fuantei keizai seichō
不安定経済成長

unstable economy
fuantei keizai
不安定経済

unstable equilibrium
fuantei kinkō
不安定均衡

untapped resources
mikaihatsu shigen
未開発資源

unused capital
miriyō shihon
未利用資本

unused labour
miriyō rōdō
未利用労働

unused productive capacity
miriyō setsubi
未利用設備

unused resources
miriyō shigen
未利用資源

ups and downs
agarisagari
上がり下がり
kōge
高下

upswing
jōshō
上昇
uwamuki
上向き

upward phase
jōshō kyokumen
上昇局面

upward trend
jōshō
上昇
uwamuki
上向き

urban concentration
toshi shūchū
都市集中

urban decay
toshi kōhai
都市荒廃

urban development
toshi kaihatsu
都市開発

urban economics
toshi keizaigaku
都市経済学

urban exodus
toshi ridatsu
都市離脱

urban planning
toshi keikaku
都市計画

urban pollution
toshi kōgai
都市公害

urban population
toshi jinkō
都市人口

urban renewal
toshi saikaihatsu
都市再開発

urbanization
toshika
都市化

user cost
shiyō hiyō
使用費用

user cost of capital
shihon no shiyō hiyō
資本の使用費用

utilitarian economic theory
kōri shugi keizai riron
功利主義経済理論

utilitarianism
kōri shugi
功利主義

utilities
(goods)
jitsuyōhin
実用品

(public services)
kōkyō jigyō
公共事業

utility
kōyō
効用

utility curve
kōyō kyokusen
効用曲線

utility function
kōyō kansū
効用関数

utilization
(capacity utilization)
kadō
稼働

(use)
riyō
利用

utilization rate
kadōritsu
稼働率

utopian socialism
kūsōteki shakai shugi
空想的社会主義

vacancies
kyūjin
求人

vacancy rate
kyūjinritsu
求人率

valuation
hyōka
評価

value
(worth)
kachi
価値

(price)
kakaku
価格

value-added
fuka kachi
付加価値

value-added tax (VAT) [UK]
fuka kachizei
付加価値税

value judgement
kachi handan
価値判断

value of currency
tsūka kachi
通貨価値

value of money
kahei kachi
貨幣価値

variable (noun)
hensū
変数

variable capital
ryūdō shihon
流動資本

variable costs
hendōhi
変動費

variable factors
kahenteki yōin
可変的要因

variable input
kahenteki tōnyūryō
可変的投入量

variable labour costs
kahenteki rōdō kosuto
可変的労働コスト

variable output
kahenteki seisanryō
可変的生産量

variable production
coefficients
kahenteki seisan keisū
可変的生産係数

variance
bunsan
分散

variance analysis
bunsan bunseki
分散分析

variation
hendō
変動

VAT (value-added tax) [UK]
fuka kachizei
付加価値税

vector
bekutoru
ベクトル

veil of money
kahei bērukan
貨幣ベール観

velocity of circulation
(tsūka no) ryūtsū sokudo
(通貨の) 流通速度

venture capital
kiken futan shihon
危険負担資本

vertical division of labour
suichokuteki bungyō
垂直的分業

vertical equity
suichokuteki kōhei
垂直的公平

vertical integration
suichokuteki tōgō
垂直的統合

vertical merger
suichokuteki gappei
垂直的合併

vertical trade
suichoku bōeki
垂直貿易

viability
seizon nōryoku
生存能力

viable economy
sonritsukanō keizai
存立可能経済

vicious circle of poverty
hinkon no akujunkan
貧困の悪循環

vicious circles
akujunkan
悪循環

virtuous circles
kōjunkan
好循環

visible balance of trade
bōeki shūshi
貿易収支

visible exports
yūkei yushutsu
有形輸出

visible imports
yūkei yunyū
有形輸入

visible trade
yūkei bōeki
有形貿易

vital statistics
jinkō dōtai tōkei
人口動態統計
jinkō tōkei
人口統計

vitality
katsuryoku
活力

volume production
ryōsan
量産

voluntary export constraint
yushutsu no jishu kisei
輸出の自主規制

voluntary saving
jihatsuteki chochiku
自発的貯蓄

voluntary unemployment
jihatsuteki shitsugyō
自発的失業

voucher
shiharaihyō
支払票

voucher schemes
shiharaihyō seido
支払票制度

wage(s)
chingin
賃金

wage bargaining
chingin kōshō
賃金交渉

wage base
chingin bēsu
賃金ベース

wage bill
chingin shiharaidaka
賃金支払高

wage-by-age
nenrei kyūyosei
年齢給与制

wage-by-job
shigotobetsu chingin
仕事別賃金

wage claims
chin'age yōkyū
賃上げ要求

wage contracts
chingin keiyaku
賃金契約

wage control
chingin tōsei
賃金統制

wage cost
chingin hiyō
賃金費用

wage curve
chingin kyokusen
賃金曲線

wage cuts
chingin kirisage
賃金切下げ

wage demands
chin'age yōkyū
賃上げ要求

wage differentials
chingin kakusa
賃金格差

wage disputes
chin'age tōsō
賃上げ闘争

wage drift
chingin dorifuto
賃金ドリフト

wage earners
chingin seikatsusha
賃金生活者

wage explosion
chingin bakuhatsu
賃金爆発

wage freeze
chingin tōketsu
賃金凍結

wage freeze policy
chingin tōketsu seisaku
賃金凍結政策

wage fund
chingin kikin
賃金基金

wage fund theory
chingin kikinsetsu
賃金基金説

wage in kind
genbutsu kyūyo
現物給与

wage incentive
shōreikyū
奨励給

wage income
chingin shotoku
賃金所得

wage increase rate
chingin jōshōritsu
賃金上昇率

wage increases
chin'age
賃上げ
chingin jōshō
賃金上昇

wage index
chingin shisū
賃金指数

wage indexation to prices
chingin no bukka suraidosei
賃金の物価スライド
制

wage inflation
chingin infurēshon
賃金インフレーション

wage labour
chinrōdō
賃労働

wage leadership
chingin sendōsei
賃金先導制

wage level
chingin suijun
賃金水準

wage movements
chingin idō
賃金移動

wage negotiations
chingin kōshō
賃金交渉

wage offensives
chingin kōsei
賃金攻勢

wage policy
chingin seisaku
賃金政策

wage-price control
chingin-bukka tōsei
賃金・物価統制

wage-price freeze
chingin-bukka tōketsu
賃金・物価凍結

wage-price guidelines
chingin-bukka gaidorain
賃金・物価ガイド
ライン

wage-price spiral
chingin-bukka no
akujunkan
賃金・物価 の悪循環

wage-push inflation
chingin atsuryoku infurēshon
賃金圧力インフレーション

wage-rate index
chingin shisū
賃金指数

wage rates
chinginritsu
賃金率

wage regulation
chingin chōsei
賃金調整

wage restraint
chingin yokusei
賃金抑制

wage scale
chingin sukēru
賃金スケール

wage settlements
chingin kettei
賃金決定

wage standardization
chingin heijunka
賃金平準化

wage structure
chingin kōzō
賃金構造

wage system
chingin taikei
賃金体系

wage theory
chinginsetsu
賃金説

wage-wage spiral
chingin-chingin no akujunkan
賃金・賃金の悪循環

wage workers
chingin rōdōsha
賃金労働者

wages and prices policy
chingin bukka seisaku
賃金物価政策

wages boards [UK]
chingin i'inkai
賃金委員会

wages classified by industries
gyōshubetsu chingin
業種別賃金

wages classified by occupations
shokubetsu chingin
職別賃金

wages councils [UK]
chingin shingikai
賃金審議会

want creation
yokubō sōshutsu
欲望創出

war economy
sensō keizai
戦争経済

war expenditure
senhi
戦費

war reparations
sensō baishō
戦争賠償

war-time budget
senji yosan
戦時予算

war-time economy
senji keizai
戦時経済

war-time shortage of goods
senjichū no busshi fusoku
戦時中の物資不足

warranted rate of growth
tekisei seichōritsu
適正成長率

warranted unemployment rate
tekisei shitsugyōritsu
適正失業率

waste
(matter)
haikibutsu
廃棄物

(squandering)
rōhi
浪費

water pollution
suishitsu osen
水質汚染

water rates
suidō ryōkin
水道料金

wave
hadō
派動

wealth
(affluence, opulence)
fuyū
富裕

(a fortune, riches)
tomi
富

(easy means, prosperity)
yūfuku
裕福

wealth distribution
tomi no bunpai
富の分配

wealth effect
tomi kōka
富効果

wealth redistribution
tomi no saibunpai
富の再分配

wealth restraint
tomi seiyaku
富制約

wealth tax
fuyūzei
富裕税

wealthy
yūfuku na
裕福な
yutaka na
豊かな

wealthy nation
fuyūkoku
富裕国

weighted average
kajū heikin
加重平均

weighted mean
kajū heikin
加重平均

weighted regression
kajū kaiki
加重回帰

welfare
(public)
fukuri kōsei
福利厚生

(well-being)
fukushi
福祉

(social)
kōsei
厚生

welfare cost(s)
fukuri kōseihi
福利厚生費

welfare economics
kōsei keizaigaku
厚生経済学

welfare expenditure
fukushi shishutsu
福祉支出

welfare expenses
fukuri kōseihi
複利厚生費

welfare facilities
fukuri setsubi
複利設備

welfare function
kōsei kansū
厚生関数

welfare indicator
fukushi shihyō
福祉指標

welfare-oriented economy
fukushi shikōgata keizai
福祉指向型経済

welfare-oriented society
fukushi shikōgata shakai
福祉指向型社会

welfare policy
fukushi seisaku
福祉政策

welfare programme
fukuri seido
複利制度

welfare society
fukushi shakai
福祉社会

welfare state
fukushi kokka
福祉国家

Western economies
seiō keizai
西欧経済

white-collar workers
howaito-karā rōdōsha
ホワイト・カラー
労働者

white paper
hakusho
白書

White Plan [US]
howaitoan
ホワイト案

wholesale
oroshiuri
卸売り

wholesale market
oroshiuri shijō
卸売市場

wholesale price index (WPI)
oroshiuri bukka shisū
卸売物価指数

wholesale prices
oroshiuri bukka
卸売物価
oroshiuri kakaku
卸売価格

wholesale trade
oroshiurigyō
卸売業

wholesalers
oroshiuri gyōsha
卸売業者

wide share ownership
kabushiki hoyū bunsan
株式保有分散

wild price rises
kyōran bukka
狂乱物価

willingness to pay
shiharai iyoku
支払意欲

windfall gain
igai no ritoku
意外の利得

windfall loss
igai no sonshitsu
意外の損失

withholding tax
gensen kazei
源泉課税

work
(labour)
rōdō
労働

(jobs)
shigoto
仕事

work committees
shokuba i'inkai
職場委員会

work councils
(factories)
kōjō kyōgikai
工場協議会

(employers and
employees)
rōshi kyōgikai
労使協議会

work in progress
shikakarihin
仕掛品

work-leisure model
shigoto-yoka moderu
仕事・余暇モデル

work permits
rōdō kyoka
労働許可

work-sharing
gappeishoku
合併職

work to rule
junpō senjutsu
順法戦術

workable competition
jikkō kyōsō
実効競争
yūkō kyōsō
有効競争

workers
rōdōsha
労働者

workers' co-operatives
rōdōsha kyōdōtai
労働者協同体

workers' participation
rōdōsha sanka
労働者参加

working age
shūgyō nenrei
就業年齢

working capital
unten shihon
運転資本

working capital ratio
unten shihon hiritsu
運転資本比率

working class
rōdōsha kaikyū
労働者階級

working conditions
rōdō jōken
労働条件

working couples
tomobataraki
共働き

working hours
rōdō jikan
労働時間

working households
kinrōsha setai
勤労者世帯

working masses
rōdō taishū
労働大衆

working population
rōdō jinkō
労働人口

working week
shūrōdō jikan
週労働時間

working women
fujin rōdōsha
婦人労働者
josei rōdōsha
女性労働者

World Bank
sekai ginkō
世界銀行

world-class skills
sekaiteki suijun ginō
世界的水準技能

world crisis
sekai kyōkō
世界恐慌

world demand
sekai juyō
世界需要

world economy
sekai keizai
世界経済

world market
sekai shijō
世界市場

world population
sekai jinkō
世界人口

world population growth rate
sekai no jinkō zōkaritsu
世界の人口増加率

world power
sekaiteki taikoku
世界的大国

world production
sekai seisan
世界生産

world recession
sekaiteki keiki kōtai
世界的景気後退

world reserves
sekai junbi
世界準備

world trade
sekai bōeki
世界貿易

world trade market
sekai bōeki shijō
世界貿易市場

worldwide inflation
sekaiteki infurēshon
世界的インフレー
ション

worldwide recession
sekaiteki fukyō
世界的不況

worth
kachi
価値

WPI (wholesale price index)
oroshiuri bukka shisū
卸売物価指数

year-end
nenmatsu
年末

year-end adjustment
nenmatsu chōsei
年末調整

yearly earnings
nenkan shūnyū
年間収入

yearly income
nenkan shotoku
年間所得

yield
(financial return)
rimawari
利回り

(production output)
seisandaka
生産高

(crop)
tsukuridaka
作り高

yield curve
rimawari kyokusen
利回り曲線

young country
shinkōkoku
新興国

young economy
shinkō keizai
新興経済

young labour
jakunen rōdō
若年労働

yuppies (young urban professionals)
yappi
ヤッピー

zero-based budgeting
zero-bēsu yosan hensei
ゼロ・ベース予算
編成

zero growth
zero seichō
ゼロ成長

zero-growth economy
zero seichō keizai
ゼロ成長経済

zero investment
zero tōshi
ゼロ投資

zero population growth
jinkō zero seichō
人口ゼロ成長

zone
chitai
地帯

zoning
toshi keikaku no chitaisei
都市計画の地帯制

agribusiness
nōgyō kanren sangyō
農業関連産業

agriculture
nōgyō
農業

air transportation industry
kōkū jigyō
航空事業

aircraft industry
kōkūki kōgyō
航空機工業

amusement industry
goraku sangyō
娯楽産業

animal husbandry
chikusangyō
畜産業

apiculture
yōhōgyō
養蜂業

apparel industry
ifuku seihin kōgyō
衣服製品工業

atomic industry
genshiryoku sangyō
原子力産業

automobile industry
jidōsha sangyō
自動車産業

banking industry
kin'yūgyō
金融業

beauty industry
biyōgyō
美容業

bee-keeping
yōhō
養蜂

beverage industry
inryō sangyō
飲料産業

brewing industry
jōzōgyō
醸造業

broadcasting industry
hōsō sangyō
放送産業

building industry
kensetsugyō
建設業

building-materials industry
kensetsu zairyō kōgyō
建設材料工業

canning industry
kanzumegyō
缶詰業

capital-goods industry
shihonzai sangyō
資本財産業

car industry
jidōsha sangyō
自動車産業

cattle-raising
bokuchikugyō
牧畜業

cement industry
semento sangyō
セメント産業

ceramic industry
yōgyō
窯業

ceramic, stone and clay products industry
yōgyō-doseki seihin kōgyō
窯業・土石製品工業

chemical industry
kagaku kōgyō
化学工業

clothing industry
hifukugyō
被服業

coal industry
sekitangyō
石炭業

coal-products industry
sekitan seihin seizōgyō
石炭製品製造業

coastal fishing
engan gyogyō
沿岸漁業

communication industry
tsūshingyō
通信業

compound industry
fukugōteki sangyō
複合的産業

computer industry
konpyūta sangyō
コンピュータ産業

construction industry
kensetsugyō
建設業

consumer goods industry
shōhizai sangyō
消費財産業

convenience food industry
benri shokuhin kōgyō
便利食品工業

cosmetics industry
keshōhin seizōgyō
化粧品製造業

cottage industry
kanai kōgyō
家内工業

cotton industry
mengyō
綿業

dairy-farming
rakunōgyō
酪農業

deep-sea fishing
en'yō gyogyō
遠洋漁業

defence industry
bōei sangyō
防衛産業

distribution industry
ryūtsū sangyō
流通産業

dyestuffs industry
somemonogyō
染物業

electrical machinery, equipment and supplies industry
denki kikai kigu seizōgyō
電気機械器具製造業

electricity industry
denki kōgyō
電気工業

electricity, water and gas supply industry
denki-gasu-suidōgyō
電気・ガス・水道業

electronics industry
denshi kōgyō
電子工業

engineering and metal-working industry
kikai kinzoku kōgyō
機械金属工業

engineering industry
enjiniaringu sangyō
エンジニアリング産業

entertainment industry
goraku sangyō
娯楽産業

extensive farming
sohō nōgyō
粗放農業

extractive industry
chūshutsu sangyō
抽出産業

farming
nōgyō
農業

fashion industry
fasshon sangyō
ファッション産業

fast-food industry
insutanto shokuhin kōgyō
インスタント食品工業

fibre industry
sen'i kōgyō
繊維工業

film industry
eiga sangyō
映画産業

fish-farming
yōgyogyō
養魚業

fishing industry
gyogyō
漁業
suisangyō
水産業

fodder industry
shiryō seizōgyō
飼料製造業

food and beverages industry
shokuryōhin kōgyō
食料品工業

food industry
shokuhin kōgyō
食品工業

food-processing industry
shokuhin kakōgyō
食品加工業

food service industry
gaishoku sangyō
外食産業

forestry
ringyō
林業

fuel industry
nenryō kōgyō
燃料工業

furniture and fixtures industry
kagu-sōbihin seizōgyō
家具・装備品製造業

glass industry
garasu kōgyō
硝子工業

grain farming
shukoku nōgyō
主穀農業

handicraft
shukōgyō
手工業

heavy industry
jūkōgyō
重工業

high-technology industry
kōdo gijutsu sangyō
高度技術産業

home industry (= cottage industry)
kanai sangyō
家内産業

housing industry
jūtaku sangyō
住宅産業

hydraulic power industry
suiryoku kōgyō
水力工業

information industry
jōhō sangyō
情報産業

insurance industry
hokengyō
保険業

intensive farming
shūteki nōgyō
集的農業

investment goods industry
tōshizai sangyō
投資財産業

iron and steel industry
tekkōgyō
鉄鋼業

iron industry
seitetsugyō
製鉄業
tekkōgyō
鉄鋼業

knowledge industry
chishiki sangyō
知識産業

lake fishing
kosui gyogyō
湖水漁業

leasing industry
riisu sangyō
リース産業
riisugyō
リース業

leather industry
hikaku kōgyō
皮革工業

leather-products industry
hikaku seihin kōgyō
皮革製品工業

leisure industry
rejā sangyō
レジャー産業

light industry
keikōgyō
軽工業

light manufacturing industry
keikōgyō
軽工業

livestock industry
chikusangyō
畜産業

lumber industry
mokuzai kōgyō
木材工業
seizaigyō
製材業

luxury goods industry
kōkyūhin seizōgyō
高級品製造業

machine-tool industry
kōsaku kikai kōgyō
工作機械工業

machinery industry
kikai kōgyō
機械工業

manual industry
shukōgyō
手工業

manufacturing industry
seizō kōgyō
製造工業
seizōgyō
製造業

meat industry
shokuniku sangyō
食肉産業

meat-processing industry
shokuniku kakōgyō
食肉加工業

meat products manufacturing industry
niku seihin kōgyō
肉製品工業

mechanical industry
kikai kōgyō
機械工業

metal mining
kinzoku kōgyō
金属工業

metal-working industry
kinzoku kōgyō
金属工業

metallurgy
yakin
冶金

mining industry
kōgyō
鉱業
kōzangyō
鉱山業

motor industry
jidōsha sangyō
自動車産業

multiple agriculture
takakuteki nōgyō
多角的農業

munitions industry
gunju kōgyō
軍需工業
heiki sangyō
兵器産業

music industry
ongaku sangyō
音楽産業

non-manufacturing industry
hiseizōgyō
非製造業

nuclear industry
kakukōgyō
核工業

ocean industry
kaiyō sangyō
海洋産業

offshore fishing
okiai gyogyō
沖合漁業

oil industry
sekiyu sangyō
石油産業

optical industry
hikari sangyō
光産業

packaging industry
hōsō sangyō
包装産業

paper-manufacturing industry
seishi kōgyō
製紙工業
seishigyō
製紙業

petrochemical industry
sekiyu kagaku kōgyō
石油化学工業
sekiyu kagaku sangyō
石油化学産業

petroleum and coal products industry
sekiyu sekitan seihin kōgyō
石油石炭製品工業

petroleum-based industry
sekiyu kanren sangyō
石油関連産業

petroleum industry
sekiyu sangyō
石油産業

pharmaceutical industry
yakuhin kōgyō
薬品工業

plantation farming
saishoku nōgyō
栽植農業

plastics industry
gōsei jushi
合成樹脂

porcelain industry
jiki seihin seizōgyō
磁器製品製造業

pottery industry
yōgyō
窯業

poultry-farming
yōkeigyō
養鶏業

power-generation industry
denryoku sangyō
電力産業

precious stone industry
hōsekigyō
宝石業

precision-instrument industry
seimitsu kōgyō
精密工業

printing and publishing industry
insatsu-shuppan sangyō
印刷・出版産業

printing industry
insatsugyō
印刷業

process industry
sōchi kōgyō
装置工業

processing industry
kakō kōgyō
加工工業

producer goods industry
seisanzai sangyō
生産財産業

public utility industry
kōeki jigyō
公益事業

publishing industry
shuppangyō
出版業

pulp and paper industry
parupu sangyō
パルプ産業

quarrying industry
saisekigyō
採石業

real-estate industry
fudōsangyō
不動産業

recycling industry
saisei kōgyō
再生工業

refining industry
seirengyō
精錬業

retail industry
kourigyō
小売業

river fishing
kasen gyogyō
河川漁業

rubber industry
gomu kōgyō
ゴム工業

rubber-products industry
gomu seihin seizōgyō
ゴム製品製造業

salt industry
seiengyō
製塩業

security industry
hoan keibi sangyō
保安警備産業

sericulture
sangyō
蚕業
yōsan
養蚕

service industry
sābisu sangyō
サービス産業
sābisugyō
サービス業

ship-building industry
zōsengyō
造船業

shipping industry
kaiungyō
海運業

shoe industry
seikagyō
製靴業

silk industry
seishigyō
製糸業

smelting industry
seirengyō
精錬業

software industry
sofutouea sangyō
ソフトウエア産業

solar power industry
taiyōnetsu denryoku kōgyō
太陽熱電力工業

space industry
uchū sangyō
宇宙産業

spinning and weaving industry
bōseki-bōshoku kōgyō
紡績・紡織工業

spinning industry
bōsekigyō
紡績業

steel industry
seikōgyō
製鋼業
tekkōgyō
鉄鋼業

stock-raising
bokuchikugyō
牧畜業
chikusangyō
畜産業

sugar industry
seitōgyō
製糖業

synthetic fibre industry
gōsei sen'i kōgyō
合成繊維工業

synthetic leather products industry
gōsei hikaku seihin kōgyō
合成皮革製品工業

synthetic pulp industry
gōsei parupu kōgyō
合成パルプ工業

synthetic rubber industry
gōsei gomu kōgyō
合成ゴム工業

tanning industry
seikakugyō
製革業

telecommunications industry
denki tsūshingyō
電気通信業

textile industry
orimono kōgyō
織物工業
sen'i kōgyō
繊維工業

tidal power industry
chōryoku denryoku kōgyō
潮力電力工業

timber industry
mokuzai sangyō
木材産業
seizaigyō
製材業

tourist industry
kankōgyō
観光業

transport industry
un'yugyō
運輸業

warehousing industry
sōkogyō
倉庫業

watch and clock industry
tokei seizōgyō
時計製造業

weapon industry
heiki sangyō
兵器産業

wholesale industry
oroshiurigyō
卸売業

wood-working industry
mokkōgyō
木工業

wool industry
yōmōgyō
羊毛業

Chapter 2

Finance

A/C (account)
kanjō
勘定
kōza
口座

A/P (advice and pay)
tsūchibarai
通知払い

ABA (American Bankers Association)
amerika ginkō gyōsha kyōkai
アメリカ銀行業者協会

absolute acceptance
tanjun hikiuke
単純引受け

acceptance [UK]
hikiuke tegata
引受手形

acceptance bank
hikiuke ginkō
引受銀行

acceptance charge
hikiuke tesūryō
引受手数料

acceptance commission
hikiuke tesūryō
引受手数料

acceptance credit
hikiuke jōkentsuki shin'yō
引受条件付き信用

acceptance for honour
sanka hikiuke
参加引受け

acceptance liability
hikiuke sekinin
引受責任

acceptance of bill
tegata hikiuke
手形引受け

acceptance payable
shiharai tegata
支払手形

acceptance rate
yunyū tegata kessai sōba
輸入手形決済相場

acceptance receivable
uketori tegata
受取手形

accepted bill
hikiuke tegata
引受手形

accepted draft
hikiuke tegata
引受手形

accepting bank
hikiuke ginkō
引受銀行

acceptor
hikiukenin
引受人

accommodation
yūzū
融通

accommodation acceptance
yūzū tegata hikiuke
融通手形引受け

accommodation acceptor
yūzū tegata hikiukenin
融通手形引受人

accommodation bill
yūzū tegata
融通手形

accommodation endorsement
yūzū tegata uragaki
融通手形裏書き

accommodation endorser
yūzū uragakinin
融通裏書人

accommodation paper
yūzū tegata
融通手形

accommodation parties
yūzū tōjisha
融通当事者

accompanying documents
tenpu shorui
添付書類

account (A/C)
kanjō
勘定
kōza
口座

account balance
kanjō zandaka
勘定残高

account holder
kanjō hoyūsha
勘定保有者

account number
kōza bangō
口座番号

accumulated interest
ruiseki rishi
累積利子

accumulated savings
ruiseki chochiku
累積貯蓄

ACH (automated clearing house)
jidōteki kōkanjo
自動的交換所

ackowledgement (confirmation, validation)
kakunin
確認

(approval)
shōnin
承認

(acknowledgement of receipt)
uketori tsūchisho
受取通知書

active account
katsudō kanjō
活動勘定

advance bill
maegashi tegata
前貸手形

advice (information, guidance, notice)
annai
案内

(notification)
tsūchi
通知

advice and pay (A/P)
tsūchibarai
通知払い

advice note
annaijō
案内状
tsūchijō
通知状

advice of bill
tegata furidashi annai
手形振出案内

advice of payment
shiharai tsūchi
支払通知

advising bank
tsūchi ginkō
通知銀行

advising charge
tsūchi tesūryō
通知手数料

affiliated bank
shimai ginkō
姉妹銀行

affix (seal) [J] (see note 7)
osu
押す

after-date
hizukego
日付後

after-date bill
hizukego tegata
日付後手形

after sight
ichirango
一覧後

after-sight bill
ichirango teikibarai tegata
一覧後定期払手形

agency bill
dairiten tegata
代理店手形

agent bank
dairi ginkō
代理銀行

AIB (Associate of the Institute of Bankers) [UK]
eikoku ginkō gyōsha kyōkai'in
英国銀行業者協会員

AIB (American Institute of Banking)
amerika ginkō kyōkai
アメリカ銀行協会

allonge
fusen
付せん

alteration of bill
tegata henkō
手形変更

alternative drawee
daikō furiatenin
代行振当人

alternative payee
daikō uketorinin
代行受取人

American Bankers Association (ABA)
amerika ginkō gyōsha kyōkai
アメリカ銀行業者協会

American Institute of Banking (AIB)
amerika ginkō kyōkai
アメリカ銀行協会

amount
kingaku
金額

amount cleared
tegata kōkandaka
手形交換高

amount deposited
yokindaka
預金高

amount of bill
tegata kingaku
手形金額

amount paid
shiharaigaku
支払額

amount payable
shiharaikin
支払金

amount to clear
kōkandaka
交換高

annual interest
nenri
年利

anonymous deposit
mukimei yokin
無記名預金

anonymous time deposit
mukimei teiki yokin
無記名定期預金

antedate (noun)
jizen hizuke
事前日付け

antedate (verb)
jizen hizuke o tsukeru
事前日付けを付ける

antedated bill
jizen hizuke tegata
事前日付け手形

antedated cheque
jizen hizuke kogitte
事前日付け小切手

approved acceptance
shōnin hikiuke tegata
承認引受手形

as per advice
tsūchi no de
通知ので

Associate of the Institute of Bankers (AIB) [UK]
eikoku ginkō gyōsha kyōkai'in
英国銀行業者協会員

associated bank
kumiai ginkō
組合銀行

at sight
ichiranbarai
一覧払い
sanchakubarai
参着払い

ATM (automatic teller machine)
genkin jidō shiharaiki
現金自動支払機

attached documents
tenpu shorui
添付書類

authority
(delegation, commission)
inin
委任

(competence, power)
kengen
権限

(approval)
kōnin
公認

(permission)
ninka
認可

authorization
(delegation, commission)
inin
委任

(delegation of legal power)
juken
授権

(approval)
kōnin
公認

authorization to pay
shiharai jukensho
支払授権書

authorize
mitomeru
認める

authorized foreign exchange bank [J][1]
gaikoku kawase kōnin ginkō[1]
外国為替公認銀行

automated clearing house (ACH)
jidōteki kōkanjo
自動的交換所

automated customer services
jutaku gyōmu
受託業務

automated teller
genkin jidō shiharaiki
現金自動支払機

automatic cash-paying machine
genkin jidō shiharaiki
現金自動支払機

automatic deposit
jidō furikomi
自動振込み
jidō yokin
自動預金

automatic teller machine (ATM)
genkin jidō shiharaiki
現金自動支払機

automatic transfer
jidō furikae
自動振替え

aval
ryūtsū shōken hoshō
流通証券保証

B/L (bill of lading)
funani shōken
船荷証券

back (= to cover payment)
hikiateru
引当てる

back-to-back credit
dōji kaisetsu shin'yō
同時開設信用

back-to-back L/C
dōji kaisetsu shin'yōjō
同時開設信用状

backdate (noun)
atohizuke
後日付け

backdate (verb)
atohizuke o tsukeru
後日付けを付ける

backdated cheque
atohizuke kogitte
後日付け小切手

backdating
atohizuke
後日付け

bad cheque
fuwatari kogitte
不渡小切手

balance
zandaka
残高

balance brought forward
kurikoshi zandaka
繰越残高

balance enquiry
zandaka shōkai
残高照会

balance of account
kanjō zandaka
勘定残高
yokin zandaka
預金残高

balance of clearing
tegata kōkanjiri
手形交換尻

bank
ginkō
銀行

bank acceptance
ginkō hikiuke tegata
銀行引受手形

bank acceptance credit
ginkō hikiuke shin'yōjō
銀行引受信用状

bank acceptance rate
ginkō hikiuke waribikiritsu
銀行引受割引率

bank accommodation
ginkō yūshi
銀行融資

bank account
ginkō kanjō
銀行勘定
ginkō kōza
銀行口座
ginkō yokin
銀行預金

bank agreement
ginkō kanjō chōseihyō
銀行勘定調整表

bank balance
ginkō yokin zandaka
銀行預金残高

bank bill
[UK]
ginkō tegata
銀行手形

[US]
ginkōken
銀行券

bank bond
kin'yūsai
金融債

bank book
ginkō tsūchō
銀行通帳

bank borrowing
ginkō kariirekin
銀行借入金

bank buying rate
ginkō kaisōba
銀行買相場

bank capital
ginkō eigyō shikin
銀行営業資金

bank card
banku-kādo
バンク・カード

bank charges
ginkō tesūryō
銀行手数料

bank charter [US]
ginkō setsuritsu menkyo
銀行設立免許

bank clearing
tegata kōkan
手形交換

bank clerk
ginkōin
銀行員

bank commission
ginkō tesūryō
銀行手数料

bank commissioner
ginkō shinsain
銀行審査員

bank confirmation [US]
ginkō kaikei hōkoku
銀行会計報告

bank crash
ginkō hatan
銀行破綻

bank credit
ginkō shin'yō
銀行信用

(loans)
ginkō kashidashi
銀行貸出し

(finance)
ginkō yūshi
銀行融資

bank debenture
kin'yūsai
金融債

bank demand
ginkō sanchakubarai
銀行参着払い

bank demand draft
ginkō sanchakubarai tegata
銀行参着払手形

bank deposit
ginkō yokin
銀行預金

bank deposit passbook
yokin tsūchō
預金通帳

bank deposits and savings
yochokin
預貯金

bank discount
ginkō waribiki
銀行割引

bank discount rate
ginkō waribiki buai
銀行割引歩合

bank draft [UK]
ginkō kawase tegata
銀行為替手形

bank endorsement
ginkō uragaki
銀行裏書き

bank examination
ginkō kensa
銀行検査

bank examiner
ginkō kensakan
銀行検査官

bank failure
ginkō hatan
銀行破綻

bank float
furōto
フロート
ryūtsū
流通

bank holding company [US]
ginkō mochikabu gaisha
銀行持株会社

bank holiday
ginkō kyūjitsu
銀行休日

bank interest
ginkō rishi
銀行利子

bank lending
(loans)
ginkō kashidashi
銀行貸出し

(finance)
ginkō yūshi
銀行融資

bank line [US]
ginkō shin'yō kyūyo
gendogaku
銀行信用給与限度額

bank liquidity
ginkō ryūdōsei
銀行流動性

bank loan
ginkō kashidashi
銀行貸出し
ginkō kashitsuke
銀行貸付け

bank merger
ginkō gōdō
銀行合同

bank money
yokin tsūka
預金通貨

bank money order
ginkō kawase
銀行為替

bank note [UK]
ginkō shihei
銀行紙幣
ginkōken
銀行券

Bank of America
amerika ginkō
アメリカ銀行

bank of deposit
yokin ginkō
預金銀行

Bank of England
eiran ginkō
英蘭銀行

Bank of Japan
nippon ginkō
日本銀行

Bank of Japan bank note
nippon ginkōken
日本銀行券

bank overdraft
ginkō karikoshi
銀行借越し

bank paper
ginkō tegata
銀行手形

Bank Rate
kōtei buai
公定歩合
waribiki buai
割引歩合

bank rate (interest)
ginkō kinri
銀行金利
ginkō riritsu
銀行利率

bank rate policy
ginkō kinri seisaku
銀行金利政策

bank reconciliation
ginkō kanjō chōseihyō
銀行勘定調整表

bank records
ginkō kiroku
銀行記録

bank reference
ginkō shin'yō shōkaisaki
銀行信用照会先

bank regulations
ginkō kisei
銀行規制

bank remittance
ginkō sōkin kawase
銀行送金為替

bank report
ginkō kaikei hōkoku
銀行会計報告

bank reserve ratio
yokin shiharai junbiritsu
預金支払準備率

bank reserves
ginkō junbikin
銀行準備金
ginkō shiharai junbikin
銀行支払準備金

bank robbery
ginkō gōtō
銀行強盗

bank's fund position
shikin pojishon
資金ポジション

bank staff
ginkōin
銀行員

bank statement
ginkō kanjō hōkokusho
銀行勘定報告書

bank teller
ginkō suitō kakari
銀行出納係

bank-to-bank transaction
ginkōkan torihiki
銀行間取引

bank transaction
ginkō torihiki
銀行取引

bank transfer
ginkō furikomi
銀行振込み

bank transport truck
genkin yusōsha
現金輸送車

bank with (verb)
(–) to torihiki suru
(–) と取引する

bankable
ginkō e tanpokanō na
銀行へ担保可能な

banker
ginkōka
銀行家

banker's acceptance [US]
ginkō hikiuke tegata
銀行引受手形

banker's acceptance credit
ginkō hikiuke shin'yōjō
銀行引受信用状

banker's acceptance rate
ginkō hikiuke tegata
waribikiritsu
銀行引受手形割引率

banker's bank
ginkō no ginkō
銀行の銀行

banker's cheque
ginkō kogitte
銀行小切手

banker's clean bill
ginkō kuriin-biru
銀行クリーン・ビル

Banker's Clearing House [UK]
tegata kōkanjo
手形交換所

banker's discount
ginkō tegata waribiki
銀行手形割引

banker's draft [UK]
ginkō kawase tegata
銀行為替手形

banker's guarantee
ginkō hoshō
銀行保証

banker's L/C
ginkō shin'yōjō
銀行信用状

bankers (a company's)
torihiki ginkō
取引銀行

bankers' association
ginkō kyōkai
銀行協会

banking
  (business)
ginkō gyōmu
銀行業務

  (system)
ginkō seido
銀行制度

  (organization)
ginkō soshiki
銀行組織

  (transaction)
ginkō torihiki
銀行取引

banking activities
kin'yū katsudō
金融活動

banking administration
ginkō gyōsei
銀行行政

banking business
ginkōgyō
銀行業

banking centre
kin'yū chūshinchi
金融中心地

banking charges
ginkō shogakari
銀行諸掛り

banking circles
ginkō gyōkai
銀行業界

banking community
ginkō gyōkai
銀行業界

banking establishment
kin'yū kikan
金融機関

banking facilities
kin'yū kikan
金融機関

banking hours
ginkō eigyō jikan
銀行営業時間

banking house
kin'yū gaisha
金融会社

banking law
ginkōhō
銀行法

banking operation
ginkō un'yō sōsa
銀行運用操作

banking panic
ginkō kyōkō
銀行恐慌

banking policy
ginkō gyōmu seisaku
銀行業務政策

banking secrecy
ginkō gyōmu himitsusei
銀行業務秘密性

banking sector
ginkō bumon
銀行部門

banking syndicate
ginkōdan
銀行団

banking system
ginkō seido
銀行制度

banking world
ginkō gyōkai
銀行業界

base rate
kijun kinri
基準金利

basic discount rate
kijun waribiki buai
基準割引歩合

bearer
jisannin
持参人

bearer cheque
jisanninbarai kogitte
持参人払小切手

beneficiary
uketorinin
受取人

bill
tegata
手形

  (paper currency) [US]
ginkōken
銀行券
shihei
紙幣

bill accepted
hikiuke tegata
引受手形

bill account
tegata kanjō
手形勘定

bill advice
tegata enki tsūchijō
手形延期通知状

bill at maturity
manki tegata
満期手形

bill at sight
ichiranbarai tegata
一覧払手形

bill bearer
tegata shojinin
手形所持人

bill book
tegata kanjō chōbo
手形勘定帳簿

bill bought
kaitori tegata
買取手形
kaitori yushutsu kawase
買取輸出為替

bill clearing
tegata kōkan
手形交換

bill collection
tegata toritate
手形取立て

bill collector
tegata toritatenin
手形取立人

bill discounted
waribiki tegata
割引手形

bill discounting
tegata waribiki
手形割引

bill dishonoured
fuwatari tegata
不渡手形

bill for acceptance
hikiuke seikyū tegata
引受請求手形

bill for collection
(daikin) toritate tegata
(代金)取立手形

bill for premature delivery
hayauke tegata
早受手形

bill for presentation
teijibarai tegata
呈示払手形

bill holder
tegata shojinin
手形所持人

bill holdings
tegata mochidaka
手形持高

bill in foreign currency
gaika kawase tegata
外貨為替手形

bill in the Japanese currency
hōka kawase tegata
邦貨為替手形

bill of exchange
kawase tegata
為替手形

bill of lading (B/L)
funani shōken
船荷証券

bill payable at a fixed date
kakuteibibarai tegata
確定日払手形

bill payable at a fixed period after sight
ichirango teikibarai tegata
一覧後定期払手形

bill payable at sight
ichiranbarai tegata
一覧払手形

bill payable in foreign currency
gaika shiharai tegata
外貨支払手形

bill payable to bearer
jisanninbarai tegata
持参人払手形

bill payable to order
sashizuninbarai tegata
指図人払手形

bill receivable discounted
waribiki tegata
割引手形

bill receivable in foreign currency
gaika uketori tegata
外貨受取手形

bill rediscounted
saiwaribiki tegata
再割引手形

bill rediscounting
tegata saiwaribiki
手形再割引

bill to bearer
jisanninbarai tegata
持参人手形

bill to order
sashizuninbarai tegata
指図人払手形

bills in a set
kumi tegata
組手形

bills in clearing
toritatemisai tegata
取立未済手形

bills on demand
sanchakubarai tegata
参着払手形
yōkyūbarai tegata
要求払手形

bills on tap
sanchakubarai tegata
参着払手形

bills payable
shiharai tegata
支払手形

bills payable book
shiharai tegatachō
支払手形帳

bills receivable
uketori tegata
受取手形

bills to be collected
daikin toritate tegata
代金取立手形

black (in the)
kuroji de
黒字で

blank acceptance
shiraji hikiuke
白地引受け

blank bill
shirajishiki tegata
白地式手形

blank cheque
shirajishiki kogitte
白地式小切手

blank endorsement
shiraji uragaki
白地裏書き

blockage of funds
shikin fūsa
資金封鎖

blocked account
fūsa kanjō
封鎖勘定

blocked cheque
fūsa kogitte
封鎖小切手

blocked deposit
fūsa yokin
封鎖預金

blocked funds
fūsa shikin
封鎖資金

bounce (bouncing)
fuwatari henkyaku
不渡返却

bouncing cheque
fuwatari kogitte
不渡小切手

branch
shiten
支店

branch banking
shiten ginkō seido
支店銀行制度

branch network
shitenmō
支店網

building society [UK]
jūtaku kin'yū kikan
住宅金融機関

business bank
shōgyō ginkō
商業銀行

business days
eigyōbi
営業日

(week-days)
heijitsu
平日

buyer's credit
baiyāzu-kurejitto
バイヤーズ・クレ
ジット

cable transfer
denshin kawase
電信為替

**cancelled cheque
(voided, crossed out)**
masshō kogitte
抹消小切手

(rendered invalid, voided)
mukō kogitte
無効小切手

(paid)
shiharaizumi kogitte
支払済小切手

carry over
kurikoshi
繰越し

cash
genkin
現金

cash bill
genkin tegata
現金手形

cash card
kyasshu-kādo
キャッシュ・カード

cash deposit
genkin yokin
現金預金

cash depositor (machine)
genkin jidō azukariki
現金自動預機

cash dispenser
genkin jidō shiharaiki
現金自動支払機

cash holdings
genkin zandaka
現金残高

cash in (verb)
genkin ni kaeru
現金に換える
genkinka suru
現金化する

cash in bank
tōza yokin
当座預金

cash in transit
unsōchū no genkin
運送中の現金

cash keeper
genkin kakari
現金係

cash L/C
kyasshu-kurejitto
キャッシュ・クレ
ジット

cash position
kyasshu-pojishon
キャッシュ・ポジ
ション

cash ratio
genkin hiritsu
現金比率
genkin junbiritsu
現金準備率

cash remittance
genkin sōkin
現金送金

cash reserve
genkin junbi
現金準備
shiharai junbi
支払準備

cash reserve ratio
genkin junbiritsu
現金準備率
shiharai junbiritsu
支払準備率

cash reserve requirements
genkin junbikin seido
現金準備金制度

cashier
suitō kakari
出納係

cashier's cheque [US]
shiharainin kogitte
支払人小切手

(banker's draft)
ginkō kawase tegata
銀行為替手形

cashing
genkinka
現金化

cashing-in
genkinka
現金化

cashpoint [UK]
genkin jidō shiharaiki
現金自動支払機

CD (certificate of deposit)
yokin shōsho
預金証書

central bank
chūō ginkō
中央銀行

central bank authorities
chūō ginkō tōkyoku
中央銀行当局

central bank credit
chūō ginkō shin'yō
中央銀行信用

central bank discount rate
chūō ginkō waribiki buai
中央銀行割引歩合

central bank governor
chūō ginkō sōsai
中央銀行総裁

central bank money
chūō ginkō tsūka
中央銀行通貨

central bank rate
chūō ginkō waribiki buai
中央銀行割引歩合

Central Reserve Bank [US]
chūō junbi ginkō
中央準備銀行

certificate of deposit (CD)
yokin shōsho
預金証書

certificate of employment[2]
zaishoku shōmei[2]
在職証明

certification of payment
shiharai hoshō
支払保証

certified cheque
hoshō kogitte
保証小切手
shiharai hoshō kogitte
支払保証小切手

certifying bank
shiharai hoshō ginkō
支払保証銀行

chain banking
rensa ginkōsei
連鎖銀行制

change (verb)
ryōgae suru
両替する

charge (noun)
(fee, rate)
ryōkin
料金

(commission)
tesūryō
手数料

charge (verb)
karikata ni kinyū suru
借方に記入する

charge for changing money
ryōgaeryō
両替料

charge for collection of a bill
tegata toritateryō
手形取立料

charge for custody
hokanryō
保管料

charge for remittance
kawase tesūryō
為替手数料

check [US] (see cheque [UK])
kogitte
小切手

checking account [US]
tōza kanjō
当座勘定
tōza yokin
当座預金

cheque [UK]
kogitte
小切手

cheque book
kogittechō
小切手帳

cheque-book money
kogitte kahei
小切手貨幣

cheque-book stub
kogittechō hikae
小切手帳控え

cheque card [UK]
kogitte hoshō kādo
小切手保証カード

cheque cashed over the counter
tentō kogitte
店頭小切手

cheque clearance
kogitte no kessai
小切手の決済

cheque deposit
kogitte yokin
小切手預金

cheque for collection
daikin toritate kogitte
代金取立小切手

cheque returned unpaid
fuwatari henkan kogitte
不渡返還小切手

cheque to bearer
jisanninbarai kogitte
持参人払小切手
shojininbarai kogitte
所持人払小切手

cheque to order
sashizuninbarai kogitte
指図人払小切手
sashizushiki kogitte
指図式小切手

cheques and bills
kitte tegata
切手手形

cheques and bills for collection
toritate kitte tegata
取立切手手形

cheques and bills in the process of collection
toritatemisai kitte tegata
取立未済切手手形

chief cashier
suitō kachō
出納課長

city bank [J]
shichū ginkō
市中銀行
toshi ginkō
都市銀行

claused bill of exchange
kurōzutsuki tegata
クローズ付手形

clean acceptance
tanjun hikiuke
単純引受け

clean bill
futsū kawase tegata
普通為替手形
kuriin-biru
クリーン・ビル

clean bill of exchange
futsū kawase tegata
普通為替手形

clean bill of lading
mukoshō funani shōken
無故障船荷証券

clean draft
shin'yō tegata
信用手形

clean L/C
mutanpo shin'yōjō
無担保信用状

clear (a bill)
(tegata o) seisan suru
(手形を) 清算する

clearing
tegata kōkan
手形交換

clearing account
tegata kōkan kanjō
手形交換勘定

clearing agent
dairi kōkan ginkō
代理交換銀行

clearing agreement
kawase seisan kyōtei
為替清算協定

clearing balance
tegata kōkanjiri
手形交換尻

clearing bank [UK]
tegata kōkan kamei ginkō
手形交換加盟銀行

clearing house
tegata kōkanjo
手形交換所

clearing house certificate
kōkanjo shōken
交換所証券

clearing house due bill
kōkanjiri furikae tegata
交換尻振替手形

clearing house in-book
ukeire kōkan tegata
hikaechō
受入交換手形控帳

clearing house inspector
tegata kōkanjo kanji
手形交換所監事

clearing house out-book
haraidashi kōkan tegata
hikaechō
払出交換手形控帳

clearing house proof
tegata kōkan kessanhyō
手形交換決算表

**clearing house settlement
sheet**
kōkanjo seisanhyō
交換所清算表

clearing house statement
kōkanjo keisansho
交換所計算書

clearing items
kōkan bukken
交換物件

clearing of bill
tegata kōkan
手形交換

clearing system
tegata kōkan seido
手形交換制度

client
kokyaku
顧客
torihikisaki
取引先

close an account
kanjō o heisa suru
勘定を閉鎖する
kanjō o kaiyaku suru
勘定を解約する

coin
kōka
硬貨

coin changer
jidō ryōgaeki
自動両替機

coin collector
jidō denryokukei
自動電力計

coin counting machine
kōka keisūki
硬貨計数機

collecting bank
toritate ginkō
取立銀行

collection
toritate
取立て

collection charge
toritateryō
取立料

commercial bank
shōgyō ginkō
商業銀行

commercial banking
shōgyō ginkōgyō
商業銀行業

commercial bill
shōgyō tegata
商業手形

commercial documents
shōgyō shorui
商業書類

commercial L/C
shōgyō shin'yōjō
商業信用状

commercial paper
shōgyō tegata
商業手形

commission
tesūryō
手数料

company's bankers
torihiki ginkō
取引銀行

company registration[3]
shōgyō tōkibo tōhon[3]
商業登記簿謄本

company seal[4]
inkan shōmei[4]
印鑑証明

compensating balance [US]
hoshō yokin
補償預金

compound interest
fukuri
複利

conditional endorsement
jōkentsuki uragaki
条件付裏書き

confidentiality
(privacy)
himitsusei
秘密性

(secret information)
kimitsusei
機密性

confidentiality of depositor
yokinsha no kimitsusei
預金者の機密性

confirmed L/C
kakunin shin'yōjō
確認信用状

consortium bank
kokusai ginkō rengō
国際銀行連合

consumer banking
koguchi kin'yū
小口金融

convertible account
tokubetsu yokin kanjō
特別預金勘定

corporate account
shayō no futsū yokin
社用の普通預金

corporate customers
hōjin torihikisaki
法人取引先

corporate deposit
hōjin yokin
法人預金

corporate savings
hōjin chochiku
法人貯蓄

correspondent
koruresusaki
コルレス先

correspondent account
koruresu kanjō
コルレス勘定

correspondent arrangement
koruresu keiyaku
コルレス契約

correspondent bank
koruresu ginkō
コルレス銀行

corset [UK]
korusetto
コルセット
yokin zōkaritsu kisei
預金増加率規制

counter
madoguchi
窓口

counter cheque
aikogitte
相小切手

counterfoil
hikae bubun
控え部分

counter-sign
(endorse, witness)
fukusho suru
副署する

(sign jointly)
rensho suru
連署する

counter-signature
(endorsement,
witnessing)
fukusho
副署

(joint signature)
rensho
連署

country bank
chihō ginkō
地方銀行

cover an overdraft
kaburi no shikin teate o
suru
過振りの資金手当て
をする

credit
(loan)
shin'yō(gashi)
信用 (貸し)

(vs. debit)
kashikata
貸方

credit advice
nyūkinzumi tsūchisho
入金済通知書

credit balance
kashikata zandaka
貸方残高

credit bank
shin'yō ginkō
信用銀行

(financing)
kin'yū ginkō
金融銀行

credit bill
shin'yō tegata
信用手形

credit department
shin'yō chōsabu
信用調査部

credit entry
kashikata kinyū
貸方記入

credit manager
shinsa buchō
審査部長

credit policy
kin'yū seisaku
金融政策

credit side
kashikata
貸方

credit slip
nyūkinhyō
入金票

credit to current account
tōza furikomi
当座振込み

crossed cheque
ōsen kogitte
横線小切手

current account [UK]
tōza kanjō
当座勘定
tōza yokin
当座預金

current deposits
tōza yokin
当座預金

custodian (institution)
hokan kikan
保管機関

custody
(keeping)
azukari
預かり

(safe-keeping)
hogo azukari
保護預かり

(trust)
hokan
保管

custody fee
hokanryō
保管料

custody of securities
shōken hokan
証券保管

customer
kokyaku
顧客
tokuisaki
得意先

(account)
torihikisaki
取引先

customer advice service
kokyaku sōdan
顧客相談

customer's acceptance
tokuisaki hikiuke tegata
得意先引受手形

customer's account
tokuisaki kanjō
得意先勘定

customer services
kokyaku sābisu
顧客サービス

DA (documents against acceptance)
hikiuke watashi
引受渡し
tegata hikiuke shorui watashi
手形引受書類渡し

date account closed
torihiki teishibi
取引停止日

date account opened
torihiki kaishibi
取引開始日

date of issue
furidashi hizuke
振出日付け
furidashibi
振出日

date of payment
shiharaibi
支払日

day of issue
furidashibi
振出日

debit (vs. credit) (noun)
karikata
借方

debit (verb)
karikata ni kinyū suru
借方に記入する

debit balance
karikata zandaka
借方残高

debit entry
karikata kinyū
借方記入

debit note
karikatahyō
借方票

debit side
karikata
借方

debit slip
karikatahyō
借方票
shiharai denpyō
支払伝票

debit voucher
karikatahyō
借方票
shiharai denpyō
支払伝票

debt (loan, borrowings)
kashikin
貸金
shakkin
借金

demand deposit [US]
yōkyūbarai yokin
要求払預金

demand draft
sanchakubarai tegata
参着払手形
yōkyūbarai tegata
要求払手形

denomination
gakumen kingaku
額面金額
tan'imei
単位名

deposit (noun)
azukekin
預け金
yokin
預金
yotaku
預託

deposit (verb)
(money, articles)
azukeru
預ける

(money)
yokin suru
預金する
yotaku suru
預託する

deposit account [UK]
yokin kanjō
預金勘定

(savings account)
chochiku yokin kanjō
貯蓄預金勘定

(fixed-term account)
teiki yokin kanjō
定期預金勘定

deposit at bank
ginkō yokin
銀行預金

deposit bank
yokin ginkō
預金銀行

deposit book
yokin tsūchō
預金通帳

deposit certificate
azukari shōken
預かり証券

deposit currency
yokin tsūka
預金通貨

deposit for safe custody
hogo azukari
保護預かり

deposit insurance
ginkō yokin hoken
銀行預金保険

deposit into current account
tōza yokin
当座預金

deposit money
kane o azukeru
金を預ける

deposit rate (Bank of Japan)
yokin riritsu
預金利率

deposit receipt
yokin shōsho
預金証書
yokin ukeireshō
預金受入証

deposit slip
yokin shōsho
預金証書

deposit-taking institution
yokin jutaku kikan
預金受託機関

deposit under an assumed name
kakūmeigi yokin
架空名義預金

deposit with notice
tsūchi yokin
通知預金

depositary
azukarinin
預かり人

(trustee)
hokannin
保管人

deposited money
yokin
預金
yotakukin
預託金

deposited securities (for safe-keeping)
hogo azukari shōken
保護預かり証券

depositing
yokin
預金
yotaku
預託

depositor
yokinsha
預金者
yotakusha
預託者

depository
hokansho
保管所

depository bank
yotaku ginkō
預託銀行

depository facilities
yotaku kikan
預託機関

direct debit
jidō furikae
自動振替え

direct debit system
jidō furikae seido
自動振替制度

direct exchange bill
chokusetsu kawase tegata
直接為替手形

disclosure
kōkai
公開

discount (noun)
waribiki
割引

discount (verb)
waribiki suru
割引する

discount at central bank
chūō ginkō waribiki
中央銀行割引

discount bank
waribiki ginkō
割引銀行

discount bill
waribiki tegata
割引手形

discount charge
waribikiryō
割引料

discount clerk
waribiki kakari
割引係

discount commission
waribiki tesūryō
割引手数料

discount operation
waribiki sōsa
割引操作

discount policy
waribiki seisaku
割引政策

discount rate
waribikiritsu
割引率

(Bank Rate)
kōtei buai
公定歩合
waribiki buai
割引歩合

discounted bill
waribiki tegata
割引手形

discounting
waribiki
割引

discounting bank
waribiki ginkō
割引銀行

discounting of bills
tegata waribiki
手形割引

dishonour (noun)
fuwatari
不渡り
hikiuke kyohi
引受拒否
hikiuke kyozetsu
引受拒絶

dishonour (verb)
fuwatari ni suru
不渡りにする

dishonoured bill
fubarai tegata
不払手形
fuwatari tegata
不渡手形

dishonoured cheque
fubarai kogitte
不払小切手
fuwatari kogitte
不渡小切手

document
shorui
書類

document attached
shorui tenpu
書類添付

documentary bill
nigawase tegata
荷為替手形

documentary bill for acceptance
nigawase hikiuke tegata
荷為替引受手形

documentary bill of exchange
nigawase tegata
荷為替手形

documentary clean bill
hadaka nigawase tegata
裸荷為替手形

documentary commercial bill
nigawase shin'yōjō
荷為替信用状

documentary credit
nigawase shin'yōjō
荷為替信用状

documentary draft
nigawase shoruitsuki tegata
荷為替書類付手形

documentary evidence
shōko shorui
証拠書類

documentary export bill
yushutsu nigawase tegata
輸出荷為替手形

documentary import bill
yunyū nigawase tegata
輸入荷為替手形

documentary L/C
nigawase shin'yōjō
荷為替信用状

documents against acceptance (DA)
hikiuke watashi
引受渡し
tegata hikiuke shorui watashi
手形引受書類渡し

documents-against-acceptance bill
hikiuke watashi tegata
引受渡手形

documents against payment (DP)
shiharai watashi
支払渡し
tegata shiharai shorui watashi
手形支払書類渡し

documents-against-payment bill
shiharai watashi nigawase tegata
支払渡荷為替手形
shiharai watashi tegata
支払渡手形

dollar account
doru kanjō
ドル勘定

domestic bill
naikoku tegata
内国手形

domestic bill of exchange
naikoku kawase tegata
内国為替手形

domestic L/C
kokunai shin'yōjō
国内信用状

domestic money order
naikoku kawase
内国為替

(remittance)
naikoku sōkin
内国送金

domicile of a bill
tegata shiharai basho
手形支払場所

domiciled bill
tashobarai tegata
他所払手形

domiciled cheque
tashobarai kogitte
他所払小切手

dormant account
kyūshi kanjō
休止勘定
suimin kōza
睡眠口座

double-name paper
fukumei tegata
複名手形

DP (documents against payment)
shiharai watashi
支払渡し
tegata shiharai shorui watashi
手形支払書類渡し

draft
kawase tegata
為替手形

draft at a tenor
kigentsuki tegata
期限付手形
teikibarai tegata
定期払手形

draft at sight
ichiranbarai tegata
一覧払手形

draft endorsee
tegata hiuragakinin
手形被裏書人

draft endorsement
tegata uragaki
手形裏書き

draft endorser
tegata uragakinin
手形裏書人

draft extension
tegata shiharai kigen enchō
手形支払期限延長

draft for collection
toritate tegata
取立手形

draft holder
tegata shojinin
手形所持人

draft holdings
tegata hoyūdaka
手形保有高

draft instructions
tegata furidashi sashizu
手形振出指図

draft on demand
yōkyūbarai tegata
要求払手形

draft payable to bearer
shojininbarai tegata
所持人払手形

draw (verb)
furidasu
振出す

draw a cheque
kogitte o furidasu
小切手を振出す

draw money
yochokin o hikidasu
預貯金を引出す

drawee
naatenin
名あて人

(of a cheque)
kogitte naatenin
小切手名あて人

(of a bill)
tegata naatenin
手形名あて人

drawer
furidashinin
振出人

(of a cheque)
kogitte furidashinin
小切手振出人

(of a bill)
tegata furidashinin
手形振出人

drawing
(issuing)
furidashi
振出し

(withdrawing)
hikidashi
引出し

drawing account
hikidashikin kanjō
引出金勘定

drawing bank
furidashi ginkō
振出銀行

drawing of bill
tegata no furidashi
手形の振出し

drawing of money
yochokin no hikidashi
預貯金の引出し

drawing place
furidashichi
振出地

drawn bill
furidashi tegata
振出手形

due date
(maturity date)
mankijitsu
満期日

(payment date)
shiharaibi
支払日

eligible bank [UK]
tekikaku ginkō
適格銀行

eligible bill
tekikaku tegata
適格手形

eligible paper [US]
tekikaku tegata
適格手形

encashment
genkinka
現金化

endorse
uragaki suru
裏書きする

endorsed bill
uragaki tegata
裏書手形

endorsee
hiuragakinin
被裏書人

endorsement
uragaki
裏書き

endorsement in blank
shiraji uragaki
白地裏書き

endorser
uragakinin
裏書人

entry
kinyū
記入

escrow
esukuro
エスクロ

escrow account
esukuro kanjō
エスクロ勘定

escrow credit
esukuro shin'yōjō
エスクロ信用状

Euro-bank
yūrōginkō
ユーロー銀行

examination
ginkō kensa
銀行検査

examiner
ginkō kensakan
銀行検査官

excess liquidity
kajō ryūdōsei
過剰流動性

excess reserves
kajō junbi
過剰準備

exchange (see foreign exchange)
kawase (gaikoku kawase)
為替 (外国為替)

exchange bank
kawase ginkō
為替銀行

exchange bill
kawase tegata
為替手形

exchange bill payable
junkawase
順為替

exchange bill receivable
gyakukawase
逆為替

exchange cover bill
kawase deai tegata
為替出合手形

EXIMBANK (Export-Import Bank of the United States)
beikoku yushutsunyū ginkō
米国輸出入銀行

export acceptance bill
yushutsu hikiuke tegata
輸出引受手形

export advance bill
yushutsu maegashi tegata
輸出前貸手形

export bill
yushutsu tegata
輸出手形

export bills bought
yushutsu tegata kaimochi
輸出手形買持ち

export draft
yushutsu tegata
輸出手形

Export-Import Bank of Japan
nihon yushutsunyū ginkō
日本輸出入銀行

Export-Import Bank of the United States (EXIMBANK)
beikoku yushutsunyū ginkō
米国輸出入銀行

export L/C
yushutsu shin'yōjō
輸出信用状

export L/C received
yushutsu shin'yōjō setsujudaka
輸出信用状接受高

export trade bill
yushutsu bōeki tegata
輸出貿易手形

export usance bill
kigentsuki yushutsu tegata
期限付輸出手形

external account (non-resident)
hikyojūsha kanjō
非居住者勘定

FDIC (Federal Deposit Insurance Corporation) [US]
renpō yokin hoken gaisha
連邦預金保険会社

Fed (Federal Reserve System) [US]
renpō junbi seido
連邦準備制度

Federal Deposit Insurance Corporation (FDIC) [US]
renpō yokin hoken gaisha
連邦預金保険会社

Federal Reserve Bank (FRB) [US]
renpō junbi ginkō
連邦準備銀行

Federal Reserve System (Fed) [US]
renpō junbi seido
連邦準備制度

Federal Savings and Loan Insurance Corporation [US]
renpō chochiku kashitsuke hoken gaisha
連邦貯蓄貸付保険会社

fee
(rate)
ryōkin
料金

(commission)
tesūryō
手数料

fill in (a form)
(yōshi o) kakikomu
(用紙を) 書込む

financial adviser
zaimu komon
財務顧問

fine bill
yūryō tegata
優良手形

first of exchange
dai'ichi kawase tegata
第一為替手形

fixed deposit
teiki yokin
定期預金

fixed-time deposit
teiki yokin
定期預金

float (verb)
furōto suru
フロートする
ryūtsū suru
流通する

for collection
daikin toritate
代金取立て

foreign bank
gaikoku ginkō
外国銀行

foreign bill
gaikoku kawase tegata
外国為替手形

foreign bill of exchange
gaikoku kawase tegata
外国為替手形

foreign bills bought
kaiire gaikoku kawase
買入外国為替

foreign bills payable
shiharai gaikoku kawase
支払外国為替

foreign bills receivable
toritate gaikoku kawase
取立外国為替

foreign bills sold
uriwatashi gaikoku kawase
売渡外国為替

foreign correspondent bank
koruresusaki ginkō
コルレス先銀行

foreign currency account
gaika kanjō
外貨勘定

foreign currency bill
gaika tegata
外貨手形

foreign currency bills bought
gaika kaiire gaikoku kawase
外貨買入外国為替

foreign currency bills payable
gaika miharai gaikoku kawase
外貨未払外国為替

foreign currency bills receivable
gaika toritate gaikoku kawase
外貨取立外国為替

foreign currency bills sold
gaika uriwatashi gaikoku kawase
外貨売渡外国為替

foreign currency deposit
gaika yokin
外貨預金

foreign currency deposit account
gaika yokin kanjō
外貨預金勘定

foreign currency L/C
gaika shin'yōjō
外貨信用状

foreign currency position
gaika mochidaka
外貨持高

foreign draft
gaika kawase tegata
外貨為替手形

foreign exchange
gaikoku kawase
外国為替

foreign exchange bank
gaikoku kawase ginkō
外国為替銀行

foreign exchange clerk
gaikoku kawase kakari
外国為替係

foreign post-office money order
gaikoku yūbin kawase
外国郵便為替

forged bill
gizō tegata
偽造手形

forged cheque
gizō kogitte
偽造小切手

forged endorsement (bill)
giuragaki
偽裏書き

forged signature
gisho
偽署

forgery
gisaku
偽作
gizō
偽造

form
yōshi
用紙

form of payment
shiharai keishiki
支払形式

fractional reserve banking
bubun junbi ginkōsei
部分準備銀行制

fraud
sagi
詐欺

FRB (Federal Reserve Bank) [US]
renpō junbi ginkō
連邦準備銀行

free reserves
jiyū junbi
自由準備

freeze
tōketsu suru
凍結する

frozen account
tōketsu kanjō
凍結勘定

fund position
shikin pojishon
資金ポジション

funds
shikin
資金

(money on deposit)
yokin
預金

general acceptance
futsū hikiuke
普通引受け

general crossed cheque
futsū ōsen kogitte
普通横線小切手

general crossing
futsū ōsen
普通横線

general L/C
tegata kaitori ginkō fushitei shin'yōjō
手形買取銀行不指定
信用状

genuine signature
honnin shinpitsu shomei
本人真筆署名

giro [UK]
yūbin furikae kawase
郵便振替為替

giro system [UK]
yūbin furikae seido
郵便振替制度

Girobank [UK]
yūbin furikae kikan
郵便振替機関

go in the red
akaji o dasu
赤字を出す

government deposit
seifu yokin
政府預金

government guarantee
seifu hoshō
政府保証

government's bank
seifu no ginkō
政府の銀行

grant an overdraft
tōza karikoshi o mitomeru
当座借越を認める

gross interest
sōrishi
総利子

group banking [US]
shūdan ginkōsei
集団銀行制

guarantee [UK] (= guaranty [US])
hoshō
保証

guarantee (person)
hihoshōnin
被保証人

guarantee (verb)
hoshō suru
保証する

guarantee of a bill
tegata shiharai hoshō
手形支払保証

guaranteed bill
hoshō tegata
保証手形

guarantor
hoshōnin
保証人

guaranty [US]
hoshō
保証

handling
toriatsukai
取扱

handling charge
toriatsukai tesūryō
取扱手数料

(for a bill)
tegata kaiire tesūryō
手形買入手数料

head cashier
suitō kachō
出納課長

high-interest bearing account
kōritsuki yokin kōza
高利付預金口座

high-street bank [UK]
shuyō na shōgyō ginkō
主要な商業銀行

high-tech banking
kōdo gijutsu ginkōsei
高度技術銀行制

holder (of bill, cheque)
shojinin
所持人

home banking
hōmu-bankingu
ホーム・バンキング

honour (a bill)
(tegata o) hikiukeru
(手形を) 引受ける
(tegata o) otosu
(手形を) 落とす

house bill
shanai tegata
社内手形

hypothec [UK]
fudōsan teitōken
不動産抵当権
teitōken
抵当権

hypothecation [US]
fudōsan teitōken
不動産抵当権
teitōken
抵当権

idle deposit
fukatsudō zandaka
不活動残高

import advance bill
yunyū maegashi tegata
輸入前貸手形

import bill
yunyū tegata
輸入手形

import draft
yunyū kawase tegata
輸入為替手形

import L/C
yunyū shin'yōjō
輸入信用状

import settlement
yunyū kessai
輸入決済

import settlement bill
yunyū kessai tegata
輸入決済手形

import trade bill
yunyū bōeki tegata
輸入貿易手形

import usance bill
kigentsuki yunyū tegata
期限付輸入手形

in the red
akaji de
赤字で

inactive account
fukatsudō kanjō
不活動勘定

income deposit
shotoku yokin
所得預金

increase in deposit
yokin zōka
預金増加

indirect exchange
kansetsu kawase
間接為替

indirect exchange bill
kansetsu kawase tegata
間接為替手形

individual bill
kojin tegata
個人手形

individual customers
kojin torihikisaki
個人取引先

individual deposit
kojin yokin
個人預金

individual saver
kojin chochikuka
個人貯蓄家

individual savings
kojin chochiku
個人貯蓄

industrial bank [UK]
kōgyō ginkō
工業銀行

industrial bill
kōgyō tegata
工業手形

ineligible bill
futekikaku tegata
不適格手形

inland bill
naikoku kawase tegata
内国為替手形

Institute of Bankers [UK]
eikoku ginkō gyōsha kyōkai
英国銀行業者協会

insufficient funds
yokin fusoku
預金不足

insufficient funds cheque
yokin fusoku kogitte
預金不足小切手

inter-bank deposit
dōgyōsha yokin
同業者預金

inter-bank exchange dealings
ginkōkan kawase torihiki
銀行間為替取引

inter-bank market
ginkōkan shijō
銀行間市場

inter-bank rate
ginkōkan sōba
銀行間相場

inter-bank transaction
ginkōkan torihiki
銀行間取引

interest
(money rates)
kinri
金利

(interest on loan or
deposit)
rishi
利子
risoku
利息

interest account
rishi kanjō
利子勘定

interest-bearing
ritsuki no
利付きの

interest-bearing account
ritsuki kanjō
利付勘定

interest-bearing checking
account
ritsuki tōza kanjō
利付当座勘定

interest-bearing deposit
ritsuki yokin
利付預金

interest-bearing deposit
account
ritsuki yokin kanjō
利付預金勘定

interest on deposit
yokin kinri
預金金利
yokin rishi
預金利子

interest on loan
kashitsukekin risoku
貸付金利息

interest on overdraft
tōza kashikoshi risoku
当座貸越利息

interest per annum
nenri
年利

interest per diem
hibu
日歩

interest rate
(money rates)
kinri
金利

(interest on loan or
deposit)
riritsu
利率
rishiritsu
利子率

interest table
rishi hayamihyō
利子早見表

international bank
kokusai ginkō
国際銀行

international banking
kokusai kin'yū
国際金融

international banking facilities
kokusai kin'yū kikan
国際金融機関

international investment bank
kokusai tōshi ginkō
国際投資銀行

investment
tōshi
投資

investment adviser
tōshi sōdannin
投資相談人

investment bank [US]
tōshi ginkō
投資銀行

investment banker [US]
tōshi ginkō
投資銀行

investment banking [US]
tōshi ginkō gyōmu
投資銀行業務

investment manager
tōshi kanrinin
投資管理人

irregular deposit
futeiki yokin
不定期預金

irrevocable L/C
torikeshifunō shin'yōjō
取消不能信用状

issue (<u>noun</u>)
(bill)
furidashi
振出し

(L/C)
hakkō
発行

issue (<u>verb</u>)
(bill)
furidasu
振出す

(L/C)
hakkō suru
発行する

issuing bank
hakkō ginkō
発行銀行

Japan Development Bank
nihon kaihatsu ginkō
日本開発銀行

joint account
kyōdō kanjō
共同勘定
kyōdō kōza
共同口座

joint deposit account
kyōdō yokin kanjō
共同預金勘定

joint depositors
kyōdō yokinsha
共同預金者

joint savings account
kyōdō chochiku kanjō
共同貯蓄勘定

kite
nareai tegata
慣れ合い手形
yūzū tegata
融通手形

L/C (letter of credit)
shin'yōjō
信用状

L/C advising bank
shin'yōjō tsūchi ginkō
信用状通知銀行

L/C applicant
hakkō irainin
発行依頼人

L/C beneficiary
shin'yōjō juekisha
信用状受益者

L/C confirming bank
shin'yōjō kakunin ginkō
信用状確認銀行

L/C confirming charge
shin'yōjō kakunin tesūryō
信用状確認手数料

L/C issued account
shin'yōjō hakkō kanjō
信用状発行勘定

L/C issuing bank
shin'yōjō hakkō ginkō
信用状発行銀行

L/C margin money
shin'yōjō kaisetsu hoshōkin
信用状開設保証金

L/C opening bank
shin'yōjō kaisetsu ginkō
信用状開設銀行

L/C opening charge
shin'yōjō kaisetsu tesūryō
信用状開設手数料

L/C parties
shin'yōjō tōjisha
信用状当事者

L/G (letter of guaranty)
shin'yō hoshōjō
信用保証状

land bank
fudōsan ginkō
不動産銀行

large bill
ōguchi tegata
大口手形

large denomination
kōgakumen
高額面

large deposit
ōguchi yokin
大口預金

large sum
tagaku
多額

last endorser
saishū uragakinin
最終裏書人

legal reserve requirement
hōtei shiharai shoyō
junbiritsu
法定支払所要準備率

lending bank
yūshi ginkō
融資銀行

letter of advice
tsūchijō
通知状

letter of authority
jukensho
授権書

letter of credit (see L/C)
shin'yōjō
信用状

letter of guaranty (L/G)
shin'yō hoshōjō
信用保証状

letter of instruction
tegata kaitori sashizusho
手形買取指図書

LIBOR (London inter-bank offered rate)
rondon ginkōkan torihiki kinri
ロンドン銀行間取引金利

line of credit [US]
kashidashi gendogaku
貸出限度額

liquid deposit
ryūdōsei yokin
流動性預金

liquid reserve
ryūdōsei junbikin
流動性準備金

liquidity of bank
ginkō ryūdōsei
銀行流動性

liquidity ratio
ryūdōsei hiritsu
流動性比率

loan
kashidashi
貸出し
kashitsuke
貸付け

loan department (of a bank)
(ginkō no) kashidashi bumon
(銀行の) 貸出部門

local bank
chihō ginkō
地方銀行

London Bankers' Clearing House
rondon tegata kōkanjo
ロンドン手形交換所

London Clearing House
rondon tegata kōkanjo
ロンドン手形交換所

London inter-bank offered rate (LIBOR)
rondon ginkōkan torihiki kinri
ロンドン銀行間取引金利

long bill
chōki tegata
長期手形

long rate
kigentsuki tegata kaisōba
期限付手形買相場

lost bill
funshitsu tegata
紛失手形

lost cheque
funshitsu kogitte
紛失小切手

made bill
uragaki tegata
裏書手形

mail transfer (MT) (transfer)
yūbin furikae
郵便振替え

(exchange)
yūbin kawase
郵便為替

main account
shuyō kanjō
主要勘定

main banker
shutorihiki ginkō
主取引銀行

maintain an account (with a bank)
(ginkō ni) kanjō o oku
(銀行に) 勘定を置く

major bank
daiginkō
大銀行

make a withdrawal
hikidasu
引出す

marked cheque
fugōtsuki kogitte
符号付小切手

mature (verb)
manki ni naru
満期になる

matured bill
manki tegata
満期手形

maximum limit of overdraft
kaburi gendo
過振限度
kashikoshi gendo
貸越限度

member bank
kamei ginkō
加盟銀行

member of the clearing house
tegata kōkanjo kumiai ginkō
手形交換所組合銀行

merchant bank
shōgyō ginkō
商業銀行

minimum reserve requirement
saitei shiharai junbiritsu
最低支払準備率

money
[general – neutral]
kane
金

(cash, specie)
genkin
現金

(coinage, currency)
kahei
貨幣

(funds)
shikin
資金

money by weight
hyōryō kahei
秤量貨幣

money center bank [US]
manē-sentā shozai ginkō
マネー・センター
所在銀行

money deposited
azukekin
預け金
yokin
預金

money market deposit account [US]
shijō kinri rendōgata futsū yokin
市場金利連動型普通
預金

money on deposit
azukekin
預け金
yokin
預金

money order
sōkin kawase
送金為替

money order form
sōkin kawase yōshi
送金為替用紙

money rates
kinri
金利

money transfer
furikae
振替え

monthly payment
tsukigake
月掛け

monthly savings
tsukigake chokin
月掛貯金

monthly statement of account
getsuji ginkō kanjō hōkokusho
月次銀行勘定報告書

mortgage
mōgejji
モーゲッジ

(house purchase loan)
jūtaku (shikin) kashitsuke
住宅 (資金) 貸付け
jūtaku kin'yu
住宅金融
fudōsan kashitsuke
不動産貸付け

(collateral)
tanpo
担保

(hypothec [UK], hypothecation [US])
teitō(ken)
抵当 (権)

mortgage bank
jūtaku kin'yū gaisha
住宅金融会社

mortgage banking
jūtaku kin'yūgyō
住宅金融業

MT (mail transfer)
yūbin furikae
郵便振替え
yūbin kawase
郵便為替

multi-national bank
takokuseki ginkō
他国籍銀行

mutilated bill
kison tegata
き損手形

mutilated cheque
kison kogitte
き損小切手

mutual loan and savings bank [US]
sōgo ginkō
相互銀行

mutual savings [US]
sōgo chochiku
相互貯蓄

mutual savings bank [US]
sōgo chochiku ginkō
相互貯蓄銀行

national bank [US]
kokuritsu ginkō
国立銀行

National Girobank [UK]
yūbin furikae kikan
郵便振替機関

national savings
kokumin chochiku
国民貯蓄

National Savings Bank (NSB) [UK]
yūbin chochiku kikan
郵便貯蓄機関

nationalized bank
kokuyūka ginkō
国有化銀行

negative interest
gyaku kinri
逆金利
mainasu no kinri
マイナスの金利

negotiable bill
ryūtsū tegata
流通手形

negotiable instrument
ryūtsū shōken
流通証券

negotiable order of withdrawal (NOW) [US]
jōtokanō yokin harai-modoshi sashizusho
譲渡可能預金払戻
指図書

negotiating bank
kaitori ginkō
買取銀行

negotiation charge
kaitori tesūryō
買取手数料

neutrality of central bank
chūō ginkō no chūritsusei
中央銀行の中立性

night depository
yakan yokin hokansho
夜間預金保管所

night safe
yakan kinko
夜間金庫

'no account'
torihiki nashi
取引なし

'no advice'
tegata no tsūchi nashi
手形の通知なし

'no funds'
yokin fusoku
預金不足
zandaka fusoku
残高不足

non-acceptance
hikiuke kyozetsu
引受拒絶

non-customer
hitorihikisaki
非取引先

non-interest bearing
murishi no
無利子の
murisoku no
無利息の

non-interest bearing account
murisoku kanjō
無利息勘定

non-member bank
hikamei ginkō
非加盟銀行

non-negotiable bill
jōtofunō tegata
譲渡不能手形

non-negotiable endorsement
uragaki kinshi tegata
裏書禁止手形

non-order bill
sashizu kinshi tegata
指図禁止手形

non-payment
fubarai
不払い
fuwatari
不渡り
shiharai kyozetsu
支払拒絶

non-payment protest
fuwatari tsūchi
不渡通知
shiharai kyozetsu shōsho
支払拒絶証書

non-resident
hikyojūsha
非居住者

non-resident account
hikyojūsha kanjō
非居住者勘定

non-resident foreign currency account
hikyojūsha gaika yokin kanjō
非居住者外貨預金勘定

non-resident free yen account [J]
hikyojūsha jiyūen kanjō
非居住者自由円勘定

nostro account
tōhō kanjō
当方勘定

not negotiable
ryūtsū kinshi
流通禁止

'not sufficient funds'
yokin fusoku
預金不足
zandaka fusoku
残高不足

note
(bank note [UK])
ginkōken
銀行券
shihei
紙幣

(negotiable instrument)
ryūtsū shōken
流通証券

notice
(advice, information)
annai
案内

(advice, notification)
tsūchi
通知

notice of acceptance
hikiuke tsūchi
引受通知

notice of dishonour
fuwatari tsūchi
不渡通知

notice of payment
nōnyū kokuchisho
納入告知書

notice of protest
shiharai kyozetsu tsūchisho
支払拒絶通知書

notification
tsūchi
通知

notifying bank
tsūchi ginkō
通知銀行

NSB (National Savings Bank) [UK]
yūbin chochiku kikan
郵便貯蓄機関

NOW (negotiable order of withdrawal) [US]
jōtokanō yokin harai-modoshi sashizusho
譲渡可能預金払戻指図書

NOW account [US]
NOW kanjō
NOW 勘定

null and void
mukō no
無効の

numbered account
mukimei yokin kanjō
無記名預金勘定

official (discount) rate [US]
kōtei buai
公定歩合

offset
sōsai
相殺

on application
seikyūbarai
請求払い

on demand
sanchakubarai
参着払い
yōkyūbarai
要求払い

on-line banking system
on-rain-bankingu-
shisutemu
オン・ライン・バン
キング・システム

one-name bill
tanmei tegata
単名手形

one-name paper
tanmei tegata
単名手形

one-year deposit
ichinen no teiki yokin
一年の定期預金

open (an account)
(kanjō o) hiraku
(勘定を) 開く
(kanjō o) kaisetsu suru
(勘定を) 開設する

open cheque
futsū kogitte
普通小切手

open credit
mujōken shin'yōjō
無条件信用状

open-end credit [US]
ōpungata shin'yō
オープン型信用

open L/C
tegata kaitori ginkō fushitei
shin'yōjō
手形買取銀行不指定
信用状

opening bank
shin'yōjō kaisetsu ginkō
信用状開設銀行

opening of account
kanjō kaisetsu
勘定開設
torihiki kaishi
取引開始

operation (banking operation)
shikin un'yō sōsa
資金運用操作

order bill
sashizushiki tegata
指図式手形

order cheque
kimeishiki kogitte
記名式小切手
sashizuninbarai kogitte
指図人払小切手

order for payment
shiharai meirei
支払命令

ordinary bank [J]
futsū ginkō
普通銀行

ordinary bill
nami tegata
並手形

ordinary deposit
futsū yokin
普通預金

ordinary deposit account
futsū yokin kanjō
普通預金勘定

original bill
miuragaki tegata
未裏書手形

original credit
genshin'yōjō
原信用状

originating bank
hakkō ginkō
発行銀行

originator
torihiki o sosei suru hito
取引を組成する人

out-of-date cheque
shikkō kogitte
失効小切手

outstanding overdraft
karikoshi zandaka
借越残高

overdraft [UK]
kaburi
過振り
karikoshi
借越し
kashikoshi
貸越し

overdraft agreement
kashikoshi keiyaku
貸越契約

overdraft facilities
kashikoshi
貸越し

overdraft limit
kaburi gendo
過振限度
kashikoshi gendo
貸越限度

overdrawing
kaburi
過振り

overdrawn account
karikoshi kanjō
借越勘定

overdrawn cheque
kaburi kogitte
過振小切手

overdue bill
kigen keika tegata
期限経過手形

overdue cheque
kigen keika kogitte
期限経過小切手

overdue interest
entai rishi
延滞利子

overdue interest per diem
entai hibu
延滞日歩

overnight safe
yakan yokin hokansho
夜間預金保管所

overseas bank
kaigai ginkō
海外銀行

overseas branch of Japanese bank
hōgin kaigaiten
邦銀海外店

paid cheque
shiharaizumi kogitte
支払済小切手

paper
(certificate)
shōken
証券

(bill)
tegata
手形

parent bank
oya ginkō
親銀行

partial acceptance
ichibu hikiuke
一部引受け

partial endorsement
ichibu uragaki
一部裏書き

parties to a bill
tegata tōjisha
手形当事者

party (parties)
tōjisha
当事者

passbook
(bank)
ginkō tsūchō
銀行通帳

(general)
yokin tsūchō
預金通帳

passbook account
yokin tsūchō kōza
預金通帳口座

past-due bill
kigen keika tegata
期限経過手形

past-due cheque
kigen keika kogitte
期限経過小切手

pay (verb)
shiharau
支払う

pay at sight
ichiranbarai o suru
一覧払いをする

pay in
furikomu
振込む
nyūkin suru
入金する

pay on application
seikyūbarai o suru
請求払いをする

pay on demand
yōkyūbarai o suru
要求払いをする

payable after date
hizukegobarai
日付後払い

payable against documents
shorui hikikaebarai
書類引換払い

payable at sight
ichiranbarai
一覧払い

payable on demand
sanchakubarai
参着払い
yōkyūbarai
要求払い

payable to bearer
jisanninbarai
持参人払い

payable to order
sashizuninbarai
指図人払い

payee
(of bill)
hishiharainin
被支払人

(beneficiary)
uketorinin
受取人

payer
shiharainin
支払人

paying bank
shiharai ginkō
支払銀行

paying book
shiharaichō
支払帳

paying-in book
yokin nyūkinchō
預金入金帳

paying-in slip
nyūkinhyō
入金票

paying teller
ginkō no shiharai kakari
銀行の支払係

payment
(repayment, settlement)
bensai
弁済

(a payment)
harai
払い
haraikomi
払込み

(disbursement)
shiharai
支払い

payment against acceptance
hikiukebarai
引受払い

payment against documents
shorui hikikaebarai
書類引換払い

payment agreement
shiharai kyōtei
支払協定

payment arrangement
shiharai kyōtei
支払協定

payment at maturity
mankibarai
満期払い

payment at sight
ichiranbarai
一覧払い

payment bill
shiharai tegata
支払手形

payment book
shiharai kinyūchō
支払記入帳

payment by acceptance
hikiukebarai
引受払い

payment by banker
ginkōbarai
銀行払い

payment by bill
tegatabarai
手形払い

payment by cheque
kogittebarai
小切手払い

payment by draft
kawase tegatabarai
為替手形払い

payment by note
yakusoku tegatabarai
約束手形払い

payment counter
shiharai madoguchi
支払窓口

payment date
shiharaibi
支払日

payment in gold
kinkabarai
金貨払い

payment on application
seikyūbarai
請求払い

payment on presentation
teijibarai
呈示払い

payment procedure
shiharai tetsuzuki
支払手続き

payment refused
shiharai kyozetsu
支払拒絶

payment stopped
shiharai teishi
支払停止

payment terms
shiharai jōken
支払条件

penal interest
iyaku rishi
違約利子

personal bill
kojin tegata
個人手形

personal checking account
kojin tōza yokin
個人当座預金

personal cheque
kojin kogitte
個人小切手

personal deposit
kojin yokin
個人預金

**personal identification number
(= PIN number)**
kojin shikibetsu bangō
(= PIN bangō)
個人識別番号
(= PIN 番号)

personal safe deposit box
kojin kashikinko
個人貸金庫

personal savings
kojin chochiku
個人貯蓄

petty savings
koguchi yochokin
小口預貯金
reisai yochokin
零細預貯金

PIN number
PIN bangō
PIN 番号

place of issue
furidashichi
振出地

place of payment
shiharaichi
支払地

post-date (verb)
jigohizuke o tsukeru
事後日付けを付ける
sakihizuke ni suru
先日付けにする

post-dated bill
jigohizuke tegata
事後日付け手形

post-dated cheque
jigohizuke kogitte
事後日付け小切手
sakihizuke kogitte
先日付け小切手

post-dating
jigohizuke
事後日付け
sakihizuke
先日付け

post-office
yūbinkyoku
郵便局

**post-office checking account
[UK]**
yūbin kogitte kanjō
郵便小切手勘定

post-office cheque
yūbin kogitte
郵便小切手

post-office deposit
yūbin chokin
郵便貯金

**post-office investment
account [UK]**
yūbin teiki yokin kanjō
郵便定期預金勘定

post-office money order
yūbin kawase
郵便為替

post-office savings
yūbin chokin
郵便貯金

post-office savings account
yūbin chokin kanjō
郵便貯金勘定

post-office savings system
yūbin chokin seido
郵便貯金制度

post-office savings tax exemption
yūbin chokin rishi hikazei seido
郵便貯金利子非課税制度

presentation for acceptance
hikiuke teiji
引受呈示

presentation for payment
shiharai yōkyū teiji
支払要求呈示

presentation of bill
tegata no teiji
手形の呈示

presentation of documents
shorui teiji
書類呈示

presenting bank
mochidashi ginkō
持出銀行

prime bill
ichiryū tegata
一流手形
yūryō tegata
優良手形

prime rate [US]
puraimu-rēto
プライム・レート

principal (person)
honnin
本人

private bank [US]
kojin ginkō
個人銀行

private bill
kojin tegata
個人手形

private deposit
kojin yokin
個人預金
minkan yokin
民間預金

private safe-deposit box
kojin kashikinko
個人貸金庫

pro-forma bill
mitsumori kawase tegata
見積り為替手形

proof of residence[5]
jūminhyō[5]
住民票

protection of depositors
yokinsha hogo
預金者保護

protest charges
hikiuke kyozetsu shōsho sakusei tesūryō
引受拒絶証書作成手数料

protest for non-acceptance
hikiuke kyozetsu shōsho
引受拒絶証書

protest waived
hikiuke kyozetsu shōsho sakusei menjo
引受拒絶証書作成免除

protested bill
hikiuke kyozetsu tegata
引受拒絶手形

protested cheque
shiharai kyozetsu kogitte
支払拒絶小切手

qualified acceptance
seigen hikiuke
制限引受け

qualified endorsement
seigen uragaki
制限裏書き

quarter days
shiharai kanjōbi
支払勘定日
shiki shiharaibi
四季支払日

quarterly interest
shihanki rishi
四半期利子

quarterly statement of account
shihanki ginkō kanjō hōkokusho
四半期銀行勘定報告書

rate of interest (money rates)
kinri
金利

(interest on loan or deposit)
riritsu
利率
rishiritsu
利子率

rate on overdraft
tōza kashikoshi risoku
当座貸越利息

receipt
uketori
受取り

(slip)
uketorishō
受取証

reclamation (correction of negotiable instrument)
gosan no teisei
誤算の訂正

red clause L/C
reddo-kurōzutsuki shin'yōjō
レッド・クローズ付信用状

redeem a dishonoured bill
fuwatari tegata o shōkan suru
不渡手形を償還する

rediscount (noun)
saiwaribiki
再割引

rediscount (verb)
saiwaribiki suru
再割引する

rediscount policy
saiwaribiki seisaku
再割引政策

rediscount rate
saiwaribiki buai
再割引歩合
saiwaribikiritsu
再割引率

rediscounted bill
saiwaribiki tegata
再割引手形

rediscounting
saiwaribiki
再割引

'refer to acceptor'
hikiukenin mawashi
引受人回し

'refer to drawer'
furidashinin mawashi
振出人回し

reference
shōmeisho
証明書

refinance bill
yunyūsha kigentsuki tegata
輸入者期限付手形

regional bank[6]
chihō ginkō[6]
地方銀行

regular checking account [US]
futsū tōza yokin
普通当座預金

rejected cheque
shiharai kyozetsu kogitte
支払拒絶小切手

rejection
kyohi
拒否
kyozetsu
拒絶

remit
sōkin suru
送金する

remit money
sōkin suru
送金する

remittance
sōkin
送金

remittance abroad
gaikoku sōkin
外国送金

remittance advice
sōkin tsūchisho
送金通知書

remittance amount
sōkingaku
送金額

remittance bank
sōkin ginkō
送金銀行

remittance bill
sōkin kawase
送金為替
sōkin tegata
送金手形

remittance by cable
denshin sōkin
電信送金

remittance by draft
kawase (tegata) sōkin
為替 (手形) 送金

remittance by mail
yūbin sōkin
郵便送金

remittance charge
sōkin tesūryō
送金手数料

remittance cheque
sōkin kogitte
送金小切手

remittance from abroad
hishimuke sōkin kawase shiharai
被仕向送金為替
支払い

remittance instruction
sōkin tsūchisho
送金通知書

remittance letter
sōkin tsūchijō
送金通知状

remittance slip
sōkin tsūchisho
送金通知書

remittee
sōkin uketorinin
送金受取人
uketorinin
受取人

remitter
furidashinin
振出人
sōkinnin
送金人

remitting bank
sōkin ginkō
送金銀行

renewal
kirikae
切替え

renewal bill
kirikae tegata
切替手形

renewal commission
kirikae tesūryō
切替手数料

rental fee (of safe deposit box)
kashikinko chingariryō
貸金庫賃借料

repurchase a dishonoured bill
fuwatari tegata o kaimodosu
不渡手形を買戻す

required reserve ratio [US]
hōtei junbiritsu
法定準備率

required reserves [US]
hōtei junbi(kin)
法定準備 (金)

reserve(s)
junbi(kin)
準備 (金)

reserve assets (Bank of England)
junbi shisan
準備資産

reserve assets ratio
junbi shisanritsu
準備資産率

reserve bank [US]
junbi ginkō
準備銀行

reserve deficiencies
junbi yokin fusoku
準備預金不足

reserve deposit
junbi yokin
準備預金

reserve ratio
junbiritsu
準備率

reserve requirement [US]
(shiharai) junbiritsu
(支払) 準備率

reserve requirement system [US]
shiharai junbiritsu seido
支払準備率制度

resident account
kyojūsha kanjō
居住者勘定

resident foreign-currency deposit account
kyojūsha gaika yokin kanjō
居住者外貨預金勘定

restricted L/C
tegata kaitori ginkō shitei shin'yōjō
手形買取銀行指定信用状

restrictive endorsement
gentei uragaki
限定裏書き

retail bank
koguchi kin'yū kikan
小口金融機関
kouri ginkō
小売銀行

retail banking
koguchi kin'yū
小口金融
kouri ginkōgyō
小売銀行業

retired bill
kaishū tegata
回収手形

returned cheque
modori kogitte
戻小切手

revocable L/C
torikeshikanō shin'yōjō
取消可能信用状

revolving credit
kaiten shin'yō
回転信用

revolving L/C
kaiten shin'yōjō
回転信用状

revolving line of credit [US]
kaiten kurejitto-rain
回転クレジット・ライン

run on banks
(ginkō) toritsuke
(銀行) 取付け

safe [UK]
hogo azukari kinko
保護預かり金庫
kashikinko
貸金庫
kinko
金庫

safe custody
hogo azukari
保護預かり

safe custody fee
hogo azukariryō
保護預かり料

safe deposit
hogo azukari
保護預かり

safe-deposit box [US]
hogo azukari kinko
保護預かり金庫
kashikinko
貸金庫
kinko
金庫

safe-deposit box holder
kashikinko hoyūsha
貸金庫保有者
kinko hoyūsha
金庫保有者

safe deposit corporation
hogo azukari gaisha
保護預かり会社
kashikinko gaisha
貸金庫会社

safe-keeping
hogo azukari
保護預かり

safe-keeping deposit
hogo azukari
保護預かり

sales bill of exchange
daikin toritate kawase tegata
代金取立為替手形

sample signature
shomei mihon
署名見本

save
chochiku suru
貯蓄する

saver
chochikuka
貯蓄家

saving
chochiku
貯蓄

savings
chochiku
貯蓄
chokin
貯金

savings account
chochiku kanjō
貯蓄勘定

savings and loan association [US]
chochiku-kashitsuke kumiai
貯蓄・貸付組合

savings bank
chochiku ginkō
貯蓄銀行

savings bank book
chochiku ginkō tsūchō
貯蓄銀行通帳

savings deposit
chochiku yokin
貯蓄預金

savings passbook
chochiku tsūchō
貯蓄通帳

seal (personal seal) [J][7]
inkan[7]
印鑑

second of exchange
daini kawase tegata
第二為替手形

secrecy
himitsusei
秘密性

secured bill
tanpotsuki tegata
担保付手形

securities subsidiaries of
foreign banks
gaikoku ginkō no shōken
kogaisha
外国銀行の証券
子会社

sender
furidashinin
振出人
sashidashinin
指出人

separate account
betsuguchi kanjō
別口勘定

servicing
ribarai
利払い

shipment of currency
genkin yusō
現金輸送

short balance
yokin zandaka fusoku
預金残高不足

short bill
tanki tegata
短期手形

short cheque
yokin fusoku kogitte
預金不足小切手

short-dated paper
tanki tegata
短期手形

short deposit balance
yokin zandaka fusoku
預金残高不足

short-term bill
tanki tegata
短期手形

short-term deposit
tanki yokin
短期預金

shortage of funds (in account)
yokin fusoku
預金不足

sight bill
ichiranbarai tegata
一覧払手形
sanchakubarai tegata
参着払手形

sight deposit [UK]
yōkyūbarai yokin
要求払預金

sight draft
ichiranbarai tegata
一覧払手形
sanchakubarai tegata
参着払手形

sight L/C
ichiranbarai tegata
shin'yōjō
一覧払手形信用状

signatory
shomeisha
署名者

signature
shomei
署名

simple discount
ginkō tegata waribiki
銀行手形割引

single bill
tan'itsu tegata
単一手形

single-name bill
tanmei tegata
単名手形

single-name paper
tanmei tegata
単名手形

sleeping account
kyūshi kanjō
休止勘定

small deposits
koguchi yokin
小口預金
reisai chokin
零細貯金

small saver
shōgaku yokinsha
小額預金者

small savings
koguchi yochokin
小口預貯金
reisai chokin
零細貯金

small sum
shōgaku
少額

sola bill
tandoku kawase tegata
単独為替手形
tan'itsu tegata
単一手形

sold bill
waribiki tegata
割引手形

sorting code
ginkō bangō
銀行番号

sound bank
shin'yō no okeru ginkō
信用のおける銀行

sound banking
kenzen ginkō shugi
健全銀行主義

sound banking principle
kenzen ginkō shugi
健全銀行主義

sound bill
ichiryū tegata
一流手形
kakujitsu tegata
確実手形

special bill
kimeishiki tegata
記名式手形

special checking account [US]
tokubetsu tōza yokin
特別当座預金

special crossed cheque
tokutei ōsen kogitte
特定横線小切手

special crossing
tokutei ōsen
特定横線

special deposit [UK]
betsudan yokin
別段預金

special endorsement
kimeishiki uragaki
記名式裏書き

special L/C
tegata kaitori ginkō shitei
shin'yōjō
手形買取銀行指定
信用状

special safe deposit
tokubetsu hogo azukari
特別保護預かり

specimen of signature
shomei mihon
署名見本

stale cheque
chien kogitte
遅延小切手
chōki keika kogitte
長期経過小切手
shikkō kogitte
失効小切手

standing order
keizoku sashizusho
継続指図書

state bank
[J]
kokuritsu ginkō
国立銀行

[US]
shūritsu ginkō
州立銀行

state-owned bank
kokuyū ginkō
国有銀行

statement of account
ginkō kanjō hōkokusho
銀行勘定報告書

status enquiry
shisan chōsa
資産調査

sterling bill
pondobarai tegata
ポンド払手形

stolen bill
tōnan tegata
盗難手形

stolen cheque book
tōnan kogittechō
盗難小切手帳

stop payment
shiharai teishi sashizu
支払停止指図

stop-payment order
shiharai teishi tsūchi
支払停止通知

stop the payment of a cheque
kogitte no shiharai o teishi
suru
小切手の支払いを
停止する

stopped cheque
shiharai teishi kogitte
支払停止小切手

stopped draft
shiharai teishi kawase
tegata
支払停止為替手形

straight L/C
tokuteinin waribiki shin'yōjō
特定人割引信用状

strong box
hogo azukari kinko
保護預かり金庫
kinko
金庫

strong room
kinkoshitsu
金庫室

stub
hikae bubun
控え部分

sub-depository bank
fukujutaku ginkō
副受託銀行

subsidiary bank
kogaisha ginkō
子会社銀行

sum of money
kingaku
金額

suspense account
karikanjō
仮勘定

suspension of payment
shiharai teishi
支払停止

suspension of transaction
torihiki teishi
取引停止

sweep facility [US]
suuiipu torikime
スウィープ取決め

syndicate
ginkōdan
銀行団

table of compound interest
fukurihyō
複利表

tax on deposit interest
yokin rishi kazei
預金利子課税

telegraphic transfer (TT)
denshin kawase
電信為替

teller
kinsen suitō kakari
金銭出納係

temporary account
ichijiteki kanjō
一時的勘定

temporary cheque book
ichijiteki kogittechō
一時的小切手帳

tenor
tegata manki made no kikan
手形満期までの期間

term bill
teikibarai tegata
定期払手形

terms of payment
shiharai jōken
支払条件

third of exchange
daisan kawase tegata
第三為替手形

thrift institution [US]
chochiku kikan
貯蓄機関

till money [UK]
madoguchi genkin
窓口現金

time account
tsūchi yokin
通知預金

time bill
kigentsuki tegata
期限付手形
teikibarai tegata
定期払手形

time deposit [US]
chochikusei yokin
貯蓄性預金
teiki yokin
定期預金

time draft
ichirango teikibarai tegata
一覧後定期払手形

total amount
sōgaku
総額

trade acceptance
bōeki hikiuke tegata
貿易引受手形

trade bill
bōeki tegata
貿易手形
shōgyō tegata
商業手形

transaction
torihiki
取引

transfer (noun)
furikae
振替え
furikomi
振込み

transfer (verb)
furikomu
振込む

transfer (an account)
(kanjō o) ikan suru
(勘定を) 移管する

transfer fee
furikaeryō
振替料

transfer of funds
shikin idō
資金移動

transfer order
furikae sashizusho
振替指図書

transfer request
furikae sashizusho
振替指図書

transfer slip
furikae denpyō
振替伝票

transfer to another bank account
furikomi
振込み

transferable credit
jōtokanō shin'yōjō
譲渡可能信用状

transferable L/C
jōtokanō shin'yōjō
譲渡可能信用状

transit number [US]
ginkō bangō
銀行番号

transit operation
tegata kōkan
手形交換

transport of bank notes and coins
gensō
現送

traveller's cheques
ryokō(sha) kogitte
旅行(者)小切手

trust
shintaku
信託

trust account
shintaku kanjō
信託勘定

trust bank [J][8]
shintaku ginkō[8]
信託銀行

trust department (of a bank)
(ginkō no) shintaku bumon
(銀行の) 信託部門

trust letter
yunyū tanpo nimotsu hokanshō
輸入担保荷物保管証

trust receipt
yunyū tanpo nimotsu hokanshō
輸入担保荷物保管証

trustee
jutakusha
受託者

(custodian, keeper)
hokannin
保管人

Trustee Savings Bank (TSB) [UK]
shintaku chochiku ginkō
信託貯蓄銀行

TSB (Trustee Savings Bank) [UK]
shintaku chochiku ginkō
信託貯蓄銀行

TT (telegraphic transfer)
denshin kawase
電信為替

two-name paper
fukumei tegata
複名手形

unclaimed balance
museikyū kanjō zandaka
無請求勘定残高

unclaimed deposit
museikyū yokin
無請求預金

unconfirmed credit
fukakunin shin'yōjō
不確認信用状

unconfirmed L/C
fukakunin shin'yōjō
不確認信用状

uncrossed cheque
musenbiki kogitte
無線引小切手

(ordinary)
futsū kogitte
普通小切手

undated
muhizuke
無日付け

undated acceptance
muhizuke hikiuke
無日付け引受け

undated bill
muhizuke tegata
無日付け手形

undated cheque
muhizuke kogitte
無日付け小切手

unit bank [US]
tandoku ginkō
単独銀行
tan'itsu ginkō
単一銀行

unit banking system [US]
tandoku ginkōsei
単独銀行制
tan'itsu ginkō seido
単一銀行制度

unpaid bill
fuwatari tegata
不渡手形

unpaid cheque
fuwatari kogitte
不渡小切手

unpaid draft
fuwatari tegata
不渡手形

unused cheque
mishiyō kogitte
未使用小切手

usance
tegata kikan
手形期間
tegata shiharai kikan
手形支払期間

usance bill
kigentsuki (kawase) tegata
期限付(為替)手形

usance bill rate
kigentsuki (kawase) tegata sōba
期限付(為替)手形相場

usance rate
kigentsuki kawase sōba
期限付為替相場

value date
tegata kessaibi
手形決済日

vault
chikashitsu
地下室
kinkoshitsu
金庫室

vault cash [US]
temoto genkin
手元現金

vostro account
kihō kanjō
貴方勘定

weekday
heijitsu
平日

wholesale banking
ōguchi kin'yū
大口金融

wholesale deposits
ōguchi yokin
大口預金

windbill
kara tegata
空手形

window
madoguchi
窓口

window-dressing
funshoku sōsa
粉飾操作

window-dressing deposits
funshoku yokin
粉飾預金

withdraw
hikidasu
引出す
yokin o orosu
預金をおろす

withdrawal
hikidashi
引出し

working days
sagyō nissū
作業日数

write out (a cheque)
(kogitte o) furidasu
(小切手を) 振出す

Notes

1. authorized foreign exchange bank (gaikoku kawase kōnin ginkō 外国為替公認銀行): bank authorized by the Japanese Ministry of Finance to carry out short-term lending and borrowing activities in foreign currencies.

2. certificate of employment (zaishoku shōmei 在職証明): usually required from individual customers in order to open an account with a Japanese bank.

3. company registration (shōgyō tōkibo tōhon 商業登記簿謄本): normally requested from corporate customers in order to open a company account with a Japanese bank.

4. company seal (inkan shōmei 印鑑証明): normally requested from corporate customers in order to open a company account with a Japanese bank.

5. proof of residence (jūminhyō 住民票): usually required from individual customers in order to open an account with a Japanese bank.

6. regional bank (chihō ginkō 地方銀行): commercial Japanese bank regionally located and dealing mostly with regional businesses.

7. seal (inkan 印鑑): usually required from individual customers in order to open an account with a Japanese bank.

8. trust bank (shintaku ginkō 信託銀行): Japanese bank offering banking as well as trust and savings facilities.

Additional expressions

go-yōken ご用件 ('your bank business') is a term used by bank staff when addressing a customer.

tōko 当行 ('our bank') is a term used by bank staff when corresponding with clients or other banks.

abolition of the official price of gold
kin no kōtei kakaku haishi
金の公定価格廃止

above par
heika ijō de
平価以上で

abrasion of coin
kōka mametsu
硬貨摩滅

acceptable currency
juryō yōnin tsūka
受領容認通貨

active circulation
ginkōken hakkōdaka
銀行券発行高

actual rate of exchange
genjitsuteki kawase sōba
現実的為替相場

adequate gold and foreign exchange reserves
tekisei gaika junbidaka
適正外貨準備高

adequate money supply
tekisei tsūkaryō
適正通貨量

adjustable peg
chōseikanō kugizuke sōba
調整可能釘付け相場

adjustable peg rate system
chōseikanō kugizuke sōba seido
調整可能釘付け相場制度

adverse exchange rate
gyaku kawase sōba
逆為替相場

agio
(charge for changing money)
tsūka no ryōgae tesūryō
通貨の両替手数料

(difference in value between two currencies)
uchibu
打歩

agiotage
gaikoku kawase e no tōki
外国為替への投機

alignment
chōsei
調整

alloy
gōkin
合金

alternative standard
kōtai hon'i
交代本位

amount
gaku
額
kingaku
金額

amount of currency in circulation
kahei no ryūtsūdaka
貨幣の流通高

amount of currency issued
kahei hakkōdaka
貨幣発行高

appreciate
tōki suru
騰貴する

appreciation
tōki
騰貴

arbitrage
kawase saitei
為替裁定

arbitrage operation
kawase saitei torihiki
為替裁定取引

arbitrageur
kawase sayatori gyōsha
為替鞘取業者

arbitrated exchange
saitei kawase
裁定為替

arbitrated exchange rate
saitei kawase sōba
裁定為替相場

assay
shikin suru
試金する

assay mark
shikin bunsekihyō
試金分析表

assay office
kōseki bunsekisho
鉱石分析所

at par
heika de
平価で

at parity
heika de
平価で

authenticity
shingi
真偽

authorized dealer
gaikoku kawase kōnin torihiki'in
外国為替公認取引員

authorized foreign exchange bank [J][9]
gaikoku kawase kōnin ginkō[9]
外国為替公認銀行

backing support
kingin junbi
金銀準備

backspread
gyakuzaya
逆鞘

ban on private ownership of gold
kinshoyū kinshi
金所有禁止

bank bill [US]
ginkō shihei
銀行紙幣
ginkōken
銀行券

bank buying rate
ginkō kaisōba
銀行買相場

bank note [UK]
ginkō shihei
銀行紙幣
ginkōken
銀行券

bank note issue
ginkōken hakkō
銀行券発行

bank note unfit for circulation
haiki ginkōken
廃棄銀行券

bank notes in circulation
ginkōken hakkōdaka
銀行券発行高

bank notes issued
hakkō ginkōken
発行銀行券

bank of issue
hakken ginkō
発券銀行

Bank of Japan bank note
nippon ginkōken
日本銀行券

bar
(1£M)
bā
バー

(gold)
bō
棒
nobebō
のべ棒

base
kijun
基準

base currency
kijun tsūka
基準通貨

basic rate of exchange
kijun kawase sōba
基準為替相場

basket of currencies
fukusū tsūka rēto
kumiawase
複数通貨レート
組合わせ

below par
heika ika de
平価以下で

bill [US]
ginkōken
銀行券
shihei
紙幣

bimetallic standard
kingin fukuhon'i(sei)
金銀複本位(制)
kingin ryōhon'i(sei)
金銀両本位(制)

bimetallism
kingin fukuhon'i(sei)
金銀複本位(制)
kingin ryōhon'i(sei)
金銀両本位(制)

blocked currency
fūsa tsūka
封鎖通貨

blocked exchange
fūsa kawase
封鎖為替

bullion
(metal)
jigane
地金

(gold and silver bullion)
kingin jigane
金銀地金

(gold bullion)
kinkai
金塊

bullion account
jigane kanjō
地金勘定

bullion broker
jigane nakagainin
地金仲買人

bullion dealer
kinginkai baibainin
金銀塊売買人

bullion holdings
jigane hoyūdaka
地金保有高

bullion market
kin shijō
金市場

bullion quotation
(metal)
jigane sōba
地金相場

(gold)
kinkai sōba
金塊相場

bullion reserve
jigane junbi
地金準備

bullion standard
jigane hon'isei
地金本位性

bullion stock
jigane sutokku
地金ストック

Bureau of the Mint [US]
zōheikyoku
造幣局

buyer's option
kaite sentaku
買手選択
kaitsukeken
買付権

buying and selling
baibai
売買

buying and selling orders
baibai chūmon dakiawase
売買注文抱合わせ

buying and selling rates
baibai sōba
売買相場

buying commission
kaitsuke tesūryō
買付手数料

buying quotation
kaikawase sōba
買為替相場

buying rate
kaisōba
買相場

carat
karatto
カラット

cash
genkin
現金

cash market
genkin shijō
現金市場

central bank intervention
chūō ginkō kainyū
中央銀行介入

central bank money
chūō ginkō tsūka
中央銀行通貨

central rate
chūshin rēto
中心レート

change (noun)
(exchange)
ryōgae
両替え

(small change)
tsurisen
釣銭

change (verb)
kaeru
変える
ryōgae suru
両替する

changing machine
tsurisen junbiki
釣銭準備機

charge for changing money
ryōgaeryō
両替料

circulation
ryūtsū
流通

circulation of bank notes
dakanken hakkōdaka
兌換券発行高
ginkōken ryūtsūdaka
銀行券流通高

circulation of money
kahei no ryūtsū
貨幣の流通

circulation period
kahei no ryūtsū kikan
貨幣の流通期間

clean float
kirei na hendō sōbasei
きれいな変動相場制
kuriin-furōto
クリーン・フロート

coin
kōka
硬貨

coin withdrawn from circulation
hikiage kahei
引揚げ貨幣

coinage
(casting, founding, mintage)
kahei chūzō
貨幣鋳造

(coin system)
kahei seido
貨幣制度

(mintage)
zōhei
造幣

commercial transaction
higinkō kawase torihiki
非銀行為替取引

commission
tesūryō
手数料

common currency
kyōtsū tsūka
共通通貨

Comptroller of the Currency [US]
tsūka kantokukan
通貨監督官

contract
yoyaku keiyaku
予約契約

contract slip
yoyaku keiyakusho
予約契約書

controlled currency
kanri tsūka
管理通貨

conversion
(convertibility)
dakan
兌換

(change)
kansan
換算

(exchangeability, transferability)
kōkan
交換

conversion note
dakan shihei
兌換紙幣

conversion rate
kansanritsu
換算率

conversion table
kawase kansanhyō
為替換算表

conversion to gold
kin dakan
金兌換

convertibility
(conversion)
dakansei
兌換性

(exchangeability, transferability)
kōkansei
交換性

convertibility into gold
kin dakansei
金兌換性
kin kōkansei
金交換性

convertible bank note
dakan ginkōken
兌換銀行券
dakanken
兌換券

convertible currency
kōkankanō tsūka
交換可能通貨

convertible gold note
dakan kinken
兌換金券

convertible paper money
dakan shihei
兌換紙幣

convertible reserve
dakan junbi
兌換準備

convertible yen
kōkankanō'en
交換可能円

counterfeit (adjective)
(dud, false, falsified)
ganzō no
贋造の

(forged, fabricated)
gizō no
偽造の

counterfeit (noun)
gizō butsu
偽造物

counterfeit (verb)
gizō suru
偽造する

counterfeit coin
ganzō kahei
贋造貨幣
gizō kahei
偽造貨幣

counterfeit money
nisegane
偽金

counterfeit note
ganzō shihei
贋造紙幣
gizō shihei
偽造紙幣

counterfeiter
niseganetsukuri
偽金造り
ganzōsha
贋造者

counterfeiting
(falsification)
ganzō
贋造

(forgery)
gizō
偽造

cover
kawase kabā
為替カバー
kawase deai
為替出合い

cover rate
deai sōba
出合相場

covering transaction
kabā torihiki
カバー取引

crawling peg
dankaiteki heika hendōsei
段階的平価変動制
heika no kokizami chōsei
平価の小刻み調整

cross rate
kurosu-rēto
クロス・レート

currency
tsūka
通貨

(agreed upon for a business transaction)
tatene
建値

currency alignment
tsūka chōsei
通貨調整

currency appreciation
tsūka kachi no tōki
通貨価値の騰貴

currency availability
tsūka aberabiritii
通貨アベイラビリティー

currency basket
tsūka basuketto
通貨バスケット

currency basket system
tsūka basuketto hōshiki
通貨バスケット方式

currency block
tsūka burokku
通貨ブロック
tsūkaken
通貨圏

currency broker
kawase burōkā
為替ブローカー
kawase nakagainin
為替仲買人

currency control
tsūka kanri
通貨管理

currency conversion
tsūka kirikae
通貨切替え

currency convertibility
tsūka kōkansei
通貨交換性

currency deflation
tsūka shūshuku
通貨収縮

currency depreciation
tsūka kachi geraku
通貨価値下落
tsūka teiraku
通貨低落

currency devaluation
tsūka kirisage
通貨切下げ

currency exchange
ryōgae
両替え

(currency agreed upon by two negotiating parties)
tatene
建値

currency flow
tsūka ryūryō
通貨流量

currency fluctuations
tsūka tōraku
通貨騰落

currency futures
tsūka sakimono torihiki
通貨先物取引

currency hoarding
tsūka taizō
通貨退蔵

currency in circulation
tsūka ryūtsūdaka
通貨流通高

currency inflation
tsūka bōchō
通貨膨張
tsūka infurēshon
通貨インフレーション

currency instability
tsūka fuan
通貨不安

currency issued
hakkō kaheiryō
発行貨幣量

currency practice
tsūka sochi
通貨措置

currency re-alignment
tsūka saichōsei
通貨再調整

currency regulation
tsūka chōsetsu
通貨調節

currency speculation
tsūka tōki
通貨投機

currency stability
tsūka anteisei
通貨安定性

currency stabilization
tsūka anteika
通貨安定化

currency support
tsūka shiji
通貨支持

currency swap
kawase no suwappu torihiki
為替のスワップ取引

currency system
tsūka seido
通貨制度

currency trader
kawase torihiki'in
為替取引員

currency unification
tsūka tōgō
通貨統合

currency unit
tsūka tan'i
通貨単位

currency value
tsūka kachi
通貨価値

currency war
tsūka sensō
通貨戦争

damaged coin
sonshō kahei
損傷貨幣

damaged note
sonshō ginkōken
損傷銀行券

dealer
diirā
ディーラー

debasement of currency
kahei kachi no teika
貨幣価値の低下

decimal coinage
jusshinhō kaheisei
十進法貨幣制

decimal currency
jusshinhō tsūka
十進法通貨

decimalization
jusshinhō
十進法

declining dollar
doruyasu
ドル安

declining pound
pondoyasu
ポンド安

defaced coin
sonshō kahei
損傷貨幣

defaced money
sonshō kahei
損傷貨幣

defence measures
bōeisaku
防衛策

defence of the dollar
doru bōei
ドル防衛

defensive intervention
bōei kainyū
防衛介入

deflation
tsūka shūshuku
通貨収縮

**demonetization
(abolition of a standard)**
haika
廃貨

**(withdrawal of a certain
currency)**
tsūka haishi
通貨廃止

demonetization of gold
kin no haika
金の廃貨

demonetize
haika suru
廃貨する

**denomination
(face value)**
gakumen kingaku
額面金額

(unit name)
tan'imei
単位名

depository bank
depojitorii ginkō
デポジトリー銀行

depreciate
tsūka no kachi o sageru
通貨の価値を下げる

depreciated currency
genka tsūka
減価通貨

depreciation
tsūka genka
通貨減価
tsūka kachi no teiraku
通貨価値の低落

designated currency
shitei tsūka
指定通貨

devaluation
heika kirisage
平価切下げ

devalue
kirisageru
切下げる

direct quotation
chokusetsu kawase sōba
直接為替相場

dirty float
dātii-furōto
ダーティー・フロート
kitanai hendō sōbasei
汚ない変動相場制

dollar
doru
ドル

dollar area
doru chi'iki
ドル地域
doruken
ドル圏

dollar bill
doru shihei
ドル紙幣

dollar bloc
doruken
ドル圏

dollar crisis
doru kiki
ドル危機

dollar exchange
doru kawase
ドル為替

dollar exchange standard
doru kawase hon'isei
ドル為替本位制

dollar gap
doru fusoku
ドル不足

dollar glut
doru kajō zandaka
ドル過剰残高

dollar-gold standard
kin-doru hon'isei
金・ドル本位制

dollar parity
doru heika
ドル平価

dollar pool
doru-pūru
ドル・プール

dollar rate
doru sōba
ドル相場

dollar rescue
doru bōei
ドル防衛

dollar reserve(s)
doru junbi
ドル準備

dollar standard
doru hon'isei
ドル本位制

dollar supporting measures
doru shiji seisaku
ドル支持政策

domestic currency
kokunai tsūka
国内通貨

(the Japanese currency)
hōka
邦貨

double standard
fukuhon'isei
複本位制

drawer
kawase furidashinin
為替振出人

dud bill [US] (= counterfeit note [UK])
ganzō shihei
贋造紙幣
gizō shihei
偽造紙幣

dud coin
ganzō kahei
贋造貨幣
gizō kahei
偽造貨幣

ECU (European Currency Unit)
ōshū tsūka tan'i
欧州通貨単位

effective exchange rate
jikkō kawase sōba
実効為替相場

EMA (European Monetary Agreement)
ōshū tsūka kyōtei
欧州通貨協定

embargo on gold
kin yushutsu kinshi
金輸出禁止

emergency currency
kinkyū tsūka
緊急通貨

EMS (European Monetary System)
ōshū tsūka seido
欧州通貨制度

EMU (European Monetary Union)
ōshū tsūka dōmei
欧州通貨同盟

Euro-currency
ōshū tsūka
欧州通貨
yūrō tsūka
ユーロー通貨

Euro-currency market
yūrō tsūka shijō
ユーロー通貨市場

Euro-dollar
yūrō-darā
ユーロー・ダラー

Euro-dollar market
yūrō-darā shijō
ユーロー・ダラー
市場

European Currency Unit (ECU)
ōshū tsūka tan'i
欧州通貨単位

European Monetary Agreement (EMA)
ōshū tsūka kyōtei
欧州通貨協定

European Monetary System (EMS)
ōshū tsūka seido
欧州通貨制度

European Monetary Union (EMU)
ōshū tsūka dōmei
欧州通貨同盟

excess currency issue
gengai hakkō
限外発行

excess note issue
ginkōken gengai hakkō
銀行券限外発行
shihei no gengai hakkō
紙幣の限外発行

excess reserves [US]
kajō junbi
過剰準備

exchange (noun)
　(foreign exchange)
kawase
為替
gaikoku kawase
外国為替

　(changing)
ryōgae
両替え

exchange (verb)
kaeru
変える
ryōgae suru
両替えする

exchange arbitrage
kawase saitei
為替裁定

exchange bank
kawase ginkō
為替銀行

exchange bill
kawase tegata
為替手形

exchange bought
kaikawase
買為替

exchange broker
kawase burōkā
為替ブローカー
kawase nakagainin
為替仲買人

exchange business
kawase gyōmu
為替業務

exchange buying
kaikawase
買為替

exchange buying rate
kaisōba
買相場

exchange clearing
kawase seisan
為替清算

exchange clearing system
kawase seisansei
為替清算制

exchange commission
ryōgaeryō
両替料

exchange contract
kawase yoyaku
為替予約

exchange control
kawase kanri
為替管理

exchange control law
kawase kanrihō
為替管理法

exchange conversion
kawase kansan
為替換算

exchange conversion rate
kawase kansanritsu
為替換算率

exchange conversion table
kawase kansanhyō
為替換算表

exchange cover
kawase deai
為替出合い

exchange dealer
kawase diirā
為替ディーラー
kawase nakagainin
為替仲買人

exchange dealing
kawase torihiki
為替取引

exchange difference
kawase sōba no hiraki
為替相場の開き

exchange discount
kawase waribiki
為替割引

exchange dumping
kawase danpingu
為替ダンピング

Exchange Equalization Account [UK]
kawase heikō kanjō
為替平衡勘定

exchange equalization operation
kawase heikō sōsa
為替平衡操作

exchange fluctuation
kawase hendō
為替変動

exchange for collection
toritate kawase
取立為替

exchange for remittance
sōkin kawase
送金為替

exchange futures
kawase sakimono
為替先物

exchange gain
kawase saeki
為替差益

exchange holdings
kawase hoyūdaka
為替保有高
kawase mochidaka
為替持高

exchange holdings restrictions
kawase hoyū seigen
為替保有制限

exchange in dollars
dorudate kawase
ドル建て為替

exchange in pounds
pondodate kawase
ポンド建て為替

exchange in yen
endate kawase
円建て為替

exchange intervention
kawase kanshō
為替干渉

exchange loss
kawase sason
為替差損

exchange operation
kawase sōsa
為替操作

exchange option
sōba no ryōdate
相場の両建て

exchange margin
kawase baibai sōba hiraki
為替売買相場開き

exchange market
kawase shijō
為替市場

exchange parity
kawase heika
為替平価

exchange payment
kawase shiharai
為替支払い

exchange pegging
kawase sōba kugitsuke
為替相場釘付け

exchange pegging policy
kawase sōba kugitsuke
seisaku
為替相場釘付け政策

exchange pegging system
kawase sōba kugitsuke
seido
為替相場釘付け制度

exchange permit
kawase kyoka
為替許可

exchange position
kawase mochidaka
為替持高

exchange profit
kawase saeki
為替差益

exchange quotation
kawase sōba
為替相場

exchange quotation table
kawase sōbahyō
為替相場表

exchange rate
kawase sōba
為替相場

exchange rate fluctuation
kawase hendō
為替変動

exchange rate movements
kawase sōba no hendō
為替相場の変動

exchange rate policy
kawase sōba seisaku
為替相場政策

exchange reserve(s)
gaika junbi
外貨準備

exchange reserve system
kawase junbi seido
為替準備制度

exchange restrictions
kawase seigen
為替制限

exchange risk
kawase risuku
為替リスク

exchange selling
urikawase
売為替

exchange selling rate
urisōba
売相場

exchange speculation
kawase tōki
為替投機

exchange speculator
kawase tōkisuji
為替投機筋

exchange spread
baibai kawase no hiraki
売買為替の開き

exchange stability
kawase antei
為替安定

exchange stabilization
kawase anteika
為替安定化

Exchange Stabilization Fund [US]
kawase antei shikin
為替安定資金

exchange standard
kawase hon'isei
為替本位制

exchange table
kawase kansanhyō
為替換算表

exchange transaction
kawase torihiki
為替取引

exchange value
kawase kachi
為替価値

external reserve
gaika junbi
外貨準備

external value
taigai kachi
対外価値

face value (bank note)
kenmengaku
券面額

faith in the dollar
doru shinnin
ドル信認

FECB (Foreign Exchange Control Board) [J]
gaikoku kawase kanri i'inkai
外国為替管理委員会

fiat money
fukan shihei
不換紙幣
meimoku shihei
名目紙幣

fiduciary issue
shin'yō hakkō
信用発行

fiduciary money
shin'yō kahei
信用貨幣

fiduciary note
mujunbi hakkō shihei
無準備発行紙幣

fiduciary paper money
shin'yō shihei
信用紙幣

fiduciary reserve
shin'yō junbi
信用準備

fine gold
junkin
純金

fineness
junbun
純分

(grade, quality)
hin'i
品位

firm tone of the dollar
dorudaka kichō
ドル高基調

fixed-date delivery
kakuteibi watashi
確定日渡し

fixed exchange rate
kotei kawase sōba
固定為替相場

fixed exchange rate system
kotei kawase sōbasei
固定為替相場制
kotei sōbasei
固定相場制

fixed par of exchange
hōtei heika
法定平価

fixing
(of a currency)
dekidakane
出来高値

(of exchange rate)
sōba tatene
相場建値

flexible currency
shinshukuteki tsūka
伸縮的の通貨

flexible exchange rate
kusshin kawase sōba
屈伸為替相場

flexible exchange rate system
kusshin kawase sōba seido
屈伸為替相場制度

flexible monetary policy
shinshukuteki kahei
seisaku
伸縮的の貨幣政策

floating exchange system
hendō kawase seido
変動為替制度

floating rate of exchange
hendō kawase sōba
変動為替相場

floating rate of exchange system
hendō kawase sōbasei
変動為替相場制

fluctuating exchange rate
hendō kawase sōba
変動為替相場

fluctuating exchange rate system
hendō kawase sōbasei
変動為替相場制

fluctuation
hendō
変動

fluctuation margin
hendō haba
変動幅

forced currency
kyōsei tsūka
強制通貨

foreign currencies futures
gaikoku tsūka sakimono
外国通貨先物

foreign currency
gaika
外貨
gaikoku tsūka
外国通貨

foreign currency deposit
gaika yokin
外貨預金

foreign currency holdings
gaika hoyūdaka
外貨保有高

foreign currency position
gaika mochidaka
外貨持高
gaika pojishon
外貨ポジション

foreign currency reserve(s)
gaika junbi
外貨準備

foreign currency reserve system
gaika junbikin seido
外貨準備金制度

foreign currency speculation
(gaikoku) kawase tōki
(外国) 為替投機

foreign-denominated
gaika
外貨

foreign exchange (see exchange)
gaikoku kawase (= kawase)
外国為替 (= 為替)

Foreign Exchange and Foreign Trade Control Law [J]
gaikoku kawase oyobi gaikoku bōeki kanrihō
外国為替および
外国貿易管理法

Foreign Exchange Bank Law [J]
gaikoku kawase ginkōhō
外国為替銀行法

Foreign Exchange Control Board (FECB) [J]
gaikoku kawase kanri i'inkai
外国為替管理委員会

foreign exchange market
gaikoku kawase shijō
外国為替市場

forged coin
ganzō kahei
贋造貨幣
gizō kahei
偽造貨幣

forged gold coin
gizō kinka
偽造金貨

forged note
ganzō shihei
贋造紙幣
gizō shihei
偽造紙幣

forger
ganzōsha
贋造者
niseganetsukuri
偽金造り

forgery
(falsification)
ganzō
贋造

(fabrication)
gizō
偽造

forward
sakimono no
先物の

forward broker
sakimono nakagainin
先物仲買人

forward business
sakimono torihiki
先物取引

forward buying
sakimono kaitsuke
先物買付け

forward contract
sakimono keiyaku
先物契約
sakimono yoyaku
先物予約

forward cover
sakimono kabā
先物カバー

forward delivery
sakigiri
先ぎり
sakiwatashi
先渡し

forward discount
sakimono deisukaunto
先物デイスカウント

forward exchange
sakimono kawase
先物為替

forward exchange contract
sakimono kawase yoyaku
先物為替予約

forward exchange dealings
sakimono kawase torihiki
先物為替取引

forward exchange market
sakimono kawase shijō
先物為替市場

forward exchange operation
sakimono kawase sōsa
先物為替操作

forward exchange rate
sakimono kawase sōba
先物為替相場

forward exchange transaction
sakimono kawase torihiki
先物為替取引

forward intervention
fōwādo kainyū
フォーワード介入

forward margin
fōwādo-mājin
フォーワード・マージン

forward market
sakimono shijō
先物市場

forward operation
sakimono torihiki
先物取引

forward position
sakimono mochidaka
先物持高

forward quotation
sakimono sōba
先物相場

forward rate
sakimono sōba
先物相場

forward rate agreement
sakimono sōba keiyaku
先物相場契約

forward transaction
sakimono torihiki
先物取引
sakiwatashi torihiki
先渡取引

free coinage
jiyū chūzō
自由鋳造

free currency
jiyū tsūka
自由通貨

free exchange market
jiyū kawase shijō
自由為替市場

free exchange rate
jiyū kawase sōba
自由為替相場

free exchange rate system
jiyū kawase sōbasei
自由為替相場制

free gold market
jiyū kin shijō
自由金市場

free reserve(s)
jiyū junbi
自由準備

full-bodied money
jittai shihei
実体紙幣

full gold standard
kanzen kinhon'isei
完全金本位制

gain on foreign exchange
gaikoku kawase saeki
外国為替差益

gold
kin
金
shōkin
正金

gold and foreign currency reserves
kin-gaika junbidaka
金・外貨準備高

gold and silver bimetallism
kingin fukuhon'isei
金銀複本位制

gold bar
bōkin
棒金
kin no nobebō
金ののべ棒

gold basis
kin hon'i kijun
金本位基準

gold bullion
kinjigane
金地金
kinkai
金塊

gold bullion market
kinjigane shijō
金地金市場
kinkai shijō
金塊市場

gold bullion quotation
kinjigane sōba
金地金相場
kinkai sōba
金塊相場

gold bullion standard
kinjigane hon'isei
金地金本位制
kinkai hon'isei
金塊本位制

gold buying
kin kōnyū
金購入

gold centre
kin no jiyū shijō
金の自由市場

gold certificate
kin shōken
金証券
kinka shōken
金貨証券

gold clause
kin yakkan
金約款

gold coin
kinka
金貨

gold coin standard
kinka hon'isei
金貨本位制

gold control
kin kanri
金管理

gold control law
kin kanrihō
金管理法

gold convertibility
kin dakansei
金兌換性

gold cover
kin junbi
金準備

gold crisis
kin kiki
金危機

gold currency
kinka
金貨

gold currency standard
kinka hon'isei
金貨本位制

gold-dollar reserve(s)
kin-doru junbi
金・ドル準備

gold drain
kin ryūshutsu
金流出

gold embargo
kin yushutsu kinshi
金輸出禁止

gold exchange
kin kawase
金為替

gold exchange reserve
kin kawase junbi
金為替準備

gold exchange standard
kin kawase hon'isei
金為替本位制

gold export
kin yushutsu
金輸出

gold export point
kin yushutsuten
金輸出点

gold fixing
kin tatene kettei
金建値決定

gold for monetary use
kaheiyō kin
貨幣用金

gold for non-monetary use
hikaheiyō kin
非貨幣用金

gold futures
kin no sakimono yoyaku
金の先物予約

gold hoarding
kin taizō
金退蔵

gold holder
kin hoyūsha
金保有者

gold holdings
kin hoyūdaka
金保有高

gold import
kin yunyū
金輸入

gold import point
kin yunyūten
金輸入点

gold ingot
kinkai
金塊

gold market
kin shijō
金市場

gold mine
kinkō
金坑

gold movement
kin ryūshutsunyū
金流出入

gold ownership
kin shoyū
金所有

gold parity
kin heika
金平価

gold point
kin gensōten
金現送点

gold policy
kin seisaku
金政策

Gold Pool
kin pūru
金プール

Gold Pool member country
kin pūru kameikoku
金プール加盟国

gold preference
kin senkō
金選好

gold price
kin kakaku
金価格

gold reserve
kin junbi
金準備

gold reserve ratio
kin junbiritsu
金準備率

gold revaluation
kin saihyōka
金再評価

gold selling
kin baikyaku
金売却

gold settlement
kin kessai
金決済

gold settlement funds
kin kessai shikin
金決済資金

gold settlement system
kin kessai seido
金決済制度

Gold Standard
kin hon'i(sei)
金本位(制)

Gold Standard system
kin hon'isei
金本位制

gold sterilization
kin futaika
金不胎化

gold sterilization policy
kin futaika seisaku
金不胎化政策

gold stock
kin hoyūdaka
金保有高

gold storage
kin chozō
金貯蔵

gold storage facility
kin chozō shisetsu
金貯蔵施設

gold tranche
gōrudo-toranshu
ゴールド・トランシュ

gold value
kin kachi
金価値

gold-value clause
kin kachi yakkan
金価値約款

government note
seifu shihei
政府紙幣

green currency [EC]
guriin tsūka
グリーン通貨

half a bar (half £M)
han bā
半バー

hard currency
(coins, metallic currency)
kōka
硬貨

(exchangeable currency)
kōkankanō tsūka
交換可能通貨

hard currency area
kōkaken
硬貨圏

higher yen quotation
endaka
円高

hoarded cash
taizō genkin
退蔵現金

hoarded currency
taizō tsūka
退蔵通貨

hoarded gold
taizō kin
退蔵金

hoarded money
taizō kahei
退蔵貨幣

hoarding
taizō
退蔵

hoarding of currency
tsūka taizō
通貨退蔵

hoarding of gold
kin taizō
金退蔵

hoarding of money
kahei taizō
貨幣退蔵

holdings
hoyūdaka
保有高
mochidaka
持高
temochi
手持ち

IMC (International Monetary Conference)
kokusai tsūka kaigi
国際通貨会議

IMF (International Monetary Fund)
kokusai tsūka kikin
国際通貨基金

immediate delivery
jikiwatashi
直渡し

inactive gold
fukatsudō kin
不活動金

inconvertibility
fukan
不換
hidakansei
非兌換性

inconvertible
dakan dekinai
兌換できない
fukan no
不換の

inconvertible bank note
fukan shihei
不換紙幣

inconvertible currency
fukan tsūka
不換通貨

inconvertible money
fukan tsūka
不換通貨

indirect exchange
kansetsu kawase
間接為替

info rate
jōhō tesūryō
情報手数料

inter-bank exchange dealings
ginkōkan kawase torihiki
銀行間為替取引

international currency reserve
kokusai tsūka junbi
国際通貨準備

international exchange
kokusai kawase
国際為替

international exchange market
kokusai kawase shijō
国際為替市場

international gold standard
kokusai kinhon'isei
国際金本位制

international monetarism
kokusai tsūka shugi
国際通貨主義

International Monetary Conference (IMC)
kokusai tsūka kaigi
国際通貨会議

international monetary co-operation
kokusai tsūka kyōryoku
国際通貨協力

International Monetary Fund (IMF)
kokusai tsūka kikin
国際通貨基金

international monetary organization
kokusai tsūka kikō
国際通貨機構

international monetary reform
kokusai tsūka seido kaikaku
国際通貨制度改革

international monetary system
kokusai tsūka seido
国際通貨制度

international official price of gold
kin no kokusai kōtei kakaku
金の国際公定価格

international re-alignment of currencies
kokusai tsūka chōsei
国際通貨調整

intervention
kainyū
介入

intervention currency
kainyū tsūka
介入通貨

intervention level
kainyū suijun
介入水準

intervention mechanism
kainyū kikō
介入機構

intervention operation
kainyū sōsa
介入操作

intervention point
kainyūten
介入点

intervention price
kainyū kakaku
介入価格

irredeemable bank note
fukan shihei
不換紙幣

irredeemable currency
fukan tsūka
不換通貨

issue (noun)
hakkō
発行

issue (verb)
hakkō suru
発行する

issue department
shihei hakkō bubun
紙幣発行部分

issuing bank
shihei hakkō ginkō
紙幣発行銀行

Japanese currency, the
hōka
邦貨

joint (currency) float
kyōdō furōto
共同フロート

key currency
kijiku tsūka
基軸通貨

key-currency countries
kijiku tsūkakoku
基軸通貨国

large denomination
kōgakumen
高額面

large sum
tagaku
多額

leading currency
shuyō tsūka
主要通貨

legal backing
tsūka no hakkō junbi
通貨の発行準備

legal money
hōtei kahei
法定貨幣

legal requirement
hōtei junbi shoyōgaku
法定準備所要額

legal reserve
hōtei junbi
法定準備

legal reserve requirement
hōtei shiharai shoyō
junbiritsu
法定支払所要準備率

legal tender
hōka
法貨
hōtei tsūka
法定通貨

liberalization of exchange control
kawase no jiyūka
為替の自由化

life of a bank note
ginkōken taiyō nensū
銀行券耐用年数

lifting of the gold embargo
kinkaikin
金解禁

limited coinage
seigen chūzō
制限鋳造
seigen tsūka
制限通貨

limited coinage issue
seigen tsūka hakkō
制限通貨発行

limited convertibility
seigentsuki kōkansei
制限付交換性

limited legal tender
yūgen hōka
有限法貨

limping Gold Standard
hakō kin hon'isei
は行金本位制

limping standard
hakō hon'isei
は行本位制

liquidity
ryūdōsei
流動性

liquidity of money
kahei no ryūdōsei
貨幣の流動性

liquidity policy
ryūdōsei seisaku
流動性政策

liquidity position
ryūdōsei jōtai
流動性状態

liquidity ratio
ryūdōsei hiritsu
流動性比率

local currency
  (area)
genchi tsūka
現地通貨

  (nation)
kokunai tsūka
国内通貨

London Bullion Market
rondon kin shijō
ロンドン金市場

London Gold Market
rondon kin shijō
ロンドン金市場

long exchange
chōki kawase
長期為替

long exchange rate
chōki kawase sōba
長期為替相場

long position
kaimochi
買持ち

lower yen quotation
en'yasu
円安

lowering of exchange rate
tatene hikisage
建値引下げ

lowest exchange rate
saitei kawase sōba
最低為替相場

maintenance of the value of a currency
tsūka kachi no iji
通貨価値の維持

major currency
shuyō tsūka
主要通貨

managed crawling peg
kanri sareta hyōka no
kokizami chōsei
管理された評価の
小刻み調整

managed currency
kanri tsūka
管理通貨

managed currency system
kanri tsūka seido
管理通貨制度

managed float
kanri furōto
管理フロート

managed floating exchange
kanri sareta hendō kawase
管理された変動為替

managed floating exchange rate
kanri sareta hendō kawase sōba
管理された変動為替相場

managed floating exchange rate system
kanri sareta hendō kawase sōbasei
管理された変動為替相場制

managed gold standard
kanri sareta kinhon'isei
管理された金本位制

margin
haba
幅
mājin
マージン

medium of exchange
kōkan shudan
交換手段

metallic coin
chūzōka
鋳造貨

metallic currency
kōka
硬貨

metallic money
kinzoku kahei
金属貨幣

metallic standard
kinzoku hon'isei
金属本位制

metallic value
kinzoku kahei kachi
金属貨幣価値

metallism
kinzoku shugi
金属主義

middle rate
chūshin sōba
中心相場

minimum gold reserve ratio
hōtei kinjunbiritsu
法定金準備率

minimum reserve
saitei junbi
最低準備

minimum reserve ratio
saitei junbiritsu
最低準備率

minimum reserve requirement
saitei shiharai junbiritsu
最低支払準備率

mint (noun)
(a foundry, a mint)
chūzōsho
鋳造所

(the Mint)
zōheikyoku
造幣局

mint (verb)
chūzō suru
鋳造する

mint par (of exchange)
hōtei heika
法定平価

mint parity
hōtei heika
法定平価

mint price
chūzō kakaku
鋳造価格

mint rate
hōtei hika
法定比価

mintage
zōhei
造幣

minting
(coinage)
chūka
鋳貨

(casting, founding)
chūzō
鋳造

(coinage, mintage)
zōhei
造幣

misalignment
fuchōsei
不調整

monetary
kahei no
貨幣の
tsūka no
通貨の

monetary agreement
tsūka kyōtei
通貨協定

monetary authorities
tsūka tōkyoku
通貨当局

monetary base
kaheiteki bēsu
貨幣的ベース

monetary control
kaheiteki tōsei
貨幣的統制

monetary crisis
tsūka kiki
通貨危機

monetary demand
kahei juyō
貨幣需要

monetary deposit
tsūkasei yokin
通貨性預金

monetary equilibrium
kaheiteki kinkō
貨幣的均衡

monetary flow
kahei no ryūtsū
貨幣の流通

monetary gold
kaheiyō kin
貨幣用金

monetary growth
tsūka kyōkyū nobiritsu
通貨供給伸び率

monetary instability
tsūka fuan
通貨不安

monetary market
tsūka shijō
通貨市場

monetary order
tsūka chitsujo
通貨秩序

monetary policy
tsūka seisaku
通貨政策

monetary reform
tsūka kaikaku
通貨改革

monetary reserve(s)
tsūka junbi
通貨準備

monetary stability
tsūka anteisei
通貨安定性

monetary stabilization
tsūka anteika
通貨安定化

monetary structure
tsūka taisei
通貨体制

monetary supply
kahei kyōkyū
貨幣供給

monetary system
(money)
kahei seido
貨幣制度

(currency)
tsūka seido
通貨制度

monetary uncertainty
tsūka fuan
通貨不安

monetary union
kahei dōmei
貨幣同盟

monetary unit
(money)
kahei tan'i
貨幣単位

(currency)
tsūka tan'i
通貨単位

monetary unrest
tsūka fuan
通貨不安

monetary upheaval
tsūkaryō no gekidō
通貨量の激動

monetary value
(money)
kahei kachi
貨幣価値

(currency)
tsūka kachi
通貨価値

monetary war
tsūka sensō
通貨戦争

monetization
kaheika
貨幣化

monetize
kaheika suru
貨幣化する

money
[general]
kane
金

(cash, specie)
genkin
現金

(coinage, currency)
kahei
貨幣

(cash, coins)
kinsen
金銭

money by weight
hyōryō kahei
秤量貨幣

money changer
(exchange bureau)
ryōgaeshō
両替商
ryōgaeya
両替屋

(change machine)
tsurisen junbiki
釣銭準備機

money circulation
kahei no ryūtsū
貨幣の流通

money creation
tsūka sōzō
通貨創造

money crisis
kahei kyōkō
貨幣恐慌

money flow
kahei no ryūtsū
貨幣の流通

money form
kahei keitai
貨幣形態

money holder
kahei hoyūsha
貨幣保有者

money holdings
kahei hoyūdaka
貨幣保有高

money in circulation
ryūtsū tsūka
流通通貨

money in reserve
yobikin
予備金

money neutrality
kahei no chūritsusei
貨幣の中立性

money shipment
kahei gensō
貨幣現送

money stock
kahei sutokku
貨幣ストック
tsūka sutokku
通貨ストック

money substitute
kahei daitaibutsu
貨幣代替物

money supply
manē-sapurai
マネー・サプライ
tsūka kyōkyūryō
通貨供給量

money withdrawn from circulation
hikiage tsūka
引揚げ通貨

monometallic standard
tanhon'i kahei seido
単本位貨幣制度
tanhon'isei
単本位制

monometallism
tanhon'i kahei seido
単本位貨幣制度
tanhon'isei
単本位制

multi-currency
fukusū tsūka
複数通貨

multi-currency intervention
fukusū tsūka kainyū
複数通貨介入

multi-currency intervention system
fukusū tsūka kainyūsei
複数通貨介入制

multinational currency alignment
takokukan tsūka chōsei
多国間通貨調整

multiple currency practice
fukusū tsūka seido
複数通貨制度

multiple currency standard
fukusū tsūka hon'isei
複数通貨本位制

multiple rates of exchange
fukusū kawase sōba
複数為替相場

mutilated bank note
sonshō ginkōken
損傷銀行券

narrow margin
shukushō hendō haba
縮小変動幅

narrower band
hendō haba shukushō seido
変動幅縮小制度

national bank note
kokuritsu ginkōken
国立銀行券

national currency
kokunai tsūka
国内通貨

(the Japanese currency) [J]
hōka
邦貨

near money
kinji kahei
近似貨幣

new monetary system
atarashii tsūka seido
新しい通貨制度

new money
shintsūka
新通貨

noble metal
kikinzoku
貴金属

nominal exchange rate
meimoku kawase sōba
名目為替相場

nominal money
meimoku kahei
名目貨幣

non-convertibility
fukan
不換
hidakansei
非兌換性

non-convertible
dakan dekinai
兌換できない
fukan no
不換の

non-convertible note
fukan shihei
不換紙幣

non-monetary
hikaheiteki
非貨幣的
hitsūkasei
非通貨性

non-monetary gold
hikaheiyō kin
非貨幣用金

note [UK]
ginkōken
銀行券
shihei
紙幣

note issue
ginkōken hakkō
銀行券発行
shihei hakkō
紙幣発行

note withdrawn from circulation
hikiage shihei
引揚げ紙幣

notes in circulation
shihei ryūtsūdaka
紙幣流通高

notes issued
ginkōken hakkōdaka
銀行券発行高
shihei hakkōdaka
紙幣発行高

numismatics
(study of coins)
kaheigaku
貨幣学

(collection of old coins)
kosen shūshū
古銭収集

official dollar reserve(s)
kōteki doru junbi
公的ドル準備

official exchange rate
kōtei kawase sōba
公定為替相場

official gold
kōteki kin
公的金

official gold and foreign currency reserves
kin-gaika junbidaka
金・外貨準備高

official gold price
kin kōteki kakaku
金公的価格

official gold reserve
kōteki kinjunbi
公的金準備

official intervention
kōteki kainyū
公的介入

official reserve
kōtei junbidaka
公定準備高

open position
ōpun-pojishon
オープン・ポジション

option
opushon keiyaku
オプション契約

option date
opushon kijitsu
オプション期日

outright cover
autoraito-kabā
アウトライト・
カバー

outright forward
autoraito-fōwādo
アウトライト・
フォーワード

outright purchase
gengai
現買い

outright sale
gen'uri
現売り

outright transaction
autoraito torihiki
アウトライト取引

overall position
ōbāōru-pojishon
オーバーオール・
ポジション

overissue
gengai hakkō
限外発行

overvaluation
kadai hyōka
過大評価

overvalued currency
kadai hyōka tsūka
過大評価通貨

paper currency
shihei
紙幣

paper gold
pēpā-gōrudo
ペーパー・ゴールド

paper money
shihei
紙幣

paper standard
shihei hon'i(sei)
紙幣本位(制)

par
heika
平価

par exchange rate
kinkō kawase sōba
均衡為替相場

par value of currency
kawase heika
為替平価

par value of exchange
kawase heika
為替平価

parity
heika
平価
hika
比価

(exchange rate)
kawase sōba
為替相場

parity adjustment
heika chōsei
平価調整

parity of gold
kin heika
金平価

parity of gold and silver
kingin hika
金銀比価

parity of silver
shirogane heika
銀平価

parity rate
saitei hika
裁定比価

pegged exchange
kotei kawase
固定為替
kugizuke kawase
釘付け為替

pegged exchange rate
kotei kawase sōba
固定為替相場

pegged exchange rate system
kotei kawase sōbasei
固定為替相場制

pegging
kugizuke
釘付け

plummet
kyūraku suru
急落する

plummeting (currency)
kyūraku
急落

plunge
kyūraku suru
急落する

position
mochidaka
持高
pojishon
ポジション

precious metals
kikinzoku
貴金属

preference for gold
kinsenkō
金選好

private gold market
minkan kin shijō
民間金市場

(free)
jiyū kin shijō
自由金市場

profit on bullion transaction
kinginkai baibai'eki
金銀塊売買益

profit on foreign exchange transaction
gaikoku kawase baibai'eki
外国為替売買益

pure gold
junkin
純金

pure gold standard
junshin kin hon'isei
純真金本位制

purity (grade, quality)
hin'i
品位

put in circulation
hakken suru
発券する

rally (noun)
hantō
反騰

rally (verb)
hantō suru
反騰する

rate of exchange
kawase sōba
為替相場

real exchange rate
jisshitsu kawase sōba
実質為替相場

real money
jisshitsu kahei
実質貨幣

real money holdings
jisshitsu kahei hoyūdaka
実質貨幣保有高

real par
jissai heika
実際平価

re-align
saichōsei suru
再調整する

re-alignment
saichōsei
再調整

redeemable paper money
dakan shihei
兌換紙幣

removal of gold embargo
kin yushutsu kaikin
金輸出解禁

renewal of exchange contract
kawase yoyaku kōshin
為替予約更新

reserve(s)
(gold and foreign currency reserves)
kin-gaika junbidaka
金・外貨準備高

(of money)
junbi(kin)
準備(金)

reserve currency
junbi tsūka
準備通貨

reserve for note issue
hakkō hoshō
発行保証

reserve requirement [US]
junbiritsu
準備率
shiharai junbiritsu
支払準備率

reserve supply of money
junbikin
準備金

retail dealing
kawase hanbaigyō
為替販売業

revaluation
heika kiriage
平価切上げ

right of note issue
ginkōken no hakkōken
銀行券の発行権

Royal Mint, the [UK]
eikoku no zōheikyoku
英国の造幣局

sale
uri
売り

save-the-dollar program
doru setsugen keikaku
ドル節減計画

scarce currency
kishō tsūka
希少通貨

scarce currency clause
kishō tsūka jōkō
希少通貨条項

SDR (Special Drawing Rights)
tokubetsu hikidashiken
特別引出権

selling
uri
売り

selling exchange
urikawase
売為替

selling quotation
urikawase sōba
売為替相場

selling rate
urisōba
売相場

sender
kawase furidashinin
為替振出人

serial number
ichiren bangō
一連番号

sharp drop (currency)
kyūraku
急落

sharp fluctuation
sōba no gekihen
相場の激変

shipment of currency
genkin yusō
現金輸送

short exchange
tanki kawase
短期為替

short exchange rate
tanki kawase sōba
短期為替相場

short position
urimochi
売持ち

short-term foreign currency
tanki gaika
短期外貨

silver
shirogane
銀

silver bullion
gin jigane
銀地金
ginkai
銀塊

silver bullion market
ginkai shijō
銀塊市場

silver certificate [US]
gin shōken
銀証券

silver coin
ginka
銀貨

silver exchange
gin kawase
銀為替

silver holder
gin hoyūsha
銀保有者

silver holdings
gin hoyū
銀保有

silver ingot
ginkai
銀塊

silver market
ginkai shijō
銀塊市場

silver standard
gin hon'isei
銀本位制

silver value
gin kachi
銀価値

single currency [EC]
EC tan'itsu tsūka
EC 単一通貨

single rate of exchange
tan'itsu kawase sōba
単一為替相場

single standard
tanhon'isei
単本位制

small note
shōgaku shihei
小額紙幣

Snake, the
sunēku
スネーク

soft currency
nanka
軟貨

(non-exchangeable)
kōkanfunō tsūka
交換不能通貨

soft currency area
nankaken
軟貨圏

soft money
fukan shihei
不換紙幣
nanka
軟貨

sound currency
kenzen tsūka
健全通貨

Special Drawing Rights (SDR)
tokubetsu hikidashiken
特別引出権

specie
(gold)
seika
正貨

(cash)
shōkin
正金

specie bank
shōkin ginkō
正金銀行

specie export
seika yushutsu
正貨輸出

specie export point
seika yusōten
正貨輸送点

specie flow mechanism
seika ryūshutsunyū kikō
正貨流出入機構

specie held abroad
zaigai seika
在外正貨

specie holdings
seika hoyūdaka
正貨保有高

specie holdings abroad
zaigai seika
在外正貨

specie import
seika yunyū
正貨輸入

specie insurance
gensō seika hoken
現送正貨保険

specie point
kin gensōten
金現送点
seika gensōten
正貨現送点
seika yusōten
正貨輸送点

specie reserve
seika junbi
正貨準備

specie shipment
gensō
現送
seika gensō
正貨現送

specie shortage
seika fusoku
正貨不足

spot
jikimono
直物

spot exchange
jikimono kawase
直物為替

spot exchange rate
jikimono kawase sōba
直物為替相場

spot exchange transaction
jikimono kawase torihiki
直物為替取引

spot operation
jikimono torihiki
直物取引

spot position
jikimono mochidaka
直物持高

spot rate
jikimono sōba
直物相場

spot transaction
jikimono torihiki
直物取引

stability
anteisei
安定性

stability of foreign exchange market
gaikoku kawase shijō no anteisei
外国為替市場の安定性

stabilization
antei(ka)
安定(化)

stabilization of currency
tsūka no antei
通貨の安定

stabilization of exchange rate
kawase sōba no antei
為替相場の安定

stabilize
antei(ka) suru
安定(化)する

stabilized currency
antei tsūka
安定通貨

stable currency
antei tsūka
安定通貨

stable exchange rate
antei kawase sōba
安定為替相場

stable money
antei kahei
安定貨幣

stable money policy
antei kahei seisaku
安定貨幣政策

standard (noun)
(basis)
hon'i(sei)
本位(制)

(norm, criterion)
hyōjun
標準

standard coin
hon'i kahei
本位貨幣

standard gold
hon'i kin
本位金

standard metal
hon'i kinzoku
本位金属

standard money
hon'i kahei
本位貨幣

standard silver
hyōjungin
標準銀

standard silver bullion
hyōjun ginjigane
標準銀地金

standard system
hon'i seido
本位制度
hon'isei
本位制

sterling
pondo
ポンド

sterling area
pondo chi'iki
ポンド地域

sterling exchange
pondo kawase
ポンド為替

sterling rate
pondo sōba
ポンド相場

sterling silver
hyōjungin
標準銀

strong currency
tsuyoi tsūka
強い通貨

strong dollar
dorudaka
ドル高

strong pound
pondodaka
ポンド高

strong yen
endaka
円高

support (noun)
shiji
支持

support (verb)
shiji suru
支持する

support buying
kaisasae
買支え

support of currency
sōba shiji
相場支持

support operation
sōba shiji sōsa
相場支持操作

support order
kaisasae chūmon
買支え注文

support point
shijiten
支持点

support rate
kaisasae sōba
買支え相場

surrender requirements
shūchū gimu
集中義務

suspension of gold-dollar convertibility
kin-doru kōkansei teishi
金・ドル交換性停止

swap
suwappu
スワップ

(central bank line of credit)
kōkan kyōtei
交換協定

swap agreement
kōkan kyōtei
交換協定
suwappu kyōtei
スワップ協定

swap arrangement
suwappu torikime
スワップ取決め

swap line
suwappu waku
スワップ枠

swap transaction
suwappu torihiki
スワップ取引

table of foreign exchange rates
kawase sōbahyō
為替相場表

target zones
mokuhyō sōbaken
目標相場圏

token money (substitute)
daiyō kahei
代用貨幣

(nominal)
meimoku kahei
名目貨幣

traded options
opushon torihiki
オプション取引

transaction
torihiki
取引

transfer (of currency)
furikae
振替え

transferable currency
furikaekanō tsūka
振替可能通貨

traveller's cheques
ryokō(sha) kogitte
旅行(者) 小切手

Treasury, the (national treasury, state coffers)
kokko
国庫

(Finance Ministry, Department of the Treasury [US], the Exchequer [UK])
ōkurashō
大蔵省

[US]
zaimushō
財務所

Treasury deposit
kokko yokin
国庫預金

Treasury note [UK]
hōtei shihei
法定紙幣

turmoil (trembling, shaking)
dōyō
動揺

(confusion, chaos)
konran
混乱

two-tier foreign exchange rate
nijū kawase sōba
二重為替相場

two-tier foreign exchange market
nijū kawase shijō
二重為替市場

two-tier foreign exchange system
nijū kawase sōbasei
二重為替相場制

two-tier gold market
kin no nijū shijō
金の二重市場

two-tier gold price
kin no nijū kakaku
金の二重価格

two-tier gold price system
kin no nijū kakakusei
金の二重価格制

undervaluation
kashō hyōka
過少評価

undervalued currency
kashō hyōka tsūka
過少評価通貨

unfavourable rate of exchange
furi na kawase sōba
不利な為替相場

universal currency
sekai tsūka
世界通貨

unlimited legal tender
museigen hōka
無制限法貨

unrestricted currency
museigen tsūka
無制限通貨

unsound currency
fukenzen tsūka
不健全通貨

unstable exchange rate
fuantei na kawase sōba
不安定な為替相場

US currency
beika
米貨

value of currency
tsūka kachi
通貨価値

value of money
kahei kachi
貨幣価値

velocity of circulation
ryūtsū sokudo
流通速度

velocity of circulation of money
kahei no ryūtsū sokudo
貨幣の流通速度

volatility
fuanteisei
不安定性

weak currency
yowai tsūka
弱い通貨

weak dollar
doruyasu
ドル安

weak pound
pondoyasu
ポンド安

weak yen
en'yasu
円安

weakening tendency
nanka keikō
軟貨傾向

wider band
waidā-bando
ワイダー・バンド

withdrawal
kaishū
回収

withdrawal of a bank note
ginkōken no kaishū
銀行券の回収

withdrawal of a coin
kōka no kaishū
硬貨の回収

withdrawal of a currency
tsūka no kaishū
通貨の回収

yen
enka
円貨

yen base
endate
円建て

yen converted from foreign currency
gaika kōkan'en
外貨交換円

yen-dollar rate
nibei kawase sōba
日米為替相場

yen exchange
enkawase
円為替

yen-pound rate
niei kawase sōba
日英為替相場

yen rate
enkawase sōba
円為替相場

yen value
enchi
円値

Note

9. authorized foreign exchange bank (gaikoku kawase kōnin ginkō 外国為替公認銀行): bank authorized by the Japanese Ministry of Finance to carry out short-term lending and borrowing activities in foreign currencies.

Algeria: dinar (DA)
arujeria: dināru
アルゼリア：
ディナール

Argentina: peso (P)
arujenchin: peso
アルゼンチン：ペソ

Australia: dollar (A$)
ōsutoraria: doru
オーストラリア：
ドル

Austria: schilling (Sch)
ōsutoria: shiringu
オーストリア：
シリング

Bahrain: dinar (BD)
bārēn: dināru
バーレーン：
ディナール

Belgium: franc (BFr)
berugii: furan
ベルギー：フラン

Bolivia: peso ($B)
boribia: peso
ボリビア：ペソ

Brazil: cruzeiro (Cr$)
burajiru: kuruzeiro
ブラジル：
クルゼイロ

Bulgaria: lev (Lv)
burugaria: rebu
ブルガリア：レブ

Canada: dollar (C$)
kanada: doru
カナダ：ドル

Chile: peso (Ch$)
chire: peso
チレ：ペソ

China (People's Republic of China): yuan
chūka jinmin kyōwakoku: yuan
中華人民共和国：元

Colombia: peso (Col$)
koronbia: peso
コロンビア：ペソ

Congo: franc de la Communauté Financière Africaine (CFA Franc)
kongo: CFA furan
コンゴ：CFA フラン

Cuba: peso (Cub$)
kyūba: peso
キューバ：ペソ

Cyprus: pound (£C)
kipurosu: pondo
キプロス：ポンド

Czechoslovakia: koruna (Kc)
chekkosurobakia: koruna
チェッコスロバキア：
コルナ

Denmark: krone (DKr)
denmāku: kurōne
デンマーク：
クローネ

Egypt: pound (£E)
ejiputo: pondo
エジプト：ポンド

Finland: mark (Fmk)
finrando: maruku
フィンランド：
マルク

France: franc (FFr) (FF)
furansu: furan
フランス：フラン

Gabon: franc de la Communauté Financière Africaine (CFA Franc)
gabon: CFA furan
ガボン：CFA フラン

Germany: mark (DM)
doitsu: maruku
ドイツ：マルク

Greece: drachma (Dr)
girisha: dorakuma
ギリシャ：ドラクマ

Guatemala: quetzal (Q)
gatemara: kezaru
ガテマラ：ケザル

Hong Kong: dollar (HK$)
honkon: doru
香港：ドル

Hungary: forint (Ft)
hangarii : forinto
ハンガリー：
フォリント

Iceland: krona (IKr)
aisurando: kurōna
アイスランド：
クローナ

India: rupee (IRe)
indo: rupii
インド：ルピー

Indonesia: rupiah (Rp)
indonesia: rupia
インドネシア：
ルピア

Iran: rial (RI)
iran: riaru
イラン：リアル

Iraq: dinar (ID)
iraku: dināru
イラク：ディナール

Ireland: pound (£Ir)
airurando: pondo
アイルランド：
ポンド

Israel: shekel (IS)
izuraeru: shekeru
イズラエル：
シェケル

Italy: lira (Lit)
Itaria: rira
イタリア：リラ

Ivory Coast: franc de la Communauté Financière Africaine (CFA Franc)
zōge kaigan: CFA furan
象げ海岸：CFA フラン

Jamaica: dollar (J$)
jamaika: doru
ジャマイカ：ドル

Japan: yen (¥)
Nihon: Yen
日本：円

Jordan: dinar (JD)
Yorudan: dināru
ヨルダン：ディナール

Kenya: shilling (KSh)
kenia: shiringu
ケニア：シリング

Kuwait: dinar (KD)
kuuēto: dināru
クウエート：
ディナール

Lebanon: pound (L£)
rebanon: pondo
レバノン：ポンド

Libya: dinar (LD)
ribia: dināru
リビア：ディナール

Luxembourg: franc (LFr)
rukusenburugu: furan
ルクセンブルグ：
フラン

Malaysia: ringgit or dollar (M$)
marēsha: doru
マレーシア：ドル

Malta: pound (£M)
maruta: pondo
マルタ：ポンド

Mexico: peso (Mex$)
mekishiko: peso
メキシコ：ペソ

Monaco: franc (Fr) (FF)
monako: furan
モナコ：フラン

Morocco: dirham (DH)
morokko: diruramu
モロッコ：ディルラム

**Netherlands: guilder (Gld),
florin (Fl)**
horanda: girudā, furorin
ホランダ：ギルダー,
フロリン

New Zealand: dollar (NZ$)
nyūjiirando: doru
ニュージーランド：
ドル

Nigeria: naira (£N)
naijiria: naira
ナイジリア：ナイラ

**North Korea (Democratic
People's Republic of Korea)**
hokusen (chōsen minshu-
shugi jinmin kyōwakoku):
wan
北鮮(朝鮮民主主義
人民共和国)：ワン

Norway: krone (NKr)
noruē : kurōne
ノルウエー：
クローネ

Oman: rial (RO)
oman: riaru
オマン：リアル

Pakistan: rupee (PRe)
pakisutan: rupii
プキスタン：ルピー

Panama: balboa (Ba)
panama: baruboa
パナマ：バルボア

Peru: sol (S/)
perū: soru
ペルー：ソル

Philippines: peso (PP)
firippin: peso
フィリッピン：ペソ

Poland: zloty (Zl)
pōrando: jiroti
ポーランド：ジロティ

Portugal: escudo (Esc)
porutogaru: esukūdo
ポルトガル：
エスクード

Romania: leu (L) (l)
rūmania: riyū
ルーマニア：リユー

Russia: rouble (Rub)
roshia: rūburu
ロシア：ルーブル

Saudi Arabia: riyal (SAR)
saujiarabia: riyāru
サウジアラビア：
リヤール

**Senegal: franc de la
Communauté Financière
Africaine (CFA Franc)**
senegaru: CFA furan
セネガル：
CFA フラン

Singapore: dollar (S$)
shingapōru: doru
シンガポール：ドル

South Africa: rand (R)
minami afurika: rando
南アフリカ：ランド

**South Korea (Republic of
Korea): wan**
nansen (daikan minkoku):
wan
南鮮(大韓民国)：ワン

Spain: peseta (Pts)
supein: peseta
スペイン：ペセタ

Sri Lanka: rupee (SCRe)
seiron: rupii
セイロン：ルピー

Sudan: pound (£Sd)
sūdan: pondo
スーダン：ポンド

Sweden: krona (kronor) (SKr)
suēden: kurōna
スウエーデン：
クローナ

Switzerland: franc (SFr)
suisu: furan
スイス：フラン

Syria: pound (£Syr)
shiria: pondo
シリア：ポンド

**Taiwan: new Taiwan dollar
(NT$)**
chūka minkoku: doru
中華民国：ドル

Thailand: baht (B), tical (Tc)
taikoku: bātsu
タイ国：バーツ

Tunisia: dinar (TD)
chunija: dināru
チュニジア：
ディナール

Turkey: lira (TL)
　toruko: rira
　トルコ：リラ

Union of Soviet Socialist Republics: rouble (Rub) [obsolete – see Russia]
　sorenpō: rūburu
　ソ連邦：ルーブル

United Arab Emirates: dirham (UD)
　yunaiteddo-arabu-emirētsu: diruramu
　ユナイテッド・
　アラブ・エミレーツ：
　ディルラム

United Kingdom: pound sterling (£)
　eikoku: pondo
　英国: ポンド

United States of America: dollar (US$)
　beikoku: doru
　米国: ドル

Venezuela: bolivar (B)
　benezuera: boribā
　ベネズエラ：
　ボリバー

Yugoslavia: dinar (Din)
　yūgosurabia: dināru
　ユーゴスラビア：
　ディナール

ability to repay
shiharai nōryoku
支払能力

abnormal risk
chōka kiken
超過危険

above-average credit rating
heikin ijō shin'yō kakuzuke
平均以上信用格付け

above par
gakumen ijō de
額面以上で

above-par value
gakumen ijō no kakaku
額面以上の価格

absolute bond
mujōken saiken
無条件債券

absorption
shōka
消化

absorption of corporate bonds
shasai shōka
社債消化

absorption of government bonds
kokusai shōka
国債消化

acceleration clause
saimu no sokuji hensai jōkō
債務の即時返済条項

acceptance
hikiuke
引受け

acceptance and guarantee
shiharai shōdaku
支払承諾

acceptance business
hikiukegyō
引受業

acceptance charge
hikiuke tesūryō
引受手数料

acceptance commission
hikiuke tesūryō
引受手数料

acceptance house [US]
tegata hikiuke gyōsha
手形引受業者
tegata hikiuke shōsha
手形引受商社

acceptance market
hikiuke shijō
引受市場

acceptance syndicate
hikiuke shinjikēto
引受シンジケート

accepting house [UK]
tegata hikiuke gyōsha
手形引受業者
tegata hikiuke shōsha
手形引受商社

account (client's)
gyoku
玉
kanjō
勘定

Account (the) [UK]
ukewatashi kikan
受渡期間

Account day [UK]
ukewatashibi
受渡日

account executive
shōken gaisha eigyōbuin
証券会社営業部員
torihiki tantōsha
取引担当者

account statement
kanjōsho
勘定書

accretion
shizen zōka
自然増加

accrue
shōjiru
生じる

accrued dividend
keika haitō
経過配当

accrued interest
keika rishi
経過利子

accrued interest payable
miharai rishi
未払利子
miharai risoku
未払利息

accrued interest receivable
mishū rishi
未収利子
mishū risoku
未収利息

accumulated capital
chikuseki shihon
蓄積資本

accumulated income
ruiseki rieki
累積利益

accumulated interest
ruiseki rishi
累積利子

accumulation
ruiseki
累積

(wealth)
chikuzai
蓄財

accumulation of capital
shihon chikuseki
資本蓄積

accumulation of wealth
chikuzai
蓄財

accumulation plan
ruiseki tōshi hōshiki
累積投資方式

accumulation trust
chikuzai shintaku
蓄財信託
ruiseki tōshi shintaku
累積投資信託

accumulative investment
ruiseki tōshi
累積投資

accumulative stock
ruiseki haitō kabu
累積配当株

acknowledgement (validation)
kakunin
確認

acknowledgement of indebtedness
fusai shōninsho
負債承認書

acquisition of shares
kabushiki shutoku
株式取得

acquittance
saimu no kaijo
債務の解除
saimu shōmetsushō
債務消滅証

across the board
zenmeigara no
全銘柄の

active account
katsudō kanjō
活動勘定

active bond
ritsuki kōsai
利付公債

active buying
kaisusumi
買進み

active debt
ritsuki kashitsuke
利付貸付け

(public debt)
nōdōteki kōsai
能動的公債

active investment
nōdōteki tōshi
能動的投資

active market
kōkyō shijō
好況市場

active stock
ninki kabushiki
人気株式

activity
katsudō
活動

actual delivery
genbutsu ukewatashi
現物受渡し

actual price
genbutsu kakaku
現物価格

actuals
genbutsu
現物

additional collateral
mashi tanpo
増担保

additional credit
tsuika shin'yō
追加信用

additional margin
tsuika shōkokin
追加証拠金

adjustable rate mortgage [US]
hendō kinrigata jūtaku kashitsuke
変動金利型住宅
貸付け

adjustment bond
seiri shasai
整理社債

ADR (American depository receipts)
beikoku yotaku shōken
米国預託証券

advance against securities
shōken tanpo kashitsuke
証券担保貸付け

advance-decline line
tōrakusen
騰落線

advance information
jizenteki jōhō
事前的情報

advance on loan
maegari
前借り

advance redemption
kuriage shōkan
繰上償還

advance refunding
(kōsai no) jizen karikae
(公債の) 事前借替え

advantageous interest rate
yūgū kinri
優遇金利

adverse factor
akuzairyō
悪材料

advisory service
tōshi komongyō
投資顧問業

after-acquired clause
jigo kakutoku zaisan jōkō
事後獲得財産条項

after-hours trading
jikangai torihiki
時間外取引

aftermarket
ryūtsū shijō
流通市場

afternoon market
goba
後場

afternoon session
goba no tachiai
後場の立会

against the box
hokan tsunagi
保管つなぎ

agency for government bonds [US]
kokusai dairiten
国債代理店

agent
(finder)
assensha
斡旋者

(commission broker, middleman)
kabushiki torihiki'in
株式取引員

(broker agent)
toritsuginin
取次人

agent bank
dairi ginkō
代理銀行

aggressive buying
kaiki ōsei
買気旺盛

agiotage
kabu e no tōki
株への投機

agreed interest rate
yakujō kinri
約定金利

agreement among underwriters
shinjikēto keiyaku
シンジケート契約

AIBD (Association of International Bond dealers)
kokusai saiken diirā kyōkai
国際債権ディーラー協会

aid fund for small businesses
chūshō kigyō josei kikin
中小企業助成基金

all or any
zenkabu mata wa nin'i no kabu hikiuke
全株または任意の株引受け

all or none
zenkabu hikiuke
全株引受け

all-time high
saikō kiroku
最高記録

all-time low
saitei kiroku
最低記録

allied member [NYSE – US]
shōken torihikijo junkai'in
証券取引所準会員

allot
wariate suru
割当てする

allotment letter
(kabushiki) wariate tsūchisho
(株式) 割当通知書

allotment of shares
bonyū
募入
kabushiki wariate
株式割当て

allottee
bonyūsha
募入者
hiwariatesha
被割当者

American depository receipts (ADR)
beikoku yotaku shōken
米国預託証券

American Stock Exchange (AMEX) (ASE)
amerikan kabushiki torihikijo
アメリカン株式取引所

AMEX (American Stock Exchange)
amerikan kabushiki torihikijo
アメリカン株式取引所

amortization [US]
bunkatsu hensai
分割返済

amortization loan [US]
bunkatsu hensai rōn
分割返済ローン

amortize [US]
bunkatsu hensai suru
分割返済する

amount issued (bond, loan)
kisaigaku
起債額

amount of loan
kashidashidaka
貸出高

amount of securities issued (value)
saiken hakkōgaku
債券発行額

(volume)
saiken hakkōryō
債券発行量

ample security
jūbun na tanpo
十分な担保

analysis
bunseki
分析

analyst
anarisuto
アナリスト

and interest
keika rishi betsuken torihiki
経過利子別権取引

animal spirits
kekki
血気

animated market
kappatsu na shikyō
活発な市況

annual interest
nenri
年利

annuity bond
nenkin shōsho
年金証書

anticipation
mikoshi
見越し

anticipation of falling market
yasune machi
安値待ち

anticipation of rising market
takane machi
高値待ち

anticipation rate
maebarai waribikiritsu
前払割引率

applicant (shares)
(kabushiki) mōshikomisha
(株式) 申込者
(kabushiki) ōbosha
(株式) 応募者

(loan)
shinseinin
申請人

application for a loan
kashidashi shinsei
貸出申請

application for shares
kabushiki mōshikomi
株式申込み
kabushiki ōbo
株式応募

application form
mōshikomi yōshi
申込用紙

application letter
mōshikomisho
申込書

application money
mōshikomikin
申込金

application procedure
mōshikomi tetsuzuki
申込手続き

application rights
mōshikomiken
申込権
ōboken
応募権

apply for a loan
kashidashi shinsei o suru
貸出申請をする

apply for shares
kabushiki o mōshikomu
株式を申込む

appraisal of assets [US]
shisan hyōka
資産評価

appraisal of securities [US]
yūka shōken hyōka
有価証券評価

appreciate
(vs. depreciate)
tōki suru
騰貴する

(increase in value)
zōka suru
増価する

appreciation
(vs. depreciation)
tōki
騰貴

(increase in price)
zōka
増価

appreciation of securities
shōken kakaku no jōshō
証券価格の上昇

approved delivery facility
ninkazumi hikiwatashi
shisetsu
認可済引渡施設

approved list (securities)
tōshi tekikaku no ichiranhyō
投資適格の一覧表

approved securities
kakujitsu shōken
確実証券

arbitrage
sayatori
鞘取り
sayatori baibai
鞘取売買

arbitrage broker
sayatori nakadachinin
鞘取仲立人

arbitrage business
sayatori torihiki
鞘取取引

arbitrage house
sayatoriya
鞘取屋

arbitrage operation
sayatori torihiki
鞘取取引

arbitrage transaction
sayatori torihiki
鞘取取引

arbitrageur
sayatori nakadachinin
鞘取仲立人
sayatori shōnin
鞘取商人
sayatori suji
鞘取筋

arbitrated interest rate
saitei kinri
裁定金利

arrear
**(arrearage, being
overdue)**
entaikin
延滞金

(payment arrears)
miharaikin
未払金

(delinquency in payment)
tainō(kin)
滞納(金)

(being in arrear)
todokōri
滞り

arrestment [UK]
sashiosae
差押さえ

artificial market
jin'i sōba
人為相場

artificial price
jin'i sōba
人為相場

**ASE (American Stock
Exchange)**
amerikan kabushiki
torihikijo
アメリカン株式
取引所

asked price [US]
uri yobine
売り呼び値
yobine
呼び値

asset(s)
shisan
資産

asset-backed financing
shisan tanpotsuki kin'yū
資産担保付金融

asset-backed securities
shisan tanpotsuki shōken
資産担保付証券

asset management
shisan kanri
資産管理
shisan un'yō
資産運用

asset value
shisan kachi
資産価値

assign
jōto suru
譲渡する

assignee
yuzuriukenin
譲受人

assignment
jōto
譲渡

assignor
jōtonin
譲渡人

assimilation
shōka
消化

Association of International Bond Dealers (AIBD)
kokusai saiken diirā kyōkai
国際債券ディーラー
協会

assumed bond
hikitsugi shasai
引継社債

at a discount
waribiki kakaku de
割引価格で

at a premium
gakumen ijō de
額面以上で

at best
mottomo yūri na nedan de
もっとも有利な値段
で
nariyuki chūmon
成行注文

at call
tanki yūshi de
短期融資で

at or better
sashine mata wa sore yori yoi kakaku de
指値またはそれより
良い価格で

at par
gakumen de
額面で

at short notice
tanki yūshi de
短期融資で

at the close
hikene de
引け値で

at the market
nariyuki de
成行で

at the opening
yoritsuki de
寄付きで

attachment
sashiosae
差押さえ

attachment of earnings [UK]
shotoku no sashiosae
所得の差押さえ

attachment order
sashiosae meirei
差押命令

attractive stock
ichiryū kabu
一流株

attractive yield
kōrimawari
好利回り

auction
kyōbai
競売

auction broker
kyōbai nakadachinin
競売仲立人
kyōbainin
競売人

auction market (securities)
kyōsō baibai shijō
競争売買市場

audit trail
kansa shōseki
監査証跡

authentification
shōnin
承認

authorize a loan
shakkan o kyōyo suru
借款を供与する

authorized dealer (recognized by the government)
seifu kōnin diirā
政府公認ディーラー

(broker)
torihiki'in
取引員

autonomous investment
dokuritsu tōshi
独立投資

average credit rating
heikin shin'yō kakuzuke
平均信用格付け

average down
nanpin de kaisagaru
難平で買下がる

average life (borrowing)
heikin shōkan kikan
平均償還期間

average price of stock
heikin kabuka
平均株価

average rate of interest
heikin kinri
平均金利

average rate of profit
heikin rijunritsu
平均利潤率

average risk
heikin kikenritsu
平均危険率

average up
nanpin de uriagaru
難平で売上がる

average yield
heikin rimawari
平均利回り

averaging
nanpin
難平

averaging down
nanpingai
難平買い

averaging up
nanpin'uri
難平売り

baby bond [US]
shōgaku saiken
小額債券

back (verb)
(assist, help, patronize)
kōen suru
後援する

(support)
shien suru
支援する

back-door financing
uraguchi kin'yū
裏口金融

back-door operation
uraguchi sōsa
裏口操作

back office
kōhō jimu bumon
後方事務部門

back-to-back credit
dōji kaisetsu shin'yōjō
同時開設信用状

backed bond
teitōtsuki saiken
抵当付債券

backed debenture
teitōtsuki saiken
抵当付債券

backer
(patron)
kōensha
後援者

(supporter)
shiensha
支援者

backing
(assistance, help,
patronage)
kōen
後援

(support)
shien
支援

(financial help)
shikin enjo
資金援助

backroom
kōhō jimu bumon
後方事務部門

backspread
gyakuzaya
逆鞘

backwardation [UK]
hikiwatashi yūyokin
引渡し猶予金

bad debt
(bad claim)
furyō saiken
不良債券

(bad loan)
furyōgashi
不良貸し

(irrecoverable debt)
kashidaore
貸倒れ

bad delivery
futō hikiwatashi
不当引渡し

bad investment
furyō tōshi
不良投資

bad loan
furyō kashitsuke
不良貸付け
furyōgashi
不良貸し

bad risk
furyō kiken
不良危険

balance certificate
zankabu shōmeisho
残株証明書

balance due
fusokugaku
不足額

balanced mutual fund
baransugata shikin
shintaku
バランス型資金信託

balloon
saishū no manki
hensaigaku
最終の満期返済額

ballot
tōhyō
投票

bang
urisabaku
売りさばく

banging the market
urikuzushi
売崩し

bank bond
kin'yūsai
金融債

bank borrowing
ginkō kariirekin
銀行借入金

bank credit
ginkō shin'yō
銀行信用

bank debenture
kin'yūsai
金融債

bank lending
(loan)
ginkō kashidashi
銀行貸出し

(credit)
ginkō shin'yō
銀行信用

(financing)
ginkō yūshi
銀行融資

bank loan
ginkō kashidashi
銀行貸出し
ginkō kashitsuke
銀行貸付け

Bank Rate
kōtei buai
公定歩合
waribiki buai
割引歩合

bank rate
ginkō riritsu
銀行利率

(money rate)
kinri
金利

bank rate policy
kinri seisaku
金利政策

bank reference
ginkō shin'yō shōkaisaki
銀行信用照会先

bargain (securities) [UK]
baibai yakujō
売買約定

bargain hunting
yasune hiroi
安値拾い

bargain stock
wariyasu kabushiki
割安株式

barometer securities
shihyō meigara
指標銘柄

barometer stock
shihyō meigara
指標銘柄

base rate
hyōjun kinri
標準金利

[UK] (= prime rate [US])
kijun kinri
基準金利
puraimu-rēto
プライム・レート

basic discount rate
kijun waribiki buai
基準割引歩合

basic interest rate
kijun kinri
基準金利

basic lending rate
kashidashi kijun kinri
貸出基準金利

basic rediscount rate
kijun saiwaribiki buai
基準再割引歩合

basis
ichi pāsento no hyakubun
no ichi
1パーセントの100分
の一

basis point
ichi pāsento no hyakubun
no ichi
1パーセントの100分
の一

basis price
kijun kakaku
基準価格

bear
yowaki
弱気

(seller)
urikata
売方

(bears, shorts)
yowaki suji
弱気筋

bear account
urigyoku
売玉
yowaki suji
弱気筋

bear covering
kaimodoshi
買戻し

bear drive
urimukai
売向い

bear market
urisōba
売相場
yowaki shijō
弱気市場

bear operator
nanpashite
軟派仕手

bear panic
fumiage
踏上げ

bear pool
urigata rengō
売方連合

bear position
tōkiteki urimochi
投機的売持ち

bear raid
urikuzushi
売崩し

bear selling
yowaki uri
弱気売り

bear spread
bea-supureddo
ベア・スプレッド

bear squeeze
urikatazeme
売方攻め

bear the market
uritataku
売叩く

bearer
jisannin
持参人

bearer bond
(public)
mukimei kōsai
無記名公債

(general)
mukimei saiken
無記名債券

bearer certificate
mukimei kabuken
無記名株券

bearer debenture
mukimei shasai
無記名社債

bearer depository receipts
mukimei yotaku shōken
無記名預託証券

bearer securities
mukimei shōken
無記名証券

bearer securities investment trust
mukimei shōken tōshi shintaku
無記名証券投資信託

bearer stock
mukimei kabu
無記名株

bearish
urikata no
売方の
yowaki no
弱気の

bearish factor
urizairyō
売材料
yowaki zairyō
弱気材料

bearish market
sagesōba
下げ相場

bearish tendency
kakō keikō
下降傾向

bearish tone
urininki
売人気
yowaki(hai)
弱気(配)

bears
nanpa
軟派

bears over
urikata kata
売方過多

bellwether bond
shihyō meigara
指標銘柄

bellwether issue
shihyō meigara
指標銘柄

below par
gakumen ika de
額面以下で

below-par value
gakumen ika no kakaku
額面以下の価格

benchmark issue
shihyō meigara
指標銘柄

beneficial owner
jueki kabunushi
受益株主

best effort [US]
saizen no doryoku
最善の努力

best-effort selling
itaku hanbai
委託販売

bid
kaitonae
買唱え

(buying price)
kaiyobine
買呼び値

(bid price, limit price)
sashine
指し値

bid and asked
yobine
呼び値

bid for a company's stock
kabushiki kaitori kōkai mōshikomi
株式買取公開申込み

bid price
tsukene
付け値

bid quotation
tsukene sōba
付け値相場

bidder
torite
取り手

bidding (public)
kōkai nyūsatsu
公開入札

Big Bang [UK]
rondon kabushiki torihikijo no tōsei kaijo
ロンドン株式取引所
の統制解除

Big Board [NYSE – US]
biggu-bōdo
ビッグ・ボード
nyūyōku kabushiki torihikijo
ニューヨーク株式
取引所

big traders
ōtesuji
大手筋

bill
(security)
shōken
証券

(statement of money owed)
tegata
手形

bill broker
tegata burōkā
手形ブローカー
tegata nakagainin
手形仲買人

bill brokerage
tegata kōsen
手形口銭

bill discounted
waribiki tegata
割引手形

bill discounter
tegata waribiki gyōsha
手形割引業者

bill discounting
tegata waribiki
手形割引

bill discounting market
tegata waribiki shijō
手形割引市場

bill rediscounted
saiwaribiki tegata
再割引手形

bill rediscounting
tegata saiwaribiki
手形再割引

bills market
tegata shijō
手形市場

Black Monday
ankoku no getsuyōbi
暗黒の月曜日

Black Thursday
ankoku no mokuyōbi
暗黒の木曜日

Black Tuesday
ankoku no kayōbi
暗黒の火曜日

blank bill
shiraji tegata
白地手形

blank bond
mukimei kōsai
無記名公債

blank transfer
shiraji jōto
白地譲渡

blank transfer of shares
kabushiki mukimei kakikae
株式無記名書換え

blanket (fidelity) bond
sōkatsu teitōkentsuki
saiken
総括抵当権付債券

blanket mortgage
sōkatsu tanpo
総括担保
sōkatsu teitō
総括抵当

block
ikkatsu baikyaku no tairyō
kabushiki
一括売却の大量株式

block trading
tairyōgyoku torihiki
大量玉取引

block transaction
tairyōgyoku torihiki
大量玉取引

blue-chip borrower
yūryō karite
優良借手

blue-chip rate
saiyūgū kinri
再優遇金利

blue-chip stock
ichiryū kabu
一流株
yūryō kabu
優良株

blue-sky laws [US]
aozorahō
青空法

blue-sky securities
aozora shōken
青空証券

boardroom
tachiaiba
立会場

bogus stock
yūrei kabu
幽霊株

bona fide creditor
zen'i no saikensha
善意の債権者

bond
(public)
kōsai
公債

(general – debt security)
saiken
債券

(corporate)
shasai
社債

(security)
shōken
証券

bond broker
saiken nakagainin
債券仲買人

bond certificate
shasaiken
社債券

bond collateral loan
kōshasai tanpo kin'yū
公社債担保金融

bond creditor
saiken kin'yū gyōsha
債券金融業者

bond dealer
saiken torihikinin
青空取引人

bond debt
shasai hakkō kariirekin
社債発行借入金

bond demand
saiken juyō
債券需要

bond discount
saiken waribiki
債券割引
shasai hakkō waribiki
社債発行割引

bond dividend
shasai haitō
社債配当

bond drawn for redemption
chūsen shōkan tōsen
shōken
抽選償還当選証券

bond expenses
shasai hakkōhi
社債発行費

bond flotation
kisai
起債

bond flotation market
kisai shijō
起債市場

bond holder
shōken shojinin
証券所持人

(public bond)
kōsai shoyūsha
公債所有者

(general – debt security)
saiken shojinin
債券所持人

(corporate bond)
shasaikensha
社債権者

bond holdings
saiken hoyūryō
債券保有量

bond indenture [US]
shasai keiyakusho
社債契約書

bond interest
saiken rishi
債券利子

bond investment
kōshasai tōshi
公社債投資

bond investment trust
kōshasai tōshi shintaku
公社債投資信託

bond issue
kisai
起債

(general)
saiken hakkō
債券発行

(corporate)
shasai hakkō
社債発行

bond-issue business
saiken hakkō gyōmu
債券発行業務

bond-issue cost
shasai hakkōhi
社債発行費

bond-issue market
kisai shijō
起債市場

bond market
kisai shijō
起債市場

(public)
kōsai shijō
公債市場

(public and corporate)
kōshasai shijō
公社債市場

(general)
saiken shijō
債券市場

(corporate)
shasai shijō
社債市場

bond payable to order
sashizuninbarai saiken
指図人払債券

bond position
saiken mochidaka
債券持高

bond price
saiken kakaku
債券価格

bond rating
(public)
kōsai kakuzuke
公債格付け

(general)
saiken kakuzuke
債券格付け

(corporate)
shasai kakuzuke
社債格付け

bond redemption
kōsai shōkan
公債償還

bond refunding
shasai karikae
社債借換え

bond register
shasai kinyūchō
社債記入帳

bond repurchase market[14]
gensaki shijō[14]
現先市場

bond sinking fund
shasaiyō gensai kikin
社債用減債基金

bond subscription
saiken ōbo
債券応募

bond swap
saiken suwappu
債券スワップ

bond to bearer
mukimei saiken
無記名債券

bond transfer
shasaiken jōto
社債券譲渡

bond underwriter
kōshasai hikiukenin
公社債引受人

bond valuation
shasai hyōka
社債評価

bond with warrant
warantotsuki shasai
ワラント付社債

bond yield
saiken rimawari
債券利回り

bonded debt
(public debt)
kōsai hakkō kariirekin
公債発行借入金

(corporate debt)
shasai hakkō kariirekin
社債発行借入金

bonds and debentures
kōshasai
公社債

bonds and debentures market
kōshasai shijō
公社債市場

bonds and securities register
yūka shōken daichō
有価証券台帳

Bonds Underwriters' Association
kōshasai hikiuke kyōkai
公社債引受協会

bonds unissued
shasai mihakkōdaka
社債未発行高

bonus issue
mushō hakkō
無償発行

bonus share
mushō kabu
無償株

book credit
urikakekin
売掛金

book-entry securities [US]
tōroku shasai
登録社債

borrow
kariire suru
借入れする
kariru
借りる

(contract a loan, obtain a loan)
shakkin suru
借金する

(apply for a loan)
shakuyō suru
借用する

borrowed capital
kariire shihon
借入資本
tanin shihon
他人資本

borrowed funds
shakuyōkin
借用金

borrowed money
shakuyōkin
借用金

(a debt, a loan of money)
kariirekin
借入金

(borrowings, liabilities)
shakkin
借金

borrowed securities
kariire yūka shōken
借入有価証券

borrowed stock
karikabu
借株

borrower
shakuyōsha
借用者

(debtor)
karite
借手

borrower country
kariirekoku
借入国
shakkinkoku
借金国

borrowing
kariire
借入れ

borrowing account
kariire kanjō
借入勘定

borrowing activity
kariire katsudō
借入活動

borrowing and lending
taishaku
貸借

borrowing capacity
kariire nōryoku
借入能力

borrowing cost
kariire kosuto
借入コスト

borrowing fee
kariire ryōkin
借入料金

borrowing from a foreign bank
gaiginkō kariire
外銀行借入れ

borrowing limit
kariire gendo
借入限度

borrowing period
kariire kikan
借入期間

borrowing rate
kariire kinri
借入金利

borrowing requirements
kariire juyō
借入需要

borrowing short
tankigari
短期借り

borrowing stock
kariirekabu
借入株

borrowings
kariirekin
借入金
shakkin
借金

bottoming-out
sokobanare
底離れ

break
sōba no bōraku
相場の暴落

break-even point
son'eki bunkiten
損益分岐点

break-out
uwabanare
上放れ

bridge financing
tsunagi yūshi
繋ぎ融資

bridge loan
tsunagi yūshi
繋ぎ融資

brisk business
kakkyō
活況

brisk market
kappatsu na shikyō
活発な市況

broad market
kōkyō shijō
好況市場

broad tape [US]
denkō jōhōban
電光情報板

broken lot
hakabu
端株

broken lot consolidation
hakabu seiri
端株整理

broker
burōkā
ブローカー

(commission agent, middleman)
nakagainin
仲買人

(authorized broker, trader, regular member)
torihiki'in
取引員

broker-dealer [UK]
burōkā-diirā
ブローカー・ディー
ラー

broker's commission
burōkā tesūryō
ブローカー手数料
nakagai tesūryō
仲買手数料

broker's fees
burōkā tesūryō
ブローカー手数料
nakagai tesūryō
仲買手数料

broker's loan
nakagainin kariirekin
仲買人借入金

broker's market
burōkā dake no tōki sōba
ブローカーだけの
投機相場

brokerage
nakagai tesūryō
仲買手数料

brokerage account
nakagai kanjō
仲買勘定

brokerage business
itaku baibai gyōmu
委託売買業務
nakagaigyō
仲買業

brokerage firm
kabushiki nakagaigyōsha
株式仲買業者
shōken gaisha
証券会社

brokerage house [US]
nakagaiten
仲買店

broking
nakadachigyō
仲立業
nakagaigyō
仲買業

bucket shop
nomiya
呑屋
yami torihiki gyōsha
ヤミ取引業者

bucket-shop operator
nomiya
呑屋
yami torihiki gyōsha
ヤミ取引業者

bucketeer
nomiya
呑屋

bucketing
mukainomi
向い呑み

**Building and Loan
Association [US]**
kenchiku shikin kin'yū
kumiai
建築資金金融組合

building society [UK]
jūtaku kin'yū kikan
住宅金融機関

bull
tsuyoki
強気

(buyer)
kaikata
買方

(bulls, longs)
tsuyoki suji
強気筋

bull account
kaigyoku
買玉
tsuyoki suji
強気筋

bull attack
kaikata no kaisusumi
買方の買進み
tsuyoki no kaisusumi
強気の買進み

bull buying
tsuyokigai
強気買い

bull-dog bond [UK]
eikokugai no hakkōsha ga
eikoku shijō de hakkō suru
saiken
英国外の発行者が
英国市場で発行する
債券

bull market
kaisōba
買相場
tsuyoki shijō
強気市場

bull operation
tsuyoki suji no sōsa
強気筋の操作

bull pool
kaikata rengō
買方連合

bull position
tōkiteki kaimochi
投機的買持ち

bull speculation
tōkigai
投機買い

bull spread
būru-supureddo
ブール・スプレッド

bull squeeze
kaishime
買占め

bull stock
tsuyoki kabu
強気株

bullet bond
kijitsu ikkatsu shōkan
saiken
期日一括償還債券

bullish
kaikata no
買方の
tsuyoki no
強気の

bullish factor
kaizairyō
買材料
tsuyoki zairyō
強気材料

bullish market
agesōba
上げ相場
jōshō sōba
上昇相場
tsuyoki sōba
強気相場

bullish sentiment
kaiki
買気

bullish support
kaiki
買気

bullish tendency
jōkō keikō
上向傾向

bullish tone
kaiki
買気
tsuyoki
強気

bunching
abiseuri
浴びせ売り

buoyancy
kabuka tōki no keikō
株価騰貴の傾向

buoyant market
tōki shijō
騰貴市場

burden of debt
saimu
債務

business borrowing
kigyō kariire
企業借入れ

business finance
kigyō kin'yū
企業金融

business lending
kigyō kashidashi
企業貸出し

business loan
kigyō kashitsuke
企業貸付け

buy
kau
買う

buy-back
kaimodoshi
買戻し

buy-back transaction
kaimodoshi sōsa
買戻し操作

buy hedge
kaihejji
買いヘッジ
kaitsunagi
買いつなぎ

buy on close
hikene de kau
引け値で買う
ōbike de kau
大引けで買う

buy on opening
yoritsuki de kau
寄付きで買う
yoritsukine de kau
寄付き値で買う

buy order
kaichūmon
買注文

buy program
kai puroguramu
買いプログラム

buy side [NYSE – US]
kikan tōshika
機関投資家

buyer
kaite
買手

(buyers)
kaikata
買方

buyer's market
kaite shijō
買手市場

buyer's option
kaite sentaku
買手選択
kaitsukeken
買付け権

buyer's risk
kaite futan
買手負担

buyers over
kaikata kata
買方過多

buying and selling
baibai
売買

buying and selling orders
baibai chūmon dakiawase
売買注文抱合わせ

buying and selling rates
baibai sōba
売買相場

buying and selling securities
saiken baibai
債券売買

buying disposition
kaiki
買気

buying drive
kaishutsudō
買出動

buying in and selling out
seriurikai
競売買い

buying interest
kaiki
買気

buying limit
kaitsuke sashine
買付け指し値

buying offer
kaimōshikomi
買申込み

buying on a falling market
oshimegai
押目買い

buying on close
hikenegai
引け値買い

buying on decline
oshimegai
押目買い

buying on margin
shin'yōgai
信用買い

buying on opening
yoritsukigai
寄付き買い

buying on reaction
oshimegai
押目買い

buying operation
kai ope
買いオペ

buying order
kaichūmon
買注文

buying price
kaisōba
買相場

buying rate
kaisōba
買相場

calendar
karendā
カレンダー

call (<u>noun</u>)
kōru
コール
saikoku
催告

(demand for payment)
haraikomi seikyū
払込請求

(collection, recovery)
kaishū
回収

call (<u>verb</u>)
(loans)
(kashidashi o) kaishū suru
(貸出しを) 回収する

(bonds)
(saiken haraikomi o) seikyū suru
(債券払込みを) 請求
する

call broker
kōru-burōkā
コール・ブローカー

call loan
kōru-rōn
コール・ローン
tanki yūshi
短期融資
tanshi
短資

call-loan broker
tanshi gyōsha
短資業者

call-loan market
kōru shijō
コール市場
tanshi shijō
短資市場

call-loan rate
kōru-rēto
コール・レート

call money
kōru-manē
コール・マネー
tanshi
短資

call-money dealer
tanshi gyōsha
短資業者

call-money market
tanshi shijō
短資市場

call option
kai opushon
買いオプション
kaitsuke sentakuken
買付け選択権
kōru-opushon
コール・オプション

call over
yobiagekata
呼上げ方

call premium
shōkan puremiamu
償還プレミアム

call price
(repurchase price)
kaimodoshi nedan
買戻値段

(redemption price)
shōkan kakaku
償還価格

call provision
kuriage shōkan jōkō
繰上償還条項

call rate
kōru hibu
コール日歩
kōru-rēto
コール・レート

call rule
kōru-rūru
コール・ルール

callable bond
shōkan kōshasai
償還公社債

calling-in
kaishū
回収

cancellation of bond
shōken haishō
証券廃消

cancelled bond
haishō shōken
廃消証券

capital
shihon
資本
shihonkin
資本金

capital accumulation
shihon chikuseki
資本蓄積

capital demand
shihon juyō
資本需要

capital export
shihon yushutsu
資本輸出

capital gains
shihon ritoku
資本利得

capital import
shihon dōnyū
資本導入

capital income
shihon shotoku
資本所得

capital-intensive investment
shihon shūyakuteki tōshi
資本集約的投資

capital interest
shihon rishi
資本利子

capital invested
tōka shihon
投下資本

capital investment
shihon tōshi
資本投資

(subscribed capital)
shusshi
出資

capital investor
shusshisha
出資者

capital liberalization
shihon jiyūka
資本自由化

capital loss
shihon sonshitsu
資本損失

capital market
shihon shijō
資本市場

capital movements
shihon idō
資本移動

capital productivity
shihon seisansei
資本生産性

capital-raising
shikin chōtatsu
資金調達

capital redemption
shihon shōkan
資本償還

capital tax
shihonzei
資本税

capital tie-up
shihon teikei
資本提携

capital transaction
shihon torihiki
資本取引

capital transfer
shihon iten
資本移転

capital transfer tax [UK]
shihon itenzei
資本移転税

carrying charge
kurinobe hibu
繰延日歩

cash account
genkin kanjō
現金勘定

cash delivery [US]
tōjitsu kessai torihiki
当日決済取引

cash in (verb)
genkinka suru
現金化する

cash market
genkin shijō
現金市場

cash on delivery (securities)
genkin hikikae
現金引換え

cash price
genbutsu kakaku
現物価格

cash redemption
genkin shōkan
現金償還

cash transaction
genkin torihiki
現金取引

cashing-in
genkinka
現金化

cats and dogs
tōki kabu
投機株

cautious
keikaiteki
警戒的

cautious mood
keikai ninki
警戒人気

CD (certificate of deposit)
yokin shōsho
預金証書

central bank credit
chūō ginkō shin'yō
中央銀行信用

**central government borrowing
requirements (CGBR) [UK]**
chūō seifu kariire juyō
中央政府借入需要

centralization of capital
shihon shūchū
資本集中

certificate
shōken
証券

certificate of deposit (CD)
yokin shōsho
預金証書

certificate of indebtedness
saimu shōsho
債務証書

certification of transfer
shōninzumi kabushiki meigi
kakikae
承認済株式名義書換え

**CFTC (Commodity Futures
Trading Commission) [US]**
beikoku no shōhin
sakimono torihiki i'inkai
米国の商品先物取引
委員会

**CGBR (central government
borrowing requirements) [UK]**
chūō seifu kariire juyō
中央政府借入需要

charge account
urikake(kin) kanjō
売掛(金)勘定

charge card
kurejitto-kādo
クレジット・カード

chart
keisen
ケイ線

chartist
keisen bunseki senmonka
ケイ線分析専門家

chattel mortgage
dōsan tanpo
動産担保

cheap credit
teiri kin'yū
低利金融

cheap money
teikinri shikin
低金利資金

cheap-money policy
teikinri seisaku
低金利政策

checking the market
shijō kakaku o shiraberu
koto
市場価格を調べる
こと

churning
korogashi
ころがし

City, the [UK]
shitii [rondon no kin'yū
machi]
シティー [ロンドンの
金融町]

City man [UK]
kin'yū gyōsha
金融業者

claim
saiken
債権

clean credit
mutanpo shin'yōjō
無担保信用状

clean loan
mutanpo kariire
無担保借入れ

client
kokyaku
顧客
tokuisaki
得意先

close money
hippaku shita kin'yū
逼迫した金融

close of the market
shijō no heisa
市場の閉鎖

closed-end fund [US]
tōshi shintaku
投資信託

**closed-end management
company**
heisashiki tōshi gaisha
閉鎖式投資会社

closed-end mortgage bond
heisa tanpotsuki shasai
閉鎖担保付社債

closed mortgage
heisashiki tanpo
閉鎖式担保

closed trade
hantai baibai
反対売買

closing
hike
引け
ōbike
大引け

closing high
takanebike
高値引け

closing low
yasunebike
安値引け

closing of account
tejimai
手仕舞い

closing of morning session
maebike
前引け

closing of session
hike
引け

closing of transfer book
kabushiki meigi kakikae
teishi
株式名義書換停止

closing price
hikene
引け値
owarine
終わり値

closing quote
hikene
引け値
owarine
終わり値

closing session
nōkai
納会

closing session of the year
dainōkai
大納会

closing tone
hikeaji
引け味

closing trade
tejimai
手仕舞い

co-financing
kyōchō yūshi
協調融資
kyōdō yūshi
共同融資

**collapse
(heavy fall, slump)**
bōraku
暴落

(crash)
hōkai
崩壊

collateral
mikaeri tanpo
見返担保
tanpo
担保

collateral bond
futai shōsho
付帯証書

collateral loan
tanpo kashitsuke
担保貸付け
tanpogashi
担保貸し

collateral security
mikaeri tanpo
見返担保

collateral value
tanpo kakaku
担保価格

collect a debt
kashidashi o kaishū suru
貸出しを回収する
kashikin o toritateru
貸金を取立てる

collection (of debt)
kashidashi no kaishū
貸出しの回収

collection bureau
furyō saiken toritate kikan
不良債権取立機関

collection business
kaishū jimu
回収事務

collection of loan
shakkan kaishū
借款回収

COMEX (Commodity Exchange of New York)
nyūyōku shōhin torihikijo
ニューヨーク商品
取引所

commercial buyers
jitsujusuji
実需筋

commercial buying
jitsujugai
実需買い

commercial credit
shōgyō shin'yō
商業信用

commercial credit company [UK]
shōgyō shin'yō gaisha
商業信用会社

commercial finance
shōgyō kin'yū
商業金融

commercial loan
shōgyō kashidashi
商業貸出し

commercial paper
shōgyō tegata
商業手形

commercial paper market
tegata shijō
手形市場

commission (fee)
tesūryō
手数料

commission broker [US]
nakagainin
仲買人
toritsuginin
取次人

commission for purchase and sale
baibai tesūryō
売買手数料

commission house
kabushiki nakagaiten
株式仲買店

commitment
yūshi keiyaku
融資契約

commitment fee
yakujōryō
約定料

commodities investment trust
shōhin tōshi shintaku
商品投資信託

commodity
shōhin
商品

commodity broker
shōhin nakagainin
商品仲買人

commodity exchange
shōhin torihikijo
商品取引所

Commodity Exchange of New York (COMEX)
nyūyōku shōhin torihikijo
ニューヨーク商品
取引所

Commodity Futures Trading Commission (CFTC) [US]
beikoku no shōhin
sakimono torihiki i'inkai
米国の商品先物取引
委員会

commodity loan
shōhin taishaku
商品貸借

commodity market
shōhin shijō
商品市場

commodity prices
bukka
物価

commodity transaction
shōhin torihiki
商品取引

common stock [US]
futsū kabu
普通株

competitive stock
kyōsōryoku aru kabu
競争力ある株

computer trading
konpyūtagata baibai torihiki
コンピュータ型売買
取引

concentrated investment
shūchū tōshi
集中投資

concentration of investment
tōshi shūchū
投資集中

conditional bond
jōkentsuki saiken
条件付債券

conditional collateral
futai jōken
付帯条件

**conditional loan
(tied loan)**
himotsuki yūshi
ひも付融資

(with conditions)
jōkentsuki yūshi
条件付融資

conditions
jōken
条件

confidential enquiry
shin'yō toiawase
信用問合わせ

confirmation
kakunin
確認

confirmed credit
kakunin shin'yō
確認信用

confirmed note
kakuninsho
確認書

conflict of interests
rigai no fuitchi
利害の不一致

**consolidated bond
(public)**
seiri kōsai
整理公債

(corporate)
seiri shasai
整理社債

consolidated debt
kakutei kōsai
確定公債

(funded public debt)
chōki kōsai
長期公債

**consolidated stock (= consols)
[UK]**
konsoru kōsai
コンソル公債

consolidation of debt
saimu tanaage
債務棚上げ

consolidation of public loans
kōsai seiri
公債整理

**consols (= consolidated stock)
[UK]**
konsoru kōsai
コンソル公債

consols market [UK]
konsoru shijō
コンソル市場

consortium
shakkandan
借款団

(international)
kokusai shakkandan
国際借款団

constant dollar plan [US]
teigaku rieki ruisekigata
tōshin
定額利益累積型投信

contango [UK]
kurikoshi hibu
繰越日歩

contango day [UK]
kurikoshi kessanbi
繰越決算日

continuous session
zaraba
ザラ場

**contract
(agreement)**
keiyaku
契約

(engagement, promise)
yakujō
約定

contract month
gengetsu
限月

contract note [UK]
baibai shōsho
売買証書

contracted interest rate
yakujō kinri
約定金利

contractual plan
keizoku rieki ruisekigata
tōshin
継続利益累積型投信

contrarian
gyakubari
逆バリ

**contribution
(donation, gift of money)**
kenkin
献金

**(gift of money,
subscription)**
kifu(kin)
寄付(金)

**conversion
(refinancing, refunding,
renewal)**
karikae
借換え

(exchange, switch-over)
tenkan
転換

conversion discount
tenkan waribiki
転換割引

conversion issue
karikae hakkō
借換発行

conversion of public loans
kōsai no karikae
公債の借換え

conversion parity
tenkan hiritsu
転換比率

conversion premium
tenkan puremiamu
転換プレミアム

conversion price
tenkan kakaku
転換価格

conversion ratio
tenkan hiritsu
転換比率

conversion rights
tenkanken
転換権

conversion stock
tenkan kabu
転換株

conversion value
tenkan kachi
転換価値

convertibility
tenkan kanōsei
転換可能性

convertible at market price
jika tenkankanō
時価転換可能

convertible bond
tenkan shasai
転換社債

convertible debenture
tenkan shasai
転換社債

convertible securities
tenkan shōken
転換証券

convertible stock
tenkan kabushiki
転換株式

convertibles
tenkan shōken
転換証券

corner the market (securities)
kabu o kaishimeru
株を買占める

cornering the market
kaishime
買占め

corporate bond
shasai
社債

corporate borrowing
kigyō kariire
企業借入れ

corporate credit
kigyō kin'yū
企業金融

corporate debenture
shasai
社債

corporate finance
kaisha kin'yū
会社金融

corporate financing
kigyō kin'yū
企業金融

corporate investment
kigyō tōshi
企業投資

corporate investment overseas
kigyō kaigai tōshi
企業海外投資

corporate raider [US]
kaisha nottorima
会社乗っ取り魔

corporate shareholder
hōjin kabunushi
法人株主

correction
(shijō no) teisei
(市場の) 訂正

corrective buying
teiseigai
訂正買い

corrective market
teisei sōba
訂正相場

corrective rise
teiseidaka
訂正高

corrective selling
teiseiuri
訂正売り

cost of funds [US]
shikin kosuto
資金コスト

counter
tentō
店頭

counter-bid
gyaku sashine
逆指し値

counter stock
tentō kabu
店頭株

coupon
risatsu
利札

coupon bond
risatsutsuki saiken
利札付債券

coupon issue [US]
risatsutsukisai
利札付債

coupon number
risatsu bangō
利札番号

coupon off
risatsuochi
利札落ち

coupon on
risatsutsuki
利札付き

coupon pass [US]
kyūpon-pasu
キューポン・パス

coupon rate
hyōmen riritsu
表面利率

coupon security [US]
risatsutsukisai
利札付債

cover
(collateral)
tanpo
担保

(repurchase)
kaimodoshi
買戻し

cover shorts
karauri kabu no kaimodoshi
空売り株の買戻し

covered bear
kaimodoshi yowakisuji
買戻し弱気筋

covering
kaimodoshi
買戻し

covering by shorts
yowaki no kaimodoshi
弱気の買戻し

covering contract
kaimodoshi keiyaku
買戻し契約

crash
(slump, heavy fall)
bōraku
暴落

(breakdown, disintegration)
hōkai
崩壊

creation of credit
shin'yō sōzō
信用創造

credit
shin'yō
信用

(financing)
kin'yū
金融

(charge)
kake
掛け

(credit facility, loan)
yūshi
融資

credit accommodation
shin'yō kyōyo
信用供与

credit account [UK]
kake kanjō
掛け勘定
urikake(kin) kanjō
売掛(金)勘定

credit agency [UK]
shōgyō kōshinjo
商業興信所

credit agency for small businesses
chūshō kigyō kin'yū kikan
中小企業金融機関

credit analysis
shin'yō bunseki
信用分析

credit association [J]10
shin'yō kinko10
信用金庫

credit availability
shin'yō no abirabiritii
信用のアベイラビリティー

credit bank
kin'yū ginkō
金融銀行
shin'yō ginkō
信用銀行

credit bureau [US]
shōgyō kōshinjo
商業興信所

credit card
kurejitto-kādo
クレジット・カード

credit ceiling
shin'yō gendo
信用限度
yūshi gendo
融資限度

(limit of loan amount)
kashidashi gendogaku
貸出限度額

credit ceiling system
kashidashi gendogaku seido
貸出限度額制度

credit company
kin'yū gaisha
金融会社

credit conditions
kin'yū jōtai
金融状態
shin'yō jōtai
信用状態

credit control [UK]
shin'yō tōsei
信用統制

credit co-operative [J]11
shin'yō kyōdō kumiai11
信用協同組合

credit creation
shin'yō sōzō
信用創造

credit crisis
shin'yō kyōkō
信用恐慌

credit customer
kakeuri tokuisaki
掛売得意先

credit department (of a bank)
(ginkō no) shin'yō chōsabu
(銀行の) 信用調査部

credit evaluation
shin'yō hyōka
信用評価

credit expansion
shin'yō kakudai
信用拡大

credit facilities
shin'yō ben'eki
信用便益

credit flow
shin'yō nagare
信用流れ

credit guarantee
shin'yō hoshō
信用保証

credit inquiry
shin'yō chōsa
信用調査
shin'yō shōkai
信用照会

credit institution
kin'yū kikan
金融機関

credit instruction
shin'yō no sashizu
信用の指図

credit instrument
shin'yō shōken
信用証券

credit limit
shin'yō gendo
信用限度

(limit of loan amount)
kashidashi gendogaku
貸出限度額

credit line
shin'yō kyōyo gendo
信用供与限度

(limit of loan amount)
kashidashi gendogaku
貸出限度額

credit loan
shin'yōgashi
信用貸し

credit management
shin'yō kanri
信用管理

credit markets
kin'yū shijō
金融市場

credit paper
shin'yō shōken
信用証券

credit policy
kin'yū seisaku
金融政策

credit rating
kakuzuke
格付け
shin'yō kakuzuke
信用格付け

**credit rationing
(limit)**
shin'yō seigen
信用制限

(allocation)
shin'yō wariate
信用割当て

credit reference
shin'yō shōkaisaki
信用照会先

credit regulations
shin'yō kisei
信用規制

credit relaxation
kin'yū kanwa
金融緩和

credit report
shin'yō hōkokusho
信用報告書

credit requirements
shikin juyō
資金需要

credit restraint
kin'yū hikishime
金融引締め

**credit restrictions
(regulations)**
shin'yō kisei
信用規制

(limits)
shin'yō seigen
信用制限

credit risk
shin'yō risuku
信用リスク

credit secured by real estate
fudōsan teitō shin'yō
不動産抵当信用

credit squeeze
kin'yū hikishime
金融引締め

credit squeeze measures
kin'yū hikishime sochi
金融引締措置

credit squeeze policy
kin'yū hikishime seisaku
金融引締政策

credit standing
shin'yō jōtai
信用状態

credit status
shin'yō jōtai
信用状態

credit terms
kakeuri jōken
掛売条件
shin'yō jōken
信用条件

credit tightening
shin'yō hikishime
信用引締め

credit union [US][J]12
shin'yō kumiai12
信用組合

credit-worthiness
shin'yōdo
信用度

credit-worthy
shin'yōdo no
信用度の

creditor
saikensha
債権者

(lender)
kashinushi
貸主

creditor nation
saikenkoku
債権国

cross order
mawashigyoku
回し玉

crossed sale
nareai baibai
なれ合い売買

crossed trade
nareai baibai
なれ合い売買

crossing
aitai baibai
相対売買

crossing orders
kuiai
食合い

crowding-out
kuraudingu-auto
クラウディング・
アウト
shimedashi
締出し

cum all
shokenritsuki
諸権利付き

cum coupon
risatsutsuki
利札付き

cum dividend
haitōtsuki
配当付き

cum new
kokabutsuki
子株付き
shinkabutsuki
新株付き

cum rights
kenritsuki
権利付き

cumulative
ruisekiteki na
累積的な

cumulative lending
ruisekiteki kashitsuke
累積的貸付け

cumulative preference shares
[UK]
ruiseki yūsen kabu
累積優先株

cumulative preferred stock
[US]
ruiseki yūsen kabu
累積優先株

Curb, the [US]
amerikan kabushiki
torihikijo
アメリカン株式
取引所

curb (see also kerb)
jōgai (shijō)
場外(市場)

curb broker
jōgai kabu nakagainin
場外株仲買人

curb dealing
jōgai torihiki
場外取引

Curb Exchange [US]
amerikan kabushiki
torihikijo
アメリカン株式
取引所

curb market
jōgai shijō
場外市場

curb stock
jōgai torihiki kabu
場外取引株

curb trading
jōgai torihiki
場外取引

currency futures
tsūka sakimono torihiki
通貨先物取引

current market conditions
genzai no shikyō
現在の市況

current monetary conditions
genzai no kin'yū jōsei
現在の金融情勢

current rate of interest
genkō rishiritsu
現行利子率

current value
jika
時価

current yield
genzai rimawari
現在利回り

cushion bond
kushonsai
クション債

cut in interest rates
kinri kirisage
金利切下げ

cut interest rates
kinri o kirisageru
金利を切下げる

cyclical stock
junkan kabu
循環株

dabble in speculation
sōba ni te o dasu
相場に手を出す

daily official list
kabushiki torihikijo kōhō
株式取引所広報

daily trading limit
nitchū nehaba seigen
日中値幅制限

damaged share certificate
kison kabuken
き損株券

date of record
kijunbi
基準日

date of redemption
shōkan kijitsu
償還期日

dated securities [UK]
shōkan kijitsutsuki shōken
償還期日付証券

day loan
tōjitsukagiri kashitsuke
当日限り貸付け

day order
tōjitsukagiri chūmon
当日限り注文

day-to-day money
yokujitsu mono
翌日物

day trader (= scalper)
kozayatori
小鞘取り

day trading
nichi kakari
日計り

days in arrear
entai nissū
延滞日数

days of grace
yūyo nissū
猶予日数

dead loan
kogetsuki yūshi
こげつき融資

deadline
shimekiribi
締切日

deadweight debt
shijūteki kōsai
死重的公債

deal
torihiki
取引

dealer
diirā
ディーラー

dealer loan
diirā-rōn
ディーラー・ローン

dealer market
gyōshakan sōba
業者間相場

dealing
baibai torihiki
売買取引

dealing business
baibai gyōmu
売買業務

dealing in futures
sakimono torihiki
先物取引

dealing within the account
teiki torihiki
定期取引

dear money
kōkinri shikin
高金利資金

dear-money policy
kōkinri seisaku
高金利政策

debenture
saiken
債券
shasai
社債

debenture bond
shasaiken
社債券

debenture certificate
saiken
債券

debenture coupon
shasai risatsu
社債利札

debenture holder
shasaiken shojinin
社債券所持人
shasaikensha
社債権者

debenture holdings
shasaiken hoyūdaka
社債券保有高

debenture in dollars
beika saiken
米貨債券

debenture in foreign currency
gaika saiken
外貨債券

debenture in pound sterling
eika saiken
英貨債券

debenture interest
saiken rishi
債券利子

debenture redemption
shasai shōkan
社債償還

debenture stock
kakuteiritsuki kabushiki
確定利付株式

(certificate [UK])
shasaiken
社債券

debenture to bearer
shojininbarai shasai
支持人払社債

debenture transfer
shasaiken jōto
社債券譲渡

debenture trust
shasaiken shintaku
社債券信託

debentures account
saiken kanjō
債券勘定

debentures issued
saiken hakkōdaka
債券発行高

debentures issued at discount
waribikisai
割引債

debt
(liabilities)
fusai
負債

(advance, loan)
kashikin
貸金

(indebtedness)
saimu
債務

(borrowings)
shakkin
借金

debt accumulation
saimu ruiseki
債務累積

debt bomb
saimu bakudan
債務爆弾

debt burden
saimu
債務

debt capital
kariire shihon
借入資本

debt collection
kashidashi no kaishū
貸出の回収
shakkin toritate
借金取立て

debt collector
kashikin toritatenin
貸金取立人
shakkin toritatenin
借金取立人

debt conversion
saimu tenkan
債務転換

debt crisis
saimu kiki
債務危機

debt finance
saiken kin'yū
債券金融

debt instrument
saimu shōsho
債務証書

debt interest charges
fusai rishi
負債利子

debt management
(national debt)
kokusai kanri
国債管理

(public debt)
kōsai kanri
公債管理

debt obligation
kariire saimu
借入債務

debt of honour
mushōsho saimu
無証書債務
mushōsho shakkin
無証書借金
shin'yōgari
信用借り

debt redemption
saimu shōkan
債務償還

debt rescheduling
shiharai teishi
支払停止

debt retirement
saimu hensai
債務返済

debt securities
saimu shōken
債務証券

debt service
ribarai
利払い

debt service ratio
saimu hensai hiritsu
債務返済比率

debt servicing
ribarai
利払い

debt servicing capacity
saimu hensai nōryoku
債務返済能力

debt swap
saimu suwappu
債務スワップ

debtor
saimusha
債務者

debtor nation
saimukoku
債務国
shakkinkoku
借金国

decline (noun)
teiraku
低落

decline (verb)
sagaru
下がる

declining market
(shijō no) rakuchō
(市場の) 落調

deed of arrangement [UK]
saimu seiri shōsho
債務整理証書

deed of transfer (shares)
jōto shōsho
譲渡証書

deed of trust
shintaku shōsho
信託証書

deep discount bond
kōritsu waribikisai
高率割引債

default (noun)
furikō
不履行
saimu furikō
債務不履行

default (verb)
fumitaosu
踏倒す
hensai o okotaru
返済を怠る

default interest
entai risoku
延滞利息

default risk
furikō kiken
不履行危険

defaulted bond
furikō shasai
不履行社債

defaulted bond interest
furikō saiken rishi
不履行債券利子

defaulter
furikōsha
不履行者

defensive buying
bōeigai
防衛買い

defensive investment
bōeiteki tōshi
防衛的投資

defensive securities
bōei shōken
防衛証券

defensive shares
bōei kabu
防衛株

deferment of payment
shiharai enki
支払延期

deferred bond
sueoki saiken
据置債券

deferred coupon note [UK]
(public)
shōkan enki kōsai
償還延期公債

(corporate)
shōkan enki shasai
償還延期社債

deferred deliveries
nobewatashi
延渡し

deferred interest bond
(public)
shōkan enki kōsai
償還延期公債

(corporate)
shōkan enki shasai
償還延期社債

deferred payment
nobebarai
延払い
sueokibarai
据置払い

delayed delivery
chien hikiwatashi
遅延引渡し

delinquency
entai
延滞

delisting
jōjō haishi
上場廃止

deliver
watasu
渡す

delivery
hikiwatashi
引渡し
ukewatashi
受渡し

delivery bill
hikiwatashi shōken
引渡証券

delivery date
ukewatashibi
受渡日

delivery day
ukewatashibi
受渡日

delivery month
gengetsu
限月

delivery of shares
kabu no ukewatashi
株の受渡し

delivery on month basis
gengetsu watashi
限月渡し

delivery price
ukewatashi nedan
受渡値段

delivery versus payment
shiharai watashi
支払渡し

demand for payment
shiharai seikyū
支払請求

demand loan
yōkyūbarai kashitsuke
要求払貸付け

denomination of shares
gakumen kingaku
額面金額

deposit (noun)
kyōtakukin
供託金

deposit (verb)
kyōtaku suru
供託する

deposit as collateral
tanpo yokin
担保預金

deposited securities
kyōtaku yūka shōken
供託有価証券

depositor
kyōtakusha
供託者

depository receipt [US]
beikoku yotaku shōken
米国預託証券

depository trust company (DTC) [US]
kabuken furikae kikan
株券振替機関

depreciation of securities
saiken hyōkason
債券評価損

depressed market
chintai shikyō
沈滞市況
fushin shikyō
不振市況

deregulate
kisei o teppai suru
規制を撤廃する

deregulation
kisei teppai
規制撤廃

deregulation policy
kisei teppai seisaku
規制撤廃政策

destroyed or lost bond
meppunshitsu shōken
滅紛失証券

development finance
kaihatsu kin'yū
開発金融

development loan
kaihatsu yūshi
開発融資

differential
hakabu tesūryō
端株手数料

difficulty in raising money
hanbōkan
繁忙感

dilution
kihakuka
希薄化

dip
nesagari
値下がり
oshime
押目

direct arbitrage
chokusetsu saitei
直接裁定

direct financing
chokusetsu kin'yū
直接金融

direct investment
chokusetsu tōshi
直接投資

direct loan
chokusetsu kashidashi
直接貸出し
chokusetsu shakkan
直接借款

direct paper
chokusetsu kawase tegata
直接為替手形

direct placement [US]
chokusetsu boshū
直接募集

direct placing [UK]
chokusetsu boshū
直接募集

direct public issue of shares
chokusetsu boshū
直接募集

direct quotation
chokusetsu sōba
直接相場

direct securities
chokusetsu shōken
直接証券

disbursement
shiharai
支払い

disclosure
kigyō naiyō kaiji
企業内容開示

discount (noun)
waribiki
割引

discount (verb)
waribiki suru
割引する

discount account
waribiki kanjō
割引勘定

discount bill
waribiki tegata
割引手形

discount bill market
tegata waribiki shijō
手形割引市場

discount bond
waribikisai
割引債

discount broker (bills)
tegata waribiki nakagainin
手形割引仲買人

discount charge
waribikiryō
割引料

discount commission
waribiki tesūryō
割引手数料

discount company
waribiki gaisha
割引会社

discount corporation
waribiki shōkai
割引商会

discount debenture
waribikisai
割引債

discount government bond
waribiki kokusai
割引国債

discount house [UK]
waribiki gyōsha
割引業者
waribiki shōsha
割引商社

discount ledger
waribiki tegata motochō
割引手形元帳

discount market
waribiki shijō
割引市場

discount of government
securities
kokusai waribikiryō
国債割引料

discount operation
waribiki sōsa
割引操作

discount rate
waribikiritsu
割引率

(Bank Rate)
kōtei buai
公定歩合
waribiki buai
割引歩合

discount rate policy
waribikiritsu seisaku
割引率政策

discount register
waribiki tegata kinyūchō
割引手形記入帳

discount window
kin'yū chōsetsu madoguchi
金融調節窓口

discounted bills
waribiki tegata
割引手形

discounted securities
waribiki saiken
割引債券

discounting
waribiki
割引

discretionary account
baibai ichinin kanjō
売買一任勘定

discretionary account
transaction
baibai ichinin kanjō torihiki
売買一任勘定取引

discretionary investment
sentakuteki tōshi
選択的投資

discretionary order
baibai ichinin chūmon
売買一任注文

discretionary trust
tōshi komontsuki shintaku
投資顧問付信託

dishonoured note
fubarai yakusoku tegata
不払約束手形

disintermediation
hikin'yū chūkaika
非金融仲介化

disposal (of securities)
shobun
処分

distress selling
nageuri
投売り

distribution (securities)
(shōken no) bunpai
(証券の) 分配

diversification
bunsan tōshi
分散投資
takaku tōshi
多角投資

diversified investment
bunsan tōshi
分散投資
takaku tōshi
多角投資

diversified investment
company
bunsan tōshigata tōshi
shintaku
分散投資型投資信託

diversified portfolio
risuku bunsangata pōtoforio
リスク分散型ポート
フォリオ

diversifier
bunsan tōshika
分散投資家

diversify
tōshi o bunsan suru
投資を分散する

divestiture
tōshi no baikyaku
投資の売却

dividend
haitō(kin)
配当(金)

dividend income
haitō shotoku
配当所得

dividend yield
haitō rimawari
配当利回り

dollar bond
beika kōsai
米貨公債

domestic bond
naikokusai
内国債
naisai
内債

domestic investment
kokunai tōshi
国内投資

domestic loan
naikokusai
内国債
naisai
内債

domestic securities [J]
honpō shōken
本邦証券

donated stock
zōyo kabushiki
贈与株式

donation
(contribution)
kifu(kin)
寄付(金)

(present)
zōyo
贈与

donation tax
zōyozei
贈与税

donator
zōyosha
贈与者

double financing
nijū kin'yū
二重金融

double option
fukugō sentakukentsuki
torihiki
複合選択権付取引
ryōdate
両建て

doubtful loan
kogetsukigashi
焦げ付貸し

Dow Jones [US]
dau
ダウ

Dow Jones commodity index
dau-jōnzu shōhin sōba shisū
ダウ・ジョーンズ
商品相場指数

Dow Jones indexes [US]
dau heikin kabuka shisū
ダウ平均株価指数

Dow Jones industrial average
dau heikin
ダウ平均

downward trend
sageashi
下げ足

drawing
chūsen shōkan
抽選償還

drawn bond
chūsenzumi saiken
抽選済債券

drop below par
gakumenware
額面割れ

drop in investment
tōshi genshō
投資減少

DTC (depository trust company) [US]
kabuken furikae kikan
株券振替機関

dual currency bond
nijū tsūka datesai
二重通貨建債

due bill [US]
shakuyō shōsho
借用証書

due date
(maturity date)
mankijitsu
満期日

(payment date)
shiharaibi
支払日

dull market
chintai shikyō
沈滞市況

dumping
nageuri
投売り

ease (verb)
teiraku suru
低落する

easing of money market
kin'yū kanwa
金融緩和

easing-off
teiraku
低落

easy credit
shin'yō kakuchō
信用拡張

easy-credit policy
shin'yō kakuchō seisaku
信用拡張政策

easy money
kanwa na kin'yū
緩和な金融
teikinri shikin
低金利資金
teiri kin'yū
低利金融

easy-money policy
kin'yū kanwa seisaku
金融緩和政策
teikinri seisaku
低金利政策

effective date
hakkō kijitsu
発効期日

effective (interest) rate
jikkō kinri
実効金利

effective yield
jikkō rimawari
実効利回り

efficient portfolio
yūkō no pōtoforio
有効のポートフォリオ

eligible collateral
tekikaku tanpo
適格担保

eligible corporate bond
tekikaku shasai
適格社債

eligible investment
tekikaku tōshi
適格投資

eligible paper
(certificate)
tekikaku shōken
適格証券

(bill)
tekikaku tegata
適格手形

eligible security
tekikaku tanpo
適格担保

emergency extension of
repayment
kinkyū enchō
緊急延長

emergency loan
kinkyū yūshi
緊急融資

end borrower
saishū kariiresha
最終借入者

equipment credit
kikai shakkan
機械借款

equipment modernization loan
setsubi kindaika shikin
kashitsuke
設備近代化資金
貸付け

equities (= ordinary shares)
[UK]
futsū kabu
普通株

equity (in mortgage or hire-
purchase contract)
zaisan bukken no junsui
kakaku
財産物件の純粋価格

equity investment
kabushiki tōshi
株式投資

equity issue
shusshi shōken
出資証券

equity kicker
kabushiki tenkan seikyūken
株式転換請求権

erratic market
rankōge shikyō
乱高下市況
sōba rankōge
相場乱高下

Euro-bond
yūrōsai
イーロー債

Euro-bond market
yūrōsai shijō
イーロー債市場

Euro-credit
yūrō shin'yō
イーロー信用

Euro-issue
yūrō shijō kisai
イーロー市場起債

Euro-loan
yūrōsai
イーロー債

Euro-market
yūrō kin'yū shijō
イーロー金融市場

even lot
baibai tan'i
売買単位

evidence of debt
saimu shōken
債務証券

ex all [US]
shokenri ochi
諸権利落ち

ex allotment
shinkabu ochi
新株落ち

ex coupon
risatsu ochi
利札落ち

ex dividend
haitō ochi
配当落ち

ex interest
riochi
利落ち

ex-interest bond
riochi saiken
利落債券

ex-interest quotation
hadaka sōba
裸相場

ex-interest transaction
hadaka torihiki
裸取引

ex new
shinkabu ochi
新株落ち

ex rights
kenri ochi
権利落ち

ex warrants
kenri ochi
権利落ち

examination of loan
application
kashidashi shinsa
貸出審査

excess margin
kitei ijō no tesūryō
規定以上の手数料

exchange (place of trading)
torihikijo
取引所

exchange broker
torihikijo nakagainin
取引所仲買人

exchange dealer
kabushiki nakagainin
株式仲買人

exchange distribution
torihikijo bunbai
取引所分売

exchange members
torihikijo kai'in
取引所会員

Exchequer bills [UK]
ōkurashō shōken
大蔵省証券

Exchequer bonds [UK]
kokko saiken
国庫債券

execution
torihiki shikkō
取引執行

exempt securities
menjo shōken
免除証券

exercise
sentaku baibai kenri kōshi
選択売買権利行使

exercise price
kenri kōshi kakaku
権利行使価格

exorbitant interest
bōri
暴利

expected interest earnings
yosō rishi shūeki
予想利子収益

expected return
yosō shūekiritsu
予想収益率

expiration of obligation
saimu shōmetsu
債務消滅

expiry notice
shikkō tsūchisho
失効通知書

exposure
kashidashi risuku
貸出しリスク

extendable maturity
enchōkanō manki
延長可能満期

extended bond [US]
(public)
shōkan enki kōsai
償還延期公債

(corporate)
shōkan enki shasai
償還延期社債

extended credit
enchō shin'yō
延長信用

extension of repayment time
hensai enki
返済延期
shiharai kigen enchō
支払期限延長

(grace)
shiharai yūyo
支払猶予

extensive investment
kakuchō tōshi
拡張投資

external bond
gaisai
外債

external debt
taigai saimu
対外債務

external financial limits [UK]
gaibu kin'yū gendo
外部金融限度

external loan
gaisai
外債

face value
gakumen kakaku
額面価格

factor (impetus)
zairyō
材料

factoring
saiken kaitori gyōmu
債券買取業務

fail position
rikōfunō pojishon
履行不能ポジション

failure to deliver
ukewatashi funō
受渡不能

(default)
ukewatashi furikō
受渡不履行

failure to receive
uketori funō
受取不能

faint recovery
ayamodoshi
あや戻し

fair market value
kōsei shijō kakaku
公正市場価格

fair return
tekisei shūeki
適正収益

fall due
manki ni naru
満期になる

falling market
kakō shikyō
下降市況

fancy stock
negasa kabu
値嵩株

favourable factor
kōzairyō
好材料

Federal funds rate [US]
renpō shikin kinri
連邦資金金利

feverish market
nekkyō sōba
熱狂相場

fictitious credit
kara shin'yō
から信用

fiduciary loan
shin'yō kashitsuke
信用貸付け

fill or kill
sokuji shikkō chūmon
即時執行注文

finance (noun)
(banking, financing)
kin'yū
金融

(credit facility, lending)
yūshi
融資

(financial affairs of a
company)
zaimu
財務

(financial affairs of the
State)
zaisei
財政

finance (verb)
(subscribe capital)
shusshi suru
出資する

(provide credit, lend
money)
yūshi suru
融資する

finance bill
kin'yū tegata
金融手形

finance company [US]
kin'yū gaisha
金融会社

finance house [UK]
kin'yū gaisha
金融会社

finance house base rate [UK]
kin'yū gaisha kijun kinri
金融会社基準金利

finance paper
kin'yū tegata
金融手形

financial ability
shiryoku
資力
zairyoku
財力

financial accommodation
yūshi
融資

financial activity
kin'yū katsudō
金融活動

financial adviser
zaimu komon
財務顧問

financial affairs
zaimu
財務

financial agreement
kin'yū kyōtei
金融協定

financial aid
kin'yū enjo
金融援助
zaisei enjo
財政援助

financial analysis
zaimu bunseki
財務分析

financial analyst
zaimu bunsekika
財務分析家

financial appraisal
zaimu satei
財務査定

financial assets
kin'yū shisan
金融資産

financial assistance
kin'yū enjo
金融援助
zaisei enjo
財政援助

financial backing
shikin enjo
資金援助

financial burden
kin'yū futan
金融負担

financial centre
kin'yū chūshinchi
金融中心地

financial circles
kin'yūkai
金融界
zaikai
財界

financial claim
kin'yū saiken
金融債権

financial climate
kin'yū jōsei
金融状勢

financial column
keizairan
経済欄

financial commodities
kin'yū shōhin
金融商品

financial company
kin'yū gaisha
金融会社

financial crisis
kin'yū kyōkō
金融恐慌

financial deregulation
kin'yū kanwa
金融緩和

financial expert
kin'yū senmonka
金融専門家

financial futures
kin'yū sakimono
金融先物

financial group
zaidan
財団

financial guarantee
kin'yūteki hoshō
金融的保証

financial help
kin'yū enjo
金融援助

financial incentives
zaimu yūin
財務誘因

financial income
zaimu shūeki
財務収益

financial inducements
kin'yūjō no yūgū sochi
金融上の優遇措置

financial institution
kin'yū kikan
金融機関

financial instrument
kin'yū shudan
金融手段

financial interests
tōshi kankeisha
投資関係者

financial intermediaries
kin'yū chūkai kikan
金融仲介機関

financial intermediation
kin'yū chūkai
金融仲介

financial liberalization
kin'yū jiyūka
金融自由化

financial loss
kin'yūjō no sonshitsu
金融上の損失

financial magnate
zaikai no ōdatemono
財界の大立者

financial management
zaimu kanri
財務管理

financial market
kin'yū shijō
金融市場

financial obligation
kin'yū saimu
金融債務

financial operation
kin'yū sōsa
金融操作

financial panic
kin'yū kyōkō
金融恐慌

financial planning
zaimu keikaku
財務計画

financial policy
kin'yū seisaku
金融政策
zaisei seisaku
財政政策

financial portfolio
kin'yū shisan
金融資産

financial power
zairyoku
財力

financial profits
kin'yūjō no rieki
金融上の利益

financial programme
zaisei keikaku
財政計画

financial provisions
kin'yūteki junbi
金融的準備

financial prudence
kenjitsu kin'yū shugi
堅実金融主義

financial regulation
kin'yū kisei
金融規制

financial requirements
shikin juyō
資金需要

financial resources
kin'yū shigen
金融資源
zaigen
財源

financial revolution
kin'yū kakumei
金融革命

financial scheme
zaisei keikaku
財政計画

Financial Services Act [UK]
shōken torihikihō
証券取引法

financial sources
shikingen
資金源

**financial stability
(financial world)**
zaikai no antei
財界の安定

(financial affairs)
zaisei antei
財政安定

**financial standing
(funds situation)**
shikin jijō
資金事情

(credit standing)
shisan jōtai
資産状態

(asset situation)
shisan jōtai
資産状態

financial status
zaisei jōtai
財政状態

financial supermarket
shōken gaisha
証券会社

financial support
kin'yū enjo
金融援助
zaisei enjo
財政援助

financial syndicate
kin'yūdan
金融団

financial system
kin'yū taikei
金融体系

**Financial Times index of
industrial ordinary shares**
finansharu-taimuzu kōgyō
kabuka shisū
フィナンシャル・
タイムズ工業株価
指数

Financial Times Stock Exchange Index
finansharu-taimuzu kabushiki torihikijo shisū
フィナンシャル・タイムズ株式取引所指数

financial transaction
kin'yū torihiki
金融取引

financial unrest
zaikai no fuan
財界の不安

financial war
kin'yū sensō
金融戦争

financial wealth
kin'yū shisan
金融資産

financial world
kin'yūkai
金融界
zaikai
財界

financier
kin'yū gyōsha
金融業者
zaiseika
財政家

financing
kin'yū chōtatsu
金融調達

financing activity
kin'yū katsudō
金融活動

financing corporation
yūshi gaisha
融資会社

financing market
hakkō shijō
発行市場

financing operations
kin'yū chōtatsu sōsa
金融調達操作

financing requirements (credit demand)
jushi
需資

(borrowing requirements)
kariire juyō
借入需要

(demand for funds)
shikin juyō
資金需要

finder
assennin
斡旋人
assensha
斡旋者

finder's fee
assen tesūryō
斡旋手数料

fine rate
yūryō tegata waribiki buai
有料手形割引歩合

firm basis
kikan shitei jōken
期間指定条件

firm bid
kakutei kaiyobine
確定買呼び値

firm commitment
kaiuke saishūteki yakusoku
買受最終的約束

firm market
shikyō kenchō
市況堅調

firm offer
kakutei uriyobine
確定売呼び値

firm order
kakutei chūmon
確定注文

firm price
kakutei kakaku
確定価格

firm quote
kakutei kakaku
確定価格

firm rate
kakutei riritsu
確定利率

firm securities
kenchō shōken
堅調証券

firm stock
baibai kakutei kabu
売買確定株

firm tone
kenchō
堅調

firm undertone
sokogatai
底堅い

first board [US]
zenba tachiai
前場立会い

first-class securities
ichiryū shōken
一流証券

first market
dai'ichi shijō
第一市場

first mortgage bond
dai'ichi tanpotsuki saiken
第一担保付債券

first preferred stock
dai'ichi yūsen kabu
第一優先株

First Section (Tokyo Stock Exchange)[13]
dai'ichibu[13]
第一部

first session of the month
hakkai
発会

first session of the year
daihakkai
大発会

fiscal agent
zaimu dairinin
財務代理人

fixed collateral
sueoki tanpo
据置担保

fixed debt
kotei kariirekin
固定借入金

fixed-income investment
kakutei shotoku tōshi
確定所得投資

fixed-income securities
kakutei shotoku shōken
確定所得証券

fixed interest
kakutei rishi
確定利子

fixed-interest bearing
kakuteiritsuki
確定利付き

fixed-interest bearing bond
kakuteiritsuki saiken
確定利付債券

fixed-interest debt
kakuteiritsuki saimu
確定利付債務

fixed-interest securities
kakuteiritsuki shōken
確定利付証券

fixed investment
kotei tōshi
固定投資

fixed-investment trust
kotei tōshi shintaku
固定投資信託

fixed loan
teiki kashitsuke
定期貸付け

fixed-rate government bond
ritsuki kokusai
利付国債

fixed-rate loan
kotei kinri kashidashi
固定金利貸出し

fixed-rate mortgage loan
kotei kinrigata jūtaku
kashitsuke
固定金利型住宅
貸付け

fixing
kakaku no jōken kettei
価格の条件決定

flat bond
murisoku kōsai
無利息公債

flat market
kakaku no ugokanai shijō
価格の動かない市場

flat quotation
hadaka sōba
裸相場

flat yield
kin'itsu rimawari
均一利回り

flexible-rate mortgage loan
hendō kinrigata jūtaku
kashitsuke
変動金利型住宅
貸付け

flight capital
tōhi shihon
逃避資本

flight from cash
genkin kara no tōhi
現金からの逃避

float (verb)
(appeal for funds)
boshū suru
募集する

(issue securities)
hakkō suru
発行する

(issue bonds, float loans)
kisai suru
起債する

floater [US]
hendōritsukisai
変動利付債

floating charge
fudō tanpo
浮動担保

floating debt
(floating liabilities)
ryūdō fusai
流動負債

(short-term government debt)
tanki kōsai
短期公債

floating public bond
ryūdō kōsai
流動公債

floating rate
hendō rishi
変動利子

floating-rate note [US]
hendōriritsusai
変動利率債

floating rate of interest
hendō rishi
変動利子

floating securities
ryūdō shōken
流動証券

floating shares
ryūdō kabu
流動株

floating stock
ryūdō kabu
流動株

floating supply
ryūdōgyoku
流動玉

floor
tachiaiba
立会場

floor broker [US]
(securities)
banai burōkā
場内ブローカー

(commodities)
shōhin torihikijo kai'in no
dairinin
商品取引所会員の
代理人

floor clerk
batachi
場立ち

floor member
shōhin torihikijo kai'in
商品取引所会員

floor price
sokone
底値

floor trader [US]
batachi
場立ち

flotation
(loan flotation)
bosai
募債

(appeal for funds)
boshū
募集

(issue of securities)
hakkō
発行

(going public)
kabushiki kōkai
株式公開

(issue of bonds, loan flotation)
kisai
起債

flotation of external loan
gaisai boshū
外債募集

flotation of government bonds
kōsai hakkō
公債発行

flotation of loan
bosai
募債
kisai
起債

fluctuation limit
nehaba seigen
値幅制限

forced liquidation
tezume
手詰め

forced market
jin'i sōba
人為相場
wanryoku sōba
腕力相場

forced quotation
jin'i sōba
人為相場
wanryoku sōba
腕力相場

forced sale
kyōbai shobun
強売処分

foreclosure
teitō nagare
抵当流れ
teitōken shikkō
抵当権執行

foreclosure proceedings
teitō nagare tetsuzuki
抵当流れ手続き

foreclosure sale
teitō nagare kōbai
抵当流れ公売

foreign bond
gaikokusai
外国債
gaisai
外債

foreign borrowing
taigai kariire
対外借入れ

foreign buying (of Japanese company shares)
gaijingai
外人買い

foreign capital
gaikoku shihon
外国資本
gaishi
外資

foreign capital inflow
gaishi dōnyū
外資導入

foreign capital invested in Japan
gaikoku shihon
外国資本

foreign capital investment
gaikoku shihon tōshi
外国資本投資

foreign capital offensive
gaishi kōsei
外資攻勢

foreign currency bond
gaikasai
外貨債

foreign currency finance
gaika kin'yū
外貨金融

foreign currency securities
gaika shōken
外貨証券

foreign currency speculation
gaikoku kawase tōki
外国為替投機

foreign debt
(foreign bond)
gaisai
外債

(external debt)
taigai saimu
対外債務

foreign exchange futures
gaikoku kawase sakimono
外国為替先物

foreign exchange loan
gaikoku kawase kashitsuke
外国為替貸付け

foreign investment
(investment from abroad)
gaikoku kara no tōshi
外国からの投資

(foreign capital)
gaishi
外資

(investment overseas)
kaigai tōshi
海外投資

foreign investment in Japanese securities
gaijin tainitsu shōken tōshi
外人対日証券投資

foreign investor
gaijin tōshika
外人投資家

foreign lender
kaigai kashidashinin
海外貸出人

foreign loan
gaisai
外債

foreign loan issue
gaisai hakkō
外債発行

foreign securities
gaikoku shōken
外国証券

foreign securities company
gaikoku shōken gaisha
外国証券会社

forfeit
sōshitsu suru
喪失する

forfeiture
sōshitsu
喪失

(loss of rights)
shikken
失権

forged bond
gizō saiken
偽造債券

forged security
gizō shōken
偽造証券

forged share certificate
gizō kabuken
偽造株券

forged stock certificate
gizō kabuken
偽造株券

forward
sakimono
先物

forward broker
sakimono nakagainin
先物仲買人

forward contract
sakimono keiyaku
先物契約
sakimono yoyaku
先物予約

forward delivery
sakigiri
先ぎり
sagiwatashi
先渡し

forward market
sakimono shijō
先物市場

forward price
sakimono nedan
先物値段

forward purchase
sakimono kaitsuke
先物買付け

forwardation [UK]
kurikoshi hibu
繰越日歩

fractional lot
hakabu
端株
hasū kabu
端数株

fractional order
hakabu chūmon
端株注文
hasū chūmon
端数注文

fractional share
hakabu
端株
hasū kabu
端数株

fraud
sagi
詐欺

free and open market
jiyū shijō
自由市場

free stocks (commodity market)
jiyū zaikohin
自由在庫品

freezing of assets
shisan tōketsu
資産凍結

front-door financing
omoteguchi kin'yū
表口金融

front-door operation
omoteguchi sōsa
表口操作

front-end fee
kisho hiyō
期初費用

front-end load
sakidori tesūryō
先取手数料

frozen account
kogetsuki kanjō
焦付き勘定

frozen credit
kogetsuki yūshi
焦付き融資

frozen loan
kogetsukigashi
焦付き貸し

fulfilment of obligation
saimu rikō
債務履行

full disclosure
(kabushiki no) kanzen kaiji
(株式の) 完全開示

full listing [UK]
zenjōjō
全上場

full renewal of loan
zengaku keizoku
全額継続

fully registered bond
kanzen tōroku shōken
完全登録証券

fully secured basis (for loan)
zengaku tanpotsuki de
全額担保付きで

fund(s)
(a fund)
kikin
基金

(capital, funds)
shikin
資金

fund management
tōshi komon
投資顧問

fund-raising
shikin chōtatsu
資金調達

fund-raising campaign
bokin undō
募金運動

funded debt
chōki fusai
長期負債

funding
shikin chōtatsu
資金調達

funding (Bank of England)
kokusai no karikae
国債の借換え

fungibles
daitaikanō shōken
代替可能証券

future delivery
sakigiri
先ぎり
sakiwatashi
先渡し

futures
sakimono
先物

futures contract
sakimono keiyaku
先物契約

futures delivery
sakiwatashi
先渡し

futures market
sakimono shijō
先物市場

futures option
sakimono opushon
先物オプション

futures price
sakimono kakaku
先物価格

futures purchase
sakimonogai
先物買い

futures quotation
sakimono sōba
先物相場

futures selling
sakimono uri
先物売り

futures trading
sakimono baibai
先物売買

futures transaction
sakimono torihiki
先物取引

gain(s)
(a profit, returns)
rieki
利益

(profit, returns)
rijun
利潤

(benefit, profit, returns)
ritoku
利得

(earnings, proceeds, a profit)
shūeki
収益

gambling
tōkiteki baibai
投機的売買

gap
gyappu
ギャップ

general mortgage
sōkatsu teitō
総括抵当

general mortgage bond
ippan tanpotsuki shasai
一般担保付社債

'gensaki' market [J][14]
gensaki shijō[14]
現先市場

gilt-edged securities (= gilts) [UK]
kinbuchi shōken
金縁証券

gilt-edged stock [UK]
yūryō kabu
優良株

global financial institutions
sekaiteki kin'yū kikan
世界的金融機関

GNMA (Government National Mortgage Association) [US]
seifu teitō kinko
政府抵当金庫

go-go fund
gōgō-fando
ゴーゴー・ファンド

go public
kabushiki kōkai suru
株式公開する

going long
omowakugai
思惑買い

going short
omowakuuri
思惑売り

gold bond
kinka saiken
金貨債券

gold-collateral loan
kintanpo shakkan
金担保借款

gold loan
kinka shakkan
金貨借款

good delivery (securities)
tekihō ukewatashi
適法受渡し

good financial standing
yūryō shisan jōtai
優良資産状態

good investment
yūryō tōshi
優良投資

good-this-month order
tōgetsu kagiri yūkō na chūmon
当月限り有効な注文

good-this-week order
tōshū kagiri yūkō na chūmon
当週限り有効な注文

good-till-cancelled order
kaiyaku made yūkō na chūmon
解約まで有効な注文

government agency bond
seifu kikan saiken
政府機関債券

government agency securities
seifu kikan shōken
政府機関証券

government bond
kokusai
国債

government bond certificate
kokusai shōken
国債証券

government bond in foreign currency
gaika kokusai
外貨国債

government borrowing
seifu kariire
政府借入れ

government broker
seifu burōkā
政府ブローカー

government debt
(national)
kokusai
国債

(public)
kōsai
公債

government financial agency
seifu kin'yū kikan
政府金融機関

government financial institution
seifu kin'yū kikan
政府金融機関

government-guaranteed bond
seifu hoshōsai
政府保証債

government investment
seifu tōshi
政府投資

government lending
seifu kashidashi
政府貸出し

government loan
(national)
kokusai
国債

(public)
kōsai
公債

Government National Mortgage Association (GNMA) [US]
seifu teitō kinko
政府抵当金庫

government obligations (= governments) [US]
seifu shōken
政府証券
seifusai
政府債

government securities
seifu shōken
政府証券

government securities market
kōsai shijō
公債市場

government sponsorship
seifu shusai
政府主催

government stock
seifu shōken
政府証券

governments (= government obligations) [US]
seifu shōken
政府証券
seifusai
政府債

grace
(shiharai) yūyo
(支払) 猶予

grace period
(shiharai) yūyo kikan
(支払) 猶予期間

grading (of commodities)
tōkyūzuke
等級付け

grain exchange
kokumotsu torihikijo
穀物取引所

granting of credit
shin'yō kyōyo
信用供与

grey market
gurē-māketto
グレー・マーケット

gross interest
sōrishi
総利子

gross investment
sōtōshi
総投資

gross margin
sōsaeki
総差益

gross spread
nezaya
値ざや

gross yield
sōrimawari
総利回り

ground-floor price
saitei hakkō kakaku
最低発行価格

group investment
dantai tōshi
団体投資

growth fund
seichō meate no tōshi shintaku
成長目当ての投資信託

growth stock
seichō kabu
成長株

guarantee (person)
hihoshōnin
被保証人

guarantee (= guaranty) (assurance)
hoshō
保証

(security, collateral)
tanpo
担保

guarantee fee
hoshōryō
保証料

guaranteed bond
hoshō saiken
保証債券
hoshōsai
保証債

guaranteed mortgage
hoshō tanpo
保証担保

guaranteed securities
hoshōtsuki shōken
保証付証券

guarantor
hoshōnin
保証人

guaranty (noun)
(assurance)
hoshō
保証

(security, collateral)
tanpo
担保

guaranty (verb)
hoshō suru
保証する

guaranty bond
hoshōsho
保証書

guidelines
shidō kijun
指導基準

hammer the market [US]
uritataku
売叩く

hammering [UK]
rondon kabushiki torihikijo
kai'in no hasan kokuchi
ロンドン株式取引所
会員の破産告知

hammering the market [US]
uritataki
売叩き

hard dollars [US]
hādo-doru (tesūryō)
ハード・ドル (手数料)

hard loan
hādo-rōn
ハード・ローン

hardening
hikishimari
引締まり

haven
ansokuchi
安息地
teihakujo
停泊所

heavy decline
bōraku
暴落

heavy market
nanjaku shikyō
軟弱市況

heavy selling
urikomi
売込み

heavy trading
ōakinai
大商内

hedge (noun)
hejji
ヘッジ
kaketsunagi
掛けつなぎ
tsunagi
つなぎ

hedge (verb)
tsunagu
つなぐ

hedge buying
kaitsunagi
買いつなぎ
kaketsunagikai
掛けつなぎ買い

hedge clause
sekinin kaihi jōkō
責任回避条項

hedge fund
hejji tōshi shintaku
ヘッジ投資信託

hedge selling
kaketsunagiuri
掛けつなぎ売り
uritsunagi
売りつなぎ

hedging
kaketsunagi
掛けつなぎ
tsunagi baibai
つなぎ売買

hedding contract
kaketsunagi keiyaku
掛けつなぎ契約

hedging market
tsunagi shijō
つなぎ市場

hedging operation
kaketsunagi sōsa
掛けつなぎ操作

hedging transaction
hejji torihiki
ヘッジ取引
kaketsunagi torihiki
掛けつなぎ取引

hefty investment
tagaku no tōshi
多額の投資

hidden loan
fukumi kashidashi
含み貸出し

high credit rating
takai shin'yō kakuzuke
高い信用格付け

high flyer
takane kabu
高値株

high-grade corporate bond
yūryō shasai
優良社債

**high-interest-bearing
debenture**
kōritsuki shasai
高利付社債

**high-interest-bearing
securities**
kōritsuki shōken
高利付証券

high-interest credit
kōkinri shikin
高金利資金

high interest rate
kōkinri
高金利

high-interest rates policy
kōkinri seisaku
高金利政策

high price
takane
高値

high-price stock
negasa kabu
値がさ株

high-tech stock
haiteku kabushiki
ハイテク株式

higher quotation at the close
hikedaka
引け高

highest credit rating
saikō shin'yō kakuzuke
最高信用格付け

highest interest rate
saikō kinri
最高金利
saikō rishiritsu
最高利子率

highest price
takane
高値

highs and lows
takane-yasune
高値・安値

hire purchase [UK]
fubarai shin'yō
賦払信用
kappu shin'yō
割賦信用

holding period
hoyū kikan
保有期間

holding the market
kaisasae
買支え

holdings
(general)
hoyūdaka
保有高

(stock)
mochikabu(sū)
持株(数)

home loan
jūtaku kashitsuke
住宅貸付け

home mortgage loan
jūtaku teitō kashitsuke
住宅抵当貸付け

home purchase loan
jūtaku kashitsuke
住宅貸付け

hot issue
ninki ga aru shinpatsu
shōken
人気がある新発証券

hot money
hotto-manē
ホット・マネー

hot stock
(popular)
ninki ga aru kabu
人気がある株

(stolen)
tōnan kabu
盗難株

House, the [UK]
rondon kabushiki torihikijo
ロンドン株式取引所

house
shōken gaisha
証券会社

house account
shōken gaisha honshiten
no kanjō
証券会社本支店
の勘定

**house maintenance
requirement**
shōken gaisha no shōkokin
ijiritsu
証券会社の証拠金
維持率

housing bond
jūtaku saiken
住宅債券

housing credit
jūtaku kin'yū
住宅金融

Housing Loan Corporation [J]
jūtaku kin'yū kōko
住宅金融公庫

hypothec [UK]
fudōsan teitōken
不動産抵当権

hypothecation [US]
(pledging of property)
fudōsan teitōken
不動産抵当権

**(pledging of securities for
margin loans)**
yūka shōken tanpo sashiire
有価証券担保差入れ

hypothecation agreement [US]
tanpo keiyaku
担保契約

idle capital
yūkyū shihon
遊休資本
yūshi
遊資

idle money
yūkin
遊金
yūkyū shikin
遊休資金

**IFC (International Finance
Corporation)**
kokusai kin'yū kōsha
国際金融公社

illiquid investments
hiryūdōsei tōshi
非流動性投資

imbalance of orders
chūmon no fukinkō
注文の不均衡

immediate delivery (securities)
jikiwatashi
直渡し

immediate or cancel order
shikyū chūmon
至急注文

immediate profit
mesaki no rieki
目先の利益

impact loan [J][15]
inpakuto-rōn[15]
インパクト・ローン

import of capital
shihon dōnyū
資本導入

import of foreign capital
gaishi dōnyū
外資導入

improvement
uwamuki
上向き

imputed interest
kizoku rishi
帰属利子

in and out trade
hihakari akinai
日計り商い
tanki tejimai
短期手仕舞い

inactive market
kansan na shijō
閑散な市場
kansan na shikyō
閑散な市況

inactive securities
fukappatsu shōken
不活発証券

inactive stock
fukappatsu kabu
不活発株
funinki kabu
不人気株

incentives
yūin
誘因

(favourable measures)
yūgū sochi
優遇措置

income
shotoku
所得

(earnings, return)
shūeki
収益

(earnings, fruit)
shūnyū
収入

income bond
shūeki saiken
収益債券

income debenture
shūeki shasai
収益社債

income-creating finance
shotoku zōshutsu kin'yū
所得造出金融

income from capital
shihon shotoku
資本所得

income from interest
rishi shotoku
利子所得

income from money in trust
kinsen shintaku shūeki
金銭信託収益

income from property
zaisan shotoku
財産所得

income from real estate
fudōsan shotoku shūnyū
不動産所得収入

income-oriented
shotoku meate no
所得目当ての

income-oriented investment
shotoku meate no tōshi
所得目当ての投資

income-producing stock
shotoku o umu kabushiki
所得を生む株式

income share
saisan kabu
採算株
shisan kabu
資産株

income stock
saisan kabu
採算株
shisan kabu
資産株

inconvertibility
fukan
不換
hikōkansei
非交換性

inconvertible
fukan no
不換の

inconvertible funds
fukan no shikin
不換の資金

inconvertible securities
fukan no shōken
不換の証券

increase in interest rates
kinri hikiage
金利引上げ
riage
利上げ

increased renewal of loan
zōgaku keizoku
増額継続

indebtedness
fusai
負債

(amount)
fusaigaku
負債額

indenture
shintaku shōsho
信託証書

independent broker [NYSE – US]
dokuritsu burōkā
独立ブローカー

index fund
indekkusu-fando
インデックス・ファンド

index-linked [UK]
infure bōei no
インフレ防衛の

index-linking [UK]
infure bōei sochi
インフレ防衛措置

index options
indekkusu-opushon
インデックス・オプ
ション

indexation [UK]
infure bōei sochi
インフレ防衛措置

indexing
indekkushingu
インデックシング

indication
shijō genzai kakaku kehai
no shiji
市場現在価格気配
の指示

indicator
shihyō
指標

indirect debt
kansetsu fusai
間接負債

indirect financing
kansetsu kin'yū
間接金融

indirect investment
kansetsu tōshi
間接投資

individual investment
kojin tōshi
個人投資

individual investor
kojin tōshika
個人投資家

individual shareholder
kojin kabunushi
個人株主

induced investment
yūhatsu tōshi
誘発投資

inducements
yūin
誘因

industrial bond
jigyōsai
事業債

industrial investment
sangyō tōshi
産業投資

industrial loan
jigyōsai
事業債

**Industrial Ordinary Shares
Index [US]**
kōgyō kabuka shisū
工業株価指数

industrial securities
kōgyō shōken
工業証券

**industrial shares (=
industrials)**
kōgyō kabu
工業株

**industrials (= industrial
shares)**
kōgyō kabu
工業株

inflation-proofing [US]
infure bōei sochi
インフレ防衛措置

initial investment
shoki tōshi
初期投資
tōsho tōshi
当初投資

initial margin
tōsho shōkokin
当初証拠金

initial public offering (IPO)
kōkai kōbo
公開公募

initial yield
tōsho rimawari
当初利回り

inquiry into financial situation
shin'yō jōtai chōsa
信用状態調査

inscribed bond
kimei saiken
記名債券

inscribed public bond
kimei kōsai
記名公債

inscribed securities
kimei shōken
記名証券

inscribed share
kimei kabu
記名株

inscribed share certificate
kimei kabuken
記名株券

inside broker
jōnai nakagainin
場内仲買人

inside information
naibu jōhō
内部情報

inside market
jōnai shijō
場内市場

inside the floor
jōnai
場内

inside the room
jōnai
場内

insider
insaidā
インサイダー
naibusha
内部者

insider dealing [UK]
insaidā no torihiki
インサイダーの取引
naibusha no torihiki
内部者の取引

insider information
kaisha naibu no jōhō
会社内部の情報
naibusha no jōhō
内部者の情報

insider trading [US]
insaidā no torihiki
インサイダーの取引
naibusha no torihiki
内部者の取引

instalment
bunkatsubarai(kin)
分割払い(金)
kappubarai(kin)
割賦払い(金)

instalment credit [US]
fubarai shin'yō
賦払信用
kappu shin'yō
割賦信用

instalment finance
kappu kin'yū
割賦金融

instalment-type loan
kappubarai kashitsuke
割賦払貸付け

institutional broker
kikan burōkā
機関ブローカー

institutional buyer
kikan kōbaisha
機関購買者

institutional buying
kikangai
機関買い

institutional investment
kikan tōshi
機関投資

institutional investor
kikan tōshika
機関投資家

institutional selling
kikan'uri
機関売り

institutional shareholder
kikan kabunushi
機関株主

instrument
shōken
証券

instrument of credit
shin'yō shōken
信用証券

intensive investment
shūyaku tōshi
集約投資

inter-business credit
kigyōkan shin'yō
企業間信用

inter-government debt
seifukan saimu
政府間債務

interchangeable bonds
kōkan saiken
交換債券

interest
(money rates)
kinri
金利

(gains, profit, returns)
rieki
利益

(interest on loans and deposits)
rishi
利子
risoku
利息

interest arbitrage
rishi saitei
利子裁定

interest-bearing
ritsuki no
利付きの

interest-bearing bond
ritsuki saiken
利付債券

interest-bearing capital
rishitsuki shihon
利子付資本

interest-bearing public bond
ritsuki kōsai
利付公債

interest-bearing securities
ritsuki shōken
利付証券

interest burden
kinri futan
金利負担
rishi futan
利子負担

interest cover(age)
kinri futan nōryoku
金利負担能力

interest differential
kinrisa
金利差

Interest Equalization Tax [US]
rishi heikōzei
利子平衡税

interest expense
shiharai rishi
支払利子

interest for delay
entai rishi
延滞利子

interest-free
murisoku no
無利息の

interest-free loan
murishi yūshi
無利子融資
murisoku no kashitsuke
無利息の貸付け

interest in arrears
chien risoku
遅延利息
entai risoku
延滞利息

interest income
rishi shotoku
利子所得

interest margin
rizaya
利鞘

interest on bond
saiken rishi
債券利子

interest on borrowing
kariirekin kinri
借入金金利

interest on debenture
shasai rishi
社債利子

interest on external bond
gaisai rishi
外債利子

interest on external loan
gaisai rishi
外債利子

interest on government securities
kokusai rishi
国債利子

interest on loan
kashidashi kinri
貸出金利

interest on public bonds
kōsai rishi
公債利子

interest on the outstanding balance
mihensai zandaka kinri
未返済残高金利

interest paid
shiharai rishi
支払利子

interest payable
kariirekin rishi
借入金利子
miharai rishi
未払利子

interest payment
ribarai
利払い
rishi shiharai
利子支払い

interest payment burden
kinri futan
金利負担

interest payment date
rishi shiharai kijitsu
利子支払期日

interest per annum
nenri
年利

interest per diem
hibu
日歩

interest period
kinri kikan
金利期間

interest rate (money rates)
kinri
金利

(interest on loans or deposits)
riritsu
利率
rishiritsu
利子率

interest rate adjustment
kinri chōsei
金利調整

interest rate control
kinri no kontorōru
金利のコントロール

interest rate deregulation
kinri jiyūka
金利自由化

interest rate mechanism
kinri kikō
金利機構

interest rate movement
kinri dōkō
金利動向

interest rate policy
kinri seisaku
金利政策

interest rate stabilization
kinri no antei
金利の安定

interest rate structure
kinri taikei
金利体系

interest rate swap
kinri no kōkan torihiki
金利の交換取引

interest rate war
kinri sensō
金利戦争

interest revenue
risoku shūnyū
利息収入

interest-sensitive
kinri ugoki ga shinkeishitsu na
金利動きが神経質な

interest-sensitive stock
kinri ugoki ga shinkeishitsu na kabu
金利動きが神経質な株

interest spread
rizaya
利鞘

interest table
rishi hayamihyō
利子早見表

interest tax
rishizei
利子税

interest unpaid
miharai rishi
未払利子

interest warrant
rishi shiharai sashizusho
利子支払指図書

interest yield
rimawari
利回り

interim finance
chūkan kin'yū
中間金融

intermediary
chūkaisha
仲介者

intermediate term
chūki
中期

intermediation
chūkai
仲介

internal debt
naibu fusai
内部負債
naisai
内債

internal rate of return (IRR)
naibu shūekiritsu
内部収益率

international bond issue
kokusaiteki saiken hakkō
国際的債券発行

international capital market
kokusai shihon shijō
国際資本市場

international capital movements
kokusai shihon idō
国際資本移動

international capital transactions
kokusai shihon torihiki
国際資本取引

international commodities
kokusai shōhin
国際商品

International Commodities Clearing House [UK]
kokusai shōhin torihikijo
国際商品取引所

international consortium
kokusai hikiukedan
国際引受団

international diversification
kokusai bunsan tōshi
国際分散投資

international finance
kokusai kin'yū
国際金融

International Finance Corporation (IFC)
kokusai kin'yū kōsha
国際金融公社

international financial market
kokusai kin'yū shijō
国際金融市場

international financial transaction
kokusai kin'yū torihiki
国際金融取引

international indebtedness
kokusai taishaku
国際貸借

international investment
kokusai tōshi
国際投資

international investment bank
kokusai tōshi ginkō
国際投資銀行

international investment trust
kokusai tōshi shintaku
国際投資信託
kokusai tōshin
国際投信

international loan market
kokusai kashitsuke shijō
国際貸付市場

international market
kokusai shijō
国際市場

international market price
kokusai shijō kakaku
国際市場価格

international money market
kokusai kin'yū shijō
国際金融市場

International Petroleum Exchange (IPE) [UK]
kokusai sekiyu torihikijo
国際石油取引所

international securities
kokusai shōken
国際証券

international shares
kokusai kabu
国際株

international stock
kokusai kabu
国際株

international syndicate
kokusai hikiukedan
国際引受団

international trading of securities
shōken no kokusai torihiki
証券の国際取引

international underwriting group
kokusai hikiukedan
国際引受団

internationally traded commodities
kokusai shōhin
国際商品

intraday
nitchū takahikune
日中高低値

intrinsic value
opushon no hongenteki kachi
オプションの本源的
価値

introduced stock
kōkai kabu
公開株

introduction [UK]
kōkai
公開

introduction of foreign capital
gaishi dōnyū
外資導入

introduction of foreign investment
gaishi dōnyū
外資導入

inventory financing
zaiko kin'yū
在庫金融

invest
tōshi suru
投資する

invested capital
tōka shihon
投下資本

investible funds
tōshikanō shikin
投資可能資金

investing activity
tōshi katsudō
投資活動

investing client
tōshikyaku
投資客

investing country
tōshikoku
投資国

investing institution
tōshi kikan
投資機関

investing public
taishū tōshika
大衆投資家

investment
tōshi
投資

(subscribed capital)
shusshi
出資

(use of capital)
un'yō
運用

investment abroad
taigai tōshi
対外投資

investment advice
tōshi sōdan
投資相談

investment adviser
tōshi komon
投資顧問

investment advisory service
tōshi komongyō
投資顧問業

investment analysis
tōshi bunseki
投資分析

investment analyst
tōshi bunseki senmonka
投資分析専門家

investment appraisal
tōshi hyōka
投資評価

investment bank [US]
tōshi ginkō
投資銀行

investment banker [US]
tōshi ginkō
投資銀行

investment banking [US]
tōshi ginkōgyō
投資銀行業

investment boom
tōshi keiki
投資景気

investment broker
tōshi chūkainin
投資仲介人

investment budget
tōshi yosan
投資予算

investment buying
tōshigai
投資買い

investment capital
tōshi shihon
投資資本

investment certificate
shusshi shōken
出資証券

investment club
tōshi kurabu
投資クラブ

investment commodity
tōshizai
投資財

investment company
tōshi gaisha
投資会社

investment credit [US]
tōshi zeikōjo
投資税控除

investment criteria
tōshi kijun
投資基準

investment currency
tōshi tsūka
投資通貨

investment drive
tōshi iyoku
投資意欲

investment effort
tōshi doryoku
投資努力

investment fund
tōshi kikin
投資基金

investment funds
tōshi shikin
投資資金

investment grade
tōshi tekikaku
投資適格

investment grant
tōshi hojokin
投資補助金

investment guarantee
tōshi hoshō
投資保証

investment in foreign securities
taigai shōken tōshi
対外証券投資

investment in Japanese stock by non-Japanese
gaijin tōshi
外人投資

investment in public utilities
kōkyō tōshi
公共投資

investment in real estate
fudōsan tōshi
不動産投資

investment in securities
shōken tōshi
証券投資

investment in shares
kabushiki tōshi
株主投資

investment in stock
kabushiki tōshi
株主投資

investment incentives
tōshi yūin
投資誘因

investment income
tōshi shotoku
投資所得

investment instrument
tōshi bukken
投資物件

investment letter
tōshi mokuteki kakuninsho
投資目的確認書

investment management
tōshi kanri
投資管理

investment manager
tōshi kanrinin
投資管理人

investment market
tōshi shijō
投資市場

(issue market)
hakkō shijō
発行市場

investment opportunity
tōshi kikai
投資機会

investment outlet
tōshi taishō
投資対象

investment plan
tōshi keikaku
投資計画

investment policy
tōshi seisaku
投資政策

investment portfolio
tōshi mokuroku
投資目録

investment programme
tōshi keikaku
投資計画

investment risk
tōshi risuku
投資リスク

investment securities
tōshi (yūka) shōken
投資(有価)証券

investment shares
tōshi kabu
投資株

investment stock
tōshi kabu
投資株

investment strategy
tōshi senryaku
投資戦略

investment tax credit [US]
tōshi zeikōjo
投資税控除

investment trust
tōshi shintaku
投資信託

investment value
tōshi kachi
投資価値

investment yield
un'yō rimawari
運用利回り

investor
tōshika
投資家

investor base
tōshika bēsu
投資家ベース

invitation to subscribe for shares
kabunushi no boshū
株主の募集

I.O.U.
shakuyōshō
借用証

IPE (International Petroleum Exchange) [UK]
kokusai sekiyu torihikijo
国際石油取引所

IPO (initial public offering)
kōkai kōbo
公開公募

IRR (internal rate of return)
naibu shūekiritsu
内部収益率

irredeemable bond
mushōkan saiken
無償還債券

irredeemable debenture
mushōkan shasai
無償還社債

irredeemable public bond
mushōkan kōsai
無償還公債

irredeemable securities
mushōkan shōken
無償還証券

irredeemable stock
mushōkan kabu
無償還株

irregular fluctuations
fukisoku hendō
不規則変動

irregular market
hakō sōba
は行相場
henchō shikyō
変調市況

issue (noun)
(issue of securities)
hakkō
発行

(flotation of loan, issue of bond)
kisai
起債

(description, title)
meigara
銘柄

issue (verb)
hakkō suru
発行する

issue against securities
hoshō junbi hakkō
保証準備発行

issue amount
kisaigaku
起債額

issue at market price
jika hakkō
時価発行

issue at par
gakumen hakkō
額面発行

issue business
hakkō jimu
発行事務

issue date
hakkōbi
発行日

issue house
hakkō gaisha
発行会社

issue limit
hakkō gendo
発行限度

issue margin
hakkō yoryoku
発行余力

issue market
(shares)
hakkō shijō
発行市場

(bonds, loans)
kisai shijō
起債市場

issue of bond
kisai
起債

issue of bond at discount
saiken waribiki hakkō
債券割引発行

issue of debenture
shasai hakkō
社債発行

issue of government bonds
kokusai hakkōdaka
国債発行高

issue of securities
saiken hakkō
債券発行

issue of shares
kabushiki hakkō
株式発行

issue of shares at the current price
kabushiki no jika hakkō
株式の時価発行

issue price
hakkō kakaku
発行価格

issue syndicate
hakkōdan
発行団

issue terms
hakkō jōken
発行条件

issue to shareholders
kabunushi wariate
株主割当て

issued shares
hakkōzumi kabushiki
発行済み株式

issued stock
hakkōzumi kabushiki
発行済み株式

issuer
hakkō shōsha
発行商社
hakkōgyōsha
発行業者
hakkōsha
発行者

issuer's cost
hakkōsha rimawari
発行者利回り

issues qualified for loans
yūshiteki kakumeigara
融資的格銘柄

issuing house [UK]
hakkō shōsha
発行商社
shōken hakkōten
証券発行店

Japanese capital invested abroad
honpō shihon
本邦資本

jobber
[UK – obsolete]
jōnai nakagainin
場内仲買人

(see market maker)
(nezuke gyōsha)
(値付業者)

jobber's turn
rizaya
利鞘

joint and several guarantee
rentai hoshō
連帯保証

joint and several obligation
rentai saimu
連帯債務

joint corporate bond
kyōdō shasaiken
共同社債券

joint debt
rentai saimu
連帯債務

joint debtor
rentai saimusha
連帯債務者

joint financing
kyōchō yūshi
協調融資

joint guarantee
rentai hoshō
連帯保証

joint investment
kyōdō tōshi
共同投資

joint promissory note
rentai yakusoku tegata
連帯約束手形

junior bond
kai no saiken
下位の債券
kōjun'i saiken
後順位債券

junior issue
kai no saiken hakkō
下位の債券発行
kōjun'i saiken hakkō
後順位債券発行

junior mortgage
kōjun'i teitō
後順位抵当

junior mortgage bond
kōjun'i tanpotsuki shasai
後順位担保付社債

junior securities
kai no shōken
下位の証券
kōjun'i shōken
後順位証券
retsugo shōken
劣後証券

junk bond [US]
kakuzuke ga hikui shōken
格付けが低い証券

kerb (see also curb)
jōgai (shijō)
場外(市場)

kerb broker
jōgai kabu nakagainin
場外株仲買人

kerb dealing
jōgai torihiki
場外取引

kerb market
jōgai shijō
場外市場

kerb stock
jōgai torihiki kabu
場外取引株

kerb trading
jōgai torihiki
場外取引

kickback
haraimodoshi
払戻し

killing
sōba no ōatari
相場の大当たり

kite-flying
yūzū tegata furidashi
融通手形振出し

laggard
deokure kabu
出遅れ株

large-lot
ōguchi
大口

large shareholder
daikabunushi
大株主

last quotation
hikene
引け値
owarine
終わり値

last session
hike
引け

last trading day
saishū nōkai
最終納会

leader (stock)
shuryoku kabu
主力株

leading operators
yūryoku suji
有力筋

leading speculators
ōtesuji
大手筋

leading stock
hanagata kabu
花形株
shuryoku kabu
主力株

legal investment
hōtei tōshi
法定投資

legal list [US]
hōtei tōshi risuto
法定投資リスト

legal rate of interest
hōtei riritsu
法定利率

legal transfer
hōtei jōto
法定譲渡

lend
kashidasu
貸出す
kashitsukeru
貸付ける
kasu
貸す

lender
dashite
出し手
kashite
貸手
kingashi gyōsha
金貸業者

lender of last resort
saishū no kashite
最終の貸手

lender's risk
kashite no kiken
貸手の危険

lending
(loan)
kashidashi
貸出し

(financing)
yūshi
融資

lending activity
yūshi katsudō
融資活動

lending attitude
yūshi taido
融資態度

lending bank
yūshi ginkō
融資銀行

lending facility
kashitsuke seido
貸付制度

lending guidelines
kashitsuke shirei
貸付指令

lending market
kashidashi shijō
貸出市場
kashitsuke shijō
貸付市場

lending operations
yūshi katsudō
融資活動

lending period
kashidashi kikan
貸出期間

lending policy
kashidashi seisaku
貸出政策

lending race
kashidashi kyōsō
貸出競争

lending rate
kashidashi kinri
貸出金利
kashidashi riritsu
貸出利率

lending restrictions
yūshi kisei
融資規制

lending securities
kashishōken
貸証券

lending stock
kashikabu
貸株

lendings
kashidashidaka
貸出高

letter of allotment
kabunushi wariate tsūchijō
株主割当通知状

letter of application
mōshikomisho
申込書

letter of intent
ikōjō
意向状

 (prospectus)
shuisho
趣意書

letter of proxy
ininjō
委任状

letter of regret
kabushiki bonyū kotowarijō
株式募入断り状

letter security
hitōroku no shibosai
非登録の私募債

leveraged investment company
rebarejiddo tōshi gaisha
レバレジッド投資会社

leveraged stock
rebarejiddo kabu
レバレジッド株

liberalization
jiyūka
自由化

liberalization of capital transactions
shihon torihiki no jiyūka
資本取引の自由化

liberalization of interest rates
kinri jiyūka
金利自由化

LIBOR (London inter-bank offered rate)
rondon ginkōkan torihiki kinri
ロンドン銀行間取引金利

lien
sakitori tokken
先取特権

lien holder
sakitori tokkensha
先取特権者

light trading
usuakinai
薄商い

limit (price)
sashine
指値

limit calculation
sashine santeihō
指値算定法

limit order
sashine chūmon
指値注文

limit order information system
sashine chūmon jōhō shisutemu
指値注文情報システム

limited convertibility
seigentsuki kōkansei
制限付交換性

liquid securities
ryūdō shōken
流動証券

liquidate (securities)
(shōken o) genkinka suru
(証券を) 現金化する

liquidation
 (cashing-in)
genkinka
現金化
kankin
換金

 (evening-up of accounts)
tejimai
手仕舞い

liquidation of bears
nanpa no tejimai
軟派の手仕舞い

liquidation of bulls
kōha no tejimai
硬派の手仕舞い

liquidation of longs
kōha no tejimai
硬派の手仕舞い
tejimaiuri
手仕舞い売り

liquidation of shorts
nanpa no tejimai
軟派の手仕舞い
tejimaigai
手仕舞い買い

list of quotations
sōbahyō
相場表

listed
jōjō sarete iru
上場されている

listed company
jōjō gaisha
上場会社

listed issue
jōjō meigara
上場銘柄

listed option
jōjō opushon
上場オプション

listed securities
jōjō shōken
上場証券

listed shares
jōjō kabu
上場株

listed stock
jōjō kabu
上場株

listed stock issue
jōjō meigara
上場銘柄

listing
jōjō
上場

listing requirements
jōjō shinsa kijun
上場審査基準

listing standard
jōjō kijun
上場基準

LME (London Metal Exchange)
rondon kinzoku torihikijo
ロンドン金属取引所

load
tesūryō
手数料

loan
kariirekin
借入金
kashitsuke(kin)
貸付け(金)
shakkan
借款

(lending)
kashidashi
貸出し

(financing)
yūshi
融資

loan account
kariirekin kanjō
借入金勘定
kashitsuke kanjō
貸付勘定

loan agreement
shakkan kyōtei
借款協定

loan application
kashitsuke mōshikomi
貸付申込み
yūshi mōshikomi
融資申込み

loan approval
kashitsuke shōnin
貸付承認

loan capital
kariire shihon
借入資本
kashitsuke shihon
貸付資本

loan clearance
taishaku kessai
貸借決済

loan commitment
kashidashi yoyaku
貸出予約

loan crowd
shōken chūkainin no nakama
証券仲介人の仲間

loan customer
yūshisaki
融資先

loan/deposit ratio
yogashiritsu
預貸率

loan extension
shakkan kyōyo
借款供与

loan flotation
kisai
起債

loan for home-owner
kojin mochiie kashitsuke
個人持家貸付け

loan holder
saikensha
債権者

loan issue
saiken hakkō
債券発行

loan on bills
tegata kashitsuke
手形貸付け

loan on deed
shōsho kashitsuke
証書貸付け

loan on deposits
yokin tanpo kashitsuke
預金担保貸付け

loan on guarantee
hoshō kashitsuke
保証貸付け

loan on insurance policy
hoken shōken tanpo kashitsuke
保険証券担保貸付け

loan on listed stock
jōjō kabushiki tanpo kashitsuke
上場株式担保貸付け

loan on security
tanpogashi
担保貸し

loan period
kashitsuke kikan
貸付期間

loan policy
kashitsuke seisaku
貸付政策

loan race
kashitsuke kyōsō
貸付競争

loan rate
kashidashi kinri
貸出金利
kashidashi riritsu
貸出利率

loan refusal
yūshi kyohi
融資拒否

loan secured by commodities collateral
shōhin tanpo kashitsuke
商品担保貸付け

loan secured by corporate debentures
shasai tanpo kashitsuke
社債担保貸付け

loan secured by government bond
kōsai tanpo kashitsuke
公債担保貸付け

loan secured by government pension
onkyū tanpo kashitsuke
恩給担保貸付け

loan secured by real estate
fudōsan teitō kashitsuke
不動産抵当貸付け

loan secured by stocks and bonds
yūka shōken tanpo kashitsuke
有価証券担保貸付け

loan security
tanpogashi
担保貸し

loan shark
kōrigashi
高利貸し

loan stock
tenkan shasai
転換社債

loan to government
seifu kashitsukekin
政府貸付金

loan value
kashidashigaku
貸出額
kashitsuke kagaku
貸付価額

loan with third-party guarantee
hoshō kashitsuke
保証貸付け

loans for small businesses
chūshō kigyō kin'yū
betsuwaku yūshi
中小企業金融別枠
融資

loans to foreign countries
taigai shakkan kyōyo
対外借款供与

loans to the public
shomin kin'yū
庶民金融

local authority stock
chihōsai
地方債

locked-in
tōketsu shita
凍結した

locked-up
son'eki no kakutei
損益の確定

locked-up capital
kogetsuki shihon
焦付資本

London inter-bank offered rate (LIBOR)
rondon ginkōkan torihiki kinri
ロンドン銀行間取引
金利

London Metal Exchange (LME)
rondon kinzoku torihikijo
ロンドン金属取引所

London Stock Exchange
rondon kabushiki torihikijo
ロンドン株式取引所

long account
kaigyoku
買玉

(bulls)
tsuyoki suji
強気筋

long bond
chōkisai
長期債

long commitment
chōki yoyaku
長期予約

long credit
chōki shin'yō
長期信用

long-dated bill
chōki tegata
長期手形

long-dated securities [UK]
chōki no shōkan kijitsutsuki shōken
長期の償還期日付
証券

long hedge
kaihejji
買いヘッジ
kaitsunagi
買いつなぎ

long liquidation
urimodoshi
売戻し

long market
kaisugi no sōba
買過ぎの相場
tsuyoki sōba
強気相場

long position
kaimochi
買持ち

long selling
tsuyokiuri
強気売り

long-term bond
chōkisai
長期債

long-term capital market
chōki shihon shijō
長期資本市場

long-term credit
chōki shin'yō
長期信用

long-term credit market
chōki kin'yū shijō
長期金融市場

long-term debenture
chōki shasai
長期社債

long-term debt
chōki kariirekin
長期借入金

long-term financing
chōki kin'yū
長期金融

long-term government bond (national)
chōki kokusai
長期国債

(public)
chōki kōsai
長期公債

long-term government securities
chōki seifu shōken
長期政府証券

long-term interest rate
chōki kinri
長期金利
chōki rishiritsu
長期利子率

long-term investment
chōki tōshi
長期投資

long-term loan
chōki kashidashi
長期貸出し
chōki kashitsuke(kin)
長期貸付け(金)
chōkisai
長期債

long-term securities
chōki shōken
長期証券

long-term trading
chōki torihiki
長期取引

long-term yield
chōki rimawari
長期利回り

longs
(government bonds [UK])
chōki kokusai
長期国債

(bulls)
tsuyokisuji
強気筋

loser (stock)
nesagari kabu
値下がり株

loss
sonshitsu
損失

loss from falling price
nesagari sonshitsu
値下がり損失

loss from redemption of bond
shasai no shōkan sason
社債の償還差損

loss from securities revaluation
yūka shōken no hyōkason
有価証券の評価損

loss on sale
baikyakuson
売却損

loss on securities sold
yūka shōken baikyakuson
有価証券売却損

lost security
funshitsu shōken
紛失証券

lost share certificate
funshitsu kabuken
紛失株券

lot (securities)
tan'i
単位

low
yasune
安値

low-dividend stock
teihai kabu
低配株

low-grade stock
tei'i kabu
低位株

low interest
teikinri
低金利
teiri
低利

low-interest credit
teikinri shikin
低金利資金

low-interest loan
teiri kashitsuke
低利貸付け

(financing)
teiri yūshi
低利融資

low interest rate
teikinri
低金利
teirishiritsu
低利子率

low-interest rates policy
teikinri seisaku
低金利政策

low-priced stock
neyasu kabu
値安株

low-value stock
teigakumen kabushiki
低額面株式

low yield
teirimawari
低利回り

low-yield bond
teirimawari saiken
低利回り債券

lower closing quotation
hikeyasu
引け安

lower quotation
shitane
下値

lowest interest rate
saitei kinri
最低金利
saitei rishiritsu
最低利子率

lull
ichijun moyō
一巡模様

mail credit
mēru-kurejitto
メール・クレジット

maintenance call
shōkokin yōkyū tsūchi
証拠金要求通知

maintenance fee
kanrihi
管理費

maintenance margin [US]
iji shōkokin
維持証拠金

maintenance requirement
shōkokin yōkyū
証拠金要求

make a market
nezuke
値付け

make a price
nezuke
値付け

make-up price
seisan kakaku
清算価格

managed account
gōdō un'yō kanjō
合同運用勘定

managed unit trust [UK]
kanri yunittogata tōshi
shintaku
管理ユニット型投資
信託

management company
tōshi gaisha
投資会社

management fee
kanri tesūryō
管理手数料

management group
hikiuke kanjidan
引受幹事団

managing underwriter
hikiuke kanji
引受幹事

manipulated quotation
jin'i sōba
人為相場

manipulation
jin'i sōsa
人為操作
sōba sōjū
相場操縦

margin
 (difference between
 buying and selling prices)
baibai kakaku no hiraki
売買価格の開き

 (spread)
nezaya
値鞘

 (profit margin)
rizaya
利鞘

 (deposit money)
shōkokin
証拠金

margin account
shōkokin kanjō
証拠金勘定

margin agreement
shōkokin keiyakusho
証拠金契約書

margin buying
shin'yōgai
信用買い

margin call
tsuika shōkokin
追加証拠金

margin money
shōkokin
証拠金

margin rate
shōkokinritsu
証拠金率

margin requirement
shōkokin shoyōgaku
証拠金所要額

margin trading
shin'yō torihiki
信用取引
shōkokin torihiki
証拠金取引

margin transaction
shin'yō torihiki
信用取引
shōkokin torihiki
証拠金取引

marginal decline
sōba no biraku
相場の微落

market
 (market place, exchange)
shijō
市場

 (market conditions, tone,
 position)
shikyō
市況

 (quotation, market price)
sōba
相場

market all-time high
shijō saikō
市場最高

market analysis
shijō bunseki
市場分析

market analyst
shijō dōkō bunseki
senmonka
市場動向分析専門家

market appraisal
shijō hyōka
市場評価

market behaviour
shijō kōdō
市場行動

market capitalization
jika sōgaku
時価総額

market conditions
shōjō
商状

 (tone, position)
shikyō
市況

 (trade market situation)
shōkyō
商況

market data
shijō jōhō
市場情報

market data system
shijō jōhō shisutemu
市場情報システム

market decline
shijō suitai
市場衰退

market discount rate
shijō waribiki buai
市場割引歩合

market disruption
shijō konran
市場混乱

market fluctuation
shika hendō
市価変動

market forces
shijō yōin
市場要因

market forecast
shijō mitōshi
市場見通し
sōbakan
相場観

market hours
tachiai jikan
立会時間

market index
shijō shisū
市場指数

market information
shijō jōhō
市場情報

market instrument
tanki saimu shōsho
短期債務証書

market interest rates
shichū kinri
市中金利

market leader
shijō no shudō kabu
市場の主導株

market-leading commodities
shikyō shōhin
市況商品

market maker [US]
nezuke gyōsha
値付業者

market movements
sōba no dōkō
相場の動向

market operation
shijō sōsa
市場操作

market order [US]
nariyuki chūmon
成行注文

market-out clause
menseki jōkō
免責条項

market position
shikyō
市況

market price
shijō kakaku
市場価格
shika
市価
sōba
相場

market quotation
shijō sōba
市場相場
shijō yobine
市場呼び値

market rally
shikyō kaifuku
市況回復

market rate
(interest)
shijō kinri
市場金利
shijō rishiritsu
市場利子率

(interbank rate)
shijō sōba
市場相場

(bills)
shijō waribiki buai
市場割引歩合

market recovery
shikyō kaifuku
市況回復

market report
shikyō hōkoku
市況報告

market research
shijō yōin bunseki
市場要因分析

market risk
shijō kakaku hendō risuku
市場価格変動リスク

market slump
sōba no bōraku
相場の暴落

market stability
shijō anteisei
市場安定性

market stabilization
kakaku antei sōsa
価格安定操作

market tone
(mood of market)
kehai
気配

(sentiment, psychology)
shijō ninki
市場人気

(conditions)
shikyō
市況

(trade market situation)
shōkyō
商況

market trend
shijō dōkō
市場動向

market value
shijō kachi
市場価値

market yield
shijō rimawari
市場利回り

marketability
ryūdōsei
流動性
shijōsei
市場性

marketable
ryūdōsei no aru
流動性のある
shijōsei no aru
市場性のある

marketable issue
shijōsei shōken
市場性証券

marketable securities
shijōsei shōken
市場性証券

massive borrowing
tairyō kariire
大量借入れ

master card
oya kādo
親カード

master credit
oya shin'yōjō
親信用状

matched orders
nareai baibai chūmon
なれ合売買注文

matured bond
manki saiken
満期債券

maturity
manki
満期

maturity date
mankijitsu
満期日

maturity repayment
mankibarai modoshikin
満期払戻金

maximum amount of issue
saikō hakkō gendo
最高発行限度

maximum limit for interest rates
furisaikō gendo
付利最高限度

maximum limit of overdraft
kashikoshi kyokudogaku
貸越極度額

mean return
kitai shūeki
期待収益

means
shiryoku
資力
zairyoku
財力

means of settlement
kessai hōhō
決済方法

medium and long-term credit
chūchōki shin'yō
中長期信用

medium and long-term interest rates
chūchōki kinri
中長期金利

medium-term
chūki no
中期の

medium-term bond
chūkisai
中期債

medium-term credit
chūki shin'yō
中期信用

medium-term loan
chūki kashidashi
中期貸出し

medium-to-long-term bonds
chūchōkisai
中長期債

mediums [UK]
chūki kokusai
中期国債

member firm
shōken torihikijo kai'in
証券取引所会員

members' rate
torihikijo kai'in sōba
取引所会員相場

middleman
chūkainin
仲介人
chūkaisha
仲介者

minimum lending rate (MLR)
saitei kashidashi buai
最低貸出歩合
saitei kashidashi kinri
最低貸出金利

minimum margin requirement
saitei shōkokinritsu
最低証拠金率

minimum rate of interest
saitei rishiritsu
最低利子率

minimum risk
saishō kiken
最小危険

minimum-risk portfolio
saishō kiken pōtoforio
最小危険ポートフォ
リオ

minimum subscription
kabushiki saishō ōbogaku
株式最小応募額

missing the market
shijō o ushinau koto
市場を失うこと

mixed market
kimayoi sōba
気迷い相場

MLR (minimum lending rate)
saitei kashidashi buai
最低貸出歩合
saitei kashidashi kinri
最低貸出金利

moderate fluctuation
shōōrai
小往来

moderate trading
ochitsuki shikyō
落着き市況

monetization of debt
kōsai no kaheika
公債の貨幣化

money
[general – neutral]
kane
金

(funds)
shikin
資金

(financing)
yūshi
融資

money at call
tanki yūshi
短期融資

money at short notice
tanki tsūchigashi
短期通知貸し

money borrowed
kariirekin
借入金

money broker
kin'yū gyōsha
金融業者

money in trust
kinsen shintaku
金銭信託

money lender
kanegashi
金貸し
kin'yū gyōsha
金融業者

money lending business
kanegashigyō
金貸業

money lent
kashikin
貸金

money market
kin'yū shijō
金融市場

money market broker
tanshi gyōsha
短資業者

money market dealer
tanshi gyōsha
短資業者

money market fund [US]
shijō kinri rendōgata tōshi shintaku
市場金利連動型投資信託

money market instrument
kin'yū shijō shōken
金融市場証券

money market intervention
kin'yū shijō e no kainyū
金融市場への介入

money market management
kin'yū shijō no un'ei
金融市場の運営

money market securities
kin'yū shijō shōken
金融市場証券

money market rate
shijō kinri
市場金利

money rate
shichū kinri
市中金利

money value (securities)
kingaku
金額

month-end delivery
getsumatsu watashi
月末渡し

month-end liquidation
getsumatsu seiri
月末整理

monthly instalment
geppu
月賦
tsukigake
月掛け

mood (market)
kehai
気配

moratorium
shiharai teishi
支払停止

morning fixing
gozen tatene kettei
午前建値決定

morning session
zenba
全場

mortgage (noun)
mōgejji
モーゲッジ

(real-estate purchase loan)
fudōsan kashitsuke
不動産貸付け

(house purchase loan)
jūtaku (shikin) kashitsuke
住宅(資金)貸付け

(house purchase financing)
jūtaku kin'yū
住宅金融

(collateral)
tanpo
担保

(hypothec [UK], hypothecation [US])
teitō(ken)
抵当(権)

mortgage (verb)
teitō ni ireru
抵当に入れる

mortgage-backed bond
teitōtsuki saiken
抵当付債券

mortgage-backed securities
tanpotsuki shōken
担保付証券

mortgage bank
jūtaku kin'yū gaisha
住宅金融会社

mortgage banking
jūtaku kin'yūgyō
住宅金融業

mortgage bond
tanpotsuki saiken
担保付債券

mortgage business
jūtaku kin'yūgyō
住宅金融業

mortgage certificate
teitō shōsho
抵当証書

mortgage company
jūtaku kin'yū gaisha
住宅金融会社

mortgage credit (home financing)
jūtaku kin'yū
住宅金融

(secured loan)
teitōgashi
抵当貸し

mortgage creditor
teitōkensha
抵当権者

mortgage debenture
teitōkentsuki shasai
抵当権付社債

mortgage debt
fudōsan teitō fusai
不動産抵当負債

mortgage debtor
teitōken setteisha
抵当権設定者

mortgage deed
tanpo shōken
担保証券

mortgage documents
teitōshō shorui
抵当証書類

mortgage loan
mōgejji kashitsuke
モーゲッジ貸付け

(real-estate purchase loan)
fudōsan kashitsuke
不動産貸付け

(home purchase loan)
jūtaku (shikin) kashitsuke
住宅(資金)貸付け

mortgage market
teitō shijō
抵当市場

mortgage pool
fukusū no tanpo
複数の担保

mortgage rate
mōgejji kashitsuke kinri
モーゲッジ貸付金利

mortgage repayment
mōgejji kashitsuke hensai
モーゲッジ貸付返済

mortgage servicing
mōgejji kashitsuke hensai kanri
モーゲッジ貸付返済管理

mortgagee
teitō saikensha
抵当債権者
teitōkensha
抵当権者

mortgager
teitōken setteisha
抵当権設定者

movement (of market prices)
shika no ashidori
市価の足取り
sōba no ashidori
相場の足取り

municipal bond
(region)
chihōsai
地方債

(town)
shisaiken
市債券

municipal debt
shisai
市債

municipal loan
(region)
chihōsai
地方債

(town)
shisai
市債

mutilated bond
kison shōken
き損証券

mutual debt
aitai saimu
相対債務

mutual fund [US]
kaishagata tōshi shintaku
会社型投資信託

naked debenture
mutanpo shasai
無担保社債

naked option
nēkiddo-opushon
ネーキッド・オプ
ション

naked position
nēkiddo-pojishon
ネーキッド・ポジ
ション

narrow margin
kozaya
小鞘

(small profits)
hakuri
薄利

narrow market
fukyō shijō
不況市場
kansan na shijō
閑散な市場

NASD (National Association of Securities Dealers) [US]
zenbei shōkengyō kyōkai
全米証券業協会

NASDAQ system (National Association of Securities Dealers Automated Quotations System) [US]
nazudakku
ナズダック

National Association of Securities Dealers (NASD) [US]
zenbei shōkengyō kyōkai
全米証券業協会

national bond
kokusai
国債

national credit
kokka shin'yō
国家信用

national debt
kokka saimu
国家債務
kokusai
国債

national debt interest
kokka saimu rishi
国家債務利子

national debt management
kokusai kanri
国債管理

national loan
naikokusai
内国債
naisai
内債

NBFI (non-bank financial intermediaries)
ginkō'igai no kin'yū kikan
銀行以外の金融機関

near delivery
kinjitsu watashi
近日渡し

near futures
kijika mono
期近物

near maturity
kinmanki
近満期

near money
ryūdō shisan
流動資産

near-panic market
kyōfu sōba
恐怖相場

near-term securities
kijikasai
期近債

nearbys
kijika mono
期近物

nearest month
saikingetsu
最近月

negative carry
gyaku kinri
逆金利

negative spread
gyakuzaya
逆鞘

negotiability
(transferability)
jōtokanōsei
譲渡可能性

(marketability)
ryūtsūsei
流通性

negotiable
(transferable)
jōtokanō
譲渡可能

(marketable)
ryūtsūsei no aru
流通性のある

negotiable bill
ryūtsū tegata
流通手形

negotiable bond
ryūtsū saiken
流通債券

negotiable certificate of deposit [US]
jōtokanō teiki yokin shōsho
譲渡可能定期預金
証書

negotiable document
ryūtsū shorui
流通書類

negotiable instrument
ryūtsū shōken
流通証券

negotiable note
ryūtsū yakusoku tegata
流通約束手形

negotiable paper
ryūtsū shōken
流通証券

negotiable securities
yūka shōken
有価証券

negotiate
(securities)
ryūtsū suru
流通する

(carry out a transaction)
torihiki suru
取引する

negotiated market
kokyaku shijō
顧客市場

negotiated transaction
aitai baibai
相対売買

negotiation (transaction)
torihiki
取引

nervousness
rōbai
狼狽

net interest (from account)
junrisoku
純利息

net investment
juntōshi
純投資

net position
junmochidaka
純持高

net present value (NPV)
jungenzai kachi
純現在価値

net price
shōmi kakaku
正味価格

net proceeds
shōmi hakkō kawarikin
正味発行代り金

net yield
junrimawari
純利回り

new financial commodities
shinkin'yū shōhin
新金融商品

new high
(record)
shinkiroku
新記録

(prices)
shintakane
新高値

new issue
shinki hakkō
新規発行

new issue market
hakkō shijō
発行市場

new issues
shinki hakkō saiken
新規発行債券

new loans
shinki kashidashi
新規貸出し

new low (prices)
shin'yasune
新安値

new shares
kokabu
子株
shinkabu
新株

new stock
kokabu
子株
shinkabu
新株

New Year session
hatsutorihiki
初取引

New York Stock Exchange (NYSE)
nyūyōku kabushiki torihikijo
ニューヨーク株式
取引所

newly introduced shares
kōkai kabu
公開株

newly issued corporate bond
shinki hakkō shasai
新規発行社債

nifty fifty [US]
ninki no aru gojū meigara no kabushiki
人気のある50銘柄
の株式

Nikkei Dow Jones Average [J]
nikkei dau
日経ダウ

Nikkei Stock Average [J]
nikkei kabushiki shisū
日経株式指数

no change
mochiai
保合い

no credit outstanding
yoshin zandaka wa nai
与信残高はない

no-limit order
nariyuki chūmon
成行注文

no-par stock
mugakumen kabushiki
無額面株式

no par value
mugakumen no
無額面の

no-par-value stock
mugakumen kabushiki
無額面株式

nominal interest rate
hyōmen kinri
表面金利

nominal price
gakumen kingaku
額面金額

nominal quotation
meimoku sōba
名目相場

nominal value
gakumen kakaku
額面価格

nominal yield
meimoku rimawari
名目利回り

nominee
meiginin
名義人

non-bank financial intermediaries (NBFI)
ginkō'igai no kin'yū kikan
銀行以外の金融機関

non-bank institutions
higinkō kin'yū kikan
非銀行金融機関

non-bearer bond
kimei saiken
記名債券

non-callable public and corporate bonds
kichū hishōkan kōshasai
期中非償還公社債

non-convertibility
fukan
不換
hikōkansei
非交換性

non-convertible
fukan no
不換の
hikōkansei
非交換性

non-convertible bond
futsūsai
普通債

non-cumulative
hiruisekiteki
非累積的

non-cumulative credit
hiruiseki shin'yōjō
非累積信用状

non-cumulative preference shares [UK]
hiruiseki yūsen kabu
非累積優先株

non-cumulative preferred stock [US]
hiruiseki yūsen kabu
非累積優先株

non-delivery
ukewatashi furikō
受渡不履行

non-dividend
muhaitō
無配当

non-dividend payer
muhai kabu
無配株

non-dividend-paying company
muhai gaisha
無配会社

non-instalment credit
ikkatsubarai shin'yō
一括払信用

non-interest-bearing
murisoku no
無利息の

non-interest-bearing bond (public)
murisoku kōsai
無利息公債

(corporate)
murisoku shasai
無利息社債

non-interest-bearing debt
murisoku saiken
無利息債券

non-interest-bearing securities
murisoku shōken
無利息証券

non-marketable securities
shijōsei no nai shōken
市場性のない証券

non-negotiable (non-marketable)
hiryūtsū no
非流通の

(non-transferable)
jōtofunō
譲渡不能

non-negotiable bill
jōtofunō tegata
譲渡不能手形

non-negotiable note
jōtofunō yakusoku tegata
譲渡不能約束手形

non-negotiable paper
jōtofunō tegata
譲渡不能手形

non-negotiable securities
jōtofunō shōken
譲渡不能証券

non-par stock
mugakumen kabushiki
無額面株式

non-public information
kaisha naibu no jōhō
会社内部の情報

non-recourse loan
hisokyūteki rōn
非遡及的ローン

non-taxable interest income
hikazei rishi shotoku
非課税利子所得

non-taxable investment
menzei tōshi mono
免税投資物

non-taxable securities
menzei yūka shōken
免税有価証券

not quoted
jōjō sarete nai
上場されてない

not rated
kakuzuke no nai
格付けのない

note (negotiable instrument)
ryūtsū shōken
流通証券

(promissory note)
yakusoku tegata
約束手形

note at sight
ichiranbarai yakusoku tegata
一覧払約束手形

note broker
yakusoku tegata nakagainin
約束手形仲買人

note discounted
waribiki yakusoku tegata
割引約束手形

note of hand
yakusoku tegata
約束手形

note payable
shiharai yakusoku tegata
支払約束手形

note receivable
uketori yakusoku tegata
受取約束手形

note to bearer
jisanninbarai yakusoku tegata
持参人払約束手形

note to order
sashizushiki yakusoku tegata
指図式約束手形

novation (replacement of party to a contract by another party)
katagawari
肩代り

(replacement of old debt by new one)
saimu no kōkai
債務の更改

NPV (net present value)
jungenzai kachi
純現在価値

nullified bond
shikkō shōken
失効証券

NYSE (New York Stock Exchange)
nyūyōku kabushiki torihikijo
ニューヨーク株式取引所

obligation (debt, liabilities)
fusai
負債

(debt, security, bond)
saiken
債券

(debt, indebtedness)
saimu
債務

odd lot
hakabu
端株
hasū
端数

odd-lot broker
hakabu no burōkā
端株のブローカー

odd-lot dealer
hakabu senmon gyōsha
端株専門業者

odd-lot differential
hakabu tesūryō
端株手数料

odd-lot investment
hakabu tōshi
端株投資

odd-lot investor
hakabu tōshika
端株投資家

odd-lot shares
hakabu
端株

odd-lot trading
hakabu torihiki
端株取引

odd-lot transaction
hakabu torihiki
端株取引

odd-lotter
hakabu torihikisha
端株取引者

off-board [US]
jōgai
場外

off-board market
jōgai shijō
場外市場

off-mart dealing
jōgai torihiki
場外取引

offer
(offering price)
kōbo kakaku
公募価格

(asked price)
urine
売値
uriyobine
売呼び値

offer by subscription
yoyaku boshū
予約募集

offer for public subscription
kōbo
公募

offer for sale [UK]
(introduction)
kōkai
公開

(placing [UK], placement [US])
boshū
募集

(direct issue)
kansetsu hakkō
間接発行

(public offering)
kōbo
公募

offer price [UK]
(offering price)
kōbo kakaku
公募価格

(asked price)
urine
売値
uriyobine
売呼び値

offer to sell
(securities)
boshū
募集

offeree
urimōshikomi ukesha
売申込受者

offerer
urimōshikomisha
売申込者

offering
boshū
募集

offering circular
boshū annai
募集案内

offering day
kōbojitsu
公募日

offering price
(public offering price)
kōbo kakaku
公募価格

(selling price)
uridashi kakaku
売出価格

(asked price)
urine
売値
uriyobine
売呼び値

official discount rate
kōtei buai
公定歩合

official list [UK]
kabushiki torihikijo kōhō
株式取引所公報

official money rates
kōtei buai
公定歩合

official prices [London Metal Exchange]
kōtei kakaku
公定価格

official quotation
kōtei sōba
公定相場

official rate
kōtei buai
公定歩合

offshore banking
ofushoa ginkō gyōmu
オフショア銀行業務

offshore banking units
ofushoa ginkō
オフショア銀行

offshore centre
ofushoa-sentā
オフショア・センター

offshore financial centres
ofushoa tōshi sentā
オフショア投資センター

(tax heavens)
zeikin hinanchi
税金避難地

offshore funds
ofushoa-fando
オフショア・ファンド

offshore investment trust
ofushoa tōshi shintaku
オフショア投資信託

old shares
kyūkabu
旧株
oyakabu
親株

old stock
kyūkabu
旧株
oyakabu
親株

on account
kakeuri
掛売り

on the curb
jōgai de
場外で

on-the-curb dealing
jōgai torihiki
場外取引

One Hundred Share Index [UK]
(finansharu taimuzu no) kabushiki torihikijo no hyaku meigara no kabushiki shisū
(フィナンシャル・タイムズの) 株式取引所の100銘柄の株式指数

open account
kakeuri
掛売り

open buying
shingikai
新規買い

open-end investment trust
ōpungata tōshi shintaku
オープン型投資信託

open-end management company
ōpungata tōshi shintaku gaisha
オープン型投資信託会社

open-end mortgage
kaihōgata tanpo
開放型担保

open-end mortgage bond
kaihōgata tanpo shasai
開放型担保社債

open-ended fund
ōpungata tōshi shintaku
オープン型投資信託

open interest
torikumi
取組み

open market (securities)
aozora shijō
青空市場

(market overt)
kōkai shijō
公開市場

(finance)
shichū
市中

open-market discount rate
shichū waribiki buai
市中割引歩合

open-market operations
kōkai shijō sōsa
公開市場操作

open-market quotation
kōkai shijō sōsa no sōba
公開市場操作の相場
shichū sōba
市中相場

open-market rates (interest rates)
shichū kinri
市中金利

open-market selling operation
uri ope
売りオペ

open mortgage
ichibu teitō
一部抵当

open-mortgage bond
sōkatsu teitō saiken
総括抵当債券

open order
mujōken chūmon
無条件注文

(good-till-cancelled order)
kaiyaku made yūkō na chūmon
解約まで有効な注文

open selling
shingiuri
新規売り

opening
yoritsuki
寄付き

opening call
yoriyobine
寄呼び値

opening high
takayori
高寄り

opening of financial markets
kin'yū shijō no kaihō
金融市場の開放

opening price (asked price US], offer price [UK])
kōbo kakaku
公募価格
urine
売り値
yobine
呼び値

(bid price, offered price)
tsukene
付け値

(opening quotation)
yoritsuki nedan
寄付き値段
yoritsukine
寄付き値

opening quotation
yoritsuki sōba
寄付相場

opening session
yoritsuki
寄付き

opening session of the year
daihakkai
大発会

opening tone
yoritsuki kehai
寄付気配

operation in bills
tegata operēshon
手形オペレーション

operation on the Stock Exchange
kabushiki torihikijo de no torihiki
株式取引所での取引

operator
(speculator, trader)
shite
仕手

(speculator, stock jobber, gambler)
sōbashi
相場師

option
opushon
オプション

(right to buy or sell)
sentaku baibaiken
選択売買権
sentakuken
選択権

(privilege)
tokken
特権

option buyer
tokken kaite
特権買い手

option period
sentakukentsuki torihiki kikan
選択権付取引期間

option premium
opushonryō
オプション料

option premium price
sentakuken no kakaku
選択権の価格

option seller
tokken urite
特権売り手

option writer
opushon no urite
オプションの売り手

optional redemption
nin'i shōkan
任意償還

order
chūmon
注文

ordinary interest
tsūjō risoku
通常利息

ordinary interest rate
tsūjō kinri
通常金利

ordinary shares [UK]
futsū kabu
普通株

ordinary shareholder
futsū kabunushi
普通株主

ordinary warrant
honshōkokin
本証拠金

original capital
genshi shihon
原始資本

original investment
genshi tōshigaku
原始投資額
tōsho tōshigaku
当初投資額

original issue discount
hakkōji waribiki
発行時割引

original issue stock
shohatsu kabu
初発株

outright purchase
gengai
現買い

outright sale
gen'uri
現売り

outside transaction
mujōken ope
無条件オペ
mujōken torihiki
無条件取引

outside applicant
ippan kabushiki ōbosha
一般株式応募者

outside broker
jōgai nakagainin
場外仲買人

outside dealing
jōgai torihiki
場外取引

outside market
jōgai shijō
場外市場

outside securities
jōgai shōken
場外証券

outside stock
hijōjō kabu
非上場株

outsider
shirōto suji
素人筋

outstanding balance of loan
mihensai zandaka
未返済残高

outstanding bond
mishōkan saiken
未償還債券

outstanding credit
kashitsuke zandaka
貸付残高

outstanding debt
miharai saimu
未払債務
misai shakkin
未済借金

outstanding loan
kiō kashidashi
既往貸出し

outstanding obligation
saimu zandaka
債務残高

outstanding principal
zanson ganpon
残存元本

outstanding public loan
mishōkan kōsai
未償還公債

outstanding securities
mishōkan shōken
未償還証券

outward investment
taigai tōshi
対外投資

over-allocation
chōka wariate
超過割当て

over-the-counter broker
gaibu burōkā
外部ブローカー

over-the-counter market
tentō shijō
店頭市場

over-the-counter stock
tentō kabu
店頭株

over-the-counter trading
tentō baibai
店頭売買

over-the-counter transaction
tentō torihiki
店頭取引

overall investment
zentai tōshi
全体投資

overbid (noun)
kakene
掛け値

overbid (verb)
kakene o suru
掛け値をする

overborrow
kado ni kariru
過度に借りる

overborrowing
kariire kata
借入過多

overbought market
kaisugi no sōba
買過ぎの相場

overbought position
kaimochi
買持ち

overbuy
kaisugiru
買過ぎる

overbuying
kaisugi
買過ぎ

overdue
entai no
延滞の
kigen keika no
期限経過の

overdue interest
entai rishi
延滞利子

overdue interest per diem
entai hibu
延滞日歩

overdue loan
kigen keika kashitsuke
期限経過貸付け

overdue note
kigen keika yakusoku
tegata
期限経過約束手形

overhang
yojō
余剰

overindebtedness
saimu chōka
債務超過

overinvestment
kajō tōshi
過剰投資

overissue
chōka hakkō
超過発行
kadai hakkō
過大発行

overnight call loan
yokujitsubarai kashitsuke
翌日払貸付け

overnight delivery
yokujitsu watashi
翌日渡し

overnight loan
yokujitsubarai kashitsuke
翌日払貸付け

overnight money
yokujitsubarai shikin
翌日払資金

overnight repo
yokujitsu mono no repo
翌日物のレポ

overnight securities
yokujitsu mono
翌日物

oversell
urisugiru
売過ぎる

overselling
urisugi
売過ぎ

oversold market
urisugi no sōba
売過ぎの相場

oversold position
urimochi
売持ち

overspeculation
katō tōki
過当投機

oversubscribed
boshū chōka no
募集超過の
mōshikomi chōka no
申込超過の
ōbo chōka no
応募超過の

oversubscription
boshū chōka
募集超過
mōshikomi chōka
申込超過
ōbo chōka
応募超過

overvalued stock
kadai hyōka no kabu
過大評価の株

owe money
shiharai gimu ga aru
支払義務がある

own shares
kabushiki o motte iru
株式を持っている

P/E ratio (price/earnings ratio)
kabuka shūekiritsu
株価収益率

panic
kyōkō
恐慌

panic market
kyōkō sōba
恐慌相場

panic price
kyōkō kakaku
恐慌価格

panic quotations
kyōkō sōba
恐慌相場

panic selling
rōbai uri
狼狽売り

paper
  (bill)
  tegata
  手形

  (securities)
  shōken
  証券

paper credit
shiken shin'yō
紙券信用

par
gakumen
額面

par bond
gakumen shasai
額面社債

par issue
gakumen hakkō
額面発行

par value
gakumen kakaku
額面価格

par-value share
gakumen kabu
額面株

par-value stock
gakumen kabu
額面株

parallel financing
heikō yūshi
平行融資

parallel loan
heikō shakkan
平行借款

partial delivery
ichibu ukewatashi
一部受渡し

partially secured basis (for loan)
ichibu tanpotsuki de
一部担保付きで

participating bond
rieki sanka shasai
利益参加社債

participating preference share [UK]
rieki haitō yūsen kabu
利益配当優先株

participating preferred stock [US]
rieki haitō yūsen kabu
利益配当優先株

participation
sanka
参加

participation certificate
sanka shōsho
参加証書

participation loan
  kyōchō yūshi
  協調融資
  kyōdō yūshi
  共同融資
  sanka kashitsuke
  参加貸付け

partly paid shares
miharaikomi kabu
未払込株

pass-through security
pasu-surū shōken
パス・スルー証券

passive bond
  (public)
  murishi kōsai
  無利子公債

  (general)
  murishi saiken
  無利子債券

  (corporate)
  murishi shasai
  無利子社債

passive debt
murisoku saimu
無利息債務

passive investment
judōteki tōshi
受動的投資

pawnbroker [UK]
shichiya
質屋

pawned article
shichimono
質物

pawning
shichiire
質入れ
shichioki
質置き

pawning ticket
shichiken
質券

pawnshop [UK]
shichiya
質屋

pay a debt
fusai o kaesu
負債を返す
shakkin o shiharau
借金を支払う

pay-back method
shihon kaishū
資本回収

pay-back period
tōshi kaishū kikan
投資回収期間

pay off (int. verb)
rieki o motarasu
利益をもたらす

pay-out period
shihon kaishū kikan
資本回収期間

payable at call
yōkyūbarai
要求払い

payable on demand
yōkyūbarai
要求払い

paying agent
shiharai dairinin
支払代理人

payment
(repayment)
bensai
弁済

(instalment)
haraikomi
払込み

(repayment,
reimbursement)
hensai
返済

(disbursement)
shiharai
支払い

payment at maturity
mankibarai
満期払い

payment date
shiharai kijitsu
支払期日

payment day
shiharaibi
支払日

payment of interest
risoku no shiharai
利息の支払い

payment record
shiharai kiroku
支払記録

payment reputation
shiharai sehyō
支払世評

payment terms
shiharai jōken
支払条件

peg (verb)
kugizuke suru
釘付けする
osaeru
抑える

pegged market
kugizuke shika
釘付市価

pegged stock
kugizuke kabu
釘付株

pegging
kugizuke
釘付け

pegging of prices
shika no kugizuke
市価の釘付け

penal interest
iyaku rishi
違約利子

penalty
iyakukin
違約金

penalty clause
iyaku jōkō
違約条項

pennant
penanto
ペナント

penny shares [UK]
penii kabu
ペニー株

penny stock [US]
penii kabu
ペニー株

PEP (Personal Equity Plan)
[UK]
kojin tōshi zeikōjo keikaku
個人投資税控除計画

per share
hitokabu atari (no)
一株当たり（の）

performance of obligation
saimu no rikō
債務の履行

performance stock
gyōseki kabu
業績株

period of grace
shiharai yūyo kikan
支払猶予期間

permanent bond
eikyū saiken
永久債券

permanent financing
chōki yūshi
長期融資

permanent public debt
eikyū kōsai
永久公債

perpetual bond
mukigen saiken
無期限債券

perpetual debenture
mukigen shasai
無期限社債

perpetual public loan
mukigen kōsai
無期限公債

personal credit
kojin shin'yō
個人信用

personal dividend income
kojin haitō shotoku
個人配当所得

Personal Equity Plan (PEP)
[UK]
kojin tōshi zeikōjo keikaku
個人投資税控除計画

personal financing planning
kojin zaimu keikaku
個人財務計画

personal-guarantee loan
kojin hoshō kashidashi
個人保証貸出し

personal interest income
kojin rishi shotoku
個人利子所得

personal liability
kojinteki fusai
個人的負債

personal loan
kojin kashitsuke
個人貸付け

[UK]
kojin no tanpotsukinai
kashitsuke
個人の担保付きない
貸付け

petty loan
koguchi kashidashi
小口貸出し

physical (noun)
genbutsu
現物

physical price
genbutsu kakaku
現物価格

pick-up
rimawari no kaizen
利回りの改善

pipeline (securities)
hakkō yotei
発行予定

place of payment
shiharaichi
支払地

place of settlement
kessaichi
決済地

placement [US]
boshū
募集

placement agent
boshū dairinin
募集代理人

placement prospectus
boshū yōkō
募集要項

placing [UK]
boshū
募集

placing of orders
hatchū
発注

plain bond
mutanpo saiken
無担保債券

planned investment
keikakuteki tōshi
計画的投資

pledge as security
tanpo toshite sashiireru
担保として差入れる

pledged assets
shichiire shisan
質入資産

pledged securities
shichiire yūka shōken
質入有価証券

pledging
shichiire
質入れ

plough back
saitōshi suru
再投資する

plough-back profit
saitōshiyō rieki
再投資用利益

ploughing back
saitōshi katei
再投資過程

polarization [UK]
nibun kyokuka
二分極化

pool of financing
kyōdō shusshi
共同出資

popular issue
ninki kabu
人気株

popular stock
hanagata kabu
花形株
ninki kabu
人気株

portfolio
pōtoforio
ポートフォリオ
yūka shōken meisaisho
有価証券明細書

portfolio investment
shisan un'yō tōshi
資産運用投資

portfolio management (asset management)
shisan kanri
資産管理

portfolio selection
shisan sentaku
資産選択

position
mochidaka
持高

post
shōken torihiki no posuto
証券取引のポスト

pound-cost averaging [UK]
teigaku rieki ruisekigata tōshin
定額利益累積型投信

pound sterling bond
eika saiken
英貨債券

preference bill
yūgū tegata
優遇手形

preference bond [UK]
yūsen kōsai shōken
優先公債証券

preference debenture [UK]
yūsen shasai
優先社債

preference dividend [UK]
yūsen haitō
優先配当

preference share [UK]
yūsen kabu
優先株

preference shareholder [UK]
yūsen kabunushi
優先株主

preferred stock [US]
yūsen kabu
優先株

preferred stockholder [US]
yūsen kabunushi
優先株主

preliminary prospectus
karimokuromisho
仮目論見書

premature delivery (futures)
hayauke watashi
早受渡し

premium

(premium over bond value)
gakumen chōkagaku warimashikin
額面超過額割増金

(option charge)
opushonryō
オプション料

(call premium)
shōkan puremiamu
償還プレミアム

(bonus)
warimashikin
割増金

premium bond [UK]
warimashikintsuki chochiku saiken
割増金付貯蓄債券

prepayment
kizen shōkan
期前償還

prepayment penalty
kizen shōkan iyakukin
期前償還違約金

price/earnings ratio (P/E ratio)
kabuka shūekiritsu
株価収益率

price of commodities
bukka
物価

price of shares
kabuka
株価

price range
nehaba
値幅

price spread
nebiraki
値開き

primary dealer [US]
seifu shōken kōnin diirā
政府証券公認ディーラー

primary distribution
ichiji bunbai
一次分売

primary market (new issue market)
hakkō shijō
発行市場

primary offering
ichiji bunbai
一次分売
uridashi
売出し

primary securities
hongenteki shōken
本源的証券

prime bill
ichiryū tegata
一流手形
yūryō tegata
優良手形

prime borrower
ōguchi kashidashisaki
大口貸出先

prime corporate bond
ichiryū shasai
一流社債

prime credit
genshin'yōjō
原信用状

prime customer
yūryō torihikisaki
優良取引先

prime interest rate
kijun kinri
基準金利

prime lending rate
kijun kinri
基準金利

prime rate [US]
kijun kinri
基準金利
puraimu-rēto
プライム・レート

prime securities
hongenteki shōken
本源的証券

prime stock
shuryoku kabu
主力株

principal

(debt)
gankin
元金
ganpon
元本

(person)
honnin
本人

principal amount
ganpon kingaku
元本金額

principal and interest
ganri
元利

principal guaranteed
ganpon hoshō
元本保証

prior-lien bond
yūsen tanpokentsuki shasai
優先担保付社債

prior redemption
mankizen shōkan
満期前償還

priority financing
yūgū kin'yū
優遇金融

private foreign capital
minkan gaishi
民間外資

private foreign investment
minkan kaigai tōshi
民間海外投資

private investment
minkan tōshi
民間投資

private investment abroad
taigai minkan tōshi
対外民間投資

private issue of shares
enko boshū
縁故募集

private offering [UK]
shibo
私募

private placement [US]
shibo
私募

private-placement bonds
hikōbosai
非公募債

private placing [UK]
shibo
私募

private subscription
enko boshū
縁故募集

proceeds from sale
baikyaku daikin
売却代金

productive capital
seisan shihon
生産資本

productive investment
seisanteki tōshi
生産的投資

productivity of capital
shihon seisansei
資本生産性

productivity of investment
tōshi seisansei
投資生産性

professional dealers
kurōto suji
玄人筋

professional speculator
sōbashi
相場師
tōki senmonka
投機専門家
tōkishi
投機師

profit
rijun
利潤

(gain, return)
rieki
利益

(earnings, return)
shūeki
収益

profit factor
rieki yōso
利益要素

profit from redemption
shōkan saeki
償還差益

profit from redemption of debentures
shasai shōkan'eki
社債償還益

profit from revaluation of securities
yūka shōken hyōka'eki
有価証券評価益

profit margin
rizaya
利鞘

profit on sale
baikyakueki
売却益

profit on securities sold
yūka shōken baikyaku'eki
有価証券売却益

profit per share
hitokabu atari rieki
一株当たり利益

profit-taking
rigui
利食い

profitability
shūekisei
収益性

profitability analysis
shūekisei bunseki
収益性分析

profitable investment
yūri na tōshi
有利な投資

program trading
konpyūtagata baibai
コンピュータ型売買

prohibition of resale
tenbai kinshi
転売禁止

project financing
keikaku yūshi
計画融資

promissory note
yakusoku tegata
約束手形

promissory note holder
yakusoku tegata shojinin
約束手形所持人

prospective return
yosō shūekiritsu
予想収益率

prospective yield
yosō rimawari
予想利回り

prospectus
mokuromisho
目論見書
setsuritsu shuisho
設立趣意書

protected bear
kaimodoshi yowakisuji
買戻し弱気筋

prudence
shinchō
慎重

prudent-man rule
shinchō na kanrisha junsoku
慎重な管理者準則

public and corporate bonds
kōshasai
公社債

public bond
kōsai
公債

public credit
kōshin'yō
公信用

public debt
kōsai
公債

public investment
kōkyō tōshi
公共投資

public investor
taishū tōshika
大衆投資家

public issue (of shares)
kōbo
公募

public issues (government's)
kōbosai
公募債

public offering [US]
kōbo
公募
kōkai
公開

public offering price
kōbo kakaku
公募価格

public placement [US]
kōbo
公募
kōkai
公開

public placing [UK]
kōbo
公募
kōkai
公開

public sector borrowing requirements
kōkyō bumon kariire juyō
公共部門借入需要

public securities
kōsai
公債

public subscription
kōbo
公募

public utility bond
kōkigyōsai
公企業債

public utility stock
kōeki kabu
公益株

publicly held stock
kōkai kabu
公開株

publicly offered shares
uridashi kabu
売出株

publicly subscribed shares
kōbo kabu
公募株

purchase fund
kihatsusai no kaiire kikin
既発債の買入基金

purchase group
kaiire gurūpu
買入れグループ

purchase note
kaiyakusho
買約書

purchase of securities
yūka shōken kaiire
有価証券買入れ

purchase order
kaichūmon
買注文

purchase price
kaiire kakaku
買入価格

purchasing redemption
kaiire shōkan
買入償還

put bond
shōkan seikyūkentsuki shasai
償還請求権付社債

put of more
tsuika kentsuki baibai
追加権付売買

put option
(bond redemption)
mankizen shōkan opushon
満期前償還オプション

(selling option)
uriopushon
売りオプション
uritsuki sentakuken
売付選択権

puts and calls
tokkentsuki baibai
特権付売買

qualitative analysis (securities)
teisei bunseki
定性分析

quantitative analysis (securities)
teiryō bunseki
定量分析

quiet market
kansan na shikyō
閑散な市況

quotation
sōba
相場

quotation after the close
hikeato kehai
引け跡気配

quotation board
sōba kokuchiban
相場告知板

quoted
jōjō sarete iru
上場されている

quoted company
jōjō gaisha
上場会社

quoted market value
shijō kakaku
市場価格

quoted value of all listed stocks
zenjōjō meigara jika sōgaku
全上場銘柄時価総額

quoting
tonae
唱え

raider
kōransha
こう乱者
rēdā
レーダー

raiding the market
urikuzushi
売崩し

raise capital
shihon o chōtatsu suru
資本を調達する

raise funds
shikin o chōtatsu suru
資金を調達する

raise interest rates
kinri o (hiki)ageru
金利を(引)上げる

rally (noun)
hantō
反騰
tachinaori
立直り

rally (verb)
(recover)
hanpatsu suru
反発する

(rebound)
hantō suru
反騰する

(recover)
kaifuku suru
回復する

(make a comeback, be revived)
morikaesu
盛り返す

rallying of the market
shikyō no hantō
市況の反騰

random walk
sōba no fukisoku na ugoki
相場の不規則な動き

range
haba
幅

rate
(per cent, commission)
buai
歩合

(per cent)
ritsu
率

rate of discount
waribikiritsu
割引率

rate of interest
(money rates)
kinri
金利

(interest on loans or deposits)
riritsu
利率
rishiritsu
利子率

rate of return
riekiritsu
利益率

rate of return on investment
tōshi riekiritsu
投資利益率

rate of yield
rimawariritsu
利回り率

rating
kakuzuke
格付け

reaction (of market)
hannō
反応
hanraku
反落

real-estate investment trust (REIT) [US]
fudōsan tōshi shintaku
不動産投資信託

real interest rate
jisshitsu kinri
実質金利

real investment
jitsubutsu tōshi
実物投資

real rate of return
jisshitsu riekiritsu
実質利益率

real share
jitsukabu
実株

real stock
jitsukabu
実株

realized investment
jitsugen shita tōshi
実現した投資

realized loss
jitsugen sonshitsu
実現損失

realized profit
jitsugen rieki
実現利益

reborrowing
karikae
借換え

rebound
hanpatsu
反発

recall of loan
kashikin no chōshū
貸金の徴収

reckless lending
hōman kashidashi
放漫貸出し

recommended issue
suishō kabu
推奨株

reconversion of stock
saitenkan
再転換

record price
takane
高値

recouping a loss
modoshi
戻し

recourse loan
sokyūkentsuki rōn
遡及権付きローン

recover
kaifuku suru
回復する

(rally)
hanpatsu suru
反発する

(rebound)
hantō suru
反騰する

recovery
(rally)
hanpatsu
反発

(market)
kaifuku
回復
tachinaori
立直り

recovery high
modori takane
戻り高値

recycle (capital)
kanryū suru
還流する

recycling (of capital)
kanryū
還流

red herring (prospectus) [US]
karimokuromisho
仮目論見書

redeem
shōkan suru
償還する

redeemability
shōkankanōsei
償還可能性

redeemable bond
(public)
zuiji shōkan kōsai
随時償還公債

(general)
zuiji shōkan saiken
随時償還債券

redeemable debenture
yūki shasai
有期社債

redeemable preferred stock
shōkan yūsen kabu
償還優先株

redeemable public debt
shōkan kōsai
償還公債

redeemable security
kaimodoshikanō shōken
買戻可能証券

redeemable stock
shōkankanō kabushiki
償還可能株式

redeemed principal and interest
shōkan kinkajitsu
償還金果実

redemption
shōkan
償還

redemption at market value
shika shōkan
市価償還

redemption at maturity
manki shōkan
満期償還

redemption at par value
gakumen shōkan
額面償還

redemption before maturity
mankizen shōkan
満期前償還

redemption by drawing
chūsen shōkan
抽選償還

redemption by instalments
kappu shōkan
割賦償還

redemption by purchase
kaiire shōkan
買入償還

redemption date
shōkan kijitsu
償還期日

redemption of debenture
shasai shōkan
社債償還

redemption of foreign bonds
gaikokusai shōkan
外国債償還

redemption of external loan
gaisai shōkan
外債償還

redemption of public bond
kōsai shōkan
公債償還

redemption of securities
saiken shōkan
債券償還

redemption premium
shōkan puremiamu
償還プレミアム

redemption price
shōkan kakaku
償還価格

redemption yield
shōkan rimawari
償還利回り

rediscount (noun)
saiwaribiki
再割引

rediscount (verb)
saiwaribiki suru
再割引する

rediscount policy
saiwaribiki seisaku
再割引政策

rediscount rate
saiwaribiki buai
再割引歩合
saiwaribikiritsu
再割引率

rediscounted bill
saiwaribiki tegata
再割引手形

rediscounting
saiwaribiki
再割引

reduced renewal of loan
gengaku keizoku
減額継続

refinancing (refunding)
karikae
借換え

refugee capital
tōhi shihon
逃避資本

refunding
karikae
借換え

refunding bond
karikae saiken
借換債券

regional stock exchanges
chihō kabushiki torihikijo
地方株式取引所

register
kirokubo
記録簿
tōrokubo
登録簿

registered bond
(public)
kimei kōsai
記名公債
tōroku kōsai
登録公債

(general)
tōroku saiken
登録債券

registered coupon bond
tōrokusai
登録債

registered debenture
kimei shasai
記名社債

registered representatives
tōroku yūka shōken
gaimu'in
登録有価証券外務員

registered securities
(inscribed)
kimei shōken
記名証券

(on record)
tōroku shōken
登録証券

registered share
kimei kabu
記名株

registered share certificate
tōroku kabuken
登録株券

registered stock
kimei kabu
記名株

registrar [UK]
meigi kakikae dairinin
名義書換代理人

registration
(document, record)
kiroku
記録
tōki
登記

(entry, record)
tōroku
登録

registration fee
tōkiryō
登記料
tōrokuryō
登録料

registration of securities
shōken tōroku
証券登録

registration statement
hakkō todokeidesho
発行届出書
yūka shōken todokeidesho
有価証券届出書

regular lot
baibai tan'i
売買単位

regular transaction
futsū torihiki
普通取引

regular-way delivery
tsūjō ukewatashi
通常受渡し

regular-way settlement
tsūjō ukewatashi
通常受渡し

regulated commodities
tōsei shōhin
統制商品

regulated interest rate
kisei kinri
規制金利

regulated investment company [US]
tōsei o uketa tōshi gaisha
統制を受けた投資
会社

regulation
(control)
kisei
規制

(rules)
kisoku
規則

(provisions, stipulations)
kitei
規定

(control, regimentation)
tōsei
統制

regulation of stock price
kabuka kisei
株価規制

regulatory control on bank lendings
kashidashi zōkagaku kisei
貸出増加額規制

rehypothecation [US]
saitanpo settei
再担保設定

re-invest
saitōshi suru
再投資する

re-investment
saitōshi
再投資

re-investment rate
saitōshi kinri
再投資金利

re-issue of debentures
shasai no saihakkō
社債の再発行

re-issue of forfeited shares
shikken kabu no saihakkō
失権株の再発行

re-issue of shares
kabushiki no saihakkō
株式の再発行

re-issued debenture
saihakkō shasai
再発行社債

re-issued shares
saihakkō kabushiki
再発行株式

REIT (Real-Estate Investment Trust) [US]
fudōsan tōshi shintaku
不動産投資信託

reject
kyozetsu suru
拒絶する

rejection
kyozetsu
拒絶

remargin
tsuika shōkokin
追加証拠金
tsuishō
追証

renew
kakikaeru
書換える

renewal
(rewriting, transfer)
kakikae
書換え

(refinancing, refunding)
karikae
借換え

(updating)
kōshin
更新

renewal bond
karikae saiken
借換債券

renewal of loan
kashidashi no karikae keizoku
貸出の借換継続

renewed bond
kōshinsai
更新債

renewed promissory note
kirikae yakusoku tegata
切替約束手形

repatriation (investment)
hongoku sōkan
本国送還

repay
(settle)
bensai suru
弁済する

(reimburse)
hensai suru
返済する

(redeem)
shōkan suru
償還する

repay a debt
shakkin o hensai suru
借金を返済する

repay a loan
kashidashi o hensai suru
貸出しを返済する

repay a loan in instalments
kappu hensai suru
割賦返済する

repayment
(settlement)
bensai
弁済

(refund)
haraimodoshi
払戻し

(money repaid)
henkin
返金

(reimbursement)
hensai
返済

repayment ability
shiharai nōryoku
支払能力

repayment at maturity
kigen henkin
期限返金

repayment date
hensai kijitsu
返済期日

repayment of debt
shakkin hensai
借金返済

repayment of loan
kashidashi hensai
貸出返済

repayment of principal and interest
ganrikyaku
元利却

repayment period
hensai kigen
返済期限

repayment terms
shiharai jōken
支払条件

repo (repurchase agreement)
kaimodoshi keiyaku
買戻契約

reporting dealer [US]
seifu shōken kōnin diirā
政府証券公認ディーラー

repudiation of debt
shiharai kyozetsu
支払拒絶

repudiation of national debt
kokusai haki
国債破棄

repudiation of public debt
kōsai haki
公債破棄

repurchase (noun)
kaimodoshi
買戻し

(re-acquisition, replacement)
saishutoku
再取得

repurchase (verb)
kaimodosu
買戻す
saishutoku suru
再取得する

repurchase agreement (repo)
kaimodoshi keiyaku
買戻契約

repurchase price
kaimodoshi nedan
買戻値段
saishutoku kakaku
再取得価格

repurchase right
kaimodoshiken
買戻権

repurchased stock
saishutoku kabu
再取得株

repurchaser
kaimodoshinin
買戻人

reputation
sehyō
世評

resale
tenbai
転売
urimodoshi
売戻し

resale before maturity
mankizen urimodoshi
満期前売戻し

rescheduling
saimu hensai kurinobe
債務返済繰延べ

residual shares
senzaiteki kabushiki
潜在的株式

resistance barrier
sōba no teikōsen
相場の抵抗線

restraint
hikishime
引締め
yokusei
抑制

restrictions on stockholdings
mochikabu seigen
持株制限

restrictive lending attitude
kashidashi yokusei taido
貸出抑制態度

restrictive lending policy
kashidashi yokusei seisaku
貸出抑制政策

retail investor
kojin tōshika
個人投資家

retired bond
kaishū shōken
回収証券

retired debt
hensai shakkin
返済借金

**retirement
(recovery, collection)**
kaishū
回収

(redemption)
shōkan
償還

(amortization)
shōkyaku
消却

**return
(profit)**
rieki
利益

(yield)
rimawari
利回り

(earnings, profit)
shūeki
収益

return on capital
shihon shūeki
資本収益

return on investment
tōshi rieki
投資利益
tōshi shūeki
投資収益

Reuter index of commodity prices
roitā shōhin shisū
ロイター商品指数

**revenue
(profit, return)**
shūeki
収益

(income, return)
shūnyū
収入

revenue bond
shūnyū tanposai
収入担保債

reversal
irekae
入替え

reverse split
kabushiki no heigō
株式の併合

revived quotation
fukine
吹き値

revolving credit
kaiten shin'yō
回転信用

**rig the market
(boost)**
kaiaoru
買あおる

(corner, monopolize)
kaishimeru
買占める

**rigger
(booster)**
kaiaorinin
買あおり人

(cornerman, monopolist)
kaishimenin
買占人

**rigging the market
(boosting)**
kaiaori
買あおり

(monopolizing)
kaishime
買占め

right of redemption
shōkan seikyūken
償還請求権

ring
tachiaiba
立会場

rising quotation
agesōba
上げ相場

risk
kiken
危険

risk analysis
kiken bunseki
危険分析

risk assessment
kiken satei
危険査定

risk-averse investment
kiken kaihigata tōshi
危険回避型投資

risk aversion
kiken kaihi
危険回避

risk averter
kiken kaihisha
危険回避者

risk bearer
kiken futansha
危険負担者

risk-bearing
kiken futan
危険負担

risk diversification
kiken bunsan
危険分散

risk diversifier
kiken bunsangata tōshika
危険分散型投資家

risk factor
kiken yōin
危険要因

risk lover
kiken aikōsha
危険愛好者

risk neutral
kiken chūritsusha
危険中立者

risk premium
kiken puremiamu
危険プレミアム

risk-taking
kiken futan
危険負担

riskless
kiken no nai
危険のない

riskless transaction
kiken no nai torihiki
危険のない取引

risky investment
bōkenteki tōshi
冒険的投資

rock bottom
ōzoko
大底

roll-over
korogashi
ころがし

roll-over credit
korogashi kashidashi
ころがし貸出し

roll-over loan
korogashi rōn
ころがしローン

round lot
tan'i kabu
単位株
torihiki tan'i
取引単位

round-trip trade
ōfuku torihiki
往復取引

round-tripping
ōfuku torihiki
往復取引

run (of market)
shikyō no sūsei
市況の趨勢

run-off
torihikijo owarine no insatsu
取引所終わり値の
印刷

running broker
tegata toritsuginin
手形取次人

safe investment
anzen tōshi
安全投資

safety
anzen
安全

safety-oriented
anzen meate no
安全目当ての

safety stock
anzen kabu
安全株

sag
sagaru
下がる

sagging
rakuchō
落調

sagging market
nesagari kehai
値下がり気配
rakuchō shijō
落調市場

sale
(disposal)
baikyaku
売却

(secondary offering of bonds)
uridashi
売出し

sale of bills
tegata uridashi
手形売出し

sale of securities on a commission basis
boshū uridashi
募集売出し

sale of securities on an underwriting basis
hikiuke uridashi
引受売出し

sales contract
baibai keiyaku
売買契約

'samurai' bond [J][16]
endate gaisai[16]
円建外債

Savings and Loan Association [US]
chochiku-kashitsuke kumiai
貯蓄・貸付組合

savings bond [US]
chochiku saiken
貯蓄債券

scale-down buying
kaisagari hōshin no kai
買下方針の買い

scale order
kizami chūmon
刻み注文

scalper [US]
kozayatori
小鞘取り

scalping
hayame rigui
早目利食い
kozaya torihiki
小鞘取引

scandal
fusei jiken
不正事件

screening
shinsa
審査

scrip
karikabuken
仮株券
karishōken
仮証券

scrip issue
mushō shinkabu
無証新株

scrutiny
shinsa
審査

SEAQ (Stock Exchange Automated Quotation System) [UK]
torihikijo no jidōteki sōba seido
取引所の自動的相場制度

seasoned securities
antei shōken
安定証券
kakujitsu shōken
確実証券

seat
kai'inken
会員権

SEC (Securities and Exchange Commission) [US]
shōken torihiki i'inkai
証券取引委員会

Second Section (Tokyo Stock Exchange)[17]
dainibu[17]
第二部

secondary distribution
saiuridashi
再売出し

secondary market
ryūtsū shijō
流通市場

secondary offering
niji bunbai
二次分売
saiuridashi
再売出し

secured advance
tanpotsuki kashitsuke
担保付貸付け

secured basis (for a loan)
tanpotsuki de
担保付きで

secured bill
tanpotsuki tegata
担保付手形

secured bond
tanpotsuki saiken
担保付債券

secured creditor
yūtanpo saikensha
有担保債権者

secured debenture
tanpotsuki shasai
担保付社債

secured debt
tanpotsuki fusai
担保付負債

secured loan (collateral loan)
tanpogashi
担保貸し
tanpotsuki kashidashi
担保付貸出し
tanpotsuki kashitsuke
担保付貸付け

secured note
tanpotsuki yakusoku tegata
担保付約束手形

securities
(yūka) shōken
(有価) 証券

securities account
yūka shōken kanjō
有価証券勘定

securities account
yūka shōken kanjō
有価証券勘定

securities analysis
shōken bunseki
証券分析

securities analyst
shōken bunsekika
証券分析家

Securities and Exchange Commission (SEC) [US]
shōken torihiki i'inkai
証券取引委員会

Securities and Exchange Law [J]
shōken torihikihō
証券取引法

Securities and Investment Board [UK]
shōken oyobi tōshi i'inkai
証券および投資委員会

Securities Association [UK]
shōkengyō kyōkai
証券業協会

securities borrowed
kariire yūka shōken
借入有価証券

securities broker
yūka shōken nakagainin
有価証券仲買人

securities broker-dealer
shōkengyōsha
証券業者

securities business
shōkengyō
証券業

securities dealer
shōken gaisha
証券会社

securities deposited as collateral
tanpo sashiire yūka shōken
担保差入有価証券

securities deposited as guarantee
hoshō sashiire yūka shōken
保証差入有価証券

securities finance corporation [J]
shōken kin'yū gaisha
証券金融会社

securities financing
shōken kin'yū
証券金融

securities holder
shōken shoyūsha
証券所有者

securities holding
hoyū shōken
保有証券

securities house
shōken gaisha
証券会社

(issuing house)
hakkō shōsha
発行商社
shōken hakkōten
証券発行店

securities in trust
azukari shōken
預かり証券

Securities Industry Association [US]
shōkengyō kyōkai
証券業協会

securities investment
shōken tōshi
証券投資

securities invesment trust
shōken tōshi shintaku
証券投資信託

securities loaned
kashitsuke yūka shōken
貸付有価証券

securities management trust
yūka shōken kanri shintaku
有価証券管理信託

securities market
shōken shijō
証券市場

securities portfolio
shōken hoyū
証券保有

securities register
yūka shōken kinyūchō
有価証券記入帳

securities registration statement
yūka shōken todokeidesho
有価証券届出書

securities reserve
yūka shōken junbi
有価証券準備

securities subsidiaries of foreign banks
gaikoku ginkō no shōken kogaisha
外国銀行の証券
子会社

securities transaction
yūka shōken torihiki
有価証券取引

securities transaction tax
yūka shōken torihikizei
有価証券取引税

securities transfer
yūka shōken iten
有価証券移転

securities transfer tax
yūka shōken itenzei
有価証券移転税

securities trust
yūka shōken shintaku
有価証券信託

securities yield
shōken rimawari
証券利回り

securitization
saiken no shōkenka
債権の証券化

securitized paper
saiken shōkenka no shōken
債権証券化の証券

security
(safety)
anzen
安全

(guarantee)
hoshō
保証

(mortgage)
tanpo
担保

(pledge)
teitō
抵当

security, a
(bond, debenture)
saiken
債券

(financial instrument)
shōken
証券

(negotiable security)
yūka shōken
有価証券

security swap
saiken no irekae
債券の入替え

seed money
tōsho tōnyū shikin
当初投入資金

selective buying (securities)
busshokugai
物色買い

selective credit control
sentakuteki shin'yō kisei
選択的信用規制

selective investment
senbetsu tōshi
選別投資

selective lending
senbetsu yūshi
選別融資

Self-Regulating Organizations (SROs) [UK]
jishu kisei kikan
自主規制機関

Self-Regulatory Organizations (SROs) [US]
jishu kisei kikan
自主規制機関

sell at a high price
takaku uru
高く売る

sell at a limit
sashine de uru
指し値で売る

sell at a loss
sonshite uru
損して売る

sell at a profit
mōkete uru
儲けて売る

sell at the best price
takane de uru
高値で売る

sell long
tsuyokiuri suru
強気売りする

sell-off
urikuzushi
売崩し

sell on margin
shin'yō de uru
信用で売る

sell-out
shobun'uri
処分売り

sell program
konpyūtagata uri
コンピュータ型売り

sell short
karauri suru
空売りする

seller
urite
売り手

seller's market
urite shijō
売手市場

seller's option
urite sentaku
売手選択

seller's rate
urisōba
売相場

sellers over
urikata kata
売方過多

selling commission
hanbai tesūryō
販売手数料

selling group
hanbaidan
販売団

selling hedge
uritsunagi
売りつなぎ

selling interest
sage ikō
下げ意向

selling limit
urisashine
売り指し値

selling long
tsuyokiuri
強気売り

selling-off
urikuzushi
売崩し

selling on recovery
modoriuri
戻売り

selling operation
uri ope
売りオペ

selling order
urichūmon
売注文

selling price
urine
売り値

selling short
karauri
空売り

selling syndicate
shōken hakkō hikiuke shinjikēto
証券発行引受けシンジケート

senior issue
jōi no saiken hakkō
上位の債券発行

senior mortgage
yūsen'i teitō
優先位抵当

senior mortgage bond
yūsen'i tanpotsuki shasai
優先位担保付社債

senior securities
yūsen shōken
優先証券

sensitive market
ugoki ga shinkeishitsu na shijō
動きが神経質な市場

(unstable)
fuantei shikyō
不安定市況

sentiment indicators
kehai no shihyō
気配の指標

serial bonds
renzoku shōkan saiken
連続償還債券

serial issue
renzoku shōkan hakkō
連続償還発行

servicing
ribarai
利払い

session (Stock Exchange)
tachiai
立会

setback (market)
gataochi
がた落ち

(pull-back quotations)
hikimodoshi
引戻し

settlement
(repayment)
bensai
弁済
hensai
返済

(payment)
harai
払い

(settlement of account)
kessai
決済

(closing of contract)
seisan
清算

(delivery)
ukewatashi
受渡し

settlement date
kessaibi
決済日

settlement day
seisanbi
清算日
ukewatashibi
受渡日

settlement of debt
saimu bensai
債務弁済

settlement of obligation
saimu bensai
債務弁済

settlement price
kessai kakaku
決済価格

(official price [UK])
kōtei kakaku
公定価格

settlement terms
kessai jōken
決済条件

shake-out
nageuri
投売り

share
kabu(shiki)
株(式)

share account
kabushiki kanjō
株式勘定

share allotment
kabushiki wariate
株式割当て

share allotment letter
kabushiki wariate tsūchi
株式割当通知

share application
kabushiki mōshikomi
株式申込み

share application form
kabushiki mōshikomi yōshi
株式申込用紙

share certificate
kabuken
株券

share certificate transfer
kabuken meigi kakikae
株券名義書換え

share covering
kaimodoshi
買戻し

share dealer
kabushiki torihiki'in
株式取引員

share index
kabuka shisū
株価指数

share indices
kabuka shisū to heikin kabuka
株価指数と平均株価

share issue
(issuing)
kabushiki hakkō
株式発行

(an issue)
kabu meigara
株銘柄

share jobber
kabushiki torihiki'in
株式取引員

share list
kabushiki sōbahyō
株式相場表

share market
kabushiki shijō
株式市場

share ownership
kabushiki hoyū
株式保有

share price
kabuka
株価

share prospectus
kabushiki mokuromisho
株式目論見書

share quotation
kabushiki sōba
株式相場

share repurchase plan
jisha kabushiki kaimodoshi keikaku
自社株式買戻計画

share transfer
kabushiki kakikae
株式書換え

share with par value
gakumen kabu
額面株

share without par value
mugakumen kabu
無額面株

sharebroker
kabushiki nakagainin
株式仲買人

sharebroking
kabushiki nakagaigyō
株式仲買業

shareholder
kabunushi
株主

shareholder's account
kabushiki kanjō
株式勘定

shareholding
mochikabu
持株

shares owned by non-Japanese [J]
gaijin hoyū kabusū
外人保有株数

sharp advance
kyūtō
急騰

sharp break
bōsage
棒下げ
kyūraku
急落

sharp decline
kyūraku
急落

sharp fall (prices)
kyūraku
急落

sharp improvement
kyūtō
急騰

sharp market fluctuation
sōba no gekihen
相場の激変

sharp rise in prices
bōtō
暴騰

sharp setback
kyūhanraku
急反落

shelf registration [US]
(SEC ni taisuru) shōken hakkō no ikkatsu tōroku
(SEC に対する) 証券発行の一括登録

short account
karauri kanjō
空売勘定
tanki mikoshi uri
短期見越売り

short bond
tanki saiken
短期債券

short coupon
tanki risatsu
短期利札

short covering [US]
kaiume
買埋め
karauri no kaimodoshi
空売りの買戻し

short credit
tanki shin'yō(gashi)
短期信用(貸し)

short hedge
urihejji
売りヘッジ
uritsunagi
売りつなぎ

short interest
karauri sōgaku
空売り総額

short loan
tanki kashitsuke
短期貸付け

short market
sagesōba
下げ相場
yowaki shikyō
弱気市況

short money
tanki kariire
短期借入れ

short-money market
tanki kin'yū shijō
短期金融市場

short position
karauri sōdaka
空売り総高
urimochi
売持ち

short purchase
(karauri no) kaimodoshi
(空売りの) 買戻し

short sale
karauri
空売り

short sellers
karaurisuji
空売筋

short-term bill
tanki tegata
短期手形

short-term bond
tanki saiken
短期債券

short-term borrowing
tanki kariire
短期借入れ

short-term capital
tanki shihon
短期資本

short-term capital market
tanki shihon shijō
短期資本市場

short-term credit
tanki shin'yō
短期信用
tanshi
短資

short-term credit broker
tanshi gyōsha
短資業者

short-term credit market
tanki kin'yū shijō
短期金融市場

short-term debenture
tanki shasai
短期社債

short-term debt
tanki fusai
短期負債

short-term financing
tanki yūshi
短期融資

short-term government bond
tanki kokusai
短期国債

short-term government securities
seifu tanki shōken
政府短期証券
tanki kokusai
短期国債

short-term interest rate
tanki kinri
短期金利
tanki rishiritsu
短期利子率

short-term investment
tanki tōshi
短期投資

short-term loan
tanki kashitsuke
短期貸付け

short-term loan market
tanki kashitsuke shijō
短期貸付市場

short-term money market
tanki kin'yū shijō
短期金融市場

short-term money rate
tanki kinri
短期金利

short-term public bond
tanki kōsai
短期公債

short-term securities
tanki shōken
短期証券

short-term yield
tanki rimawari
短期利回り

shorts
(government bonds [UK])
tanki kokusai
短期国債

(bears)
yowaki suji
弱気筋

sight note
ichiranbarai yakusoku
tegata
一覧払約束手形

simple debenture
mutanpo shasai
無担保社債

simple interest
tanri
単利

simple option
tanjun tokkentsuki baibai
単純特権付売買

sinking fund
gensai kikin
源債基金

skip-day [US]
yokuyokujitsu kessai
翌々日決済

sky-rocket
kyūtō suru
急騰する

sky-rocketing
kyūtō
急騰

slack market
kanman na shikyō
緩慢な市況

slight advance
shōtō
小騰

slight decline
shōraku
小落

slight recovery of the market
komodoshi
小戻し

slight steadying of the market
kojikkari shōjō
小じっかり商状

sluggish market
donchō shikyō
鈍調市況
nanjaku shikyō
軟弱市況

slump
bōraku
暴落
gataochi
がた落ち

small bond [US]
shōgaku saiken
少額債券

small government bond
shōgaku kokusai
少額国債

small investor
koguchi tōshika
小口投資家

small loan
koguchi yūshi
小口融資

small loan company [US]
koguchi kin'yū gaisha
小口金融会社

small-lot sale
koguchiuri
小口売り

small-lot traders
koguchisuji
小口筋

small shareholder
kokabunushi
小株主

small stock
kogata kabu
小型株

small stockholder
kokabunushi
小株主

soaring market
kōtō shikyō
高騰市況

soft dollars [US]
sofuto-doru (tesūryō)
ソフト・ドル(手数料)

soft loan
sofuto-rōn
ソフト・ローン

soft market
nanchō shikyō
軟調市況

soiled certificate
osen shōken
汚染証券

sold-out
uriichijun
売一巡

sound financing
kenjitsu yūshi
堅実融資

sound investment
kenzen tōshi
健全投資

sound investor
kenzen tōshika
健全投資家

special loan
tokushu kashitsuke
特殊貸付け

special offering [US]
tokubetsu uridashi
特別売出し

specialist
[J][18]
saitori[18]
才取り

[US]
supesharisuto
スペシャリスト

specialist block purchase [US]
supesharisuto ga okonau
ōguchi no kaitsuke
スペシャリストが
行なう大口の買付け

specialist block sale [US]
supesharisuto ga okonau
ōguchi no uritsuke
スペシャリストが
行なう大口の売付け

specified issue
tokutei meigara
特定銘柄

speculate
omowaku o suru
思惑をする
tōki suru
投機する

speculation
omowaku
思惑
tōki
投機

speculation on the stock market
kabushiki tōki
株式投機

speculative boom
tōkiteki būmu
投機的ブーム

speculative buyers
omowakugaisuji
思惑買い筋

speculative buying
omowakugai
思惑買い

(on anticipation)
mikoshigai
見越買い

speculative gain
tōki rijun
投機利潤

speculative interest
kaininki
買人気
omowakugai ninki
思惑買人気

speculative interests
omowakusuji
思惑筋

speculative investment
omowaku tōshi
思惑投資

speculative market
omowaku shikyō
思惑市況
tōki shijō
投機市場

speculative mood
omowaku kibun
思惑気分

speculative operation
omowaku torihiki
思惑取引
tōki torihiki
投機取引

speculative profit
tōkiteki rijun
投機的利潤

speculative purchase
omowakugai
思惑買い

speculative sale
omowaku'uri
思惑売り

speculative selling
omowaku'uri
思惑売り
tōki uri
投機売り

speculative shares
shite kabu
仕手株
tōki kabu
投機株

speculative stock
shite kabu
仕手株
tōki kabu
投機株

speculative trading
omowaku torihiki
思惑取引
tōkiteki torihiki
投機的取引

(on anticipation)
mikoshi akinai
見越商い

speculative transaction
omowaku torihiki
思惑取引
tōkiteki torihiki
投機的取引

speculator(s)
tōkika
投機家
omowakushi
思惑師

(speculative interests)
omowakusuji
思惑筋

[J]
sōbashi
相場師

(professionals)
tōkisuji
投機筋

spilling stock
nagemono
投げ物

split
kabushiki bunkatsu
株式分割

split order
bunkatsu chūmon
分割注文

split quotation
bunkatsu sōba
分割相場

split rating
bunkatsu kakuzuke
分割格付け

split sale
bunkatsu uri
分割売り

sponsor
kōensha
後援者
shiensha
支援者

sponsorship
kōen
後援
shien
支援

spot
genbutsu
現物

spot broker
genbutsu nakagainin
現物仲買人

spot commodity
genbutsu
現物
jikimono
直物

spot contract
genbutsu sokuji watashi
yakujō
現物即時渡約定

spot dealers
jitsukabu suji
実株筋

spot delivery
genbutsu watashi
現物渡し

spot market
genbutsu shijō
現物市場

spot price
genbutsu kakaku
現物価格

spot rate
genbutsu sōba
現物相場

spot share
genkabu
現株
jitsukabu
実株

spot transaction
genbutsu torihiki
現物取引
jitsubutsu torihiki
実物取引

spotty market
mura no aru shijō
むらのある市場

spread
(double option, straddle)
fukugō sentakukentsuki
torihiki
複合選択権付取引
ryōdate
両建て

(difference between prices)
hiraki
開き
nebiraki
値開き

(price range, price fluctuations)
nehaba
値幅

(interest margin)
rizaya
利鞘

(of interest rates)
supureddo
スプレッド

squeeze
kin'yū hikishime
金融引締め

SROs (Self-Regulating Organizations) [UK]
jishu kisei kikan
自主規制機関

SROs (Self-Regulatory Organizations) [US]
jishu kisei kikan
自主規制機関

stable market
antei shikyō
安定市況

stag
shitesuji
仕手筋

stagnant market
nanchō shikyō
軟調市況

Standard and Poor's Index [US]
sutandādo-pua kabuka
shisū
スタンダード・プア
株価指数

standard rate of interest
hyōjun kinri
標準金利

standard stock
hyōjun kabu
標準株

standard yield
hyōjun rimawari
標準利回り

standby credit
sutandobai-kurejitto
スタンドバイ・クレ
ジット

standstill (market)
ashibumi
足踏み

state bond
kokusai
国債

status
shisan jōtai
資産状態

status enquiry
shisan chōsa
資産調査

steady market
kenchō na shikyō
堅調な市況

Sterling bond
eikabarai shōken
英貨払い証券

stock
(shares [UK] [US])
kabu(shiki)
株(式)

(fixed-interest security [UK])
kakuteiritsuki shōken
確定利付証券

stock account
kabushiki kanjō
株式勘定

stock acquisition
kabushiki shutoku
株式取得

stock arbitrage
kabushiki saitei torihiki
株式裁定取引

stock at par
gakumen kabu
額面株

stock certificate
kabuken
株券

stock certificate transfer
kabuken meigi kakikae
株券名義書換え

stock clearing
kabushiki seisan
株式清算

stock company
kabushiki gaisha
株式会社

stock corporation
kabushiki gaisha
株式会社

stock dealings
kabushiki torihikidaka
株式取引高

stock discount
kabushiki waribiki
株式割引

Stock Exchange
(shares)
kabushiki torihikijo
株式取引所

(securities)
shōken torihikijo
証券取引所

Stock Exchange Automated Quotation System (SEAQ) [UK]
torihikijo no jidōteki sōba seido
取引所の自動的相場制度

Stock Exchange clearing house
kabushiki seisanjo
株式清算所

Stock Exchange Daily Official List [UK]
kabushiki torihikijo kōhō
株式取引所公報

Stock Exchange holiday
kabushiki torihikijo kyūjitsu
株式取引所休日

Stock Exchange listing requirements
kabushiki torihikijo kijun
株式取引所基準

Stock Exchange member
kabushiki torihikijo kai'in
株式取引所会員

Stock Exchange panic
kabushiki kyōkō
株式恐慌

Stock Exchange placement [UK]
kabushiki torihikijo kōkai
株式取引所公開

Stock Exchange placing [US]
kabushiki torihikijo kōkai
株式取引所公開

Stock Exchange regulations
kabushiki torihikijo kisoku
株式取引所規則

stock index
kabuka shisū
株価指数

stock index future
kabuka shisū sakimono
株価指数先物

stock indexes and averages
kabuka shisū to heikin kabuka
株価指数と平均株価

stock investment
kabushiki tōshi
株式投資

stock investment trust [J]
kabushiki tōshi shintaku
株式投資信託

stock issue
(an issue)
kabu meigara
株銘柄

(issuing)
kabushiki hakkō
株式発行

stock jobber [UK]
kabuya
株屋

stock jobbing
kabushiki baibai(gyō)
株式売買(業)

stock list
(shares)
kabushiki sōbahyō
株式相場表

(securities)
kehaijō
気配状

stock loan
kashikabu
貸株

stock loan market
kashikabu shijō
貸株市場

stock manipulation
kabuka sōsa
株価操作
kabushiki sōsa
株式操作

stock market
kabushiki shijō
株式市場

stock market crash
kabushiki shijō no hōkai
株式市場の崩壊

stock market quotations
kabushiki sōba
株式相場

stock option
kabushiki kaitori sentakuken
株式買取選択権

stock owner
kabushiki shoyūsha
株式所有者

stock ownership
kabushiki shoyū
株式所有

stock portfolio
yūka shōken meisaisho
有価証券明細書

stock price
kabuka
株価

stock price average
kabuka heikin
株価平均

stock price index
kabuka shisū
株価指数

stock price movements
kabuka sui'i
株価推移

stock purchase right
shinkabu hikiukeken
新株引受権

stock purchase warrant
shinkabu hikiukeken
shōsho
新株引受権証書

**stock purchased on the
market**
shijō keiyu kabushiki
市場経由株式

stock quotation
kabushiki sōba
株式相場

stock rating
kabushiki no kakuzuke
株式の格付け

stock receipt
kabuken jōtoshō
株券譲渡証

stock record book
kabushiki daichō
株式台帳

stock record date
kabushiki meigi kakikae
teishibi
株式名義書換停止日

stock redemption
kabushiki shōkan
株式償還

stock register
kabunushi meibo
株主名簿

stock repurchase
jisha kabu kaimodoshi
自社株買戻し

stock right
kabushiki hikiukeken
株式引受権

stock split [US]
kabushiki bunkatsu
株式分割

stock subscription
kabushiki mōshikomi
株式申込み
kabushiki ōbo
株式応募

stock transfer
kabushiki jōto
株式譲渡
kabushiki meigi kakikae
株式名義書換え

stock transfer form
kabushiki meigi kakikae
yōshi
株式名義書換用紙

stock transfer register
kabushiki meigi kakikae
kinyūbo
株式名義書換記入簿

stock turnover
kabushiki kaitenritsu
株式回転率

stock with par value
gakumen kabu
額面株

stock without par value
mugakumen kabu
無額面株

stock yield
kabushiki rimawari
株式利回り

stockbroker [UK]
kabushiki nakagainin
株式仲買人

stockbroking
kabushiki nakagaigyō
株式仲買業

stockholder
kabunushi
株主

stockholding
kabushiki hoyū
株式保有

**stockholding limit for foreign
investors [J]**
gaijin mochikabu seigen
外人持株制限

stockholding ratio
kabushiki hoyūritsu
株式保有率

**stockholding ratio of
foreigners [J]**
gaijin mochikabu hiritsu
外人持株比率

stop-limit order
sashine chūmon
指し値注文

stop loss
gyaku sashine
逆指し値

stop-loss order
gyaku sashine chūmon
逆指し値注文

stop-loss selling
iyakenage
嫌気投げ

stop order
gyaku sashine chūmon
逆指し値注文

stop price
gyaku nedan
逆値段

straddle
fukugō sentakukentsuki torihiki
複合選択権付取引
ryōdate
両建て

straight bond
futsū shasai
普通社債

straight climb
bōage
棒上げ

straight fall
bōsage
棒下げ

strategic investment
senryakuteki tōshi
戦略的投資

street price
hikego sōba
引け後相場

strike price
kenri kōshi kakaku
権利行使価格

stringency
hippaku
逼迫

stringent market
hippaku shikyō
逼迫市況

strong market
tsuyoki shikyō
強気市況

strong shareholder
antei kabunushi
安定株主
anzen kabunushi
安全株主

strong tone
tsuyofukumi
強含み

structure of interest rates
kinri kōzō
金利構造

subordinated bond
retsugo shasai
劣後社債

subordinated debt
retsugo saimu
劣後債務

subscribe
(for shares)
(kabushiki o) hikiukeru
(株式を) 引受ける
(kabushiki o) mōshikomu
(株式を) 申込む
(kabushiki o) ōbo suru
(株式を) 応募する

(for a loan)
(saiken ni) ōzuru
(債券に) 応ずる

subscribed shares
hikiukezumi kabushiki
引受済株式

subscriber
(share applicant)
(kabushiki) hikiukenin
(株式) 引受人
(kabushiki) mōshikomisha
(株式) 申込者
(kabushiki) ōbosha
(株式) 応募者

(capital investor)
shusshisha
出資者

subscription
(offer to sell, placement [US], placing [UK])
boshū
募集

(application)
mōshikomi
申込み
ōbo
応募

(capital investment)
shusshi
出資

subscription certificate
shusshi shōsho
出資証書

subscription form
mōshikomi yōshi
申込用紙

subscription list
kabushiki mōshikomi ichiranhyō
株式申込一覧表

subscription money
mōshikomikin
申込金

subscription price
ōbo kakaku
応募価格

subscription right
shinkabu hikiukeken
新株引受権

subscription to government securities
kokusai ōbo
国債応募

subscription to securities
shōken ōbo
証券応募

subscription warrant
shinkabu hikiukeken shōsho
新株引受権証書

subsidiary collateral
fukutanpo
副担保

substitution (collateral)
tanpo no sashikae
担保の差替え

sub-underwriter
shita hikiuke gaisha
下引受会社

sub-underwriting
shita hikiuke
下引受け

supply of necessary funds
hitsuyō shikin no kyōkyū
必要資金の供給

support
(help)
enjo
援助

(backing)
kōen
後援

(maintenance)
shiji
支持

support level
shiji suijun
支持水準

supporting the market
bōsengai
防戦買い

surrender of shares
kabushiki no bosshū
株式の没収
kabushiki no shikken
株式の失権

surrendered shares
shikken kabu
失権株

suspended trading
tachiai teishi
立会停止

suspension of interest payment
ribarai teishi
利払停止

suspension of transactions
torihiki teishi
取引停止

swap
suwappu
スワップ

(securities)
(saiken no) irekae
(債券の)入替え

(interest rate)
(kinri no) kōkan
(金利の)交換

swap transaction
irekae torihiki
入替取引
kōkan torihiki
交換取引
suwappu torihiki
スワップ取引

switching
tōshi shintakukan furikae
投資信託間振替え

syndicate
(underwriting group)
hikiukedan
引受団

(consortium)
shakkandan
借款団
shinjikēto
シンジケート

(financing group)
kyōchō yūshidan
協調融資団
kyōyūdan
協融団

syndicate contract
shinjikēto keiyaku
シンジケート契約

syndicated credit
kyōchō yūshi
協調融資

syndicated loan
shinjikēto-rōn
シンジケート・
ローン

syndication
kokusai kyōchō yūshi
国際協調融資

systematic risk
shijō kakaku hendō risuku
市場価格変動リスク

T-bill (Treasury Bill) [US]
zaimushō shōken
財務省証券

take-over (noun)
(acquisition, buy-out)
baishū
買収

(acquisition, purchase)
kaitori
買取り

(of a company)
nottori
乗っ取り

take over (verb)
(buy out)
baishū suru
買収する

(acquire, purchase)
kaitoru
買取る

(a company)
nottoru
乗っ取る

take-over bid
kabushiki kōkai kaitsuke
株式公開買付け

taking delivery
ukewatashi o ukeru koto
受渡を受けること

tap stock [UK]
tappu hakkō
タップ発行

target price
(securities)
baibai kakaku
売買価格

(take-over)
baishū kakaku
買収価格

tax-exempt bond
menzeisai
免税債

tax-exempt securities
menzei shōken
免税証券

tax-free investment
menzei tōshi
免税投資

tax havens
zeikin hinanchi
税金避難地

tax shelters
zeikin hinan shudan
税金避難手段

taxable income
kazei shotoku
課税所得

technical analysis
shijō naibu yōin bunseki
市場内部要因分析

technical factor
shijō naibu yōin
市場内部要因

technical rally
ayamodoshi
あや戻し

technical reaction
ayaoshi
あや押し

technician
keisen'ya
ケイ線屋

temporary advance
ichiji tatekae
一時立替え

temporary borrowing
ichiji kariirekin
一時借入金

temporary investment
ichiji tōshi
一時投資

temporary lending
ichiji kashitsuke
一時貸付け

temporary loan
ichiji kashitsukekin
一時貸付金

tender
(take-over bid)
kabushiki kōkai kaitsuke
株式公開買付け

(bid)
nyūsatsu
入札

tender offer [US]
kabushiki kōkai kaitsuke
株式公開買付け

term
(time limit, repayment period)
kigen
期限

(period)
kikan
期間

(fixed term)
teiki
定期

term bond
teiki shasai
定期社債

term loan
kigentsuki kashidashi
期限付貸出し

term of loan
taishaku kigen
貸借期限

term of payment
shiharai kigen
支払期限

terms and conditions of loan
kashitsuke jōken
貸付条件

terms of loan flotation
bosai jōken
募債条件

terms of transaction
baibai jōken
売買条件

thin market
kansan na shikyō
閑散な市況

third market
kabushiki daisan shijō
株式第三市場

thrifts [US]
chochiku kin'yū kikan
貯蓄金融機関

tick (noun)
shōken kakaku kizami
証券価格きざみ

ticker
kabushiki sōba hyōjiki
株式相場表示機

ticker tape
kabushiki sōba hyōtēpu
株式相場表テープ

tied loan
himotsuki yūshi
ひもつき融資

tight market
hippaku shikyō
逼迫市況

tight money
kin'yū hikishime
金融引締め

tight-money policy
kin'yū hikishime seisaku
金融引締政策

tightening (of market)
hippaku
逼迫

tightening of monetary restraint
hikishime seisaku kyōka
引締政策強化

time loan
teiki kashitsuke
定期貸付け

time value
jikanteki kachi
時間的価値

tip
(information)
jōhō
情報

(leak)
riiku
リーク

Tokyo Stock Exchange
tōkyō shōken torihikijo
東京証券取引所

Tokyo Stock Exchange stock price average index
tōshō kabuka heikin shisū
東証株価平均指数

tombstone
boseki kōkoku
墓石広告

tone (of market) (atmosphere, sentiment)
fukumi
含み

(mood)
kehai
気配

(conditions, movements, position)
shikyō
市況

total return
sōrimawari
総利回り
sōshūeki
総収益

trade investment
eigyō tōshi
営業投資

trade on one's own account
tebari
手張り

trader (securities)
shōkengyōsha
証券業者

trading (business)
akinai
商い

(buying and selling)
baibai
売買

(transaction)
torihiki
取引

trading account
baibai kanjō
売買勘定

trading day
torihikibi
取引日

trading floor
tachiaiba
立会場

trading limit
mochidaka gendo
持高限度

trading pattern
keikōsen
傾向線

trading pit
tachiaiba
立会場

trading post
tachiai posuto
立会ポスト

trading range
takane-yasune no haba
高値・安値の幅

trading ring
tachiaiba
立会場

trading unit
torihiki tan'i
取引単位

trading volume
kabushiki torihikidaka
株式取引高

tranche
hakkōbun
発行分

transaction
torihiki
取引

transaction fee
torihiki tesūryō
取引手数料

transaction on dealers' basis
shikiri baibai
仕切売買

transaction on the exchange
shōken torihikijo no torihiki
証券取引所の取引

transfer (assign)
jōto suru
譲渡する

transfer (assignment)
jōto
譲渡

(renewal)
kakikae
書換え

(name transfer)
meigi kakikae
名義書換え

transfer agent [US]
meigi kakikae dairinin
名義書換代理人

transfer book
meigi kakikae daichō
名義書換台帳

transfer book closed
meigi kakikae teishi
名義書換停止

transfer book open
meigi kakikae kaishi
名義書換開始

transfer day
meigi kakikaebi
名義書換日

transfer fee
jōtoryō
譲渡料
meigi kakikaeryō
名義書換料

transfer of securities
yūka shōken no jōto
有価証券の譲渡

transfer of share certificate
kabuken meigi kakikae
株券名義書換え

transfer order
jōto sashizusho
譲渡指図書

transferable
(assignable)
jōtokanō
譲渡可能

(marketable, negotiable)
ryūtsūsei no aru
流通性のある

transferee
yuzuriukenin
譲受人

transferor
jōtonin
譲渡人

Treasury bill
[UK]
ōkurashō shōken
大蔵省証券

[US] (= T-bill)
zaimushō shōken
財務省証券

Treasury bill rate
ōkurashō shōken kinri
大蔵省証券金利

Treasury bills issued
ōkurashō shōken hakkō-daka
大蔵省証券発行高

Treasury bond [US]
kokko saiken
国庫債券

trend (of market)
ashidori
足取り
keikō
傾向

trend analysis
keikō bunseki
傾向分析

trend line
keikōsen
傾向線

trust
shintaku
信託

trust account
shintaku kanjō
信託勘定

trust agreement
shintaku keiyaku
信託契約

trust business
shintakugyō
信託業

trust deed [US]
shintaku keiyakusho
信託契約書
shintaku shōsho
信託証書

trustee
hishintakusha
被信託者
jutakusha
受託者

(custodian, keeper)
hokannin
保管人

turn
jōnai nakagainin no rizaya
場内仲買人の利鞘

two-generation loan
oyako rōn
親子ローン

type of loan
kashidashi hōhō
貸出方法

uncertainty (market)
kimayoi ninki
気迷い人気

unclaimed bond
mikōfu shōken
未交付証券

unclaimed share
museikyū kabu
無請求株
shikken kabu
失権株

unclaimed share certificate
museikyū kabuken
無請求株券

unclaimed stock
museikyū kabu
無請求株
shikken kabu
失権株

unclaimed stock certificate
museikyū kabuken
無請求株券

uncollectible loan
kogetsuki yūshi
こげつき融資

unconditional call loan
mujōken mono kōru-rōn
無条件ものコール・
ローン

unconditional debt
mujōken saimu
無条件債務

unconditional loan
mujōkengashi
無条件貸し

unconditionally guaranteed loan
mujōken hoshō kashitsuke
無条件保証貸付け

unconditionals
mujōken mono
無条件物

undated securities [UK]
shōkan kijitsutsukinai shōken
償還期日付ない証券

underinvestment
kashō tōshi
過少投資

undersubscribed
boshū kashō no
募集過少の
mōshikomi kashō no
申込過少の

undersubscription
kashō boshū
過少募集
kashō mōshikomi
過少申込み

undertone
ba'aji
場味

underwrite
hikiukeru
引受ける

underwriter(s)
hikiuke gyōsha
引受業者

underwriting
hikiuke
引受け

underwriting agreement
hikiuke keiyaku
引受契約

underwriting business
hikiuke gyōmu
引受業務

underwriting by the Bank of Japan
nichigin hikiuke
日銀引受け

underwriting commission
hikiuke tesūryō
引受手数料

underwriting company
hikiuke gaisha
引受会社

underwriting contract
hikiuke keiyaku
引受契約

underwriting group
hikiukedan
引受団

underwriting of government securities
kokusai hikiuke
国債引受け

underwriting syndicate
hikiukedan
引受団

undigested securities
mishōka shōken
未消化証券

undigested stock
urenokori
売れ残り

unearned interest
mikeika rishi
未経過利子

unemployed capital
yūkyū shihon
遊休資本
yūshi
遊資

uneven market
haran shijō
波乱市場

unfunded public debt
ryūdō kōsai
流動公債

uninscribed bond
mukimei shōken
無記名証券

uninscribed share
mukimei kabu
無記名株

uninscribed share certificate
mukimei kabuken
無記名株券

uninscribed stock
mukimei kabu
無記名株

uninscribed stock certificate
mukimei kabuken
無記名株券

unit trust [UK]
yunittogata tōshi shintaku
ユニット型投資信託

unlisted
hijōjō no
非上場の

unlisted company
hijōjō gaisha
非上場会社

unlisted securities
hijōjō shōken
非上場証券

unlisted securities market [US]
tentō shijō
店頭市場

unlisted shares
hijōjō kabushiki
非上場株式

unlisted stock
hijōjō kabushiki
非上場株式

unload (securities)
tairyō shobun suru
大量処分する

unloading
tairyō shobun
大量処分

unpaid debt
miharai saimu
未払債務

unpaid interest
miharai rishi
未払利子

unpaid note
fuwatari yakusoku tegata
不渡約束手形

unproductive capital
hiseisanteki tōshi
非生産的投資

unquoted companies
hijōjō gaisha
非上場会社

unregistered bond (public)
mukimei kōsai
無記名公債

(corporate)
mukimei shasai
無記名社債

unregistered certificate
mukimei kabuken
無記名株券

unregistered debenture
mukimei shasaiken
無記名社債券

unregistered note
mukimei yakusoku tegata
無記名約束手形

unsecured
mutanpo no
無担保の

unsecured advance
mutanpo kashitsuke
無担保貸付け

unsecured bill
shin'yō tegata
信用手形

unsecured bond
(public)
mutanpo kōsai
無担保公債

(general)
mutanpo saiken
無担保債券

(corporate)
mutanpo shasai
無担保社債

unsecured credit
shin'yōgashi
信用貸し

unsecured creditor
mutanpo saikensha
無担保債権者

unsecured debenture
mutanpo shasai
無担保社債

unsecured discount bill
mutanpo waribiki tegata
無担保割引手形

unsecured loan
mutanpo kashidashi
無担保貸出し
mutanpo kashitsuke
無担保貸付け
mutanpogashi
無担保貸し

unsecured note
mutanpo shasaiken
無担保社債券

unsettled market
kimayoi shikyō
気迷い市況

unsound finance
fukenzen zaisei
不健全財政

unsound investment
fukenzen tōshi
不健全投資

untied loan
fukōsoku yūshi
不拘束融資

unused balance (of loan)
gendo yoyūgaku
限度余裕額

upward tendency
sōba no uwamuki
相場の上向き

upward trend
ageashi
上げ足

US dollar bond
beitsūka kōsai
米通貨公債

usurer
bōriya
暴利屋
kōrigashi
高利貸し

usurious interest
bōri
暴利
kōri
高利

usurious loan
kōri no kashitsuke
高利の貸付け

usurious rate of interest
kōriritsu
高利率

usury
kōri
高利

valuation of assets
shisan hyōka
資産評価

valueless stock
kachi no nai kabu
価値のない株

variable interest rate
hendō riritsu
変動利率

variable rate bond
fukakuteiritsukisai
不確定利付債
hendōritsukisai
変動利付債

variable rate securities
fukakuteiritsuki shōken
不確定利付証券
hendōritsukisai
変動利付債

variable-rate mortgage loan
hendō kinrigata jūtaku
kashitsuke
変動金利型住宅
貸付け

voided bond
shikkō shōken
失効証券

volatile market
kimagure shikyō
気紛れ市況

volatility
kakaku hendōritsu
価格変動率

volume (of trading)
baibaidaka
売買高
torihikidaka
取引高

waiting period
fusakui kikan
不作為期間

waiver of obligation
saimu menjo
債務免除

wallflower
ninki ga nakunakatta kabu
人気がなくなった
株

war bond
gunji kōsai
軍事公債

warehouse receipt
(commodities)
azukari shōken
預かり証券
sōko shōken
倉庫証券

warehousing
sōko hoyū
倉庫保有

warrant
(subscription right)
kabushiki kaitoriken shōsho
株式買取権証書

(share warrant)
shusshi shōken
出資証券

warrant bond
kabushiki kaitoriken shasai
株式買取権社債

wash
nareai torihiki
なれ合い取引

wash sale [US]
nareai baibai
なれ合い売買

watch list
yōkeikai meigara
要警戒銘柄

watched stock
chūmoku kabu
注目株

weak market
yowaki shikyō
弱気市況

weak shareholder
fudō kabunushi
浮動株主

weak stockholder
fudō kabunushi
浮動株主

weak tone
nanchō
軟調

weakening market
rakuchō
落調

'when issued' transaction
hakkōbi torihiki
発行日取引

'when issued' transaction loan
hakkōbi torihiki kashitsuke
発行日取引貸付け

wide margin
ōzaya
大鞘

wide share ownership
kabushiki hoyū bunsan
株式保有分散

widow-and-orphan stock
antei haitō kabu
安定配当株
shisan kabu
資産株

wild fluctuation (market)
rankōge
乱高下

window
madoguchi
窓口

window guidance [J]19
madoguchi shidō19
窓口指導

wire house
burōkā gyōsha
ブローカー業者

with warrant
kenritsuki
権利付き

without-par-value shares
mugakumen kabu
無額面株

without-par-value stock
mugakumen kabu
無額面株

world financial centre
sekai no kin'yū chūshinchi
世界の金融中心地

world market
kokusai shijō
国際市場

world market commodities
kokusai shōhin
国際商品

write-off (loan)
chōkeshi
帳消し

Yankee bond [US]
beikoku de hakkō beidoru gaisai
米国で発行米ドル外債

yearly interest rate
nenri
年利

yen-based financing
enbēsu kin'yū
円ベース金融

yen-based investment
enbēsu tōshi
円ベース投資

yen credit
enshakkan
円借款

yen-denominated bond
endatesai
円建債

yen-denominated securities
enbarai shōken
円払証券

yield
rimawari
利回り

yield gap
rimawari kakusa
利回り較差

yield on investment
un'yō rimawari
運用利回り

yield rate
rimawariritsu
利回り率

yield spread
rimawari kakusa
利回り較差

yield to maturity
manki rimawari
満期利回り
saishū rimawari
最終利回り

yield to subscribers
ōbosha rimawari
応募者利回り

zero-coupon bond
zero-kūponsai
ゼロ・クーポン債

Notes

10. credit association (shin'yō kinko 信用金庫): Japanese banking institution offering credit facilities to small businesses.

11. credit co-operative (shin'yō kyōdō kumiai 信用協同組合): similar to the 'credit association' described in note 10, but serving very small businesses.

12. credit union (shin'yō kumiai 信用組合): similar to the 'credit association' described above in note 10, but serving very small businesses.

13. First Section (dai'ichibu 第一部): section of the Tokyo Stock Exchange that deals in prime securities (see also note 17).

14. 'gensaki' market (gensaki shijō 現先市場): bond market run by Japanese securities houses in the secondary market with a repurchase agreement, competing with bank-run markets that deal in certificates of deposits and call money.

15. impact loan (inpakuto-rōn インパクト・ローン): loan issued in a foreign currency by an authorized foreign exchange bank.

16. 'samurai' bond (endate gaisai 円建外債): yen-denominated bond issued in Japan by foreign issuing houses.

17. Second Section (dainibu 第二部): section of the Tokyo Stock Exchange which is concerned with lower-rated securities (see also note 13).

18. specialist (saitori 才取り): intermediary dealing only between members of the Stock Exchange. Unlike the New York Exchange specialist, he is not allowed to buy or sell on his own account.

19. window guidance (madoguchi shidō 窓口指導): informal guidelines issued by the Bank of Japan with regard to bank lending policies.

absentee landlord
fuzai jinushi
不在地主

absentee landowner
fuzai jinushi
不在地主

absentee owner
fuzai shoyūsha
不在所有者

absentee ownership
fuzai shoyūken
不在所有権

absentee system
fuzai shoyūsei
不在所有制

abstract of title
kenri shōmei yōkakusho
権利証明要約書

accommodation
jūtaku
住宅

accommodation information (in newspaper)
jūtaku jōhō
住宅情報

accrued rent
miharai chinshakuryō
未払賃借料
mishū kachin
未収家賃

acquisition of property
zaisan no shutoku
財産の取得

acquisition of real estate
fudōsan shutoku
不動産取得

acreage allotment [UK]
sakuzuke wariate
作付割当て

adjustable rate mortgage [US]
hendō kinrigata jūtaku
kashitsuke
変動金利型住宅
貸付け

administration of an estate
isan kanri
遺産管理

administrator of an estate
isan kanrinin
遺産管理人

administrator of property
zaisan kanrinin
財産管理人

agency
(fudōsan) dairinin
(不動産) 代理人
fudōsan'ya
不動産屋

agent
(fudōsan) dairinin
(不動産) 代理人

agent commission
(fudōsan) dairinin tesūryō
(不動産) 代理人
手数料

agent fee
(fudōsan) dairinin tesūryō
(不動産) 代理人
手数料

agreement (contract)
keiyaku
契約

agricultural land
nōchi
農地

air-conditioned
reibō sōchi no
冷房装置の

air conditioning
reibō sōchi
冷房装置

alien property
gaikokujin zaisan
外国人財産

alienation of property
zaisan no jōto
財産の譲渡

allotment [UK]
sakuzuke wariate
作付割当て

alterations
kaichiku
改築

amenities
kaitekisa
快適さ

apartment [US]
apāto
アパート

apartment complex
apāto danchi
アパート団地

apartment house
apāto jūtaku
アパート住宅

apartment owner
apāto shoyūsha
アパート所有者

**appliances
(fixtures and fittings)**
bihin
備品

(utensils)
kigu
器具

(gadgets)
shikake
仕掛け

appraisal [US]
hyōka
評価

appraisal of real estate
fudōsan hyōka
不動産評価

appraised value
hyōka kakaku
評価価格

**appraiser
(valuer)**
hyōkanin
評価人

(expert)
kanteinin
鑑定人

appreciate
zōka suru
増価する

appreciation
zōka
増価

arable land
kōchi
耕地

architect
kenchiku gishi
建築技師
kenchikuka
建築家

architectural design
kenchiku sekkei
建築設計

architectural style
kenchiku yōshiki
建築様式

architecture
kenchiku
建築

area
chi'iki
地域

area development
chi'iki kaihatsu
地域開発

area redevelopment
chi'iki saikaihatsu
地域再開発

area rehabilitation
chi'iki fukkō
地域復興

area survey
chi'iki chōsa
地域調査

**area within commuting
distance**
tsūkinkanō ku'iki
通勤可能区域

asking price
kibō baikyaku kakaku
希望売却価格

assessed valuation
hyōka kachi
評価価値

assessed value of land
kōtei chika
公定地価

assessment
hyōka
評価

association
kumiai
組合

attachment of property
zaisan no sashiosae
財産の差押さえ

auction (noun)
kyōbai
競売
seriuri
競り売り

auction (verb)
kyōbai ni dasu
競売に出す
kyōbai ni suru
競売にする

auction broker
kyōbainin
競売人

auction company
seriuri gaisha
競り売り会社

auction house
kyōbaijō
競売場

auction notice
kyōbai tsūchi
競売通知

auction price
kyōbai kakaku
競売価格

auction procedure
kyōbai tetsuzuki
競売手続き

auction room
kyōbaijō
競売場

auction sale
kyōbai
競売

auctioneer (noun)
kyōbainin
競売人

auctioneer (verb)
kyōbai suru
競売する

auctioneer's commission
kyōbai tesūryō
競売手数料

**back rent
(land)**
tainō chidai
滞納地代
(house)
tainō yachin
滞納家賃

bailiff
shikkōri
執行吏

behind with one's rent
yachin ga todokotte iru
家賃が滞っている

bid at auction
kyōraku
競落

bidder at auction
kyōrakunin
競落人

blanket mortgage
sōkatsu teitō
総括抵当

block [US]
kukaku
区画

board and room
shukuhakuryō
宿泊料

boarder
shukuhakunin
宿泊人

borough [UK]
jichi toshi
自治都市

breach of contract
keiyaku ihan
契約違反

build
kenchiku suru
建築する
kizuku
築く

builder
kenchiku gyōsha
建築業者
kenchikusha
建築者

building
kenchiku
建築
kensetsu
建設

building, a
biru
ビル
kenchikubutsu
建築物
tatemono
建物

building and fixtures
tatemono oyobi fuzoku setsubi
建物および付属設備

Building and Loan Association [US]
kenchiku shikin kin'yū kumiai
建築資金金融組合

building appreciation
tatemono zōka
建物増価

building area
kenchiku menseki
建築面積

building association [US]
jūtaku kumiai
住宅組合

building company
kenchiku gaisha
建築会社

building construction
kenchiku kōzō
建築構造

building contract
kenchiku ukeoi
建築請負

building contractor
kenchiku ukeoigyōsha
建築請負業者
kenchiku ukeoinin
建築請負人

building cost
kenchikuhi
建築費

building land
takuchi
宅地

building law
kenchiku hōki
建築法規

building lot
kenchikuyōchi
建築用地

building maintenance expenses
tatemono ijihi
建物維持費

building materials
kenchiku zairyō
建築材料

building permit
kenchiku kyoka
建築許可

building regulation
kenchiku tōsei
建築統制

building repair expenses
tatemono shūrihi
建物修理費

building repairs
tatemono shūri
建物修理

building site
kenchiku shikichi
建築敷地

building society [UK]
jūtaku kin'yū kikan
住宅金融機関

building tax
kenchikuzei
建築税

building under construction
kenchikuchū no tatemono
建築中の建物

buy
kau
買う

buyer
kainushi
買主
kaite
買手

buying offer
kaimōshikomi
買申込み

buying price
kaine
買値

cancellation of contract
keiyaku hōki
契約放棄

cash purchase
genkin kōnyū
現金購入

cash transaction
genkin torihiki
現金取引

central heating (apparatus)
chūō danbō sōchi
中央暖房装置

(system)
chūō danbōhō
中央暖房法

chattel
dōsan
動産

chattel mortgage
dōsan teitō
動産抵当

cheap land
yasui yōchi
安い用地

city land price
shigaichi kakaku
市街地価格

client
kokyaku
顧客

closed mortgage
heisashiki teitō
閉鎖式抵当

coal
sekitan
石炭

coal supply
kyūtan
給炭

collective ownership
kyōdō shoyū(ken)
共同所有(権)

collective responsibility
shūdan sekinin
集団責任
shūgō sekinin
集合責任

commission sale
tesūryō baibai
手数料売買

common expenses
kyōdō hiyō
共同費用

common ownership
kyōyū(ken)
共有(権)

common property
kyōyū zaisan
共有財産

community
kyōdōtai
共同体

community property (husband and wife's)
fūfu kyōyū zaisan
夫婦共有財産

commute
tsūkin suru
通勤する

commuter
tsūkinsha
通勤者

commuting
tsūkin
通勤

conditions of tenure
hoyū shoken
保有諸権

construct
kensetsu suru
建設する
kizuku
築く

construction
kenchiku
建築
kensetsu
建設

construction, a
kenchikubutsu
建築物
kensetsubutsu
建設物

construction company
kenchiku gaisha
建築会社
kensetsu gaisha
建設会社

construction contract
kensetsu keiyaku
建設契約

construction cost
kenchikuhi
建築費
kensetsuhi
建設費

construction work
kenchiku kōji
建築工事

contract (noun)
keiyaku
契約

contract (verb)
keiyaku suru
契約する

contract date
keiyaku hizuke
契約日付け

contract period
keiyaku kigen
契約期限

contracting parties
keiyaku tōjisha
契約当事者

contractor
dokengyōsha
土建業者

conventional mortgage loan
tsūjōgata fudōsan kashidashi
通常型不動産貸出し

conversion
kaichiku
改築

conveyance
zaisan jōto
財産譲渡

conveyance of estate
zaisan jōto
財産譲渡

conveyancer
fudōsan jōto toriatsukainin
不動産譲渡取扱人

conveyancing (business)
fudōsan jōto gyōmu
不動産譲渡業務

(procedure)
fudōsan jōto tetsuzuki
不動産譲渡手続き

co-owner
kyōdō shoyūsha
共同所有者

co-ownership
kyōdō shoyūken
共同所有権

corporate estate
hōjin zaisan
法人財産

corporate property
hōjin zaisan
法人財産

cottage
inakaya
田舎家

covenant
keiyaku jōkō
契約条項
natsuin shōsho keiyaku
捺印証書契約

crown land (imperial estate) [J]
goryōchi
御料地

cultivated land
kōchi
耕地

current market value
genzai shijō kakaku
現在市場価格

current value
genzai kachi
現在価値

damp
shikke/shikki
湿気

deed
natsuin shōsho
捺印証書
shōsho
証書

deed of conveyance
jōto shōsho
譲渡証書

deed of sale
baikyaku shōsho
売却証書

deed of title
  (land)
chiken
地権

  (real estate)
fudōsan kenri shōsho
不動産権利証書

deed of trust
shintaku shōsho
信託証書

default (noun)
furikō
不履行

  (breach of contract)
iyaku
違約

default (verb)
fumitaosu
踏倒す

default risk
furikō kiken
不履行危険

defaulter
furikōsha
不履行者
iyakusha
違約者

defective work
shisonji sagyō
仕損じ作業

degradation
akka
悪化

deposit (key money)
shikikin
敷金
tetsukekin
手付金

depreciation
genka
減価

depreciation of land
tochi genka
土地減価

depressed area
teitai chi'iki
停滞地域

detached house
jibun no ie
自分の家

deterioration
akka
悪化

develop
kaihatsu suru
開発する

developed area
kikaihatsu chi'iki
既開発地域

developer
kaihatsu gyōsha
開発業者

development
kaihatsu
開発

development area
kaihatsu chi'iki
開発地域

development company
chi'iki kaihatsu gaisha
地域開発会社

development project
kaihatsu keikaku
開発計画

dilapidation (run-down state)
kōhai
荒廃

dispose of one's possessions
zaisan o shobun suru
財産を処分する

disposition of one's estate
fudōsan no jōto
不動産の譲渡

document(s)
  (note, letter)
bunsho
文書

  (papers)
shorui
書類

  (deed, certificate)
shōsho
証書

documentation
bunsho tenpu
文書添付

domain (private)
tochi shoyūken
土地所有権

domicile
jūsho
住所

draw (a deed)
(shōsho o) sakusei suru
(証書を) 作成する

draw up (a contract)
(keiyaku o) teiketsu suru
(契約を) 締結する

drawing (of a deed)
sakusei
作成

drawing up (of a contract)
teiketsu
締結

dry rot
kansō fukyū
乾燥腐朽

dwelling
(residence, address)
jūkyo
住居

(accommodation, residence)
jūtaku
住宅

eagerness to buy
kōbai iyoku
購買意欲

eagerness to sell
baikyaku iyoku
売却意欲

earnings from property
fudōsan shūnyū
不動産収入

electrical appliances
denki kigu
電気器具

electricity
denki
電気

electricity charges
denki ryōkin
電気料金
denryokuhi
電力費

electricity company
denryoku gaisha
電力会社

electricity rates
denki ryōkin
電気料金

electricity supply
kyūden
給電

elevator [US]
erebētā
エレベーター

escheat
(real estate)
fudōsan fukkiken
不動産復帰権

(land)
tochi fukkiken
土地復帰権

estate
(land)
chisho
地所

(real estate)
fudōsan
不動産

estate agent [UK]
fudōsangyōsha
不動産業者

(houses-for-rent finding agency)
kashiya shūsengyō
貸家周旋業

estate contract
fudōsan keiyaku
不動産契約

estate development
shikichi kaihatsu
敷地開発

estate duty
isanzei
遺産税

estate income
isan shotoku
遺産所得

estate planning
shisan keikaku
資産計画

estate tax
(inheritance tax)
isanzei
遺産税

(succession tax) (= death duty [UK])
sōzokuzei
相続税

estimate
mitsumori
見積り

estimated value
santei kakaku
算定価格

evaluate
hyōka suru
評価する

evaluation
hyōka
評価

evict
oitateru
追立てる

eviction
oitate
追立て
tachinoki
立退き

eviction order
tachinoki meirei
立退命令

exclusive residential area
sen'yō jūtaku chi'iki
専用住宅地域

execute (contracts, deeds) (complete)
kansei suru
完成する

(draw)
sakusei suru
作成する

execution of sales contract
baibai keiyaku kansei
売買契約完成

exorbitant prices
futō kakaku
不当価格
hōgai na nedan
法外な値段

expectation of inheritance
sōzoku kitai
相続期待

expiration date
mankijitsu
満期日

expiration of a contract
keiyaku manki
契約満期

expire
kireru
切れる

expired contract
manki keiyaku
満期契約

exploitation of land
tochi kaihatsu
土地開発

expropriation
(land)
(tochi no) shūyō
(土地の) 収用

(repossession)
(shoyūken no) toriage
(所有権の) 取上げ

extension of contract
keiyaku enchō
契約延長

facilities
setsubi
設備

factory site
(land for industrial
development)
kōjō kensetsuyōchi
工場建設用地

(industrial area)
kōjō shikichi
工場敷地

family estate
katoku
家督

farming land
kōchi
耕地
nōchi
農地

fiduciary estate
shintaku zaisan
信託財産

final price
saishū kakaku
最終価格

fire-proof building
taika kenchikubutsu
耐火建築物

first mortgage
dai'ichi teitō
第一抵当
ichiban teitō
一番抵当

first-time buyer
hajimete no kainushi
初めての買主

fixed-rate mortgage loan
kotei kinrigata jūtaku
kashitsuke
固定金利型住宅貸付け

fixtures and fittings
bihin
備品
kagu jūki
家具什器

flat [UK]
apāto
アパート

flat owner
apāto shoyūsha
アパート所有者

flat-sit (verb)
apāto o mamoru
アパートを守る

flexible-rate mortgage loan
hendō kinrigata jūtaku
kashitsuke
変動金利型住宅貸付け

floor space
tatetsubo
建坪

for-rent sign
kashiya fuda
貸家札

for-sale sign
uriya fuda
売家札

forced repossession
kyōsei toriage
強制取上げ

forced sale
kōbai
公売

foreclosure
teitō nagare
抵当流れ
teitōken shikkō
抵当権執行
ukemodoshiken sōshitsu
受戻権喪失

foreclosure sale
teitō nagare kōbai
抵当流れ公売

freehold
jiyū hoyūken
自由保有権

freehold land
shoyūchi
所有地

freehold landlord
(tochi shoyūsei no) jinushi
(土地所有制の) 地主

freeholder
(tochi shoyūsei no) jinushi
(土地所有制の) 地主

furnished house
kagutsuke kashiya
家具付貸家

furnished house to let
zōsakutsuki kashiya
造作付貸家

furnishings
bihin
備品

furniture
kagu
家具

garden
niwa
庭

garden city
den'en toshi
田園都市

gas
gasu
ガス

gas company (public) [J]
gasu kōsha
ガス公社

gas range
gasu-renji
ガス・レンジ

general mortgage
sōkatsu teitō
総括抵当

grant
hojokin
補助金

grazing land
bokusōchi
牧草地

green belt
ryokuchitai
緑地帯

ground rent [UK]
shakuchiryō
借地料

habitat
(residence)
jūsho
住所

(home)
seisokuchi
生息地

(centres of population)
shūraku
集落

habitation
jūsho
住所
jūtaku
住宅

have one's property repossessed
shoyūchi o toriagerareru
所有地を取上げられる

heating
danbō
暖房

heating apparatus
danbō sōchi
暖房装置

heating system
danbōhō
暖房法

heir
sōzokunin
相続人

heir to property
zaisan sōzokunin
財産相続人

heirship
sōzokuken
相続権

hereditary property
seshū zaisan
世襲財産

high density area
kōmitsudo chi'iki
高密度地域

high mortgage rates
kōkinri jūtaku kashitsuke
高金利住宅貸付け

high-rise apartment house
kōsō jūtaku
高層住宅

high-rise building
kōsō kenchiku
高層建築

hired house
kariya
借家

home
(one's own home)
jika
自家

(a house, dwelling, residence)
jūkyo
住居

(one's abode)
jūsho
住所

(accommodation, housing)
jūtaku
住宅

(household)
katei
家庭

home address
jūshō
住所

home loan
jūtaku kashitsuke
住宅貸付け

home owner
jika shoyūsha
自家所有者

home ownership
jitaku shoyū
自宅所有

home purchase loan
jūtaku kashitsuke
住宅貸付け

house
ie
家

(accommodation, housing)
jūtaku
住宅

(a building)
kaoku
家屋

house agent
kaoku shūsennin
家屋周旋人

house broker
kaoku shūsennin
家屋周旋人

house for rent
kashiya
貸家

house for sale
uriya
売家

house furnishings
katei yōhin
家庭用品

house-hunting
kashiya sagashi
貸家捜し

house maintenance
kaoku iji
家屋維持

house maintenance expenses
kaoku ijihi
家屋維持費

house owner
yanushi
家主

house owners' association
kashiya kumiai
貸家組合

house rent
shakuryō
借料
yachin
家賃

house repair expenses
kaoku shūzenhi
家屋修繕費

house repairs
kaoku shūzen
家屋修繕

house running expenses
kaoku kanrihi
家屋管理費

house-sit (verb)
ie o mamoru
家を守る

house tax
kaokuzei
家屋税

house to let
kashiya
貸家

household
katei
家庭
kazoku
家族

household appliances
katei yōgu
家庭用具

household effects
kazai
家財

household expenses
kakeihi
家計費

householder
kaoku shoyūsha
家屋所有者

housing
jūtaku
住宅

housing complex
danchi
団地

housing construction
jūtaku kensetsu
住宅建設

housing development
jūtaku haihatsu
住宅開発

housing estate
danchi
団地

housing land
takuchi
宅地

housing loan
jūtaku kashitsuke
住宅貸付け

Housing Loan Corporation [J]
jūtaku kin'yū kōko
住宅金融公庫

housing market
jūtaku shijō
住宅市場

housing project
danchi keikaku
団地計画

housing shortage
jūtakunan
住宅難

housing standards
kyojū suijun
居住水準

housing units
ikkodate jūtaku
一戸建住宅

hypothec [UK]
fudōsan teitō
不動産抵当
teitōken
抵当権

hypothecation [US]
fudōsan teitō
不動産抵当
teitōken
抵当権

idle land
asonde iru tochi
遊んでいる土地

idle properties
yūkyū jūtaku
遊休住宅

immovable property
fudōsan
不動産

improvements
kairyō
改良

income from property
zaisan shotoku
財産所得

income from real estate
fudōsan shotoku
不動産所得

increase in value
zōka
増価

increased value
zōka kachi
増価価値

individual house owner
jika shoyūsha
自家所有者

individual property
kojin zaisan
個人財産

industrial area
kōgyō chi'iki
工業地域

industrial complex
kōgyō danchi
工業団地

industrial district
kōgyō chitai
工業地帯

industrial site
kōjō kensetsuyōchi
工場建設用地
kōjō shikichi
工場敷地

industrial zone
kōgyō chitai
工業地帯

industrialized area
sangyō chi'iki
産業地域

industrialized urban area
sangyō toshi chi'iki
産業都市地域

inflated value of land
chika no bōtō
地価の暴騰

inhabitant(s)
(resident population)
jūmin
住民

(dwellers, residents)
jūnin
住人

inhabitant's tax
jūminzei
住民税

inherit
sōzoku suru
相続する
tsugu
継ぐ

inheritance
(property left, legacy)
isan
遺産

(succession)
sōzoku
相続

inheritance of family estate
katoku sōzoku
家督相続

inheritance of property
isan
遺産
zaisan sōzoku
財産相続

inheritance property
sōzoku zaisan
相続財産

inheritance tax [UK]
isan shutokuzei
遺産取得税
sōzokuzei
相続税

inherited property
sōzoku zaisan
相続財産

inspection
kensa
検査

inspector
kensa'in
検査員

intestate estate
muyuigon zaisan
無遺言財産

invalid contract
mukō no keiyaku
無効の契約

inventory
zaisan mokuroku
財産目録

investment in real estate
fudōsan tōshi
不動産投資

itemized bill
kōmokubetsu kanjōsho
項目別勘定書

joint estate
kyōyū zaisan
共有財産

joint heirs
kyōdō sōzokunin
共同相続人

joint mortgage
kyōdō tanpo
共同担保

joint owner
kyōyūsha
共有者

joint ownership
kyōyūken
共有権

joint property
kyōyū zaisan
共有財産

joint purchase
kyōdō kōnyū
共同購入

junior mortgage
kōjun'i teitō
後順位抵当

key money [US]
shikikin
敷金
tetsukekin
手付金

knock down
torikowasu
取りこわす

land
tochi
土地

land acquisition
tochi shutoku
土地取得

land acquisition price
tochi shutoku kakaku
土地取得価格

land agency
(administrators,
managers)
tochi kanrinin
土地管理人

(commission agency)
tochi shūsengyō
土地周旋業

land agent
tochi shūsengyōsha
土地周旋業者

land allotment sale
bunjōchi
分譲地

land and building(s)
tochi oyobi tatemono
土地および建物

land appreciation
tochi zōka
土地増価

land broker
tochi burōkā
土地ブローカー

land classification
tochi kubun
土地区分

land developer
tochi kaihatsu gyōsha
土地開発業者

land development
tochi kaihatsu
土地開発

land expropriation
tochi shūyō
土地収用

land for rent
kashichi
貸地

land for sale
hanbaiyō tochi
販売用土地

land for sale in lots
bunjōchi
分譲地

land grant [US]
tochi haraisage
土地払下げ

land improvement
tochi kairyō
土地改良

land laws
tochi shoyūhō
土地所有法

land lease
tochi chintaiken
土地賃貸権

land leaseholder
shakuchinin
借地任

land management
tochi kanri
土地管理

land ownership
tochi shoyū(ken)
土地所有(権)

land price
chika
地価
tochi kakaku
土地価格

land productivity
tochi seisansei
土地生産性

land proprietor
jinushi
地主

land rate [UK]
chiso
地租

land re-allocation
tochi kukaku seiri
土地区画整理

land reclamation
tochi zōsei
土地造成

(farm land)
nōchi zōsei
農地造成

land reclamation for housing
development
takuchi zōsei
宅地造成

land register
tochi daichō
土地台帳

land registration
tochi tōki
土地登記

land registry
tochi tōkisho
土地登記所

land rent
chidai
地代

land rental revenue
tochi chingariryō
土地賃借料

land revenue
tochi shūeki
土地収益

land-saving
tochi setsuyakuteki
土地節約的

land settlement
tochi settei
土地設定

land steward
chisho kanrinin
地所管理人

land system
tochi seido
土地制度

land tax
chiso
地租

land tenancy
tochi shakuyō
土地借用

land tenant
tochi hoyūsha
土地保有者

land tenure
tochi hoyū(ken)
土地保有(権)

land to let
kashichi
貸地

land transaction
tochi torihiki
土地取引

land transfer
tochi shoyūken iten
土地所有権移転

land use
tochi riyō
土地利用

land-using
tochi shiyōteki
土地使用的

land utilization
tochi riyō
土地利用

land valuation system
chika kōji seido
地価公示制度

land value
chika
地価
tochi kakaku
土地価格

landed class
jinushi kaikyū
地主階級

landed estate
tochi fudōsan
土地不動産

landed interest
(landowners' class)
jinushi kaikyū
地主階級

(landowners)
jinushitachi
地主たち

landed property
chisho
地所
shoyūchi
所有地

landed proprietor
tochi shoyūsha
土地所有者

landholder
tochi shoyūsha
土地所有者

landholding
tochi shoyū
土地所有

landlady
(land owner)
jinushi
地主
tochi shoyūsha
土地所有者

(of rented property)
kashinushi
貸主

landlord
(land owner)
jinushi
地主
tochi shoyūsha
土地所有者

(of rented property)
kashinushi
貸主

landlord's agent
sahainin
差配人

landlord's liability
jinushi sekinin
地主責任

landlords' association
kashiya kumiai
貸家組合

landowner
jinushi
地主
tochi shoyūsha
土地所有者

large landowner
daijinushi
大地主

lease (noun)
(let)
chingashi
賃貸し

(leasehold)
shakuchiken
借地権

lease (verb)
(to hold)
chingari suru
賃借りする

(to let)
chingashi suru
賃貸しする

leasehold
(leased land)
chinshakuchi
賃借地

(right of lease)
chinshakuken
賃借権

(a lease)
shakuchiken
借地権

(fixed-period lease)
teiki chinshakuken
定期賃借権

leasehold ground rent
shakuchidai
借地代

leasehold land
kariirechi
借入地
shakuchi
借地

leasehold property
chinshaku fudōsan
賃借不動産

leaseholder
(lessee)
chinshakunin
賃借人

(tenant)
shakuchinin
借地人

leaseholding
teiki shakuchi
定期借地

leave a deposit (on a house)
(ie ni) tetsukekin o utsu
(家に) 手付金を打つ

legacy
isan
遺産

legal expenses
bengoshi hiyō
弁護士費用

lessee
(leaseholder)
chinshakunin
賃借人

(tenant)
karinushi
借主

(land leaseholder)
shakuchinin
借地人

(house leaseholder)
shakuyanin
借家人

lessor
(land lessor)
kashichinin
貸地人

(landlady, landlord)
kashinushi
貸主

(house lessor)
kashiyanin
貸家人

let (verb)
kasu
貸す

let a house
ie o kasu
家を貸す

let a room
kashima o kasu
貸間を貸す

letting
chingashi
賃貸し

life lease
(real estate)
shūshin fudōsanken
終身不動産権

(land)
shūshin shakuchiken
終身借地権

life tenant
(real estate)
shūshin fudōsankensha
終身不動産権者

(land)
shūshin shakuchinin
終身借地人

living in rented accommodation
kashiyazumai
貸家住まい

local rates [UK]
chihōzei
地方税

local tax
(area)
chihōzei
地方税

(inhabitant's tax)
jūminzei
住民税

location
(area, place, spot)
basho
場所

(site)
ichi
位置

location (of property)
shozaichi
所在地

lodger
(room-mate, paying guest)
dōkyonin
同居人

(room tenant)
magarinin
間借人

(boarder)
shukuhakunin
宿泊人

lodgings
shukuhakujo
宿泊所

long lease
chōki chingashi keiyaku
長期賃貸契約
chōki shakuchi keiyaku
長期借地契約

look after a house
ie o mamoru
家を守る

look for a house to rent
kashiya o sagasu
貸家を捜す

loss on sale of property
zaisan baikyakuson
財産売却損

loss on sale of real estate
fudōsan baikyakuson
不動産売却損

lowering of price
kakaku hikisage
価格引下げ

maintenance
iji
維持

maintenance charges
ijihi
維持費

maintenance cost
ijihi
維持費

maintenance expenses
ijihi
維持費

make an offer
tsukene suru
付け値する

marginal land (unproductive land)
fumōchi
不毛地

material property
yūkei zaisan
有形財産

means
shiryoku
資力

(assets)
shisan
資産

(property)
zaisan
財産

means test
shiryoku chōsa
資力調査
shisan chōsa
資産調査

model apartment
moderu-apāto
モデル・アパート

model building
moderu-biru
モデル・ビル

moderate price
kakuyasu nedan
格安値段
renka
廉価

modernization
kindaika
近代化

modest house
shisso na jūkyo
質素な住居

mortgage
mōgejji
モーゲッジ

(real estate purchase
loan)
fudōsan kashitsuke
不動産貸付け

(hypothec [UK],
hypothecation [US])
fudōsan teitō
不動産抵当
teitōken
抵当権

(house purchase loan)
jūtaku kashitsuke
住宅貸付け

mortgage agreement
mōgejji keiyaku
モーゲッジ契約

mortgage bank
teitō ginkō
抵当銀行

mortgage business
jūtaku kin'yūgyō
住宅金融業

mortgage clause
teitōkensha tokuyaku jōkō
抵当権者特約条項

mortgage company
fudōsan kin'yū gaisha
不動産金融会社
jūtaku kin'yū gaisha
住宅金融会社
mōgejji gaisha
モーゲッジ会社

mortgage credit
jūtaku kin'yū
住宅金融

mortgage creditor
teitōkensha
抵当権者

mortgage debt
fudōsan teitō fusai
不動産抵当負債

mortgage debtor
teitōken setteisha
抵当権設定者

mortgage documents
teitōshō shorui
抵当証書類

mortgage finance
fudōsan kin'yū
不動産金融

mortgage holder
teitōken setteisha
抵当権設定者

mortgage insurance
teitō hoken
抵当保険

mortgage lender
teitōkensha
抵当権者

mortgage loan
fudōsan kashitsuke
不動産貸付け
jūtaku (shikin) kashitsuke
住宅(資金)貸付け
mōgejji kashitsuke
モーゲッジ貸付け

mortgage on land and
buildings (company's)
tochi-tatemono teitō shasai
土地・建物抵当社債

mortgage protection
insurance
teitō shikin hoken
抵当資金保険

mortgage rate
mōgejji kashitsuke kinri
モーゲッジ貸付金利

mortgage repayment
mōgejji kashitsuke hensai
モーゲッジ貸付返済

mortgage sale
teitōbutsu baikyaku
抵当物売却

mortgage settlement
teitōken settei
抵当権設定

mortgagee
teitō saikensha
抵当債権者
teitōkensha
抵当権者

mortgager
teitōken setteisha
抵当権設定者

move (change residence)
sumikaeru
住替える

municipal tax
(residential tax)
jūminzei
住民税

(cities, towns, villages) [J]
shichōsonzei
市町村税

(city tax)
shizei
市税

national property
kokuyū zaisan
国有財産

neglect (noun)
mushi
無視

negotiation
(bargaining)
kōshō
交渉

(business talks)
shōdan
商談

neighbourhood
kinjo
近所

(vicinity)
fukin
付近

non-fulfilment of contract
keiyaku furikō
契約不履行

non-resident landlord
fuzai jinushi
不在地主

non-resident landowner
fuzai jinushi
不在地主

non-taxable exchange of
property
hikazei no shūyōkōkanchi
非課税の収用交換地

non-taxable property
menzei zaisan
免税財産

non-visible property
mukei zaisan
無形財産

notice of sale
baikyaku tsūchi
売却通知

nuisance
kōan bōgai
公安妨害

occupancy
(residence, habitation)
kyojū
居住

(exclusive possession)
sen'yū
占有

occupant
sen'yūsha
占有者

occupier
(resident, inhabitant)
kyojūsha
居住者

(resident with exclusive
possession right)
sen'yūsha
占有者

occupy
(reside)
kyojū suru
居住する

(have exclusive
possession)
sen'yū suru
占有する

offer to buy
kaimōshikomi
買申込み

offer for sale (verb)
uri ni dasu
売りに出す

offered price
tsukene
付値

one-family house
nokidate no ie
軒建ての家

open land
kūkanchi
空閑地

open mortgage
ichibu teitō
一部抵当

overvalue
kadai hyōka suru
過大評価する

overvalued
kadai hyōka no
過大評価の

overvaluation
kadai hyōka
過大評価

own house
mochiie
持家

owner
shoyūsha
所有者

(proprietor)
mochinushi
持主

owner-occupied home
jika
自家
mochiie
持家

owner of a house
yanushi
家主

ownership
shoyūken
所有権

part-owner
kyōyūsha
共有者

parties to a contract
keiyaku tōjisha
契約当事者

parties to a sale
baibai tōjisha
売買当事者

patrimony
seshū zaisan
世襲財産

period of contract
keiyaku kigen
契約期限

period of lease
shakuyō kikan
借用期間

period of tenancy
shakuyō kikan
借用期間

perpetual lease
eitai shakuchiken
永代借地権

personal assets (movables)
dōsan
動産

personal effects
shojihin
所持品
temawarihin
手回品

personal estate
dōsan
動産

personal income from property
kojin fudōsan shotoku
個人不動産所得

personal property
dōsan
動産
jinteki zaisan
人的財産
kojin zaisan
個人財産

personal property tax
kojin dōsanzei
動産動産税

personal rental income
kojin chintairyō shotoku
個人賃貸料所得

planning
keikaku
計画

planning agreement
keikaku kyōtei
計画協定

planning authorities
keikaku kikan
計画機関
keikaku tōkyoku
計画当局

planning permission
keikaku kyoka
計画許可

planning permit
keikaku kyokashō
計画許可証

plant site
kōjō ritchi
工場立地

plot
kukaku shita tochi
区画した土地

poll tax
jintōzei
人頭税

**possession
(occupancy)**
sen'yū
占有

(ownership)
shoyū
所有

possession of property
shisan no shoyū
資産の所有

possession right
sen'yūken
占有権

possessions
shoyūbutsu
所有物
zaisan
財産

possessor
shoyūsha
所有者

potential buyer
senzaiteki kainushi
潜在的買主

potential seller
senzaiteki urite
潜在的売手

prefabricated house
purehabu jūtaku
プレハブ住宅

present address
genjūsho
現住所

present domicile
genjūsho
現住所

present occupier
genjūsha
現住者

present residence
genjūsho
現住所

present value
genzai kakaku
現在価格

**price
(cost, value)**
kakaku
価格

(a figure, a price)
nedan
値段

price cut
kakaku kirisage
価格切下げ

price increase
kakaku hikiage
価格引上げ

prior lien on property
zaisan senshuken
財産先取権

private housing
minkan jūtaku
民間住宅

private property
shiyū zaisan
私有財産

private transaction
minkan torihiki
民間取引

proceeds from sale
uriage kingaku
売上金額

profit from real estate
fudōsan shūeki
不動産収益

profit on disposal of property
dōsan shobun'eki
動産処分益

profit on disposal of real estate
fudōsan shobun'eki
不動産処分益

profit on sale of property
zaisan baikyakueki
財産売却益

profit on sale of real estate
fudōsan baikyakueki
不動産売却益

property
(chattel, movables)
dōsan
動産

(real estate)
fudōsan
不動産

(premises, domicile)
kataku
家宅

(assets)
shisan
資産

(landed property)
shoyūchi
所有地

(estate, fortune)
zaisan
財産

property, a
(a house)
kaoku
家屋

(a possession)
shoyūbutsu
所有物

(land)
tochi
土地

property developer
takuchi kaihatsu gyōsha
宅地開発業者

property in land
tochi no shoyūken
土地の所有権

property inventory
zaisan mokuroku
財産目録

property man
zaisanka
財産家

property management
zaisan kanri
財産管理

property market
fudōsan shijō
不動産市場

property owner
(land)
jinushi
地主

(house)
yanushi
家主

property prices
fudōsan kakaku
不動産価格

property rights
zaisanken
財産権

property tax
zaisanzei
財産税

property valuation
zaisan hyōka
財産評価

proprietary
shoyūken no
所有権の

proprietary rights
shoyūken
所有権

proprietor
shoyūsha
所有者

prospective buyer
mikomi kaite
見込み買手

provisions of lease
chintaishaku kitei
賃貸借規定

public auction
kōbai
公売

public land
kōyūchi
公有地

public property
kōkyō zaisan
公共財産

publicly-owned land
kōkyō shoyūchi
公共所有地

pull down (a house)
(ie o) torikowasu
(家を)取りこわす

purchase (acquisition)
shutoku
取得

purchase price
kaine
買値

purchaser
kainushi
買主
kaite
買手

quality housing
jūtaku no shitsu
住宅の質

quality of environment
kankyō no shitsu
環境の質

rateable value
kazei mitsumori kakaku
課税見積価格

ratepayer
chihōzei nōzeisha
地方税納税者

rates
sozei
租税

[UK]
chihōzei
地方税

(inhabitant's tax)
jūminzei
住民税

real estate
fudōsan
不動産

real-estate acquisition
fudōsan shutoku
不動産取得

real-estate agent
fudōsan dairinin
不動産代理人
fudōsangyōsha
不動産業者

real estate and properties
shoyū dōsan fudōsan
所有動産不動産

real-estate appraiser
fudōsan kanteishi
不動産鑑定士

real-estate broker
fudōsan burōkā
不動産ブローカー

real-estate business
fudōsangyō
不動産業

real-estate credit
fudōsan teitō shin'yō
不動産抵当信用

real-estate development
fudōsan kaihatsu
不動産開発

real estate in trust
fudōsan shintaku
不動産信託

real-estate income
fudōsan shotoku
不動産所得

real-estate investment
fudōsan tōshi
不動産投資

Real Estate Investment Trust (REIT) [US]
fudōsan tōshi shintaku
不動産投資信託

real-estate loan
fudōsan kashitsuke
不動産貸付け

real-estate management
fudōsan kanri
不動産管理

real-estate mortgage
fudōsan teitō
不動産抵当

real-estate mortgage loan
fudōsan teitō kashitsuke
不動産抵当貸付け

real-estate speculation
fudōsan tōki
不動産投機

real-estate tax
fudōsanzei
不動産税

real-estate trust
fudōsan shintaku
不動産信託

real estate under offer
hanbaiyō fudōsan
販売用不動産

realtor [US]
fudōsangyōsha
不動産業者

realtor's office
fudōsan'ya
不動産屋

realty [US]
fudōsan
不動産

realty business
fudōsangyō
不動産業

realty company
fudōsan gaisha
不動産会社

rebuild
kizukinaosu
築直す

reclaimed land
tsukiji
築地

reconstruction
kaichiku
改築

reconstruction work
kaichiku kōji
改築工事

redevelopment
saikaihatsu
再開発

redevelopment company
saikaihatsu gaisha
再開発会社

refundable deposit
haraimodoshikanō na shikikin
払戻可能な敷金
haraimodoshikanō na tetsukekin
払戻可能な手付金

REIT (Real Estate Investment Trust) [US]
fudōsan tōshi shintaku
不動産投資信託

reject an offer
teikyō o shazetsu suru
提供を謝絶する

renewal of contract
keiyaku kōshin
契約更新

rent (noun)
(house, land)
chinshakuryō
賃借料

(house)
yachin
家賃

rent (verb)
kariru
借りる

rent control
yachin tōsei
家賃統制

rent day
yachin shiharaibi
家賃支払日

rent-free
yachin nashi no
家賃なしの

rent-free apartment
yachin tada no apāto
家賃ただのアパート

rent in advance
maebarai yachin
前払家賃

rent in arrears
entai yachin
延滞家賃
yachin no todokōri
家賃の滞り

rent in kind
jitsubutsu chidai
実物地代

rent income
yachin shotoku
家賃所得

rent increase
yachin hikiage
家賃引上げ

rent of land and building(s)
tochi tatemono chinshaku-ryō
土地建物賃借料

rent payable
miharai yachin
未払家賃
miharai chinshakuryō
未払賃借料

rent payment
chinshakuryō shiharai
賃借料支払い
yachin shiharai
家賃支払い

rent receipt
chinshakuryō juryō
賃借料受領
yachin juryō
家賃受領

rent strike
yachin fubarai dōmei
家賃不払同盟
yachin fubarai undō
家賃不払運動

rental income
yachin shotoku
家賃所得

rental market value
yachin sōba
家賃相場

rented house
shakuya
借家

rented room
karima
借間

renting
chingari
賃借り

renting a room
magari
間借り

renting regulations
yachin kisei
家賃規制

renting tenant
chingarinin
賃借人

repair (verb)
(alter, reconstruct)
kaichiku suru
改築する

(rebuild)
kizukinaosu
築直す

(make individual repairs)
shūri suru
修理する

(recondition)
shūzen suru
修繕する

repair and maintenance
shūzen-iji
修繕・維持

repair and maintenance expenses
shūzen-ijihi
修繕・維持費

repair and modernization
jūtaku shūri kindaika
住宅修理近代化

repair expenses
shūzenhi
修繕費

repair work
shūri kōji
修理工事

repairman
shūzenkō
修繕工

repairs
shūri
修理

repossess
toriageru
取上げる

repossessed property
toriage kaoku
取上家屋

repossession
toriage
取上げ

repossession proceedings
toriage tetsuzuki
取上手続き

(legal proceedings for vacation of property)
akewatashi seikyū soshō
明渡請求訴訟

residence, a
(dwelling, address, house)
jūkyo
住居

(domicile, one's abode)
jūsho
住所

(house, accommodation)
jūtaku
住宅

(place of residence, habitation)
kyojū
居住

(dwelling house)
kyotaku
居宅

residence (stay)
chūzai
駐在

resident
kyojūsha
居住者

(occupant of house)
jūnin
住人

resident owner
kyojū shoyūsha
居住所有者

(current)
genjū shoyūsha
現住所有者

resident ownership
kyojūsha shoyū
居住者所有

resident registration
jūmin tōroku
住民登録

resident tax
jūminzei
住民税

residential area
jūtaku chi'iki
住宅地域

(district)
jūtaku ku'iki
住宅区域

residential construction
jūtaku kensetsu
住宅建設

residential land
takuchi
宅地

residential suburbs
kōgai jūtakuchi
郊外住宅地

residuary estate
zan'yo zaisan
残余財産

revaluation of land
chika shūsei
地価修正

reversion
fudōsan fukki
不動産復帰

revert
fukki suru
復帰する

reverting of property
fudōsan fukki
不動産復帰

right of inheritance
sōzokuken
相続権

right of lease
chinshakuken
賃借権

right of ownership
shoyūken
所有権

right of tenure
hoyūken
保有権

room
heya
部屋

room rent
heyadai
部屋代

room to let
kashima
貸間

room-to-let sign
kashima fuda
貸間札

rot
kusare
腐れ

rundown
kōhai sareta
荒廃された

sale
baikyaku
売却

sale by agent
dairiten hanbai
代理店販売

sale by auction
kyōbai
競売

sales contract
baibai keiyaku
売買契約

sales value
baikyaku kakaku
売却価格

second mortgage
niban teitō
二番抵当

sell
uru
売る

seller
baikyakunin
売却人
urite
売手

selling point
seringu-pointo
セリング・ポイント

selling price
baikyaku kakaku
売却価格

selling real estate
fudōsan hanbaigyō
不動産販売業

semi-detached house
nokitsuzuki no ie
軒続きの家

senior mortgage
yūsen teitō
優先抵当

separate property
tokuyū zaisan
特有財産

separation of property
zaisan bunri
財産分離

service flat
makanaitsuki apāto
まかない付きアパート

settle down
sumitsuku
住着く

several ownership
bunkatsu shoyūken
分割所有権

site
ichi
位置
shikichi
敷地
yōchi
用地

site value
shikichi kagaku
敷地価額

slum
suramu
スラム

slum clearance
suramu no kaishō
スラムの解消

small landowner
kojinushi
小地主

sold
baikyakuzumi
売却済み

solicitor
bengoshi
弁護士

solicitor's fees
bengoshi hōshū
弁護士報酬

squat (noun)
mudan kyojū
無断居住
sukatto
スカット

squat (verb)
mudan kyojū suru
無断居住する
sukatto suru
スカットする

squatter
mudan kyojūsha
無断居住者
sukattā
スカッター

squatter group
sukattā-gurūpu
スカッター・グループ

squatter-proof
sukattā bōei no
スカッター防衛の

standard contract
hyōjun keiyaku
標準契約

state land
kan'yūchi
官有地

state-owned property
kokuyū zaisan
国有財産

storage
sōko
倉庫

storage charges
kurashikiryō
倉敷料

storage company
sōko gaisha
倉庫会社

sublease
matagashi
又貸し
tengashi
転貸し

sublessee
matagarinin
又借人
tenshakunin
転借人

sublessor
matagashinin
又貸人
tengashinin
転貸人

sublet
matagashi
又貸し
tengashi
転貸し

subletting
matagashi
又貸し
tengashi
転貸し

subtenancy
matagari
又借り
tenshaku
転借

subtenant
matagarinin
又借人
tenshakunin
転借人

suburban
kōgai no
郊外の

suburbanite
kōgai kyojūsha
郊外居住者

suburbs
kōgai
郊外

succession
sōzoku
相続

succession dispute
sōzoku arasoi
相続争い

succession tax
sōzokuzei
相続税

succession to property
isan sōzoku
遺産相続

successor
sōzokusha
相続者

survey
(expert opinion, appraisal)
kantei
鑑定

(land measurement)
sokuryō
測量

surveyor
  (expert)
  kanteinin
  鑑定人

  (land measurement expert)
  sokuryōshi
  測量士

surveyor's fee
  kanteiryō
  鑑定料

surveyor's report
  kantei hōkokusho
  鑑定報告書
  kanteisho
  鑑定書

take a lodger
  dōkyonin o oku
  同居人を置く

take lodgings (in someone's house)
  ie o kamaeru
  家を構える

tax on house
  kaokuzei
  家屋税

taxable property
  kazei zaisan
  課税財産

tenancy
  (house tenancy)
  kaoku shakuyō
  家屋借用

  (farming tenancy)
  kosakunō
  小作農

tenancy dispute
  (farming tenancy)
  kosaku sōgi
  小作争議

  (house tenancy)
  shakuya sōgi
  借家争議

tenancy of land in common
  kyōdō shakuchi
  共同借地

tenancy period
  shakuyō kikan
  借用期間

tenant
  chingarinin
  賃借人
  karinushi
  借主

  (land tenant)
  shakuchinin
  借地人

  (house tenant)
  shakuyanin
  借家人

tenant farm land
  kosakuchi
  小作地

tenant farmer
  kosakunin
  小作人
  shakuchi nōgyōsha
  借地農業者

tenant for life
  (farming tenant)
  shūshin kosakunin
  終身小作人

  (land tenant)
  shūshin shakuchinin
  終身借地人

tenant rights (land)
  shakuchiken
  借地権

tenantry
  (farming tenants)
  kosakunin
  小作人

  (land tenants)
  shakuchinin
  借地人

  (house tenants)
  shakuyanin
  借家人

tenants' association
  shakuyanin kumiai
  借家人組合

tenure
  hoyū
  保有

  (right of tenure)
  hoyūken
  保有権

tenure for life (land)
  shūshin tochi hoyūken
  終身土地保有権

termor
  teiki fudōsankensha
  定期不動産権者

testament
  yuigonsho
  遺言書

testator
  yuigonsha
  遺言者

title deed
  fudōsan kenri shōsho
  不動産権利証書

title to a property
  zaisanken
  財産権

transfer of ownership
  shoyūken iten
  所有権移転

transfer of title to a property
  zaisanken iten
  財産権移転

trespass (verb)
  shinnyū suru
  侵入する

trespasser
  (kataku) shingaisha
  (家宅)侵害者

trespassing
  kataku shingai
  家宅侵害
  kataku shinnyū
  家宅侵入

  (legal offence)
  fuhō shingai
  不法侵害

trust
  shintaku
  信託

trust deed [US]
shintaku keiyakusho
信託契約書
shintaku shōsho
信託証書

trust estate
shintaku zaisan
信託財産

trust property
shintaku zaisan
信託財産

undervaluation
kashō hyōka
過少評価

undervalue
kashō hyōka suru
過少評価する

undervalued
kashō hyōka no
過少評価の

undeveloped area
mikaihatsu chi'iki
未開発地域

unencumbered
futan no nai
負担のない

unfurnished house
kagutsukenai kashiya
家具付けない貸家

unoccupied land
akichi/kūchi
空地

unpleasant (surroundings, etc.)
suminikui
住難い

unused building
yūkyū tatemono
遊休建物

unused land
yūkyū tochi
遊休土地

upkeep (of a house)
(kaoku no) iji
(家屋の) 維持

upkeep expenses
ijihi
維持費

urban area
tokaichi
都会地
toshi chi'iki
都市地域

urban community
toshi kyōdōtai
都市共同体

urban decay
toshi kōhai
都市荒廃

urban development
toshi kaihatsu
都市開発

urban land
shigaichi
市街地
tokaichi
都会地

urban land value
shigaichi chika
市街地地価

urban redevelopment
toshi saikaihatsu
都市再開発

urban renewal
toshi kaizō
都市改造

urbanization
toshika
都市化

utilities (facilities)
setsubi
設備

vacant estate
sōzokunin no nai zaisan
相続人のない財産

vacant ground
akichi/kūchi
空地

vacant house
akiya
空家

vacant land
akichi/kūchi
空地
kūkanchi
空閑地

vacant land tax
kūkanchizei
空閑地税

vacant lot
akichi/kūchi
空地
sarachi
さら地

vacant property
akiya
空家

vacate a house
akiya ni suru
空家にする
ie o akeru
家を明ける

valuation [UK]
hyōka
評価
kachi handan
価値判断

(evaluation)
mitsumori
見積り

valuation of land
tochi no mitsumori
土地の見積り

valuation of property (real estate)
fudōsan no mitsumori
不動産の見積り

(estate, fortune)
zaisan hyōka
財産評価

value of land
chika
地価

valuer
hyōkasha
評価者

variable-rate mortgage loan
hendō kinrigata jūtaku
kashitsuke
変動金利型住宅
貸付け

vendor
baikyakunin
売却人
urite
売手
urinushi
売主

verbal agreement
kōtō keiyaku
口頭契約

village
mura
村

village community
sonraku kyōdōtai
村落共同体

voluntary repossession
nin'i toriage
任意取上げ

wasteland
(wild)
arechi
荒れ地

(uncultivated)
mikaikonchi
未開墾地

water
mizu
水

water charges
suidōryōkin
水道料金

water, lighting and heating expenses
suidōkōatsuhi
水道光熱費

water quality
suishitsu
水質

water rates
suidōryō
水道料

(for amount of water used)
kyūsuiryō
給水料

water supply
kyūsui
給水

(amount supplied)
kyūsuiryō
給水量

water tank
kyūsuitō
給水塔

wear and tear
mason
磨損
sonmō
損耗

wear-and-tear expenses
masonhi
磨損費
sonmōhi
損耗費

western-style appartment [J]
yōshiki apāto
様式アパート

wife's separate estate
tsuma no zaisan
妻の財産

will
yuigonsho
遺言書

written agreement
shomen keiyaku
書面契約

written contract
seibun keiyaku
成分契約

written estimate
mitsumorisho
見積書

Chapter 3

Insurance

acceptance
hoken mōshikomisho no ninka
保険申込書の認可

accident
jiko
事故
saigai
災害
shōgai
傷害

accident and indemnity insurance
shōgai hoshō hoken
傷害補償保険

accident and sickness insurance
shōgai shippei hoken
傷害疾病保険

accident insurance
saigai hoken
災害保険
shōgai hoken
傷害保険

accident policy
shōgai hoken shōken
傷害保険証券

act of God
fuka kōryoku
不可抗力

actuarial cost method
hoken sūriteki hiyō keisanhō
保険数理的費用計算法

actuarial department
sūribu
数理部

actuarial value
hoken sūriteki kachi
保険数理的価値

actuary
hoken keirinin
保険経理人
hoken sūrishi
保険数理士

additional insurance
tsuika hoken
追加保険

advice of loss
songai tsūchi
損害通知

against all risks
zenkiken tanpo de
全危険担保で
zenson kiken tanpo de
全損危険担保で

age group
nenrei kaisō
年齢階層
nenreisō
年齢層

agreed-value policy
hoken hyōkagaku
保険評価額

agricultural insurance
nōgyō hoken
農業保険

all-risks insurance
sōgō hoken
総合保険

all-risks insurance policy
sōgō hoken shōken
総合保険証券

amount covered
hoken kingaku
保険金額

amount insured
hoken kingaku
保険金額

amount of damage
songaigaku
損害額

annual premium
nenbarai hokenryō
年払保険料

annuitant
nenkin jukyūsha
年金受給者
nenkin uketorinin
年金受取人

annuity
nenkin
年金

annuity insurance
nenkin hoken
年金保険

annuity option
nenkin no sentaku
年金の選択

annuity table
nenkin jukyūshahyō
年金受給者表
nenkin seimeihyō
年金生命表

applicant
hoken mōshikomisha
年金申込者

application for insurance
hoken mōshikomisho
年金申込書

appraisal [US]
hyōka
評価
kantei
鑑定

appraisal clause
hyōka yakkan
評価約款

appraisal of damage
songai hyōka
損害評価

appraised value
hyōka kachi
評価価値

appraiser
hoken kanteinin
保険鑑定人
hyōkanin
評価人

appreciation in value
zōka
増価

approval
ninka
認可

approve
ninka suru
認可する

arson
hōka
放火

assessed value
satei kagaku
査定価額

**assessment
(valuation, rating)**
hyōka
評価

(investigation, revision)
satei
査定

assessment of damage
songai hokengaku no satei
損害保険額の査定

**assessment of insurance
claim**
tenpo seikyūgaku no satei
てん補請求額の査定

assessor
hyōkanin
評価人

assigned risk
wariate kiken buntan
割当危険分担

assignee
yuzuriukenin
譲受人

assignment
jōto
譲渡

assignor
jōtonin
譲渡人

assumed risk
ninchi sareta kiken soshō
認知された危険訴訟

assumption of risk
kiken futan no ninchi
危険負担の認知
kiken hikiuke
危険引受け

assurance
hoken
保険

assurance company
hoken gaisha
保険会社

assured, the
hihokensha
非保険者
hokenkin uketorinin
保険金受取人

assurer
hokengyōsha
保険業者

attestation clause
sensei yakkan
宣誓約款

automatic coverage
jidō tanpo
自動担保

**automatic extension of
coverage**
jidō enki
自動延期

automatic reinsurance
jidōteki saihoken
自動的再保険

**automobile accident
insurance**
jidōsha jiko hoken
自動車事故保険

automobile body insurance
jidōsha shatai hoken
自動車車体保険

automobile liability insurance
jidōsha sekinin hoken
自動車責任保険

**automobile liability insurance
certificate**
jidōsha sekinin hoken
shōmeisho
自動車責任保険
証明書

**automobile liability insurance
policy**
jidōsha sekinin hoken
shōken
自動車責任保険証券

automobile insurance
jidōsha hoken
自動車保険

automobile insurance policy
jidōsha hoken shōken
自動車保険証券

average
kaison
海損

average life
heikin jumyō
平均寿命

bad debt insurance
kashidaore hoken
貸倒れ保険

bad risk
furyō kiken
不良危険

**bank burglary-robbery
insurance**
ginkō tōnan hoken
銀行盗難保険

**bank burglary-robbery
insurance policy**
ginkō tōnan hoken shōken
銀行盗難保険証券

beneficiary
hokenkin uketorinin
保険金受取人

blanket clause
sōkatsuteki jōkō
総括的条項

blanket insurance
sōkatsu hoken
総括保険

blanket insurance policy
sōkatsu hoken shōken
総括保険証券

**bodily injury liability
insurance**
shintai shōgai sekinin
hoken
身体傷害責任保険

bond [UK]
ichibarai hokenryō shōken
一払保険料証券

breakage clause
hason songai tenpo yakkan
破損損害てん補約款

breakage insurance
hason hoken
破損保険

building insurance
kenchiku hoken
建築保険
tatemono hoken
建物保険

burglar alarm system
tōnan yobō keihōki
盗難予防警報器
yatō keihō sōchi
夜盗警報装置

burglary insurance
tōnan hoken
盗難保険

business insurance
jigyō hoken
事業保険

business interruption insurance
eigyō rieki hoken
営業利益保険
kyūgyō hoken
休業保険

business liability insurance
kigyō sekinin hoken
企業責任保険

casualty
saigai
災害
shōgai
傷害

casualty insurance
saigai hoken
災害保険
shōgai hoken
傷害保険

casualty insurance claim
shōgai hokenkin
傷害保険金

casualty insurance money
shōgai hokenkin
傷害保険金

casualty insurance premium
shōgai hokenryō
傷害保険料

catastrophe
daisaigai
大災害

catastrophe insurance
hijō daisaigai hoken
非常大災害保険

catastrophe risks
hijō kiken
非常危険

certificate of insurance
hoken shōmeisho
保険証明書

change of beneficiary
hokenkin uketorinin no shitei henkō
保険金受取人の指定変更

claim
hoken(kin) seikyū
保険(金)請求

claim assessment
songai satei
損害査定

claim department
songai sateibu
損害査定部

claim paid
shiharaizumi hoshōkin
支払済補償金

claim payable
tenpokin
てん補金

claim settlement
hoshō shiharai
補償支払い

claimant
seikyūnin
請求人

clause
jōkō
条項
yakkan
約款

claused insurance policy
jōkentsuki hoken shōken
条件付保険証券

client
kokyaku
顧客

co-insurance
kyōdō hoken
共同保険

co-insurance money
kyōdō hokenkin
共同保険金

co-insurer
kyōdō hokensha
共同保険者

collective accident insurance
shūdan shōgai hoken
集団傷害保険

collective insurance
shūdan hoken
集団保険

collision insurance
shōtotsu hoken
衝突保険

commercial burglary insurance
shōhin tōnan hoken
商品盗難保険

commercial insurance
eiri hoken
営利保険

company liability insurance
kaisha sekinin hoken
会社責任保険

company policy
kaisha hakkō hoken shōken
会社発行保険証券

company's risk
kaisha kiken mochi
会社危険持ち

compensation for damages
songai baishō(kin)
損害賠償(金)

compensation for death
shibō hoshōkin
死亡補償金

compensation for injury
fushō hoshōkin
負傷補償金

compensation for loss
songai baishō
損害賠償

compensation insurance
hoshō hoken
補償保険

compound insurance
sōgō hoken
総合保険

comprehensive coverage
sōgō tanpo hoken shōken
総合担保保険証券

comprehensive general liability insurance
sōgōteki ippan sekinin hoken
総合的一般責任保険

comprehensive general liability insurance policy
sōgōteki ippan sekinin hoken shōken
総合的一般責任保険証券

comprehensive house insurance
sōgōteki jūtaku hoken
総合的住宅保険

comprehensive house insurance policy
sōgōteki jūtaku hoken shōken
総合的住宅保険証券

comprehensive insurance
sōgō hoken
総合保険

comprehensive insurance policy
sōgō hoken shōken
総合保険証券

comprehensive motorcar insurance
sōgō jidōsha hoken
総合自動車保険

comprehensive motorcar insurance policy
sōgō jidōsha hoken shōken
総合自動車保険証券

comprehensive personal liability insurance
sōgōteki kojin sekinin hoken
総合的個人責任保険

comprehensive personal liability insurance policy
sōgōteki kojin sekinin hoken shōken
総合的個人責任保険証券

compromised settlement
dakyō shiharai
妥協支払い

compulsory health insurance
kyōsei kenkō hoken
強制健康保険

compulsory insurance
kyōsei hoken
強制保険

compulsory liability insurance
kyōsei baishō sekinin hoken
強制賠償責任保険

compulsory motorcar liability insurance
kyōsei jidōsha baishō sekinin hoken
強制自動車賠償責任保険

concealment
fukokuchi
不告知

conditions life insurance
seimei hoken yakkan
生命保険約款

consequential damage
kansetsu songai
間接損害

consequential damage insurance
kansetsu songai hoken
間接損害保険

consequential loss
kansetsu songai
間接損害

contingency insurance
gūhatsu jiken hoken
偶発事件保険

continuation clause
kikan enchō jōkō
期間延長条項

continuous coverage
keizokuteki saihoken
継続的再保険

contract
keiyaku
契約

contractual liability insurance
keiyaku sekinin hoken
契約責任保険

contribution clause
songai buntan jōkō
損害分担条項

convertible insurance
kahen hoken
可変保険

cover (verb)
(— ni) hoken o tsukeru
(—に) 保険をつける

coverage
hoken tanpo
保険担保

covered against/for (—)
(— ni) hoken o kakeru
(—に) 保険をかける

credit insurance
shin'yō hoken
信用保険

crop insurance
sakumotsu hoken
作物保険

current value of annuity
nenkin genka
年金現価

damage
  (harm)
  higai
  被害

  (loss)
  songai
  損害

  (injury)
  sonshō
  損傷

damage by fire
  kasai ni yoru songai
  火災による損害

damage by vermin
  chūgai
  虫害

damage by water
  suigai
  水害

damage evaluation
  songai hyōka
  損害評価

damage incurred
  higai
  被害

damage insurance
  songai hoken
  損害保険

damage to property
  zaisan songai
  財産損害

date of expiry
  keiyaku mankibi
  契約満期日

day insurance
  hibu hoken
  日歩保険

death and dismemberment
  saigai shibō
  災害死亡

death benefits
  shibō hokenkin
  死亡保険金
  shibō kyūfu
  死亡給付

death claim
  shibō hokenkin seikyū
  死亡保険金請求

deferred annuity
  sueoki nenkin
  据置年金

depreciation insurance
  torikaehi hoken
  取替費保険

devastated area
  kōhaichi
  荒廃地

devastation
  kōhai
  荒廃

  (heavy damage)
  sangai
  惨害

direct business
  chokusetsu hokengyō
  直接保険業

disability
  haishitsu
  廃疾

disability benefit
  haishitsu kyūfu
  廃疾給付

disability clause
  haishitsu jōkō
  廃疾条項

disability insurance
  shintai shōgai hoken
  身体傷害保険

disability provisions
  haishitsu kitei
  廃疾規定

disablement
  fugu
  不具

disclosure
  kokuchi
  告知

discretion
  sairyō
  裁量

document
  shorui
  書類

double endowment insurance
  baigaku yōrō hoken
  倍額養老保険

double indemnity
  baigaku hoshō shiharai
  倍額補償支払い

double insurance
  jūfuku hoken
  重複保険

driving insurance
  jidōsha hoken
  自動車保険

duration of policy
  hoken keiyaku kikan
  保険契約期間

earthquake
  jishin
  地震

earthquake-covered clause
  jishin kiken tanpo tokubetsu
  yakkan
  地震危険担保特別
  約款

earthquake insurance
  jishin hoken
  地震保険

employer's liability insurance
  koyōsha sekinin hoken
  雇用者責任保険

endowment
  yōrō hoken
  養老保険
  yōrō shikin
  養老資金

endowment annuity
  yōrō nenkin
  養老年金

endowment annuity insurance
  yōrō seimei hoken
  養老生命保険

endowment assurance
seizon hoken
生存保険
yōrō hoken
養老保険
yōrō nenkin tokuyaku
hoken
養老年金特約保険

endowment policy
yōrō hoken shōken
養老保険証券

estimated damage
songai mikomi
損害見込み
suitei songaigaku
推定損害額

excluded risks
menseki kiken
免責危険

exclusion
jogai
除外

exclusion clause
jogai jōkō
除外条項

expiration of term
manki
満期

explosion
bakuhatsu
爆発

explosion clause
bakuhatsu kiken tanpo
tokubetsu yakkan
爆発危険担保特別
約款

explosion insurance
bakuhatsu hoken
爆発保険

exposure
kikendo
危険度

extended coverage
kakuchō tanpo
拡張担保

extended coverage insurance
kakuchō kiken hoken
拡張危険保険

extended insurance
keizoku hoken
継続保険

extended medical payment insurance
kakuchō iryōhi hoken
拡張医療費保険

extended policy
enchō hoken keiyaku
延長保険契約

extended-term insurance
enchō hoken
延長保険

extra premium
warimashi hokenryō
割増保険料

facultative reinsurance
nin'i saihoken
任意再保険

family protection insurance
kazoku hoshō hoken
家族保証保険

fine arts insurance
bijutsu kōgeihin hoken
美術工芸品保険

fine arts insurance policy
bijutsu kōgeihin hoken
shōken
美術工芸品保険証券

fire
kasai
火災

fire hazards
kasai kiken
火災危険

fire insurance
kasai hoken
火災保険

flexible retirement scheme
nanshiki teinensei
軟式定年制

floater
hōkatsu hoken keiyaku
包括保険契約

floating policy
hōkatsu hoken shōken
包括保険証券

flood damages
suigai
水害

flood insurance
kōzui hoken
洪水保険

force majeure
fuka kōryoku
不可抗力

force majeure clause
fuka kōryoku jōkō
不可抗力条項

forcible entry
fuhō shinnyū
不法侵入

freezer insurance
reitōki hoken
冷凍機保険

freight insurance
unchin hoken
運賃保険

frost insurance
sōgai hoken
霜害保険

full coverage
zenbu tanpo
全部担保

full disclosure clause
kanzen kokuchi jōkō
完全告知条項

full insurance
zenbu hoken
全部保険
zengaku hoken
全額保険

full protection policy
zengaku futan hoken
shōken
全額負担保険証券

fully insured person
kanzen hihokensha
完全被保険者

fully paid policy
hokenryō haraikomizumi keiyaku
保険料払込済契約

general average
buntan kaison
分担海損
kyōdō kaison
共同海損

general clause
ippan yakkan
一般約款

general conditions
futsū yakkan
普通約款

general cover
ikkatsu hoken
一括保険

general insurance
futsū hoken
普通保険

general insurance clauses and conditions
futsū hoken yakkan
普通保険約款

general liability
futsū baishō sekinin
普通賠償責任

general risk
futsū kiken bukken
普通危険物件

general terms and conditions
ippan jōken
一般条件

good risk
yūryō kiken
優良危険

gross premium
eigyō hokenryō
営業保険料

group accident insurance
dantai shōgai hoken
団体傷害保険

group annuity
dantai nenkin
団体年金

group endowment insurance
dantai yōrō hoken
団体養老保険

group health insurance plan
shūdan kenkō hoken seido
集団健康保険制度

group hospitalization insurance
dantai nyūinhi hoken
団体入院費保険

group insurance
dantai hoken
団体保険

group insurance policy
dantai hoken shōken
団体保険証券

group life insurance
dantai seimei hoken
団体生命保険

group medical expense insurance
dantai iryōhi hoken
団体医療費保険

group pension
dantai nenkin
団体年金

group permanent insurance
dantai chōki hoken
団体長期保険
dantai shūshin hoken
団体終身保険

group term insurance
dantai teiki hoken
団体定期保険

guaranteed income contract [US]
kakuteiritsuki hoken keiyaku
確定利付保険契約

hail storm insurance
hyōgai hoken
ひょう害保険

hazardous goods
kiken kamotsu
危険貨物

hazards
kiken
危険

health insurance
kenkō hoken
健康保険

health insurance doctor
kenkō hoken'i
健康保険医

health insurance premium
kenkō hokenryō
健康保険料

hijacking
nottori
乗っ取り

hold-harmless agreement
menseki tokuyaku
免責特約

home contents floater
kazai hōkatsu hoken
家財包括保険

home contents package policy
jūtaku sōgō hoken shōken
住宅総合保険証券

homeowner's insurance
jūtaku shoyūsha hoken
住宅所有者保険

homeowner's insurance policy
jūtaku shoyūsha hoken shōken
住宅所有者保険証券

hospital
byōin
病院

hospital expenses
nyūinhi
入院費

hospital professional liability insurance
byōin sekinin hoken
病院責任保険

hospitalization
nyūin kikan
入院期間

hospitalization insurance
nyūin hiyō hoken
入院費用保険

hospitalization insurance policy
nyūin hiyō hoken shōken
入院費用保険証券

housebreaking
jūkyo shinnyū
住居侵入

household goods insurance
kazai hoken
家財保険

household insurance
katei hoken
家庭保険

householder's comprehensive insurance
jūtaku sōgō hoken
住宅総合保険

householder's comprehensive insurance policy
jūtaku sōgō hoken shōken
住宅総合保険証券

housing loan insurance
jūtaku yūshi hoken
住宅融資保険

impairment
haishitsu
廃疾

important clause
songai kensa tōyakkan
損害検査等約款

increased rate
teizō hokenryō
逓増保険料

increased value
zōchi kagaku
増値価額

increased value insurance
zōchi hoken
増値保険

increasing premium plan
hokenryō ruika hoken
保険料累加保険

indemnify
tsugunau
償う

indemnity
baishōkin
賠償金

indemnity insurance
songai hoken
損害保険

individual accident insurance
kojin shōgai hoken
個人傷害保険

individual annuity policy plan
kojin nenkin keiyaku hōshiki
個人年金契約方式

individual insurance
futsū hoken
普通保険

individual insurance premium
kobetsu hokenryō
個別保険料

industrial accident
gyōmu saigai
業務災害

industrial insurance
rōdō hoken
労働保険
sangyō hoken
産業保険

(for industrial personnel)
kōgyō jūgyōin hoken
工業従業員保険

inherent hazards insurance
naibu kiken tanpo hoken
内部危険担保保険

inherent hazards insurance policy
naibu kiken tanpo hoken shōken
内部危険担保保険証券

innocent concealment
zen'i no fukokuchi
善意の不告知

inspection
tenken
点検

inspection report
tenken hōkoku
点検報告

instalment insurance
nenpu hoken
年賦保険

insurability
hoken kanōtai
保険可能体

insurable
hokenkanō na
保険可能な

insurable interest
hoken kagaku
保険価額

insurable property
hihoken bukken
被保険物件
hokenkanō zaisan
保険可能財産

insurable risk
hoken jiko
保険事故

insurable value
hoken kagaku
保険価額

insurance
hoken
保険

insurance account
hoken kanjō
保険勘定

insurance accounting
hoken kaikei
保険会計

insurance adjuster
hoken seisannin
保険清算人

insurance adviser
hoken komon
保険顧問

insurance against disability
haishitsu hoken
廃疾保険

insurance against fire
kasai hoken
火災保険

insurance against loss or damage
songai hoken
損害保険

insurance against theft
tōnan hoken
盗難保険

insurance agent
(person)
hoken dairinin
保険代理人

(agency)
hoken dairiten
保険代理店

insurance amount
hoken kingaku
保険金額

insurance appraiser
hoken kanteinin
保険鑑定人

insurance benefits
hokenkin
保険金

insurance binder
hoken karikeiyakusho
保険仮契約書

insurance broker
hoken burōkā
保険ブローカー
hoken chūkainin
保険仲介人

insurance business
hokengyō
保険業

insurance carrier
hokengyōsha
保険業者

insurance certificate
hoken hikiukeshō
保険引受証
hoken shōmeisho
保険証明書

insurance claim
hokenkin seikyū
保険金請求

insurance claims
mishū hokenkin
未収保険金

insurance claims unsettled
mikessan hokenkin
未決算保険金

insurance clauses
hoken jōkō
保険条項
hoken yakkan
保険約款

insurance company
hoken gaisha
保険会社

insurance contract
hoken keiyaku
保険契約

insurance contractor
hoken keiyakusha
保険契約者

insurance cost
hoken genka
保険原価

insurance cover(age)
hoken tanpo
保険担保

insurance documents
hoken shorui
保険書類

insurance fraud
hoken sagi
保険詐欺

insurance fund
hoken tsumitatekin
保険積立金

insurance market
hoken shijō
保険市場

insurance money
hokenkin
保険金

insurance on someone's life
tanin no seimei hoken keiyaku
他人の生命保険契約

insurance policy
hoken shōken
保険証券

insurance policy valuation
hoken hyōkagaku
保険評価額

insurance premium
hoken kakekin
保険掛金
hokenryō
保険料

insurance premium rate
hokenryōritsu
保険料率

insurance premium reduction
hokenryō kōjo
保険料控除

insurance rate
hokenryōritsu
保険料率

insurance surveyor
hoken kensanin
保険検査人

insurance underwriter
hokengyōsha
保険業者
hokensha
保険者

insurance value
hoken kagaku
保険価額

insurance with medical examination
yūshinsa hoken
有診査保険

insurance without medical examination
mushinsa hoken
無診査保険

insure
(someone)
hoken suru
保険する

(take out an insurance)
hoken ni ireru
保険に入れる

insured, the
hihokensha
被保険者

insured amount
hoken kingaku
保険金額

insured articles
hihokenbutsu
被保険物

insured property
hihokenbutsu
被保険物

insured value
hoken kagaku
保険価額

insurer
hokengyōsha
保険業者
hokensha
保険者

invalid claim
mukō no hoken seikyū
無効の保険請求

joint annuity
kyōdō nenkin
共同年金

joint insurance
rentai hoken
連帯保険

joint insurance policy
rentai hoken shōken
連帯保険証券

joint life annuity
kyōdō shōgai nenkin
共同生涯年金

joint life insurance
rentai seimei hoken
連帯生命保険

key-man insurance
kei'eisha hoken
経営者保険
kigyō kanbu hoken
企業幹部保険

landlords and tenants' insurance
jinushi-chingarinin sekinin hoken
地主・賃借人責任保険

lapsed policy
kigen keika hoken shōken
期限経過保険証券

last survivor
saishū seizonsha
最終生存者

last survivor annuity
saishū seizonsha nenkin
最終生存者年金

last survivor insurance
saishū seizonsha hoken
最終生存者保険

leakage
rōdatsu
漏脱

legal liability insurance
hōtei sekinin hoken
法定責任保険

liability
sekinin
責任

liability insurance
sekinin hoken
責任保険

libel insurance
meiyo kisonnin hoken
名誉き損任保険

life annuity
shūshin nenkin
終身年金

life assurance
seimei hoken
生命保険

life insurance
seimei hoken
生命保険

life insurance claim
seimei hokenkin
生命保険金

life insurance company
seimei hoken gaisha
生命保険会社

life insurance contract
seimei hoken keiyaku
生命保険契約

life insurance fund
seimei hoken tsumitatekin
生命保険積立金

life insurance money
seimei hokenkin
生命保険金

life insurance policy
seimei hoken shōken
生命保険証券

life insurance premium
seimei hokenryō
生命保険料

life insurance syndicate
seihodan
生保団

limited insurance policy
seigentsuki hoken shōken
制限付保険証券

limited payment insurance
yūgen haraikomi hoken
有限払込保険

limited-payment insurance policy
yūgen haraikomi hoken shōken
有限払込保険証券

limited policy
seigentsuki hoken shōken
制限付保険証券

livestock insurance
kachiku hoken
家畜保険

livestock insurance policy
kachiku hoken shōken
家畜保険証券

loaded premium
eigyō hokenryō
営業保険料

location of property insured
hihokenbutsu shozaichi
被保険物所在地

long-term insurance
chōki hoken
長期保険

loss
songai
損害

loss assessment
songai hyōka
損害評価

loss assessor
songai hyōkanin
損害評価人

loss department
songai sateibu
損害査定部

loss report
songai tsūchi
損害通知

lump sum
sōkatsu kingaku
総括金額

lump-sum payment
ichijibarai
一時払い

lump-sum settlement
hokenkin ichijibarai
保険金一時払い

machine breakdown insurance
kikai hason hoken
機械破損保険

machine insurance
kikai hoken
機械保険

machine insurance policy
kikai hoken shōken
機械保険証券

major loss
shuyō songai
主要損害

major medical expense insurance
kōgaku iryōhi hoken
高額医療費保険

malicious damage insurance
hikō hoken
非行保険

malpractice coverage
hikō kiken hoken
非行危険保険

malpractice insurance
senmonshoku sekinin hoken
専門職責任保険
shokugyōteki hikō hoken
職業的非行保険

manufacturer's liability insurance
seizōgyōsha sekinin hoken
製造業者責任保険

marine insurance
kaijō hoken
海上保険

marine insurance contract
kaijō hoken keiyaku
海上保険契約

marine insurance policy
kaijō hoken shōken
海上保険証券

maximum amount of insurance
saikō hoken kingaku
最高保険金額

medical examination
kenkō shindan
健康診断
shinsa
診査

medical expenses
iryōhi
医療費

medical insurance
iryō hoken
医療保険

medical professional liability insurance
iryō shokugyō sekinin hoken
医療職業責任保険

merchandise insurance
shōhin hoken
商品保険

middleman
chūkaisha
仲介者
chūkan gyōsha
中間業者

minimum loss clause
saishō songai yakkan
最小損害約款

minimum premium
saitei hokenryō
最低保険料

misstatement
gohō
誤報

mixed insurance
kongō hoken
混合保険

mixed policy
kongō hoken shōken
混合保険証券

monthly premium
tsukigake hokenryō
月掛け保険料

moral hazard
dōtokuteki kiken
道徳的危険

mortality
shibōritsu
死亡率

mortgage insurance
teitō hoken
抵当保険

mortgage repayment insurance
jūtaku shikin hoken
住宅資金保険

motor insurance
jidōsha hoken
自動車保険

movables all-risk insurance
dōsan sōgō hoken
動産総合保険

multi-location risk insurance
tasū shozaichi kiken tanpo hoken
多数所在地危険担保保険

mutual insurance
sōgo hoken
相互保険

mutual insurance company
sōgo hoken gaisha
相互保険会社

named risk
tokutei kiken
特定危険

named risk insurance
tokutei kiken hoken
特定危険保険

natural risk
shizenteki kiken
自然的危険

nature of risk
kiken no seishitsu
危険の性質

negligence liability insurance
kashitsu sekinin hoken
過失責任保険

net premium
shōmi hokenryō
正味保険料

no claim
mujiko
無事故

no-claim bonus
muji modoshi
無事戻し

no-claim rebate
mujiko modoshi
無事故戻し

nomination of beneficiary
hokenkin uketorinin no shitei
保険金受取人の指定

nominee
uketori meiginin
受取名義人

non-deductible franchise
mukōjo menseki
無控除免責

not insured
hoken no kakete nai
保険のかけてない

obligation to disclose
kokuchi gimu
告知義務

officers and directors liability insurance
yakuin sekinin hoken
役員責任保険

on-the-job accident
gyōmujō no jiko
業務上の事故

open cover
hōkatsu yotei hoken keiyaku
包括予定保険契約

open policy
hōkatsu yotei hoken shōken
包括予定保険証券

optional insurance
nin'i hoken
任意保険

optional insurance plan
nin'i hoken seido
任意保険制度

ordinary branch
futsū hoken
普通保険

ordinary life insurance
fūtsū seimei hoken
普通生命保険

overestimation
kadai hyōka
過大評価

overinsurance
chōka hoken
超過保険

overinsured
hoken kagaku kadai no
保険価額過大の

overvaluation
kadai hyōka
過大評価

overvalue
kadai hyōka suru
過大評価する

overvalued
kadai hyōka no
過大評価の

owner's liability insurance
shoyūsha sekinin hoken
所有者責任保険

paid-up insurance
haraikomizumi hoken
払込済保険

paid-up insurance policy
haraikomizumi hoken shōken
払込済保険証券

partial disability
bubun haishitsu
部分廃疾

partial disablement
ichibu fugu
一部不具

partial insurance
bubun hoken
部分保険

partial loss
bunson
分損

partial redemption
kaiyaku
解約

participating companies
sanka gaisha
参加会社

particular average
tandoku kaison
単独海損
tokutan bunson
特担分損

particular average warranty
bunson yakkan
分損約款

partnership insurance
kumiai hoken
組合保険

passenger insurance
jōkyaku hoken
乗客保険

passenger liability insurance
jōkyaku shōgai sekinin hoken
乗客傷害責任保険

past medical history
kiōshō
既往症

patent insurance
tokkyoken hoken
特許権保険

payment of claim
hokenkin shiharai
保険金支払い

payment of premium
hokenryō haraikomi
保険料払込み

pension
nenkin
年金

pension insurance
nenkin hoken
年金保険

pension plan
nenkin keikaku
年金計画
nenkin seido
年金制度

pension scheme
nenkin seido
年金制度

pension trust
nenkin shintaku
年金信託

peril
kiken
危険

permanent health insurance
iryō hoken
医療保険

period of coverage
hoken kikan
保険期間

period of risk
kiken futan kikan
危険負担期間

period-of-risk clause
kiken kikan jōkō
危険期間条項

person insured
hihokensha
被保険者

personal accident insurance
kojin shōgai hoken
個人傷害保険

personal annuity scheme
kojin nenkin keiyaku hōshiki
個人年金契約方式

personal health care
kojin iryō
個人医療

personal insurance
kojin hoken
個人保険

personal liability insurance
kojin sekinin hoken
個人責任保険

personal pension
kojin nenkin seido
個人年金制度

policy
hoken shōken
保険証券

policy clause
hoken yakkan
保険約款

policy conditions
hoken yakkan
保険約款

policy contract
hoken keiyaku
保険契約

policy form
shōken yōshi
証券用紙

policy holder
hoken keiyakusha
保険契約者

policy value
hoken kagaku
保険価額

portable pension
iten nenkin seido
移転年金制度

premium
hokenryō
保険料

premium adjustment
ryōkin chōsetsu
料金調節

premium discount
hokenryō waribiki
保険料割引

premium discount for good risk
yūryō bukken waribiki
優良物件割引

premium income
hokenryō shūnyū
保険料収入

premium level
hokenryō suijun
保険料水準

premium rate
hokenryōritsu
保険料率

private annuity
minkan nenkin
民間年金

private business insurance
shiei hoken
私営保険

private insurance
shihoken
私保険

private pension
shiteki nenkin
私的年金

(vs. state)
minkan nenkin
民間年金

private pension plan
shiteki nenkin keikaku
私的年金計画

professional liability insurance
senmon shokugyō sekinin hoken
専門職業責任保険

professional liability insurance policy
senmon shokugyō sekinin hoken shōken
専門職業責任保険証券

proof of death
shibō shōmei
死亡証明

proof of loss
songai shōmei
損害証明

property damage
zaisan songai
財産損害

property damage liability insurance
zaibutsu sonkai sekinin hoken
財物損壊責任保険

property depreciation
zaibutsu genka
財物減価

property depreciation insurance
zaibutsu genka hoken
財物減価保険

property insurance
zaibutsu hoken
財物保険

(movables)
dōsan hoken
動産保険

provision(s)
kitei
規定

public liability insurance
ippan baishō sekinin hoken
一般賠償責任保険

re-appraisal [US]
saihyōka
再評価

recovery
kaishū
回収

reference number
shōgō bangō
照合番号

reinsurance
saihoken
再保険

reinsurance agreement
saihoken keiyaku
再保険契約

reinsurance clause
saihoken jōkō
再保険条項

reinsurance money
saihokenkin
再保険金

reinsurance premium
saihokenryō
再保険料

renewal of policy
keiyaku keizoku
契約継続

renewal policy
keizoku keiyaku
継続契約

renewal premium
keizoku hokenryō
継続保険料

renewal receipt
keizoku keiyakusho
継続契約書

replacement
saishutoku
再取得
torikae
取替え

replacement cost
torikae hiyō
取替費用

replacement insurance
saishutoku hoken
再取得保険
torikae hoken
取替保険

replacement value
saishutoku kachi
再取得価値
torikae kachi
取替価値

retirement
taishoku
退職

retirement income insurance policy
taishoku nenkin hoken shōken
退職年金保険証券

retroactive insurance
sokyū hoken
遡及保険

return premium
hokenryō haraimodoshi
保険料払戻し

risk(s)
kiken
危険

risk-bearing
kiken futan
危険負担

risk cost
kiken hiyō
危険費用

risk-covering insurance
kiken hoken
危険保険

risk disclosure
kiken kaiji
危険開示

risk disclosure statement
kiken kaijisho
危険開示書

risk premium
kiken hokenryō
危険保険料
kiken uchibu
危険打部

risk-taking
kiken futan
危険負担

robbery insurance
tōnan hoken
盗難保険

schedule of insurance amount
kyūbetsu hoken kingaku
級別保険金額

selection of risk
kiken no sentei
危険の選定

self-employment insurance
jieigyō hoken
自営業保険

settlement of claim
hoshō shiharai
補償支払い

short-term insurance
tanki hoken
短期保険

short-term insurance rates
tanki hokenryōritsu
短期保険料率

sickness insurance
shippei hoken
疾病保険

signature
shomei
署名

single liability
tan'itsu sekinin
単一責任

single premium
ichijibarai hokenryō
一時払保険料
tan'itsu hokenryō
単一保険料

single risk
tokubetsu kiken
特別危険

special insurance
tokutei hoken
特定保険

specific insurance
kobetsu hoken
個別保険

sports insurance
supōtsu hoken
スポーツ保険

sports insurance policy
supōtsu hoken shōken
スポーツ保険証券

sports liability insurance
supōtsu sekinin hoken
スポーツ責任保険

sports liability insurance policy
supōtsu sekinin hoken shōken
スポーツ責任保険証券

spread loss cover
chōki renzoku songai tenpo
長期連続損害てん補

standard annuity mortality table
hyōjun nenkinhyō
標準年金表

standard disability provisions
hyōjun haishitsu kitei
標準廃疾規定

standard insurance
hyōjun hoken
標準保険

standard provisions
hyōjun kitei
標準規定

strike insurance
suto hoken
スト保険

subject matter of insurance
hoken no mokuteki
保険の目的

sub-standard insurance
hyōjun kahon hoken
標準下本保険

substantial damages
jisshitsuteki songai
実質的損害

substantial damages compensation
jisshitsuteki songai baishōkin
実質的損害賠償金

sum insured
hoken kingaku
保険金額

sum reinsured
saihoken kingaku
再保険金額

superannuation
chōnenkin
超年金

supplementary pension plan
hosoku nenkin seido
補足年金制度

surgical expenses insurance
shujutsuhi hoken
手術費保険

surrender an insurance policy
hoken keiyaku o kaijo suru
保険契約を解除する

surrender value
hokenryō haraimodoshi
保険料払戻し

survivor
izoku
遺族
seizonsha
生存者

survivor's annuity
izoku nenkin
遺族年金

survivor's annuity insurance
izoku nenkin hoken
遺族年金保険

survivor's benefit
izoku fujoryō
遺族扶助料

survivor's insurance
seizon hoken
生存保険

take out an insurance
hoken o tsukeru
保険をつける

term insurance
teiki hoken
定期保険

term insured
hoken kikan
保険期間

term life insurance
teiki seimei hoken
定期生命保険

terms and conditions of a contract
keiyaku jōken
契約条件

terms of insurance
hoken jōken
保険条件

terms of policy
hoken yakkan
保険約款

third party
daisansha
第三者

third party, fire and theft car insurance
daisansha-kasai-tōnan jidōsha hoken
第三者・火災・盗難
自動車保険

third-party insurance
taidaisansha hoken
対第三者保険

third-party liability
taidaisansha sekinin
対第三者責任

third-party liability insurance
taidaisansha sekinin hoken
対第三者責任保険

time policy
kikan hoken
期間保険

total loss
zenson
全損

transfer of policy
hoken keiyaku no iten
保険契約の移転

transport insurance
unsō hoken
運送保険

travel insurance
ryokōsha shōgai hoken
旅行者傷害保険

travel insurance policy
ryokōsha shōgai hoken shōken
旅行者傷害保険証券

treaty reinsurance
tokuyaku saihoken
特約再保険

umbrella cover
hōkatsu keiyaku
包括契約

unapproved insurance
mumenkyo hoken
無免許保険

unavoidable risks
fukahiteki kiken
不可避的危険

under-insurance
fusoku hoken
不足保険

under-insured
hoken kagaku kashō no
保険価額過少の

undersigned, the
shomeisha
署名者

undervaluation
kashō hyōka
過少評価

undervalue
kashō hyōka suru
過少評価する

undervalued
kashō hyōka no
過少評価の

underwrite
hoken o hikiukeru
保険を引受ける

underwriter(s)
hokengyōsha
保険業者

underwriting
hoken hikiuke
保険引受け

unemployment insurance
shitsugyō hoken
失業保険

unexpired insurance
mikeika hoken
未経過保険

uninsurability
hoken funōtai
保険不能体

uninsurable
hoken funō na
保険不能な

uninsured
muhoken no
無保険の

unit-linked life assurance [UK]
yunittogata seimei hoken
ユニット型生命保険

unknown risk
fusoku no kiken
不足の危険

unoccupied building insurance
akiya hoken
空家保険

unvalued policy
mihyōka hoken
未評価保険

valued policy
teigaku hoken shōken
定額保険証券

variable annuity
hendō nenkin
変動年金
hengaku nenkin
変額年金
kahen nenkin
可変年金

variable annuity plan
kahen nenkin seido
可変年金制度

voluntary health insurance
nin'i kenkō hoken seido
任意健康保険制度

voluntary insurance
nin'i hoken
任意保険

voluntary reinsurance
nin'i saihoken
任意再保険

waiver clause
kiken yakkan
棄権約款

war risks
sensō kiken
戦争危険

war risks insurance
sensō hoken
戦争保険

water damage
suigai
水害

water damage insurance
suigai hoken
水害保険

wear and tear
mason
磨損
sonmō
損耗

whole insurance
zengaku hoken
全額保険

whole life insurance
shūshin seimei hoken
終身生命保険

whole reinsurance
zengaku saihoken
全額再保険

windstorm and flood insurance
fūsuigai hoken
風水害保険

workers' accident insurance
rōsai hoken
労災保険

workmen's compensation insurance
rōdōsha saigai hoshō hoken
労働者災害補償保険

yearly renewable premium
shizen hokenryō
自然保険料

Chapter 4

Business; Company law

ability to compete
kyōsōryoku
競争力

abortive enterprise
funin kigyō
不妊企業

absentee director
fuzai jūyaku
不在重役
hijōkin jūyaku
非常勤重役

absentee management
fuzai kei'eisha
不在経営者

absorption
kyūshū
吸収

　(merger and acquisition)
　kyūshū gappei
　吸収合併

abuse of power
kenryoku no ran'yō
権力の濫用

accompanying documents
tenpu shorui
添付書類

accredited
shinnin sareta
信任された

acknowledge a signature
shomei o shōnin suru
署名を承認する

acquire a business
kigyō o kaitoru
企業を買取る

acquire a company
　(buy out)
kaisha o baishū suru
会社を買収する

　(purchase)
　kaisha o kaitoru
　会社を買取る

acquired rights
kitokuken
既得権

acquirer
shutokusha
取得者

acquisition (of a company)
　(buy-out)
baishū
買収

　(purchase)
　kaitori
　買取り

　(absorption)
　kyūshū
　吸収

　(merger and acquisition)
　kyūshū gappei
　吸収合併

　(take-over)
　nottori
　乗っ取り

act for the company
kaisha ni kawatte kōdō
subeku
会社に代わって行動
すべく

act of incorporation
setsuritsuhō
設立法

acting director
dairi torishimariyaku
代理取締役

acting president
shachō dairi
社長代理

actionable fraud
sagi
詐欺

active partner
gyōmu tantō shain
業務担当社員

activity analysis
kei'ei bunseki
経営分析

actual partner
genshain
現社員

address (company's)
kigyō shozaichi
企業所在地

administration
　(control, supervision)
kanri
管理

　(management, running)
　kei'ei
　経営

　(control, rule)
　shihai
　支配

administration committee
kanri i'inkai
管理委員会

administrative ability
kanri nōryoku
管理能力
kei'ei shuwan
経営手腕

administrative improvement
kei'ei kaizen
経営改善

administrative structure
kei'ei soshiki
経営組織

administrator
torishimariyaku
取締役

affiliate [US]
　(collateral company,
　subsidiary)
bōkei gaisha
傍系会社

　(related company)
　kankei gaisha
　関係会社
　kanren gaisha
　関連会社

　(subsidiary) (see note 20)
　keiretsu gaisha (see note
　20)
　系列会社
　kogaisha
　子会社

affiliated company [US]
(collateral company)
bōkei gaisha
傍系会社

(related company)
kankei gaisha
関係会社
kanren gaisha
関連会社

(subsidiary) (see note 20)
keiretsu gaisha (see note 20)
系列会社
kogaisha
子会社

affiliated corporation [US]
kankei gaisha
関係会社

affiliated enterprise [US]
kankei gaisha
関係会社
kanren gaisha
関連会社

affiliated group
kigyō no kanren gurūpu
企業の関連グループ

affiliated organization
keitō kikan
系統機関

affiliated person
tokubetsu rigai kankeinin
特別利害関係人

affiliation
(relation)
kankei
関係

[J]20
keiretsu20
系列

(tie-up)
teikei
提携

agency
dairiten
代理店

agent (for the company)
daihyōsha
代表者

alien company
gaikoku gaisha
外国会社
gaikoku kigyō
外国企業

alien corporation
gaikoku gaisha
外国会社
gaikoku hōjin
外国法人

alteration
(change)
henkō
変更

(revision)
kaisei
改正

amalgamate
gappei suru
合併する

amalgamated company
gappei gaisha
合併会社

amalgamation
(absorption, merger, consolidation)
gappei
合併

(combination, union, joint partnership)
gōdō
合同

amalgamation procedure
gappei tetsuzuki
合併手続き

amend
(change)
henkō suru
変更する

(correct)
teisei suru
訂正する

amendment
henkō
変更
teisei
訂正

amendment of articles
teikan henkō
定款変更

anonymous association
tokumei kumiai
匿名組合

antecedents
(history, development)
enkaku
沿革

(background)
keireki
経歴

applicable law
junkyohō
準拠法

applicant
shinseinin
申請人

application for registration
(company)
kiroku shinsei(sho)
記録申請(書)

(patent)
tōroku shinsei(sho)
登録申請(書)

appoint
ninmei suru
任命する

appointment (to a post)
ninmei
任命

appointment of directors
torishimariyaku no ninmei
取締役の任命

area of operation (= field)
torihiki bun'ya
取引分野

articles of association [UK]
kaisha teikan
会社定款
teikan
定款

articles of company
tsūjō teikan
通常定款

articles of incorporation [US]
kaisha teikan
会社定款
teikan
定款

articles of partnership
kumiai kiyaku
組合規約
kumiai teikan
組合定款

associate[21]
kumiai'in[21]
組合員
teikeisha
提携者

associated company [UK]
(collateral company)
bōkei gaisha
傍系会社

(related company)
kankei gaisha
関係会社
kanren gaisha
関連会社

(subsidiary) (see note 20)
keiretsu gaisha (see note 20)
系列会社
kogaisha
子会社

association
(guild, partnership)[22]
kumiai[22]
組合
kyōdō kumiai
共同組合

(league, society)
kyōkai
協会

(joint partnership)
noriai
乗合い
gōdō
合同

(corporation)
shadan
社団

association clause
boshū jōkō
募集条項

authentification
shōnin
承認

authority
kengen
権限

authority to represent the company
daihyō kengen
代表権限

authorization (powers)
kengen
権限

authorized representative
daihyō kengen o yūsuru torishimariyaku
代表権限を有する
取締役

authorized signatories
daihyō kengen o yūsuru shomeisha
代表権限を有する
署名者

automonous body
jichitai
自治体

background
(history, development)
enkaku
沿革

(career)
keireki
経歴

bad business
furi na jigyō
不利な事業

bad performance
nozomashiku nai gyōseki
望ましくない業績

benevolent association
sōgo fujo kumiai
相互扶助組合

benevolent institution
jizen kyōkai
慈善協会

big business
daishōbai
大商売

(large corporation)
daikigyō
大企業

big merger
ōgata gappei
大型合併

blank power of attorney
hakushi ininjō
白紙委任状

blue-chip company
yūryō gaisha
優良会社

Board of Directors
torishimariyakukai
取締役会

board of managing directors
jōmukai
常務会

body
dantai
団体

body corporate
hōjin
法人

bogus company
yūrei gaisha
幽霊会社

branch network
shitenmō
支店網

branch office
shisha
支社
shiten
支店

(vs. head-office)
shibu
支部

(agency, outpost)
shutchōjo
出張所

Branch Register [UK]
shisha tōkibo
支社登記簿

bubble company
hōmatsu gaisha
泡沫会社

build up a business
shōbai o kizukiageru
商売を築上げる

building
tatemono
建物

business
(operation, work)
gyōmu
業務

(operation, trade)
eigyō
営業

(industry)
jitsugyō
実業

(commerce, trade)
shōbai
商売
shōgyō
商業

(transaction)
torihiki
取引

business, a
(enterprise, venture)
jigyō
事業

(company)
kaisha
会社

(an enterprise)
kigyō
企業

(commercial company)
shōji gaisha
商事会社

(trading company)
shōsha
商社

business activity
eigyō katsudō
営業活動

business address
kigyō shozaichi
企業所在地

business administration
kigyō kei'ei
企業経営

business affiliation
jigyō kankei
事業関係

business agent
dairiten
代理店

business ailments
kigyō no byōjō
企業の病状

business analysis
kei'ei bunseki
経営分析

business census
shōgyō sensasu
商業センサス

business centre
shōgyō chūshinchi
商業中心地

business circles
jitsugyōkai
実業界

business collaboration
jigyō teikei
事業提携

business combination
kigyō gōdō
企業合同

business competitor
shōbai gataki
商売敵

business concern
shōji gaisha
商事会社

business concession
eigyō menkyo
営業免許

business confidence
kigyōka no kakushin
企業家の確信

business connections
torihiki kankei
取引関係

business consultant
kei'ei kanrishi
経営管理士
kei'ei komon
経営顧問

business customary practice
shōkanshū
商慣習

business day
eigyōbi
営業日

business diagnosis
kei'ei shindan
経営診断

business diversification
gyōmu tayōka
業務多様化

business diversification programme
gyōmu tayōka keikaku
業務多様化計画

business documents
kenri shorui
権利書類

business engagements
shōyō
商用

business enterprise
kigyō
企業

business establishment
jigyōsho
事業所

business expansion
gyōmu kakuchō
業務拡張
jigyō kakuchō
事業拡張

business expertise
jigyō no senmon chishiki
事業の専門知識

business field
eigyō bun'ya
営業分野
jigyō bun'ya
事業分野

business giant
kyodai kigyō
巨大企業

business group
jitsugyō dantai
実業団体
kigyō shūdan
企業集団

business hours
eigyō jikan
営業時間

business infrastructure
eigyō kiban
営業基盤

business licence
eigyō menkyo
営業免許

business management
gyōmu kanri
業務管理
kei'ei kanri
経営管理
kigyō kei'ei
企業経営

business matter
yōken
用件

business modernization
(rationalization)
kigyō gōrika
企業合理化

business name
shōgō
商号

business objectives
kei'ei mokuteki
経営目的

business operation
eigyō
営業
jigyō un'ei
事業運営

business opportunity
shōki
商機

business organization
(set-up)
gyōmu soshiki
業務組織

(group)
jitsugyō dantai
実業団体

business outlook
gyōkyō
業況

business performance
eigyō jisseki
営業実績
(kigyō) gyōseki
(企業) 業績

business performance report
gyōseki hōkokusho
業績報告書

business person
(trader)
gyōsha
業者

(entrepreneur)
jitsugyōka
実業家
kigyōka
企業家

business plan
kigyō keikaku
企業計画

business planning
(project)
jigyō keikaku
事業計画

(management planning)
kei'ei keikaku
経営計画

business policy
kigyō seisaku
企業政策

(management policy)
kei'ei hōshin
経営方針

business practice
(management)
kei'ei jissen
経営実践

(trade)
shōkankō
商慣行
shōkanshū
商慣習

business proprietor
jigyōnushi
事業主

business rationalization
kigyō gōrika
企業合理化

business report
eigyō hōkokusho
営業報告書

(performance report)
gyōseki hōkokusho
業績報告書

business results analysis
gyōseki kentō
業績検討

business scale
jigyō kibo
事業規模

business scheme
jigyō keikaku
事業計画

business status
eigyō jōtai
営業状態

business strategy
kei'ei senryaku
経営戦略

business structure
kigyō kōzō
企業構造
kigyō taishitsu
企業体質

business woman
josei jimuka
女性事務家
josei jitsugyōka
女性実業家

business world
jitsugyōkai
実業界

**businessman
(trader)**
gyōsha
業者

(entrepreneur)
jitsugyōka
実業家
kigyōka
企業家

buy-out (noun)
baishū
買収

buy out (verb)
baishū suru
買収する

by-laws
shasoku
社則

capital clause
shihon jōkō
資本条項

CEO (chief executive officer)
kei'ei saikō sekininsha
経営最高責任者

**certificate of incorporation
[US]**
hōjin setsuritsu ninkashō
法人設立認可証
kaisha setsuritsu kyokashō
会社設立認可証

certificate of registration
shōgyō tōkibo tōhon
商業登記簿謄本

**certificate to commence
business**
sōgyō kaishi kyokashō
創業開始許可証

certified copy
ninshō tōhon
認証謄本

certified translation
ninshō hon'yaku
認証翻訳

chain
chēn
チェーン

(store)
rensaten
連鎖店

chain operation
chēn-operēshon
チェーン・オペレー
ション

chairman
kaichō
会長

**Chairman of the Board of
Directors**
torishimariyaku kaichō
取締役会長

**change in organization
structure**
kikōjō no henkō
機構上の変更

**change of address
(company's)**
shozaichi henkō
所在地変更

change of business name
kigyō kaishō
企業改称

change of line of business
gyōshu henkō
業種変更

change of name (company's)
shōgō kaishō
商号改称

change of trade name
shōgō henkō
商号変更

charitable corporation
kōeki hōjin
公益法人

charitable enterprise
jizen jigyō
慈善事業

charitable organization
jizen kikan
慈善機関

charitable trust
kōeki zaidan
公益財団

charter
teikan
定款

chartered company [UK]
tokkyo gaisha
特許会社

chartered corporation [UK]
tokkyo gaisha
特許会社

chief controller
keiri buchō
経理部長

chief director
rijichō
理事長

chief executive
sōmu buchō
総務部長

chief executive officer (CEO)
kei'ei saikō sekininsha
経営最高責任者

classification of companies
kigyō bunrui
企業分類

close one's business
shōbai o yameru
商売を止める

**clause
(article)**
jōkō
条項

(stipulation)
jōkan
条款

close company [UK]
heisa gaisha
閉鎖会社
hikōkai gaisha
非公開会社

closed corporation [US]
heisa gaisha
閉鎖会社
hikōkai gaisha
非公開会社

combination of companies
kaisha rengō
会社連合

combine (noun)
kigyō gōdō
企業合同

commercial business
shōgyō
商業

(profit-making business)
eiri jigyō
営利事業

commercial company
eiri gaisha
営利会社
eiri kigyō
営利企業

commercial directory
shōgyōnin meibo
商業人名簿

commercial enterprise
eiri jigyō
営利事業

commercial establishment
shōkai
商会
shōsha
商社

commercial partnership
eiri kumiai
営利組合

commission agency business
ton'yagyō
問屋業

commission agent
itaku hanbainin
委託販売人

common seal [UK]
inkan shōmei
印鑑証明
shain
社印

Companies Act [UK]
kaishahō
会社法

company
kaisha
会社

(a business, an enterprise)
kigyō
企業

(commercial establishment)
shōkai
商会
shōsha
商社

company chairman
kaichō
会長

company incorporated abroad
genchi hōjin
現地法人
genchi kigyō
現地企業

company law [UK]
kaishahō
会社法

company letterhead
kaisha no shokan'yōshi tōbu
会社の書簡用紙頭部

company limited by guarantee
hoshō sekinin gaisha
保証責任会社

company limited by shares
kabushiki gaisha
株式会社

company name
kaishamei
会社名
shamei
社名

company of the same parentage
dōkei no kaisha
同系の会社

company organization
kaisha soshiki
会社組織

company policy
kaisha seisaku
会社政策

company registration
shōgyō tōki
商業登記

company registration certificate
shōgyō tōkibo tōhon
商業登記簿謄本

company regulations
shasoku
社則

company reorganization
kaisha kōsei
会社更生

company seal
inkan shōmei
印鑑証明
shain
社印

company secretary
kaisha no kanji
会社の幹事

company standard
shanai kikaku
社内規格

company's charter
kaisha setsuritsu kyokashō
会社設立許可証

company's solicitors
kaisha komon bengoshi
会社顧問弁護士

competitive
kyōsōteki na
競争的な

competitiveness
kyōsōryoku
競争力

competitor
kyōsō aite
競争相手

comply with the rules
kikaku o shitagau
規格を従う

concern
  (a company)
  kaisha
  会社

  (a business, an enterprise)
  kigyō
  企業

  (commercial establishment)
  shōkai
  商会

  (trading company)
  shōsha
  商社

conduct business
  jigyō o kei'ei suru
  事業を経営する

conglomerate
  fukugō kigyō
  複合企業

consolidated subsidiary
  renketsu kogaisha
  連結子会社

consolidation
  shinsetsu gappei
  新設合併

consolidation group
  renketsu shūdan
  連結集団

consolidation of companies
  kaisha no shinsetsu gappei
  会社の新設合併

consortium
  konsōshiamu
  コンソーシアム

contest for corporate control
  kaisha shihaiken no kyōsō
  会社支配権の競争

control
  (administration, management)
  kanri
  管理

  (rule, domination)
  shihai
  支配

control person
  tokubetsu rigai kankeinin
  特別利害関係人

controlled company
  hishihai gaisha
  被支配会社

controlled foreign company
  hishihai gaikoku gaisha
  被支配外国会社

controlling company
  shihai gaisha
  支配会社

  (parent company)
  oyagaisha
  親会社

controlling interests
  shihaiteki riken
  支配的利権

co-owner
  kyōdō shoyūsha
  共同所有者

co-ownership
  kyōdō shoyū
  共同所有

co-partner
  kyōdō kumiai'in
  共同組合員
  kyōdōsha
  共同者

co-partnership
  kyōdō kumiai
  共同組合

copy of document
  shorui tōhon
  書類謄本

corporate
  hōjin soshiki no
  法人組織の

corporate body
  hōjin
  法人
  hōjin dantai
  法人団体

corporate business
  hōjin kigyō
  法人企業

corporate business sector
  hōjin kigyō bumon
  法人企業部門

corporate control
  shihaiken
  支配権

corporate directors
  hōjin riji
  法人理事
  kaisha torishimariyaku
  会社取締役

corporate enterprise (corporate business, corporation)
  hōjin kigyō
  法人企業

  (group)
  shūdan kei'ei
  集団経営

corporate entity
  kigyōtai
  企業体

corporate form
  hōjin keitai
  法人形態

corporate identity
  kaisha shikibetsu
  会社識別

corporate image
  kigyō imēji
  企業イメージ

corporate juridical person
  shadan hōjin
  社団法人

corporate lawyer
  kaisha komon bengoshi
  会社顧問弁護士
  kigyō komon bengoshi
  企業顧問弁護士

corporate manager
  kei'eisha
  経営者

corporate member
  hōjin kai'in
  法人会員
  kaisha kai'in
  会社会員

corporate name
(legal person)
hōjin meigi
法人名義

(company)
kaishamei
会社名
shamei
社名

(business)
shōgō
商号

corporate officer
kaisha yakuin
会社役員

corporate organization
(legal person)
hōjin soshiki
法人組織

(company)
kaisha soshiki
会社組織

corporate person
hōjin
法人

corporate reorganization
kaisha kōsei
会社更生

corporate reorganization
procedure
kaisha kōsei tetsuzuki
会社更生手続き

corporate responsibility
kyōdō sekinin
共同責任

corporate rights
hōjinken
法人権

corporate staff
kōporēto-sutaffu
コーポレート・
スタッフ

corporate structure
kaisha taishitsu
会社体質

corporation
(group)
dantai
団体

(legal person)
hōjin
法人

(joint-stock company)
kabushiki gaisha
株式会社

(company)
kaisha
会社
kigyō
企業

corporation aggregate
ippan hōjin
一般法人
shadan hōjin
社団法人

corporation charter
kaisha teikan
会社定款

corporation controller
kaisha kansayaku
会社監査役

corporation law [US]
kaishahō
会社法

corporation lawyer
kaisha komon bengoshi
会社顧問弁護士
kigyō komon bengoshi
企業顧問弁護士

corporation seal
inkan shōmei
印鑑証明
shain
社印

corporation sole
tandoku hōjin
単独法人

corrupt practices
fusei kōi
不正行為

co-signatory
renshonin
連署人

co-signatory powers
renshonin no kengen
連署人の権限

counter-sign
(endorse, witness)
fukusho suru
副署する

(sign jointly)
rensho suru
連署する

counter-signature
(endorsement,
witnessing)
fukusho
副署

(joint signature)
rensho
連署

country
kuni
国

create a company
kaisha o seiritsu suru
会社を成立する

curtailment of operations
sōgyō tanshuku
操業短縮

custody of the common seal
shain no hokan
社印の保管

damage to document
shorui kison
書類き損

damaged document
kison shorui
き損書類

date of establishment
setsuritsu nengappi
設立年月日

date of start of business
sōgyō nengappi
操業年月日

day-to-day business
nichijō gyōmu
日常業務

decentralized management
bunkenteki kanri
分権的管理

decentralized management organization
bunkenteki kanri soshiki
分権的管理組織

decision
kettei
決定

decision-maker
ishi ketteisha
意思決定者

decision-making
ishi kettei
意思決定

deed
shōsho
証書

deed of partnership
kumiai keiyaku shōsho
組合契約証書

delegation of authority
kengen ijō
権限委譲
kengen inin
権限委任

delegation of powers
kengen ijō
権限委譲
kengen inin
権限委任

delegation of responsibility
kengen ijō
権限委譲

deputy chairman
fukushachō
副社長

deputy managing director [UK]
fukushachō
副社長

detached office
shussen no jimusho
出先の事務所

direct control
kantoku
監督

director
torishimariyaku
取締役

(executive, officer)
jūyaku
重役

director's fee
yakuin hōshū
役員報酬

director's remuneration
yakuin hōshū
役員報酬

director's report
torishimariyaku no hōkoku
取締役の報告

disclosure
kōkai
公開

dissolution
kaishō
解消

dissolution of partnership
teikei no kaishō
提携の解消

dissolve
kaishō suru
解消する

diversification management
takaku kei'ei
多角経営

diversification of business
gyōmu tayōka
業務多様化
jigyō tayōka
事業多様化

diversification operation
takaku kei'ei
多角経営

divestiture
kogaisha no baikyaku
子会社の売却

division (in a company)
jigyōbu
事業部

do business
torihiki suru
取引する

document
shorui
書類

document of right
kenri shōken
権利証券

domestic business
naikoku kigyō
内国企業

domestic company
naikoku gaisha
内国会社

domestic corporation
naikoku hōjin
内国法人

domicile
kigyō shozaichi
企業所在地

dormant company
tokumei gaisha
匿名会社

**dormant partner
(minor)**
jakushō shain
弱小社員

(anonymous)
tokumei kumiai'in
匿名組合員
tokumei shain
匿名社員

draft (noun)
sakusei
作成

draft (verb)
sakusei suru
作成する

drawing up the Articles of Incorporation
teikan no sakusei
定款の作成

dummy company
damii gaisha
ダミー会社

dummy director
meigi torishimariyaku
名義取締役

(outside director)
shagai jūyaku
社外重役

duplicate
fukuhon
副本
tōhon
謄本

duties
(office, functions, tasks)
ninmu
任務

(extent of responsibility)
sekinin han'i
責任範囲

(functions, job, work)
shokumu
職務
tantō gyōmu
担当業務

efficiency of management
kei'ei kōritsu
経営効率

employed director
koyō jūyaku
雇用重役

employed executive
koyō kei'eisha
雇用経営者

empower
kengen o ataeru
権限を与える

empowered to (—)
(—) kengen o fuyo sarete
iru
(—) 権限を付与され
ている

enter into business (with)
(to no) gyōmu teikei o
teiketsu suru
(との) 業務提携を
締結する

enterprise
(undertaking, project)
jigyō
事業

(business, company)
kigyō
企業

entrepreneur
jigyōka
事業家
kigyōka
企業家

entrepreneur spirit
kigyōka seishin
企業家精神
kigyōshin
企業心

entrepreneurial
kigyōka no
企業家の

entrepreneurial skill
kei'ei gijutsu
経営技術

entrepreneurship
kigyōka seishin
企業家精神
kigyōshin
企業心

establish
(found, institute)
setchi suru
設置する

(found, form, set up)
setsuritsu suru
設立する

established
setsuritsu sareta
設立された

establishment (of a company)
(formation, setting up)
setsuritsu
設立

(inauguration, start of business)
sōgyō
創業

examination of documents
shorui no kensa
書類の検査

exclusive distributor
itte hanbaiten
一手販売店

exclusive distributorship
itte hanbaiken
一手販売権

execute a deed
shōsho o chōin suru
証書を調印する

executive (noun)
kei'eisha
経営者

executive ability
kei'ei nōryoku
経営能力

executive board
jōmukai
常務会
shikkō i'inkai
執行委員会

executive committee
shikkō i'inkai
執行委員会

executive director
jōmu torishimariyaku
常務取締役

executive duties
kei'ei gimu
経営義務

executive management
kei'ei kanbu
経営幹部

executive officer
shikkō shain
執行社員
shikkōkan
執行官

(highest-ranking)
saikō shokuin
最高職員

executive responsibility
kanri sekinin
管理責任

executive staff
(kei'ei) kanbu
(経営) 幹部

executive vice-president [US]
fukushachō
副社長

exempted corporation
hikazei hōjin
非課税法人

exempted private company
tokurei shigaisha
特例私会社

existing company
kison kigyō
既存企業

expansion
kakuchō
拡張

expansion of business
jigyō kakuchō
事業拡張

expansion programme
kakuchō keikaku
拡張計画

experience in management
kei'ei keiken
経営経験

experienced management
keiken yūka na kei'eisha
経験有価な経営者

expert manager
senmon kei'eisha
専門経営者

expiration of power of attorney
ininken no shūryō
委任権の終了

exploitation efficiency
genkai nōritsu
限界能率

factory
kōjō
工場

factory owner
kōjōnushi
工場主

false representation
fushinjitsu na hyōji
不真実な表示

false signature
gihitsu shomei
偽筆署名

falsification
shorui gizō
書類偽造

family concern
dōzoku gaisha
同族会社

file (an application)
mōshitate o suru
申立てをする
shinseisho o teishutsu suru
申請書を提出する

filing of documents
shorui no shinsei
書類の申請

firm
  (company)
  kaisha
  会社

  (business)
  kigyō
  企業

  (concern)
  shōsha
  商社

first-class company
ichiryū no kaisha
一流の会社

flourishing business
keiki no ii kaisha
景気のいい会社

foreign affiliate
gaishikei kigyō
外資系企業

foreign-backed enterprise
gaishikei kigyō
外資系企業

foreign company
gaikoku gaisha
外国会社
gaikoku kigyō
外国企業

foreign corporate body
gaikoku hōjin
外国法人

foreign corporation
gaikoku gaisha
外国会社
gaikoku hōjin
外国法人

foreign-owned company
gaishikei kigyō
外資系企業

foreign subsidiary
kaigai jūzoku gaisha
海外従属会社

forged seal (company's)
gizō shain
偽造社印

forged signature
gisho
偽署

forgery of document
bunsho gizō
文書偽造

forgery of seal (company's)
shain gizō
社印偽造

form a company
kaisha o okosu
会社を起こす
kaisha o setsuritsu suru
会社を設立する

form of business organization
gyōtai
業態
kigyō keitai
企業形態

form of enterprise
kigyō keitai
企業形態

formation of a company
kaisha setsuritsu
会社設立

found
(create, institute)
setchi suru
設置する

(set up)
setsuritsu suru
設立する

(establish, start business)
sōgyō suru
創業する

foundation, a
(group)
dantai
団体

(association)
kyōkai
協会

founder
setsuritsusha
設立者
sōgyōsha
創業者

(promoter)
hokkinin
発起人

founding
(establishment)
setsuritsu
設立

(start of business)
sōgyō
創業

franchise
furanchaizu
フランチャイズ

(business concession)
eigyō menkyo
営業免許

(business rights)
eigyōken
営業権

(sale rights) [US]
itte hanbaiken
一手販売権

franchise agreement
furanchaizu keiyaku
フランチャイズ契約

franchise rights
eigyōken
営業権

franchisee
eigyōken hoyūsha
営業権保有者
furanchaizu o ataerareru
hito
フランチャイズを
与えられる人

franchisor
furanchaizu o ataeru hito
フランチャイズを
与える人

fraudulent act
fusei kōi
不正行為

fraudulent misrepresentation
akui fujitsu hyōji
悪意不実表示

friendly buyer
yūkōteki na baishūsha
友好的な買収者.

friendly take-over
yūkōteki na nottori
友好的な乗っ取り

fulfil one's duties
shokumu o hatasu
職務を果たす

functions
ninmu
任務
shokumu
職務

fusion
(merger)
gappei
合併

(joint partnership)
gōdō
合同

Gazette, the
kanpō
官報

general affairs committee
sōmu i'inkai
総務委員会

general management
sōkatsu kei'eisō
総括経営層

**general management
executives**
sōkatsu kei'eisō
総括経営層

general partner
mugen sekinin shain
無限責任社員

general partnership
(unlimited)
gōmei gaisha
合名会社

(ordinary)
tsūjō kumiai
通常組合

general power of attorney
zenken ininjō
全権委任状

general trading company [J]
sōgō shōsha
総合商社

giant firm
kyodai kigyō
巨大企業

giant merger
ōgata gappei
大型合併

go into partnership
teikei suru
提携する

going concern
eigyōchū no kigyō
営業中の企業
keizoku kigyō
継続企業

good reputation
kōhyō
好評

governing board
rijikai
理事会

government corporation
kōsha
公社
seifu kigyō
政府企業

government enterprise
kangyō
官業
seifu kigyō
政府企業

government institution
seifu kikan
政府機関

government-owned corporation
kōyū gaisha
公有会社
seifu shoyū gaisha
政府所有会社

government ownership
kokuyū
国有

hand over a business
shōbai o yuzuru
商売を譲る

head-office
honsha
本社
honten
本店

headquarters
eigyō no honkyo
営業の本拠

high-growth enterprise
kōseichō kigyō
高成長企業

holding company
mochikabu gaisha
持株会社

horizontal integration
suiheiteki tōgō
水平的統合

horizontal merger
suiheiteki gappei
水平的合併

hostile take-over
tekitaiteki na nottori
敵対的な乗っ取り

improvement of business operations
jimu kaizen
事務改善

inaugurate
hossoku suru
発足する
kaishi suru
開始する

inauguration
hossoku
発足

(opening of business)
kaigyōshiki
開業式

incoming partner
shinnyūshain
新入社員

incompetent management
setsuretsu na kei'ei
拙劣な経営

incorporate
hōjin soshiki ni suru
法人組織にする

(form, set up)
setsuritsu suru
設立する

incorporated
hōjin soshiki no
法人組織の
hōjin toshite setsuritsu sareta
法人として設立された

(inc., with limited liability)
yūgen sekinin no
有限責任の

incorporated association
shadan hōjin
社団法人

incorporated business
hōjin kigyō
法人企業

incorporated company
hōjin gaisha
法人会社

[US]
yūgen sekinin gaisha
有限責任会社

incorporated foundation
zaidan hōjin
財団法人

incorporation
hōjin soshiki no setsuritsu
法人組織の設立
kaisha setsuritsu
会社設立

incorporation certificate
setsuritsu shōsho
設立証書

incorporation procedure
kaisha setsuritsu tetsuzuki
会社設立手続き

incorporator
hōjin setsuritsusha
法人設立者
kaisha setsuritsusha
会社設立者

independent business
jieigyō
自営業

independent company
dokuritsu no kaisha
独立の会社

individual enterprise
kojin kigyō
個人企業

individual firm
kobetsu kigyō
個別企業

individual name
kojinmei
個人名

individual proprietor
jieigyōsha
自営業者

individual proprietorship
kigyō no tandoku shoyū
企業の単独所有

individually owned firm
jiei no kigyō
自営の企業

industrial concern
kōgyō gaisha
工業会社

industrial group
kōgyō shūdan
工業集団

industrial property
kōgyō shoyūken
工業所有権

industrial rights
kōgyō shoyūken
工業所有権

infringement of patent right
tokkyoken shingai
特許権侵害

infringement of trademark
shōhyōken shingai
商標権侵害

inherited firm
sōzoku gaisha
相続会社

inspection of corporate records
kaisha kiroku no kensa
会社記録の検査

inspection of documents
bunsho no etsuran
文書の閲覧

institute (noun)
kyōkai
協会

institution
kikan
機関

integrated management
sōgō un'ei
総合運営

integration
tōgō
統合

international company
kokusai gaisha
国際会社

international corporation
kokusai gaisha
国際会社

international enterprise
kokusai kigyō
国際企業

international organization
kokusai kikō
国際機構

international reputation
kokusaiteki na seika
国際的な声価

interruption of business
eigyō teishi
営業停止

irresponsible management
hōman kei'ei
放漫経営

irrevocable power of attorney
kakutei ininjō
確定委任状

irrevocable proxy
kakutei ininjō
確定委任状

joint and several liability
rentai sekinin
連帯責任

joint business
gōdō kigyō
合同企業

joint business venture
gōben gaisha
合弁会社

joint company
gōben gaisha
合弁会社

joint concern
gōben gaisha
合弁会社

joint control
kyōdō kanri
共同管理
kyōdō shihai
共同支配

joint enterprise
kyōdō kigyō
共同企業

(combined business)
gōdō kigyō
合同企業

(joint partnership)
noriai
乗合い

joint international venture
kokusai kyōdō shusshi gaisha
国際共同出資会社

joint liability
rentai sekinin
連帯責任

joint management
gōdō kei'ei
合同経営
kyōdō kei'ei
共同経営

joint operation
kyōdō kei'ei
共同経営

joint owner
kyōyūsha
共有者

joint ownership
kyōyūken
共有権

joint responsibility
kyōdō sekinin
共同責任

joint-stock company
[US]
gōshi gaisha
合資会社

[UK]
kabushiki gaisha
株式会社

joint-stock limited partnership
kabushiki gōshi gaisha
株式合資会社

joint undertaking
kyōdō jigyō
共同事業

joint venture
gōben jigyō
合弁事業

joint-venture company
gōben gaisha
合弁会社

junior partner
kakyū shain
下級社員

juridical person
hōjin
法人

laboratory
kenkyūjo
研究所

large corporation
daikigyō
大企業

large-scale enterprise
daikibo kigyō
大規模企業

large-scale merger
ōgata gappei
大型合併

latecomer
kōhatsu kigyō
後発企業

lateral integration
sokumen tōgō
側面統合

leading company
sendō kigyō
先導企業
shudō kigyō
主導企業

leading firm
sendō kigyō
先導企業
shudō kigyō
主導企業

legal documents
hōritsu shorui
法律書類

legal person
hōjin
法人

legal power
hōteki kenryoku
法的権力

legal representative
hōtei dairinin
法定代理人

legal status (of company)
(kigyō no) hōteki seikaku
(企業の) 法的性格

letter of proxy
ininjō
委任状

letterhead
kashiragaki
頭書き

liability
sekinin
責任

liability limited by guarantee
hoshō sekinin
保証責任

liability limited by shares
kabushiki sekinin
株式責任

licence
(permit, permission)
kyoka
許可
menkyo
免許

(patent right)
tokkyoken
特許権

licence fee
menkyoryō
免許料
tokkyoken shiyōryō
特許権使用料

licencing
menkyosei
免許制

licensee
hikyokasha
被許可者

licensor
ken'etsusha
検閲者

limitation of liability
sekinin seigen
責任制限

limited company [UK]
yūgen (sekinin) gaisha
有限(責任)会社

limited liability
yūgen sekinin
有限責任

limited-liability company
yūgen (sekinin) gaisha
有限(責任)会社

limited partner
yūgen sekinin shain
有限責任社員

limited partnership
(company)
gōshi gaisha
合資会社

(association)
yūgen sekinin kumiai
有限責任組合

line of business
eigyō bun'ya
営業分野
gyōshu
業種

list of members
kai'in meibo
会員名簿

local branch
chihō shiten
地方支店

local business
genchi kigyō
現地企業

local office
chihō jimusho
地方事務所

location of branch offices
shiten no bunpu
支店の分布

location of business
eigyōsho
営業所

loss of document
bunsho no funshitsu
文書の紛失

lost document
funshitsu bunsho
紛失文書

lower management
kakyū kei'eisō
下級経営層

lucrative business
yūri na jigyō
有利な事業

main business
hongyō
本業

major control
kahansū shihai
過半数支配
tasū shihai
多数支配

majority-owned subsidiary
kahansū shoyū jūzoku
gaisha
過半数所有従属会社

majority ownership
kahansū shoyū
過半数所有

majority representation
tasū daihyō
多数代表

majority shareholder
tasū kabunushi
多数株主

manage
  (control)
kanri suru
管理する

  (run)
kei'ei suru
経営する

management
  (control)
kanri
管理

  (administration, running)
kei'ei
経営

  (staff)
kei'eisha
経営者

  (level of management, strata)
kanrisō
管理層
kei'eisō
経営層

management advisory service
kei'ei jogen
経営助言

management consultant
kei'eishi
経営士

management consulting
kei'ei shindan
経営診断
kigyō shindan
企業診断

management control
kei'eisha shihai
経営者支配

management development
kanrisha keihatsu
管理者啓発

management development programme
kanrisha keihatsu keikaku
管理者啓発計画

management education
kei'ei kyōiku
経営教育

management efficiency
kei'ei kōritsu
経営効率

management hierarchy
kei'ei kaisō
経営階層

management information system
kei'ei jōhō kanri seido
経営情報管理制度

management of affairs
jimu kanri
事務管理

management organization
kei'ei kanri soshiki
経営管理組織

management performance
kei'ei gyōseki
経営業績
kei'ei jisseki
経営実績

management planning
kei'ei keikaku
経営計画

management policy
kei'ei hōshin
経営方針

management responsibilities
kei'ei sekinin
経営責任

management review
kei'ei kansa
経営監査

management revolution
kei'eisha kakumei
経営者革命

management rights
kei'eiken
経営権

management strategy
kei'ei senryaku
経営戦略

management standards
kanri hyōjun
管理標準

management structure
kei'ei soshiki
経営組織

management system
kei'ei soshiki
経営組織

management technique
kanri gijutsu
管理技術
kei'ei gijutsu
経営技術

management training programme
kanrisha kunren keikaku
管理者訓練計画

manager [UK]
fukushachō
福社長

managerial control
kei'eiteki tōsei
経営的統制

managerial function
kanrinin no shokumu
管理人の職務

managerial know-how
kei'ei gijutsu
経営技術

managerial standards
kanri hyōjun
管理標準

managing Board of Directors
kanri torishimariyakukai
管理取締役会

managing committee
jōmu i'inkai
常務委員会

managing director
[J]
jōmu torishimariyaku
常務取締役
senmu torishimariyaku
専務取締役

[UK]
shachō
社長

managing executive
jimu kyokuchō
事務局長

managing partner
gyōmu shikkō shain
業務執行社員

marginal enterprise
genkai kigyō
限界企業

marginal entrepreneur
genkai kigyōka
限界企業家

marginal firm
genkai kigyō
限界企業

medium and small enterprises
chūshō kigyō
中小企業

medium-sized enterprise
chūken kigyō
中堅企業

member
shain
社員

member company
kai'in gaisha
会員会社

member's bankruptcy
shain no hasan
社員の破産

member's death
shain no shibō
社員の死亡

members of the Board
kōsei'in
構成員

Memorandum of Association
kitai yakkan
基体約款

merge (with)
(to) gappei suru
(と)合併する

merger
(fusion)
gappei
合併

(joint partnership)
gōdō
合同

(absorption, merger and acquisition)
kyūshū gappei
吸収合併

merger activity
gappei katsudō
合併活動

merger agreement
gappei no dōi
合併の同意

merger on equal terms
taitō gappei
対等合併

merger terms
gappei jōken
合併条件

middle management
chūkan kei'eisō
中間経営層

minor enterprise
chūshō kigyō
中小企業

minor executives
kakyū kanbu shokuin
下級幹部職員

Minute Book
gijirokubo
議事録簿

minutes
gijiroku
議事録

misconduct
futō kei'ei
不当経営

misleading name (of a company)
shōgō no fumeiryō
商号の不明瞭

misrepresentation
fujitsu hyōji
不実表示

multi-company
tagyōshu gaisha
多業種会社

multi-industry firm
tagyōshu kigyō
多業種企業

multi-market corporation
takaku kei'ei gaisha
多角経営会社

multi-market firm
tasū shijō kigyō
多数市場企業

multi-merger
takakuteki gappei
多角的合併

multi-national, a
takokuseki kigyō
多国籍企業

multi-plant company
takōjō gaisha
多工場会社

multiple management
takaku kei'ei
多角経営

multi-product firm
tasū shōhin seizō gaisha
多数商品製造会社

mushroom company
tanmei gaisha
短命会社

mutilated document
kison bunsho
き損文書

mutilation of document
bunsho kison
文書き損

name of company
kigyōmei
企業名

　(business name)
shōgō
商号

nameplate
hyōsatsu
標札／表札

national company
kokunai kigyō
国内企業

nationality
kokuseki
国籍

nationally owned firm
kokuyū kigyō
国有企業

nationalization
kokuyūka
国有化

nationalize
kokuyūka suru
国有化する

nationalized company
kokuei kigyō
国営企業

nature of business
jigyō no shurui
事業の種類

neglect one's duties
shokumu o okotaru
職務を怠る

new business
shinsetsu kigyō
新設企業

newcomer
kōhatsu kigyō
後発企業

newly established corporation
shinsetsu kigyō
新設企業

nominal partner
hyōgenteki shain
表現的社員

non-productive business
hiseisanteki jigyō
非生産的事業

non-profit business
hi'eiri kigyō
非営利企業

non-profit company
hi'eiri gaisha
非営利会社

non-profit corporation
hi'eiri hōjin
非営利法人

non-profit foundation
hi'eiri zaidan
非営利財団

non-profit institution
hi'eiri kikan
非営利機関

non-profit organization
hi'eiri dantai
非営利団体

non-taxable corporation
kōkyō hōjin
公共法人

notice
tsūchi
通知

notification
todoke
届け
tsūchijō
通知状

notification of change of address
jūsho henkō todoke
住所変更届け

notify
tsūchi o ataeru
通知を与える

number of directors
yakuinsū
役員数

number of employees
jūgyōinsū
従業員数

objectives
kamoku
科目
mokuteki
目的

objects (of a company)
eigyō kamoku
営業科目

objects clause
kamoku jōkō
科目条項

office
　(place of business)
jimusho
事務所

　(post)
shūnin
就任

office building
eigyōyō kaoku
営業用家屋

office management
jimu kanri
事務管理

office manual
jimu kitei
事務規程

office regulations
shūgyō kisoku
就業規則

office routine
kei'ei jimu
経営事務

officer of a company
yakuin
役員

offshoot
kogaisha
子会社

old firm (shop)
rōho
老舗

one-man business
hitori kigyō
一人企業

one-man company
hitori gaisha
一人会社

one-man operation
hitori kei'ei
一人経営

open corporation
kabushiki kōkai gaisha
株式公開会社

opening hours
eigyō jikan
営業時間

operate
eigyō suru
営業する
itonamu
営む

operating business
eiri gaisha
営利会社

operating company
eigyō gaisha
営業会社

operating philosophy
kei'ei tetsugaku
経営哲学

operating rate
sōgyōritsu
操業率

(capacity)
kadōritsu
稼働率

operating ratio
eigyō (katsudō) hiritsu
営業(活動)比率

operating report
gyōmu hōkokusho
業務報告書

operating results
eigyō jisseki
営業実績
eigyō seiseki
営業成績
gyōseki
業績

operation
(a business operation)
eigyō
営業

(business, work)
gyōmu
業務

(an enterprise)
jigyō
事業

(management, running)
kei'ei
経営

(work)
sagyō
作業
sōgyō
操業

(conduct, management, administration)
un'ei
運営

operation standard
sagyō hyōjun
作業標準

operational company
eigyō gaisha
営業会社
jigyō gaisha
事業会社

operational control
gyōmu kanri
業務管理

operator
kei'eisha
経営者
un'eisha
運営者

opportunity
kikai
機会

ordinary partnership (= unlimited)
gōmei gaisha
合名会社

organization
(group)
dantai
団体

(institution)
kikan
機関

(structure)
kikō
機構

(association)
kyōkai
協会

(set-up)
soshiki
組織

organization chart
kaisha kikōzu
会社機構図
soshikizu
組織図

organization committee
sōritsu i'inkai
創立委員会

organization control
soshiki taisei
組織体制

organization man
soshikinin
組織人

organization process
setsuritsu tetsuzuki
設立手続き

organization structure
kikō
機構
soshiki kōzō
組織構造

organizational ability
soshiki nōryoku
組織能力

organizational improvement
soshikijō no kaizen
組織上の改善

original company
motouke gaisha
元受け会社

original document
seihon
正本

outpost
desaki
出先
shussen no jimusho
出先の事務所

outside director
shagai jūyaku
社外重役

overall control
sōkatsu kei'ei
総括経営

overall efficiency
zenkōritsu
全校率

overall management
sōkatsu kei'ei
総括経営

overall reorganization
zenmenteki hensei
全面的編成

overseas affiliate
kaigai kanren gaisha
海外関連会社

overseas branch
kaigai shiten
海外支店

overseas firm
kaigai kigyō
海外企業

overseas holding company
kaigai mochikabu gaisha
海外持株会社

overseas operation
kaigai jigyō
海外事業

own site (company's)
jisha no shikichi
自社の敷地

owner
(kigyō) shoyūsha
(企業) 所有者

owner control
shoyūsha shihai
所有者支配

owner-controlled firm
shoyūsha kigyō
所有者企業

owner-managed
kojin kei'ei no
個人経営の

owner-manager
shoyū kei'eisha
所有経営者

owner of business
jigyōnushi
事業主

owner-operator
jiei sagyōsha
自営作業者

ownership
(kigyō) shoyūken
(企業) 所有権

parent company
oyagaisha
親会社

part-owner
kigyō kyōyūsha
企業共有者

part-time business
pātotaimugyō
パートタイム業

part-time director
hijōkin jūyaku
非常勤重役

partially owned
bubun shoyū no
部分所有の

participation in management
kei'ei sanka
経営参加

partner
(co-partner)[21]
kumiai'in[21]
組合員

(joint business operators)
kyōdō kei'eisha
共同経営者

(joint capital investor)
kyōdō shusshisha
共同出資者

(member of company)
shain
社員

partner with limited liability
yūgen sekinin shain
有限責任社員

partner with unlimited liability
mugen sekinin shain
無限責任社員

partnership
(general, unlimited)
gōmei gaisha
合名貴社

(limited)
gōshi gaisha
合資会社

(association)[22]
kumiai[22]
組合

(combined businesses)
tōgō kigyō
統合企業

partnership agreement
kumiai keiyaku
組合契約

partnership articles
kumiai keiyakusho
組合契約書

patent
tokkyo
特許

patent applicant
tokkyo shutsugannin
特許出願人

patent application
tokkyo shutsugan
特許出願

patent applied for
tokkyo shutsuganchū
特許出願中

patent assignment
tokkyoken jōto
特許権譲渡

patent fee
tokkyoryō
特許料

patent grant
tokkyo kyoka
特許許可

patent holder
tokkyoken hojisha
特許権保持者

patent infringement
tokkyoken shingai
特許権侵害

patent law
tokkyohō
特許法

patent licence
tokkyo raisensu
特許ライセンス

patent licensing
tokkyo jitchi kyodaku
特許実地許諾

patent office
tokkyokyoku
特許局

patent pending
tokkyo shutsuganchū
特許出願中

patent right
tokkyoken
特許権

patent tax
tokkyozei
特許税

patentability
tokkyo shikaku
特許資格

patentee
tokkyokensha
特許権者

patentor
tokkyoken juyosha
特許権授与者

performance
gyōseki
業績

(actual results, record of achievement)
jisseki
実績

(merit, result)
seiseki
成績

performance evaluation
gyōseki hyōka
業績評価

permanent power of attorney
jōnin ininjō
常任委任状

permission to deal
sōgyō menkyo
創業免許

personnel
jin'in
人員
shokuin
職員

place of business
eigyōsho
営業所
jigyōsho
事業所

planning
keikaku
計画
kikaku
企画

planning ability
keikaku nōryoku
計画能力
kikakuryoku
企画力

plant
kōjō shisetsu
工場施設

plant capacity
kōjō setsubi nōryoku
工場設備能力

plant closure
kōjō heisa
工場閉鎖

plant location
kōjō ritchi
工場立地

plant management
setsubi kanri
設備管理

plc (public limited company) [UK]
kōkai yūgen sekinin gaisha
公開有限責任会社

power of attorney
(dairi) ininjō
(代理)委任状
ininken
委任権

power of representation
dairiken
代理権

powers
kengen
権限

premises
(place, office)
jimusho
事務所

(building)
tatemono
建物

president [US]
shachō
社長

prime business
yūryō kigyō
優良企業

principal members
shuyō na shain
主要な社員

principal place of business
eigyō no honkyo
営業の本拠

private company
(closed corporation [US])
kabushiki hikōkai gaisha
株式非公開会社

(non-governmental)
minkan kigyō
民間企業

(= limited) [UK]
shigaisha
私会社
yūgen gaisha
有限会社

private concern
kojin kigyō
個人企業

private corporation (= closed corporation) [US]
kabushiki hikōkai gaisha
株式非公開会社

private enterprise
(undertaking, business)
min'ei jigyō
民営事業

(company)
minkan kigyō
民間企業

private firm
minkan kigyō
民間企業

private non-profit organization
minkan hi'eiri dantai
民間非営利団体

privately operated business
min'ei jigyō
民営事業

privately owned company
hikōkai gaisha
非公開会社

privatization
min'eika
民営化

privatize
min'eika suru
民営化する

productive business
seisanteki jigyō
生産的事業

profit-making business
eiri jigyō
営利事業

profit-making company
eiri gaisha
営利会社

profit-making corporation
eiri hōjin
営利法人

profit-making enterprise
eiri kigyō
営利企業

profit-making institution
eiri kikan
営利機関

profit-making organization
eiri dantai
営利団体

profitable business concern
kōrijun no shōsha
高利潤の商社
mōkaru shōbai
もうかる商売
yūri na jigyō
有利な事業

promoter
hokkinin
発起人

proprietor
(kigyō) shoyūsha
(企業)所有者
kigyōnushi
企業主
kigyōsha
企業者

proprietorship
kojin kigyō
個人企業

prospectus
mokuromisho
目論見書
setsuritsu shuisho
設立趣意書

provincial branch
chihō shisha
地方支社

proxy
(representation)
dairi
代理

(representation right)
dairiken
代理権

(person)
dairinin
代理人

proxy form
dairi ininjō
代理委任状

public body
kōkyō dantai
公共団体

public company [UK]
kabushiki kōbo gaisha
株式公募会社

(limited company)
yūgen gaisha
有限会社

public corporation [US]
kōkyō kigyō
公共企業

public enterprise
kōei kigyō
公営企業
kōkyō kigyō
公共企業

public entity
kōkyō dantai
公共団体

public group
kōkyō dantai
公共団体

public-interest corporation
kōeki hōjin
公益法人

public limited company (plc) [UK]
kōkai yūgen sekinin gaisha
公開有限責任会社

public organization
kōkyō dantai
公共団体

public service company
kōeki jigyō gaisha
公益事業会社

public utility company
kōeki gaisha
公益会社
kōkyō jigyō dantai
公共事業団体

public utility corporation
kōeki dantai
公益団体

public utility enterprise
kōeki kigyō
公益企業

publicly held company
kabushiki kōkai gaisha
株式公開会社

purchase (of a company)
baishū
買収
kaitori
買取り

quorum provision
teisokusū no kitei
定足数の規定

racket (extortion)
yusuri
強請り

racketeer (intimidator)
kyōhakusha
脅迫者

racketeering
yusuri
強請り

rate of operation
sōgyōritsu
操業率

rationalization
gōrika
合理化

rationalization investment
gōrika tōshi
合理化投資

rationalization measures
gōrika sochi
合理化措置

rationalization of business
kei'ei gōrika
経営合理化

rationalization of enterprise
kigyō gōrika
企業合理化

rationalization of management
kei'ei gōrika
経営合理化

rationalize
gōrika suru
合理化する

recently established
saikin setsuritsu no
最近設立の

recovery
kaifuku
回復

regional office
chihō shiten
地方支店

regional representation
chihō daihyō
地方代表

register (noun)
  (name register)
meibo
名簿

  (official record)
tōkibo
登記簿

  (roster)
tōrokubo
登録簿

register (verb)
tōki suru
登記する
tōroku suru
登録する

register of companies
shōgyō tōkibo
商業登記簿

Register of Directors and Secretaries
torishimariyaku oyobi kanji meibo
取締役および幹事名簿

Register of Members
shain meibo
社員名簿

Register of Shareholders
kabunushi meibo
株主名簿

registered
tōkizumi
登記済み

registered as (—)
(— toshite) tōki sareta
(—として)登記された

registered company
hōjin gaisha
法人会社

registered design
tōroku ishō
登録意匠

registered office
honsha jimusho
本社事務所

registered owner
tōroku meiginin
登録名義人

registered patent
kōnin tokkyo
公認特許

registered representative
tōroku daihyōsha
登録代表者

registered trademark
tōroku shōhyō
登録商標**

Registrar of Companies [UK]
tōroku kikan
登録機関
tōrokukan
登録官

registration
(official record)
tōki
登記

(entry, record)
tōroku
登録

registration certificate
tōroku shōmeisho
登録証明書

registration department (of company)
tōroku bubun
登録部分

registration fee
tōkiryō
登記料
tōrokuryō
登録料

registration fee stamp [UK]
tōroku inshizei
登録印紙税

registration formalities
tōki tetsuzuki
登記手続き

registration of business name
shōgō tōroku
商号登録

registration of company
kaisha setsuritsu tōki
会社設立登記

registration of design
ishō tōroku
意匠登録

registration of incorporation
setsuritsu tōki
設立登記

registration of patent
tokkyo tōroku
特許登録

registration tax
tōrokuzei
登録税

related company
kankei gaisha
関係会社
kanren gaisha
関連会社
keiretsu gaisha (see note 20)
系列会社

rename
kaishō suru
改称する

renaming
shamei no kaishō
社名の改称

reorganization
saihensei
再編成

(reconstitution)
saikōsei
再構成

(reorganization of the company)
seiri kōsei
整理構成

reorganization and consolidation
seiri tōgō
整理統合

reorganization proceedings
kōsei tetsuzuki
構成手続き

reorganize
saihensei suru
再編成する

report
hōkokusho
報告書

represent
(act for)
daihyō suru
代表する

(be a proxy for, stand for someone)
dairi suru
代理する

representation
daihyō
代表
dairi
代理

representative
daihyōsha
代表者

representative agency
dairiten
代理店

representative director
daihyō torishimariyaku
代表取締役

representative member
daihyō shain
代表社員

representative office
daihyōbu
代表部

representative partner
daihyō shain
代表社員

reputation
(fame)
hyōban
評判

(good)
seibō
声望

(popularity)
seika
声価

resignation of Chairman
shachō no jinin
社長の辞任

responsibilities
ninmu
任務

responsibility
(duties)
gimu
義務

(liability)
sekinin
責任

responsibility of operation
gyōmu suikō sekinin
業務遂行責任

restrictive business practices
seigenteki shōkankō
制限的商慣行
seigenteki shōkanshū
制限的商慣習

results of operations
kei'ei seiseki
経営成績

retiring partner
taishoku shain
退職社員

revocation of power of attorney
kaininjō
解任状

right of representation
daihyōken
代表権

rights
(authority, power)
kengen
権限

(claim, privilege)
kenri
権利

rival business
shōbai gataki
商売敵

rival company
kyōsō gaisha
競争会社

run a business
jigyō o kei'ei suru
事業を経営する

run a company
kaisha o torishikiru
会社を取仕切る

safe-keeping of documents
shorui no hokan
書類の保管

scope of authority
kengen no han'i
権限の範囲

Seal
inkan shōmei
印鑑証明
shain
社印

sealing of document
natsuin
捺印

Secretary
kaisha no kanji
会社の幹事

Secretary's signature
kanji no shomei
幹事の署名

self-regulating organizations
jishu kisei kikan
自主規制機関

semi-public corporation
hankōkyō kigyō
半公共企業

senior company
oyagaisha
親会社

senior executive
jōkyū kei'eisha
上級経営者

senior executive director
senmu torishimariyaku
専務取締役

senior management
jōkyū kei'eisō
上級経営層

senior managing director
senmu torishimariyaku
専務取締役

senior partner
kosan shain
古参社員

senior vice-president [US]
fukushachō
副社長

set up business
shōbai o kizuku
商売を築く

several ownership
bunkatsu shoyūken
分割所有権

several responsibility
rentai sekinin
連帯責任

severally liable
kobetsu sekinin no
個別責任の

shell company
betsudō gaisha
別動会社

sideline
kengyō
兼業

sign
chōin suru
調印する
shomei suru
署名する

signatories
shomeisha
署名者

signature
shomei
署名

signature and seal
jisho ōin
自署押印

signed and sealed
shomei natsuin
署名捺印

signing of documents
shorui no chōin
書類の調印

silent partner
tokumei shain
匿名社員

simplification (streamlining)
kansoka
簡素化

single firm
tan'itsu kigyō
単一企業

sister company
shimai gaisha
姉妹会社

site
shikichi
敷地

size of business
kei'ei kibo
経営規模

size of firm
kigyō kibo
企業規模

sleeping partner
kyūmin shain
休眠社員
tokumei shain
匿名社員

small and medium-size businesses
chūshō kigyō
中小企業

small business
shōkibo kigyō
小規模企業
shōkigyō
小企業

small concern
shōkigyō
小企業

small enterprise
shōkigyō
小企業

small firm
shōkigyō
小企業

small incorporated family firm
shōkibo no dōzoku kigyō
小規模の同族企業

sole director
kojin jūyaku
個人重役

sole ownership
tandoku shoyūken
単独所有権

sole proprietor
kojin jigyōnushi
個人事業主

sole proprietorship
kojin gaisha
個人会社

sole trader
kojin shōnin
個人商人

solicitor [UK]
bengoshi
弁護士

sound business
kenzen kigyō
健全企業

sound company
kenjitsu gaisha
堅実会社

sound management
kenjitsu kei'ei
堅実経営

special power of attorney
tokutei ininjō
特定委任状

special report
tokubetsu hōkoku
特別報告

specialization (business)
tokka
特化

specimen of signature
shomei mihon
署名見本

sphere of business
eigyō han'i
営業範囲

staff and functional organization
sanbō shokkai soshiki
参謀職階組織

staff and line organization
sanbō chokkeishiki soshiki
参謀直系式組織

start a business
jigyō o okosu
事業を起こす

start a new business
shinjigyō o hajimeru
新事業を始める

start of business
(kigyō) sōgyō
(企業)創業
sōgyō kaishi
創業開始

state control
kokuyū
国有

state enterprise
kokuei kigyō
国営企業

state-owned enterprise
kokuyū kigyō
国有企業

state-run business
kokuei kigyō
国営企業

status (business)
eigyō jōtai
営業状態

statutory books
hōrei zensho
法令全書

statutory company
kokusaku kōsha
国策公社

statutory instrument
hōritsu no shudan
法律の手段

statutory provisions
hōritsu no kitei
法律の規定

stock company
kabushiki gaisha
株式会社

streamlining
kansoka
簡素化

structure
taisei
体制

sub-office
shutchōjo
出張所

subsidiary
kogaisha
子会社
jūzoku gaisha
従属会社

(affiliate)
bōkei gaisha
傍系会社

subsidiary business
fukugyō
副業

substratum
eigyō kamoku
営業科目

successful business
seikō shita jigyō
成功した事業

suspension of rights
kenri teishi
権利停止

take-over (noun)
nottori
乗っ取り

(buy-out)
baishū
買収

(acquisition)
kaitori
買取り

(succession)
keishō
継承

take over (verb)
nottoru
乗っ取る

(buy out)
baishū suru
買収する

(acquire, purchase)
kaitoru
買取る

(succeed to)
keishō suru
継承する

take over a business
kigyō o hikitoru
企業を引取る
kigyō o hikitsugu
企業を引継ぐ
kigyō o keishō suru
企業を継承する

take-over bid
kabushiki kōkai kaitsuke
株式公開買付け

take over the management
kei'ei o hikitsugu
経営を引継ぐ

target company
baishū taishō gaisha
買収対象会社

temporary business office
karijimusho
仮事務所

top executive
saikō kei'eisha
最高経営者

top management
saikō kei'eisō
最高経営層

trade directory
dōgyōsha jinmeiroku
同業者人名録

trade name
shōgō
商号

(trademark)
shōhyōmei
商標名

trade register
shōgyō tōki
商業登記

trade right
shōken
商権

trademark
shōhyō
商標

trademark infringement
shōhyōken shingai
商標権侵害

trademark registration
shōhyō tōroku
商標登録

trademark right
shōhyōken
商標権

trading company
shōji gaisha
商事会社
shōsha
商社

trading concern
bōeki gaisha
貿易会社
shōsha
商社

trading corporation
shōji gaisha
商事会社
shōsha
商社

trading house
shōsha
商社

trading licence
shōhyō raisensu
商標ライセンス

transfer of business
eigyō jōto
営業譲渡

Transfer Register [UK]
meigi kakikae daichō
名義書換台帳

transfer registration
tōroku henkō
登録変更

transferee
yuzuriukenin
譲受人

transferor
jōtonin
譲渡人

trust company
shintaku gaisha
信託会社

trust corporation
shintaku gaisha
信託会社

type of business
gyōshu
業種

type of enterprise
kigyō keitai
企業形態

unconsolidated subsidiary
hirenketsu kogaisha
非連結子会社

undertaking
(business venture)
jigyō
事業

(company)
kigyō
企業

unincorporated
hihōjin no
非法人の

unincorporated business
hihōjin kigyō
非法人企業

unincorporated company
hihōjin gaisha
非法人会社

unit for counting companies [J]
tsu
つ

unlimited company [UK]
mugen sekinin gaisha
無限責任会社

unlimited liability
mugen sekinin
無限責任

unlimited liability company
mugen sekinin gaisha
無限責任会社

unlimited partner
mugen sekinin shain
無限責任社員

unlimited partnership
mugen sekinin kumiai
無限責任組合

unproductive business
fuseisanteki jigyō
不生産的事業
hiseisanteki jigyō
非生産的事業

unsound company
fukenzen na kigyō
不健全な企業

usual practice
kanshū
慣習

vacation of office
jishoku
辞職

variance in signature
shomei no fuitchi
署名の不一致

venture (risky)
bōkenteki jigyō
冒険的事業

vertical integration
suichokuteki tōgō
垂直的統合

vertical merger
suichokuteki gappei
垂直的合併

vice-president [US]
fukushachō
副社長

voting power
giketsuken
議決権
tōhyōken
投票権

voting right
giketsuken
議決権
tōhyōken
投票権

white knight
yūkōteki na baishūsha
友好的な買収者

wholly owned
kanzen shoyū no
完全所有の
zenbu shoyū no
全部所有の
zengaku shusshi no
全額出資の

wholly owned affiliate
kanzen shoyū kankei gaisha
完全所有関係会社

wholly owned company
kanzen shoyū gaisha
完全所有会社
zenbu shoyū gaisha
全部所有会社

wholly owned subsidiary
kanzen shoyū kogaisha
完全所有子会社
zenbu shoyū kogaisha
全部所有子会社
zengaku shusshi kogaisha
全額出資子会社

wilful misrepresention
akui fujitsu hyōji
悪意不実表示

withdrawal from a company
taisha
退社

withdrawal from a partnership
taishoku
退職

witness (noun)
shōnin
承認

witness (verb)
shōnin toshite shomei suru
承認として署名する

working partner
rōmu shusshi shain
労務出資社員

worldwide enterprise
sekai kigyō
世界企業

written notice
tsūchi
通知

'zaibatsu' [J][23]
zaibatsu[23]
財閥

'zaibatsu' dissolution
zaibatsu kaitai
財閥解体

Notes

20. affiliation (keiretsu 系列): company group formed by interlocking shareholdings including a bank which is not the group's holding company.

21. associate, partner (kumiai'in 組合員): note that 'kumiai'in' can also be used for 'rōdō kumiai'in', meaning a member of a trade-union or labour union.

22. association, partnership (kumiai 組合): note that 'kumiai' can also be used for 'rōdō kumiai', meaning trade-union or labour union.

23. 'zaibatsu' (財閥): sometimes translated as 'financial clique' or 'industrial conglomerate', the 'zaibatsu' is a large interlocking group of Japanese companies dominated by a bank holding controlling interests in the other members of the group. Because of the restrictions imposed by Japanese legislation since the Second World War, the 'zaibatsu' has gradually been replaced by the 'keiretsu' (see note 20).

above the line
kakusenjō
画線上

absorbed cost
kaishūzumi genka
回収済原価

absorbed overheads [US]
kaishūzumi kansetsuhi
回収済間接費

absorption
kaishū
回収

absorption costing
zenbu genka keisan
全部原価計算

absorption rate
kaishūritsu
回収率

abstract (noun)
tekiyōsho
摘要書

accelerated amortization
kasoku shōkyaku
加速償却

accelerated depreciation
kasoku genka shōkyaku
加速原価償却
kasoku shōkyaku
加速償却

account
kanjō
勘定

(bill)
kanjōsho
勘定書

(statement)
keisansho
計算書

account books
chōbo
帳簿
kaikeibo
会計簿
suitōbo
出納簿

account headings
kanjō kamoku
勘定科目

account stated
kakutei kanjōsho
確定勘定書

account statement
kanjōsho
勘定書
keisansho
計算書

account title
kanjō kamoku
勘定科目

accountant
kaikeigakari
会計係

(certified public accountant)
kaikeishi
会計士

(public accountant)
keirishi
計理士

accountant's certificate
kansa hōkokusho
監査報告書

accountant's liability
kaikeigakari no sekinin
会計係の責任

accountant's report
kaikei hōkoku(sho)
会計報告(書)

accounting
keiri
経理

(accounts)
kaikei
会計

(settlement of accounts)
kaikei kessan
会計決算
kessan
決算

(calculations)
keisan
計算

accounting bases
kaikei kijun
会計基準

accounting books
kaikei chōbo
会計帳簿

accounting code
keiri kijun
経理基準

accounting date
kaikeibi
会計日

accounting entity
kaikei jittai
会計実体
kaikei shutai
会計主体

(unit)
kaikei tan'i
会計単位

accounting firm
kaikei gaisha
会計会社

accounting for external reporting
gaibu hōkoku kaikei
外部報告会計

accounting for internal reporting
naibu hōkoku kaikei
内部報告会計

accounting for management
kanri kaikei
管理会計

accounting information system
kaikei jōhō shisutemu
会計情報システム

accounting method
kaikei hōshiki
会計方式
kaikeihō
会計法

accounting officer
suitōyaku
出納役

accounting operations
kaikei sagyō
会計作業

accounting period
kaikei kikan
会計期間

(tax year)
kaikei nendo
会計年度

accounting policy
kaikei shori hōshin
会計処理方針

accounting practice
kaikei jitsumu
会計実務

accounting principles
kaikei gensoku
会計原則

accounting procedure
kaikei tetsuzuki
会計手続き

accounting processing
kaikei shori
会計処理

accounting records
kaikei kiroku
会計記録

accounting regulations
kaikei kisoku
会計規則

accounting report
kaikei hōkoku(sho)
会計報告(書)

accounting rules
kaikei tsūsoku
会計通則

accounting standard
kaikei kijun
会計基準

accounting statement
keisansho
計算書

accounting subject
kaikei kamoku
会計科目

accounting system
kaikei seido
会計制度

(accounting method)
kaikeihō
会計法

(calculation system)
keisan shisutemu
計算システム

accounting technique
kaikei hōshiki
会計方式

accounting terminology
kaikei yōgo
会計用語

accounting unit
kaikei tan'i
会計単位

accounting valuation
kaikeiteki hyōka
会計的評価

accounting year
kaikei nendo
会計年度

(business year)
jigyō nendo
事業年度

accounts
kaikei
会計

accounts coding system
kaikei yōgo no kigō seido
会計用語の記号制度

accounts for financial year
kaikei nendo no kaikei
会計年度の会計

accounts payable
kaikakekin
買掛金
miharaikin
未払金
miharai kanjō
未払勘定

accounts payable ledger
kaikakekin motochō
買掛金元帳

accounts processing
kaikei shori
会計処理

accounts receivable
urikakekin
売掛金
uketori kanjō
受取勘定

accounts receivable ledger
urikakekin motochō
売掛金元帳

accretion
shizen zōka
自然増加

accrual
hassei
発生
mishūshi kanjō
未収支勘定

accrual account
hassei kōmoku
発生項目

accrual accounting
hassei shugi kaikei
発生主義会計

accruals basis
hassei shugi
発生主義

accruals method
hassei shugi
発生主義

accrued assets
mikoshi shisan
見越資産

accrued depreciation
hassei genka
発生減価

accrued dividend
keika haitō(kin)
経過配当(金)

accrued expenses
miharai hiyō
未払費用

accrued income
mishū shūeki
未収収益

accrued liability
mikoshi fusai
見越負債

accrued payroll
miharai chingin
未払賃金
miharai kyūryō
未払給料

accrued revenue
miharai shūeki
未払収益
mishū shūeki
未収収益

accrued salaries
miharai kyūryō
未払給料

accrued wages
miharai chingin
未払賃金

accumulate
ruiseki suru
累積する

accumulated depreciation
genka shōkyaku
ruisekigaku
減価償却累積額

accumulated dividend
ruiseki haitō(kin)
累積配当(金)

accumulated earnings [US]
rieki ryūhokin
利益留保金
ryūho rieki
留保利益

accumulated fund
tsumitatekin
積立金

accumulated income
ruiseki rieki
累積利益

accumulated profits
rieki jōyokin
利益剰余金
ryūho riekikin
留保利益金

accumulated reserves [UK]
rieki ryūhokin
利益留保金
ryūho rieki
留保利益

accumulation
rieki jōyokin
利益剰余金
ryūho riekikin
留保利益金

accumulation of capital
shihon chikuseki
資本蓄積

acid ratio
sansei hiritsu
酸性比率

acid-test ratio
sansei shiken hiritsu
酸性試験比率

acquire a business
kigyō o kaitoru
企業を買取る

acquire a company
kaisha o kaitoru
会社を買取る

acquire an interest in a company
kaisha no kabushiki o shutoku suru
会社の株式を取得する

acquire assets
shisan o hikitsugu
資産を引継ぐ

acquisition (of a company)
kaitori
買取り

(buy-out)
baishū
買収

(absorption)
kyūshū
吸収

acquisition accounting
kyūshū kaikei
吸収会計

acquisition cost
baishū kakaku
買収価格

acquisition of proprietary interest
mochibun shutoku
持分取得

acquisition of shares
kabushiki shutoku
株式取得

acquisition price (company)
baishū kakaku
買収価格

action (= equity stake)
mochibun
持分

active assets
katsudō shisan
活動資産
seisan shisan
生産資産

active capital
katsudō shihon
活動資本

activity accounting
katsudō kaikei
活動会計

activity cost
gyōmu katsudō genka
業務活動原価

actual-basis accounting
jissai shugi kaikei
実際主義会計

actual-cost accounting (system)
jissai genka keisan (seido)
実際原価計算(制度)

actual-cost method
jissai genka keisanhō
実際原価計算法

additional capital
zōka shihon
増加資本

additional paid-in capital
zōka haraikomi shihonkin
増加払込資本金

additional reserve
zōka sekinin junbikin
増加責任準備金

additional working capital
zōka unten shihon
増加運転資本

additional working funds
zōka unten shikin
増加運転資金

adequate liquidity
tekisei ryūdōsei
適正流動性

adjust
(reconcile)
chōsei suru
調整する

(re-adjust)
seiri suru
整理する

(liquidate)
seisan suru
精算する

(correct)
shūsei suru
修正する

adjusted trial balance
seirigo shisanhyō
整理後試算表

adjusting entry
seiri kinyū
整理記入
shūsei kinyū
修正記入

adjustment
(reconciliation)
chōsei
調整

(re-adjustment)
seiri
整理

(liquidation)
seisan
清算

(correction)
shūsei
修正

adjustment at term end
kimatsu seiri
期末整理

adjustment for instalment sales
kappu hanbai rieki modoshiiregaku
割賦販売利益戻入額

adjustment of accounts
chōbo seiri
帳簿整理

administration cost
kanrihi
管理費

administrative accounting
kanri kaikei
管理会計

administrative audit
jizen kansa
事前監査

administrative balance sheet
kei'ei taishaku taishōhyō
経営貸借対照表

administrative budget
kanri yosan
管理予算

administrative expenses
kanrihi
管理費
kei'eihi
経営費

advance
maebarai
前払い
tatekaekin
立替金

advances received
maeukekin
前受金

advertisement for subscription
boshū kōkoku
募集広告

advertising budget
kōkoku yosan
広告予算

advertising expenses
kōkokuhi
広告費

after-tax income
zeibiki shotoku
税引所得

after-tax profit
zeibiki rieki
税引利益
zeibiki rijun
税引利潤

after-tax profit rate
zeibiki riekiritsu
税引利益率

all-purpose balance sheet
mannō taishaku taishōhyō
万能貸借対照表

all-purpose financial statement
tamokuteki zaimu shohyō
多目的財務諸表

allocation
haibunhō
配分法

allocation certificate
kabushiki wariate shōsho
株式割当証書

allocation of costs
genka haifu
原価配付

allocation of expenses
keihi wariate
経費割当て

allot
wariate suru
割当てする

allotment
bonyū
募入
kabushiki wariate
株式割当て

allotment letter
kabushiki wariate tsūchisho
株式割当通知書

allotment of shares
kabushiki wariate
株式割当て

allotment of shares to relatives
enkosha wariate
縁故者割当て

allotment sheet
haifuhyō
配付表

allotment to shareholders
kabunushi wariate
株主割当て

allotment value
wariategaku
割当額

allotted share capital
hakkōzumi kabushiki shihonkin
発行済株式資本金

allottee
bonyūsha
募入者
hiwariatesha
被割当者

allowable tax deductions
seitō na zeikōjo
正当な税控除

**allowance
(provision, reserve)**
hikiatekin
引当金
junbikin
準備金

(compensation, perk)
hōshū
報酬
teate
手当

allowance audit
hikiatekin kansa
引当金監査

allowance for bad debts
kashidaore hikiatekin
貸倒引当金
kashidaore junbikin
貸倒準備金

allowance for depreciation
genka shōkyaku hikiatekin
原価償却引当金

allowance for doubtful accounts [UK]
kashidaore hikiatekin
貸倒引当金
kashidaore junbikin
貸倒準備金

allowance for sales discounts [UK]
uriage waribiki hikiatekin
売上割引引当金

allowed depreciation
shōkyaku han'igaku
償却範囲額

amortization [UK]
(genka) shōkyaku
(原価)償却

amortize [UK]
shōkyaku suru
償却する

amortized cost
shōkyakubiki genka
償却引原価

amount carried forward
jiki e no kurikoshidaka
次期への繰越高

amount carried over
jiki e no kurikoshidaka
次期への繰越高

amount in arrear
miharai kingaku
未払金額

amount of capital
shihongaku
資本額
shihonkingaku
資本金額

amount of capital invested
shusshigaku
出資額

amount of capital to be raised
boshūgaku
募集額

amount of share capital
shusshigaku
出資額

amount subscribed
ōbo kingaku
応募金額
ōbogaku
応募額

analysis of balance sheet
taishaku taishōhyō bunseki
貸借対照表分析

analysis of financial statement
zaimu shohyō bunseki
財務諸表分析

ancillary expenses
fuzui hiyō
付随費用

annual accounts
nenji kessan
年次決算

annual audit
nendo kansa
年度監査

annual balance sheet
nendo taishaku taishōhyō
年度貸借対照表

annual budget
nenkan yosan
年間予算

annual closing of books
nendo chōbo shimekiri
年度帳簿締切り

annual depreciation allowance [UK]
nenkan genka shōkyaku
年間原価償却

annual dividend
futsū haitō
普通配当

annual expenditure
nenkan shishutsu
年間支出

annual report
nenhō
年報
nenji hōkokusho
年次報告書

annual report and accounts
nenji hōkokusho to kaikei
年次報告書と会計

annual return
nenji hōkokusho
年次報告書

annual revenue
nenkan shūnyū
年間収入

annual running expenditure
nenkan keihi
年間経費
nenkan un'eihi
年間運営費

annual statement
nenji eigyō hōkokusho
年次営業報告書
nenji kei'ei hōkokusho
年次経営報告書

anticipated cost
mikomi genka
見込原価

anticipated profits
mikomi rieki
見込利益

applicant (for shares)
(kabushiki) mōshikomisha
(株式)申込者
(kabushiki) ōbōsha
(株式)応募者

application account
mōshikomi shōkokin kanjō
申込証拠金勘定

application and allotment
book
mōshikomi-wariatechō
申込・割当帳

application for shares
kabushiki mōshikomi
株式申込み
kabushiki ōbo
株式応募

application form
mōshikomi yōshi
申込用紙

application letter
mōshikomisho
申込書

application money
mōshikomi shōkokin
申込証拠金
mōshikomikin
申込金

application procedure
mōshikomi tetsuzuki
申込手続き

application rights
mōshikomiken
申込権
ōboken
応募権

applied overheads [UK]
kaishūzumi kansetsuhi
回収済間接費

apply for shares
kabushiki o mōshikomu
株式を申込む

apportionment
haitō
配当
wariate
割当て

appraisal [US]
hyōka
評価

appraisal of assets [US]
shisan hyōka
資産評価

appraisal rights
kabushiki kaitori seikyūken
株式買取請求権

appraisal surplus [US]
hyōka taijōyokin
評価替剰余金

appropriation
jūtō(kin)
充当(金)

(on balance sheet)
shobun
処分

appropriation account
shūeki haitō kanjō
収益配当勘定

appropriation budget
keihi yosan
経費予算

arrearage
(being overdue)
entaikin
延滞金

(payment arrears)
miharaikin
未払金

arrears
entaikin
延滞金
miharaikin
未払金

arrears of dividend
chien haitōkin
遅延配当金

asset(s)
shisan
資産

asset register
shisan tōrokubo
資産登録簿

asset revaluation
shisan saihyōka
資産再評価

asset valuation
shisan hyōka
資産評価

asset value
shisan kakaku
資産価格

assets and liabilities
shisan to fusai
資産と負債

assets statement
shisan mokuroku
資産目録

assets structure
shisan kōsei
資産構成

assign
jōto suru
譲渡する

assignee
yuzuriukenin
譲受人

assigned stock
jōto shitei kabu
譲渡指定株

assignment
jōto
譲渡

assignor
jōtonin
譲渡人

audit (noun)
kaikei kansa
会計監査
kansa
監査

audit (verb)
kansa suru
監査する

audit adjustment
kansa shūsei
監査修正

audit certificate
kansa shōmeisho
監査証明書

audit company
kaikei kansa gaisha
会計監査会社

audit fee
kansaryō
監査料

audit instruction
kansa sashizusho
監査指図書

audit of financial statement
zaimu shohyō kansa
財務諸表監査

audit opinion
kansa hōkokusho
監査報告書

audit period
kansa kikan
監査期間

audit procedure
kansa tetsuzuki
監査手続き

audit report
kansa hōkokusho
監査報告書

audit staff (of a company)
kansa yakuin
監査役員

audit standard
kansa kijun
監査基準

audit techniques
kansa gijutsu
監査技術

audit trail
kansa shōseki
監査証跡

audit year
kansa nendo
監査年度

auditing
kansa
監査

auditing officer
kansayaku
監査役

auditing rules
kansa gensoku
監査原則

auditing standard
kansa kijun
監査基準

auditing system
kansa shisutemu
監査システム

auditor
(independent)
kaikei kansanin
会計監査人

(government)
kaikei kensakan
会計検査官

(corporate)
kansayaku
監査役

auditor's certificate
kansayaku shōmeisho
監査役証明書

auditor's opinion
kansanin no iken
監査人の意見

auditor's report
kansa hōkokusho
監査報告書

authorized auditor
hōtei kansanin
法定監査人

authorized capital [UK]
juken shihon
授権資本

authorized capital stock [US]
juken shihon
授権資本

authorized shares
juken kabu
授権株

auxiliary capital
hojo shihon
補助資本

auxiliary ledger
hojo motochō
補助元帳

available assets
jiyū shisan
自由資産

available profit
shobunkanō riekikin
処分可能利益金

avoidable costs
kaihikanō genka
回避可能原価

bad debt(s)
kashidaore
貸倒れ

bad debt loss
kashidaore sonshitsu
貸倒損失

bad debt provision
kashidaore hikiatekin
貸倒引当金
kashidaore junbikin
貸倒準備金

bad debt reserve
kashidaore hikiatekin
貸倒引当金
kashidaore junbikin
貸倒準備金

bad debts written off
kashidaore shōkyaku
貸倒償却

bail out (a company)
beiru-auto suru
ベイル・アウトする

balance
(difference)
sagaku
差額

(remaining sum)
zandaka
残高

balance an account
kanjō o kessan suru
勘定を決算する

balance at the beginning of a period
kishu zandaka
期首残高

balance book
zandakachō
残高帳

balance brought forward
kurikoshi zandaka
繰越残高

balance brought over from the last period
zenki kurikoshikin
前期繰越金

balance carried forward
kurikoshi zandaka
繰越残高

balance in ledger
motochō zandaka
元帳残高

balance sheet
taishaku taishōhyō
貸借対照表

balance sheet analysis
taishaku taishōhyō bunseki
貸借対照表分析

balance sheet audit
taishaku taishōhyō kansa
貸借対照表監査

balance sheet date
taishaku taishōhyō no hizuke
貸借対照表の日付け

balance sheet item
taishaku taishōhyō kamoku
貸借対照表科目

balance sheet total
taishaku taishōhyō sōkei
貸借対照表総計

balance the books
chōbo o shimekiri suru
帳簿を締切りする

balanced budget
kinkō yosan
均衡予算

balancing figure
chōsei sūji
調整数字

balancing item
chōsei kōmoku
調整項目

ballot (draw for shares)
tōhyō
投票

basic cost method
genka keisan hōshiki
原価計算方式

basis of apportionment
wariate kijun
割当基準

batch cost
batchi genka
バッチ原価

batch costing [UK]
batchi genkahō
バッチ原価法

bearer certificate
mukimei kabuken
無記名株券

bearer stock
mukimei kabu
無記名株

before-tax profit
zeikomi rieki
税込利益

beginning balance
kishu zandaka
期首残高

beginning of fiscal year
nendo hajime
年度初め

beginning of period
kishu
期首

beginning of the year
kishu
期首

below the line
kakusenka
画線下

benefit/cost ratio
hiyō-ben'eki hiritsu
費用・便益比率

benefits
rieki
利益

bid for company's stock
kabushiki kaitori kōkai mōshikomi
株式買取公開申込み

bill
(statement of account)
kanjōsho
勘定書

(invoice)
okurijō
送状

bills payable (on balance sheet)
shiharai tegata
支払手形

black figures
kuroji
黒字

blank transfer of shares
kabushiki mukimei kakikae
株式無記名書換え

bogus dividend
tako haitō
タコ配当

bonus (dividend)
rieki haitō
利益配当

bonus dividend
tokubetsu haitō(kin)
特別配当(金)

bonus issue
mushō hakkō
無償発行
shihonkin kumiire hakkō
資本金組入発行

bonus share
mushō wariate kabu
無償割当株
tokubetsu haitō kabu
特別配当株

bonuses
bōnasu
ボーナス
shōyokin
賞与金

bonuses for directors and auditors
yakuin shōyokin
役員賞与金

book account
chōbojō no taishaku kanjō
帳簿上の貸借勘定

book audit
chōbo kansa
帳簿監査

book balance
chōbo zandaka
帳簿残高

book cost
chōbo genka
帳簿原価

book credit
kakeurikin
掛売金

(credit side)
chōbojō no kashikata
帳簿上の貸方

book date
chōbo hizuke
帳簿日付け

book debit
chōbojō no karikata
帳簿上の借方

book debt
kaikakekin
買掛金

book entry
chōbo kinyū
帳簿記入

book inventory
chōbo tanaoroshi
帳簿棚卸し

book inventory method
chōbo tanaoroshihō
帳簿棚卸法

book-keeper
bokigakari
簿記係

book-keeping
boki
簿記

book-keeping system
boki seido
簿記制度

book loss
chōbojō no sonshitsu
帳簿上の損失

book price
chōbo kagaku
帳簿価額

book profit
chōbojō no rieki
帳簿上の利益

book surplus
chōbojō no jōyokin
帳簿上の剰余金

book system
chōbo seido
帳簿制度

book valuation
chōbo hyōka
帳簿評価

book value
boka
簿価
chōbojō no kakaku
帳簿上の価格

book value per share
hitokabu atari boka
一株当たり簿価

books
chōbo
帳簿
kaikeibo
会計簿

borrowed capital
kariire shihon
借入資本
tanin shihon
他人資本

borrowing requirements
kariire juyō
借入需要

bottom line
shūshi kessan
収支決算

bought day book
shiirechō
仕入帳

bought ledger
shiire motochō
仕入元帳

branch accounts
shiten kanjō
支店勘定

(accounting)
shiten kaikei
支店会計

break-even analysis
son'eki bunki bunseki
損益分岐分析

break-even chart
son'eki bunki zuhyō
損益分岐図表

break-even point
son'eki bunkiten
損益分岐点

break-up value
seisan kachi
清算価値
seisan kagaku
清算価額

breakdown of total
gōkei no uchiwake
合計の内訳

brought forward
kurikoshi
繰越し

brought forward account
kurikoshi kanjō
繰越勘定

budget
yosan
予算

budget account
yosan kanjō
予算勘定

budget allocations
yosan wariategaku
予算割当額

budget centre
yosan sentā
予算センター

budget cost allowance
yosan genka hikiatekin
予算原価引当金

budget deficit
akaji yosan
赤字予算

budget for the coming year
rainendo no yosan
来年度の予算

budget items
yosan kōmoku
予算項目

budget period
yosan kikan
予算期間

budget planning
yosan keikaku
予算計画

budget report
yosan hōkokusho
予算報告書

budget sheet
yosanhyō
予算表

budget surplus
yosan jōyo
予算剰余

budgetary control
yosan kanri
予算管理

budgeted balance sheet
mitsumori taishaku
taishōhyō
見積貸借対照表

budgeted cost
yosan genka
予算原価

budgeting
yosan hensei
予算編成

budgeting system
yosan seido
予算制度

buildings (on balance sheet)
tatemono
建物

burden [UK]
seisan kansetsuhi
生産間接費

business accounting
kigyō kaikei
企業会計

**business accounting
principles**
kigyō kaikei gensoku
企業会計原則

business audit
gyōmu kansa
業務監査

business borrowing
kigyō kariire
企業借入れ

business capital
kigyō shihon
企業資本

business costs
kigyō hiyō
企業費用

business earnings
kigyō shūeki
企業収益

business equipment
kigyō setsubi
企業設備

business equity
kigyō no mochibun
企業の持分

business expenditure
eigyōhi
営業費

**business expenses
(office expenses)**
eigyōhi
営業費

(operating expenses)
jigyōhi
事業費

business finance
kigyō zaimu
企業財務

business income
eigyō shotoku
営業所得
kigyō shotoku
企業所得
kigyō shūnyū
企業収入

business income tax
eigyō shotokuzei
営業所得税

business investment
kigyō tōshi
企業投資

business liquidity
kigyō no temoto ryūdōsei
企業の手許流動性

business loan
kigyō kashitsuke
企業貸付け

business profit tax
eigyō ritokuzei
営業利得税
eigyō shūekizei
営業収益税

business profits
kigyō rieki
企業利益

business report
eigyō hōkokusho
営業報告書

business results
eigyō seiseki
営業成績
gyōseki
業績

business tax
eigyōzei
営業税
jigyōzei
事業税

business year
eigyō nendo
営業年度
jigyō nendo
事業年度

(financial year)
kaikei nendo
会計年度

buy-out (noun)
baishū
買収

buy out (verb)
baishū suru
買収する

calculation(s)
keisan
計算

calculation of dividend
haitō keisan
配当計算

call
haraikomi saikoku
払込催告
haraikomi seikyū
払込請求

call account
haraikomi kanjō
払込勘定

call in shares
kabushiki o kaishū suru
株式を回収する

call letter
haraikomi seikyū tsūchisho
払込請求通知書

call list
haraikomi seikyū risuto
払込請求リスト

call on shareholders
kabushiki haraikomi seikyū
株式払込請求

call on shares
kabushiki haraikomi saikoku
株式払込催告
kabushiki haraikomi seikyū
株式払込請求

call-up
haraikomi saikoku
払込催告
haraikomi seikyū
払込請求

capital
shihon
資本
shihonkin
資本金

(own capital, proprietary capital)
jiko shihon
自己資本

(owner's equity)
shoyūnushi mochibun
所有主持分

(subscribed capital)
shusshi
出資

capital account
shihon kanjō
資本勘定

capital adjustment
shihon shūsei
資本修正

capital allowance
shihon hikiate
資本引当て

capital appreciation
shihon zōka
資本増加

capital appropriation
shihon shobun
資本処分

capital appropriation account
shihon shobun kanjō
資本処分勘定

capital assets [UK]
shihon shisan
資本資産

(fixed assets [US])
kotei shisan
固定資産

capital availability
shihon no riyō kanōsei
資本の利用可能性

capital budget
shihon yosan
資本予算

capital budgeting
shihon no yosan hensei
資本の予算編成

capital composition
shihon kōsei
資本構成

capital consumption
shihon shōmō
資本消耗

capital consumption allowance
shihon shōmō hikiate
資本消耗引当て

capital decrease
genshi
源資

capital depletion
shihon genka
資本減価

capital employed
shiyō shihongaku
使用資本額

capital expenditure
shihon shishutsu
資本支出

capital expenditure appraisal
shihon shishutsu satei
資本支出査定

capital expenditure budget
shihon shishutsu yosan
資本支出予算

capital fund
shihonkin
資本金

capital gain
shihon ritoku
資本利得

(capital profit)
shihon rijun
資本利潤

capital gains tax
shihon ritokuzei
資本利得税

capital gearing
giaringu
ギアリング

capital increase
zōshi
増資

capital inflow
shihon ryūnyū
資本流入

capital introduced
dōnyū shihon
導入資本

capital invested (= capital subscribed)
shusshi
出資

capital investment
shusshi
出資

capital investor
shusshisha
出資者

capital issue
shihon kōbo
資本公募

capital issued
kōbo shihonkin
公募資本金

capital/liabilities ratio
shihon-fusai hiritsu
資本・負債比率

capital loss
shihon sonshitsu
資本損失

capital maintenance
shihon iji
資本維持

capital outflow
shihon ryūshutsu
資本流出

capital outlay
shihon shishutsu
資本支出

capital padding
kadai zōshi
過大増資

capital participation
shihon sanka
資本参加

capital profit
shihon rijun
資本利潤

capital-raising
shikin chōtatsu
資金調達

capital ratio
shihon kaitenritsu
資本回転率

capital rationing
shihon seigen
資本制限

capital recovery
shihon kaishū
資本回収

capital redemption
shihon shōkan
資本償還

capital redemption reserve fund
shihon shōkan tsumitatekin
資本償還積立金

capital reduction
genshi
減資

capital reduction due to merger
gappei ni yoru genshi
合併による減資

capital requirements
shihon juyō
資本需要

capital reserve
shihon junbikin
資本準備金

capital spending
shihon shishutsu
資本支出

capital stock
kabunushi shihon
株主資本
kabushiki shihon
株式資本

capital stock issued
kabushiki hakkōgaku
株式発行額

capital stock of subsidiaries and affiliated companies
jūzoku gaisha oyobi kankei gaisha shusshikin
従属会社および関係会社出資金

capital stock outstanding
shihonkin genzaidaka
資本金現在高

capital stock subscribed
hikiukezumi shihonkin
引受済資本金

capital stock unissued
kabushiki mihakkōgaku
株式未発行額

capital stock unpaid
miharaikomi shihonkin
未払込資本金

capital structure
shihon kōsei
資本構成

capital subscribed
hikiukezumi shihonkin
引受済資本金
shusshikin
出資金

capital subscription
shusshi
出資

capital surplus
shihon jōyokin
資本剰余金

capital surplus reserve
shihon junbikin
資本準備金

capital turnover
shihon kaiten
資本回転

capital turnover ratio
shihon kaitenritsu
資本回転率

capital unissued
shihon mihakkōbun
資本未発行分

capital watering
kadai zōshi
過大増資
shihon mizumashi
資本水増し

capitalization
shihon kumiire
資本組入れ
shihonka
資本化

capitalization issue
shihonkin kumiire hakkō
資本金組入発行

capitalization value
shihon kangen kachi
資本還元価値
shihon kingaku
資本金額

capitalize
shihonka suru
資本化する
shusshi suru
出資する

carried-over surplus
zennendo jōyokin ukeire
前年度剰余金受入れ

carry
kurikoshi
繰越し

carry-back (noun)
kurimodoshi
繰戻し

carry back (verb)
kurimodosu
繰戻す

carry-back of losses
kessonkin no kurimodoshi
欠損金の繰戻し

carry-forward (noun)
kurikoshi
繰越し

carry forward (verb)
kurikosu
繰越す

carry forward to the next term
jiki e no kurikoshi
次期への繰越し

carry-over (noun)
kurikoshi
繰越し

carry over (verb)
kurikosu
繰越す

carry-over of losses
kessonkin no kurikoshi
欠損金の繰越し

carrying amount
shōmi chōbo kagaku
正味帳簿価額
junchōbo kagaku
純帳簿価額

carrying cost
mochikoshi hiyō
持越費用

cash account
genkin kanjō
現金勘定

cash and deposits (on balance sheet)
genkin-yokin
現金・預金

cash assets
genkin shisan
現金資産

cash at bank
tōza yokin
当座預金

cash audit
genkin kansa
現金監査

cash balances
genkin zandaka
現金残高

cash-balances accounting
genkin zandaka kaikei seido
現金残高会計制度

cash basis
genkin shugi
現金主義

cash-basis accounting
genkin shugi kaikei
現金主義会計

cash book
genkin suitōbo
現金出納簿
genkin suitōchō
現金出納帳

cash budget
genkin (shūshi) yosan
現金(収支)予算

cash discount
genkin waribiki
現金割引

cash dividend
genkin haitō
現金配当

cash earnings
genkin shūnyū
現金収入

cash expenses
genkin keijōhi
現金経常費

cash flow
genkin ryūdō
現金流動
kasshu-furō
カヤッシュ・フロー

cash-flow budget
genkin (shūshi) yosan
現金(収支)予算

cash-flow statement
genkin shūshi ichiranhyō
現金収支一覧表

cash forecasts
genkin shūshi mitsumori
現金収支見積り

cash fund
genkin shikin
現金資金

cash in hand [UK]
temoto genkin
手許現金

cash income
genkin shotoku
現金所得

cash inflow
genkin ryūnyū
現金流入

cash item
genkin kōmoku
現金項目

cash journal
genkin shiwakechō
現金仕訳帳

cash-journal method
genkinshiki shiwakehō
現金式仕訳法

cash liabilities
genkin fusai
現金負債

cash limit
genkin seigen
現金制限

cash needs
genkin juyō
現金需要

cash on hand [US]
temoto genkin
手許現金

cash outflow
genkin ryūshutsu
現金流出

cash payment
genkin shiharai
現金支払い

cash payments book
genkin shiharaichō
現金支払帳

cash payments budget
genkin shiharai yosan
現金支払予算

cash payments journal
genkin shiharaichō
現金支払帳

cash ratio
genkin hiritsu
現金比率

cash receipt
genkin uketori
現金受取り

cash receipts book
genkin uketori shiwakechō
現金受取仕訳帳

cash receipts journal
genkin uketori shiwakechō
現金受取仕訳帳

cash sales book
genkin uriagechō
現金売上帳

cash statement
genkin keisansho
現金計算書

certificate (share)
karikabuken
仮株券

certification of transfer
shōninzumi kabushiki meigi
kakikae
承認済株式名義
書換え

certified accountant [UK]
ninkyo kaikeishi
認許会計士

certified financial statement
kansazumi zaimu shohyō
監査済財務諸表

**certified public accountant
(CPA) [US]**
kōnin kaikeishi
公認会計士

chairman's statement
kaichō no hōkoku
会長の報告

chart of accounts
kanjō kamokuhyō
勘定課目表

chartered accountant [UK]
tokkyo kaikeishi
特許会計士

check-off
chekku-ofu
チェック・オフ

chief accountant
shunin kaikeikan
主任会計官

chief controller
keiri buchō
経理部長

circulating assets
ryūdō shisan
流動資産

circulating capital
ryūdō shihon
流動資本

classes of shares
kabushu
株種

**classification of balance sheet
items**
taishaku taishōhyō kōmoku
no bunrui
貸借対照表項目
の分類

**classified profit and loss
statement**
kubun son'eki keisansho
区分損益計算書

clear profit
jun'eki
純益

clearance of bad debts
furyō shisan kirisute
不良資産切捨て

close accounts
kanjō o shimekiru
勘定を締切る

close the books
chōbo o shimekiru
帳簿を締切る

close subscription lists
boshū o shimekiru
募集を締切る

closed accounts
shimekirizumi kanjō
締切済勘定

closing adjustment
kessan seiri
決算整理

closing audit
kessan kansa
決算監査

closing balance
kessan zandaka
決算残高
shimekiri zandaka
締切残高

closing day
kessanbi
決算日
shimekiribi
締切日

closing entry
kessan kinyū
決算記入
kessan shiwake
決算仕訳

closing of accounts
kanjō no shimekiri
勘定の締切り
kessan
決算

closing of accounts for the first half of the year
zenki kessan
前期決算

closing of accounts for the second half of the year
kōki kessan
後期決算

closing of accounts for the year
nenji kessan
年次決算

closing of expenditure accounts
keihi kessan
経費決算

closing of subscription
boshū shimekiri
募集締切り

closing of the books
chōbo no shimekiri
帳簿の締切り
kessan
決算

closing procedure
kessan tetsuzuki
決算手続き

closing trial balance
shimekiri shisanhyō
締切試算表

collection
chōshū
徴収

column
keta
桁

column book
taketashiki chōbo
多桁式帳簿

column cash book
taketashiki genkin suitōbo
多桁式現金出納簿

column ledger
taketashiki motochō
多桁式元帳

combined balance sheet
gappei taishaku taishōhyō
合併貸借対照表
ketsugō taishaku taishōhyō
結合貸借対照表

combined financial statement
ketsugō zaimuhyō
結合財務表

combined income statement
gappei son'eki keisansho
合併損益計算書

combined profit and loss statement
gappei son'eki keisansho
合併損益計算書

commemorative dividend
kinen haitō
記念配当

commercial accounting
shōgyō kaikei
商業会計

commission account
tesūryō kanjō
手数料勘定

commissions received account
uketori tesūryō kanjō
受取手数料勘定

common costs
kyōtsū keihi
共通経費

common dividend
futsū haitō
普通配当

common stock [US] (ordinary shares)
futsū kabu
普通株

(on balance sheet)
shihonkin
資本金

company accounting
kaisha kaikei
会社会計

company financing
kaisha kin'yū
会社金融

company with reduced capital
genshi gaisha
減資会社

company's auditors
kansayaku
監査役

company's bankers
torihiki ginkō
取引銀行

company's brokers
kaisha no burōkā
会社のブローカー

comparative balance sheet
hikaku taishaku taishōhyō
比較貸借対照表

comparative income statement
hikaku son'eki keisansho
比較損益計算書

comparative profit and loss statement
hikaku son'eki keisansho
比較損益計算書

comparative statement
hikaku keisansho
比較計算書

compensating error [UK]
sōsai goki
相殺誤記

complete audit
kanzen kansa
完全監査

completed audit
kimatsu kaikei kansa
期末会計監査

compound entry
fukugō kinyū
複合記入

compound journal entry
fukugō shiwake kinyū
複合仕訳記入

compound trial balance
gappei shisanhyō
合併試算表

conditions of issue
hakkō jōken
発行条件

consolidated accounts
tōgō kanjō
統合勘定

consolidated balance sheet
renketsu taishaku taishōhyō
連結貸借対照表

consolidated financial statements
renketsu zaimu shohyō
連結財務諸表

consolidated income and expenditure account
renketsu son'eki keisansho
連結損益計算書

consolidated income statement
renketsu son'eki keisansho
連結損益計算書

consolidated profit and loss account
renketsu son'eki keisansho
連結損益計算書

consolidated surplus
renketsu jōyokin
連結剰余金

consolidated work sheet
renketsu seisanhyō
連結精算表

consolidated working fund
renketsu unten shikin
連結運転資金

consolidation
(merger)
gappei
合併

(accounts)
renketsu
連結
tōgō
統合

(liquidation, arrangement)
seiri
整理

consolidation fund
seiri kikin
整理基金

consolidation ledger
renketsu motochō
連結元帳

consolidation of accounts
kanjō no renketsu
勘定の連結

consolidation of share capital
kabushiki gappei
株式合併
kabushiki no tōgō
株式の統合

consolidation of stock
kabushiki no tōgō
株式の統合

constant capital
fuhen shihon
不変資本

constant cost(s)
fuhen hiyō
不変費用
koteihi
固定費

constant expenses
fuhen hiyō
不変費用
koteihi
固定費

constant returns
shūeki ittei
収益一定

construction in progress (on balance sheet)
kensetsu karikanjō
建設仮勘定

contingency
gūhatsu jiken
偶発事件

contingency fund
gūhatsu jiken junbikin
偶発事件準備金

contingency reserve
gūhatsu sonshitsu tsumitatekin
偶発損失積立金

contingent gain
gūhatsu rieki
偶発利益

contingent liability
gūhatsu saimu
偶発債務

contingent loss
gūhatsu sonshitsu
偶発損失

continuous audit
keizoku kaikei kansa
継続会計監査

contributed capital
kyoshutsu shihon
拠出資本

control account
tōsei kanjō
統制勘定

control period
kanri kikan
管理期間

controllable cost
kanrikanōhi
管理可能費

controller
kansayaku
監査役

conversion
tenkan
転換

conversion rights
tenkanken
転換権

conversion stock
tenkan kabushiki
転換株式

convertibility
tenkan kanōsei
転換可能性

convertible preference shares
tenkan yūsen kabu
転換優先株

convertible preferred stock
tenkan yūsen kabu
転換優先株

cooked accounts
kaisaku kanjō
改作勘定

co-ownership of shares
kabushiki no kyōyū
株式の共有

corporate accounting
kigyō kaikei
企業会計

corporate accounting principles
kigyō kaikei gensoku
企業会計原則

corporate assets
hōjin shisan
法人資産

corporate bond
hōjin saiken
法人債券
shasai
社債

corporate book-keeping
kaisha boki
会社簿記

corporate borrowing
kigyō kariire
企業借入れ

corporate business results
kessan kaisha gyōseki
決算会社業績

corporate capital
kaisha shihon
会社資本

corporate debenture
shasai
社債

corporate earnings
kigyō shūeki
企業収益

corporate estate
hōjin zaisan
法人財産

corporate expenses
shahi
社費

corporate finance
kigyō zaimu
企業財務

corporate financial statement
kaisha zaimu shohyō
会社財務諸表

corporate financing
kigyō kin'yū
企業金融

corporate growth
kigyō seichō
企業成長

corporate income
hōjin shotoku
法人所得

corporate income tax
hōjin shotokuzei
法人所得税

corporate investment
kigyō tōshi
企業投資

corporate investment overseas
kigyō kaigai tōshi
企業海外投資

corporate liquidity
kigyō ryūdōsei
企業流動性

corporate performance
kigyō gyōseki
企業業績

corporate profit
kigyō rieki
企業利益
kigyō rijun
企業利潤
kigyō shūeki
企業収益

corporate profit after tax
zeibikigo hōjin rijun
税引後法人利潤

corporate profit before tax
zeibikizen hōjin rijun
税引前法人利潤

corporate profit tax
hōjin rijunzei
法人利潤税

corporate property
hōjin zaisan
法人財産

corporate raider [US]
kaisha nottorima
会社乗っ取り魔

corporate report
kigyō hōkokusho
企業報告書

corporate retained earnings
hōjin ryūho
法人留保

corporate saving(s)
hōjin chochiku
法人貯蓄

corporate securities
hōjin shōken
法人証券

corporate shareholder
hōjin kabunushi
法人株主

corporate stock
kaisha kabushiki
会社株式

corporate tax
hōjinzei
法人税

corporate trust [US]
hōjin shintaku
法人信託

corporation profit tax
hōjin ritokuzei
法人利得税

corporation's own stock
jisha kabu
自社株

corporation tax
hōjinzei
法人税

corporation tax credit
hōjinzeikōjo
法人税控除

cost
kosuto
コスト

(prime cost)
genka
原価

(expenses)
hiyō
費用

cost absorption
genka kyūshū
原価吸収

cost accountant
genka keisanshi
原価計算士

cost accounting
genka keisan
原価計算

cost accounting method
genka keisan hōshiki
原価計算方式

cost accounting period
genka keisan kikan
原価計算期間

cost accounting standards
genka keisan kijun
原価計算基準

cost accounting system
genka keisan seido
原価計算制度

cost accounts
genka kanjō
原価勘定

cost allocation
genka haifu
原価配布

cost analysis
genka bunseki
原価分析

cost apportionment
genka wariate
原価割当て

cost audit
genka kansa
原価監査

cost basis
(base)
genka kijun
原価基準

(principle)
genka shugi
原価主義

cost behaviour
genka no dōkō
原価の動向

cost-benefit analysis
hiyō-ben'eki bunseki
費用・便益分析

cost-benefit ratio
hiyō-ben'eki hiritsu
費用・便益比率

cost book
genka chōbo
原価帳簿

cost calculation
genka santei
原価算定

cost centre
genka chūshinten
原価中心点

cost control
genka kanri
原価管理

cost control account
keihi tōsei kanjō
経費統制勘定

cost department
genka bumon
原価部門

cost-effective
hiyō yūkōdo no
費用有効度の

cost-effectiveness
hiyō yūkōdo
費用有効度

cost-effectiveness analysis
hiyō yūkōdo bunseki
費用有効度分析

cost estimates
genka mitsumori
原価見積り

cost factor
genka yōso
原価要素

cost finding
genka keisan
原価計算
hiyō keisan
費用計算

cost keeper
genka keisanshi
原価計算士

cost keeping
genka keisan
原価計算

cost ledger
genka motochō
原価元帳

cost management
genka kanri
原価管理

cost method
genkahō
原価法

cost minimization
hiyō kyokushōka
費用極小化

cost of capital
shihon kosuto
資本コスト

cost of equipment
setsubihi
設備費

cost of funds [US]
shikin kosuto
資金コスト

cost of insurance
hoken genka
保険原価

cost of maintenance
ijihi
維持費

cost of marketing
shijō hiyō
市場費用

cost of production
seisanhi
生産費

(manufacturing)
seizō genka
製造原価

cost of purchase
shiire genka
仕入原価

cost of repairs
shūzenhi
修繕費

cost of sales
uriage genka
売上原価

cost reduction
genka hikisage
原価引下げ
genka kirisage
原価切下げ

cost report
genka hōkokusho
原価報告書

cost-saving
keihi setsuyaku
経費節約

cost-saving measures
keihi setsuyakusaku
経費節約策

cost sheet
genka keisanhyō
原価計算表

cost system
genka keisan seido
原価計算制度

cost unit
genka tan'i
原価単位

costing [UK]
genka keisan
原価計算

costing method
genka keisan hōshiki
原価計算方式

costing period
genka keisan kikan
原価計算期間

costing system
genka keisan seido
原価計算制度

costing unit
genka keisan tan'i
原価計算単位

CPA (certified public accountant) [US]
kōnin kaikeishi
公認会計士

credit balance
kashikata zandaka
貸方残高

credit entry
kashikata kinyū
貸方記入

credit side
kashikata
貸方

creditors' ledger
saikensha no motochō
債権者の元帳

cum dividend
haitōtsuki
配当付き

cum new
kokabutsuki
子株付き
shinkabutsuki
新株付き

cum rights
kenritsuki
権利付き

cumulative
ruisekiteki na
累積的な

cumulative accounting
ruisekiteki keisan
累積的計算

cumulative dividend
ruiseki haitō
累積配当

cumulative income statement
ruisekiteki son'eki keisansho
累積的損益計算書

cumulative preference shares [UK]
ruiseki yūsen kabu
累積優先株

cumulative preferred stock [US]
ruiseki yūsen kabu
累積優先株

cumulative profit and loss statement
ruisekiteki son'eki keisansho
累積的損益計算書

cumulative stock
ruisekiteki yūsen kabu
累積的優先株

current assets
ryūdō shisan
流動資産

current assets/total deposits ratio
ryūdō shisan hiritsu
流動資産比率

current balance
keijō kanjō
経常勘定

current budget
keijō yosan
経常予算

current business year
genjigyō nendo
現事業年度

current cost
genzai no genka
現在の原価

current expenditure
keijō shishutsu
経常支出

(expenditure for the current term)
tōki shishutsu
当期支出

current expenses
genzai no hiyō
現在の費用

(ordinary expenses, running expenses)
keijōhi
経常費

current expenses/current income ratio
keijō shūshiritsu
経常収支率

current financial year [UK]
genkaikei nendo
現会計年度

current fiscal year [US]
genkaikei nendo
現会計年度

current liabilities
ryūdō fusai
流動負債

current liabilities/net worth ratio
ryūdō fusai hiritsu
流動負債比率

current loans payable
tōza karikoshi
当座借越し

current loans receivable
tōza kashikoshi
当座貸越し

current net earnings
tōki junshūeki
当期純収益

current net income
tōki junshotoku
当期純所得

current net profit
tōki junrieki
当期純利益

current period
tōki
当期

current period net income
tōki junrieki
当期純利益

current position
unten shihon jōtai
運転資本状態

current ratio
ryūdō hiritsu
流動比率

current revenue
keijō shūnyū
経常収入

current surplus
keijō kuroji
経常黒字

current term
tōki
当期

current-term net income
tōki junrieki
当期純利益

current-term net loss
tōki junsonshitsu
当期純損失

current-term net profit
tōki junrieki
当期純利益

current-term settlement
tōki kessan
当期決算

current transaction
keijō torihiki
経常取引

current year
tōnen
当年

curtailment of expenditure
keihi setsugen
経費節減

cut costs (verb)
hiyō o kiritsumeru
費用を切詰める

cutbacks
(economizing)
kiritsume
切詰め

(axing, trimming down)
sakugen
削減

(economy, retrenchment)
setsugen
節減

(curtailment, diminuation)
shukushō
縮小

cutting down on expenses
keihi setsugen
経費節減

daily cash balance book
genkin zandaka nichiji kinyūchō
現金残高日次記入帳

daily trial balance
nichiji shisanhyō
日次試算表

damaged share certificate
kison kabuken
き損株券

debenture
shasai
社債

debenture capital
kariire shihonkin
借入資本金

debenture certificate
saiken
債券

debenture stock [UK]
shasaiken
社債券

debenture stock certificate
shasaiken
社債券

debit balance
karikata zandaka
借方残高

debit entry
karikata kinyū
借方記入

debit side
karikata
借方

debt capital
fusai shihon
負債資本

debt/equity ratio
fusai-shihon hiritsu
負債・資本比率

debt ratio
fusai hiritsu
負債比率

declaration of dividend
haitō no happyō
配当の発表

declaration of solvency
shiharai nōryoku no senkoku
支払能力の宣告

decrease in capital
genshi
減資

decreasing costs
hiyō teigen
費用逓減

deductions
kōjo
控除
tenbiki
天引き

deferment
kurinobe
繰延べ

deferred account
kurinobe kanjō
繰延勘定

deferred assets
kurinobe shisan
繰延資産

deferred charge
kurinobe hiyō
繰延費用

deferred credit
kurinobe kashikata
繰延貸方

deferred debit
kurinobe karikata
繰延借方

deferred dividend
kurinobe haitōkin
繰延配当金
sueoki haitōkin
据置配当金

deferred expenditure
kurinobe shishutsu
繰延支出

deferred expenses
kurinobe hiyō
繰延費用
kurinobe keihi
繰延経費

deferred income
kurinobe shūeki
繰延収益

deferred liabilities
kurinobe fusai
繰延負債
sueoki fusai
据置負債

deferred payment
nobebarai
延払い
sueokibarai
据置払い

deferred profits
rieki kurinobekin
利益繰延金

deferred revenue
kurinobe shūeki
繰延収益

deferred settlement
kurinobe kessai
繰延決済

deferred shares [UK]
kōhai kabu
後配株

deferred stock [US]
kōhai kabu
後配株

deferred tax
sueokizei
据置税

deficiency
fusokugaku
不足額
fusokukin
不足金

deficiency account
fusokukin kanjō
不足金勘定

deficit
(red figures)
akaji
赤字

(amount of loss)
kessongaku
欠損額
kessonkin
欠損金

deficit at the beginning of the period
zenki kurikoshi kessonkin
前期繰越欠損金

deficit carried forward
jiki kurikoshi kessonkin
次期繰越欠損金

denomination of shares
gakumen kingaku
額面金額

departmental accounting
bumonbetsu kaikei
部門別会計

departmental accounts
bumonbetsu kaikei
部門別会計

departmental budget
bumon yosan
部門予算

departmental cost accounting
bumonbetsu genka keisan
部門別原価計算

departmental expenses
bumonhi
部門費

departmental summary sheet
bumonhi shūkeihyō
部門費集計表

depletion allowance
genka hikiate
原価引当て

depletion of capital
shihon no kokatsu
資本の枯渇

deposits received (on balance sheet)
shoazukarikin
諸預り金

depreciable amount
genka shōkyakugaku
原価償却額

depreciable assets
genka shōkyaku shisan
原価償却資産

depreciable cost
genka shōkyaku kiso genka
原価償却基礎原価

**depreciation
(decrease in value)**
genka
減価

(amortization [UK])
genka shōkyaku
原価償却

depreciation account
genka shōkyaku kanjō
原価償却勘定

depreciation accounting
genka shōkyaku kaikei
原価償却会計

depreciation adjustment
genka shōkyaku chōsei
原価償却調整

depreciation allowance
genka shōkyaku hikiatekin
原価償却引当金

depreciation cost
genka shōkyakuhi
原価償却費

depreciation expenses
genka shōkyakuhi
原価償却費

depreciation fund
genka shōkyaku kikin
原価償却基金

depreciation method
genka shōkyakuhō
原価償却法

depreciation of assets
shisan shōkyaku
資産償却

depreciation rate
genka shōkyakuritsu
原価償却率

depreciation reserve
genka shōkyaku hikiatekin
原価償却引当金

depreciation unit
genka shōkyaku tan'i
原価償却単位

detailed audit
seimitsu kansa
精密監査

direct cost
chokusetsu genka
直接原価
chokusetsuhi
直接費

direct cost centre
chokusetsuhi sentā
直接費センター

direct cost method
chokusetsu genkahō
直接原価法

direct costing
chokusetsu genka keisan
直接原価計算

direct depreciation
chokusetsu shōkyaku
直接償却

direct expenses
chokusetsu keihi
直接経費
chokusetsuhi
直接費

direct labour cost
chokusetsu rōdōhi
直接労働費

direct liabilities
chokusetsu fusai
直接負債

direct material cost
chokusetsu zairyōhi
直接材料費

direct placement [US]
chokusetsu boshū
直接募集

direct placing [UK]
chokusetsu boshū
直接募集

direct public issue of shares
chokusetsu boshū
直接募集

director's bonus
yakuin shōyo
役員賞与

director's fee
yakuin teate
役員手当

director's remuneration
yakuin hōshū
役員報酬

disclosure
kigyō naiyō kaiji
企業内容開示

discount account
waribiki kanjō
割引勘定

discount ledger
waribiki motochō
割引元帳

discounts (on balance sheet)
waribikiryō
割引量

distributable profits
haitōkanō rieki
配当可能利益

distribution
(split)
bunpai
分配

(allocation, division)
haibun
配分

(apportionment, dividend)
haitō
配当

distribution cost
ryūtsū keihi
流通経費

distribution expenses [US]
hanbaihi
販売費

distribution of assets
shisan no haibun
資産の配分

distribution of net profits
rieki shobun
利益処分

distribution of profits
rieki haitō
利益配当

distribution of shareholders
kabunushi no bunpai
株主の分配

distribution overheads
ryūtsūhi
流通費

distribution policy
bunpaihō
分配法

divestment
kenri sōshitsu
権利喪失

dividend(s)
haitōkin
配当金

(allotment, apportionment)
haitō
配当

(on balance sheet)
rieki haitōkin
利益配当金

dividend account
haitō kanjō
配当勘定

dividend balance
haitō jūtō zandaka
配当充当残高

dividend book
haitōchō
配当帳

dividend check [US]
haitōken
配当券

dividend cover
haitō bairitsu
配当倍率

dividend credit
haitō kōjo
配当控除

dividend cut
genpai
減配

dividend equalization fund
haitō heikin junbikin
配当平均準備金

dividend equalization reserve
haitō heikin tsumitatekin
配当平均積立金

dividend in arrear
entai haitōkin
延滞配当金
miharai haitōkin
未払配当金

dividend increase
zōhai
増配

dividend list
haitō shiharaihyō
配当支払表

dividend notice
haitō tsūchisho
配当通知書

dividend off
haitōochi
配当落ち

dividend on
haitōtsuki
配当付き

dividend on common stock
futsū kabu haitōkin
普通株配当金

dividend on preference shares [UK]
yūsen kabu haitōkin
優先株配当金

dividend on preferred stock [US]
yūsen kabu haitōkin
優先株配当金

dividend pay-out
haitō shiharai
配当支払い

dividend pay-out ratio
haitō shiharairitsu
配当支払率

dividend payable
miharai haitōkin
未払配当金

dividend per share
hitokabu atari haitō
一株当たり配当

dividend preference
haitō yūsen
配当優先

dividend rate
haitōritsu
配当率

dividend receivable
mishū haitōkin
未収配当金

dividend received
uketori haitōkin
受取配当金

dividend register
haitō kinyūchō
配当記入帳

dividend re-investment plan
haitōkin saitōshi shikumi
配当金再投資仕組み

dividend reserve
haitō junbi tsumitatekin
配当準備積立金

dividend rights
haitōken
配当権

dividend unclaimed
miharai haitōkin
未払配当金

dividend warrant [UK]
haitōkin shiharaishō
配当金支払証

dividend yield
haitō rimawari
配当利回り

dividends per share
hitokabu atari haitōkin
一株当たり配当金

double-account system
fukushiki kaikei seido
複式会計制度

double entry
fukushiki kichōhō
複式記帳法

double-entry book-keeping
fukushiki boki
複式簿記

double taxation
nijū kazei
二重課税

earned legal reserves (on balance sheet)
rieki junbikin
利益準備金

earned revenue
jitsugen shūeki
実現収益

earned surplus [US] (see retained earnings)
rieki jōyokin
利益剰余金

earned surplus reserves
rieki junbikin
利益準備金

earning assets
shūeki shisan
収益資産

earning power
shūekiryoku
収益力

earning rate
shūekiritsu
収益率

earning ratio
kigyō shūekiritsu
企業収益率

earnings
shūeki
収益

(profit)
rieki
利益

earnings basis
shūeki bēsu
収益ベース

earnings/dividends ratio
riekikin-haitō hiritsu
利益金・配当比率

earnings on assets
shisan shotoku
資産所得

earnings per share
hitokabu atari rieki
一株当たり利益
hitokabu atari shūeki
一株当たり収益

earnings report
shūeki hōkokusho
収益報告書

earnings statement [US]
son'eki keisansho
損益計算書

earnings yield
shūeki rimawari
収益利回り

embezzle
ōryō suru
横領する
tsukaikomu
使込む

embezzlement
ōryō
横領
tsukaikomi
使込み

embezzler
ōryō hannin
横領犯人

emergency fund
gūhatsu sonshitsu junbikin
偶発損失準備金
hijō shikin
非常資金

emoluments, salaries and allowances
hōshū oyobi kyūyo
報酬および給与

employed capital
shiyō shihon
使用資本

employees' welfare cost
fukushi kōseihi
福祉厚生費

employment cost (wage expenses)
chingin hiyō
賃金費用

(personnel expenses)
jinkenhi
人件費

end of the month
getsumatsu
月末

enterprise with foreign capital
gaishikei kigyō
外資系企業

entertainment expense account
kōsaihi kanjō
交際費勘定
settaihi kanjō
接待費勘定

entertainment expenses
kōsaihi
交際費
settaihi
接待費

entry
kinyū
記入

equipment fund
setsubi shikin
設備資金

equipment investment
setsubi tōshi
設備投資

equities (= ordinary shares) [UK]
futsū kabu
普通株

equity
(share holdings)
kabushiki hoyū
株式保有

(holding interest)
mochibun
持分

equity accounting
mochibun kaikei
持分会計

equity capital
jiko shihon
自己資本
kabunushi shihon
株主資本

equity dilution
mochikabu hiritsu no teika
持株比率の低下

equity financing
mochibun shihon chōtatsu
持分資本調達

equity funding
mochibun shihon chōtatsu
持分資本調達

equity investment
shusshi
出資

equity issue
shusshi shōken
出資証券

equity ownership
mochibun hoyūken
持分保有権

equity participation
shihon sanka
資本参加

equity shareholder
mochibun hoyūsha
持分保有者

error
gosa
誤差

estimated balance sheet
mitsumori taishaku taishōhyō
見積貸借対照表

estimated cost
mitsumori genka
見積原価

estimated cost accounting
mitsumori genka keisan
見積原価計算

estimated financial statement
mitsumori zaimu shohyō
見積財務諸表

estimated funds statement
mitsumori shikinhyō
見積資金表

estimated loss
mitsumori sonshitsugaku
見積損失額

estimated profit
mitsumori rieki
見積利益

estimated profit and loss
mitsumori son'eki
見積損益

estimated profit and loss statement
mitsumori son'eki keisansho
見積損益計算書

ex-dividend
haitōochi
配当落ち

ex-rights
kenriochi
権利落ち

ex-warrants
kenriochi
権利落ち

examination of financial statement
zaimu shohyō kansa
財務諸表監査

examine the books
chōbo o kansa suru
帳簿を監査する

excess profit
chōka ritoku
超過利得

existing assets
kizon shisan
既存資産

existing shareholders
genkabunushi
現株主

expected profit
kitai rieki
期待利益
yosō rieki
予想利益

expenditure
shishutsu
支出

expense(s)
hiyō
費用

(business expenses)
eigyōhi
営業費

(operating expenses)
kei'eihi
経営費

(outlay, spending)
keihi
経費

expense account
(business expenses)
keihi kanjō
経費勘定

(entertainment expenses)
kōsaihi kanjō
交際費勘定
settaihi kanjō
接待費勘定

expense allowance
keihikyū
経費給

expense analysis
hiyō bunseki
費用分析

expense analysis sheet
keihi uchiwakehyō
経費内訳表

expense book
keihi uchiwakechō
経費内訳帳

expense budget
keihi yosan
経費予算

expense control
keihi kanri
経費管理

expense item
himoku
費目

expense ledger
keihi motochō
経費元帳

expense report
keihi hōkokusho
経費報告書

expense voucher
kōsaihi denpyō
交際費伝票

external audit
gaibu kansa
外部監査

external auditor
gaibu kansanin
外部監査人

external capital
gaibu shihon
外部資本

external financing
gaibu chōtatsu
外部調達

extra allowance
tokubetsu teate
特別手当

extra dividend
tokubetsu haitō
特別配当

extra expenditure
rinjihi
臨時費

extraordinary budget
rinji yosan
臨時予算

extraordinary expenditure
rinji shishutsu
臨時支出

extraordinary income
rinji shotoku
臨時所得

extraordinary item
rinji kōmoku
臨時項目

extraordinary loss
tokubetsu sonshitsu
特別損失

extraordinary profit
tokubetsu rieki
特別利益

extraordinary profit and loss
tokubetsu son'eki
特別損益

extraordinary revenue
rinji shūnyū
臨時収入

face value
gakumen kakaku
額面価格

facilities (on balance sheet)
kōchikubutsu
構築物

false accounting [UK]
ayamatta keisan
誤った計算

fictitious assets
gisei shisan
擬制資産

fictitious capital
gisei shihon
擬制資本

final accounts
nenji kessan
年次決算

final adjustments
saishū no chōsei
最終の調整

final audit
kimatsu kansa
期末監査

final balance
kimatsu zandaka
期末残高

final cost
sōgenka
総原価

final dividend
saishū haitō
最終配当

final trial balance
saishū shisanhyō
最終試算表

finance a business
jigyō ni shusshi suru
事業に出資する

finance committee
zaimu i'inkai
財務委員会

financial accounting
zaimu kaikei
財務会計

financial accounts
zaimu kanjō
財務勘定

financial adviser
zaimu komon
財務顧問

financial affairs
zaimu
財務

financial analysis
zaimu bunseki
財務分析

financial assets
kin'yū shisan
金融資産

financial audit
zaimu kansa
財務監査

financial budget
shikin yosan
資金予算

financial control
zaimu kanri
財務管理

financial deficit
shikin fusoku
資金不足

financial department
zaimu bumon
財務部門

financial difficulty
zaimu konnan
財務困難

financial figures
zaimu keisū
財務計数

financial insolvency
zaimu funō
財務不能

financial liabilities
kin'yū fusai
金融負債

financial management
zaimu kanri
財務管理

financial planning
zaimu keikaku
財務計画

financial position
zaimu jōtai
財務状態

**financial position statement
(balance sheet)**
taishaku taishōhyō
貸借対照表

financial ratio
zaimu hiritsu
財務比率

financial reorganization
kin'yū saihensei
金融再編成

financial report
kaikei hōkoku(sho)
会計報告(書)

financial requirements
shikin juyō
資金需要

financial resources
zaigen
財源

financial results
zaimuteki kekka
財務的結果

financial retrenchment
keihi setsugen
経費節減

financial review
keiri gainen
経理概念

financial situation
zaimu jōtai
財務状態

financial solvency
zaimu ryūdōsei
財務流動性

financial standing
zaimu jōtai
財務状態

  (funds situation)
shikin jijō
資金事情

  (asset situation)
shisan jōtai
資産状態

financial statement
zaimu shohyō
財務諸表

financial statement analysis
zaimu shohyō bunseki
財務諸表分析

financial statement audit
zaimu shohyō kansa
財務諸表監査

financial status
zaimu jōtai
財務状態

financial straits
zaimu konnan
財務困難

financial strength
shin'yōryoku
信用力

financial structure
zaimu kōsei
財務構成

financial year [UK]
kaikei nendo
会計年度

financing (= procurement)
(shikin) chōtatsu
(資金)調達

financing requirements
shikin juyō
資金需要

**finished goods (on balance
sheet)**
seihin
製品

first half of the year
kamihanki
上半期
zenki
前期

first preferred stock
dai'ichi yūsen kabu
第一優先株

first quarter
dai'ichi shihanki
第一四半期

fiscal year [US]
kaikei nendo
会計年度

fixed assets [US]
kotei shisan
固定資産

fixed assets/debt ratio
kotei shisan-fusai hiritsu
固定資産・負債比率

fixed assets ledger
kotei shisan daichō
固定資産台帳

fixed assets/long-term capital ratio
kotei shisan-chōki shihon hiritsu
固定資産・長期資本
比率

fixed assets/net worth ratio
kotei shisan-seika hiritsu
固定資産・正価比率

fixed assets ratio
kotei shisan hiritsu
固定資産比率

fixed assets turnover ratio
kotei shisan kaitenritsu
固定資産回転率

fixed budget
kotei yosan
固定予算

fixed capital
kotei shihon
固定資本

fixed capital investment
kotei shihon tōshi
固定資本投資

fixed charges
koteihi
固定費

fixed costs
koteihi
固定費

fixed expenses
koteihi
固定費

fixed liabilities
kotei fusai
固定負債

fixed liabilities/long-term capital ratio
kotei fusai-chōki shihon hiritsu
固定負債・長期資本
比率

fixed liabilities/net worth ratio
kotei fusai hiritsu
固定負債比率

fixed overheads
koteihi
固定費

floating assets
ryūdō shisan
流動資産

floating capital
ryūdō shihon
流動資本

floating charge
fudō tanpo
不動担保

floating fund
ryūdō shikin
流動資金

floating liabilities
ryūdō fusai
流動負債

forecast
(anticipation)
yosō
予想

(prediction)
yosoku
予測

forecast balance sheet
yosō taishaku taishōhyō
予想貸借対照表

forecast budget
yosoku yosan
予測予算

forecast cost
yosoku genka
予測原価

foreign assets
gaikoku shisan
外国資産

foreign buying of Japanese company shares
gaijingai
外人買い

foreign capital
gaikoku shihon
外国資本
gaishi
外資

forfeit
sōshitsu suru
喪失する

forfeited shares
shikken kabu
失権株

forfeiture
sōshitsu
喪失

(loss of rights)
shikken
失権

forfeiture of shares
kabushiki no bosshū
株式の没収
kabushiki no shikken
株式の失権

forged share certificate
gizō kabuken
偽造株券

forged stock certificate
gizō kabuken
偽造株券

forged transfer of shares
gizō kabuken meigi kakikae
偽造株券名義書換え

founder's profit
sōgyōsha ritoku
創業者利得

founder's shares
hokkinin kabu
発起人株

fraudulent gains
fusei ritoku
不正利得

free share
mushō kabu
無償株

full disclosure
(kabushiki no) kanzen kaiji
(株式の)完全開示

fully depreciated
genka shōkyakuzumi
原価償却済み

fully paid capital stock
zengaku haraikomizumi kabu
全額払込済株

fully paid-up shares
zengaku haraikomizumi kabu
全額払込済株

fund
kikin
基金

fund accounting
shikin kaikei
資金会計

fund control
shikin tōsei
資金統制

fund management
shikinguri
資金繰り

fund position of the company
kigyō temoto ryūdōsei
企業手許流動性

funds
shikin
資金
zaigen
財源

funds in hand [UK]
temoto shikin
手許資金

funds on hand [US]
temoto shikin
手許資金

furniture and fittings (on balance sheet)
kigu-bihin
器具・備品

gains
(profit, returns)
rieki
利益
rijun
利潤

(benefit, profit, returns)
ritoku
利得

(earnings, proceeds, profit)
shūeki
収益

gains from capital reduction
genshi saeki
源資差益

gains from revaluation of fixed assets
kotei shisan hyōkaeki
固定資産評価益

gains from sale of fixed assets
kotei shisan baikyakueki
固定資産売却益

gearing [UK]
giaringu
ギアリング
teiritsu
挺率

gearing ratio
fusai-shihon hiritsu
負債・資本比率

general accounting
ippan kaikei
一般会計

general accounting principles
ippan kaikei gensoku
一般会計原則

general accounts
ippan kaikei
一般会計

general administrative costs
ippan kanrihi
一般管理費

general administrative expenses
ippan kanrihi
一般管理費

general administrative expenses budget
ippan kanrihi yosan
一般管理費予算

general audit
futsū kansa
普通監査
ippan kansa
一般監査

general auditing standard
kansa ippan kijun
監査一般基準

general balance sheet
ippan taishaku taishōhyō
一般貸借対照表

general book-keeping
ippan boki
一般簿記

general budget
sōyosan
総予算

general closing
tsūjō kessan
通常決算

general cost
ippan genka
一般原価

general expenses
ippan keihi
一般経費

general expenses/current income ratio
ippan keihiritsu
一般経費率

general fund
ippan shikin
一般資金

general journal
ippan shiwakechō
一般仕訳帳

general ledger
sōkanjō motochō
総勘定元帳

general ledger account
sōkanjō motochō kanjō
総勘定元帳勘定

general operating expenses
ippan eigyōhi
一般営業費

general operating funds
ippan eigyō shikin
一般営業資金

general overheads
ippan kansetsuhi
一般間接費

general profit and loss account
son'eki kanjō
損益勘定

general reserve
betto tsumitatekin
別途積立金

go public
kabushiki kōkai suru
株式公開する

going concern value
keizoku kigyō kachi
継続企業価値

good financial standing
yūryō shisan jōtai
優良資産状態

gross assets
sōshisan
総資産

gross capital
sōshihon
総資本

gross cash flow
gurosu-kyasshu-furō
グロス・キャッシュ・フロー

gross cost
sōgenka
総原価

gross earnings
sōshūeki
総収益

gross expenditure
sōshishutsu
総支出

gross income
sōshotoku
総所得
sōshūnyū
総収入

(for tax declaration)
hōjin no ekikin
法人の益金

gross loss
sōsonshitsu
総損失

gross margin [US]
sōrieki
総利益
sōrijun
総利潤

gross profit [UK]
sōrieki
総利益
sōrijun
総利潤

gross profit analysis
sōrieki bunseki
総利益分析

gross profit on sales
uriage sōrieki
売上総利益

gross profit ratio
sōekiritsu
総益率

gross revenue
sōshūeki
総収益

gross working capital
sōunten shihon
総運転資本

gross worth
sōzaisan
総財産

group accounts
kigyō shūdan zaimuhyō
企業集団財務表

group financial statement
kigyō shūdan zaimuhyō
企業集団財務表

grouping of accounts
kanjō no sōkatsu
勘定の総括

growth
seichō
成長

growth forecasting
seichō yosoku
成長予測

guaranteed stock
(haitō no) hoshō kabu
(配当の)保証株

half yearly settlement of accounts
hanki kessan
半期決算

hidden assets
fukumi shisan
含み資産
intoku shisan
隠匿資産

hidden reserve
intoku tsumitatekin
隠匿積立金

high dividend
kōritsu haitō
高率配当

hiring cost (recruitment cost)
saiyōhi
採用費

holdings
kabushiki hoyū
株式保有
mochikabusū
持株数

illiquid assets
hiryūdōsei shisan
非流動性資産

illiquid capital
hiryūdōsei shihon
非流動性資本

illiquid funds
hiryūdōsei shikin
非流動性資金

illiquidity
hiryūdōsei
非流動性

incidental cost
zappi
雑費

incidental expenses
rinjihi
臨時費

income
shotoku
所得

(corporate income)
hōjin shotoku
法人所得

(profits)
rieki
利益
shūeki
収益

(return, revenue)
shūnyū
収入

income at liquidation
seisan shotoku
清算所得

income before tax (on balance sheet)
zeibiki maetōki rieki
税引前当期利益

income from business
jigyō shotoku
事業所得

income from operations
eigyō rieki
営業利益

income retention
shanai ryūho
社内留保

income statement
son'eki keisansho
損益計算書

income statement audit
son'eki keisansho kansa
損益計算書監査

income taxes (on balance sheet)
hōjinzei oyobi jūminzei
法人税および住民税

incorporated accountant
hōjin kaikeishi
法人会計士

increase of capital
zōshi
増資

increased costs
zōka hiyō
増加費用

increased profits
zōeki
増益

independent accountant
dokuritsu kaikeishi
独立会計士

independent accountant's opinion
dokuritsu kaikeishi no ikensho
独立会計士の意見書

independent accounting
dokuritsu kaikei
独立会計

independent audit
kaikei kansa
会計監査

independent auditor
kaikei kansanin
会計監査人

independent auditor's opinion
kaikei kansanin no ikensho
会計監査人の意見書

indirect costs
kansetsuhi
間接費

indirect depreciation
kansetsu shōkyaku
間接償却

indirect expenses
kansetsuhi
間接費

individual shareholder
kojin kabunushi
個人株主

influx of capital
shihon ryūnyū
資本流入

initial audit
shodo kansa
初度監査

initial budget
tōsho yosan
当初予算

initial capital
kishu shihon
期首資本

initial cost
genka
原価

initial cost of business
kaigyōhi
開業費

initial depreciation
shoki shōkyaku
初期償却

initial expenditure
sōgyōhi
創業費

initial expenses
sōgyōhi
創業費

initial loss
sōgyōki kesson
創業期欠損

initial outlay
tōsho shishutsu
当初支出

initial public offering
kōkai kōbo
公開公募

injection of capital
shihon dōnyū
資本導入

inscribed share
kimei kabu
記名株

inscribed share certificate
kimei kabuken
記名株券

inside information
naibu jōhō
内部情報

insider
insaidā
インサイダー
naibusha
内部者

installation cost
kasetsuhi
架設費

instalment
kappubarai
割賦払い

instalment account
kappu kanjō
割賦勘定

instalment accounting
kappu kaikei
割賦会計

instalment accounts payable
kappubarai shiharai kanjō
割賦払支払勘定

instalment accounts receivable
kappubarai toritate kanjō
割賦払取立勘定

instalment customer account
kappubarai tokuisaki kanjō
割賦払得意先勘定

instalment payment
kappubarai
割賦払い

institutional shareholder
kikan kabunushi
機関株主

instructions to accountant
kaikeishi e no shirei
会計士への指令

insufficient liquidity
kashō ryūdōsei
過少流動性

intangible assets
mukei shisan
無形資産

intangible capital
mukei shihon
無形資本

intangible fixed assets
mukei kotei shisan
無形固定資産

inter-business credit
kigyōkan shin'yō
企業間信用

interest (rights)
riken
利権

interest and dividends received (on balance sheet)
uketori risoku oyobi haitōkin
受取利息および
配当金

interest expenses (on balance sheet)
shiharai rishi
支払利子

interim account
chūkan kanjō
中間勘定

interim audit
chūkan kansa
中間監査

interim closing
chūkan kessan
中間決算

interim dividend
chūkan haitō
中間配当

interim report
chūkan hōkokusho
中間報告書

interim statement
chūkan keisansho
中間計算書

internal analysis
naibu bunseki
内部分析

internal audit
naibu kansa
内部監査

internal audit report
naibu bunseki hōkokusho
内部分析報告書

internal audit standard
naibu kansa kijun
内部監査基準

internal audit system
naibu kansa seido
内部監査制度

internal auditing
naibu kansa
内部監査

internal auditing department
naibu kansabu
内部監査部

internal auditor
naibu kansanin
内部監査人

internal business analysis
naibu kei'ei bunseki
内部経営分析

internal financial management
naibu zaimu kanri
内部財務管理

internal financing
naibu kin'yū
内部金融

**inventory
(stock-taking)**
tanaoroshi
棚卸し

(stock-taking list)
tanaoroshihyō
棚卸表

(stock)
zaiko
在庫

inventory accounting
tanaoroshi shisan kaikei
棚卸資産会計

inventory assets
tanaoroshi shisan
棚卸資産

inventory audit
tanaoroshi kansa
棚卸監査

inventory loss
tanaoroshison
棚卸損

inventory profit
tanaoroshi shisan rieki
棚卸資産利益

inventory reserve
tanaoroshi shisan hikiatekin
棚卸資産引当金

inventory/sales ratio
zaiko-uriage hiritsu
在庫・売上比率

inventory turnover
tanaoroshi shisan
kaitenritsu
棚卸資産回転率

inventory valuation
tanaoroshi hyōka
棚卸評価

inventory value
tanaoroshi kagaku
棚卸価額

investible funds
tōshikanō shikin
投資可能資金

investment
tōshi
投資

(subscribed capital)
shusshi
出資

(use of capital)
un'yō
運用

investment account
shisan shūeki kanjō
資産収益勘定

investment budget
tōshi yosan
投資予算

investment capital
tōshi shihon
投資資本

investment certificate
shusshi shōken
出資証券

investment cost
tōshi hiyō
投資費用

investment expenditure
tōshi shishutsu
投資支出

investment fund
tōshi kikin
投資基金

investment funds
tōshi shikin
投資資金

investment in plant and equipment
setsubi tōshi
設備投資

investment ledger
yūka shōken motochō
有価証券元帳

investment reserve
tōshi junbikin
投資準備金

investments and advances (on balance sheet)
tōshitō
投資等

investments in subsidiaries
kogaisha shusshikin
子会社出資金

invisible assets
mukei shisan
無形資産

invitation to subscribe for shares
kabunushi no boshū
株主の募集

invoice
okurijō
送状

invoice amount
okurijō kingaku
送状金額

invoice book
okurijō shiirechō
送状仕入帳
okurijō shikirichō
送状仕切帳

invoice number
okurijō bangō
送状番号

invoice register
okurijō kinyūchō
送状記入長

issue (noun) (issuing)
hakkō
発行

(an issue, title)
meigara
銘柄

issue (verb)
hakkō suru
発行する

issue at par
gakumen hakkō
額面発行

issue date
hakkōbi
発行日

issue of shares
kabushiki hakkō
株式発行

issue of shares at the current price
kabushiki no jika hakkō
株式の時価発行

issue price
hakkō kakaku
発行価格

issue procedure
hakkō tetsuzuki
発行手続き

issue syndicate
hakkōdan
発行団

issue terms
hakkō jōken
発行条件

issue to shareholders
kabunushi wariate
株主割当て

issue value
hakkō kakaku
発行価格

issued capital
boshū shihon
募集資本
hakkōzumi kabushiki
shihonkin
発行済株式資本金

issued capital stock
hakkōzumi kabushiki
shihonkin
発行済株式資本金

issued shares
hakkōzumi kabushiki
発行済株式

issuer
hakkōsha
発行者

issuer's cost
hakkōsha rimawari
発行者利回り

issuing company
hakkō gaisha
発行会社

issuing corporation
hakkō hōjin
発行法人

item
kōmoku
項目

item of account
kanjō kōmoku
勘定項目

itemization
(details)
meisai
明細

(breakdown)
uchiwake
内訳

itemize an account
kanjō no meisaisho o
tsukuru
勘定の明細書を作る

itemized account
meisai kanjō
明細勘定
shiwake kanjō
仕訳勘定

itemized accounts
meisai seisansho
明細精算書

itemized bill
kōmokubetsu kanjōsho
項目別勘定書

job costing [US]
batchi genkahō
バッチ原価法

joint audit
kyōdō kansa
共同監査

joint capital
kyōdō shihon
共同資本

joint financing
kyōdō shusshi
共同出資

joint stock
kyōdō shihon
共同資本
gōshi
合資

journal
shiwakechō
仕訳帳

journal entry
shiwakechō kinyū
仕訳帳記入

journal-form ledger
shiwakechōshiki motochō
仕訳帳式元帳

journal transfer method
kansetsu shimekirihō
間接締切法

key ledger
sōkanjō motochō
総勘定元帳

labour cost
rōdōhi
労働費
rōmuhi
労務費

lack of capital
shikin fusoku
資金不足

land (on balance sheet)
tochi
土地

large amount of capital
tagaku no shikin
多額の資金

large capital stock
ōgata kabu
大型株

large shareholder
daikabunushi
大株主

ledger
motochō
元帳

(register)
daichō
台帳

(original register)
genbo
原簿

ledger account
motochō kanjō
元帳勘定

ledger assets
motochō shisan
元帳資産

ledger balance
motochō zandaka
元帳残高

ledger control
motochō tōsei
元帳統制

ledger keeper
motochō kakari
元帳係

ledger transfer
motochō furikae
元帳振替え

ledger transfer method
motochō no chokusetsu shimekirihō
元帳の直接締切法

legal capital
hōtei shihon
法定資本

legal earned reserves
rieki junbikin
利益準備金

letter of allotment
kabunushi wariate tsūchijō
株主割当通知状

letter of application
mōshikomisho
申込書

letter of intent
ikōjō
意向状
shuisho
趣意書

letter of regret
kabushiki bonyū kotowarijō
株式募入断り状

leverage [US]
rebarejjido
レバレッジド
teiritsu
挺率

leveraged buy-out
rebarejjido-baiauto
レバレッジド・バイ
アウト

leveraged company
rebarejjido gaisha
レバレッジド会社

liabilities
fusai
負債

liabilities and capital
fusai oyobi shihon
負債および資本

liabilities/net worth ratio
fusai-shihon hiritsu
負債・資本比率

liable capital
sekinin shihon
責任資本

limited audit
gentei kansa
限定監査

liquid assets
ryūdō shisan
流動資産

liquid capital
ryūdō shihon
流動資本

liquid funds
ryūdō shikin
流動資金

liquid position
ryūdōsei aru jōtai
流動性ある状態

liquid ratio
ryūdō hiritsu
流動比率

liquid reserve
ryūdō junbikin
流動準備金

liquidate
seisan suru
清算する

liquidation
seisan
清算

liquidation accounts
seisan kanjō
清算勘定

liquidation balance sheet
seisan taishaku taishōhyō
清算貸借対照表

liquidation income
seisan shotoku
清算所得

liquidation procedure
seisan tetsuzuki
清算手続き

liquidation profit and loss statement
seisan son'eki keisansho
清算損益計算書

liquidation sale
tezume uri
手詰売り

liquidation tax
seisan shotokuzei
清算所得税

liquidation value
seisan kachi
清算価値

liquidator
seisannin
清算人

liquidity
ryūdōsei
流動性

liquidity basis
ryūdōsei bēsu
流動性ベース

liquidity crisis
ryūdōsei kiki
流動性危機

liquidity position
ryūdōsei jōtai
流動性状態

liquidity problems
ryūdōsei mondai
流動性問題

liquidity ratio
ryūdōsei hiritsu
流動性比率

list of shareholders
kabunushi meibo
株主名簿

listing requirements
jōjō shinsa kijun
上場審査基準

listing standard
jōjō kijun
上場基準

loan book
kashitsuke kinyūchō
貸付記入帳

loan capital
kashitsuke shihon
貸付資本

loan ledger
kashitsuke motochō
貸付元帳

loans to affiliates
kankei gaisha kashi-tsukekin
関係会社貸付金

long-term capital
chōki shihon
長期資本

long-term liabilities
chōki fusai
長期負債

long-term loans payable
chōki kariirekin
長期借入金

long-term loans receivable
chōki kashitsukekin
長期貸付金

long-term solvency
chōki shiharai nōryoku
長期支払能力

loss
sonshitsu
損失

loss and gain account
son'eki kanjō
損益勘定

loss and gain statement
son'eki keisansho
損益計算書

loss carried forward
kurikoshi sonshitsukin
繰越損失金

loss for the current term
tōki sonshitsukin
当期損失金

loss from bad debts
kashidaore sonshitsu
貸倒損失

loss from capital reduction
genshi sason
減資差損

loss from inventory
tanaoroshi genmō sonshitsu
棚卸減耗損失

loss from merger
gappei sason
合併差損

loss of capital
shihon sonshitsu
資本損失

loss on investments and credits
tōshi-saiken hyōkason
投資・債券評価損

loss on revaluation of fixed assets
kotei shisan hyōkason
固定資産評価損

loss on sale of fixed assets
kotei shisan baikyakuson
固定資産売却損

loss provision
sonshitsu hikiatekin
損失引当金

lost share certificate
funshitsu kabuken
紛失株券

low-dividend stock
teihai kabu
低配株

machinery and equipment (on balance sheet)
kikai-sōchi
機械・装置

main account
shuyō kanjō
主要勘定

main book
genbo
原簿

main budget
kihonteki yosan
基本的予算

main expenses
shuyō hiyō
主要費用

maintenance cost
ijihi
維持費

maintenance expenses
ijihi
維持費

major shareholder
shuyō kabunushi
主要株主

major stockholder
shuyō kabunushi
主要株主

majority control
kahansū shihai
過半数支配

majority-owned
kahansū shoyū no
過半数所有の

majority ownership
kahansū shoyū
過半数所有

making up losses
sonshitsu hoten
損失補填

management accounting
kanri kaikei
管理会計

management audit
kei'ei kansa
経営監査

management buy-out
kei'eisha baishū
経営者買収

management expenses
kanri hiyō
管理費用

management stock
yakuin kabu
役員株

managing expenses
kei'eihi
経営費

marginal cost
genkai genka
限界原価

marginal costing
genkai genka keisan
限界原価計算

marginal expenses
genkai hiyō
限界費用

marginal income
genkai rieki
限界利益

marginal income statement
genkai son'eki keisansho
限界損益計算書

marginal proceeds
genkai uriagedaka
限界売上高

marginal profit
genkai rieki
限界利益
genkai rijun
限界利潤

marginal returns
genkai shūeki
限界収益

marginal revenue
genkai shūnyū
限界収入

marketable securities (on balance sheet)
yūka shōken
有価証券

marketing cost
hanbaihi
販売費
ryūtsūhi
流通費

marketing cost accounting
hanbai genka kaikei
販売原価会計

material assets
yūkei shisan
有形資産

materials
zairyō
材料

materials accounting
zairyō kaikei
材料会計

materials and supplies account
zairyō oyobi chozōhin kanjō
材料および貯蔵品勘定

materials cost
zairyōhi
材料費

materials cost analysis
zairyōhi bunseki
材料費分析

materials cost basis
zairyōhihō
材料費法

materials cost budget
zairyōhi yosan
材料費予算

maximization of profits
rijun kyokudaika
利潤極大化

merchandise
shōhin
商品

minimization of cost
hiyō kyokushōka
費用極小化

minimum subscription
kabushiki saishō ōbogaku
株式最小応募額

minority control
shōsū shihai
少数支配

minority equity
shōsū kabunushi mochibun
少数株主持分

minority interest
shōsū kabunushi mochibun
少数株主持分

minority shareholder [UK]
shōsū kabunushi
少数株主

minority shareholders' rights [UK]
shōsū kabunushiken
少数株主権

minority stockholder [US]
shōsū kabunushi
少数株主

minority stockholders' rights [US]
shōsū kabunushiken
少数株主権

misappropriation of funds
futō shishutsu
不当支出

miscellaneous accounts
zatsukanjō
雑勘定

miscellaneous accounts payable
shomiharaikin
諸未払金

miscellaneous accounts receivable
shomishūkin
諸未収金

miscellaneous assets
zatsushisan
雑資産

miscellaneous deposits
betsudan yokin
別段預金

miscellaneous expenditure
zatsushishutsu
雑支出

miscellaneous expenses
zappi
雑費

miscellaneous gains
zatsueki
雑益

miscellaneous income
zatsushūnyū
雑収入

miscellaneous losses
zatsusonshitsu
雑損失

miscellaneous profits
zatsueki
雑益

miscellaneous receipts
zatsushūnyū
雑収入

miscellaneous receivables
zatsuuketori kanjō
雑受取勘定

miscellaneous services
zatsumu
雑務

miscellaneous wages and salaries
zatsukyū
雑給

money capital
kahei shihon
貨幣資本

money-losing company
akaji no kigyō
赤字の企業

month end
getsumatsu
月末

monthly accounting
getsuji kessan
月次決算

monthly balance
getsuji zandaka
月次残高

monthly balance sheet
getsuji taishaku taishōhyō
月次貸借対照表

monthly budget
getsuji yosan
月次予算

monthly payroll sheet
getsuji chingin kyūryō keisansho
月次賃金給料計算書

monthly profit and loss statement
getsuji son'eki keisansho
月次損益計算書

monthly statement
getsuji keisansho
月次計算書

monthly trial balance
getsuji shisanhyō
月次試算表

names of shareholders
kabunushimei
株主名

necessary expenses
hitsuyō keihi
必要経費

net asset value
shōmi shisan kagaku
正味資産価額

net asset worth
shōmi shisan kachi
正味資産価値

net assets
junshisan
純資産

net assets per share
hitokabu atari junshisan
一株当たり純資産

net book value
junchōbo kagaku
純帳簿価額

net business saving
junkigyō chochiku
純企業貯蓄

net capital
junshihon
純資本

net cash flow
netto-kyasshu-furō
ネット・キャッシュ・
フロー

net cost
jungenka
純原価

net current assets
shōmi ryūdō shisan
正味流動資産

net earnings
junshūnyū
純収入

net equity assets
shōmi mochibun shisan
正味持分資産

net financial assets
junkin'yū shisan
純金融資産

net income
junshotoku
純所得

(profits)
junrieki
純利益

net income after tax
zeibikigo no junrieki
税引後の純利益

net income for the year
tōki junrieki
当期純利益

net income ratio
shotokuritsu
所得率

net liabilities
junfusai
純負債

net loss
junsonshitsu
純損失

net loss on sales
uriage junsonshitsu
売上純損失

net operating earnings
keijō jun'ekigaku
経常純益額

net operating loss
junsonshitsu
純損失

net operating profit
jun'eigyō rieki
純営業利益

net profit(s)
junrieki
純利益

net profit after depreciation
shōkyakugo no junrieki
償却後の純利益

net profit and loss account
junson'eki keisan
純損益計算

net profit before depreciation
shōkyakuzen junrieki
償却前純利益

net profit before tax
hōjin zeikōjozen junrieki
法人税控除前純利益

net profit for the year
tōki junrieki
当期純利益

net profit margin
uriage junriekiritsu
売上純利益率

net profit/net worth ratio
shōmi unten shihon riekiritsu
正味運転資本利益率

net profit on book basis
chōbo shōmi rieki
帳簿正味利益

net profit on cash basis
genkin shōmi rieki
現金正味利益

net profit on sales
uriage junrieki
売上純利益

net profit ratio
jun'ekiritsu
純益率

net profits/capital ratio
shihon-riekiritsu
資本・利益率

net profits/sales ratio
uriagedaka-junriekiritsu
売上高・純利益率

net receipts
shōmi uketorikin
正味受取金

net reserve
junjunbi
純準備

net sales
shōmi uriagedaka
正味売上高

net surplus
junjōyokin
純剰余金

net working capital
jun'unten shihon
純運転資本

net worth
shōmi shisan
正味資産

　(equity capital)
　jiko shihon
　自己資本

net worth/debts ratio
shihon-fusai hiritsu
資本・負債比率

net worth/fixed capital ratio
shihon kotei hiritsu
資本固定比率

net worth/liabilities ratio
shihon-fusai hiritsu
資本・負債比率

net worth ratio
jiko shihon hiritsu
自己資本比率

net worth/total capital ratio
jiko shihon hiritsu
自己資本比率

net worth value per share
hitokabu atari junshisan
一株当たり純資産

new issue
shinki hakkō
新規発行

new share
shinkabu
新株

newly introduced shares
kōkai kabu
公開株

next closing of account
jiki kessan
次期決算

next term
jiki
次期

no-par stock
mugakumen kabushiki
無額面株式

no-par value
mugakumen no
無額面の

no-par-value stock
mugakumen kabushiki
無額面株式

nominal account
meimoku kanjō
名目勘定

nominal assets
meimoku shisan
名目資産

nominal capital
meimoku shihon
名目資本

nominal income
meimoku shūnyū
名目収入

nominal profit
meimoku rieki
名目利益

nominal value of shares
kabushiki gakumen kakaku
株式額面価格

non-cash assets
higenkin shisan
非現金資産

non-consolidated balance sheet
hirenketsu taishaku taishōhyō
非連結貸借対照表

non-cost items
higenka kōmoku
非原価項目

non-cumulative dividend
hiruiseki haitō
非累積配当

non-cumulative preference shares [UK]
hiruiseki yūsen kabu
非累積優先株

non-cumulative preferred stock [US]
hiruiseki yūsen kabu
非累積優先株

non-dividend payer
muhai kabu
無配株

non-dividend-paying company
muhai gaisha
無配会社

non-financial assets
hikin'yū shisan
非金融資産

non-issuance of stock certificate
kabuken fuhakkō
株券不発行

non-ledger assets
chōbogai shisan
帳簿外資産

non-operating assets
eigyōgai shisan
営業外資産

non-operating expenses
eigyōgai hiyō
営業外費用

non-operating income
eigyōgai shūeki
営業外収益
eigyōgai shūnyū
営業外収入

non-operating loss
eigyōgai sonshitsu
営業外損失

non-operating profit
eigyōgai rieki
営業外利益
eigyōgai rijun
営業外利潤

non-operating profit and loss
eigyōgai son'eki
営業外損益

non-operating revenue
eigyōgai shūnyū
営業外収入

non-par stock
mugakumen kabushiki
無額面株式

non-payment of calls
kabushiki shiharai funō
株式支払不能

non-recurring expense
rinji shishutsu
臨時支出

non-recurring gain
kei'eigai ritoku
経営外利得

non-recurring income
rinji shūnyū
臨時収入

non-recurring loss
kei'eigai sonshitsu
経営外損失

non-recurring profit
rinji rieki
臨時利益

non-subscribed shares
mōshikomi sarenakatta kabu
申込みされなかった株

non-voting shares
mugiketsuken kabu
無議決権株

non-voting stock
mugiketsuken kabu
無議決権株

normal depreciation
seijō genka shōkyaku
正常原価償却

normal profits
seijō rijun
正常利潤

notes and accounts payable
shiharai saimu
支払債務

notes and accounts receivable
uketori saiken
受取債券

notes and bills discounted
waribiki tegata
割引手形

notes and bills payable
shiharai tegata
支払手形

notes and bills receivable
uketori tegata
受取手形

notes and bonds (on balance sheet)
shasai
社債

notice of forfeiture
shikken tsūchisho
失権通知書

number of outstanding shares
hakkō kabushikisū
発行株式数

number of shareholders
kabunushisū
株主数

number of shares
kabushikisū
株式数

number of shares held
mochikabusū
持株数

number of shares issued
hakkōzumi kabushikisū
発行済株式数

number of shares remaining
zanzon kabushikisū
残存株式数

obsolete assets
chinpuka shisan
陳腐化資産

obsolete stock
chinpuka tanaoroshi shisan
陳腐化棚卸資産

offer by subscription
yoyaku boshū
予約募集

offer by tender
kabushiki kōkaitsuki seido
株式公開付制度

offer for public subscription
kōbo
公募
kōkai
公開

**offer for sale [UK]
(placing)**
boshū
募集

(direct issue)
kansetsu hakkō
間接発行

(public offering)
kōbo
公募

(public introduction)
kōkai
公開

offer price
kōbo kakaku
公募価格

offering
boshū
募集
kōbo
公募

offering circular
boshū annai
募集案内

offering day
kōbojitsu
公募日

offering price
kōbo kakaku
公募価格

office equipment maintenance and repair expenses
eigyōyō jūki bihin hoshu shūzenhi
営業用什器備品保守修繕費

office expenses
eigyōhi
営業費
jimuhi
事務費

office expenses account
eigyōhi kanjō
営業費勘定

office expenses book
eigyōhi uchiwakechō
営業費内訳帳

office management expenses
jimu kanrihi
事務管理費

office rental
jimusho chingariryō
事務所賃借料

office supplies expenses
jimu yōhinhi
事務用品費

officer's bonus
yakuin shōyo
役員賞与

officers' salaries account
yakuin hōkyū kanjō
役員俸給勘定

offset
sōsai
相殺

offset account
sōsai kanjō
相殺勘定

offset item
sōsai kōmoku
相殺項目

offset reserve
sōsai hikiatekin
相殺引当金

offsetting error [UK]
sōsai gosa
相殺誤差

old shares
kyūkabu
旧株
oyakabu
親株

omit dividend
muhai ni suru
無配にする

one-year budget
tannendo yosan
単年度予算

open ledger
mikessan motochō
未決算元帳

opening accrual
kurikoshi mishūshi kanjō
繰越未収支勘定

opening balance
kurikoshi zandaka
繰越残高

opening entry
kurikoshi kichō
繰越記帳

opening pre-payment
kurikoshi maebaraikin
繰越前払金

operating account
eigyō kanjō
営業勘定

operating assets
eigyō shisan
営業資産
un'yō shisan
運用資産

operating audit
gyōmu kansa
業務監査

operating budget
eigyō yosan
営業予算

operating capital
eigyō shihon
営業資本
unten shihon
運転資本

operating costs
eigyō hiyō
営業費用
eigyōhi
営業費
unten hiyō
運転費用
untenhi
運転費

operating expenses
eigyō hiyō
営業費用
eigyōhi
営業費
unten hiyō
運転費用
untenhi
運転費

operating expenses book
eigyōhi uchiwakechō
営業費内訳帳

operating expenses ledger
eigyōhi motochō
営業費元帳

operating expenses/sales ratio
uriagedaka-eigyōhi hiritsu
売上高・営業費比率

operating funds
unten shikin
運転資金

operating gains
eigyō ritoku
営業利得

operating income
eigyō shūnyū
営業収入

operating income after depreciation
shōkyakugo keijō rieki
償却後経常利益

operating ledger
eigyō motochō
営業元帳

operating loss
eigyō sonshitsu
営業損失

operating profit
eigyō rieki
営業利益
eigyō rijun
営業利潤

operating profit and loss
eigyō son'eki
営業損益

operating profit ratio
eigyō riekiritsu
営業利益率

operating reserve
eigyō junbikin
営業準備金
eigyō tsumitatekin
営業積立金

operating revenue
eigyō shūeki
営業収益
eigyō shūnyū
営業収入

operating statement
eigyō keisansho
営業計算書

operating surplus
eigyō jōyo
営業剰余

operation audit
gyōmu kansa
業務監査

operation cost
sagyōhi
作業費
untenhi
運転費

operation funds
unten shikin
運転資金

operational accounting
operēshonaru-akauntingu
オペレーショナル・
アカウンティング

operational budget
jikkō yosan
実行予算

operational costs
sagyōhi
作業費
untenhi
運転費

opportunity cost
kikai hiyō
機会費用

optional dividend
sentaku haitō
選択配当

ordinary assets
futsū shisan
普通資産

ordinary budget
keijō yosan
経常予算

ordinary capital
keijō shihon
経常資本

ordinary depreciation
futsū shōkyaku
普通償却

ordinary dividend
futsū haitō
普通配当

ordinary expenditure
keijō hiyō
経常費用
keijōhi
経常費

ordinary expenses
keijō hiyō
経常費用
keijōhi
経常費

ordinary loss
keijō sonshitsu
経常損失

ordinary profit
keijō rieki
経常利益

ordinary shareholders
futsū kabunushi
普通株主

ordinary shares
futsū kabu
普通株

ordinary warrant
honshōkokin
本証拠金

organization cost
sōgyōhi
創業費

organization expenses
sōgyōhi
創業費

organization expenses amortized
setsuritsu shōkyakuhi
設立償却費

original budget
tōsho yosan
当初予算

original capital
genshi shihon
原始資本

original cost
genshi genka
原始原価

original entry
genshi kinyū
原始記入

original investment
genshi tōshigaku
原始投資額

original issue stock
shohatsu kabu
初発株

other assets
hoka no shisan
他の資産

other expenses
eigyōgai hiyō
営業外費用

other income
eigyōgai shūeki
営業外収益

other liabilities
hoka no fusai
他の負債

other reserves
betto tsumitatekin
別途積立金

other revenue
zatsushūnyū
雑収入

out-of-books assets
bogai shisan
簿外資産

out-of-pocket expenses
genkin shishutsu hiyō
現金支出費用

outgoings
shishutsu
支出
shutsuhi
出費

outlay
(expenses)
hiyō
費用

(running expenses)
keihi
経費

(expenditure)
shishutsu
支出

output cost
seisakuhi
製作費

outside applicant
ippan kabushiki ōbosha
一般株式応募者

outside capital
gaibu shihon
外部資本
tanin shihon
他人資本

outstanding account
miharai kanjō
未払勘定
mikessan kanjō
見決算勘定

outstanding amount
genzaidaka
現在高

outstanding balance
miharai zandaka
未払残高

outstanding borrowings
mihensai kariire
見返済借入れ

outstanding capital
hakkōzumi shihon
発行済資本

outstanding capital stock
kabushiki hakkōdaka
株式発行高

outstanding dividends
miharai haitōkin
未払配当金

outstanding issue
hakkō zandaka
発行残高

outstanding liabilities
mishōkan fusai
未償還負債

outstanding shares
hakkōzumi kabushiki
発行済株式
shagai kabushiki
社外株式

outstanding stock
hakkōzumi kabushiki
発行済株式
shagai kabushiki
社外株式

overall accounts
sōgō kanjō
総合勘定

overall budget
sōgō yosan
総合予算

overcapitalization
kadai shihon
過大資本
shihon kajō
資本過剰

overcapitalized
kadai shihon no
過大資本の
shihon kajō no
資本過剰の

overdue account
kigen keika kanjō
期限経過勘定

overhead cost
kansetsuhi
間接費

overheads
(indirect expenses)
kansetsuhi
間接費

(various charges)
shogakari
諸掛り

(total running expenses)
sōkeihi
総経費

overissue
chōka hakkō
超過発行
kadai hakkō
過大発行

overlapping account
jūfuku kanjō
重複勘定

overseas investment reserve
kaigai tōshitō sonshitsu
tsumitatekin
海外投資等損失積立金

overstock (noun)
zaika kajō
在荷過剰

oversubscribed
boshū chōka no
募集超過の
mōshikomi chōka no
申込超過の
ōbo chōka no
応募超過の

oversubscription
boshū chōka
募集超過
mōshikomi chōka
申込超過
ōbo chōka
応募超過

own capital
jiko shihon
自己資本

own capital ratio
jiko shihon hiritsu
自己資本比率

own funds
jiko shikin
自己資金

owner's capital
jiko shihon
自己資本

owner's equity
jigyōnushi mochibun
事業主持分
shoyūsha mochibun
所有者持分

owner's interest
jigyōnushi mochibun
事業主持分
shoyūsha mochibun
所有者持分

owner's salary
jigyōnushi hōshū
事業主報酬

ownership capital
kabunushi shihon
株主資本

ownership interest
jigyōnushi mochibun
事業主持分
shoyūsha mochibun
所有者持分

ownership separated from capital
kei'ei to bunri shita shoyūken
経営と分離した所有権

paid-cash book
genkin shiharaichō
現金支払帳

paid-up amount
haraikomizumi kingaku
払込済金額

paid-up capital
haraikomizumi shihon(kin)
払込済資本(金)

paid-up shares
haraikomizumi kabu
払込済株

paper profit
chōbojō no rieki
帳簿上の利益

par issue
gakumen hakkō
額面発行

par value
gakumen kakaku
額面価格

par-value capital stock
gakumen kabushiki shihonkin
額面株式資本金

par-value share
gakumen kabu
額面株

par-value stock
gakumen kabu
額面株

partial audit
bubun kansa
部分監査

participating dividend
sanka haitō
参加配当

participating preference shares [UK]
rieki haitō yūsen kabu
利益配当優先株

participating preferred stock [US]
rieki haitō yūsen kabu
利益配当優先株

participating stock
rieki haitō kabu
利益配当株

participation
sanka
参加

participation certificate
sanka shōsho
参加証書

participation in profits
rijun sanka
利潤参加

partly paid shares
miharaikomi kabu
未払込株

parts (on balance sheet)
bubunhin
部分品

pass a dividend
muhai ni suru
無配にする

passed dividend
horyū haitō
保留配当

pay (verb)
harau
払う
shiharau
支払う

pay a dividend
haitō suru
配当する

pay for shares
kabukin o haraikomu
株金を払込む

pay-out period
kaishū kikan
回収期間

pay-out ratio
haitō seikō
配当性向

pay sheet
kyūryō shiharaihyō
給料支払表

paymaster
kyūryō shiharai kakari
給料支払係

payment
harai
払い
shiharai
支払い

payment book
shiharai kinyūchō
支払記入帳

payment date (for shares)
shiharai kijitsu
支払期日

payment for shares
kabushiki no haraikomi
株式の払込み

payment in arrear
harainokori
払残り

payment of dividend
haitō no shiharai
配当の支払い

payment received
shiharai ryōshūzumi
支払領収済み

payment record for dividends
haitō shiharai chōsho
配当支払調書

payroll
(book)
chingin daichō
賃金台帳
kyūryō shiharai meibo
給料支払名簿

(amount of salaries)
kyūyo shiharai sōgaku
給与支払総額

payroll audit
kyūryō kansa
給料監査

payroll book
chingin daichō
賃金台帳

payroll deductions
chingin kōjo
賃金控除

payroll period
chingin shiharai kikan
賃金支払期間

payroll records
kyūyo kiroku
給与記録

payroll register
chingin-kyūryō shiharaibo
賃金・給料支払簿

payroll tax
kyūyozei
給与税

pension fund
nenkin kikin
年金基金

per share
hitokabu atari (no)
一株当たり(の)

percentage balance sheet
hyakubun taishaku taishōhyō
百分貸借対照表

percentage of profits
sōriekiritsu
総利益率

percentage statement
hyakubunritsu zaimu shohyō
百分率財務諸表

period
kikan
期間

period budget
kotei yosan
固定予算

period cost
kikan genka
期間原価

period of account
kaikei kikan
会計期間

period planning
kikan keikaku
期間計画

periodic accounting
kimatsu keisan
期末計算

periodic audit
teiki kansa
定期監査

periodic balance sheet
teiki taishaku taishōhyō
定期貸借対照表

periodic inventory [US]
teiki tanaoroshi
定期棚卸し

periodic stock-taking [UK]
teiki tanaoroshi
定期棚卸し

periodic trial balance
kimatsu shisanhyō
期末試算表

permanent assets
eikyū shisan
永久資産

permanent auditor
jōnin kansayaku
常任監査役

personnel expenditure
jinkenhi
人件費

personnel expenses
jinkenhi
人件費

petty cash
kogaku genkin
小額現金
koguchi genkin
小口現金

petty cash account
koguchi genkin kanjō
小口現金勘定

petty cash-book
koguchi genkin suitōbo
小口現金出納簿

petty cash funds
koguchi genkin shikin
小口現金資金

petty cash payments
koguchi genkin shiharai
小口現金支払い

petty cash slip
koguchi genkin denpyō
小口現金伝票

petty cash system
koguchi genkin seido
小口現金制度

petty expenses
zappi
雑費

placement [US]
boshū
募集

placement agent
boshū dairinin
募集代理人

placement prospectus
boshū yōkō
募集要項

placing [UK]
boshū
募集

planned obsolescence
keikakuteki chinpuka
計画的陳腐化

planning accounting
keikaku kaikei
計画会計

plant and equipment
setsubi
設備

plant and equipment budget
setsubi yosan
設備予算

plant and equipment investment
setsubi tōshi
設備投資

pooling of capital
shihon no gōdō
資本の合同

post (verb)
shiwake suru
仕訳する
tenki suru
転記する

post into the ledger
motochō ni tenki suru
元帳に転記する

post up accounts
kichō suru
記帳する

postage
yūbin ryōkin
郵便料金

post-audit
jigo kansa
事後監査

post-closing entry
shimekirigo kinyū
締切後記入

post-closing trial balance
kurikoshi shisanhyō
繰越試算表

posting
tenki
転記

posting book
tenkibo
転記簿

posting error
tenki no ayamari
転記の誤り

pre-depreciation profit
shōkyakuzen rieki
償却前利益

pre-emption
sakigaiken
先買権
yūsen kaitoriken
優先買取権

pre-emptive rights
sakigaiken
先買権
yūsen kaitoriken
優先買取権

preference dividend [UK]
yūsen haitō
優先配当

preference shareholder [UK]
yūsen kabunushi
優先株主

preference shares [UK]
yūsen kabu
優先株

preferential dividend [UK]
yūsen haitō
優先配当

preferential right
yūsenken
優先権

preferred dividend [US]
yūsen haitō
優先配当

preferred stock [US]
yūsen kabu
優先株

preferred stockholder [US]
yūsen kabunushi
優先株主

preliminary audit
yobi kansa
予備監査

preliminary balance sheet
yobi taishaku taishōhyō
予備貸借対照表

preliminary prospectus
karimokuromisho
仮目論見書

prepaid expenses
maebarai hiyō
前払費用

prepayments (on balance sheet)
maebaraikin
前払金

pre-tax
zeibikimae
税引前

pre-tax profit
zeibikimae rieki
税引前利益

previous financial year
zennendo
前年度

previous term
zenki
前期

prime cost
genka
原価

prior claim
sakitoriken
先取権

priority of debts
shakkin no sakitoriken
借金の先取権

private capital
minkan shihon
民間資本
shiteki shihon
私的資本

private capital formation
minkan shihon keisei
民間資本形成

private funds
shizai
私財

private issue of shares
enko boshū
縁故募集

private offering [UK]
shibo
私募

private placement [US]
shibo
私募

private placing [UK]
shibo
私募

private subscription
enko boshū
縁故募集

pro-forma accounting report
mitsumori kaikei hōkoku
見積会計報告

pro-forma balance sheet
mitsumori taishaku taishōhyō
見積貸借対照表

pro-forma financial statement
mitsumori zaimu shohyō
見積財務諸表

pro-forma invoice
mitsumori okurijō
見積送状

processing of accounts
kaikei shori
会計処理

production overhead cost [US]
seisan kansetsuhi
生産間接費

profit(s)
(money-making)
eiri
営利

(gain, return)
rieki
利益
rijun
利潤

(earnings, return)
shūeki
収益

profit after tax
zeibiki rieki
税引利益

profit and loss
son'eki
損益

profit and loss account [UK]
son'eki kanjō
損益勘定

profit and loss for the previous period
zenki son'eki
前期損益

profit and loss report
son'eki hōkoku
損益報告

profit and loss statement [US]
son'eki keisansho
損益計算書

profit and loss summary account
shūgō son'eki kanjō
集合損益勘定

profit appropriation
rieki shobun
利益処分

profit before tax
zeikomi rieki
税込利益

profit brought forward from previous term
zenki kurikoshi riekikin
前期繰越利益金

profit/capital ratio
shihon-riekiritsu
資本・利益率

profit for the current term
tōki riekikin
当期利益金

profit forecasting
rieki yosoku
利益予測

profit from amalgamation
gappei saeki
合併差益

profit from capital reduction
genshi saeki
減資差益

profit from consolidation
gappei saeki
合併差益

profit from merger
gappei saeki
合併差益

profit from valuation
hyōkaeki
評価益

profit increase
zōeki
増益

profit-making business (for tax purposes)
shūeki jigyō
収益事業

profit margin
rieki haba
利益幅

profit maximization
rijun kyokudaika
利潤極大化

profit not yet realized
mijitsugen rieki
未実現利益

profit per share
hitokabu atari rieki
一株当たり利益

profit prior to consolidation
renketsumae rieki
連結前利益

profit prior to incorporation
kaisha setsuritsumae rieki
会社設立前利益

profit projection
rieki yosoku
利益予測

profit ratio
riekiritsu
利益率
rijunritsu
利潤率

profit ratio of operating capital
kei'ei shihon riekiritsu
経営資本利益率

profit ratio of paid-up capital
haraikomi shihon riekiritsu
払込資本利益率

profit ratio of total capital
sōshihon riekiritsu
総資本利益率

profit reserve
rieki junbikin
利益準備金

profit sharing
rieki bunpai
利益分配
rijun bunpai
利潤分配

profit-sharing bond
rieki sanka shasai
利益参加社債

profit-sharing ratio
rieki bunpairitsu
利益分配率

profit-sharing securities
rijun shōken
利潤証券

profit-sharing stock
rijun bunpai kabu
利潤分配株

profit-taking
rijun kakutoku
利潤獲得

profits available for distribution
haitōkanō rieki
配当可能利益

profits/net worth ratio
jiko shihon riekiritsu
自己資本利益率

profits on the sale of fixed assets
kotei shisan baikyakueki
固定資産売却益

profits on the sale of investment securities
tōshi yūka shōken baikyaku'eki
投資有価証券売却益

profits paid to shareholders
kabunushi ni shiharaizumi rieki
株主に支払済利益

profits position
shūeki jōkyō
収益状況

profits tax
ritokuzei
利得税
shūekizei
収益税

progressive ledger
renzoku motochō
連続元帳

projected balance sheet
mitsumori taishaku taishōhyō
見積貸借対照表

projected financial statement
mitsumori zaimu shohyō
見積財務諸表

projected funds statement
mitsumori shikinhyō
見積資金表

projected income statement
mitsumori son'eki keisansho
見積損益計算書

promoter's profit
hokkinin rijun
発起人利潤

promoter's shares
hokkinin kabu
発起人株

promotion expenses
sōgyōhi
創業費

property ledger
zaisan daichō
財産台帳

proprietor's equity
kigyōnushi mochibun
企業主持分

proprietor's income
kigyōnushi shotoku
企業主所得

proprietor's investment
kigyōnushi shusshigaku
企業主出資額

proprietor's salary
kigyōnushi hōkyū
企業主俸給

proprietory interest
kigyōnushi mochibun
企業主持分

provision for discounts allowable [US]
uriage waribiki junbikin
売上割引準備金

provision for doubtful debts [US]
kashidaore hikiatekin
貸倒引当金
kashidaore junbikin
貸倒準備金

provision for repairs
shūzenhi hikiatekin
修繕費引当金

proxy for dividend
haitō ininjō
配当委任状

public issue (of shares)
(kabushiki no) kōbo
(株式の) 公募

public offering
kōbo
公募

public offering price
kōbo kakaku
公募価格

public placement [US]
kōbo
公募
kōkai
公開

public placing [UK]
kōbo
公募
kōkai
公開

public subscription
kōbo
公募

public utility stock
kōeki kabu
公益株

publicly held stock
kōkai kabu
公開株

publicly offered shares
uridashi kabu
売出株

publicly subscribed shares
kōbo kabu
公募株

purchase
　(buying)
kōbai
購買

　(laying-in of stock)
shiire
仕入れ

purchase account
shiire kanjō
仕入勘定

purchase analysis
kōbai bunseki
購買分析

purchase book
shiirechō
仕入帳

purchase budget
shiire yosan
仕入予算

purchase cost
shiire genka
仕入原価

purchase discounts
shiire waribiki
仕入割引

purchase invoice
shiire okurijō
仕入送状

purchase journal
shiire shiwakechō
仕入仕訳帳
shiirechō
仕入帳

purchase ledger
shiire motochō
仕入元帳

purchase of company's equity
kaitori
買取り

purchase price
　(of a business)
baishū kakaku
買収価格

　(of shares)
kaiire kakaku
買入価格

purchasing expenses
shiire hiyō
仕入費用

purpose of funds
shikin shito
資金使途

pyramiding
rinose
利乗せ

qualification shares
shikaku kabu
資格株

qualified audit certificate
gentei kansa hōkokusho
限定監査報告書

quarter
shihanki
四半期

quick assets
tōza shisan
当座資産

quick capital
tōza shihon
当座資本

quick liabilities
tanki fusai
短期負債

quick ratio
tōza hiritsu
当座比率

quick sales at small profits
hakuritabai
薄利多売

raise capital
shihon o chōtatsu suru
資本を調達する

raise cash
genkinka suru
現金化する

raise funds
shikin o chōtatsu suru
資金を調達する

rate of depreciation
genka shōkyaku hiritsu
原価償却比率

rate of depreciation to total assets
sōshisan shōkyakuritsu
総資産償却率

rate of dividend
haitōritsu
配当率

rate of earnings on total capital
sōshihon riekiritsu
総資本利益率

rate of profit
rijunritsu
利潤率

rate of return over cost
hiyō chōka shūekiritsu
費用超過収益率

ratio analysis
hiritsu bunseki
比率分析

rationalization investment
gōrika tōshi
合理化投資

re-acquired shares
saishutoku kabu
再取得株

re-adjusting
shūsei
修正

re-adjusting entries
shūsei kinyū
修正記入

re-appraisal [US]
saihyōka
再評価

real assets
fudōsan
不動産

real capital
jitsubutsu shihon
実物資本

realizable assets
baikyakukanō shisan
売却可能資産
kankakanō shisan
換価可能資産
kankinkanō shisan
換金可能資産

realization
kanka
換価
kankinka
換金化

realization account
kanka kanjō
換価勘定

realized appreciation
jitsugen zōkagaku
実現増価額

realized depreciation
jitsugen genka shōkyaku
実現原価償却

realized profit
jitsugen rieki
実現利益

recapitalization
shihon kōsei no kaihen
資本構成の改変
shihon kumiire
資本組入れ
shihon saikōsei
資本再構成

receipt (for expenses incurred)
ryōshūsho
領収書
uketorishō
受取証

receipt book
uketorichō
受取帳

receipts and payments
shūshi
収支

receipts and payments book-keeping
shūshi boki
収支簿記

receipts/payments ratio
ukeharairitsu
受払率

receivable account
uketori kanjō
受取勘定

receive a dividend
haitō o ukeru
配当を受ける

recommended issue
suishō kabu
推奨株

reconciliation
shōsa
照査

  (adjustment)
chōsei
調整

reconciliation items
chōsei kōmoku
調整項目

recruiting expenses
saiyō hiyō
採用費用

recurring profit
keijō rieki
経常利益

recurring profit and loss
keijō son'eki
経常損益

red herring (prospectus) [US]
karimokuromisho
仮目論見書

redeemable preference shares [UK]
shōkan yūsen kabu
償還優先株

redeemable preferred stock [US]
shōkan yūsen kabu
償還優先株

redeemable stock
shōkankanō kabushiki
償還可能株式

reduction in costs
genka kirisage
原価切下げ

reduction in expenditure
keihi setsugen
経費節減

reduction of capital
genshi
減資

reduction of dividend
genpai
減配

redundancy payment
yojō rōdōsha hoshōkin
余剰労働者補償金

registered capital
tōki shihonkin
登記資本金

registered share
kimei kabu
記名株

registered share certificate
tōroku kabuken
登録株券

registered stock
kimei kabu
記名株

registering a deficit
sonshitsu keijō
損失計上

registrar [UK]
meigi kakikae dairinin
名義書換代理人

regular dividend
tsūjō haitō
通常配当

reinvested profit
rieki jōyokin
利益剰余金

re-issue of forfeited shares
shikken kabu no saihakkō
失権株の再発行

re-issue of shares
kabushiki no saihakkō
株式の再発行

re-issued shares
saihakkō kabushiki
再発行株式

release of funds
shikin hōshutsu
資金放出

repairs and maintenance expenses
hoshu shūzenhi
保守修繕費

replacement cost
torikae genka
取替原価

research and development expenses
kenkyū kaihatsuhi
研究開発費

reserve
hikiatekin
引当金
junbikin
準備金
tsumitatekin
積立金

reserve account
junbikin kanjō
準備金勘定
tsumitatekin kanjō
積立金勘定

reserve assets
junbi shisan
準備資産

reserve for bad debts
kashidaore hikiatekin
貸倒引当金
kashidaore junbikin
貸倒準備金

reserve for corporate tax
hōjin zeibiki hikiatekin
法人税引引当金

reserve for depreciation
genka shōkyaku hikiatekin
原価償却引当金

reserve for dividends
haitō junbi tsumitatekin
配当準備積立金

reserve for employees' retirement allowance
jūgyōin taishoku kyūyo hikiatekin
従業員退職給与引当金

reserve for foreign exchange fluctuations
kawase hendō junbi tsumitatekin
為替変動準備積立金

reserve for losses
kesson tsumitatekin
欠損積立金

reserve for overseas investment
kaigai tōshitō sonshitsu tsumitatekin
海外投資等損失積立金

reserve for repairs
shūzen junbikin
修繕準備金

reserve for research and development
kenkyū kaihatsu tsumitatekin
研究開発積立金

reserve for retirement allowance
taishoku kyūyo hikiatekin
退職給与引当金

reserve for unissued stock
hikiate mihakkō kabu
引当未発行株

reserve funds
junbi shikin
準備資金
yobikin
予備金

retail accounting
kouri kaikei
小売会計

retained earnings
ryūho rieki
留保利益

retained income
ryūho rieki
留保利益

retained profit
ryūho rieki
留保利益

(internal reserve)
naibu ryūho
内部留保

retained surplus
ryūho rieki
留保利益

retentions
ryūho
留保

retirement fund
taishokukin
退職金

retrenchment
keihi setsugen
経費節減

return on equity
mochibun rieki
持分利益

revaluation
saihyōka
再評価

revaluation of assets
shisan saihyōka
資産再評価

revaluation reserve
saihyōka tsumitatekin
再評価積立金

revenue
(gains, profits)
rieki
利益

(profit, return)
shūeki
収益

(earnings, income)
shūnyū
収入

revenue from operations (on balance sheet)
eigyō shūeki
営業収益

revenue reserve
rieki junbikin
利益準備金

revised budget
shūsei yosan
修正予算

rigging of accounts
funshoku kessan
粉飾決算

risk capital
kiken futan shihon
危険負担資本

rough balance sheet
gaisan taishaku taishōhyō
概算貸借対照表

rough profit and loss statement
gaisan son'eki keisansho
概算損益計算書

royalties on patent right
tokkyoken shiyōryō
特許権使用料

running cost
ranningu-kosuto
ラッニング・コスト

running expenses
keijōhi
経常費
untenhi
運転費

salaries
(remuneration)
kyūyo
給与

(monthly pay)
kyūryō
給料

salaries and allowances
hōshū oyobi kyūyo
報酬および給与

salaries and wages account
kyūryō-chingin kanjō
給料・賃金勘定

sales
uriage
売上げ

(sales and marketing)
hanbai
販売

sales account
uriage kanjō
売上勘定

sales accounting
uriage hanbai kaikei
売上販売会計

sales amount
uriagedaka
売上高

sales analysis
uriage bunseki
売上分析

sales book
uriagechō
売上帳

sales budget
hanbai yosan
販売予算

sales cost
uriage genka
売上原価

sales discounts
uriage waribiki
売上割引

sales earnings
eigyō shūnyū
営業収入

sales expenses
hanbai keihi
販売経費
hanbaihi
販売費

sales forecasting
uriagedaka yosoku
売上高予測

sales invoice
uriage okurijō
売上送状

sales journal
uriage shiwakechō
売上仕訳帳

sales ledger
uriage motochō
売上元帳

sales profit
uriage rieki
売上利益

sales promotion expenses
hanbai sokushinhi
販売促進費

sales revenue [US]
sōuriagedaka
総売上高
uriage shūeki
売上収益

schedule of financial statement
zaimu shohyō fuzoku meisaihyō
財務諸表付属明細表

scheduled cost
hyōji genka
表示原価

scope of audit
kansa han'i
監査範囲

scrip
karikabuken
仮株券

scrip certificate
karikabuken
仮株券

scrip dividend
shōsho haitō
証書配当

scrip issue
mushō hakkō
無償発行

second half of the year
kōki
後期
shimohanki
下半期

second quarter
daini shihanki
第二四半期

secret assets
bogai shisan
簿外資産

securities ledger
yūka shōken motochō
有価証券元帳

self-financing
jiko kin'yū
自己金融

semi-annual dividend
hanki haitō
半期配当

senior issue
jōi no kabushiki
上位の株式

setting-up expenses
sōgyōhi
創業費

setting-up cost
sōgyōhi
創業費

settlement (payment)
harai
払い
shiharai
支払い

settlement discount
genkin waribiki
現金割引

settlement of accounts
kessan
決算

settlement of accounts for the latter half of the year
kōki kessan
後期決算

settlement of bills
kessai
決済

settlement period
kessanki
決算期

settlement sheet
kessanhyō
決算表

shaky financial condition
fuan na shikin jijō
不安な資金事情

share
kabu
株
kabushiki
株式

share alloment
kabushiki wariate
株式割当て

share allotment letter
kabushiki wariate tsūchi
株式割当通知

share application
kabushiki mōshikomi
株式申込み

share application form
kabushiki mōshikomi yōshi
株式申込用紙

share bonus
kabushiki bōnasu
株式申込ボーナス

share capital
kabushiki shihon
株式申込資本

share certificate
kabuken
株券

share certificate transfer
kabuken meigi kakikae
株券名義書換え

share consolidation
kabushiki gappei
株式合併

share dividend
kabushiki haitō(kin)
株式配当(金)

share issue
(issuing)
kabushiki hakkō
株式発行

(an issue)
kabu meigara
株式銘柄

share ledger
kabushiki motochō
株式元帳

share prospectus
kabushiki mokuromisho
株式目論見書

share qualification
kabushiki shikaku
株式資格

share register
kabunushi meibo
株式名簿

share transfer
kabushiki kakikae
株式書換え

share warrant [UK]
mukimei kabuken
無記名株券

share warrants register [UK]
mukimei kabuken kinyūbo
無記名株券記入簿

share with par value
gakumen kabu
額面株

share without par value
mugakumen kabu
無額面株

shareholder [UK]
kabunushi
株主

shareholder's account
kabushiki kanjō
株式勘定

shareholder's equity
jiko shihon
自己資本
kabunushi mochibun
株主持分

(on balance sheet)
shihon shukanjō
資本主勘定

shareholder's right to inspect the books
kabunushi no chōbo etsuranken
株主の帳簿閲覧権

shareholder's rights
kabunushiken
株主権

shareholders' ledger
kabunushi motochō
株主元帳

shareholders' list
kabunushi meibo
株主名簿

shareholders' register
kabunushi meibo
株主名簿

shareholding
kabushiki hoyū
株式保有
mochikabu
持株

shareholding ratio
kabushiki hoyūritsu
株式保有率

shares outstanding
hakkōzumi kabushiki
発行済株式

short-form audit report [US]
tanbunshiki kansa hōkokusho
短文式監査報告書

short-form report
tanbunshiki hōkokusho
短文式報告書

short of capital (to be)
shikin fusoku (o kitasu)
資金不足(を来す)

short of funds
shikinnan
資金難

short-term capital
tanki shihon
短期資本

short-term liabilities
tanki fusai
短期負債

short-term loans payable
tanki kariirekin
短期借入金

short-term loans receivable
tanki kashitsukekin
短期貸付金

short-term notes (on balance sheet)
tanki saiken
短期債券

shortage of funds
shikin fusoku
資金不足

simple account
tanjun kanjō
単純勘定

simple account form
tanjun kanjōshiki
単純勘定式

simple accounting
tanshiki boki
単式簿記

simple cost accounting
tanjun sōgō genka keisan
単純総合原価計算

simple journal
tanjun shiwakechō
単純仕訳帳

single account system
tanshiki kaikeihō
単式会計法

single balance sheet
tan'itsu no taishaku taishōhyō
単一の貸借対照表

single book-keeping
tanshiki boki
単式簿記

single entry
tanshiki kinyū
単式記入

single-entry book-keeping
tanshiki boki
単式簿記

sinking fund
shōkyaku tsumitatekin
償却積立金

slip book-keeping
denpyōshiki boki
伝票式簿記

slip system of accounting
denpyōshiki kaikeihō
伝票式会計法

small business financing
chūshō kigyō kin'yū
中小企業金融

small capital
shōshihon
小資本

small capital stock
kogata kabu
小型株

small shareholder
kokabunushi
子株主

small stockholder
kokabunushi
子株主

social security contributions
shakai hoshōhi
社会保障費

soiled share certificate
osen kabuken
汚染株券

sole shareholder
kojin kabunushi
個人株主

solvency
shiharai nōryoku
支払能力

solvent
shiharai nōryoku ga aru
支払能力がある

sound finance
kenzen zaisei
健全財政

sound financial standing
kenzen na shisan jōtai
健全な資産状態

source of capital
shihon shussho
資本出所

special account
tokubetsu kanjō
特別勘定

special allowance
tokubetsu teate
特別手当

special assets
tokutei shisan
特定資産

special audit
tokubetsu kansa
特別監査

special bad debts reserve
saiken shōkyaku tokubetsu kanjō
債券償却特別勘定

special contingency reserve
tokubetsu gūhatsu sonshitsu junbikin
特別偶発損失準備金

special depreciation reserve
tokubetsu shōkyaku tsumitatekin
特別償却積立金

special discounts
tokubetsu waribiki
特別割引

special dividend
tokubetsu haitō
特別配当

special expenses
tokubetsu hiyō
特別費用

special fund
tokubetsu shikin
特別資金

special ledger
tokushu motochō
特殊元帳

special losses
tokubetsu sonshitsu
特別損失

special profits
tokubetsu rieki
特別利益

special profits and losses
tokubetsu son'eki
特別損益

special-purpose financial statement
tokutei mokutekiyō zaimu shohyō
特定目的用財務諸表

specified issue
tokutei meigara
特定銘柄

specified rate of dividend
tokutei haitōritsu
特定配当率

split
kabushiki bunkatsu
株式分割

split-ledger account
bunkatsu motochō kanjō
分割元帳勘定

sponsorship(s)
kōen
後援
shien
支援

standard cost
(prime cost)
hyōjun genka
標準原価

(production cost)
hyōjun seisanhi
標準生産費

standard cost accounting
hyōjun genka keisan
標準原価計算

standard cost method
hyōjun genkahō
標準原価法

standard cost sheet
hyōjun genkahyō
標準原価表

standard cost system
hyōjun genka keisan seido
標準原価計算制度

standard costing
hyōjun genka keisan
標準原価計算

standard income statement
hyōjun son'eki keisansho
標準損益計算書

standard labour cost
hyōjun rōmuhi
標準労務費

standing
shisan jōtai
資産状態

standing auditor
jōnin kansayaku
常任監査役

standing cost
koteihi
固定費

start-up cost
sōgyōhi
創業費

stated capital
kakutei shihon
確定資本

stated liabilities
hyōji fusai
表示負債

stated value
hyōmenjō kachi
表面上価値

state of the company's affairs
zaimu jōtai
財務状態

statement (financial)
zaimu shohyō
財務諸表

statement analysis
zaimu shohyō bunseki
財務諸表分析

statement of account
kanjōsho
勘定書

statement of assets and liabilities [US]
shisan-fusaihyō
資産・負債表

statement of income and expenses
shūshi ichiranhyō
収支一覧表

statement of income and retained earnings
son'eki oyobi jōyokin ketsugō keisansho
損益および剰余金
結合計算書

statement of items
uchiwakesho
内訳書

statement of operating earnings
keijō rieki keisansho
経常利益計算書

statement of realization and liquidation
shobun-seisan keisansho
処分・清算計算書

statement of stockholders' equity
kabunushi mochibun keisansho
株主持分計算書

status
  (asset situation)
  shisan jōtai
  資産状態

  (financial)
  zaimu jōtai
  財務状態

statutory audit
hōtei kansa
法定監査

stock
  (shares)
  kabu
  株
  kabushiki
  株式

  (goods)
  zaikohin
  在庫品

stock certificate [US]
kabuken
株券

stock certificate transfer
kabuken meigi kakikae
株券名義書換え

stock dividend
kabushiki haitō(kin)
株式配当(金)

stock equity
kabushiki mochibun kakaku
株式持分価格

Stock Exchange placement [US]
kabushiki torihikijo kōkai
株式取引所公開

Stock Exchange placing [UK]
kabushiki torihikijo kōkai
株式取引所公開

stock issue
  (an issue)
  kabu meigara
  株式銘柄

  (issuing)
  kabushiki hakkō
  株式発行

stock issue cost
kabushiki hakkōhi
株式発行費

stock ledger
  (shares)
  kabushiki motochō
  株式元帳

  (goods)
  zaikohin motochō
  在庫品元帳

stock of affiliated companies
kankei gaisha kabushiki
関係会社株式

stock purchase right
shinkabu hikiukeken
新株引受権

stock purchase warrant
shinkabu hikiukeken shōsho
新株引受権証書

stock receipt
kabuken jōtoshō
株券譲渡証

stock register
kabunushi meibo
株主名簿

stock repurchase
jisha kabu kaimodoshi
自社株買戻し

stock right
kabushiki hikiukeken
株式引受権

stock split [US]
kabushiki bunkatsu
株式分割

stock subscription
kabushiki mōshikomi
株式申込み
kabushiki ōbo
株式応募

stock transfer
kabushiki jōto
株式譲渡
kabushiki meigi kakikae
株式名義書換え

stock transfer book
kabushiki meigi kakikae kinyūbo
株式名義書換記入簿

stock transfer form
kabushiki meigi kakikae yōshi
株式名義書換用紙

stock transfer register
kabushiki meigi kakikae kinyūbo
株式名義書換記入簿

stock turnover
zaikohin kaitenritsu
在庫品回転率

stock valuation
zaikohin hyōka
在庫品評価

stock watering
kadai zōshi
過大増資
kabushiki mizumashi
株式水増し
kabushiki mizuwari
株式水割り

stock with equity option
kabushiki kaitorikentsuki shasai
株式買取権付社債

stock with par value
gakumen kabu
額面株

stock without par value
mugakumen kabu
無額面株

stockholder
kabunushi
株主

stockholder's equity
kabunushi mochibun
株主持分

stockholder's rights
kabunushiken
株主権

stockholders' ledger
kabunushi motochō
株主元帳

stockholders' list
kabunushi meibo
株主名簿

stockholding
kabushiki hoyū
株式保有

stockholding cost
mochikoshi hiyō
持越費用

stockholding ratio
kabunushi hoyūritsu
株主保有率

subscribe for shares
kabushiki o hikiukeru
株式を引受ける

(apply)
kabushiki o mōshikomu
株式を申込む
kabushiki o ōbo suru
株式を応募する

(invest capital)
shusshi suru
出資する

subscribed capital
ōbo shikin
応募資金
shusshi
出資

subscribed capital stock
hikiukezumi kabushiki
引受済株式

subscribed shares
hikiukezumi kabushiki
引受済株式

subscriber
kabushiki hikiukenin
株式引受人

(applicant)
kabushiki mōshikomisha
株式申込者
kabushiki ōbosha
株式応募者

(capital investor)
shusshisha
出資者

subscriber's yield
ōbosha rimawari
応募者利回り

subscription
kabushiki hikiuke
株式引受け

(application)
kabushiki mōshikomi
株式申込み
kabushiki ōbo
株式応募

(capital investment)
shusshi
出資

subscription book closed
kabushiki boshū shimekiri
株式募集締切み

subscription book open
kabushiki boshū kaishi
株式募集開始

subscription certificate
shusshi shōken
出資証券

subscription clause
boshū jōkō
募集条項

subscription form
mōshikomi yōshi
申込用紙

subscription list
kabushiki mōshikomi ichiranhyō
株式申込一覧表

subscription money
mōshikomikin
申込金

subscription price
ōbo kakaku
応募価格

subscription right
kabushiki mōshikomiken
株式申込権
kabushiki ōboken
株式応募権

(shareholders' right to new shares)
shinkabu hikiukeken
新株引受権

subscription to capital
shusshi
出資

subscription to the increased capital
zōshi haraikomikin
増資払込金

subscription warrant
shinkabu hikiukeken shōsho
新株引受権証書

subscriptions receivable account
kabushiki hikiuke kanjō
株式引受勘定

subsidiary accounts
hojo kanjō
補助勘定

subsidiary journal
hojo kinyūchō
補助記入帳

subsidiary ledger
hojo motochō
補助元帳

subsidized company
hojo gaisha
補助会社

sub-underwriters
shita hikiuke gaisha
下引受会社

sub-underwriting
shita hikiuke
下引受け

sufficient capital
jūbun na shihon
十分な資本

sufficient funds
jūbun na shikin
十分な資金

summarization
sōkatsu
総括

summarizing account
shūgō kanjō
集合勘定

summary journal
sōgō shiwakechō
総合仕訳帳

summary sheet
shūkeihyō
集計表

sundries
zappi
雑費

sundry account
zatsukanjō
雑勘定

sundry allowances
zatsuteate
雑手当

sundry income
zatsushūnyū
雑収入

sundry losses
zatsusonshitsu
雑損失

sundry profits
zatsueki
雑益

sundry receipts
zatsushūnyū
雑収入

superfluous expenses
jōhi
冗費

supplementary budget
tsuika yosan
追加予算

supplementary cost
hojoteki hiyō
補助的費用

supplies
chozōhin
貯蔵品

surplus
jōyokin
剰余金

surplus account
jōyokin kanjō
剰余金勘定

surplus adjustment
jōyokin shūsei
剰余金修正

surplus analysis
jōyokin bunseki
剰余金分析

surplus appropriation
jōyokin shobun
剰余金処分

surplus appropriation statement
jōyokin shobun keisansho
剰余金処分計算書

surplus assets
yojō shisan
余剰資産

surplus at beginning of the period
zenki kurikoshi riekikin
jōyokin
前期繰越利益金
剰余金

surplus at date of acquisition
shutokutoki jōyokin
取得時剰余金

surplus at liquidation
seisan jōyokin
清算剰余金

surplus at opening of new period
kishu jōyokin
期首剰余金

surplus available for dividends
haitōkanō jōyokin
配当可能剰余金

surplus balance
jōyokin
剰余金

surplus for redemption fund
shōkan jōyokin
償還剰余金

surplus from capital reduction
genshi jōyokin
減資剰余金

surplus from forfeited shares
shikken kabushiki jōyokin
失権株式剰余金

surplus from merger
gappei saeki
合併差益

surplus from retirement of capital stock
genshi saeki
減資差益

surplus from revaluation
saihyōka jōyokin
再評価剰余金

surplus funds
jōyokin
剰余金

surplus profit
jōyo rieki
剰余利益

surplus reserves
jōyo tsumitatekin
剰余積立金

(on balance sheet)
rieki junbikin
利益準備金

surplus statement
jōyokin keisansho
剰余金計算書

surplus statement account
jōyokin keisansho kanjō
剰余金計算書勘定

surrender of shares
kabushiki no bosshū
株式の没収
kabushiki no shikken
株式の失権

surrendered shares
shikken kabu
失権株

suspense account
karikanjō
仮勘定
mikessan kanjō
未決算勘定

take-over bid
kabushiki kōkai kaitsuke
株式公開買付け

tangible assets
yūkei shisan
有形資産

tangible net worth
yūkei shōmi shisan
有形正味資産

target price (take-over)
baishū kakaku
買収価格

tax adviser
zeimu komon
税務顧問

tax audit
zeimu kansa
税務監査

tax cuts for businesses
kigyō genzei
企業減税

tax documents
zeimu shorui
税務書類

tax enquiry
zeimu chōsa
税務調査

tax-free business
hikazei kigyō
非課税企業

tax-free corporation
hikazei hōjin
非課税法人

tax loss
sozei no sonshitsu
租税の損失

tax minimization
sozei kyokushōka
租税極小化

tax on business
eigyōzei
営業税
kigyō kazei
企業課税

tax on profits
ritokuzei
利得税

tax on undistributed profits
ryūho shotokuzei
留保所得税

tax planning
zeimu keikaku
税務計画

**tax shelters
(measures)**
zeikin hinan shudan
税金避難手段

(places)
zeikin hinanchi
税金避難地

telephone expenses
denwa hiyō
電話費用

temporary insolvency
ichijiteki shiharai funō
一時的支払不能

tentative balance sheet
karitaishaku taishōhyō
仮貸借対照表

term (period)
kikan
期間

term end
kimatsu
期末

term-end account
kimatsu kanjō
期末勘定

term-end adjustments
kimatsu seiri
期末整理

term-end balance
kimatsu zandaka
期末残高

term-end closing of accounts
kimatsu kessan
期末決算

time limit for share applications
kabushiki mōshikomi kigen
株式申込期限

title of account
kanjō kamoku
勘定科目

tools (on balance sheet)
kōgu
工具

total (grand total)
sōkei
総計

total amount
sōgaku
総額
zengaku
全額

total amount amortized
shōkanzumi sōgaku
償還済総額

total amount depreciated
genka shōkyaku sōgaku
原価償却総額

total amount of capital invested
shusshi sōgaku
出資総額

total amount subscribed
ōbo sōgaku
応募総額

total amount written off
shōkyaku sōgaku
償却総額

total assets
shisan sōkei
資産総計

total capital
shihonkin gōkei
資本金合計
sōshihon
総資本

total capital and liabilities
shihon-fusai gōkei
資本・負債合計

total cost
zenbu genka
全部原価

total costing
zenbu genka keisan
全部原価計算

total earnings
sōshūeki
総収益

total equity
junshisan
純資産

total expenditure
sōshishutsu
総支出

total expenses
sōhiyō
総費用

total expenses/total revenue ratio
junshūeki hiritsu
純収益比率

total gains
zenshūeki
全収益

total income
sōshotoku
総所得

total liabilities
fusai gōkei
負債合計

total liabilities/net worth ratio
fusaikaritsu
負債化率

total receipts
sōshūnyū
総収入

total revenue
sōshūnyū
総収入

total shareholders' equity (on balance sheet)
shihon gōkei
資本合計

training expenses
kunrenhi
訓練費

transfer
(assignment)
jōto
譲渡

(name transfer)
meigi kakikae
名義書換え

transfer agent [US]
meigi kakikae dairinin
名義書換代理人

transfer of share certificate
kabuken meigi kakikae
株券名義書換え

transfer receipt
meigi kakikaehyō
名義書換表

transfer register
meigi kakikae daichō
名義書換台帳

transferee
yuzuriukenin
譲受人

transferor
jōtonin
譲渡人

Treasurer
zaimu buchō
財務部長

trial balance
boki no shisanhyō
簿記の試算表

trial balance sheet
shisanhyō
試算表

turnover [UK]
sōuriagedaka
総売上高

turnover of capital
shihon kaiten(ritsu)
資本回転(率)

turnover ratio
kaitenritsu
回転率

turnover tax
sōuriagezei
総売上税

unamortized
mishōkyaku no
未償却の

unamortized cost
mishōkyaku genka
未償却原価

unamortized share-issuing expenses
mishōkyaku shinkabu hakkōhi
未償却新株発行費

unappropriated deficit
mishobun sonshitsukin
未処分損失金

unappropriated earned surplus
mishobun rieki jōyokin
未処分利益剰余金

unappropriated profits
mishobun rieki jōyokin
未処分利益剰余金

unappropriated retained earnings
mishobun riekikin
未処分利益金

unappropriated retained income
mishobun ryūho riekikin
未処分留保利益金

unappropriated surplus
mishobun rieki
未処分利益

unavoidable costs
kaihifunō genka
回避不能原価

unbalanced account
mikessan kanjō
未決算勘定

unbalanced book
mikessan chōbo
未決算帳簿

unbalanced budget
fukinkō yosan
不均衡予算

uncalled capital
miharaikomi shihon(kin)
未払込資本(金)

unclaimed dividend
museikyū haitō
無請求配当

unclaimed share
museikyū kabu
無請求株

unclaimed share certificate
museikyū kabuken
無請求株券

unclaimed stock
museikyū kabu
無請求株

unclaimed stock certificate
museikyū kabuken
無請求株券

undercapitalization
kashō shusshi
過少出資

undercapitalized
kashō shusshi no
過少出資の

undersubscribed
boshū kashō no
募集過少の
mōshikomi kashō no
申込過少の

undersubscription
kashō boshū
過少募集
kashō mōshikomi
過少申込み

underwrite
hikiukeru
引受ける

underwriters
hikiuke gyōsha
引受業者

underwriting
bosai hikiuke
募債引受け

underwriting agreement
hikiuke keiyaku
引受契約

underwriting commission
hikiuke tesūryō
引受手数料

underwriting company
hikiuke gaisha
引受会社

underwriting contract
hikiuke keiyaku
引受契約

underwriting syndicate
hikiukedan
引受団

undistributable reserves
haitōfunō rieki
配当不能利益

undistributed corporate profits
mibunpai hōjin rijun
未分配法人利潤

undistributed profits
mihaitō rieki
未配当利益
mishobun rieki
未処分利益

undivided profits
mibunpai rieki
未分配利益
mihaitō rieki
未配当利益

(retained profit)
naibu ryūho
内部留保

unearned dividend (bogus dividend)
tako haitō
たこ配当

unearned income (on balance sheet)
maeuke shūekikin
前受収益金

unemployed capital
yūkyū shihon
遊休資本
yūshi
遊資

uninscribed share
mukimei kabu
無記名株

uninscribed share certificate
mukimei kabuken
無記名株権

uninscribed stock
mukimei kabu
無記名株

uninscribed stock certificate
mukimei kabuken
無記名株権

unissued capital
mihakkō shihon
未発行資本

unissued capital stock
mihakkō shihonkin
未発行資本金

unissued certificate
yobi kabuken
予備株券

unissued share
mihakkō kabu
未発行株

unissued stock
mihakkō kabu
未発行株

unit cost
tanka
単価

unit costing
tan'itsu genka keisan
単一原価計算

unit depreciation
kobetsu shōkyaku
個別償却

unliquidated
seisan sarete nai
清算されてない

unlisted assets
bogai shisan
簿外資産

unpaid account
miharai kanjō
未払勘定

unpaid call
miharaikomi kabu
未払込株

unpaid capital
miharaikomi shihon(kin)
未払込資本(金)

unpaid dividend
miharai haitōkin
未払配当金

unpaid shares
miharaikomi kabu
未払込株

unpaid stock
miharaikomi kabu
未払込株

unproductive capital
fuseisanteki shihon
不生産的資本

unrealizable assets
kankafunō shisan
換価不能資産

unrealized appreciation
mijitsugen zōka
未実現増価

unrealized profits
mijitsugen rieki
未実現利益

unregistered certificate
mukimei kabuken
無記名株券

unsettled account
mikessan kanjō
未決算勘定

unsettled bills
mikessan no kanjōsho
未決算の勘定書

unused capital
miriyō shihon
未利用資本

use of funds
shikin no shito
資金の使途

valuation [UK]
hyōka
評価

valuation account
hyōka kanjō
評価勘定

valuation at cost
genkahō
原価法

value as a going concern
keizoku kigyō kachi
継続企業価値

value of business
kigyō kachi
企業価値

variable budget
hendō yosan
変動予算

variable costing
hendō genka keisan
変動原価計算

variable capital
kahen shihon
可変資本
ryūdō shihon
流動資本

variable costs
hendōhi
変動費
kahen hiyō
可変費用

vehicles and transport (on balance sheet)
sharyō unpangu
車両運搬具

venture capital
kiken futan shihon
危険負担資本

visible assets
yūkei shisan
有形資産

voting stock
giketsuken kabushiki
議決権株式

voucher
shiharai denpyō
支払伝票
shiharaihyō
支払票
shōhyō
証票

voucher invoice
shōhyō shikirijō
証票仕切状

voucher invoice book
shōhyō shikirijōchō
証票仕切状帳

voucher receipt
shōhyō ryōshūsho
証票領収書

voucher receipt book
shohyō ryōshūshochō
証票領収書帳

voucher system
shiharaihyō seido
支払票制度

wage cost
chingin hiyō
賃金費用

wages
chingin
賃金

wages account
chingin kanjō
賃金勘定

wages and salaries
chingin-kyūryō
賃金・給料

wages and salaries book
chingin-kyūryō shiharaibo
賃金・給料支払簿

wages and salaries cost
chingin kosuto
賃金コスト

wages ledger
chingin motochō
賃金元帳

wages payable
miharai chingin
未払賃金

warrant
(subscription right)
kabushiki kaitoriken shōsho
株式買取権証書

(share warrant)
shusshi shōken
出資証券

wasteful expenditure
shippi
失費

watered assets
mizumashi shisan
水増資産
mizuwari shisan
水割資産

watered capital
mizuwari shihon
水割資本

(fictitious)
gisei shihon
擬制資本

watered stock
mizumashi kabu
水増株
mizuwari kabu
水割株

watering
mizumashi
水増し

weekly accounting
shūji kessan
週次決算

weekly trial balance
shūkan shisanhyō
週間試算表

wholesale accounting
oroshiuri kaikei
卸売会計

widening of capital
shihon kakuchō
資本拡張

windfall profits
igai no rijun
意外の利潤

window-dressing
funshoku kessan
粉飾決算

window-dressing settlement
funshoku kessan
粉飾決算

with warrant
kenritsuki
権利付き

without-par-value shares
mugakumen kabu
無額面株

without-par-value stock
mugakumen kabu
無額面株

work in progress [UK]
shikakehin
仕掛品

work sheet
seisanhyō
精算表

(employees')
sagyōhyō
作業票

working assets
un'yō shisan
運用資産

working balances
un'yō zandaka
運用残高

working budget
jikkō yosan
実行予算

working capital
unten shihon
運転資本

working capital ratio
unten shihon hiritsu
運転資本比率

working expenditure
un'eihi
運営費

working expenses
eigyōhi
営業費
jigyōhi
事業費
kei'eihi
経営費
un'eihi
運営費

working funds
unten shikin
運転資金

working reserve
keijō junbi
経常準備

working trial balance
shisanhyō
試算表

worth (= assets)
shisan
資産

worth and fixed assets ratio
shihon-kotei shisan hiritsu
資本・固定資産比率

worth/debt ratio
shihon-fusai hiritsu
資本・負債比率

write down
(amortize [UK], depreciate)
genka shōkyaku o suru
原価償却をする

(lower book value of assets)
chōbo kakaku o hikisageru
帳簿価格を引下る

write off
(cancel)
chōkeshi suru
帳消しする

(amortize [UK], depreciate)
genka shōkyaku o suru
原価償却をする

write up (raise book value of assets)
chōbo kakaku o hikiageru
帳簿価格を引上げる

writing-down
(lowering book value of assets)
chōbo kakaku hikisage
帳簿価格引下げ
hyōkagen
評価減

(amortization [UK], depreciation)
genka shōkyaku
原価償却

writing-off
chōbo kakaku hikisage
帳簿価格引下げ

(cancellation)
chōkeshi
帳消し

(amortization [UK], depreciation)
genka shōkyaku
原価償却

writing-off of bad debts
kashidaorekin shōkyaku
貸倒金償却

writing-up
(raising book value of assets)
chōbo kakaku hikiage
帳簿価格引上げ
hyōkamashi
評価増し

year end
nenmatsu
年末

year-end adjustment
nenmatsu chōsei
年末調整

year-end dividend
nendomatsu haitō
年度末配当

year-end report
nenmatsu hōkokusho
年末報告書

year-end settlement
nenmatsu kessan
年末決算

yield
rimawari
利回り

yield to subscribers
ōbosha rimawari
応募者利回り

absentee voting
fuzaisha tōhyō
不在者投票

absolute majority
zettai tasū
絶対多数

abstain from voting
kiken suru
棄権する

abstention
tōhyō no kiken
投票の棄権

acknowledge a proxy
ininjō o kakunin suru
委任状を確認する

adjourn a meeting
heikai suru
閉会する
sōkai o enki suru
総会を延期する

adjournment
heikai
閉会

adopted unanimously
zen'in ikkatsu no giketsu ni
yoru saitaku sareta
全員一括の議決に
よる採択された

adoption
kaketsu
可決

advance notice
jizen tsūkoku
事前通告

**advertise notice of a
resolution**
ketsugi tsūchi o kōkoku suru
決議通知を広告する

agenda
giji
議事

AGM (annual general meeting)
nenji sōkai
年次総会

agree unanimously
ikkatsu shite sansei suru
一括して賛成する

annual general meeting (AGM)
nenji sōkai
年次総会

approval
kaketsu
可決

assenting vote
sansei tōhyō
賛成投票

attend a meeting
kaigi ni shusseki suru
会議に出席する

attention
chūi
注意

attest a proxy
ininjō o ninshō suru
委任状を認証する

ballot
tōhyō
投票
tōhyō yōshi
投票用紙

ballot box
tōhyōbako
投票箱

be present
shusseki shite iru
出席している

become invalid
mukō ni naru
無効になる

board meeting
jūyaku kaigi
重役会議
torishimariyakukai
取締役会

break up (int. verb)
kaisan suru
解散する

call a meeting
shōshū suru
召集する

candidate
kōhosha
候補者

canvass of votes
tōhyō kensa
投票検査

carried by a majority
tasū de kaketsu sareta
多数で可決された

carry a resolution
ketsui o tsūka suru
決意を通過する

cast one's vote
ikko no tōhyō o suru
一個の投票をする

casting a vote
ketteihyō
決定票

chair a meeting
kaigi o shikai suru
会議を司会する

chairman (at meeting)
gichō
議長

change one's vote
tōhyō o henkō suru
投票を変更する

close a meeting
heikai suru
閉会する

closed ballot
kimei tōhyō
記名投票

constitute a quorum
teisokusū to suru
定足数とする

convene
shōshū suru
召集する

convened
shōshū sareta
召集された

convocation
shōshū
召集
shūkai
集会

corporate election
kaisha no senkyo
会社の選挙

count votes
tōhyō o keisan suru
投票を計算する

counting of votes
tōhyō keisan
投票計算

cumulate votes
giketsuken o ruiseki suru
議決権を累積する

cumulation of votes
tōhyō no ruiseki
投票の累積

cumulative voting
ruiseki tōhyō
累積投票

decision by majority
tasūketsu
多数決

decision of general meeting
sōkai no ketsugi
総会の決議

directors' meeting
torishimariyaku shōshū
取締役召集

directors' vote
torishimariyaku no ketsugi
取締役の決議

discuss
kentō suru
検討する

discussion
kentō
検討
tōgi
討議

dissenting vote
hantai tōhyō
反対投票

elect by ballot
hyōketsu suru
票決する

elected by a majority vote
kahansū giketsu ni yotte
sennin sareta
過半数議決によって
選任された

election
senkyo
選挙

election inspectors
senkyo kensanin
選挙検査人

election officers
senkyo tantōkan
選挙担当官

exercise the right to vote
giketsuken o kōshi suru
議決権を行使する

extra session
rinjikai
臨時会

extraordinary general meeting
rinji sōkai
臨時総会

extraordinary meeting
rinji sōkai
臨時総会

extraordinary resolution [UK]
rinji ketsugi
臨時決議

form a quorum
teisokusū to suru
定足数とする

general meeting
sōkai
総会

general proxy
hōkatsuteki ininjō
包括的委任状

general vote
ippan giketsu
一般議決

hold a meeting
kai o moyōsu
会を催す

illegal vote
ihō na tōhyō
違法な投票

insufficient notice
fujūbun na tsūchi
不十分な通知

irrevocable proxy
torikeshifunō ininjō
取消不能委任状

issue notice (verb)
tsūchi o hassuru
通知を発する

legal notice
hōritsujō no tsūchi
法律上の通知

majority decision
tasūketsu
多数決

majority quorum
teisokusū no kahansū
定足数の過半数

majority vote
kahansū giketsu
過半数議決

managing directors' meeting [J]
jōmukai
常務会

meeting
sōkai
総会

(conference)
kaigi
会議

members
kai'in
会員

minority voting
shōsū hyōketsu
小数票決

minutes of meeting
gijiroku
議事録

motion
dōgi
動議

non-cumulative voting
hiruisekiteki tōhyō
非累積的投票

non-voter
kikensha
棄権者

notice of meeting
shōshū tsūchi
召集通知

notification
tsūchi
通知

notify
tsūchi o hassuru
通知を発する

objection
hantai
反対

obtain direct representation on the Board of Directors
torishimariyakukai ni chokusetsu daihyō o ukeru
取締役会に直接代表を受ける

obtain votes
tōhyō o eru
投票を得る

officers' meeting
yakuinkai
役員会

ordinary resolution
tsūjō ketsugi
通常決議

pass a resolution
ketsugi o suru
決議をする

percentage of voting shares
pāsento no giketsukentsuki kabushiki
パーセントの議決権付株式

place of meeting
sōkai no basho
総会の場所

plurality vote
tasū giketsu
多数議決

pooling of voting power
giketsuken no pūru
議決権のプール

presence of quorum
teisokusū no shusseki
定足数の出席

proposal
teian
提案

propose
teian suru
提案する

proxy
inin
委任

proxy form
ininjō
委任状

put forward a motion
dōgi o teishutsu suru
動議を提出する

qualified to vote
giketsu suru shikaku no
議決する資格の

quorum
teisokusū
定足数

regular general meeting
kabunushi sōkai
株主総会

regular meeting
teiki sōkai
定期総会

reject a vote
tōhyō o kyohi suru
投票を拒否する

rejection of proxy
ininjō kyohi
委任状拒否

resolution
ketsui
決意
ketsugi
決議

result of the counting of votes
tōhyō keisan no kekka
投票計算の結果

revocation of proxy
ininjō torikeshi
委任状取消し

session
kaigi
会議

shareholders' meeting
kabunushi sōkai
株主総会

solicitation of proxy
ininjō kan'yū
委任状勧誘

special resolution
tokubetsu ketsugi
特別決議

special vote
tokubetsu giketsu
特別議決

statutory meeting
hōtei kabunushi sōkai
法定株主総会

statutory quorum
hōtei teisokusū
法定定足数

subject for discussion
wadai
話題

unanimous vote
ikkatsu no giketsu
一括の議決

unlawful meeting
ihō sōkai
違法総会

unqualified proxy
shikaku no nai ininjō
資格のない委任状

unrestricted proxy
museigen no ininjō
無制限の委任状

valid
yūkō no
有効の

validity
yūkō
有効

views (opinions)
iken
意見

void
mukō no
無効の

vote (noun)
tōhyō
投票

  (resolution)
giketsu
議決

  (decision)
hyōketsu
票決

vote (verb)
tōhyō suru
投票する

vote against (—)
(—) ni hantai tōhyō suru
(—)に反対投票する

vote against a resolution
ketsugi ni hantai tōhyō suru
決議に反対投票する

vote by ballot
tōhyō yōshi ni yoru hyōketsu
投票用紙による票決

vote by machine
kikai tōhyō
機械投票

vote by proxy
dairinin ni yoru giketsuken kōshi
代理人による議決権行使
dairinin ni yoru tōhyō
代理人による投票

vote by share
kabushiki ni yoru hyōketsu
株式による票決

vote by the head
tōsū ni yoru hyōketsu
頭数による票決

vote forgery
tōhyō gizō
投票偽造

vote in favour of (—)
(—) ni sansei tōhyō suru
(—)に賛成投票する

vote in person
jishin ni yoru giketsuken kōshi
自身による議決権行使

vote on (—)
(—) ni giketsu suru
(—)に議決する

voting power
giketsuken
議決権

voting right
giketsuken
議決権

voting slip
tōhyō yōshi
投票用紙

waive
kenri hōki suru
権利放棄する

waiver
kenri hōkisho
権利放棄書

waiving
kenri hōki
権利放棄

accountant in bankruptcy
hasan seisannin
破産清算人

act of bankruptcy
hasan kōi
破産行為

act of insolvency
shiharai funō kōi
支払不能行為

adjudicate
hasan senkoku suru
破産宣告する

adjudication
senkoku
宣告

adjudication of bankruptcy
hasan senkoku
破産宣告

adjudication order
hasan meirei
破産命令

administered in bankruptcy
hasan ni yoru kanri sareta
破産による管理された

administration in bankruptcy
hasan kanzai
破産管財

administration order
kanzai meirei
管財命令

administrator in bankruptcy
hasan kanrinin
破産管理人
hasan kanzainin
破産管財人

after-acquired property
hasan ketteigo kakutoku
zaisan
破産決定後獲得財産

after-acquired property clause
jigo kakutoku zaisan jōkō
爾後獲得財産条項

all-out liquidation
sōtokeai
総解合い

appeal
sogan
訴願

appellant
sogannin
訴願人

application
shinsei
申請

**application for an attachment
(against —)**
(— ni taisuru) sashiosae
no shinsei
(—に対する)差押さえ
の申請

**appointment of trustee in
bankruptcy**
hasan kanzainin no ninmei
破産管財人の任命

assignment in bankruptcy
hasanchū no jōto
破産中の譲渡

attachment
sashiosae
差押さえ

attorney [US]
bengoshi
弁護士

bankrupt (noun)
hasansha
破産者

bankrupt (to be made)
hasan o senkoku suru
破産を宣告する

bankrupt's estate
hasan zaidan
破産財団

bankruptcy
hasan
破産
tōsan
倒産

Bankruptcy Act
hasanhō
破産法

bankruptcy committee
hasan kanzai i'in
破産管財委員

bankruptcy court
hasan saibansho
破産裁判所

bankruptcy creditor
hasan saikensha
破産債権者

bankruptcy debtor
hasan saimusha
破産債務者

bankruptcy law
hasanhō
破産法

bankruptcy notice
hasan kokuchi
破産告知

bankruptcy order
hasan meirei
破産命令

bankruptcy petition
hasan shinsei
破産申請

bankruptcy proceedings
hasan tetsuzuki
破産手続き

become bankrupt
hasan suru
破産する

business failure
kei'ei hatan
経営破綻
kigyō tōsan
企業倒産

calculated bankruptcy
keikaku tōsan
計画倒産

cause of failure
hasan gen'in
破産原因

cessation of business
eigyō teishi
営業停止

chain-reaction bankruptcy
rensa tōsan
連鎖倒産

claims in bankruptcy
hasan saiken
破産債権

clear all debts
saimu zengaku o hensai
suru
債務全額を返済する

commit an act of bankruptcy
hasan kōi o suru
破産行為をする

company bankruptcy
kigyō tōsan
企業倒産

company in liquidation
seisangaisha
清算会社

company rehabilitation
kaisha kōsei
会社更生

company rehabilitation procedure
kaisha kōsei tetsuzuki
会社更生手続き

composition procedures
wagi tetsuzuki
和議手続き

compulsory auction
kyōsei kyōbai
強制競売

compulsory liquidation
kyōsei seisan
強制清算

compulsory winding-up
kyōsei kaisan
強制解散

contemplated bankruptcy
hasan yoki
破産予期

controller in bankruptcy
hasan kansakan
破産監査官

court
saibansho
裁判所

court's decision
saibansho no senkoku
裁判所の宣告

creditor in bankruptcy
hasan saikensha
破産債権者

creditors
saikensha
債権者

creditors' meeting
saikensha no sōkai
債権者の総会

debtor
saimusha
債務者

debtor in bankruptcy
hasan saimusha
破産債務者

debts
hasan saimu
破産債務
saimu
債務

debts discharged in bankruptcy
hasansha no menseki
破産者の免責

debts provable in bankruptcy
hasan saimu
破産債務

declaration of bankruptcy
hasan senkoku
破産宣告

declared bankrupt (to be)
hasansha no senkoku o ukeru
破産者の宣告を受ける
hasansha to senkoku sareru
破産者と宣告される

decree of insolvency
shiharai funō hanketsu
支払不能判決

decree of completion of bankruptcy proceedings
hasan shūketsu kitei
破産終結規定

deed of arrangement
saimu seiri shōsho
債務整理証書

default (noun)
(saimu) furikō
(債務)不履行

default (verb)
saimu furikō ni ochiiru
債務不履行に陥る

default order
furikō meirei
不履行命令

discharge of a bankrupt
hasansha no menseki
破産者の免責

discharged bankruptcy
saimu shōmetsu hasan
債務消滅破産

dismiss proceedings
tetsuzuki o kyakka suru
手続きを却下する

dispose of collateral
tanpobutsu o shobun suru
担保物を処分する

disposition of collateral
tanpobutsu no shobun
担保物の処分

dissolution of company
kaisan
解散

dissolved (to be)
kaisan suru koto ni naru
解散することになる

escape one's obligations
saimu o manukareru
債務を免かれる

estimated claims
mitsumori saiken
見積り債権

fail
hatan o kitasu
破綻を来す

failure
hatan
破綻

failure to commence business
kigyō no sōgyō funō
企業の創業不能

file (verb)
mōshitate o suru
申立てをする

file an application for bankruptcy
hasan no mōshitate o suru
破産の申立てをする
hasan shinsei o suru
破産申請をする

financial difficulties
shikinnan
資金難

force a firm into involuntary bankruptcy
kaisha o kyōsei hasan ni oikomu
会社を強制破産に追込む

forced auction
kyōsei kyōbai
強制競売

forced liquidation
kyōsei hasan
強制破産
kyōsei seisan
強制清算

fraudulent bankruptcy
sagi hasan
詐欺破産

fraudulent business
sagi
詐欺

go into bankruptcy
hasan ni hairu
破産に入る

go into liquidation
seisan ni hairu
清算に入る

go into receivership
hasan kanri o ukete iru
破産管理を受けている

going out of business
misejimai
店任舞い

'habitual' bankrupt
jōshūteki hasansha
常習的破産者

in the hands of creditors (to be)
saikensha no kanri shita ni aru
債権者の管理下にある

in the hands of the bank (to be)
ginkō no kanri shita ni aru
銀行の管理下にある

in the hands of the receivers (to be)
hasan kanzainin no kanri shita ni aru
破産管財人の管理下にある

inability to pay one's debts
hensai funō
返済不能

initiation of procedure
tetsuzuki no kaishi
手続きの開始

insolvency
shiharai funō
支払不能

insolvency of debtor
sekininsha no shiharai funō
責任者の支払不能

insolvent (adjective)
shiharai funō no
支払不能の

insolvent (noun)
hasansha
破産者

insolvent corporation
shiharai funō gaisha
支払不能会社

insolvent debtor
hasansha
破産者

insolvent winding-up
shiharai funō hasan
支払不能破産

inspection
kensa
検査

inspection committee
kensa i'in
検査委員

involuntary bankruptcy
kyōsei hasan
強制破産

involuntary insolvency
kyōsei shiharai funō
強制支払不能

involuntary liquidation
kyōsei hasan
強制破産

involuntary petition
kyōseiteki mōshitate
強制的申立て

joint debtor
rentai saimusha
連帯債務者

judgement credit
hanketsu saiken
判決債権

judgement creditor
hanketsu saikensha
判決債権者

judgement debt
hanketsu saimu
判決債務

judgement debtor
hanketsu saimusha
判決債務者

legal action
sotsui
訴追

legal case
soshō jiken
訴訟事件

legal proceedings
soshō tetsuzuki
訴訟手続き

legally enforceable debts
hōritsujō kyōsei dekiru saimu
法律上強制できる債務

liabilities
fusai
負債

liquidated company
seisan gaisha
清算会社

liquidated partnership
seisan shain
清算社員

liquidation
seisan
清算

(dissolution, break-up)
kaisan
解散

(winding-up)
(kaisha) seiri
(会社)整理

liquidation procedure
seiri tetsuzuki
整理手続き

liquidation without court involvement
naiseiri
内整理

liquidator
seisannin
清算人

litigant
soshō tōjisha
訴訟当事者

litigation
soshō
訴訟

litigation costs
soshō hiyō
訴訟費用

make an assignment in bankruptcy
hasanchū no jōto o okonau
破産中の譲渡を行なう

negligent bankruptcy
katai hasan
過怠破産

official receiver
kōnin kanzainin
公認管財人

official receiver's report
kōnin kanzainin no hōkokusho
公認管財人の報告書

on the verge of bankruptcy
hatan rotei
破綻露呈

order (from the court)
meirei
命令

overindebtedness
saimu chōka
債務超過

party in bankruptcy
hasan kankeinin
破産関係人

pay one's creditors in full
saikensha no taishite zengaku shiharau
債権者の対して全額支払う

payment
shiharai
支払い

payment in instalments
bunkatsubarai
分割払い

petition for review (verb)
saishinri o motomeru
再審理を求める

petition hearing
hasan saibansho tetsuzuki
破産裁判所手続き

petition in bankruptcy
hasan no mōshitate
破産の申立て
hasan shinsei
破産申請

petitioner in bankruptcy
hasan no mōshitatenin
破産の申立人

plaintiff
soshōnin
訴訟人

preferential claims in bankruptcy
hasan yūsen saiken
破産優先債権

preferential creditor
yūsen saikensha
優先債権者

preferential debt
yūsen saiken
優先債権

preferential payments in bankruptcy
hasan yūsen shiharai
破産優先支払い

preferred creditor
yūsen saikensha
優先債権者

preferred debt
yūsen saiken
優先債権

prior claim
sakitoriken
先取権

priority of debts
shakkin no sakitoriken
借金の先取権

proceedings
tetsuzuki
手続き

proceeds from the disposition of collateral
tanpobutsu no shobun kagaku
担保物の処分価額

property of the bankrupt
hasansha no zaisan
破産者の財産

property reached in bankruptcy
hasan ni yotte hosoku sareta zaisan
破産によって捕捉された財産

provisional attachment
karisashiosae
仮差押さえ

provisional liquidator
kariseisannin
仮清算人

receiver
hasan kanzainin
破産管財人
kanzainin
管財人

receiver in bankruptcy
hasan kanzainin
破産管財人

receiver's certificate
kanzainin shōsho
管財人証書

receivership
hasan kanri
破産管理

receiving order
hasan kanzainin ninmeisho
破産管財人任命書

referee
shinrinin
審理人

referee in bankruptcy
hasan shinrinin
破産審理人

release from debt
saimu menjo
債務免除

repeated bankruptcy
kurikashi hasan
繰返破産

review
saishinri
再審理

senior creditor
sakijun'i saikensha
先順位債権者

senior debt
yūsen bensai saimu
優先弁済債務

shaky financial condition
fuan na shikin jijō
不安な資金事情

solvent winding-up
shiharai nōryoku no aru hasan
支払能力のある破産

statement of affairs
shisan jōtai hōkoku
資産状態報告

statement of liquidation
hasan seisansho
破産清算書

summons
reijō
令状

supervision
kantoku
監督

supervision of the court
saibansho no kantoku
裁判所の監督

supervision order
kantoku meirei
監督命令

suspend payment
shiharai o teishi suru
支払いを停止する

suspension of banking transactions
ginkō torihiki teishi
銀行取引停止

suspension of business
eigyō teishi
営業停止

suspension of payments to creditors
saikensha e no shiharai teishi
債権者への支払停止

take legal action
saibansho ni oite tetsuzuki o toru
裁判所において手続きを取る

take to court
sochin suru
訴陳する

trustee in bankruptcy
hasan kanzainin
破産管財人

vacate the declaration of bankruptcy
hasan senkoku o torikesu
破産宣告を取消す

voluntary bankrupt
jihatsuteki hasansha
自発的破産者

voluntary bankruptcy
jihatsuteki hasan
自発的破産
jiko hasan
自己破産
nin'i hasan
任意破産

voluntary insolvency
nin'i shiharai funō
任意支払不能

voluntary liquidation
jishu kaisan
自主解散
jishu seisan
自主清算
nin'i seisan
任意清算

voluntary petition
jihatsuteki mōshitate
自発的申立て

voluntary petition and proceedings
jiko hasan
自己破産

voluntary winding-up
nin'i hasan
任意破産
nin'i kaisan
任意解散

warrant in bankruptcy
hasansha zaisan sashiosae reijō
破産者財産差押令状

wind up
hasan suru
破産する

winding-up
(bankruptcy procedure)
hasan tetsuzuki
破産手続き

(suspension of business)
jigyō teishi
事業停止

(dissolution, break-up)
kaisan
解散

(liquidation)
kaisha seiri
会社整理

(business closure)
kigyō heisa
企業閉鎖

winding-up by the court
kyōsei kaisan
強制解散

winding-up of business
haigyō
廃業

winding-up order
hasan meirei
破産命令

winding-up petition
hasan no mōshitate
破産の申立て
hasan shinsei
破産申請

winding-up procedure
hasan no tetsuzuki
破産の手続き

winding-up rules
hasan kisoku
破産規則

Chapter 5

Employment; Personnel

academic record (personal history)
gakureki
学歴

active recruitment policy
sekkyokuteki koyō seisaku
積極的雇用政策

advertisement (ad)
kōkoku
広告

age
nenrei
年齢

age limit
nenrei seigen
年齢制限

alma mater
bokō
母校

annual recruitment
teiki saiyō
定期採用

applicant
(candidate)
kōhosha
候補者

(entrant)
ōbosha
応募者

(aspirant)
shibōsha
志望者

application
(trying one's luck with employers)
mōshikomi
申込み

(in response to an advertisement)
ōbo
応募

application form
mōshikomi yōshi
申込用紙
ōbo yōshi
応募用紙

apply
mōshikomu
申込む
ōbo suru
応募する

appointment (for interview)
yakusoku
約束

aptitude test
tekisei kensa
適性検査

asset
tsuyomi
強味

Bachelor of Arts (BA)
gakushi
学士

Bachelor of Science (BS [US], BSc [UK])
gakushi
学士

background
bakkuguraundo
バックグラウンド
haikei
背景
keireki
経歴

background knowledge
haikeiteki na chishiki
背景的な知識

biggest asset
saidai no tsuyomi
最大の強味

business administration (study of)
kei'eigaku
経営学

business college
jitsumu gakkō
実務学校

business education
jitsumu kyōiku
実務教育

business management studies
kei'eigaku
経営学

business training
jitsugyō kyōiku
実業教育

candidate
kōhosha
候補者

career
kyaria
キャリア

(occupation, profession)
shokugyō
職業

career counselling
shokugyō hodō
職業補導
shokugyō sōdan
職業相談

career counsellor
shokugyō shidōsha
職業指導者
shokugyō sōdannin
職業相談人

career plan
kyaria-puran
キャリア・プラン

change jobs
[less formal]
shoku o kaeru
職を変える

(change companies)
tensha suru
転社する

[formal]
tenshoku suru
転職する

change of jobs
tenshoku
転職

classified advertisements
annai kōkoku
安内広告

commercial school
shōgyō gakkō
商業学校

composure (cool nerves)
reisei na shinkei
冷静な神経

conditions of employment
koyō jōken
雇用条件

corporate entrance exam
nyūsha shiken
入社試験

curriculum vitae (CV) [UK]
rirekisho
履歴書

degree
gakui
学位

discrimination
sabetsu
差別

discrimination on the basis of race
shusabetsu
種差別

discrimination on the basis of sex
seisabetsu
性差別

Doctorate (PhD)
hakasegō/hakushigō
博士号

education
kyōiku
教育

educational background
gakureki
学歴

employment
koyō
雇用

　(work)
　shūgyō
　就業

employment agency
shokugyō shōkaijo
職業紹介所

employment bureau (of Japanese schools)
shokugyō shidōka
職業指導課
shūshokuka
就職課

employment exchange
shokugyō shōkaijo
職業紹介所

employment opportunity
koyō kikai
雇用機会

employment policy
koyō seisaku
雇用政策

employment prospects
koyō mitōshi
雇用見通し

employment seeker
kyūshokusha
求職者

equal employment opportunity
koyō kikai kintō
雇用機会均等

equal opportunity
kikai kintō
機会均等

equal opportunity employer [UK]
kikai kintō koyōsha
機会均等雇用者

evaluate
hyōka suru
評価する

experience
keiken
経験

experienced
keiken jūbun na
経験十分な
keiken yutaka na
経験豊かな

explanatory meeting[24]
setsumeikai[24]
説明会

family dependents
fuyō kazokusū
扶養家族数

female (adjective)
josei (no)
女性(の)

fill a vacancy
ketsuin o hojū suru
欠員を補充する
kūseki o jūsoku suru
空席を充足する
shigoto no aki o umeru
仕事の空きを埋める

find employment
shūshoku suru
就職する

formal education
seiki no kyōiku
正規の教育

forte
tokui
得意

general capabilities
ippanteki nōryoku
一般的能力
sōgōteki nōryoku
総合的能力

general education
futsū kyōiku
普通教育

general knowledge
ippanteki chishiki
一般的知識

get a job
shūshoku suru
就職する

graduate (noun)
sotsugyōsha
卒業者

graduate (verb)
sotsugyō suru
卒業する

headhunter
heddohantā
ヘッドハンター
jinzai sukauto
人材スカウト
kyūjin sukauto
求人スカウト

headhunting
heddohantingu
ヘッドハンティング

headhunting firm
jinzai gaisha
人材会社

help find a job
shūshoku no sewa o shite
yaru
就職の世話をしてやる

help-wanted advertisement
kyūjin kōkoku
求人広告

high school
kōkō
高校

higher education
kōtō kyōiku
高等教育

hire
[formal]
saiyō suru
採用する

[less formal]
yatou
雇う

hiring
[formal]
saiyō
採用

[less formal]
yatoire
雇いれ

hiring standards
koyō hyōjun
雇用標準

individual visit (see note 24)
kobetsu hōmon (see note 24)
個別訪問

industrial technical school
kōgyō gakkō
工業学校

industrial technical training
kōgyō kyōiku
工業教育

interview (noun)
mensetsu
面接

interview (verb)
mensetsu suru
面接する

interviewee
mensetsusha
面接者

interviewer
kyūshokugakari
求職係

interviewing
mensetsu
面接

interviewing technique
mensetsu no tekunikku
面接のテクニック

IQ (intelligence quotient)
chinō shisū
知能指数

IQ test
aikyū-tesuto
アイキュー・テスト

job
(job of work, task)
shigoto
仕事

(occupation, profession)
shokugyō
職業

(function, post)
shokumu
職務

job applicant
kyūshokusha
求職者

job application
kyūshoku
求職
kyūshoku mōshikomi
求職申込み
shūshoku mōshikomi
就職申込み

job centre [UK]
shokugyō shōkaijo
職業紹介所

job creation
koyō sōshutsu
雇用創出
shokugyō sōshutsu
職業創出

job description
[less formal]
shigoto no naiyō
仕事の内容

(written description)
shokumu kijutsusho
職務記述書

[formal]
shokumu no naiyō
職務の内容

job experience
shokugyō keiken
職業経験
shokumu keiken
職務経験

job hopper
[less formal]
hinpan ni shoku o kaeru hito
頻繁に職を変える人

[formal]
jōshū tenshokusha
常習転職者

job hunter
kyūshokusha
求職者

job hunting
kyūshoku (katsudō)
求職 (活動)

job interview
kyūshoku mensetsu
求職面接

job introduction
shokugyō shōkai
職業紹介

job market
kyūjin shijō
求人市場
shūshoku shijō
就職市場

job offer
kyūjin
求人

job opening
shūshokuguchi
就職口

[less formal]
shigoto no aki
仕事の空き
tsutomeguchi
勤め口

job opportunity
koyō kikai
雇用機会

job placement
shūshoku
就職

job requirements
shokumu shikaku
職務資格

job search
kyūshoku
求職

job search channels
kyūshoku rūto
求職ルート

job seeker
kyūshokusha
求職者

job shopping
jobu-shoppingu
ジョブ・ショッピング

job specifications
shokumu naiyō
職務内容

job vacancy
ketsuin
欠員
kyūjin
求人

knowledge
chishiki
知識

labour exchange
shokugyō shōkaijo
職業紹介所

labour market
rōdō shijō
労働市場

leaving vacancies unfilled
ketsuin fuhojū
欠員不補充

letter of introduction
shōkaijō
紹介状

letter of recommendation
suisenjō
推薦状

local labour market
chihō rōdō shijō
地方労働市場

look for a job
kyūshoku suru
求職する

main asset
saidai no tsuyomi
最大の強味

main weakness
saidai no tansho
最大の短所

major employers
daikoyōnushi
大雇用主

major subject of study
senkō kamoku
専攻科目

male (adjective)
dansei (no)
男性(の)

management science
kei'eigaku
経営学

marital status
kon'in no jōkyō
婚姻の状況

married
kekkon shite iru
結婚している

Master of Arts (MA)
shūshi
修士

Master of Science (MS [US], MSc [UK])
shūshi
修士

Master's Degree in Business Administration (MBA)
kei'eigaku shūshi
経営学修士

nationality
kokuseki
国籍

nationality at birth
shusshōtoki no kokuseki
出生時の国籍

new hiring
shinki saiyō
新規採用

new job offers
shinki kyūjin
新規求人

new school graduates on the labour market
shinki gakusotsu rōdōryoku
新規学卒労働力

occasional recruitment[25]
chūto saiyō[25]
中途採用

occupational change
tengyō
転業

occupational guidance
shokugyō shidō
職業指導

old boys' network
ōbii
オービー

opening, an
hatarakiguchi
働き口
kyūjinguchi
求人口
shūshokuguchi
就職口
tsutomeguchi
勤め口

opportunity
(possibility)
kanōsei
可能性

(chance)
kikai
機会

part-time work
pāto-taimu-wāku
パート・タイム・
ワーク

(students)
arubaito
アルバイト

pass an exam
gōkaku suru
合格する

personal connections
kojinteki na tsunagari
個人的なつながり

personal history
(experience)
keireki
経歴

(curriculum vitae)
rirekisho
履歴書

personality
(force of one's
personality)[26]
haragei[26]
腹芸

(character, personal
qualities)
hitogara
人柄

(character, good
qualities)
jinkaku
人格

(character, nature)
seikaku
性格

personality test
seikaku kensa
性格検査

personnel recruitment
jin'in hojū
人員補充

place (verb)
shūshoku saseru
就職させる

placement
shūshoku shōkai
就職紹介

placement agency
shūshoku shōkaijo
就職紹介所

placement bureau
(universities')
shūshokubu
就職部

placement fee
shūshoku shōkai tesūryō
就職紹介手数料

placement officer
(head of placement
bureau)
shūshoku buchō
就職部長

(placement clerk)
shūshoku tantōsha
就職担当者

position
(status, office, post)
chii
地位

(job, work)
shoku
職

post
posuto
ポスト

(position, office)
chii
地位

(place of appointment)
ninchi
任地

post-graduate school
daigakuin
大学院

practical utility
jitsuyōsei
実用性

preferential hiring
kumiai'in yūsen koyō
組合員優先雇用

preferential hiring system
kumiai'in yūsen koyō seido
組合員優先雇用制度

professional education
shokugyō kyōiku
職業教育

(specialist)
senmon kyōiku
専門教育

professional school
senmon gakkō
専門学校

professional skills
senmon gijutsu
専門技術

professional training
(specialized education)
senmon shokugyō kyōiku
専門職業教育

(specialized training)
senmonteki kunren
専門的訓練

professional woman
shokugyō fujin
職業婦人

qualifications
shikaku
資格

qualified
(meeting requirements)
shikaku no aru
資格のある

(suitable, eligible)
tekikaku no
適格の

qualified for (—)
(—) ni teki shite iru
(—) に適している

recruit (verb)
(invite applications)
boshū suru
募集する

(fill a vacancy, replace)
hojū suru
補充する

(engage, take on)
saiyō suru
採用する

recruiting
boshū
募集
saiyō
採用

recruiting new employees
shinki saiyō
新規採用

recruitment
saiyō
採用

(filling a vacancy, replacing)
hojū
補充

(inviting applications)
shinki boshū
新規募集

recruitment method
boshū hōhō
募集方法
hojū hōhō
補充方法

recruitment programme
boshū puroguramu
募集プログラム
hojū puroguramu
補充プログラム

recruitment technique
boshū no tekunikku
募集のテクニック
hojū no tekunikku
補充のテクニック

recruitment test
saiyō shiken
採用試験

regular recruitment (see note 25)
teiki saiyō (see note 25)
定期採用

rehire (verb)
saikoyō suru
再雇用する

rehiring
saikoyō
再雇用

replacement (person)
daihyōsha
代表者

resume [US]
rirekisho
履歴書

school leaver (high-school graduate)
gakusotsusha
学卒者

select
erabu
選ぶ

shortcoming
tansho
短所

single
dokushin no
独身の

situation vacant
ketsuin
欠員

situation-vacant column
kyūjin kōkokuran
求人広告欄

situation wanted
kyūshoku
求職

situation-wanted advertisement
kyūshoku kōkoku
求職広告

skill(s)
jukuren
熟練

(ability)
ginō
技能

(technical)
gijutsuteki jukuren
技術的熟練
gikō
技巧

special ability
senmon nōryoku
専門能力

special skill(s)
senmon gijutsu
専門技術

speciality [UK]
senmon
専門

specialize in (—)
(—) o senkō suru
(—) を専攻する

specialized education
senmon kyōiku
専門教育

specialized school
senmon gakkō
専門学校

specialty [US]
senmon
専門

staff recruitment
shain saiyō
社員採用

strong point
tokui
得意
tsuyomi
強味

study abroad
ryūgaku suru
留学する

subject of study (= major)
senkō kamoku
専攻科目

suitability
tekisei
適性

technical education
jitsugyō kyōiku
実業教育

technical school
jitsugyō gakkō
実業学校

technical skills
gijutsuteki jukuren
技術的熟練

technical training
gijutsu kunren
技術訓練

(education)
gijutsu kyōiku
技術教育

terms of employment
koyō jōken
雇用条件

test (noun)
shiken
試験
tesuto
テスト

test (verb)
shiken suru
試験する
tesuto suru
テストする

top graduate
ichiban yūshū na
sotsugyōsha
一番優秀な卒業者

trip for study abroad
ryūgaku tokō
留学渡航

unfilled vacancy
mijūsoku kyūjin
未充足求人

university
daigaku
大学

university graduate
daigaku sotsugyōsha
大学卒業者

vacancy
kyūjin(guchi)
求人(口)

(vacant position)
ketsuin
欠員

('vacant seat')
kūseki
空席

(opening)
shūshokuguchi
就職口

vacant position
ketsuin
欠員
kūseki
空席
kyūjin(guchi)
求人(口)

vocation
shokugyō tekisei
職業適性

vocational aptitude
shokugyō tekisei
職業適性

vocational counselling
shokugyō sōdan
職業相談

vocational counsellor
shokugyō shidōsha
職業指導者
shokugyō sōdannin
職業相談人

vocational education
shokugyō kyōiku
職業教育

vocational guidance
shokugyō shidō
職業指導

vocational school
shokugyō gakkō
職業学校

vocational test
shokugyō tekisei kensa
職業適性検査

vocational training
shokugyō kunren
職業訓練

weak point (lack of aptitude for a particular thing)
nigate
苦手

word-of-mouth recommendation
kuchi kara kuchi e no
suisen
口から口への推薦

work experience
shigotoreki
仕事歴
shokureki
職歴

work permit
rōdō kyoka
労働許可

written exam
hikki shiken
筆記試験

yearly recruitment
teiki saiyō
定期採用

Notes

24. explanatory meeting (setsumeikai 説明会): these meetings are part of the Japanese graduate-recruitment process and are held at the various companies that advertise jobs at universities in an effort to attract graduates. They are the first recruitment step and are usually followed by 'individual visits' (kobetsu hōmon 個別訪問) by those graduates that have answered the companies' university advertisements.

25. occasional recruitment (chūto saiyō 中途採用): hiring of new staff on an as-needed basis to fill specific posts, as opposed to the yearly or 'regular recruitment' (teiki saiyō 定期採用) of university graduates carried out by Japanese corporations.

26. personality (haragei 腹芸): the force of one's personality that enables someone to convey their intentions to another person by making the right psychological use of that person's own personality, knowledge and expectations.

Additional expressions

aotagai 青田買い ('buying a paddy field') and aotagari 青田刈り ('reaping a green paddy field'): in a business context these expressions describe the intensive graduate-recruitment methods used by companies in Japan which literally 'harvest' schools and universities for new 'crops' of graduates every year and make advance contracts of employment with certain students who are to graduate the following year.

hikinuki 引抜き ('plucking'): because of the lifetime employment principle Japanese companies do not as a rule employ people who have worked for other companies. However, occasionally a company may urgently require someone with highly specialized skills or experience and so may try to tempt this particular person away from his firm.

rōnin 浪人 ('a samurai without a master'): in a business context 'rōnin' is sometimes used to describe someone who willingly remains unemployed until he has found the particular job that he is looking for. It can also refer to a high-school graduate who has failed to get into university and who is waiting for another chance to do so.

ability
 (capability, faculties)
 nōryoku
 能力

 (gift, talent)
 sainō
 才能

able
 yūnō na
 有能な

able person
 (person of talent)
 jinzai
 人材

 (go-getter)
 yarite
 やり手

absence
 kekkin
 欠勤

absence rate
 kekkinritsu
 欠勤率

absence without permission
 mutodoke kekkin
 無届欠勤

absentee
 kekkinsha
 欠勤者

absenteeism
 kekkin
 欠勤

 (habitual absence)
 jōshūteki kekkin
 常習的欠勤

 (planned absence)
 keikakuteki kekkin
 計画的欠勤

absenteeism rate
 kekkinritsu
 欠勤率

abuse of power
 kenryoku no ran'yō
 権力の濫用

accountability
 kei'ei sekinin
 経営責任

accountant
 kaikeigakari
 会計係
 kaikeishi
 会計士
 keirishi
 計理士

accounting department
 kaikeibu
 会計部
 keiribu
 経理部

accounts manager
 kaikei buchō
 会計部長

acting director
 dairi torishimariyaku
 代理取締役

acting general manager
 buchō dairi
 部長代理

acting manager
 kachō dairi
 課長代理

acting president
 shachō dairi
 社長代理

active
 kappatsu na
 活発な

active employment policy
 sekkyokuteki koyō seisaku
 積極的雇用政策

adaptability
 tekiōsei
 適応性

adaptable
 tekiōsei no aru
 適応性のある

administration
 (control, supervision)
 kanri
 管理

 (management)
 kei'ei
 経営

administration department
 kanri bumon
 管理部門
 kanribu
 管理部

administrative ability
 kanri nōryoku
 管理能力
 kei'ei shuwan
 経営手腕

administrative staff
 kanri shokuin
 管理職員

administrator
 (supervisor, manager)
 kanrinin
 管理人

 (management)
 kei'eisha
 経営者

advancement
 shōshin
 昇進

advertising department
 kōkokubu
 広告部
 sendenbu
 宣伝部

advertising manager
 kōkoku buchō
 広告部長

aggressive
 sekkyokuteki na
 積極的な

agricultural worker
 nōgyō rōdōsha
 農業労働者

allocation of responsibilities
 sekinin buntan
 責任分担

ambition
 yashin
 野心

ambitions
 nerai
 狙い

ambitious
yashinteki na
野心的な

analyst
bunsekika
分析家

appoint
ninmei suru
任命する

appointed (to be)
ninmei sareru
任命される

appointment (to a post)
ninmei
任命

apprentice
minarai
見習い
totei
徒弟

apprenticeship
minarai seido
見習い制度
toteisei
徒弟制

apprenticeship period
totei kikan
徒弟期間

apprenticeship training
totei yōsei
徒弟養成

aptitude
tekisei
適性

area manager
chi'iki tantō shihainin
地域担当支配人

artisan
shokunin
職人

assertiveness training
jiko shuchō kunren
自己主張訓練

assigned to (—)
(—) ni haizoku sareru
(—) に配属される

assignment
ninmu
任務

assistant
joshu
助手

assistant general manager
fukusōshihainin
副総支配人

assistant manager
fukushihainin
副支配人

attendance
shukkin
出勤

attendance book
shukkinbo
出勤簿

auditing department
kansabu
監査部

auditor
kansayaku
監査役

authority
kengen
権限

authorization (= power)
kengen
権限

average
heikinteki na
平均的な

back-office force
naikinshokuin
内勤職員

behaviour outside the office
kaisha igai no kōdō
会社以外の行動

blue-collar worker
nikutai rōdōsha
肉体労働者

book-keeper
bokigakari
簿記係

boss [informal]
bosu
ボス

brain work
chiteki rōdō
知的労働
seishin rōdō
精神労働

brain worker
chishiki rōdōsha
知識労働者

branch manager
shishachō
支社長
shitenchō
支店長

break (rest)
burēki
ブレーキ
kyūkei
休憩
yasumi
休み

business card
meishi
名刺

business research department
chōsabu
調査部

busy
isogashii
忙しい

('have things to do')
yōji ga aru
用事がある

capability
(efficiency)
nōritsu
能率

(ability, capacity)
nōryoku
能力

capable
yūnō na
有能な

capable person
jinzai
人材

career
kyaria
キャリア
shokugyō
職業

career ambition
kyaria ni taisuru yashin
キャリアに対する野心

career improvement
kyaria no kōjō
キャリアの向上

career programme
keireki kanri seido
経歴管理制度

career woman
josei kanrishokuin
女性管理職員
shokugyō fujin
職業婦人

carte-blanche
hakushi
白紙

casual employment
rinji koyō
臨時雇用

casual labour
(irregular)
futeiki rōdō
不定期労働

(day)
hiyatoi rōdō
日雇労働

(free)
jiyū rōdō
自由労働

casual labourer
futeiki rōdosha
不定期労働者
hiyatoi rōdosha
日雇労働者
jiyū rōdosha
自由労働者

casual work
(irregular)
futeiki rōdō
不定期労働

(day)
hiyatoi rōdō
日雇労働

(free)
jiyū rōdō
自由労働

casual worker
futeiki rōdōsha
不定期労働者
hiyatoi rōdōsha
日雇労働者
jiyū rōdōsha
自由労働者

CEO (chief executive officer)
kei'ei saikō sekininsha
経営最高責任者

certificate of employment
zaishoku shōmei
在職証明

chairman
kaicho
会長

Chairman of the Board of Directors
torishimariyaku kaichō
取締役会長

challenge
charenji
チャレンジ

change
idō
異動

character
hada
肌

cheap labour
teichingin rōdōryoku
低賃金労働力

cheap labour policy
teichingin rōdō seisaku
低賃金労働政策

cheerful
yōki na
陽気な

chief accountant
shunin kaikeikan
主任会計官

chief buyer
kōbai shunin
購買主任

chief clerk
jimuchō
事務長
kakarichō
係長

chief controller
keiri buchō
経理部長

chief executive
shuseki
主席

chief executive officer (CEO)
kei'ei saikō sekininsha
経営最高責任者

chief operation officer
gyōmu saikō sekininsha
業務最高責任者

chief sales executive
hanbai tantō jūyaku
販売担当重役

civil servant
kōmuin
公務員

clerical staff
jimu shokuin
事務職員

clerical work
jimu
事務

clerk
jimuin
事務員

clock (verb)
jikan o hakaru
時間を計る

clock card
shukkinhyō
出勤表

closed union
heisateki kumiai
閉鎖的組合

coffee break
kōhii-burēki
コーヒー・ブレーキ
kyūkei
休憩

colleague
dōryō
同僚
shigoto nakama
仕事仲間

collective agreement
dantai kyōyaku
団体協約
shūdan kyōyaku
集団協約

commercial traveller
gyōshōnin
行商人

company employee[27]
kaisha no shain
会社の社員
kaishain
会社員
shain[27]
社員

company newsletter
shanai shinbun
社内新聞

company secretary
kaisha no kanji
会社の幹事

company spirit
kaisha no seishin
会社の精神

company union
kigyōbetsu rōdō kumiai
企業別労働組合

[US]
goyō kumiai
御用組合

competition
kyōsō
競争

competition among employees
shain aida ni no kyōsō
社員間にの競争

conditions of employment
koyō jōken
雇用条件

consultant
konsarutanto
コンサルタント

contact (rapport)
sesshoku
接触

contentment
manzoku
満足

continuous service
kinzoku nensū
勤続年数

continuous training
keizoku kunren
継続訓練

contract
keiyaku
契約

contract immigrant labour
keiyaku imin rōdō
契約移民労働

contract labour
keiyaku rōdō
契約労働

contracted labourer
keiyaku rōdōsha
契約労働者

contribution
kōkendo
貢献度

corporate anthem[28]
shaka[28]
社歌

corporate planning office
kikakushitsu
企画室

dangerous occupation
kiken na shokugyō
危険な職業

dangerous work
kiken na shigoto
危険な仕事

day duty
hiruma kinmu
昼間勤務

day labourer
hiyatoi rōdōsha
日雇労働者

day-shift worker
hiruma sagyōin
昼間作業員

day work
hiruma kinmu
昼間勤務
hiruma shūgyō
昼間就業

day worker
hiyatoi rōdōsha
日雇労働者

dedicated to one's work
shigoto ni taisuru kōkendo ga aru
仕事に対する貢献度
がある

dedication
kōkendo
貢献度

degree of loyalty
chūsei no teido
忠誠の程度

delegation of responsibility
kengen ijō
権限委譲

demotion[29]
kōtō
降等
sasen[29]
左遷

department
bu
部
bumon
部門

departmental manager
buchō
部長

departmental staff member
buin
部員

dependents
fuyōsha
扶養者

(family)
fuyō kazoku
扶養家族

deputy chairman
fukukaichō
副会長

deputy general manager
jichō
次長

deputy manager
fukushihainin
副支配人

deputy managing director [UK]
fukushachō
副社長

design department
sekkei bumon
設計部門

desk (seat)
seki
席

development office
kaihatsushitsu
開発室

diligence
kinben
勤勉

diligent
kinben na
勤勉な

director
jūyaku
重役
torishimariyaku
取締役

disciplinary rules
shokuba kiritsu
職場規律

discrimination
sabetsu
差別

discrimination on the basis of race
shusabetsu
種差別

discrimination on the basis of sex
seisabetsu
性差別

discriminatory practices
sabetsuteki koyō kankō
差別的雇用慣行

disincentive to work
rōdō iyoku o yokusei suru mono
労働意欲を抑制する
もの

dissatisfaction
fumanzokukan
不満足感

dissatisfied
fumanzokukan ga aru
不満足感がある

distinguished service
kōrō
功労

division
jigyōbu
事業部

domestic work
kanai rōdō
家内労働

duration of employment
koyō kikan
雇用期間

duties
(office, functions, tasks)
ninmu
任務

(extent of responsibility)
sekinin han'i
責任範囲

(office, functions, work, job)
shokumu
職務

eager-beaver
hitasura ni hataraku ningen
ひたすらに働く人間

eagerness to work
kinrō iyoku
勤労意欲

educated manpower
kyōiku ga aru jinteki shigen
教育がある人的資源

efficiency
kōritsu
効率

efficiency of labour
rōdō nōritsu
労働能率

efficiency rating
kinmu hyōtei
勤務評定

efficiency rating system
kinmu hyōtei seido
勤務評定制度

efficient
kōritsu na
効率な

effort
doryoku
努力

eight-hour day
ichinichi hachijikansei
1日8時間制

employ (to be in employ)
shūshoku shite iru
就職している

employ (verb)
koyō suru
雇用する

employed director
koyō jūyaku
雇用重役

employed labourer
koyō rōdōsha
雇用労働者

employed person [statistical]
hikoyōsha
被雇用者

employed worker
koyō rōdōsha
雇用労働者

employee
[formal, statistical]
hikoyōsha
被雇用者

[general]
jūgyōin
従業員

[informal]
yatoinin
雇い人

(member of white-collar staff)
shokuin
職員

employee counselling
jūgyōin sōdan
従業員相談

employee handbook
jūgyōin benran
従業員便覧

employee rating
jūgyōin kōka
従業員孝課

employee relations
jūgyōin kankei
従業員関係

employee representation
jūgyōin daihyō
従業員代表

employee representative
jūgyōin daihyōsha
従業員代表者

employee services
kōseibu
厚生部
fukushibu
福祉部

employee skills inventory
jūgyōin tekizai kiroku
従業員適材記録

employee training
jūgyōin kunren
従業員訓練

employee transferred to another branch or company[30]
shukkō shain[30]
出向社員

employee turnover
rishokuritsu
離職率
taishokuritsu
退職率

employee's annual report
jūgyōin'yō nenpō
従業員用年報

employee's attitude
jūgyōin no taido
従業員の態度

employee's past record
jūgyōin no kako no kiroku
従業員の過去の記録

employees of the company
kaisha no shain
会社の社員

employees' association
jūgyōin kumiai
従業員組合

employees' attendance record
kaisha no shukkinbo
会社の出勤簿

employees' attitude survey
jūgyōin no taido chōsa
従業員の態度調査

employees' opinion poll
jūgyōin iken chōsa
従業員意見調査

employer
[formal, statistical]
koyōsha
雇用者

[less formal]
yatoinushi
雇い主

(the management)
kei'eisha
経営者

employer and employee relations
koyōsha tai jūgyōin no kankei
雇用者対従業員の関係

employment
(having on the payroll)
koyō
雇用

(work)
shūgyō
就業

employment conditions
koyō jōken
雇用条件

employment contract
koyō keiyaku
雇用契約

employment policy
koyō seisaku
雇用政策

employment practices
koyō kankō
雇用慣行
koyō shūkan
雇用習慣

employment system
koyō keitai
雇用形態

engineer
gijutsuka
技術家
gishi
技師

engineering department
gijutsubu
技術部

executive
kei'eisha
経営者

(director)
jūyaku
重役

(leading executive)
kanbu shokuin
幹部職員
kei'ei kanbu
経営幹部

(officer)
yakuin
役員

executive ability
kei'ei nōryoku
経営能力

executive director
jōmu torishimariyaku
常務取締役
senmu torishimariyaku
専務取締役

executive duties
kei'ei shokumu
経営職務

executive job
kanri shokumu
管理職務
kanrishoku
管理職

executive managing director
senmu torishimariyaku
専務取締役

executive officer
saikō shokuin
最高職員
shikkō shain
執行社員

executive personnel
kanri shokuin
管理職員

executive position
jūyakushoku
重役職
kanri shokui
管理職位

executive secretary
jimu kyokuchō
事務局長

executive staff
kanbu (shokuin)
幹部(職員)
kei'ei kanbu
経営幹部

executive vice-president [US]
fukushachō
副社長

expatriate
kaigai chūzaiin
海外駐在員

experience
keiken
経験

experience rating
keiken hyōka
経験評価

exploitation of labour
rōdō sakushu
労働搾取

export department
yushutsubu
輸出部

export manager
yushutsu buchō
輸出部長

extra work
jikangai rōdō
時間外労働

extra worker
yojō rōdōsha
余剰労働者

factory manager
kōjō kantoku
工場監督
kōjōchō
工場長

factory worker
[general]
kōin
工員

(employee)
kōjō jūgyōin
工場従業員

(labourer)
kōjō rōdōsha
工場労働者

failure
shippai
失敗

fair employment practices
kōsei koyō kankō
公正雇用慣行

family worker
kazoku rōdōsha
家族労働者

farm work
nōgyō rōdō
農業労働

farm worker
nōgyō rōdōsha
農業労働者

fellow worker
shigoto nakama
仕事仲間

female employee
joshi jūgyōin
女子従業員

female worker
joshi rōdōsha
女子労働者

field personnel
eigyōin
営業員

field representative
eigyō daihyōsha
営業代表者

field supervisor
eigyō shidōin
営業指導員

finance department
zaimubu
財務部

financial director
zaimu kanrisha
財務管理者

five-day week (system)
shūkyū futsukasei
週休2日制

flexi-time system
furekkusu-taimu seido
フレックス・タイム
制度
shinshukuteki rōdō jikan
seido
伸縮的労働時間制度

foreman
shokuchō
職長

forty-hour week system
shūyonjū jikansei
週40時間制

free labourer
jiyū rōdōsha
自由労働者

(non-unionized)
hikumiai rōdōsha
非組合労働者

freelance work
jiyūgyō
自由業

freelancer
jiyū keiyakusha
自由契約者
jiyūgyōsha
自由業者

freshman orientation
shinnyūshain kyōiku
新入社員教育

frustration
rakutan
落胆

fulfil one's duties
shokumu o hatasu
職務を果たす

full employment (once probation period is over)
honsaiyō
本採用

full-time
jōkin no
常勤の

full-time employment
jōkin koyō
常勤雇用

full-time labour force
jōyō rōdōryoku
常用労働力

full-time union officer
kumiai senjūsha
組合専従者

full-time worker
senjūsha
専従者

fully staffed
zen'in ga sorotte iru
全員が揃っている

function(s)
(duties, office, tasks)
ninmu
任務

(duties, job, work)
shokumu
職務

general affairs department
sōmubu
総務部

general management
sōkatsu kei'eisō
総括経営層
zenpan kei'eisō
全般経営層

general manager
sōshihainin
総支配人

general training
ippanteki kunren
一般的訓練

general union
ippan kumiai
一般組合

get on with people
hito to umaku yatte yuku
人とうまくやって行く

go-getter
yarite
やり手
yashinteki na jinbutsu
野心的な人物

going to the office
shussha
出社

government employee
kōmuin
公務員

grievance
kujō
苦情

grievance committee
kujō shori i'inkai
苦情処理委員会

grievance procedure
kujō shori tetsuzuki
苦情処理手続き

grievance settlement
kujō shori
苦情処理

grievance settlement system
kujō shori seido
苦情処理制度

group chief
kakarichō
係長

group interaction
shūdan sōgo sayō
集団相互作用

group loyalty
shūdan chūseishin
集団忠誠心

group training
shūdan kunren
集団訓練

group unity
danketsu
団結

guarantee of employment
koyō hoshō
雇用保証

guaranteed employment plan
koyō hoshō seido
雇用保証制度

gymnastics[31]
taisō[31]
体操

half-time
hannichi
半日

half-timer
hannichi rōdōsha
半日労働者

handle (verb)
toriatsukau
取扱う

hard worker
hatarakimono
働き者

harmony
shōwa
昭和

hazardous work
kiken na shigoto
危険な仕事

heavy work
[less formal]
chikara shigoto
力仕事

[formal]
jūrōdō
重労働

hierarchy
kei'ei kaisō
経営階層

high morale
takai kinrō iyoku
高い勤労意欲

high performer
sugureta eigyō tantōin
優れた営業担当員

high-quality (staff)
ryōshitsu no
良質の

hired agricultural worker
nōgyō chingin rōdōsha
農業賃金労働者

hired hand
yatoinin
雇い人

hot job
kinkyū shigoto
緊急仕事

human depreciation
ningen no genka
shōkyakuhi
人間の原価償却費

human investment
jinteki tōshi
人的投資

human relations
ningen kankei
人間関係

human relations management
ningen kankei kanri
人間関係管理

human resources
jinteki shigen
人的資源

human skills
jinteki jukuren
人的熟練

human valuation
ningen hyōka
人間評価

human value
jinteki kachi
人的価値

identity with group
ittaikan
一体感

idle
taida na
怠惰な

idleness
taida
怠惰

illegal worker
yami rōdōsha
闇労働者

immigrant worker
imin rōdōsha
移民労働者

import department
yunyūbu
輸入部

import manager
yunyū buchō
輸入部長

in charge of (—)
(—) o tantō shite iru
(—) を担当している

in-house training
shanai kunren
社内訓練

in-house union [J]32
kigyōnai rōdō kumiai32
企業内労働組合

inadequately employed worker
fukanzen shūgyōsha
不完全就業者

incentive
(encouragement, motivation)
shōrei
奨励

(incentive pay)
shōreikin
奨励金

incentive to work
shūgyō shōrei
就業奨励

incompetence
munō
無能

incompetent
jisseki no nai
実績のない
munō na
無能な

increase in efficiency
nōritsu zōshin
能率増進

independent worker
dokuritsu rōdōsha
独立労働者

industrial relations
rōshi kankei
労使関係

industrial relations management
rōshi kankei kanri
労使関係管理

industrial training
sangyō kunren
産業訓練

industrial union
sangyō kumiai
産業組合

industrial worker
sangyō rōdōsha
産業労働者

industrious
kinben na
勤勉な

inefficiency
hinōritsu
非能率

inefficient
hinōritsu na
非能率な

inequality
fubyōdō
不平等

instructor
kōshi
講師

intelligence
chinō
知能
chiryoku
知力

intelligent
chinōteki na
知能的な
zunō na
頭脳な

interaction
sōgo sayō
相互作用

inter-company transfer
jigyōbukan tenkin
事業部門転勤
naibu tenkin
内部転勤

internal training
shanai kunren
社内訓練

international communications department
kokusai kōryūbu
国際交流部

international division
kaigaibu
海外部

inter-relations in the workplace
shokuba ni okeru ningen kankei
職場における人間関係

jack-of-all-trades
nandemoya
何でも屋

job
(task, work)
shigoto
仕事

(occupation, profession)
shokugyō
職業

(function, post)
shokumu
職務

job content
[less formal]
shigoto no naiyō
仕事の内容

[formal]
shokumu naiyō
職務内容

job description
[less formal]
shigoto no naiyō
仕事の内容

(written description)
shokumu kijutsusho
職務記述書

[formal]
shokumu naiyō
職務内容

job dissatisfaction
shigoto ni taisuru no fumanzokukan
仕事に対するの不満足感

job evaluation
shokumu hyōka
職務評価

job holder
teishokusha
定職者

job performing ability
shokunō
職能

job promotion
shokushunai shōshin
職種内昇進

job rating
shokumu hyōka
職務評価

job requirements
shokumu shikaku
職務資格

job retraining
shokugyō saikunren
職業再訓練

job rotation
(personnel rotation)
jinji idō
人事異動

(position rotation)
shokuba haichi tenkan
職場配置転換

job satisfaction
shigoto ni taisuru no manzokukan
仕事に対するの満足感

job security
shigoto antei
仕事安定

job stability
shigoto anteisei
仕事の安定性

job title
shigoto no katagaki
仕事の肩書き

job training
shokugyō kunren
職業訓練

join a company
kaisha ni hairu
会社に入る
nyūsha suru
入社する

junior
kōhai
後輩

junior clerk
kakyū shokuin
下級職員

junior employee
junshain
準社員

junior executive
kakyū kanrisha
下級管理者

key executive
chūshin kei'eisha
中心経営者

key job
kijun shokumu
基準職務

key worker
shuyō rōmusha
主要労務者

knowledge of the job
shokumu chishiki
職務知識

laboratory
kenkyūjo
研究所

labour
kinrō
勤労
rōdō
労働
rōmu
労務

labour agreement
rōdō kyōyaku
労働協約

labour contract
rōdō keiyaku
労働契約

labour control
rōmu kanri
労務管理

labour delegate
rōdō daihyōsha
労働代表者

labour force
rōdōryoku
労働力

labour intensification
rōdō kyōka
労働強化

labour leader
rōdō kumiai shidōsha
労働組合指導者

labour management
rōdō kanri
労働管理
rōmu kanri
労務管理

labour-management
rōshi
労使

labour-management conference system
rōshi kyōgisei
労使協議制

labour-management relations
rōshi kankei
労使関係

labour-management talk
rōshi kyōgi
労使協議

labour official
rōdō kumiai kanbu
労働組合幹部

labour practices
rōdō kankō
労働慣行
rōdō kanshū
労働慣習
rōdō kōi
労働行為

labour relations
rōdō kankei
労働関係

labour relations department
rōmubu
労務部

labour shortage
rōdōryoku fusoku
労働力不足

labour turnover
rōdō idō
労働移動

labour union [US]
rōdō kumiai
労働組合

labourer
rōdōsha
労働者

large-scale staff reshuffle
daikibo na jinji idō
大規模な人事異動

lawyer (company lawyer)
kaisha komon bengoshi
会社顧問弁護士

laziness
taida
怠惰

lazy
taida na
怠惰な

lazy person
namakemono
怠け者

leaving certificate
taishoku shōmeisho
退職証明書

leaving the office
taisha
退社

legal department
hōkibu
法規部

liberal profession
jiyūgyō
自由業

lifetime employment
shūshin koyō
終身雇用

light labour
keirōdō
軽労働

litigation department
hōkibu
法規部

**local labour
(zone)**
chihō rōdō
地方労働

(native)
dochaku rōdō
土着労働

local union
chiku rōdō kumiai
地区労働組合

long hours
chōjikan rōdō
長時間労働

low morale
hikui kinrō iyoku
低い勤労意欲

lower management
kakyū kei'eisō
下級経営層

lower rank
kasō kaikyū
下層階級

lowly occupation
iyashii shokugyō
卑しい職業

loyalty to the company
kaisha ni taisuru chūseishin
会社に対する忠誠心

lunch break
chūshoku jikan
昼食時間

major staff reshuffle
ōkii idō
大きい異動

male employee
danshi jūgyōin
男子従業員

man-hour
hitori ichijikan no shigotoryō
一人一時間の仕事量

management
**(administration, running,
control)**
kanri
管理
kei'ei
経営

(administrators)
kanrisha
管理者
kei'eisha
経営者

(vs. employees)
kei'eishasoku
経営者側

**management training
programme**
kanrisha kunren keikaku
管理者訓練計画

manager
kanrisha
管理者
shihainin
支配人

[UK]
fukushachō
副社長

(section chief)
kachō
課長

managerial position
kanrishoku
管理職

managerial staff
kanrishokuin
管理職員

managing director
jōmu torishimariyaku
常務取締役
senmu torishimariyaku
専務取締役

[UK]
shachō
社長

manpower
(human resources)
jinteki shigen
人的資源

(labour force)
rōdōryoku
労働力

manpower development
jinteki shigen kaihatsu
人的資源開発

manpower management
rōdōryoku kanri
労働力管理

manpower policy
jinteki shigen seisaku
人的資源政策

manpower shortage
jinteki shigen fusoku
人的資源不足
rōdōryoku fusoku
労働力不足

manual labour
kinniku rōdō
筋肉労働
nikutai rōdō
肉体労働
rōmu
労務

manual piecework[33]
naishoku[33]
内職

manual work
kinniku rōdō
筋肉労働
nikutai rōdō
肉体労働
rōmu
労務

manual worker
kinniku rōdōsha
筋肉労働者
nikutai rōdōsha
肉体労働者

marginal employee
genkai hikoyōsha
限界被雇用者

marginal employer
genkai koyōsha
限界雇用者

marginal worker
genkai rōdōsha
限界労働者

marketing department
hanbaibu
販売部

marketing manager
hanbai buchō
販売部長

maximum number of hours
saikō shūgyō jikan
最高就業時間

member of staff
shoin
所員
shokuin
職員

members of the company
kaisha kai'in
会社会員

merit
(worth)
kachi
価値

(work merit)
kōrō
功労

merit rating
jinji kōka
人事考課

merit rating system
jinji kōkasei
人事考課制

merit system
jisseki seido
実績制度

middle management
chūkan kei'eisō
中間経営層

middle management executive
chūkan kanbu
中間幹部

migrant worker
imin rōdōsha
移民労働者

migratory worker
kisetsu rōdōsha
季節労働者

minor executive
kakyū kanbu shokuin
下級幹部職員

minor staff reshuffle
shōidō
小異動

misallocation of labour
ayamatta rōdō haibun
誤った労働配分

monday-morning blues
getsuyōbi no asa no
yūutsubyō
月曜日の朝の憂鬱病

monotonous work
tanchō rōdō
単調労働
tanjun sagyō
単純作業

moonlighting
fukugyō
副業
rinji yakan kinmu
臨時夜間勤務

morale
kinrō iyoku
勤労意欲
shiki
士気

morale survey
shiki chōsa
士気調査

morning assembly[34]
chōrei[34]
朝礼

motivated
yaru ki no aru
やる気のある

motivation
dōki
動機

nameplate
nēmupurēto
ネームプレート

neglect one's duties
shokumu o okotaru
職務を怠る

negligent
zubora na
ずぼらな

new appointment (post)
funin
赴任

new employee
shinnyūshain
新入社員

new post
funin
赴任

newly hired worker
shinki shūgyōsha
新規就業者

night duty
yagyō
夜業
yakan kinmu
夜間勤務
yakin
夜勤

night shift
yagyō
夜業
yakan sagyō
夜間作業
yakin
夜勤

night-shift hours
yakin jikan
夜勤時間

night-shift worker
yakan sagyōin
夜間作業員
yakin rōdōsha
夜勤労働者
yakinsha
夜勤者

night work
yakan kinmu
夜間勤務
yakan shūgyō
夜間就業

non-manual work
zunō rōdō
頭脳労働

non-manual worker
zunō rōdōsha
頭脳労働者

non-productive employee
hiseisanteki jūgyōin
非生産的従業員

non-productive labour
hiseisanteki rōdō
非生産的労働

non-productive worker
hiseisanteki rōdōsha
非生産的労働者

non-union shop
hirōdō kumiai kōjō
非労働組合工場

non-union worker
hikumiai rōdōsha
非組合労働者

notification[35]
jirei[35]
辞令

normal working week
hyōjun rōdōshū
標準労働週

number of days worked
shūgyō nissū
就業日数

number of employees
jūgyōinsū
従業員数

occupation
shokugyō
職業
shokumu
職務

occupational classification
shokumu bunrui
職務分類

occupational groups
shokugyō shūdan
職業集団
shokushu
職種

odd hand
rinjiyatoi
臨時雇い

odd job
rinji shigoto
臨時仕事

off duty (to be)
kinmu ga akeru
勤務が明ける

off-the-job training
shokubagai kunren
職場外訓練

office
(place of work)
jimusho
事務所

(room)
heya
部屋

(department, room)
shitsu
室

(post)
shokumu
職務

office clerk
jimuin
事務員

office code of conduct
shafū
社風

office customs
shafū
社風

office duties
jimu
事務

office force
jimusho zenshokuin
事務所全職員
shoin
所員

office hours
kinmu jikan
勤務時間
shūgyō jikan
就業時間

office management
jimu kanri
事務管理

office manager
jimuchō
事務長

office personnel
jimu shokuin
事務職員
shoin
所員

office politics
shanai no jinmyaku arasoi
社内の人脈争い
shanai no seiji
社内の政治

office regulations
shanai kitei
社内規定

office staff
shoin
所員

office work
jimu
事務

office worker
jimu keitō
事務系統
jimuin
事務員

officer of the company
yakuin
役員

official employment (once the probation period is over)
honsaiyō
本採用

on duty (to be)
kinmuchū de aru
勤務中である

on-the-job training
jitchi kunren
実地訓練
shokubanai kenshū
職場内研修
shokubanai kunren
職場内訓練

one-job skill
tannō jukuren
単能熟練

open-plan office
ōbeya
大部屋

open union
kōkai kumiai
公開組合

operative
genba shokuin
現場職員
kōin
工具

organization
soshiki
組織

organization chart
kaisha kikōzu
会社機構図

organizational ability
soshiki nōryoku
組織能力

organized labour
soshiki rōdōsha
組織労働者

organized worker
soshiki rōdōsha
組織労働者

orientation
orientēshon
オリエンテーション

output
seisandaka
生産高

overall efficiency
sōgō nōritsu
総合能率
zenkōritsu
全効率

overseas assignment
kaigai kinmu
海外勤務

overtime work
zangyō
残業

(extra work)
chōka kinmu
超過勤務

(out-of-hours work)
jikangai rōdō
時間外労働

overwork (noun)
kajū rōdō
過重労働
yobun no shigoto
余分の仕事

overwork (verb)
kado ni hataraku
過度に働く

part-time
hijōkin no
非常勤の
pāto-taimu
パート・タイム

part-time director
hijōkin jūyaku
非常勤重役

part-time employee
hijōkin kinmusha
非常勤勤務者

part-time work
pāto-taimu-wāku
パート・タイム・
ワーク

(students)
arubaito
アルバイト

part-time worker
hijōkin rōdōsha
非常勤労働者

part-timer
pāto-taimā
パート・タイマー

passive
shōkyokuteki na
消極的な

paternalism
kazoku shugi
家族主義
onjō shugi
温情主義

paternalistic
kazoku shugiteki na
家族主義的な
onjō shugiteki na
温情主義的な

performance
(achievements,
contributions, results)
gyōseki
業績

(actual results, record of
achievement)
jisseki
実績

(merit, results)
seiseki
成績

(execution)
suikō
遂行

performance assessment
shokunō kōka
職能孝果

performance of duties
shigoto no suikō
仕事の遂行
shokumu no suikō
職務の遂行

performance of duty
sekinin no suikō
責任の遂行

performance rating
kōka
孝課
shokunō kōka
職能孝課

period of employment
koyō kikan
雇用期間

periodic job rotation
teikiteki na jinji idō
定期的な人事異動

permanent employee
shūshin yatoinin
終身雇い人

permanent employment
shūshin koyō
終身雇用

person in charge
kakari
係
tantōsha
担当者

personnel
jin'in
人員
shokuin
職員

personnel administration
jinji kanri
人事管理

personnel affairs
jinji
人事

personnel changes
jinji no henkō
人事の変更

personnel composition
jin'in kōsei
人員構成

personnel cuts
jin'in sakugen
人員削減
jin'in seiri
人員整理

personnel department
jinjibu
人事部

personnel evaluation
jinji hyōka
人事評価

personnel interchange
jinji kōryū
人事交流

personnel management
jinji kanri
人事管理

personnel manager
jinji kanrisha
人事管理者
jinji tantō jūyaku
人事担当重役

personnel rating
jinji kōka
人事孝課

personnel records
jinji kiroku
人事記録

personnel reduction
jin'in sakugen
人員削減
jin'in seiri
人員整理

personnel reshuffle
jinji idō
人事異動

personnel review
jinji kōka
人事孝課

personnel structure
jinji soshiki
人事組織

physical work
nikutai rōdō
肉体労働

piece work
chinshigoto
賃仕事
dekidakabarai no shigoto
出来高払いの仕事

piece worker
chinshigotonin
賃仕事人
dekidakabarai shokunin
出来高払職人

planning department
kikakubu
企画部

plant manager
kōjōcho
工場長

position
(status, office, post)
chii
地位

(job, work)
shoku
職

(opening; position)
tsutomeguchi
勤め口

positive
sekkyokuteki na
積極的な

post
posuto
ポスト

(status, office)
chii
地位

(place of appointment)
ninchi
任地

posted (to be)
funin suru
赴任する

posted abroad (to be)
chūzai suru
駐在する

PR (public relations)
dairi
代理
piiāru
ピーアール

practical experience
jitchi keiken
実地経験

practical on-the-job training
jitchi kenshū
実地研修

president [US]
shachō
社長

private office
kojin'yō no ofisu
個人用のオフィス

probation period
shiyō kikan
試用期間

procurement department
chōtatsubu
調達部

procurement manager
chōtatsu buchō
調達部長

product development office
shōhin kaihatsu shitsu
商品開発室

production control department
seisan kanribu
生産管理部

production department
seizōbu
製造部

productive
seisanteki na
生産的な

productive employee
seisanteki jūgyōin
生産的従業員

productive labour
seisanteki rōdōryoku
生産的労働力

productive worker
seisanteki rōdōsha
生産的労働者

productivity
seisansei
生産性

productivity clause
seisansei jōkō
遺産性条項

productivity deal
seisansei kyōyaku
生産性協約

productivity drive
seisansei kōjō undō
生産性向上運動

productivity of labour
rōdō seisansei
労働生産性

profession
shokugyō
職業

professional (noun)
chiteki shokugyōka
知的職業家

professional employee
senmonka shokuin
専門家職員

professional job
senmonshoku
専門職

professionalism
puro konjō
プロ根性

promoted to (—)
(—) o noboru
(—) を昇る

promotion
shōshin
昇進

promotion by seniority
nenkōjoretsusei no shōshin
年功序列性の昇進

promotion ladder
hashigo
梯子

promotion opportunities
shōshin no kikai
昇進の機会

promotion race
kaisha no shussekaidō
会社の出世街道

prospects
(hope, promise)
mikomi
見込み

(future possibilities)
shōraisei
将来性

public affairs department
kōhōshitsu
広報室

public employee
kōmuin
公務員

public relations (PR)
dairi
代理
piiāru
ピーアール

public relations department
dairibu
代理部
kōhōbu
広報部

public relations work
senden katsudō
宣伝活動

purchasing department
kōbaibu
購買部

purchasing manager
kōbai shunin
購買主任

qualified instructor
shikaku no aru kōshi
資格のある講師

racial discrimination
jinshu sabetsu
人種差別

rank
kaikyū
階級

rank and file
ippan jūgyōin
一般従業員

ranking
junjozuke
順序付け

rapport
itchi kyōryoku
一致協力

rationalization
jin'in seiri
人員整理

re-assignment
haiten
配転
idō
異動

receptionist
uketsuke
受付け

recognition (official acknowledgement)
hyōshō
表彰

reduced hours
tanshuku jikan
短縮時間

reduction in working hours
rōdō jikan no tanshuku
労働時間の短縮
rōdō jikansū no genshō
労働時間数の減少

regional manager
chihō shitenchō
地方支店長

regular employee
jōji jūgyōsha
常時従業者
seiki no shain
正規の社員

regular employment
jōyō koyō
常用雇用

regular worker
jōyō rōdōsha
常用労働者

rehire (verb)
saikoyō suru
再雇用する

rehiring
saikoyō
再雇用

remunerative work
rieki no aru shigoto
利益のある仕事

representative director
daihyō torishimariyaku
代表取締役

request for transfer
tennin negai
転任願い

research department
kenkyūshitsu
研究室

reshuffle
jinji idō
人事異動

responsibilities
ninmu
任務
sekinin han'i
責任範囲

responsibility (duties)
gimu
義務

(liability)
sekinin
責任

retrain
saikunren suru
再訓練する

retraining
saikunren
再訓練

right-hand man[36]
futokorogatana[36]
懐刀

right to work
rōdōken
労働権

routine work
kimari kitta shigoto
きまり切った仕事

sales and marketing department
eigyōbu
営業部
hanbaibu
販売部

sales department
eigyōbu
営業部
hanbaibu
販売部

sales force
eigyō hanbairyoku
営業販売力

salesman
hanbaigakari
販売係
sērusuman
セールスマン

satisfaction
manzoku
満足

satisfied
manzoku ga aru
満足がある

seasonal employment
kisetsu koyō
季節雇用

seasonal labour
kisetsu rōdō
季節労働

seasonal labourer
kisetsu rōdōsha
季節労働者

seasonal migrant labour
kisetsu ryūnyū rōdōryoku
季節流入労働力

seasonal migration
kisetsu imin
季節移民

seasonal work
kisetsu rōdō
季節労働

seasonal worker
kisetsu rōdōsha
季節労働者

secretarial office
hishoshitsu
秘書室

secretary
hisho
秘書

section
ka
課

section chief
kachō
課長

sedentary occupation
ijoku
居職

selective employment
sentaku koyō
選択雇用

self-employed (to be)
jiei suru
自営する

self-employed person
jieigyōsha
自営業者

self-employment
jieigyō
自営業
jiko koyō
自己雇用

semi-skilled labour
hanjukuren rōdō
半熟練労働

semi-skilled labour force
hanjukuren rōdōryoku
半熟練労働力

semi-skilled work
hanjukuren rōdō
半熟練労働

semi-skilled worker
hanjukuren rōdōsha
半熟練労働者
hanjukurenkō
半熟練工

semi-skilled workforce
hanjukuren rōdōryoku
半熟練労働力

senior
senpai
先輩

senior executive
jōkyū kanrisha
上級管理者

senior executive director
senmu torishimariyaku
専務取締役

senior management
jōkyū kei'eisō
上級経営層

senior managing director
senmu torishimariyaku
専務取締役

senior vice-president [US]
fukushachō
副社長

seniority
(long service)
nenkō
年功

(ranking)
senninjun
専任順

(right)
senninken
専任権

seniority-based promotion system
nenkōjoretsusei
年功序列制

seniority-conscious
nenkōjoretsu no ishiki
年功序列の意識

seniority practices
nenkōjoretsusei
年功序列制

seniority system
nenkōjoretsu seido
年功序列制度

sent abroad (to be)
kaigai ni haken sareru
海外に派遣される

separate office
betsu na heya
別な部屋

separation of functions
shokunō bunri
職能分離

sex discrimination
seisabetsu
性差別

sexual harassment
seiteki iyagarase
性的いやがらせ

sharp person
kiremono
切れ者

shift
kōtai
交替

shift operations
kōtai sagyō
交替作業

shift system
kōtaisei
交替制

shop assistant [UK]
ten'in
店員

shop committee
shokuba i'inkai
職場委員会

shop-floor worker
genba shokuin
現場職員

shop steward
shokuba daihyōsha
職場代表者

shop worker
ten'in
店員

side job
fukugyō
副業

sideline
fukugyō
副業
naishoku (see note 33)
内職

sign in and out
shussha taisha o kinyū suru
出社退社を記入する

simple work
tanjun rōdō
単純労働

site supervisor
genba kantoku
現場監督

six-month trial period
rokkagetsu no shiyō kikan
6か月の試用期間

skilled labour
jukuren rōdō
熟練労働

skilled labour force
jukuren rōdōryoku
熟練労働力

skilled work
jukuren rōdō
熟練労働

skilled worker
jukuren rōdōsha
熟練労働者
jukurenkō
熟練工

skilled workforce
jukuren rōdōryoku
熟練労働力

slave driver
mugoi yatoinushi
惨い雇い主

specialist
senmonka
専門家

speciality [UK]
senmon
専門

specialization
senmonka
専門化

specialty [US]
senmon
専門

stability of employment
koyō antei
雇用安定

stable
antei no
安定の

stable labour force
antei rōdōryoku
安定労働力

staff
jin'in
人員
shoin
所員
shokuin
職員
sutaffu
スタッフ

staff organization
shokusei
職制
sutaffu soshiki
スタッフ組織

staff re-assignment
jinji idō
人事異動

staff reshuffle
jinji idō
人事異動

**staff training
(manual, technical)**
shain kunren
社員訓練

**(young recruits' general
training)**
shain kyōiku
社員教育

staggered work schedule
jisa shukkin
時差出勤

standard weekly hours
hyōjun rōdōshū jikan
標準労働週時間

standard working hours
hyōjun rōdō jikan
標準労働時間

standard working week
hyōjun rōdōshū
標準労働週

start a new job
atarashii shigoto o hajimeru
新しい仕事を始める

stepping-stone (job)
koshikake
腰掛け

stop-gap job
koshikake
腰掛け

store clerk [US]
ten'in
店員

stress
sutoresu
ストレス

subordinate (noun)
buka
部下

subordinate post
kakyūshoku
下級職

successor
kōnin(sha)
後任(者)

suitable employment
tekishoku
適職

superior
jōshi
上司

**supervision
(control)**
kanri
管理

(overseeing)
kantoku
監督

(guidance)
shidō
指導

**supervisor
(overseer,
superintendent)**
kantokusha
監督者

(instructor, adviser)
shidōin
指導員

supervisory position
kantokusha no chii
監督者の地位

supervisory staff
kanri shokuin
管理職員
kantoku shokuin
監督職員

supervisory training
kantokusha kunren
監督者訓練

support staff
shomugakari
庶務係

support work
shomu
庶務

surplus staff
yojō jin'in
余剰人員

surplus workforce
kajō rōdōryoku
過剰労働力

sweat-shop
sakushu kōjō
搾取工場

sweated labour
kukan rōdōsha
苦汗労働者
sakushu rōdōsha
搾取労働者

task
ninmu
任務
shigoto
仕事
shokumu
職務
tasuku
タスク

technical training
gijutsu kunren
技術訓練

temperament
hada
肌

temporary employee (temp)
rinji jūgyōin
臨時従業員

temporary employment (temping)
ichiji koyō
一時雇用
rinji yatoi
臨時雇い

temporary job
rinji shigoto
臨時仕事

temporary work
ichiji no shigoto
一時の仕事

tenacious
konjō ga aru
根性がある

tenacity
konjō
根性

termination of contract
keiyaku shūketsu
契約終結

terms of employment
koyō jōken
雇用条件

time work
jikanbarai shigoto
時間払仕事
jikankyū rōdō
時間給労働

time worker
jikankyū rōdōsha
時間給労働者

title
katagaki
肩書き

'title-less' staff [J]
hirashain
平社員

top executive
saikō kei'eisha
最高経営者

top job
(top notch job)
ichiryū no shokugyō
一流の職業

(key job)
shuyō posuto
主要ポスト

top management
saikō kei'eisō
最高経営層

total workforce
zenrōdōsha
全労働者

trade-union [UK]
kumiai (see note 22)
組合
rōdō kumiai
労働組合

trade-union activities
kumiai katsudō
組合活動
kumiai undō
組合運動

trade-union leader
kumiai shidōsha
組合指導者

trade-union member
kumiai'in (see note 21)
組合員

trade-union membership (affiliation)
kumiai kamei
組合加盟

(number of members)
kumiai'insū
組合員数

trade-union official
kumiai kanbu
組合幹部
kumiai yakuin
組合役員

trade-unionist
rōdō kumiai'in
労働組合員

train (verb)
kunren suru
訓練する

trainee
kenshūsei
研修生

(apprentice)
jisshūsei
実習生

[less formal]
(student apprentice)
minaraisei
見習生

training
kunren
訓練

(practical training)
jisshū
実習

(study)
kenshū
研修

(general training for young recruits)
kyōiku
教育

(study and training)
renshū
練習

training period
kunren kikan
訓練期間

training programme
kunren keikaku
訓練計画

training scheme
kunren keikaku
訓練計画

transfer
tenkin
転勤
tennin
転任

transfer request
tennin negai
転任願い

transferred to (—)
(—) ni tenkin suru
(—) に転勤する

travelling salesman
gyōshōnin
行商人

treasurer
zaimu buchō
財務部長

trial period
shiyō kikan
試用期間

trouble-maker
mondai o okosu jūgyōin
問題を起こす従業員

two shifts
nikōtaisei
二交替制

typist
taipisuto
タイピスト

undermanned
jin'in fusoku no
人員不足の

unemployed skills
ginō no mochigusare
技能の持ちぐされ

unexcused absence
mutodoke kekkin
無届欠勤

unfair labour practices
futō rōdō kōi
不当労働行為

uniform
seifuku
制服

union (see note 22)
kumiai (see note 22)
組合

union activities
kumiai katsudō
組合活動

union card
kumiai'inshō
組合員証

union charter
kumiai kiyaku
組合規約

union contract
kumiai kiyaku
組合規約

union dues
kumiaihi
組合費

union executive
kumiai yakuin
組合役員

union fund
kumiai kikin
組合基金

union leader
kumiai shidōsha
組合指導者

union member
kumiai'in
組合員

union membership (affiliation)
kumiai kamei
組合加盟

(number of members)
kumiai'insū
組合員数

union official
kumiai kanbu
組合幹部
kumiai yakuin
組合役員

union organizer
kumiai orugu
組合オルグ

union representative
kumiai daihyōsha
組合代表者

union shop
yunion-shoppu
ユニオン・ショップ

unionize
kumiai o soshiki suru
組合を組織する

unionized labour force
rōdō kumiai kamei
rōdōryoku
労働組合加盟労働力

unneeded workers
yojō jin'in
余剰人員

unorganized labour force
misoshiki rōdōryoku
未組織労働力

unorganized workers
misoshiki rōdōsha
未組織労働者

unproductive
fuseisanteki na
不生産的な

unproductive employee
fuseisanteki jūgyōin
不生産的従業員

unproductive labour
fuseisanteki rōdōryoku
不生産的労働力

unproductive worker
fuseisanteki rōdōsha
不生産的労働者

unscheduled hours worked
shoteigai rōdō jikan
所定外労働時間

unskilled labour
mijukuren rōdō
未熟練労働
tanjun rōdō
単純労働

unskilled labour force
mijukuren rōdōryoku
未熟練労働力

unskilled labourer
mijukuren rōdōsha
未熟練労働者
mijukurenkō
未熟練工

unskilled occupation
jukuren fuyō no shigoto
熟練不要の仕事

unskilled work
mijukuren rōdō
未熟練労働
tanjun rōdō
単純労働

unskilled worker
mijukuren rōdōsha
未熟練労働者
mijukurenkō
未熟練工

unskilled workforce
mijukuren rōdōryoku
未熟練労働力

unstable employment
fuantei koyō
不安定雇用

unsuitable work
hada ni awasenai shigoto
肌に合わせない仕事

untrained
[formal]
fujukuren no
不熟練の
[less formal]
jukuren shite inai
熟練していない
kunren sarete inai
訓練されていない

untrained labour
fujukurenkō
不熟練工

untrained worker
fujukurenkō
不熟練工

vacation of office
jishoku
辞職

vice-president [US]
fukushachō
副社長

warning
keikoku
警告

white-collar worker
seishin rōdōsha
精神労働者
zunō rōdōsha
頭脳労働者

willingness to work
kinrō iyoku
勤労意欲
rōdō iyoku
労働意欲

'woman's work'
fujin rōdō
婦人労働

work (noun)
kinmu
勤務

(labour)
rōdō
労働

(job of work, task)
shigoto
仕事

work (verb)
hataraku
働く

work attitude
kinmu taido
勤務態度

work committee
shokuba i'inkai
職場委員会

work council
(factories)
kōjō kyōgikai
工場協議会

(employer and
employees)
rōshi kyōgikai
労使協議会

work day
kinmuhi
勤務日
rōdōhi
労働日
shūgyōhi
就業日

work for (—)
(—) ni tsutomete iru
(—) に勤めている

work habits
shigoto no yarikata
仕事のやり方

work incentive
shūgyō shōrei
就業奨励

work incentive programme
shūgyō shōrei keikaku
就業奨励計画

work load
shigotoryō
仕事量

work permit
rōdō kyoka
労働許可

work regulations
shūgyō kisoku
就業規則

work-sharing
gappeishoku
合併職

work volume
jimuryō
事務量
shigotoryō
仕事量

work week
rōdōshū
労働週

workaholic
hataraki chūdoku
働き中毒

worker
rōdōsha
労働者

workers' co-operatives
rōdōsha kyōdōtai
労働者共同体

workers' participation in management
rōdōsha no kei'ei sanka
労働者の経営参加

workers' union
jūgyōin kumiai
従業員組合

workforce
rōdōryoku
労働力

working committee
un'ei i'inkai
運営委員会

working conditions
kinmu jōken
勤務条件
rōdō jōken
労働条件

working environment [formal]
sagyō kankyō
作業環境

[less formal]
shigoto no kankyō
仕事の環境

working hours
kinmu jikan
勤務時間
rōdō jikan
労働時間
shūgyō jikan
就業時間

working week
shūrōdō jikan
週労働時間

workman
kōin
工員

workplace (office, place of employment)
kinmusaki
勤務先

(office, working place)
shigotoba
仕事場

(post)
shokuba
職場

workshop
kōba
工場
shigotoba
仕事場

worth
kachi
価値

years of service
kinmu nensū
勤務年数

Notes

27. company employee (shain 社員): 'shain' can also mean 'partner'.

28. corporate anthem (shaka 社歌): the company anthem is sung by the employees of large Japanese corporations before starting the day's work or on certain occasions, such as the anniversary of the founding of the company, to promote company spirit and a feeling of corporate identity among the workforce.

29. demotion (sasen 左遷): 'sasen' can also be the transfer of an employee to a regional office without his rank actually being lowered.

30. employee transferred to another branch or company (shukkō shain 出向社員): it sometimes happens that an employee is 'on loan' from one company to another or from one branch of the company to another. Although this is a temporary transfer and the employee is expected to return to his original place of employ, he may however decide to remain in the new branch or company until retirement.

31. gymnastics (taisō 体操): limbering-up exercises carried out in Japanese corporations at certain times of the day by the workforce.

32. in-house union (kigyōnai rōdō kumiai 企業内労働組合): an in-house – or in-company – union organized within each Japanese corporation and run by full-time officials who have their own offices in the company building. Although these officials are on the company payroll, they are independent and act on behalf of all the company employees regardless of the management's policies. It is the basic unit of trade-union organization in Japan.

33. manual piecework (naishoku 内職): the work done by Japanese housewives at home.

34. morning assembly (chōrei 朝礼): a brief talk given by a supervisor to his section employees before starting the work day or week to encourage the right work attitude and enhance group identity.

35. notification (jirei 辞令): 'jirei' is the official letter issued by the personnel department of a Japanese company announcing the hiring, re-assignment, transfer, promotion, dismissal or retirement of employees.

36. right-hand man (futokorogatana 懐刀): the 'futokorogatana', a dagger carried close to the body and used in feudal Japan for the 'seppuku' 切腹 (better known as 'harakiri' 腹切り) ritual to defend one's honour, has come to mean someone close to a person of authority and who can be relied upon to uphold that person's interests.

Additional expressions

dōki 同期 ('same class') is a term applied to employees recruited at the same time by the company they are working for.

dokushin kizoku 独身貴族 ('the unmarried aristocracy') is the name given by married company employees to young single colleagues who do not have the responsibility of a family and can enjoy their salaries and leisure time freely.

dosamawari どさ回り ('touring the provinces') is usually applied to a theatrical group on tour in the provinces, but in a business context it describes the successive re-assignments of a company employee from one regional office of the company to another. Very often such a person has very little hope of ever getting back to the head-office.

gebahyō 下馬評 ('getting-off-the-horse comment') dates back to feudal Japan when retainers would dismount their horses outside a castle and exchange gossip or speculate about personnel changes in the government. When used in a modern business context, 'gebahyō' means rumours or idle speculation about forthcoming personnel changes in a company.

haenuki 生え抜き ('born and bred') describes an employee who was recruited straight out of university and who has stayed on with the same company.

hiyameshikui 冷飯食い ('cold rice eaters') are employees kept in unduly low positions without necessarily deserving such treatment.

kissui 生粋 ('pure', 'trueborn', 'genuine') is an employee recruited straight out of university who has stayed not only in the same company but also in the same occupational group.

kogai 子飼い ('raising a pet animal') refers to a loyal and trusted employee who enjoys the protection of the superior under whom he has served since he joined the company.

miyako ochi 都落ち ('leaving the capital') refers to the transfer of an employee from the Tokyo head-office to a regional office.

nurumayu ぬるま湯 ('tepid water') applies to an employee who is quite content with a 'tepid' job and who has no ambition to achieve a 'hotter', more stimulating position.

shimanagashi 島流し ('banishment to an island') has a similar meaning to 'miyako ochi' but emphasizes the feelings of punishment and loneliness.

tanshin funin 単身赴任 ('business bachelor') is a Japanese male employee posted away from home and whose family has to remain behind.

tenkin no aisatsu 転勤の挨拶 ('paying one's respects upon transferral') is the round of courtesy calls made by the transferred employee to business contacts to thank them for their co-operation and to introduce his successor.

tobasu 飛ばす ('to let fly', 'to send flying') is to transfer an employee to an isolated branch office.

tozama 外様 ('outsider') was the name given to a retainer entering a feudal lord's service half-way through his adult life rather than as a child trainee. It is now used to describe an employee who worked for another company before joining his current one.

uchi 内 ('inside', 'home') is the keyword expressing the Japanese sense of group identity and solidarity. 'Uchi' is used in the expression 'uchi no kaisha' 内の会社 meaning 'my' or 'our' company.

across-the-board pay rise
issei no shōkyū
一斉の昇給

adjusted earned income
chōseizumi kinrō shotoku
調整済勤労所得

advance on salary
kyūryō maebarai
給料前払い

after-tax income
zeibiki shotoku
税引所得

agricultural wages
nōgyō chingin
農業賃金

allowable tax deductions
seitō na zeikōjo
正当な税控除

**allowance
(compensation)**
hōshū
報酬

(perquisite)
teate
手当

allowance for long service
nenkō kahō
年功加俸

allowance for surviving family
izoku teate
遺族手当

amount deducted
kōjogaku
控除額

annual allowance
nenkan teate
年間手当

annual income
nenkan shotoku
年間所得
nenshū
年収

annual leave
nenji kyūka
年次休暇

annual-leave request form
nenji kyūka negai
年次休暇願い

annual paid holidays
yūkyū kyūka
有給休暇

annual wage agreement
nenkan chingin kyōtei
年間賃金協定

annual wages
nenkan chingin
年間賃金

area allowance
kinmuchi teate
勤務地手当

attached hospital [J]
fuzoku byōin
付属病院

attendance fee
shuttō teate
出頭手当

attendance money
shuttō teate
出頭手当

average wage(s)
heikin chingin
平均賃金

average weekly earnings
shūatari heikin shūnyū
週当たり平均収入

average yearly earnings
nenkan heikin shūnyū
年間平均収入

bachelor dormitories [J]
tanshinryō
単身寮

bargaining
kōshō
交渉

base rate
bēsu-rēto
ベース・レート

base wage
kihon chingin
基本賃金

base-wage increase
bēsu-appu
ベース・アップ

basic pay
kihonkyū
基本給

basic salary
kihonkyū
基本給

basic wage
kihon chingin
基本賃金

basic wage rate
kihon chinginritsu
基本賃金率

benefits
kyūfu
給付

before-tax income
zeikomi shotoku
税込所得

bonus
bōnasu
ボーナス
shōyo(kin)
賞与(金)

break (rest)
burēki
ブレーキ
kyūkei
休憩
yasumi
休み

cafeteria
shain shokudō
社員食堂
shokudō
食堂

call-back pay
kōrubakku-pei
コールバック・ペイ

Christmas bonus
kurisumasu-bōnasu
クリスマス・ボーナス

collective agreement
dantai kyōyaku
団体協約
shūdan kyōyaku
集団協約

collective bargaining
dantai kōshō
団体交渉

commuting allowance
tsūkin teate
通勤手当

commuting expenses
tsūkinhi
通勤費

company dormitories [J]
kaisha no ryō
会社の寮
shainryō
社員寮

company housing
shataku
社宅

company responsibility
kaisha no futan
会社の負担

company-sponsored
kaisha enjo no
会社援助の
kaisha futan no
会社負担の

compensation
kyūyo
給与

contracted wage
keiyaku chingin
契約賃金

contractual wages
keiyaku chingin
契約賃金
kyōtei chingin
協定賃金

contributions (deductions)
tenbiki
天引き

cost-of-living allowance
seikeihi teate
生計費手当

cultural-entertainment expenses
kyōyō gorakuhi
教養娯楽費

current wages
genkō chingin
現行賃金

daily allowance
nittō
日当

daily wage
nikkyū
日給

(daily pay, payment per diem)
nittō
日当

danger allowance
kiken teate
危険手当

day-care centre
ho'ikuen
保育園
ho'ikujo
保育所

day off
kyūjitsu
休日

deduct
tenbiki suru
天引きする

deductions
(deductions from wages)
chingin kōjo
賃金控除

(withholding)
tenbiki
天引き

dependents allowance (allowance) [J]
fuyō kazoku teate
扶養家族手当

(tax deduction)
fuyō kōjo
扶養控除

direct credit system for payroll
jidō furikomi seido
自動振込制度

director's bonus
yakuin shōyo
役員賞与

director's fee
yakuin teate
役員手当

director's remuneration
yakuin hōshū
役員報酬

dormitory
(kaisha no) ryō
(会社の) 寮

dormitory fee deduction [J]
ryōhi
寮費

double taxation
nijū kazei
二重課税

earn a living
seikeihi o eru
生計費を得る

earned income
kinrō shotoku
勤労所得

earnings
shūnyū
収入

(income)
shotoku
所得

efficiency wages
nōritsu chingin
能率賃金

employee benefit fund
jūgyōin fukuri shikin
従業員福利資金

employee benefit plan
jūgyōin fukuri seido
従業員福利制度

employee benefits
jūgyōin kyūfu
従業員給付

employee counselling
jūgyōin sōdan seido
従業員相談制度

employee saving [J]
jūgyōin chochiku
従業員貯蓄

employee saving association [J]
jūgyōin chochiku kumiai
従業員貯蓄組合

employee stock-ownership plan
jūgyōin mochikabu seido
従業員持株制度

employee welfare
jūgyōin fukuri
従業員福利

employee welfare facilities
jūgyōin fukushi shisetsu
従業員福祉施設

employee welfare fund
jūgyōin fukushi kōsei kikin
従業員福祉厚生基金

employee welfare programme
jūgyōin fukuri seido
従業員福利制度

end-of-year bonus
nenmatsu no bōnasu
年末のボーナス
nenmatsu shōyo
年末賞与

equal pay
dōitsu chingin
同一賃金
dōitsu kyūyo
同一給与

equal pay for equal work
dōitsu rōdō dōitsu chingin
同一労働同一賃金

executive dining-room
yakuin shokudō
役員食堂

extra-curricular activities
kinmujikango no katsudō
勤務時間後の活動

extra pay
warimashi chingin
割増賃金

extra wage
warimashi chingin
割増賃金
kakyūkin
加給金

fair wages
kōsei chingin
公正賃金

family allowance [J]
kazoku teate
家族手当

family housing [J]
shataku
社宅

fat paycheck
tagaku no kyūryō
多額の給料

five-figure income
goketa no shūnyū
5桁の収入

fixed salary
koteikyū
固定給

fixed wage
koteikyū
固定給

flexible money wage policy
shinshukuteki kahei chingin seisaku
伸縮的貨幣賃金政策

flexible money wages
shinshukuteki kahei chingin
伸縮的貨幣賃金

flexible wage policy
shinshukuteki chingin seisaku
伸縮的賃金政策

flexible wage rate
shinshukuteki chinginritsu
伸縮的賃金率

freeze salaries
chingin o tōketsu suru
賃金を凍結する

fringe benefits
fuka kyūfu
付加給付
futai kyūfu
付帯給付

full pay
zengaku kyūyo
全額給与
zenkyū
全給

going wages
genkō chingin
現行賃金

good pay
yoi kyūyo
よい給与

gross earnings
sōshūnyū
総収入

gross hourly earnings
jikan atari sōshūnyū
時間当たり総収入

gross income
sōshotoku
総所得

gross monthly earnings
gekkan sōshūnyū
月間総収入

gross pay
zeikomi kyūyo
税込給与

gross weekly earnings
shūatari sōshūnyū
週当たり総収入

gross yearly earnings
nenkan sōshūnyū
年間総収入

group annuity
dantai nenkin
団体年金

group endowment insurance
dantai yōrō hoken
団体養老保険

group health insurance
dantai kenkō hoken
団体健康保険

group health plan
dantai kenkō hoken seido
団体健康保険制度

group hospital expense insurance
dantai nyūinhi hoken
団体入院費保険

group hospitalization insurance
dantai nyūin hoken
団体入院保険

group insurance
dantai hoken
団体保険

group life insurance
dantai seimei hoken
団体生命保険

group medical expense insurance
dantai iryōhi hoken
団体医療費保険

group pension
dantai nenkin
団体年金

group permanent insurance
dantai chōki hoken
団体長期保険
dantai shūshin hoken
団体終身保険

guaranteed annual wage
hoshō nenkan chingin
保証年間賃金

guaranteed minimum wage
saitei hoshō chingin
最低保証賃金

guaranteed wages
hoshō chingin
保証賃金

guaranteed wages plan
chingin hoshōsei
賃金保証制

half pay
hankyū
半給

handsome salary
kanari no kyūryō
かなりの給料

hazard bonus
kiken teate
危険手当

health facilities
kenkō shisetsu
健康施設

health insurance
kenkō hoken
健康保険

health-insurance card
kenkō hokenshō
健康保険証

health-insurance deduction
kenkō hokenryō
健康保険料

high income
kōgaku shotoku
高額所得
kōshotoku
高所得

high-income bracket
kōshotokusō
高所得層

high salary
kōkyū
高給

high wages
kōchingin
高賃金

holiday(s)
kyūka
休暇

[less formal]
yasumi
休み

holiday-studded period
renkyū
連休

holiday with pay
yūkyū kyūka
有給休暇

hourly earnings
jikan atari shūnyū
時間当たり収入
jikanshū
時間収

hourly wage(s)
jikan atari chingin
時間当たり賃金
jikan atari kyūyo
時間当たり給与
jikankyū
時間給

hours worked
jitsudō jikan
実働時間

housing allowance
jūkyo teate
住居手当
jūtaku teate
住宅手当

housing rental fee deduction [J]
shataku no yachin
社宅の家賃

illness
byōki
病気

in-house infirmary
naibu no shinryōjo
内部の診療所

incentive pay
shōreikin
奨励金

incentive wage
shōrei chingin
奨励賃金

incentive wage system
shōrei chinginsei
奨励賃金制

income
shotoku
所得

(earnings)
shūnyū
収入

income after tax
zeibiki shotoku
税引所得

income before tax
zeikomi shotoku
税込所得

income bracket
shotoku kaisō
所得階層
shotokusō
所得層

income from work
kinrō shotoku
勤労所得

income level
shotoku suijun
所得水準

income tax
shotokuzei
所得税

income tax filing deadline
shotokuzei shinkoku
shimekiri kijitsu
所得税申告締切期日

income tax rate
shotokuzeiritsu
所得税率

income tax return
shotokuzei shinkoku
所得税申告

(form)
shotokuzei shinkokusho
所得税申告書

income tax schedule
shotokuzeihyō
所得税表

income tax withheld at source
gensen shotokuzei
源泉所得税

increase in salary
shōkyū
昇給

increase in wages
chin'age
賃上げ
chingin jōshō
賃金上昇

increment
zōka
増加

index-linked minimum wage
infuremiai no saitei chingin
インフレ見合いの
最低賃金

individual bargaining
kojin kōshō
個人交渉

individual income tax
kojin shotokuzei
個人所得税

individual bargaining
kojin kōshō
個人交渉

individual income tax
kojin shotokuzei
個人所得税

industry-wide bargaining
sangyōbetsu dankō
産業別団交

inequality of salary
chingin no fubyōdō
賃金の不平等

inflation-compensating pay rise
infuremiai no chin'age
インフレ見合いの
賃上げ

initial salary
shoninkyū
初任給

insurance
hoken
保険

job wage
shokumukyū
職務給

just wage(s)
kōsei chingin
公正賃金

legal minimum wage
hōtei saitei chingin
法定最低賃金

living wage
seikatsu chingin
生活賃金

low basic pay
yasui kihonkyū
やすい基本給

low income
teishotoku
低所得

low-income bracket
teishotokusō
低所得層

low-paid worker
teichingin rōdōsha
低賃金労働者

low wages
teichingin
低賃金

lower and medium income groups
chūtei shotokusō
中低所得層

luncheon vouchers
chūshokuken
昼食券
shokuken
食券

maternity benefits
shussan kyūfu
出産給付

maternity leave
sankyū
産休
shussan kyūka
出産休暇

maternity-leave request
shussan kyūka negai
出産休暇願い

maximum wage
saikō chingin
最高賃金

maximum wage increase
saikō chin'age
最高賃上げ

medical attention
shinsatsu
診察

medical benefits
iryō kyūfu
医療給付

medical care
iryō
医療

medical check-up
kenkō shindan
健康診断

medical examination
kenkō shindan
健康診断

medical expenses
iryōhi
医療費

medical insurance
iryō hoken
医療保険

menstrual leave [J]
seiri kyūka
生理休暇

merit bonus
kōrō shōyo
功労賞与

middle-income bracket
chūshotokusō
中所得層

minimum guaranteed rate
saitei hoshō chinginritsu
最低保証賃金率

minimum wage
saitei chingin
最低賃金

minimum wage rate
saitei chinginritsu
最低賃金率

moderate raise
yuruyaka na shōkyū
緩やかな昇給

moderate wage
teichingin
低賃金

money wage
genkin chingin
現金賃金
kahei chingin
貨幣賃金

monthly pay
gekkyū
月給

monthly pay packet
gekkyūbukuro
月給袋

monthly payroll sheet
getsuji chingin kyūryō
keisansho
月次賃金給料計算書

monthly salary
gekkyū
月給

monthly wages
gekkyū
月給

moving expenses
hikkoshi hiyō
引越し費用

National Insurance contributions [UK]
kokumin hoken futan
国民保険負担

National Insurance deduction [UK]
kokumin hokenryō
国民保険料

net earnings
junshūnyū
純収入

net hourly earnings
jikan atari junshūnyū
時間当たり純収入

net income
junshotoku
純所得

net pay
(take-home pay)
tedori chingin
手取賃金

(after-tax pay)
zeibiki kyūryō
税引給料

net weekly earnings
shūatari junshūnyū
週当たり純収入

net yearly earnings
nenkan junshūnyū
年間純収入

night-duty allowance
yakin teate
夜勤手当

night-shift hours
yakin jikan
夜勤時間

night-work allowance
yakin teate
夜勤手当

nominal income
meimoku shūnyū
名目収入

nominal wages
meimoku chingin
名目賃金

occasional income
ichiji shotoku
一時所得

occupational risk allowance
kiken teate
危険手当

officer's bonus
yakuin shōyo
役員賞与

officer's salary
yakuin hōkyū
役員俸給

overpaid
chingin shiharai chōka no
賃金支払超過の
chingin shiharaisugi
賃金支払過ぎ

overtime allowance
chōka kinmu teate
超過勤務手当
jikangai kinmu teate
時間外勤務手当
zangyō teate
残業手当

overtime hours worked
jikangai rōdō jikan
時間外労働時間

overtime pay
jikangai chingin
時間外賃金

overtime premium rate
jikangai teate shikyūritsu
時間外手当支給率

paid employee
yūkyū jūgyōin
有給従業員

paid holidays
yūkyū kyūka
有給休暇

paid labour
yūkyū rōdō
有給労働

paid labourer
yūkyū rōdōsha
有給労働者

paid leave
yūkyū kyūka
有給休暇

paid sick leave
yūkyū byōki kyūka
有給病気休暇

paid vacation
yūkyū kyūka
有給休暇

paid worker
yūkyū rōdōsha
有給労働者

partial pay
ichibu shikyū
一部支給

pay (noun)
(wages and salaries)
hōkyū
俸給

(salary)
kyūryō
給料

(remuneration)
kyūyo
給与

(payment, provision)
shikyū
支給

pay according to ability
nōryokukyū
能力給

pay according to job performing ability
shokunōkyū
職能給

pay according to post
shokumukyū
職務給

pay according to seniority
nenkō joretsugata chingin
年功序列型賃金

pay-as-you-earn (PAYE) [UK]
gensen chōshū shotokuzei
源泉徴収所得税
gensen kazei
源泉課税

pay ceiling
chingin saikō gendo
賃金最高限度

pay cheque
kyūryō shiharai kogitte
給料支払小切手

pay cut
chingin kirisage
賃金切下げ
genpō
減俸

pay day
hōkyūbi
俸給日
kyūryōbi
給料日

pay excluding tax
zeibiki kyūyo
税引給与

pay freeze
chingin tōketsu
賃金凍結

pay including tax
zeikomi kyūyo
税込給与

pay increase
chin'age
賃上げ
chingin hikiage
賃金引上げ
chingin jōshō
賃金上昇
shōkyū
昇給

pay level
kyūyo suijun
給与水準

pay load
kyūryō futan
給料負担

pay packet
hōkyūbukuro
俸給袋

pay pause [UK]
chingin tōketsu
賃金凍結

pay policy
chingin seisaku
賃金政策

pay rise
chin'age
賃上げ
chingin jōshō
賃金上昇
shōkyū
昇給

pay sheet
kyūryō shiharaihyō
給料支払表

pay talks
chingin kōshō
賃金交渉

PAYE (pay-as-you-earn) [UK]
gensen chōshū shotokuzei
源泉徴収所得税
gensen kazei
源泉課税

paymaster
kyūryō shiharai kakari
給料支払係

payment by results
nōritsukyū
能率給

payment of salary
kyūryō shiharai
給料支払

payroll
(total amount of salaries paid)
kyūyo shiharai sōgaku
給与支払総額

(payroll book)
chingin daichō
賃金台帳
kyūryō shiharai meibo
給料支払名簿

payroll book
chingin daichō
賃金台帳
kyūryō shiharai meibo
給料支払名簿

payroll deductions
chingin kōjo
賃金控除

pension
nenkin
年金

pension fund
nenkin kikin
年金基金

pension plan
nenkin keikaku
年金計画
nenkin seido
年金制度

pension scheme
nenkin seido
年金制度

perquisites
rinji teate
臨時手当

perquisites incidental to one's position
yakutoku
役得

personal exemptions (tax)
shotokuzei no kiso kōjo
所得税の基礎控除

personal income tax
kojin shotokuzei
個人所得税

personal income tax exemption
kojin shotokuzei menjo
個人所得税免除

personnel expenses
jinkenhi
人件費

physical check-ups
kenkō shindan
健康診断

piece wage
dekidaka chingin
出来高賃金

(contracted work)
ukeoi chingin
請負賃金

piece wage rate
dekidaka chinginritsu
出来高賃金率

piece work payment
dekidakabarai
出来高払い

piece-work rate
dekidakabarai chinginritsu
出来高賃金率

poorly paid job
kyūryō no yasui shigoto
給料のやすい仕事

prevailing wages
genkō chingin
現行賃金
ippan chingin
一般賃金

prevailing wages by occupation
shokushubetsu chingin
職種別賃金

private health insurance
shiteki kenkō hoken
私的健康保険

productivity bargaining
purodakutibiti-bāgeningu
プロダクティビティ・
バーゲニング

profit-sharing
rieki bunpai
利益分配

profit-sharing scheme
rieki(kin) bunpai kikō
利益(金)分配機構
rieki(kin) bunpai seido
利益(金)分配制度

profit-sharing wage plan
rieki kintensei chingin
利益均てん制賃金

public holiday
kōkyūbi
公休日

raise
chin'age
賃上げ
chingin jōshō
賃金上昇
shōkyū
昇給

rate of wage growth
chingin zōkaritsu
賃金増加率

recreational facilities
kōsei shisetsu
厚生施設

regular pay rises
teiki shōkyū
定期昇給

regular physical check-ups
teiki kenkō shindan
定期健康診断

regular salary
honkyū
本給

**remuneration
(reward, honorarium)**
hōshū
報酬

**(compensation, salaries
and allowances)**
kyūyo
給与

request form
negai
願い

responsibility (company's)
futan
負担

salaried employee
teigakukyū jūgyōin
定額給従業員

**salaried person
(wage earner)**
chingin seikatsusha
賃金生活者

(monthly salary)
gekkyūtori
月給とり

salaries and allowances
kyūryō oyobi kyūyo
給料および給与

salaries and wages
kyūryō oyobi chingin
給料および賃金

salary
sararii
サラリー

(pay, payroll)
hōkyū
俸給

(monthly pay)
kyūryō
給料

(remuneration)
kyūyo
給与

salary in kind
genbutsu kyūyo
現物給与

salary increase
shōkyū
昇給

salary man
chingin seikatsusha
賃金生活者
sarariiman
サラリーマン

salary scale
kyūyo taikei
給与体系

salary study
kyūyo no chōsa
給与の調査

saving scheme [J]
kigyō chochiku seido
企業貯蓄制度
shanai yokin seido
社内預金制度

savings deducted at source [J]
tenbiki chokin
天引貯金

seniority allowance
kinzoku teate
勤続手当

seniority-based wage
nenkō chingin
年功賃金
nenkōjoretsugata chingin
年功序列型賃金

seniority-based wage system
nenkōjoretsugata chingin
seido
年功序列型賃金制度
nenkōjoretsugata chingin
taikei
年功序列型賃金体系

seniority bonus
nenkō kahō
年功加俸

separate taxation
bunri kazei
分離課税

severance pay
kaikokin
解雇金

sick leave
byōki kyūka
病気休暇

(absence due to illness)
byōketsu
病欠
byōki kekkin
病気欠勤

sick-leave request
byōki kekkin negai
病気欠勤願い

sick leave with pay
yūkyū byōki kyūka
有給病気休暇

sickness benefits
shippei teate
疾病手当

six-figure income [UK] [US]
rokuketa no shūnyū
6桁の収入

sliding-scale wages
suraidosei no chingin
スライド制の賃金

small salary
yasugekkyū
安月給

**social security contributions
(paid by employee)**
shakai hokenryō
社会保険料

(paid by employer)
shakai hoshōhi
社会保証費

social security deduction
shakai hokenryō
社会保険料

source of income
shotokugen
所得源

special allowance
tokubetsu teate
特別手当

special bonus
tokubetsu shōyo
特別賞与

specific duty allowance
tokubetsu kinmu teate
特別勤務手当

stability of income
shotoku no anteisei
所得の安定性

stable wage
antei chingin
安定賃金

standard rate of pay
hyōjun chinginritsu
標準賃金率
kitei no tsūjō kyūyo
規定の通常給与

standard wage
hyōjun chingin
標準賃金

standard wage rate
hyōjun chinginritsu
標準賃金率

starting salary
shoninkyū
初任給

starvation wage
kiga chingin
飢餓賃金

stock ownership plan
jūgyōin mochikabu seido
従業員持株制度

stress management programme
sutoresu kanri keikaku
ストレス管理計画

subsidized by the company
kaisha enjo no
会社援助の

subsistence income
saitei seikatsu suijun shotoku
最低生活水準所得
seizon suijun shotoku
生存水準所得

subsistence wage
seikatsu iji chingin
生活維持賃金
seizon chingin
生存賃金

summer holiday
kaki kyūka
夏季休暇

take-home pay
tedori
手取り

(wages)
tedori chingin
手取賃金

(salary)
tedori kyūryō
手取給料

tax adviser
zeimu komon
税務顧問

tax assessment
kazei satei
課税査定

tax assessment basis
kazei kijun
課税基準

tax base
kazei kijun
課税基準

tax bracket
zeiritsu tōkyū
税率等級

tax break
zeisei yūgū sochi
税制優遇措置

tax credit
zeigaku kōjo
税額控除

tax cuts
genzei
減税

tax declaration
nōzei shinkoku
納税申告

tax deduction for dependents
fuyō kōjo
不要控除

tax deductions
kazei kōjo
課税控除
sozei kōjo
租税控除

tax documents
zeimu shorui
税務書類

tax dodger
datsuzeisha
脱税者

tax dodging
datsuzei
脱税

tax enquiry
zeimu chōsa
税務調査

tax minimization
sozei kyokushōka
租税極小化

tax office
zeimusho
税務所

tax payment
nōzei
納税

tax payment date
nōzei kijitsu
納税期日

tax payment notice
nōzei tsūchisho
納税通知書

tax planning
zeimu keikaku
税務計画

tax rate
kazeiritsu
課税率
zeiritsu
税率

tax rebate
sozei kanpu(kin)
租税還付(金)

tax refund
modoshizei
戻し税
sozei kanpukin
租税還付金

tax relief
(tax cut)
genzei
減税

(favourable tax measures)
zeisei yūgū sochi
税制優遇措置

tax return
[general]
nōzei shinkokusho
納税申告書

(income tax)
shotokuzei shinkoku
所得税申告

(form)
shotokuzei shinkokusho
所得税申告書

tax return filing deadline
shotokuzei shinkoku
shimekiri kijitsu
所得税申告締切期日

tax schedule
zeiritsuhyō
税率表

taxable income
kazei shotoku
課税所得

taxes
zeikin
税金

time and a half
gowarimashi no chōka
kinmu teate
5割増しの超過勤務
手当

time-and-a-half pay
gowarimashikyū
5割増給

time sheet
sagyō jikan yoteihyō
作業時間予定表
sagyōhyō
作業表

time wage(s)
jikan chingin
時間賃金
jikankyū
時間給

time wage rate
jikan chinginritsu
時間賃金率

total income
sōshotoku
総所得

underpaid
fujūbun na chingin shiharai
不十分な賃金支払い
hakkyū no
薄給の

unemployment insurance deduction
shitsugyō hokenryō
失業保険料

unfair wage policy
fukōsei chingin seisaku
不公正賃金政策

unfair wages
fukōsei chingin
不公正賃金

uniform bonus system
tōitsu shōyosei
統一賞与制

uniform wages
kin'itsu chingin
均一賃金

union bargaining
kumiai kōshō
組合交渉

union dues
kumiaihi
組合費

unpaid job
mukyū no shigoto
無給の仕事

unpaid labour
mukyū rōdō
無給労働

unpaid labourer
mukyū rōdōsha
無給労働者

unpaid work
mukyū rōdō
無給労働

unpaid worker
mukyū rōdōsha
無給労働者

unscheduled hours worked
shoteigai rōdō jikan
所定外労働時間

vacation
kyūka
休暇

[less formal]
yasumi
休み

voucher
shiharaihyō
支払票

voucher scheme
shiharaihyō seido
支払票制度

wage(s)
chingin
賃金

wage agreement
chingin kyōtei
賃金協定

wage bargaining
chingin kōshō
賃金交渉

wage base
chingin bēsu
賃金ベース

wage-by-age
nenrei kyūyosei
年齢給与制

wage-by-job
shigotobetsu chingin
仕事別賃金

wage claims
chin'age yōkyū
賃上げ要求

wage cuts
chingin kirisage
賃金切下げ

wage demands
chin'age yōkyū
賃上げ要求

wage discrimination
chingin sabetsu
賃金差別

wage discrimination on the basis of race
shu o riyū to shita chingin sabetsu
種を理由とした賃金差別

wage discrimination on the basis of sex
sei o riyū to shita chingin sabetsu
性を理由とした賃金差別

wage dispute
chin'age tōsō
賃上げ闘争

wage freeze
chingin tōketsu
賃金凍結

wage in kind
genbutsu kyūyo
現物給与

wage incentive
shōreikyū
奨励給

wage income
chingin shotoku
賃金所得

wage increase
chin'age
賃上げ
chingin hikiage
賃金引上げ
chingin jōshō
賃金上昇

wage increase rate
chingin jōshōritsu
賃金上昇率

wage inequality
chingin fubyōdō
賃金不平等

wage negotiations
chingin kōshō
賃金交渉

wage offensive
chingin kōsei
賃金攻勢

wage payment
chingin shiharai
賃金支払い

wage payment system
chingin shiharai seido
賃金支払制度

wage plan
chingin seido
賃金制度

wage policy
chingin seisaku
賃金政策

wage rate
chinginritsu
賃金率

wage revision
chingin kaitei
賃金改訂

wage scale
chingin sukēru
賃金スケール

wage settlement
chingin kettei
賃金決定

wage system
chingin taikei
賃金体系

weekly earnings
shūatari shūnyū
週当たり収入

weekly income
shūkan shotoku
週間所得

weekly salary
shūkyū
週給

weekly wages
shūatari chingin
週当たり賃金

well-paid employee
kōchingin jūgyōin
高賃金従業員

well-paid job
kyūryō no yoi shigoto
給料のよい仕事

well-paid labour
kōchingin rōdō
高賃金労働

well-paid work
kōchingin rōdō
高賃金労働

well-paid worker
kōchingin rōdōsha
高賃金労働者

well-remunerated
kyūryō no yoi
給料のよい

with pay
yūkyū
有給

withholding
tenbiki
天引き

worksheet
sagyōhyō
作業表

yearly earnings
nenkan shūnyū
年間収入

yearly income
nenkan shotoku
年間所得

yearly salary
nenkyū
年給

yearly wages
nenkan chingin
年間賃金

accommodation
shukuhaku
宿泊

accommodation expenses
shukuhakuhi
宿泊費

bill
kanjōsho
勘定書

(invoice)
okurijō
送状

business dinner
bijinesu-dinā
ビジネス・ディナー

business entertaining
shayō kōsai
社用交際
shayō settai
社用接待

business lunch
bijinesu-ranchi
ビジネス・ランチ

business lunch or dinner with foreign visitors [J][37]
yokomeshi[37]
横飯し

business travel
gyōmu tokō
業務渡航
shutchō
出張

business traveller
shutchōsha
出張者

business trip
shutchō
出張

company excursion
shain ryokō
社員旅行

complimentary tickets
yūtaiken
優待券

cultural-entertainment expenses
kyōyō gorakuhi
教養娯楽費

dinner party
enkai
宴会

end-of-year party[38]
bōnenkai[38]
忘年会

entertainment
kōsai
交際
settai
接待

entertainment expense account
kōsaihi kanjō
交際費勘定
settaihi kanjō
接待費勘定

entertainment expenses
kōsaihi
交際費
settaihi
接待費

expense account
(general)
keihi kanjō
経費勘定

(entertainment)
shayō kōsaihi kanjō
社用交際費勘定

expense allowance
keihikyū
経費給

expense report
keihi hōkokusho
経費報告書

expense voucher
kōsaihi denpyō
交際費伝票

expenses
(general)
hiyō
費用

(business expenses)
keihi
経費

farewell party
sōbetsukai
送別会

food expenses
shokuryōhi
食料費

hotel accommodation
hoteru shūyō
ホテル収容

hotel expenses
shukuhakuhi
宿泊費

invoice
okurijō
送状

invoice amount
okurijō kingaku
送状金額

itemized bill
kōmokubetsu kanjōsho
項目別勘定書

itinerary
ryotei
旅程

meal allowance
shokuji teate
食事手当

new year party[39]
shinnenkai[39]
新年会

out-of-pocket expenses
genkin shiharai hiyō
現金支払費用

overseas business trip
kaigai shutchō
海外出張

petty cash
koguchi genkin
小口現金

petty cash account
koguchi genkin kanjō
小口現金勘定

petty cash book
koguchi genkin suitōbo
小口現金出納簿

petty cash payments
koguchi genkin shiharai
小口現金支払

petty cash slip
koguchi genkin denpyō
小口現金伝票

petty expenses
zappi
雑費

receipt
reshiito
レシート
ryōshūsho
領収書
uketorishō
受取証

red-carpet treatment
taigū
待遇

seating order
sekiji
席次

social contacts
shakō no settai
社交の接待

socializing[40]
tsukiai[40]
付合い

sports event
undōkai
運動会

transportation expenses
kōtsūhi
交通費

welcome party
kangeikai
歓迎会

welcome and farewell party[41]
kansōgeikai[41]
歓送迎会

Notes

37. business lunch or dinner with foreign visitors (yokomeshi 横飯し): 'yoko' probably refers to the horizontal way of writing used by Westerners. It somewhat implies that such a lunch or dinner is more of an ordeal than a pleasure to Japanese businessmen because they have to use a foreign language and concentrate on the business at hand during such occasions.

38. end-of-year party (bōnenkai 忘年会), or 'forget-the-year' party: held in Japanese offices at the end of the year to celebrate the year's successes and forget past failures with 'sake' and good food.

39. new year party (shinnenkai 新年会): held upon the reopening of the office, following the Christmas recess, to celebrate the new year and make corporate new-year resolutions. A Japanese company will usually have either a 'bōnenkai' or a 'shinnenkai' but rarely both.

40. socializing (tsukiai 付合い): an important part of a Japanese employee's life who is expected to socialize with colleagues and other members of the company after working hours.

41. welcome and farewell party (kansōgeikai 歓送迎会): held for both a departing member of staff and a newcomer at the same time.

Additional expressions

aisatsu mawari 挨拶回り ('round of greetings') is the round of new-year greeting calls made by Japanese employees to colleagues and clients on the first business day of the year.

bureikō 無礼講 ('free and informal party') is an informal gathering of company employees regardless of rank or title. This is particular to the end or beginning-of-the-year parties, but although a lack of formality is tolerated during such occasions, superiors are still addressed by their organizational titles rather than by their surnames.

chotto ippai ちょっと一杯 ('just a drink') is frequently heard among Japanese businessmen and suggests an informal business gathering rather than a real drinking session. An employee may be taken aside by his boss and told 'chotto ippai', or 'let's have a little talk'.

hashigo sake 梯子酒 ('bar hopping') is similar to the English 'pub crawl'. Groups of Japanese workers go drinking together after work, moving from one bar to another until very late. This important ritual is carried out at the personal expense of the senior member of the group as part of the unofficial duties of his rank.

kakushigei 隠し芸 ('hidden talent') refers to a personal entertaining ability which Japanese workers are called upon to display at informal gatherings. This amateur talent show is thought to·promote camaraderie and to liven up a party.

karaoke 空オケ ('empty orchestra') is a favourite relaxing activity among Japanese businessmen. It consists of singing songs to musical accompaniment recorded and played back on cassette tapes in bars that offer this 'amateur night' facility for the added pleasure of their customers.

o-cha o nomu お茶を飲 ('to drink tea'): apart from the regular refreshments taken by company employees during their work day, tea drinking is a way of exchanging business information informally. 'O-cha o nomimasen ka', 'shall we have a cup of tea?', is often heard among colleagues and implies a quiet business tête-à-tête.

shayōzoku 社用族 ('the expense-account tribe') refers to the company employees who can enjoy the good life on a company expense account.

sōritsu kinenbi 創立記念日 ('anniversary of the company's foundation'): a milestone in the history of the firm, such as a 20th or 25th anniversary, is usually celebrated with a formal party during which the president makes a speech to thank all the people connected with the company for their support. On a lesser year, employees may be given a day off or enjoy an informal get-together.

uchiage 打上げ ('launching', 'last theatrical performance') is a celebration party held by Japanese businessmen following the successful completion of a project. This kind of drinking party is yet another means of promoting group spirit and solidarity among company employees, and could be translated by 'grand finale'.

accident
jiko
事故

(disaster)
saigai
災害

(injury)
shōgai
傷害

claim
seikyū
請求

claim for damage
songai baishō seikyū
損害賠償請求

cleanliness
sōji
掃除

company liability
kaisha sekinin
会社責任

compensate
oginau
補う
tsugunau
償う

compensation
baishō
賠償
hoshō
補償

compensation for damages
songai baishō(kin)
損害賠償(金)

compensation for death
shibō hoshō(kin)
死亡補償(金)

compensation for injury
fushō hoshō(kin)
負傷補償(金)

compensation money
baishōkin
賠償金
hoshōkin
補償金

contingency
furyo no jiko
不慮の事故

contingency plan
kinkyū keikaku
緊急計画

crisis
kiki
危機

crisis management
kiki kanri
危機管理

damage
higai
被害
sonshō
損傷

(loss)
songai
損害

disablement
fugu haishitsu
不具廃疾

earthquake
jishin
地震

emergency
kinkyū
緊急

emergency evacuation
kinkyū hinan
緊急避難

emergency exit
hijō deguchi
非常出口

emergency manual
kinkyūji manyuaru
緊急時マニュアル

emergency stairs
hijō kaidan
非常階段

employer's liability
koyōsha sekinin
雇用者責任

explosion
bakuhatsu
爆発

fire
kaji
火事
kasai
火災

fire alarm
kasai keihō
火災警報

fire box
kashitsu
火室

fire door
shōbōto
消防戸

fire drill
shōbō enshū
消防演習
shōbō kunren
消防訓練

fire escape
(emergency stairs)
hijō kaidan
非常階段

(ladder)
kasaiyō hinan hashigo
火災用避難梯子

fire extinguisher
hikeshi
火消し
shōkaki
消火器

fire hazard
kaji kiken
火事危険
kasai kiken
火災危険

fireproof
taika
耐火

fireproof material
taikazai
耐火材

first aid
ōkyū teate
応急手当

get-away exit
hijō deguchi
非常出口
hinan deguchi
避難出口

hazard(s)
kiken
危険

hazardous work
kiken na sagyō
危険な作業

health hazard
kenkōjō no kiken
健康上の危険

hygiene
sōji
掃除

impairment
haishitsu
廃疾

indemnify
tsugunau
償う

indemnity
baishōkin
賠償金

industrial accident
gyōmu saigai
業務災害
rōmu saigai
労務災害

industrial disability
rōdō funō
労働不能

industrial disability pension
gyōmu saigai nenkin
業務災害年金

industrial disease
shokugyōbyō
職業病

industrial hazard
sangyōteki kiken
産業的危険

industrial illness
shokugyōbyō
職業病

industrial safety
sangyō anzen
産業安全

injury
fushō
負傷
kega
怪我
shōgai
傷害

invalid claim
mukō no seikyū
無効の請求

job-related accident
gyōmujō no jiko
業務上の事故

leakage
rōshutsu
漏出

liability
sekinin
責任

loss
songai
損害

loudspeaker
kakusei sōchi
拡声装置

lump-sum compensation
hoshō ichijikin
補償一時金

lump-sum settlement
hoshōkin ichijibarai
補償金一時払い

measures against disasters
saigai taisaku
災害対策

medical supplies
iyakuhin
医薬品

message broadcast
mesēji hōsō
メセージ放送

negligence
kashitsu
過失

noise
shokuba sōon
職場騒音

noise level
sōon kijun
騒音基準

noise limit
sōon seigen
騒音制限

noise pollution
sōon kōgai
騒音公害

noise suppressor
sōon yokushiki
騒音抑止器

non-inflammable
moenikui
燃え難い

occupational accident
gyōmu saigai
業務災害

occupational disease
shokugyōbyō
職業病

occupational hazard
shokugyōjō no kiken
職業上の危険

occupational risk
shokugyōjō no kiken
職業上の危険

on-the-job accident
gyōmujō no jiko
業務上の事故
gyōmujō no saigai
業務上の災害

partial disablement
ichibu fugu
一部不具

pollutant
haikibutsu
廃棄物

precautions
yobōhō
予防法

protection from fire
hiyoke
火除け

public-address system
kakusei sōchi
拡声装置

raging fire
rekka
烈火

risk(s)
kiken
危険

safe
anzen na
安全な

safety
anzen
安全

safety-first campaign
anzen undō
安全運動

safety programme
anzen keikaku
安全計画

safety record
anzen kiroku
安全記録

safety standards
anzen kijun
安全基準

serious injury
ōkega
大怪我

settlement of claim
hoshō shiharai
補償支払い

shutdown
kōjō heisa
工場閉鎖

simulated-crisis situation
shimyurēshon o tsukatta
kiki no jōkyō
シミュレーションを
使った危機の状況

spreading fire
hiashi
火脚

temporary partial disablement
ichiji bubun fugu
一時部分不具

temporary total disablement
ichiji zenbu fugu
一時全部不具

total disablement
zenbu fugu
全部不具

violent earthquake
resshin
烈震

workman's compensation
rōdōsha saigai hoshō
労働者災害補償

aging workforce
rōreika suru rōdōryoku
老齢化する労働力

amicable resignation[42]
enmantaisha[42]
円満退社

annual pension
nenkin
年金

compulsory retirement[43]
kyōsei taishoku
強制退職
teinen (taishoku)[43]
定年(退職)

compulsory retirement system
teinensei
定年制

corporate pension
kigyō nenkin
企業年金

early retirement
sōki taishoku
早期退職

employees' pension fund
jūgyōin nenkin kikin
従業員年金基金

extra retirement allowance
tokubetsu na taishoku teate
特別な退職手当

formal resignation
jihyō
辞表

full pension
kanzen nenkin
完全年金

golden years
rōgo no seikatsu
老後の生活

individual pension
kojinteki nenkin
個人的年金

informal resignation[44]
shintai ukagai[44]
進退伺い

leave one's current position
genzai no shoku o kaeru
現在の職を変える

leave the company
kaisha o saru
会社を去る
kaisha o yameru
会社を辞める

letter of resignation
jihyō
辞表

lump-sum retirement allowance
ichijikin no taishoku teate
一時金の退職手当

multi-employer pension
tasū yatoinushi nenkin
多数雇主年金

non-contributory pension
mukyoshutsu nenkin
無拠出年金

non-regular staff formed by retired workers [J]
shokutaku
嘱託

optional retirement
nin'i taishoku
任意退職

pension
nenkin
年金

pension fund
nenkin kikin
年金基金

pension funds
nenkin shikin
年金資金

pension insurance
nenkin hoken
年金保険

pension plan
nenkin keikaku
年金計画

pension scales
nenkin taikei
年金体系

pension scheme (corporate)
kigyō nenkin seido
企業年金制度

(individual)
kojinteki nenkin seido
個人的年金制度

(national pension for the self-employed) [J]
kokumin nenkin seido
国民年金制度

(state pension through a company)
kōsei nenkin seido
厚生年金制度

(state pension, public pension)
kōteki nenkin seido
公的年金制度

[general]
nenkin seido
年金基金

(government employees' pension) [J]
onkyū seido
恩給制度

(private)
shiteki nenkin seido
私的年金制度

pension trust
nenkin shintaku
年金信託

pensioner
nenkin jukyūsha
年金受給者

(government employee)
onkyū juryōsha
恩給受領者

postponed retirement
enki taishoku
延期退職

private pension
shiteki nenkin
私的年金

public pension
kōteki nenkin
公的年金

resign
jinin suru
辞任する
jishoku suru
辞職する

resign from (—)
(—) o jishoku suru
(—)を辞職する
(—) o yameru
(—)を辞める

resignation
jinin
辞任
jishoku
辞職

retiree
(teinen) taishokusha
(定年)退職者

retirement
taishoku
退職

(compulsory)
teinen taishoku
定年退職

(government employees)
onkyū
恩給

retirement age
taishoku teinen
退職定年
teinen
定年

retirement allowance
taishoku kyūyo
退職給与
taishoku teate
退職手当
taishokukin
退職金

(in lump sum)
taishoku ichijikin
退職一時金

retirement annuity
taishoku nenkin
退職年金

retirement fund
taishokukin
退職金

retirement pension
taishoku nenkin
退職年金

retiring employee
taishokusha
退職者

State-Earnings Related Pensions Scheme (SERPS) [UK]
kokumin hoken no taishoku nenkin seido
国民保険の退職年金制度

temporary retirement
kyūshoku
休職

union pension
kumiai nenkin
組合年金

voluntary resignation[45]
jihatsu jinin
自発辞任
jihatsu taishoku[45]
自発退職
jiko taishoku[45]
自己退職

voluntary retirement[46]
kibō taishoku[46]
希望退職
nin'i taishoku
任意退職

Notes

42. amicable resignation (enmantaisha 円満退社): the acceptance by a Japanese company of an employee's formal letter of resignation. Although voluntary resignation ('jihatsu' or 'jiko taishoku') is a rare occurrence in a Japanese company, it sometimes happens that an employee wishes to leave for personal reasons. The company may not agree to let him go, even if there is no lifetime employment binding contract between employer and employee, and may place him in a difficult social position. If the resignation is accepted it is viewed as an amicable parting and has no negative social consequence for the resigning employee.

43. compulsory retirement (teinen 定年): the retirement age in Japan varies from one company to another, but it is usually 55 or 60 regardless of the retiring employee's mental or physical condition.

44. informal resignation (shintai ukagai 進退伺い): this kind of resignation is submitted by a member of staff whose personal conduct or actions have somehow tarnished his company's image or jeopardized his company's interests. This admission of wrong doing and the willingness to face the consequences are often accepted with magnanimity, and punishment may take the form of a suspended pay rise or a lowering of rank.

45. voluntary resignation (jihatsu taishoku 自発退職 ; jiko taishoku 自己退職): <u>see</u> notes 42 and 46.

46. voluntary retirement (kibō taishoku 希望退職): encouraged by Japanese companies in periods of economic hardship in order to avoid the unpleasantness of laying off. Generous inducement allowances are usually given to the employees who take advantage of this offer. Although the word 'kibō' implies a personal wish to retire, it is nevertheless different from 'jihatsu' or 'jiko taishoku' which means resignation for personal reasons and which is frowned upon by Japanese employers in view of the lifetime employment system.

Additional expression

taishoku no aisatsu 退職の挨拶 ('paying respects upon resignation') is the round of courtesy calls made by the leaving employee to business contacts to thank them for their co-operation and custom and to introduce his successor.

abolition of night shifts
yagyō teppai
夜業撤廃

arbitration
chūsai
仲裁

(mediation)
chōtei
調停

arbitration agreement
chūsai keiyaku
仲裁契約

black leg
higyōyaburi
罷業破り
sutoyaburi
スト破り

closure
(place of business)
jigyōsho heisa
事業所閉鎖

(factory)
kōjō heisa
工場閉鎖

company-based union
kigyōbetsu rōdō kumiai
企業別労働組合

company union
kigyōnai rōdō kumiai
企業内労働組合

concessions
jōho
譲歩

conciliation
assen
斡旋
rōdō sōgi assen
労働争議斡旋

conflict between labour and management
rōshikan no tōsō
労使間の闘争

confrontation
taiketsu
対決

cooling-off period
reikyaku kikan
冷却期間

cutbacks (in manpower)
('weight reducing')
genryō
減量

(personnel cuts)
jin'in sakugen
人員節減

(rationalization)
jin'in seiri
人員整理

('decapitation')
kubikiri
首切り

(reduction in manpower)
rōdōryoku no setsugen
労働力の節減

deadlock
ikizumari
行詰まり

decision by arbitration
chūsai saitei
仲裁裁定

discharge
kaiko suru
解雇する

discharged dishonourably
fumeiyo ni kaiko sareru
不名誉に解雇される

disciplinary dismissal
chōkai menshoku
懲戒免職

discontent
fuman
不満

dishonourable discharge
fumeiyo na kaiko
不名誉な解雇

dismiss
kaiko suru
解雇する

dismissal
kaiko
解雇

dismissal notice
kaiko tsūchisho
解雇通知書

dispute
sōgi
争議
tōsō
闘争

dole (to be on the)
shitsugyō teate (o ukete iru)
失業手当 (を受けて
いる)

dole money
shitsugyō teate
失業手当

duration of unemployment
shitsugyō kikan
失業期間

fink
higyōyaburi
罷業破り
sutoyaburi
スト破り

fire (verb)
kubi o kiru
首を切る
yamesaseru
辞めさせる

fired (to be)
kubi(kiri) ni naru
首(切り)になる
kubi o kirerareru
首を切られる

general strike
sōhigyō
総罷業

go on strike
sutoraiki ni totsunyū suru
ストライキに突入する

go-slow
taigyō
怠業

go-slow campaign
junpō tōsō
順法闘争

grievance(s)
fuheifuman
不平不満
kujō
苦情

grievance committee
kujō shori i'inkai
苦情処理委員会

grievance procedure
kujō shori tetsuzuki
苦情処理手続き

grievance settlement
kujō shori
苦情処理

grievance settlement system
kujō shori seido
苦情処理制度

grounds for dismissal
kaiko no konkyo
解雇の根拠
kaiko no riyū
解雇の理由

illegal strike
fuhō higyō
不法罷業

improvement of work conditions
kinmu jōken no kaizen
勤務条件の改善

in-house union [J] (see note 32)
kigyōnai rōdō kumiai (see note 32)
企業内労働組合

industrial arbitration
rōdō chōtei
労働調停

industrial conflict
rōshi tōsō
労使闘争

industrial dispute
rōshi sōgi
労使争議

industrial relations court
sangyō kankei hōtei
産業関係法廷

industrial unrest
sangyō fuan
産業不安

industry-wide bargaining
sangyōbetsu dankō
産業別団交

industry-wide issue(s)
sangyōkyōtsū mondai
産業共通問題

involuntary unemployment
hijihatsuteki shitsugyō
非自発的失業
kyōsei shitsugyō
強制失業

job loss(es)
shisshoku
失職

jobless person
shisshokusha
失職者
shitsugyōsha
失業者

labour cuts
rōdōryoku no setsugen
労働力の節減

('weight reducing')
genryō
減量

(rationalization)
jin'in seiri
人員整理

('decapitation')
kubikiri
首切り

labour delegate
rōdō daihyōsha
労働代表者

labour demands
rōdōsha no yōkyū
労働者の要求

labour dispute
rōdō sōgi
労働争議

labour issue
rōdō mondai
労働問題

labour leaders
rōdō kumiai shidōsha
労働組合指導者

labour-management confrontation
rōshitairitsu
労使対立

labour-management talk
rōshi kyōgi
労使協議

labour offensive
rōdō kōsei
労働攻勢
tōsō
闘争

labour officials
rōdō kumiai kanbu
労働組合幹部

labour trouble (controversy, dispute)
rōdō fungi
労働紛議

(quarrel, complications)
rōdō funsō
労働紛争

labour unrest
rōdō fuan
労働不安

laid off (to be) (see note 47)
kikyū sareru (see note 47)
帰休される
reiofu sareru
レイオフされる

laid-off worker
ichiji kaiko rōdōsha
一時解雇労働者
rinji shitsugyōsha
臨時失業者

lay-off (noun)
reiofu
レイオフ

(temporary dismissal)
ichiji kaiko
一時解雇

(temporary release)[47]
kikyū[47]
帰休

(temporary unemployment)
rinji shitsugyō
臨時失業

lay off (verb)
reiofu suru
レイオフする

lay-off rate
ichiji kaikoritsu
一時解雇率

local strike
chi'iki tōsō
地域闘争

lock-out
rokku-auto
ロック・アウト

(place of work)
jigyōsho heisa
事業所閉鎖

(factory)
kōjō heisa
工場閉鎖

lose one's job
rishoku suru
離職する

mass meeting
taikai
大会

mediation
chōtei
調停

(arbitration)
chūsai
仲裁

mediation in labour dispute
rōdō sōgi chōtei
労働争議調停

mediator
chūsainin
仲裁人

negotiations
kōshō
交渉

notice of dismissal
kaiko tsūchisho
解雇通知書

organizer
rōdō kumiai soshikisha
労働組合組織者
rōso no orugu
労組のオルグ

out of work
shisshokuchū
失職中
shitsugyōchū
失業中

pay talks
chingin kōshō
賃金交渉

personnel cuts
jin'in sakugen
人員削減

personnel reduction (cuts)
jin'in sakugen
人員削減

(rationalization)
jin'in seiri
人員整理

picket
pike
ピケ

picket line
piketto-rain
ピケット・ライン

pressure from union (pushfulness)
kumiai no atsuryoku
組合の圧力

protest against a worker's dismissal
kubikiri hantai tōsō
首切反対闘争

rally
taikai
大会

rationalization
jin'in seiri
人員整理

recall (noun)
saikoyō
再雇用

recall (verb)
saikoyō suru
再雇用する

reduced hours
tanshuku jikan
短縮時間

reduction in working hours
rōdō jikan no tanshuku
労働時間の短縮
rōdō jikansū no genshō
労働時間数の減少

redundancy (surplus of labour)
rōdōsha no yojō
労働者の余剰

(a redundant person)
yojō rōdōsha
余剰労働者

redundancy indemnity
yojō rōdōsha hoshō
余剰労働者補償

redundancy payment
yojō rōdōsha hoshōkin
余剰労働者補償金

redundant
yojō
余剰

redundant labour force
yojō rōdōryoku
余剰労働力

redundant worker
yojō rōdōsha
余剰労働者

repeated warnings
saisan ni wataru keihō
再三にわたる警報

return to work
shokuba fukki
職場復帰

right of dismissal
kaikoken
解雇権

right-of-dismissal abuse
kaikoken ran'yō
解雇権乱用

right to strike
higyōken
罷業権
sutoken
スト権

right-to-work demonstration
shoku yokose undō
職よこせ運動

sack
kubi o kiru
首を切る
yamesaseru
辞めさせる

sacked (to be)
kubi(kiri) ni naru
首(切り)になる
kubi o kirareru
首を切られる

sacking
kubikiri
首切り

scab
sutoyaburi
スト破り

seasonal unemployment
kisetsuteki shitsugyō
季節的失業

secret ballot
mukimei tōhyō
無記名投票

severance pay
kaikokin
解雇金

shop steward
shokuba daihyōsha
職場代表者

sit-down strike
suwarikomi higyō
座込み罷業

sit-down striker
suwarikomi higyōsha
座込み罷業者

sit-in strike
suwarikomi higyō
座込み罷業

slow-down strike
sōtan higyō
操短罷業
taigyō
怠業

solidarity dispute
danketsu sōgi
団結争議

solidarity strike
dōjō higyō
同情罷業

spot strike
chi'iki higyō
地域罷業

spring labour offensive [J][48]
shuntō[48]
春闘

strike (noun)
suto(raiki)
スト(ライキ)
higyō
罷業

strike (verb)
sutoraiki suru
ストライキする

strike breaker
higyōyaburi
罷業破り
sutoyaburi
スト破り

strike breaking
higyōyaburi
罷業破り
sutoyaburi
スト破り

strike committee
higyō i'inkai
罷業委員会

strike declaration
higyō senden
罷業宣伝

strike fund
higyō kikin
罷業基金
tōsō kikin
闘争基金

strike measures
higyō taisaku sochi
罷業対策措置

strike order
higyō shirei
罷業指令
sutoraiki shirei
ストライキ指令

strike pay
higyō teate
罷業手当

strikers
higyōsha
罷業者

striking worker
sutochū no rōdōsha
スト中の労働者

supplementary unemployment benefits
hojoteki shitsugyō kyūfu
補助的失業給付

surplus workers
yojō jin'in
余剰人員

sympathy strike
dōjō higyō
同情罷業

temporarily laid-off worker
ichiji kaiko rōdōsha
一時解雇労働者

temporary dismissal
ichiji kaiko
一時解雇

temporary lay-off
ichiji kaiko
一時解雇

temporary release from work
ichijiteki taishoku
一時的退職

temporary unemployment
ichijiteki shitsugyō
一時的失業

termination
kaiko
解雇

total number of days lost
sonshitsu nissū
損失日数

trade dispute
rōdō sōgi
労働争議

trade union activities
rōdō kumiai katsudō
労働組合活動
rōdō kumiai undō
労働組合運動

trade union leader [UK]
rōdō kumiai shidōsha
労働組合指導者

trade-union official
rōdō kumiai kanbu
労働組合幹部
rōdō kumiai yakuin
労働組合役員

trade-unionist [UK]
rōdō kumiai'in
労働組合員

Trades Union Congress (TUC) [UK]
igirisu rōdō kumiai kaigi
イギリス労働組合会議

TUC (Trades Union Congress) [UK]
igirisu rōdō kumiai kaigi
イギリス労働組合会議

unemployable person
koyō futekikakusha
雇用不適格者
koyōfunōsha
雇用不能者

unemployed (to be)
shitsugyō shite iru
失業している

unemployed person
shisshokusha
失職者
shitsugyōsha
失業者

unemployed worker
shitsugyō rōdōsha
失業労働者

unemployment
shisshoku
失職
shitsugyō
失業

unemployment benefits
shitsugyō kyūfu
失業給付
shitsugyō teate
失業手当

unemployment compensation
shitsugyō hoshō
失業補償
shitsugyō teate
失業手当

unfair dismissal
futō kaiko
不当解雇

union activities
kumiai katsudō
組合活動
kumiai undō
組合運動

union bargaining
kumiai kōshō
組合交渉

union opposition
kumiai no hantai
組合の反対

unrest
fuan
不安

voluntary unemployment
jihatsuteki shitsugyō
自発的失業

vote
tōhyō
投票

wage arbitration
chingin chūsai
賃金仲裁

wage claims
chin'age yōkyū
賃上げ要求

wage demands
chin'age yōkyū
賃上げ要求

wage dispute
chin'age tōsō
賃上げ闘争

wage negotiations
chingin kōshō
賃金交渉

wage offensive
chingin kōsei
賃金攻勢

wage settlement
chingin kettei
賃金決定

walk-out (<u>noun</u>)
higyō
罷業

walk out (<u>verb</u>)
shokuba o ridatsu suru
職場を離脱する

walk-out strike
shokuba hōki
職場放棄

warning
keihō
警報

wildcat strike
yamaneko suto
山猫スト

work-to-rule campaign
junpō tōso
順法闘争

work-to-rule tactics
junpō senjutsu
順法戦術
noronoro senjutsu
のろのろ戦術

workshop meeting
shokuba taikai
職場大会

wrongful dismissal
futō kaiko
不当解雇

Notes

47. lay-off (kikyū 帰休): military expression meaning a soldier's temporary release before his term of service has expired.

48. spring labour offensive (shuntō 春闘): the traditional wage offensive carried out by Japanese unions every spring. Organized by the two largest federations in Japan, sōhyō 総評 and dōmei 同盟, it is followed by many small in-house unions who cannot conduct industry-wide offensives by themselves.

Additional expression

tennōzan 天王山 is a decisive battle in the history of Japan sometimes used to describe the final negotiations between management and trade-union in a wage dispute.

Japanese-English index

abiseuri
  bunching 205
ābusōpushon-apurōchi
  absorption approach 3
agarisagari
  fluctuations 40; ups and downs
  116
ageashi
  upward trend 285
agesōba
  bullish market 205; rising
  quotation 267
āgonomikkusu
  ergonomics 34
aikogitte
  counter cheque 141
aikokuteki na warekoso
  nationalistic one-upmanship
  72
aikyū-tesuto
  IQ test 443
airo sangyō
  bottle-neck industry 11
airurando
  Ireland 189
aisatsu mawari
  'round of greetings' 488
aisurando
  Iceland 189
aitai baibai
  crossing 213; negotiated
  transaction 250
aitai saimu
  mutual debt 249
ajia kyokutō keizai i'inkai
  Economic Commission for Asia
  and the Far East (ECAFE) 29
akaji
  deficit (red figures) 24, 385
  akaji o dasu
    go in the red 148
akaji de
  in the red 149
akaji hoten
  covering of deficit 21
akaji no kigyō
  money-losing company (-ies)
  70, 402
akaji tan'i
  deficit units 24
akaji yosan
  budget deficit 374; deficit
  budget 24
akaji zaisei
  deficit financing 24
akaji zandaka
  deficit balance 24
akajikoku
  deficit country 24
akewatashi seikyū soshō
  repossession proceedings
  (legal) 307
akichi
  unoccupied land 311; vacant
  ground 311; vacant land 311;
  vacant lot 311
akinai
  trading (business) 282
akiya
  vacant house 311; vacant
  property 311
  akiya ni suru
    vacate a house 311

akiya hoken
  unoccupied building insurance
  330
akka
  degradation 293; deterioration
  25, 293
akka yōin
  adverse factors 4
akui fujitsu hyōji
  fraudulent misrepresentation
  347; wilful misrepresentation
  363
akujunkan
  vicious circles 117
akusei infure
  bad inflation 9; inflationary
  spiral 54
akuzairyō
  adverse factor 194
amerika ginkō
  Bank of America 135
amerika ginkō gyōsha kyōkai
  American Bankers Association
  (ABA) 131, 132
amerika ginkō kyōkai
  American Institute of Banking
  (AIB) 132
amerikan kabushiki torihikijo
  American Stock Exchange
  (AMEX) (ASE) 195, 196;
  Curb, the [US] 214; Curb
  Exchange [US] 214
anarisuto
  analyst 7, 195
ankēto chōsa
  enquiry 33; questionnaire
  survey 90; survey 106
ankoku no getsuyōbi
  Black Monday 201
ankoku no kayōbi
  Black Tuesday 201
ankoku no mokuyōbi
  Black Thursday 201
ankutaddo
  United Nations Conference on
  Trade and Development
  (UNCTAD) 114, 115
anmokuteki hiyō
  implicit cost 49
annai
  advice 131; notice 153
annai kōkoku
  classified advertisements 441
annaijō
  advice note 132
ansokuchi
  haven 230
antei
  stability 102; stabilization 185
antei chingin
  stable wage(s) 103, 484
antei chinginsei
  stable wage system 103
antei haitō kabu
  widow-and-orphan stock 286
antei kabunushi
  strong shareholder 279
antei kahei
  stable money 185
antei kahei seisaku
  stable money policy 185
antei kakaku
  stable prices 103

antei kawase sōba
  stable exchange rate 185
antei keikaku
  stabilization programme 103
antei keizai
  stable economy 103
antei keizai seichō
  stable economic growth 1 03
antei kinkō
  stable equilibrium 103
antei kōka
  stabilizing effect 103
antei no
  stable 468
antei rōdōryoku
  stable labour force 468
antei seichō
  stable growth 103
antei seichō rosen
  stable growth path 103
antei shikyō
  stable market 276
antei shita
  stable 103
antei shōken
  seasoned securities 269
antei sōchi
  stabilizer 103
antei suru
  stabilize 103, 185
antei tsūka
  stabilized currency 185;
  stable currency 185
anteika
  stabilization 103, 185
anteika kinō
  stabilization function 103
anteika seisaku
  stabilization policy 103
anteika suru
  stabilize 185
anteisei
  stability 102, 185
anteiseiryoku
  stabilizing force 103
anzen
  safety 268, 493; security 270
anzen kabu
  safety stock 268
anzen kabunushi
  strong shareholder 279
anzen keikaku
  safety programme 493
anzen kijun
  safety standards 493
anzen kiroku
  safety record 493
anzen meate no
  safety-oriented 268
anzen na
  safe 493
anzen tōshi
  safe investment 268
anzen undō
  safety-first campaign 493
aotagai
  'buying a paddy field' 448
aotagari
  'reaping a green paddy field'
  448
aozora shijō
  open market (securities) 254

aozora shōken
  blue-sky securities 201
aozorahō
  blue-sky laws [US] 201
apāto
  apartment [US] 289; flat [UK]
  295
  apāto o mamoru
    flat-sit (verb) 295
apāto danchi
  apartment complex 289
apāto jūtaku
  apartment house 289
apāto shoyūsha
  apartment owner [US] 289;
  flat owner [UK] 295
arechi
  wasteland (wild) 312
arubaito
  part-time work (students) 445,
  463
arujenchin
  Argentina 189
arujeria
  Algeria 189
ashibumi
  standstill (market) 276
ashidori
  trend (of market) 283
assen
  conciliation 499
assen tesūryō
  finder's fee 224
assennin
  finder 224
assensha
  agent 194; finder 224
asshuku
  squeeze (noun) 103
atarashii infurēshon
  new inflation 74
atarashii tsūka seido
  new monetary system 181
atohizuke
  backdate (noun) 133;
  backdating 133
  atohizuke o tsukeru
    backdate (verb) 133
atohizuke kogitte
  backdated cheque 133
atsuryoku
  pressure 82
atsuryoku dantai
  pressure groups 82
autoraito-fōwādo
  outright forward 182
autoraito-kabā
  outright cover 182
autoraito torihiki
  outright transaction 182
autosaido-ragu
  outside lag 77
ayamatta keisan
  false accounting [UK] 390
ayamatta rōdō haibun
  misallocation of labour 461
ayamodoshi
  faint recovery 221; technical
  rally 281
ayaoshi
  technical reaction 281

azukari
custody (keeping) 142
azukari shōken
deposit certificate 143;
securities in trust 270;
warehouse receipt 285
azukarinin
depositary 143
azukekin
deposit 142; money deposited
152; money on deposit 152
azukeru
deposit (verb) (money, articles)
142

bā
bar (1£M) 166
ba'aji
undertone 284
baibai
buying and selling 166, 205;
trading 282
baibai chūmon dakiawase
buying and selling orders 166,
205
baibai gyōmu
dealing business 215
baibai ichinin chūmon
discretionary order 218
baibai ichinin kanjō
discretionary account 218
baibai ichinin kanjō torihiki
discretionary account
transaction 218
baibai jōken
terms of transaction 281
baibai kakaku
target price (securities) 280
baibai kakaku no hiraki
margin (difference between
buying and selling prices) 245
baibai kakutei kabu
firm stock 224
baibai kanjō
trading account 282
baibai kawase no hiraki
exchange spread 172
baibai keiyaku
sales contract 268, 308
baibai keiyaku kansei
execution of sales contract 294
baibai shōsho
contract note [UK] 210
baibai sōba
buying and selling rates 166,
205
baibai tan'i
even lot 220; regular lot 265
baibai tesūryō
commission for purchase and
sale 209
baibai tōjisha
parties to a sale 303
baibai torihiki
dealing 215
baibai yakujō
bargain (securities) [UK] 199
baibaidaka
volume (of trading) 285
baigaku hoshō shiharai
double indemnity 319

baigaku yōrō hoken
double endowment insurance
319
baika keisei
cost-plus pricing 21
baikyaku
sale (disposal) 268, 308
baikyaku daikin
proceeds from sale 261
baikyaku iyoku
eagerness to sell 294
baikyaku kakaku
sales value 308; selling price
308
baikyaku shōsho
deed of sale 293
baikyaku tsūchi
notice of sale 303
baikyakueki
profit on sale 261
baikyakukanō shisan
realizable assets 414
baikyakunin
seller 308; vendor 312
baikyakuson
loss on sale 244
baikyakuzumi
sold 309
baishō
compensation 491; reparation
94
baishō kyōtei
reparation treaty 94
baishōkin
compensation money 491;
indemnity 322, 492
baishū
acquisition (of a company) 335,
367; buy-out 13, 340, 375;
purchase (of a company) 358;
take-over 280, 362
baishū kakaku
acquisition cost (of a company)
367; acquisition price (of a
company) 367; purchase price
(of a business) 413; target
price (take-over) 280, 423
baishū suru
buy out (verb) 340, 375;
take over (verb) 280, 362
baishū taishō gaisha
target company 362
baiyāzu-kurejitto
buyer's credit 138
bakkuguraundo
background 441
bakuhatsu
explosion 320, 491
bakuhatsu hoken
explosion insurance 320
bakuhatsu kiken tanpo tokubetsu yakkan
explosion clause 320
banai burōkā
floor broker (securities) [US]
225
bandowagon kōka
bandwagon effect 9
banku-kādo
bank card 134
bapponteki sochi
radical measures 90

baransugata shikin shintaku
balanced mutual fund 198
bārēn
Bahrain 189
baruboa (panama)
balboa (Panama) 190
basho
location (area, place, spot) 301
bātā
barter 10
bātā bōeki
barter trade 10
bātā keizai
barter economy 10
bātā kyōtei
barter agreements 10
batachi
floor clerk 225; floor trader [US]
226
batchi genka
batch cost 372
batchi genkahō
batch costing [UK] 372;
job costing [US] 398
bātsu (taikoku)
baht (Thailand) 190
bea-supureddo
bear spread 199
bebii-būmu
baby boom 9
bebii-būmu sedai
baby boomers 9
beika
US currency 186
beika kōsai
dollar bond 219
beika saiken
debenture in dollars 215
beikeizai gakkai
American Economic
Association (AEA) 4, 7
beikoku
United States of America 191
beikoku de hakkō beidoru gaisai
Yankee bond [US] 286
beikoku no shōhin sakimono torihiki i'inkai
Commodity Futures Trading
Commission (CFTC) [US] 207,
209
beikoku tōkei kyōkai
American Statistical Association
(ASA) 7
beikoku yotaku shōken
American depository receipts
(ADR) 194, 195; depository
receipt [US] 217
beikoku yushutsunyū ginkō
Export-Import Bank of the
United States (EXIMBANK)
146
beiru-auto suru
bail out (a company) 372
beitsūka kōsai
US dollar bond 285
bekutoru
vector 117
benezuera
Venezuela 191
benchi-māku
benchmark 11
bengi
expedience (expediency) 35

bengoshi
attorney [US] 433; solicitor
[UK] 309, 361
bengoshi hiyō
legal expenses 301
bengoshi hōshū
solicitor's fees 309
benri shokuhin kōgyō
convenience food industry 123
bensai
payment 155, 258; repayment
266; settlement 272
bensai suru
repay (settle) 266
berugii
Belgium 189
bēsu-appu
base-wage increase 475
bēsu-rēto
base rate 475
betsu na heya
separate office 467
betsudan yokin
miscellaneous deposits 401;
special deposit [UK] 161
betsudō gaisha
shell company 360
betsuguchi kanjō
separate account 160
betto tsumitatekin
general reserve 394; other
reserves 407
bibun
differentiation (function) 26
bichiku
stockpiling (stocking for
emergency) 104
bichōsei
finetuning 39
biggu-bōdo
Big Board [NYSE – US] 200
bihin
appliances 289; fixtures and
fittings 295; furnishings 295
bijinesu-dinā
business dinner 487
bijinesu-ranchi
business lunch 487
bijutsu kōgeihin hoken
fine arts insurance 320
bijutsu kōgeihin hoken shōken
fine arts insurance policy 320
binbō
poverty (destitution) 82
binbō na
poor 81
binbōkoku
poor countries 81
binbōsen
poverty line 82
binjō neage
price hikes 83
biru
building, a 291
bishiteki keizai moderu
micro-economic model 68
bishiteki keizai seisaku
micro-economic policy 68
bishiteki keizaigaku
micro-economics 68

bubun chōsei
partial adjustment 78
bubun dokusen
partial monopoly 78
bubun haishitsu
partial disability 326
bubun hoken
partial insurance 326
bubun junbi ginkōsei
fractional reserve banking 147
bubun kansa
partial audit 408
bubun keizai
sub-economy 105
bubun kinkō
partial equilibrium 78
bubun kinkō bunseki
partial equilibrium analysis 78
bubun shoyū no
partially owned 355
bubunhin
parts (on balance sheet) 408
bubunteki kōgyōka
limited industrialization 63
buchō
departmental manager 452
buchō dairi
acting general manager 449
buin
departmental staff member 453
buka
subordinate (noun) 468
bukka
commodity prices 17, 209;
price(s) 83; price of
commodities 260
bukka antei
price stability 84
bukka anteika
price stabilization 84
bukka anteika seisaku
price-stabilization policy 84
bukka atsuryoku
price pressures 83
bukka bakuhatsu
price explosion 83
bukka-chingin akujunkan
price-wage spiral 84
bukka chōsei
price adjustment 83
bukka chōsetsu
price regulation 84
bukka dōkō
price trends 84
bukka geraku
decline in prices 23
bukka hendō
price fluctuations 84
bukka hendō chōsei no
inflation-adjusted 54
bukka hikisage
price reduction 83; reduction in
prices 93
bukka hikisage seisaku
rollback 97
bukka infurēshon
price inflation 83
bukka jōshō
price increase 83; price rise
84; rising prices 96
bukka jōshōritsu
rate of price increase 91

bukka kugizuke
price-pegging 83
bukka mitōshi
price forecast 83
bukka seisaku
price policy 83
bukka shisū
price index 83
bukka shisū suraidosei
indexing 51
bukka suijun
price level 83
bukka tōketsu
price freeze 83
bukka tōki
price increase 83; rising prices
96
bukka tōsei
price control 83
bukka tōsei i'inkai
Price Commission [UK] 83
bukka tōsei kaijo
price decontrol 83
bumon
department 452; sector 99
bumon yosan
departmental budget 386
bumonbetsu genka keisan
departmental cost accounting
386
bumonbetsu kaikei
departmental accounting 386;
departmental accounts 386
bumonhi
departmental expenses 386
bumonhi shūkeihyō
departmental summary sheet
386
būmu
boom 11
bungyō
division of labour 27
bunjōchi
land allotment sale 299;
land for sale in lots 299
bunkatsu chūmon
split order 276
bunkatsu hensai
amortization [US] 195
bunkatsu hensai rōn
amortization loan [US] 195
bunkatsu hensai suru
amortize [US] 195
bunkatsu kakuzuke
split rating 276
bunkatsu motochō kanjō
split-ledger account 419
bunkatsu shoyūken
several ownership 309, 360
bunkatsu sōba
split quotation 276
bunkatsu uri
split sale 276
bunkatsubarai
instalment 234; payment in
instalments 436
bunkatsubaraikin
instalment 234
bunkenka
decentralization 23

bunkenteki kanri
decentralized management
344
bunkenteki kanri soshiki
decentralized management
organization 344
bunkenteki seisaku kettei
decentralized decision-taking
23
bunpai
distribution (split) 27, 387;
distribution (securities) 218
bunpai kinō
distribution function 27
bunpai kokumin shotoku
national income distributed 72
bunpai no riron
distribution 27; theory of
distribution 110
bunpaihō
distribution policy 387
bunpairon
distribution (theory of) 27
bunpu no ragu
distributed lags 27
bunri kazei
separate taxation 483;
separation of taxation 99
bunrui
classification 16
bunsan
variance 117
bunsan bunseki
analysis of variance (ANOVA)
7; variance analysis 117
bunsan tōshi
diversification 218; diversified
investment 218
bunsan tōshigata tōshi shintaku
diversified investment company
218
bunsan tōshika
diversifier 218
bunseki
analysis 7, 195
bunsekika
analyst 7, 450
bunsho
document(s) 293
bunsho gizō
forgery of document 346
bunsho kison
mutilation of document 353
bunsho no etsuran
inspection of documents 349
bunsho no funshitsu
loss of document 351
bunsho tenpu
documentation 293
bunson
partial loss 326
bunson yakkan
particular average warranty
326
buntan kaison
general average 321
buppinzei
sales tax (commodity tax,
excise tax) [UK] 97
burajiru
Brazil 189

burasseru kanzei jōkyohyō
Brussels Tariff Nomenclature
12
bureikō
'free and informal party' 488
burēki
break (rest) 450, 475
buretton-uzzu kyōtei
Bretton Woods agreement 12
burōkā
broker 203
burōkā dake no tōki sōba
broker's market 204
burōkā-diirā
broker-dealer [UK] 204
burōkā gyōsha
wire house 286
burōkā tesūryō
broker's commission 204;
broker's fees 204
burokku keizai
block economy 11
būru-supureddo
bull spread 204
burugaria
Bulgaria 189
busshitsu shugi
materialism 67
busshitsu shugisha
materialist 67
busshokugai
selective buying (securities)
270
butaiura de no gōi
behind-the-scenes consensus
10
butsubutsu kōkan
barter 10
butsubutsu kōkan keizai
barter economy 10
butsunōzei
levies in kind 62
butsuryō kanri
physical controls 80
butsuteki genkai seisan-butsu
marginal physical product 66
butsuteki shigen
material resources 67
butsuteki tōnyū
physical inputs 80
byōin
hospital 321
byōin sekinin hoken
hospital professional liability
insurance 321
byōketsu
sick leave (absence due to
illness) 483
byōki
illness 478
byōki kekkin
sick leave (absence due to
illness) 483
byōki kekkin negai
sick-leave request form 483
byōki kyūka
sick leave 483

chingin-kyūryō shiharaibo
payroll register 409; wages and salaries book 427
chingin motochō
wages ledger 427
chingin no bukka suraidosei
wage indexation to prices 118
chingin no fubyōdō
inequality of salary 479
chingin no genkai seisan ryokusetsu
marginal productivity theory of wages 66
chingin rōdōsha
wage workers 119
chingin sabetsu
wage discrimination 486
chingin saikō gendo
pay ceiling 79, 481
chingin seido
wage plan 486
chingin seikatsusha
salaried person 483; salary man 483; wage earners 118
chingin seisaku
pay policy 481; wage policy 118, 486
chingin sendōsei
wage leadership 118
chingin shiharai
wage payment 486
chingin shiharai chōka no
overpaid 480
chingin shiharai kikan
payroll period 409
chingin shiharai seido
wage payment system 486
chingin shiharaidaka
wage bill 118
chingin shiharaisugi
overpaid 480
chingin shingikai
wages councils [UK] 119
chingin shisū
wage index 118; wage-rate index 119
chingin shotoku
wage income 118, 486
chingin suijun
wage level 118
chingin sukēru
wage scale 119, 486
chingin taikei
wage system 119, 486
chingin tessoku
iron law of wages 58
chingin tōketsu
pay freeze 79, 481; pay pause [UK] 79, 481; wage freeze 118, 486
chingin tōketsu seisaku
wage freeze policy 118
chingin tōsei
wage control 118
chingin yokusei
wage restraint 119
chingin zōkaritsu
rate of wage growth 482
chinginritsu
wage rate(s) 119, 486
chinginsetsu
wage theory 119

chinō
intelligence 458
chinō shisū
IQ (intelligence quotient) 443
chinpuka
obsolescence 75
chinpuka shita
obsolete 75
chinpuka shisan
obsolete assets 404
chinpuka tanaoroshi shisan
obsolete stock 404
chinrōdō
wage labour 118
chinshaku fudōsan
leasehold property 300
chinshakuchi
leasehold 300
chinshakuken
leasehold 300; right of lease 308
chinshakunin
leaseholder 300; lessee 301
chinshakuryō
rent (verb) 306
chinshakuryō juryō
rent receipt 307
chinshakuryō shiharai
rent payment 307
chinshigoto
piece work 464
chinshigotonin
piece worker 464
chintai shikyō
depressed market 217; dull market 219
chintaishaku kitei
provisions of lease 305
chire
Chile 189
chiriteki henkyō
geographic frontier 43
chiryoku
intelligence 458
chishiki
knowledge 60, 444
chishiki rōdōsha
brain worker 450
chishiki sangyō
knowledge industry 124
chishiki shūyakuteki sangyō
knowledge-intensive industries 60
chisho
estate (land) 294; landed property 300
chisho kanrinin
land steward 299
chiso
land rate [UK] 299; land tax 61, 299
chitai
zone 122
chiteki rōdō
brain work 450
chiteki shokugyōka
professional (noun) 465

chōbo
account books 365; books 373
chōbo o kansa suru
examine the books 389
chōbo o shimekiri suru
balance the books 372
chōbo o shimekiru
close the books 379
chōbo genka
book cost 373
chōbo hizuke
book date 373
chōbo hyōka
book valuation 373
chōbo kagaku
book price 373
chōbo kakaku hikiage
writing-up (raising book value of assets) 428
chōbo kakaku o hikiageru
write up (raise book value of assets) 428
chōbo kakaku hikisage
writing-down (lowering book value of assets) 428; writing-off 428
chōbo kakaku o hikisageru
write down (lower book value of assets) 427
chōbo kansa
book audit 373
chōbo kinyū
book entry 373
chōbo no shimekiri
closing of the books 379
chōbo seido
book system 373
chōbo seiri
adjustment of accounts 368
chōbo shōmi rieki
net profit on book basis 403
chōbo tanaoroshi
book inventory 373
chōbo tanaoroshihō
book inventory method 373
chōbo zandaka
book balance 373
chōbogai shisan
non-ledger assets 404
chōbojō no jōyokin
book surplus 373
chōbojō no kakaku
book value 373
chōbojō no karikata
book debit 373
chōbojō no kashikata
book credit (credit side) 373
chōbojō no rieki
book profit 373; paper profit 408
chōbojō no sonshitsu
book loss 373
chōbojō no taishaku kanjō
book account 373
chochiku
saving(s) 97, 159; thrift 110
chochiku ginkō
savings bank 159
chochiku ginkō tsūchō
savings bank book 160
chochiku kanjō
savings account 159

chochiku kansū
savings function 98
chochiku-kashitsuke kumiai
Savings and Loan Association [US] 159, 269
chochiku keihatsu
saving motivation 98
chochiku kikan
thrift institution [US] 162
chochiku kin'yū kikan
thrifts [US] 281
chochiku saiken
savings bond [US] 269
chochiku seikō
propensity to save 88
chochiku shōrei
saving encouragement 97; savings promotion 98
chochiku shōrei undō
savings promotion campaign 98
chochiku-shotoku hiritsu
savings/income ratio 98
chochiku suishin undō
savings drive 98
chochiku suru
save 159
chochiku-tōshi bunseki
saving-investment analysis 98
chochiku-tōshi no shotoku ketteiron
saving-investment theory of income determination 98
chochiku-tōshi ronsō
saving-investment controversy 98
chochiku tsūchō
savings passbook 160
chochiku yokin
savings deposit 160
chochiku yokin kanjō
deposit account [UK] (savings account) 143
chochiku yūgū sochi
preferential tax treatment for savings 82
chochikuka
saver 159
chochikuritsu
savings rate 98
chochikusei yokin
time deposit [US] 162
chochikushin
saving mentality 98; thrift mentality 110
chōin suru
sign 360
chōinfurēshon
run-away inflation 97
chōjikan rōdō
long hours 460
chōka hakkō
overissue 256, 407
chōka hoken
overinsurance 326
chōka kiken
abnormal risk 193
chōka kinmu
overtime 78; overtime work 463
chōka kinmu teate
overtime allowance 481

chūka jinmin kyōwakoku
People's Republic of China 189

chūka minkoku
Taiwan 190

chūkai
intermediation 235

chūkainin
middleman 247

chūkaisha
intermediary 235; middleman 247, 325

chūkan gijutsu
intermediate technology 55

chūkan gyōsha
middleman 325

chūkan haitō
interim dividend 396

chūkan hōkokusho
interim report 396

chūkan juyō
intermediate demand 55

chūkan kaikyū
middle class 68

chūkan kanbu
middle management executive 461

chūkan kanjō
interim account 396

chūkan kansa
interim audit 396

chūkan kei'eisō
middle management 352, 461

chūkan keisansho
interim statement 396

chūkan kessan
interim closing 396

chūkan kin'yū
interim finance 235

chūkan ragu
intermediate lag 55

chūkan seisanbutsu
intermediate products 55

chūkan shotoku kaisō
middle-income bracket 68

chūkanzai
intermediate goods 55

chūken kigyō
medium-sized enterprise 352

chūki
intermediate term 235

chūki kashidashi
medium-term loan 247

chūki keizai tenbō
medium-term economic outlook 68

chūki keizai yosoku
medium-term economic forecast 68

chūki kokusai
mediums [UK] 247

chūki no
medium-term 68, 247

chūki shin'yō
medium-term credit 247

chūki tōshi junkan
medium-term investment cycle 68

chūki yosoku
medium-term forecast 68

chūki zaimu senryaku
medium-term financial strategy 68

chūkisai
medium-term bond 247

chūmoku kabu
watched stock 286

chūmon
order 255

chūmon no fukinkō
imbalance of orders 231

chunija
Tunisia 190

chūnyū
injections 54

chūō danbō sōchi
central heating (apparatus) 291

chūō danbōhō
central heating (system) 291

chūō ginkō
central bank 15, 138

chūō ginkō kainyū
central bank intervention 15, 167

chūō ginkō no chūritsusei
neutrality of central bank 152

chūō ginkō shin'yō
central bank credit 15, 139, 207

chūō ginkō sōsai
central bank governor 139

chūō ginkō tōkyoku
central bank authorities 139

chūō ginkō tsūka
central bank money 139, 167

chūō ginkō waribiki
discount at central bank 143

chūō ginkō waribiki buai
Bank Rate 10; central bank discount rate 139; central bank rate 139

chūō junbi ginkō
Central Reserve Bank [US] 139

chūō keikaku
central planning 16

chūō keikaku keizai
centrally planned economies 16

chūō seifu kariire juyō
central government borrowing requirements (CGBR) [UK] 16, 207

chūō tōkeitōkyoku
Central Statistical Office (CSO) [UK] 16, 22

chūō zaisei
central government finance 16

chūritsu kahei
neutral money 73

chūritsu yosan
neutral budget 73

chūritsugata kin'yū seisaku
neutral monetary policy 73

chūritsuteki gijutsu shinpo
neutral technical progress 74

chūritsuteki rishiritsu
neutral rate of interest 74

chūsai
arbitration 499; mediation 501

chūsai keiyaku
arbitration agreement 499

chūsai saitei
decision by arbitration 499

chūsainin
mediator 501

chūsei no teido
degree of loyalty 452

chūsen shōkan
drawing 219; redemption by drawing 264

chūsen shōkan tōsen shōken
bond drawn for redemption 201

chūsenzumi saiken
drawn bond 219

chūshin kei'eisha
key executive 459

chūshin rēto
central rate 167

chūshin sōba
middle rate 179

chūshō kigyō
medium and small enterprises 352; minor enterprise 352; small and medium-size businesses 361

chūshō kigyō josei kikin
aid fund for small businesses 195

chūshō kigyō kin'yū
small business financing 418

chūshō kigyō kin'yū betsuwaku yūshi
loans for small businesses 243

chūshō kigyō kin'yū kikan
credit agency for small businesses 212

chūshō sangyō
minor industries 69

chūshō shōkōgyōsha
medium and small manufacturers 68

chūshoku jikan
lunch break 460

chūshokuken
luncheon vouchers 479

chūshotokukoku
middle-income nations 68

chūshotokusō
middle-income bracket 68, 480

chūshutsu sangyō
extractive industry 124

chūtei shotokusō
lower and medium income groups 65, 479

chūto saiyō
occasional recruitment 444, 448 (note 25)

chūzai
residence (stay) 308

chūzai suru
posted abroad (to be) 464

chūzō
minting (casting, founding) 179

chūzō kakaku
mint price 179

chūzō suru
mint (verb) 179

chūzōka
metallic coin 179

chūzōsho
mint (noun) (a foundry, a mint) 179

daichō
ledger (register) 398

daigaku
university 447

daigaku sotsugyōsha
university graduate 447

daigakuin
post-graduate school 445

daiginkō
major bank 151

daihakkai
first session of the year 224; opening session of the year 254

daihyō
representation (acting for, standing for) 359

daihyō sōba
authority to represent the company 337

daihyō kengen o yūsuru shomeisha
authorized signatories 337

daihyō kengen o yūsuru torishimariyaku
authorized representative 337

daihyō shain
representative member 359; representative partner 359

daihyō suru
represent (act for) 359

daihyō torishimariyaku
representative director 359, 466

daihyōbu
representative office 359

daihyōken
right of representation 360

daihyōsha
agent (for the company) 336; replacement (person) 446; representative 359

daihyōteki kigyō
representative firm 94

dai'ichi kawase tegata
first of exchange 146

dai'ichi shihanki
first quarter 39, 391

dai'ichi shijō
first market 224

dai'ichi tanpotsuki saiken
first mortgage bond 224

dai'ichi teitō
first mortgage 295

dai'ichi yūsen kabu
first preferred stock 224, 391

dai'ichibu
First Section [J] 224, 287 (note 13)

dai'ichiji kahei
primary money 84

dai'ichiji koyō
primary employment 84

dai'ichiji rōdōsha
primary workers 84

dai'ichiji sangyō
primary industry 84

dai'ichiji sanpin
primary commodities 84; primary goods 84; primary products 84

dai'ichiji shijō
primary market 84

deal sōba
cover rate 168
defure
deflation 24
defure-gyappu
deflationary gap 24
defure keikō
deflationary trend 24
defure ronsha
deflationist 24
defure seisaku
deflationary policy 24
defurēshon
deflation 24
defurētā
deflator 24
dekidaka chingin
piece wage 482
dekidaka chinginritsu
piece wage rate 482
dekidakabarai
piece work payment 482
dekidakabarai chinginritsu
piece-work rate 482
dekidakabarai no shigoto
piece work 464
dekidakabarai shokunin
piece worker 464
dekidakane
fixing (of a currency) 173
demando-puru-infurēshon
demand-pull inflation 25
demando-shifuto-infurēshon
demand-shift inflation 25
den'en toshi
garden city 296
denki
electricity 294
denki-gasu-suidōgyō
electricity, water and gas supply
industry 124
denki kigu
electrical appliances 294
denki kikai kigu seizōgyō
electrical machinery equipment
and supplies industry 124
denki kōgyō
electricity industry 124
denki ryōkin
electricity charges 294;
electricity rates 294
denki tsūshingyō
telecommunications industry
127
denkō jōhōban
broad tape [US] 203
denmāku
Denmark 189
denpyōshiki boki
slip book-keeping 418
denpyōshiki kaikeihō
slip system of accounting 418
denryoku gaisha
electricity company 294
denryoku sangyō
power-generation industry 126
denryokuhi
electricity charges 294
denshi kōgyō
electronics industry 124

denshin kawase
cable transfer 138; telegraphic
transfer (TT) 161, 163
denshin sōkin
remittance by cable 158
dentōteki bumon
traditional sectors 112
denwa hiyō
telephone expenses 423
deokure kabu
laggard 240
depojitorii ginkō
depository bank 169
desaki
outpost(s) 77, 355
dēta
data 23
dināru
**(arujeria, bārēn, chunija,
iraku, kuuēto, ribia, yorudan,
yugosurabia)**
dinar (Algeria, Bahrain, Tunisia,
Iraq, Kuwait, Libya, Jordan,
Yugoslavia) 189, 190, 191
diirā
dealer 169, 214
diirā-rōn
dealer loan 214
diruramu
**(morokko, yunaiteddo-arabu-
emirētsu)**
dirham (Morocco, United Arab
Emirates) 190, 191
disuinfurēshon
disinflation 27
dochaku rōdō
local labour (native) 64, 459
dōgaku
dynamics 28
dōgaku moderu
dynamic model 28
dōgi
motion 431
dōgi o teishutsu suru
put forward a motion 431
dōgyō kumiai
trade association (same
business) 111
dōgyōsha jinmeiroku
trade directory 362
dōgyōsha no dantai
guilds 45
dōgyōsha yokin
inter-bank deposit 149
doitsu
Germany 189
dōitsu chingin
equal pay 34, 477
dōitsu kyūyo
equal pay 477
dōitsu rōdō dōitsu chingin
equal pay for equal work 34,
477
dōji kaisetsu shin'yō
back-to-back credit 133
dōji kaisetsu shin'yōjō
back-to-back credit 198;
back-to-back L/C 133
dōji kansū
homogeneous functions 47
dōjiseido
degree of homogeneity (of a
function) 24

dōjō higyō
solidarity strike 502; sympathy
strike 503
dojō osen
soil contamination 102
dōjō sutoraiki
solidarity strike 102
dōkansū
derivative (noun) 25
dōkei no kaisha
company of the same
parentage 341
dōkengyōsha
contractor 292
dōki
'same class' 473
dōki
motivation 461
dōkō
trend (movement) 113
dōkokujin
nationals (of a country) 72
dokuritsu burōkā
independent broker [NYSE –
US] 232
dokuritsu hensū
autonomous variable(s) 8;
independent variable 51
dokuritsu kaikei
independent accounting 395
dokuritsu kaikeishi
independent accountant 395
dokuritsu kaikeishi no ikensho
independent accountant's
opinion 395
dokuritsu no kaisha
independent company 348
dokuritsu rōdōsha
independent worker 457
dokuritsu shishutsu
autonomous expenditures 8
dokuritsu shotoku
independent income 51
dokuritsu tōshi
autonomous investment 8, 197
dokusen
monopoly 70
dokusen kinshihō
anti-trust laws 7
dokusen rijun
monopoly profit 71
dokusen ronsha
monopolist 70
dokusen shihon
monopoly capital 71
dokusen shihon shugi
monopoly capitalism 71
dokusen to gappei i'inkai
Monopolies and Mergers
Commission [UK] 70
dokusen to gappeihō
Monopolies and Mergers Act
[UK] 70
dokusenryoku
monopoly power 71
dokusenteki kyōsō
monopolistic competition 70
dokusenteki shijō
monopolistic market 70
dokushin kizoku
'the unmarried aristocracy' 473

dokushin no
single 446
dokushinsha
single persons 100
dōkyonin
lodger (room-mate, paying
guest) 301
dōkyonin o oku
take a lodger 310
dōminzoku kokka
homogeneous nation 47
donchō shikyō
sluggish market 274
donka
deceleration 23; slowdown
101
dōnyū shihon
capital introduced 376
dorakuma (girisha)
drachma (Greece) 189
dorei rōdōsha
slave labour 101
doru
**(beikoku, honkon, jamaika,
kanada, nyūjirando;
ōsutoraria; shingapōru)**
dollar (United States of
America, Hong Kong, Jamaica,
Canada, New Zealand;
Australia; Singapore) 170, 189,
190, 191
(chūka minkoku, marēsha)
new Taiwan dollar (Taiwan)
190; ringgit or dollar (Malaysia)
190
doru bōei
defence of the dollar [US] 169;
dollar rescue 170
doru chi'iki
dollar area 170
doru fusoku
dollar gap 170
doru heika
dollar parity 170
doru hon'isei
dollar standard 170
doru junbi
dollar reserve(s) 170
doru kajō zandaka
dollar glut 170
doru kanjō
dollar account 144
doru kawase
dollar exchange 170
doru kawase hon'isei
dollar exchange standard 170
doru kiki
dollar crisis 170
doru-pūru
dollar pool 170
doru setsugen keikaku
save-the-dollar program 183
doru shihei
dollar bill 170
doru shiji seisaku
dollar supporting measures
170
doru shinnin
faith in the dollar 172
doru sōba
dollar rate 170
dorudaka
strong dollar 185

eiri gaisha
commercial company 341;
operating business 354;
profit-making company 357

eiri hōjin
profit-making corporation 357

eiri hoken
commercial insurance 317

eiri jigyō
commercial business 341;
commercial enterprise 341;
profit-making business 357

eiri kigyō
commercial company 341;
profit-making enterprise 357

eiri kikan
profit-making institution 357

eiri kumiai
commercial partnership 341

eirisei
profitability (money-making) 87

eirisei gensoku
principle of profitability 84

eitai shakuchiken
perpetual lease 304

ejiputo
Egypt 189

ekonomisuto
economist 31

enbarai shōken
yen-denominated securities
286

enbēsu kin'yū
yen-based financing 286

enbēsu tōshi
yen-based investment 286

enchi
yen value 187

enchō hoken
extended-term insurance 320

enchō hoken keiyaku
extended policy 320

enchō shin'yō
extended credit 221

enchōkanō manki
extendable maturity 221

endaka
higher yen quotation 176;
strong yen 185

endate
yen base 187

endate gaisai
'samurai' bond [J] 268, 287
(note 16)

endate kawase
exchange in yen 172

endatesai
yen-denominated bond 286

enerugii
energy 33

enerugii hogo
energy conservation 33

enerugii shōhi
energy consumption 33

engan gyogyō
coastal fishing 123

enjiniaringu sangyō
engineering industry 124

enjo
aid 6; support (help) 280;
assistance 8

enjokoku
aid-giving country 6

enka
yen 187

enkai
dinner party 487

enkaku
antecedents 336; background
(history, development) 337

enkawase
yen exchange 187

enkawase sōba
yen rate 187

enki taishoku
postponed retirement 496

enko boshū
private issue of shares 260,
411; private subscription 261,
411

enkosha wariate
allotment of shares to relatives
369

enmantaisha
amicable resignation 495, 496
(note 42)

enshakkan
yen credit 286

entai
delinquency 216

entai haitōkin
dividend in arrear 387

entai hibu
overdue interest per diem 154,
256

entai nissū
days in arrear 214

entai no
overdue 256

entai rishi
interest for delay 234;
overdue interest 154, 256

entai risoku
default interest 216; interest in
arrears 234

entai yachin
rent in arrears 307

entaikin
arrear(s) 196, 370; arrearage
370

en'yasu
lower yen quotation 178;
weak yen 187

en'yō gyogyō
deep-sea fishing 123

erabu
select 446

erebētā
elevator [US] 294

esukarētā jōkō
escalators 34

esukūdo (porutogaru)
escudo (Portugal) 190

esukuro
escrow 145

esukuro kanjō
escrow account 146

esukuro shin'yōjō
escrow credit 146

fasshon sangyō
fashion industry 124

**finansharu-taimuzu kabushiki
torihikijo shisū**
Financial Times Stock
Exchange Index 224

**finansharu-taimuzu kōgyō
kabuka shisū**
Financial Times index of
industrial ordinary shares 223

**finansharu-taimuzu no
kabushiki torihikijo no hyaku
meigara no kabushiki shisū**
One Hundred Share Index [UK]
254

finrando
Finland 189

firippin
Philippines 190

firippusu kyokusen
Phillips curve 80

forinto (hangarii)
forint (Hungary) 189

fōwādo kainyū
forward intervention 174

fōwādo-mājin
forward margin 174

fu no chochiku
dissaving 27

fu no kōyō
disutility (negative utility) 27

fuan
unrest 116, 503

fuan na shikin jijō
shaky financial condition 417

fuantei
instability 55

fuantei keizai
unstable economy 116

fuantei keizai seichō
unstable economic growth 116

fuantei kinkō
unstable equilibrium 116

fuantei kōka
destabilizing effect 25

fuantei koyō
unstable employment 471

fuantei na kawase sōba
unstable exchange rate 186

fuantei shikyō
sensitive market (unstable) 271

fuantei yōin
destabilizing factor 25

fuanteika
destabilization (lack of stability)
25

fuanteisei
volatility 187

fubai undō
boycott movement 11

fubaidōmei
boycott (not buying) 11

fubarai
non-payment 153

fubarai kogitte
dishonoured cheque 144

fubarai shin'yō
hire purchase [UK] 231;
instalment credit [US] 234

fubarai tegata
dishonoured bill 144

fubarai yakusoku tegata
dishonoured note 218

fubyōdō
inequality 54, 458

fuchōsei
misalignment 69, 179

fudō kabunushi
weak shareholder 286;
weak stockholder 286

fudō tanpo
floating charge 225, 392

fudōsan
estate (real estate) 294;
immovable property 297;
property 305; real estate 306;
realty [US] 306; real assets
414

fudōsan baikyakueki
profit on sale of real estate 305

fudōsan baikyakuson
loss on sale of real estate 301

fudōsan burōkā
real-estate broker 306

fudōsan dairinin
agency 289; agent 289;
real-estate agent 306

fudōsan dairinin tesūryō
agent commission 289;
agent fee 289

fudōsan fukki
reversion 308; reverting of
property 308

fudōsan fukkiken
escheat (real estate) 294

fudōsan gaisha
realty company 306

fudōsan ginkō
land bank 150

fudōsan hanbaigyō
selling real estate 308

fudōsan hyōka
appraisal of real estate 289

fudōsan jōto gyōmu
conveyancing (business) 292

fudōsan jōto tetsuzuki
conveyancing (procedure) 292

fudōsan jōto toriatsukainin
conveyancer 292

fudōsan kaihatsu
real-estate development 306

fudōsan kakaku
property prices 305

fudōsan kanri
real-estate management 306

fudōsan kanteishi
real-estate appraiser 306

fudōsan kashitsuke
mortgage 152, 302; mortgage
loan 249, 302; real-estate loan
306

fudōsan keiyaku
estate contract 294

fudōsan kenri shōsho
deed of title (real estate) 293;
title deed 310

fudōsan kin'yū
mortgage finance 302

fudōsan kin'yū gaisha
mortgage company 302

fudōsan no jōto
disposition of one's estate 293

fudōsan no mitsumori
valuation of property (real
estate) 311

fudōsan shijō
property market 305

fudōsan shintaku
real estate in trust 306;
real-estate trust 306

fukushi
welfare (well-being) 120
fukushi jukyū tokuten gensoku
entitlement principle 33
fukushi kokka
welfare state 120
fukushi kōseihi
employees' welfare cost 388
fukushi seisaku
welfare policy 120
fukushi shakai
welfare society 120
fukushi shihyō
welfare indicator 120
fukushi shikōgata keizai
welfare-oriented economy 120
fukushi shikōgata shakai
welfare-oriented society 120
fukushi shishutsu
welfare expenditure 120
fukushibu
employee services 454
fukushihainin
assistant manager 450;
deputy manager 453
fukushiki boki
double-entry book-keeping 388
fukushiki kaikei seido
double-account system 388
fukushiki kichōhō
double entry 388
fukusho
counter-signature (endorsement, witnessing) 141, 343
fukusho suru
counter-sign (endorse, witness)
141, 343
fukusōshihainin
assistant general manager 450
fukusū kawase sōba
multiple rates of exchange 181
fukusū no tanpo
mortgage pool 249
fukusū tsūka
multi-currency 181
fukusū tsūka hon'isei
multiple currency standard 181
fukusū tsūka kainyū
multi-currency intervention 181
fukusū tsūka kainyūsei
multi-currency intervention
system 181
fukusū tsūka rēto kumiawase
basket of currencies 166
fukusū tsūka seido
multiple currency practice 181
fukutanpo
subsidiary collateral 279
fukyō
decline (bad business) 23;
depression 25; recession 92;
slump 101
fukyō chi'iki
depressed areas 25;
depressed regions 25
fukyō gyōshu
depressed businesses and
industries 25
fukyō no chūkan chi'iki
grey areas [UK] 44;
intermediate areas 55
fukyō sangyō
depressed industries 25

fukyō shijō
narrow market 249
fukyō taisaku
anti-recession policy 7
fukyōji
bad times (depression, slump)
9; hard times 46; period of
recession 79
fukyū
diffusion 26
fuman
discontent 499
fumanzokukan
dissatisfaction 453
fumanzokukan ga aru
dissatisfied 453
fumeiyo na kaiko
dishonourable discharge 499
fumeiyo ni kaiko sareru
discharged dishonourably 499
fumiage
bear panic 199
fumitaosu
default (verb) 216, 293
fumōchi
marginal land (unproductive
land) 301
funani shōken
bill of lading (B/L) 133, 137
funin
new appointment 461;
new post 461
funin kigyō
abortive enterprise 335
funin suru
posted (to be) 464
funinki kabu
inactive stock 232
funshitsu bunsho
lost document 351
funshitsu kabuken
lost share certificate 244, 400
funshitsu kogitte
lost cheque 151
funshitsu shōken
lost security 244
funshitsu tegata
lost bill 151
funshoku kessan
rigging of accounts 416;
window-dressing 427; window-
dressing settlement 427
funshoku sōsa
window-dressing 163
funshoku yokin
window-dressing deposits 163
furan
(berugii, furansu, monako,
rukusenburugu, suisu)
franc (Belgium, France,
Monaco, Luxembourg,
Switzerland) 189, 190
furanchaizu
franchise 347
furanchaizu o ataerareru hito
franchisee 347
furanchaizu o ataeru hito
franchisor 347
furanchaizu keiyaku
franchise agreement 347
furansu
France 189

furekkusu-taimu seido
flexi-time system 455
furi na jigyō
bad business 337
furi na kawase sōba
unfavourable rate of exchange
186
furidashi
drawing (issuing) 145;
issue (bill) 150
furidashi ginkō
drawing bank 145
furidashi hizuke
date of issue 142
furidashi tegata
drawn bill 145
furidashibi
date of issue 142; day of issue
142
furidashichi
drawing place 145; place of
issue 156
furidashinin
drawer 145; remitter 158;
sender 160
furidashinin mawashi
'refer to drawer' 158
furidasu
draw (verb) 145; issue (verb)
(bill) 150
furidasu (kogitte o)
write out (a cheque) 163
furikae
transfer (noun) 162; money
transfer 152; transfer (of a
currency) 186
furikae denpyō
transfer slip 162
furikae kakaku keisei
transfer pricing 113
furikae sashizusho
transfer order 162; transfer
request 162
furikae shotoku
transfer incomes 113
furikaekanō tsūka
transferable currency 186
furikaeryō
transfer fee 162
furikō
default (noun) 216, 293, 434
furikō kiken
default risk 216, 293
furikō meirei
default order 434
furikō saiken rishi
defaulted bond interest 216
furikō shasai
defaulted bond 216
furikomi
transfer (noun) 162; transfer to
another bank account 162
furikomu
pay in 155; transfer (verb) 162
furikōsha
defaulter 216; 293
furisaikō gendo
maximum limit for interest rates
247
furō
flow 40
furō bunseki
flow analysis 40

furorin (horanda)
florin (Netherlands) 190
furōshotoku
non-labour income 74;
unearned income 114
furōshotoku seikatsusha
rentiers (non-work income) 94
furōto
bank float 134
furōto suru
float (verb) 146
furu-kosuto
full cost 42
furu-kosuto gensoku
full-cost principle 42
furu-kosuto kakaku keisei
full-cost pricing 42
furyō kashitsuke
bad loan 198
furyō kiken
bad risk 198, 316
furyo no jiko
contingency 491
furyō saiken
bad debt (bad claim) 198
furyō saiken toritate kikan
collection bureau 209
furyō shisan kirisute
clearance of bad debts 378
furyō tōshi
bad investment 198
furyōgashi
bad debt 198; bad loan 198
furyoku
buoyancy (buoyant force) 12
fūsa
blockade 11
fūsa kanjō
blocked account 137
fūsa kawase
blocked exchange 166
fūsa keizai
closed economy 16
fūsa kogitte
blocked cheque 137
fūsa ku'iki
blockade zone 11
fūsa seisaku
blockade policy 11
fūsa shikin
blocked funds 137
fūsa tsūka
blocked currency 166
fūsa yokin
blocked deposit 137
fusai
debt 215; indebtedness 232;
liabilities 399, 436; obligation
252
fusai o kaesu
pay a debt 257
fusai gōkei
total liabilities 424
fusai hiritsu
debt ratio 385
fusai oyobi shihon
liabilities and capital 399
fusai rishi
debt interest charges 215
fusai shihon
debt capital 385

fusai-shihon hiritsu
debt/equity ratio 385; gearing ratio 42, 393; liabilities/net worth ratio 399

fusai shōninsho
acknowledgment of indebtedness 194

fusaigaku
indebtedness (amount) 232

fusaikaritsu
total liabilities/net worth ratio 424

fusakui kikan
waiting period 285

fusei jiken
scandal 269

fusei kōi
corrupt practices 343; fraudulent act 347

fusei ritoku
fraudulent gains 392

fuseisanteki jigyō
unproductive business 363

fuseisanteki jūgyōin
unproductive employee 470

fuseisanteki na
unproductive 116, 470

fuseisanteki rōdōryoku
unproductive labour 116, 470

fuseisanteki rōdōsha
unproductive worker 470

fuseisanteki shihon
unproductive capital 426

fusen
allonge 132

fushin
slump (dullness, inactivity) 101; stagnation 103

fushin shikyō
depressed market 25, 217

fushinjitsu na hyōji
false representation 346

fushinki
period of depressed activity 79

fushō
injury 492

fushō hoshō(kin)
compensation for injury 318, 491

fusoku
deficit (shortage) 24; insufficiency 55; scarcity 98; shortage 100

fusoku hoken
under-insurance 330

fusoku no infurēshon
unanticipated inflation 114

fusoku no kiken
unknown risk 330

fusokubarai
deficiency payments 24

fusokugaku
balance due 198; deficiency 385; shortfall 100

fusokukin
deficiency 385

fusokukin kanjō
deficiency account 385

fūsuigai hoken
windstorm and flood insurance 331

futai jōken
conditional collateral 209

futai kyūfu
fringe benefits 477

futai shōsho
collateral bond 208

futaketa no
double-digit 27

futaketa no infurēshon
double-digit inflation 28; two-digit inflation 113

futaketa no shitsugyō
double-digit unemployment 28; two-digit unemployment 113

futan
responsibility (company's) 483

futan no nai
unencumbered 311

futei shikibetsu
underidentification 114

futeiki rōdō
casual labour 451; casual work 451

futeiki rōdōsha
casual labourer 451; casual worker 451

futeiki yokin
irregular deposit 150

futekikaku tegata
ineligible bill 149

futekisei haibun
misallocation 69

futō hikiwatashi
bad delivery 198

futō kaiko
unfair dismissal 503; wrongful dismissal 504

futō kakaku
exorbitant prices 295

futō kei'ei
misconduct 352

futō ritoku kōi
profiteering (excessive profits) 87

futō ritokusha
profiteer 87

futō rōdō kōi
unfair labour practices 115, 470

futō shishutsu
misappropriation of funds 401

futokorogatana
right-hand man 466, 473 (note 36)

futsū baishō sekinin
general liability 321

futsū ginkō
ordinary bank [J] 154

futsū haitō
annual dividend 369; common dividend 379; ordinary dividend 406

futsū hikiuke
general acceptance 147

futsū hoken
general insurance 321; individual insurance 322; ordinary branch 326

futsū hoken yakkan
general insurance clauses and conditions 321

futsū kabu
common stock [US] 209, 379; equities [UK] 220, 389; ordinary shares [UK] 255, 406

futsū kabu haitōkin
dividend on common stock 387

futsū kabunushi
ordinary shareholder(s) 255, 406

futsū kansa
general audit 393

futsū kawase tegata
clean bill 140; clean bill of exchange 140

futsū kiken bukken
general risk 321

futsū kogitte
open cheque 154; uncrossed cheque (ordinary) 163

futsū kyōiku
general education 442

futsū ōsen
general crossing 148

futsū ōsen kogitte
general crossed cheque 147

futsū seimei hoken
ordinary life insurance 326

futsū shasai
straight bond 279

futsū shisan
ordinary assets 406

futsū shōkyaku
ordinary depreciation 406

futsū torihiki
regular transaction 265

futsū tōza yokin
regular checking account [US] 158

futsū yakkan
general conditions 321

futsū yokin
ordinary deposit 154

futsū yokin kanjō
ordinary deposit account 154

futsūsai
non-convertible bond 251

fuwatari
dishonour 144; non-payment 153

fuwatari ni suru
dishonour (verb) 144

fuwatari henkan kogitte
cheque returned unpaid 139

fuwatari henkyaku
bounce (bouncing) 138

fuwatari kogitte
bad cheque 133; bouncing cheque 138; dishonoured cheque 144; unpaid cheque 163

fuwatari tegata
bill dishonoured 137; dishonoured bill 144; unpaid bill 163; unpaid draft 163

fuwatari tegata o kaimodosu
repurchase a dishonoured bill 158

fuwatari tegata o shōkan suru
redeem a dishonoured bill 157

fuwatari tsūchi
non-payment protest 153; notice of dishonour 153

fuwatari yakusoku tegata
unpaid note 284

fuyō kazoku
dependents (family) 453

fuyō kazoku teate
dependents allowance [J] 476

fuyō kazokusū
family dependents 442

fuyō kōjo
dependents allowance 476; tax deduction for dependents 484

fuyōsha
dependents 453

fuyū
wealth (affluence, opulence) 119

fuyūkoku
rich countries 96; wealthy nation 119

fuyūzei
wealth tax 119

fuzai jinushi
absentee landlord 289; absentee landowner 289; non-resident landlord 303; non-resident landowner 303

fuzai jūyaku
absentee director 335

fuzai kei'eisha
absentee management 335

fuzai shoyūken
absentee ownership 289

fuzai shoyūsei
absentee system 289

fuzai shoyūsha
absentee owner 289

fuzaisha tōhyō
absentee voting 429

fuzoku byōin
attached hospital [J] 475

fuzui hiyō
ancillary expenses 369

gabon
Gabon 189

gaibu burōkā
over-the-counter broker 256

gaibu chōtatsu
external financing 390

gaibu fukeizai
external diseconomies 37

gaibu hōkoku kaikei
accounting for external reporting 365

gaibu kahei
outside money 77

gaibu kansa
external audit 390

gaibu kansanin
external auditor 390

gaibu keizai
external economies 37

gaibu keizai to kibo no fukeizai
external economies and diseconomies of scale 37

gaibu kin'yū gendo
external financial limits [UK] 221

gaibu kōka
externalities 37

gaibu rōdō shijō
external labour market 37

gaibu seichō
external growth 37

gaibu shihon
external capital 390; outside capital 407

gaidoposuto
guideposts 45

gaidorain
guidelines 45

gaienteki hatten
extensive development 37

gaiginkō kariire
borrowing from a foreign bank 203

gaijin hoyū kabusū
shares owned by non-Japanese [J] 273

gaijin mochikabu hiritsu
stockholding ratio of foreigners [J] 278

gaijin mochikabu seigen
stockholding limit for foreign investors [J] 278

gaijin tainitsu shōken tōshi
foreign investment in Japanese securities 226

gaijin tōshi
investment in Japanese stock by non-Japanese 237

gaijin tōshika
foreign investor 226

gaijingai
foreign buying of Japanese company shares 226, 392

gaiju
foreign demand 41

gaika
foreign currency 40, 173; foreign-denominated 173

gaika haiseki
boycott of foreign goods 11

gaika hoyūdaka
foreign currency holdings 173

gaika junbi
exchange reserve(s) 172; external reserve(s) 37, 172; foreign currency reserve(s) 173

gaika junbikin seido
foreign currency reserve system 173

gaika kaiire gaikoku kawase
foreign currency bills bought 147

gaika kanjō
foreign currency account 147

gaika kawase tegata
bill in foreign currency 137; foreign draft 147

gaika kin'yū
foreign currency finance 226

gaika kōkan'en
yen converted from foreign currency 187

gaika kokusai
government bond in foreign currency 229

gaika miharai gaikoku kawase
foreign currency bills payable 147

gaika mochidaka
foreign currency position 173

gaika pojishon
foreign currency position 173

gaika saiken
debenture in foreign currency 215

gaika shiharai tegata
bill payable in foreign currency 137

gaika shin'yōjō
foreign currency L/C 147

gaika shōken
foreign currency securities 226

gaika tegata
foreign currency bill 147

gaika toritate gaikoku kawase
foreign currency bills receivable 147

gaika uketori tegata
bill receivable in foreign currency 137

gaika uriwatashi gaikoku kawase
foreign currency bills sold 147

gaika yokin
foreign currency deposit(s) 40, 147, 173

gaika yokin kanjō
foreign currency deposit account 147

gaikasai
foreign currency bond 226

gaikō seisaku
foreign policy 41

gaikoku bōeki
foreign trade 41

gaikoku bōeki izon
dependence on foreign trade 25

gaikoku bōeki jōsū
foreign trade multiplier 41

gaikoku bōeki seisaku
foreign trade policy 41

gaikoku gaisha
alien company 336; alien corporation 336; foreign company 346; foreign corporation(s) 40, 346; foreign firm(s) 41

gaikoku ginkō
foreign bank 147

gaikoku ginkō no shōken kogaisha
securities subsidiaries of foreign banks 160, 270

gaikoku hōjin
alien corporation 336; foreign corporate body 346; foreign corporation 346

gaikoku kara no kyōsō
foreign competition 40

gaikoku kara no tōshi
foreign investment (investment from abroad) 41, 226

gaikoku kawase
foreign exchange 41, 171, 173

gaikoku kawase baibai'eki
profit on foreign exchange transaction 183

gaikoku kawase e no tōki
agiotage 165

gaikoku kawase ginkō
foreign exchange bank 147

gaikoku kawase ginkōhō
Foreign Exchange Bank Law [J] 173

gaikoku kawase kakari
foreign exchange clerk 147

gaikoku kawase kanri i'inkai
Foreign Exchange Control Board (FECB) [J] 172, 173

gaikoku kawase kashitsuke
foreign exchange loan 226

gaikoku kawase kōnin ginkō
authorized foreign exchange bank [J] 133, 164 (note 1), 165, 187 (note 9)

gaikoku kawase kōnin torihiki'in
authorized dealer 165

gaikoku kawase oyobi gaikoku bōeki kanrihō
Foreign Exchange and Foreign Trade Control Law [J] 173

gaikoku kawase saeki
gain on foreign exchange 174

gaikoku kawase sakimono
foreign exchange futures 226

gaikoku kawase shijō
foreign exchange market 173

gaikoku kawase shijō no anteisei
stability of foreign exchange market 185

gaikoku kawase tegata
foreign bill 147; foreign bill of exchange 147

gaikoku kawase tōki
foreign currency speculation 173, 226

gaikoku kigyō
alien company 336; foreign company 346; foreign corporations(s) 40; foreign firm(s) 41

gaikoku no bōeki shōheki
foreign trade barriers 41

gaikoku no fukōsei kankō
unfair foreign trade practices 115

gaikoku seihin
foreign manufactured goods 41; foreign products 41

gaikoku shihon
foreign capital 226, 392; foreign capital invested in Japan 226

gaikoku shihon tōshi
foreign capital investment 226

gaikoku shisan
foreign assets 40, 392

gaikoku shōken
foreign securities 227

gaikoku shōken gaisha
foreign securities company 227

gaikoku sōkin
remittance abroad 158

gaikoku tsūka
foreign currency 173

gaikoku tsūka sakimono
foreign currencies futures 173

gaikoku yūbin kawase
foreign post-office money order 147

gaikokuhin
foreign goods 41

gaikokujin zaisan
alien property 289

gaikokusai
foreign bond 226

gaikokusai shōkan
redemption of foreign bonds 264

gainenteki juyō
notional demand 75

gaisai
external bond 221; external loan 221; foreign bond 226; foreign debt 41, 226; foreign loan 226

gaisai boshū
flotation of external loan 226

gaisai hakkō
foreign loan issue 227

gaisai rishi
interest on external bond 234; interest on external loan 235

gaisai shōkan
redemption of external loan 264

gaisan son'eki keisansho
rough profit and loss statement 416

gaisan taishaku taishōhyō
rough balance sheet 416

gaishi
foreign capital 40, 226, 392; foreign investment 226

gaishi dōnyū
foreign capital inflow 226; import of foreign capital 232; introduction of foreign capital 236; introduction of foreign investment 236

gaishi kōsei
foreign capital offensive 226

gaishi ryūnyū
influx of foreign capital 54

gaishi yunyū
foreign-capital import 40

gaishikei kigyō
enterprise with foreign capital 346, 388; foreign affiliate 346; foreign-backed enterprise 346; foreign-owned company 346

gaishoku sangyō
food service industry 124

gakai
collapse 16

gakkō kyō'iku
public education 89

gaku
amount 165

gakui
degree 442

gakumen
par 257

gakumen chōkagaku warimashikin
premium (premium over bond value) 260

gakumen de
at par 197

gakumen hakkō
issue at par 238, 397; par issue 257, 408

gakumen ijō de
above par 193; at a premium 197

gakumen ijō no kakaku
above-par value 193

gakumen ika de
below par 200

genka motochō
cost ledger 383
genka no dōkō
cost behaviour 382
genka santei
cost calculation 382
genka shōkyaku
amortization [UK] 369;
depreciation 386; writing-down
428; writing-off 428
genka shōkyaku o suru
write down (amortize [UK],
depreciate) 427; write off 428
genka shōkyaku chōsei
depreciation adjustment 386
genka shōkyaku hikiatekin
allowance for depreciation 369;
depreciation allowance 386;
depreciation reserve 386;
reserve for depreciation 415
genka shōkyaku hiritsu
rate of depreciation 413
genka shōkyaku kaikei
depreciation accounting 386
genka shōkyaku kanjō
depreciation account 386
genka shōkyaku kikin
depreciation fund 386
genka shōkyaku kisō genka
depreciable cost 386
genka shōkyaku ruisekigaku
accumulated depreciation 367
genka shōkyaku shisan
depreciable assets 386
genka shōkyaku sōgaku
total amount depreciated 424
genka shōkyaku tan'i
depreciation unit 386
genka shōkyakugaku
depreciable amount 386
genka shōkyakuhi
depreciation cost 386;
depreciation expenses 386
genka shōkyakuhō
depreciation method 386
genka shōkyakuritsu
depreciation rate 386
genka shōkyakuzumi
fully depreciated 393
genka shugi
cost basis (principle) 382
genka tan'i
cost unit 383
genka tsūka
depreciated currency 169
genka wariate
cost apportionment 382
genka yōso
cost factor 21, 382
genkabu
spot share 276
genkabunushi
existing shareholders 389
genkahō
cost method 383; valuation at
cost 426
genkai
margin 66
genkai bunseki
marginal analysis 66
genkai chochiku seikō
marginal propensity to save 66

genkai daitairitsu
marginal rate of substitution
(MRS) 66, 71
genkai fukōyō
marginal disutility 66
genkai genka
marginal cost 66, 400
genkai genka keisan
marginal costing 400
genkai henkeiritsu
marginal rate of transformation
66
genkai hikoyōsha
marginal employee 460
genkai hiyō
marginal expenses 66, 401
genkai hiyō kakaku keisei
marginal cost pricing 66
genkai kigyō
marginal enterprise 352;
marginal firm 352
genkai kigyōka
marginal entrepreneur 352
genkai kōyō
marginal utility 67
genkai kōyō teigen
diminishing marginal utility 26
genkai kōyō teigen no hōsoku
law of diminishing marginal
utility 61
genkai koyōsha
marginal employer 460
genkai nōritsu
exploitation efficiency 346
genkai rieki
marginal income 401; marginal
profit 401
genkai rijun
marginal profit 401
genkai rōdō
marginal labour 66
genkai rōdōsha
marginal worker(s) 67, 460
genkai rōdōsha kasetsu
additional worker hypothesis 4
genkai seisanbutsu
marginal product 66
genkai seisanhi
marginal cost of production 66
**genkai seisanryoku teigen no
hōsoku**
law of diminishing marginal
productivity 61
genkai seisanryokusetsu
marginal productivity doctrine
66
**genkai shihon-sanshutsudaka
hiritsu**
incremental capital/output ratio
(ICOR) 48, 51
genkai shōhi
marginal consumption 66
genkai shōhi seikō
marginal propensity to consume
(MPC) 66, 71
genkai shōhisha
marginal consumer 66
genkai shūeki
marginal returns 401
genkai shūnyū
marginal revenue 66, 401
genkai shūnyū seisanbutsu
marginal revenue product 67

genkai shutoku hiyō
marginal cost of acquisition 66
genkai son'eki keisansho
marginal income statement
401
genkai sozei seikō
marginal propensity to tax 66
genkai tan'i
marginal unit 67
genkai uriagedaka
marginal proceeds 401
genkai yunyū seikō
marginal propensity to import
66
genkai zeiritsu
marginal rate of tax 66
genkaikei nendo
current financial year [UK] 384;
current fiscal year [US] 384
genkin
cash 138, 167; money (specie)
70, 151, 180
genkin ni kaeru
cash in (verb) 138
genkin chingin
money wage(s) 70, 480
genkin fusai
cash liabilities 378
genkin haitō
cash dividend 377
genkin hikikae
cash on delivery (securities)
207
genkin hiritsu
cash ratio 138, 378
genkin jidō azukariki
cash depositor (machine) 138
genkin jidō shiharaiki
automated teller 133; automatic cash-paying machine
133; automatic teller machine
(ATM) 132, 133; cash
dispenser 138; cashpoint [UK]
138
genkin junbi
cash reserve 138
genkin junbikin seido
cash reserve requirements 138
genkin junbiritsu
cash ratio 138; cash reserve
ratio 138
genkin juyō
cash needs 378
genkin kakari
cash keeper 138
genkin kanjō
cash account 207, 377
genkin kansa
cash audit 377
genkin kara no tōhi
flight from cash 225
genkin keijōhi
cash expenses 377
genkin keisansho
cash statement 378
genkin kōmoku
cash item 378
genkin kōnyū
cash purchase 291
genkin ryūdō
cash flow 377
genkin ryūnyū
cash inflow 378

genkin ryūshutsu
cash outflow 378
genkin seigen
cash limit 15, 378
genkin shiharai
cash payment 378
genkin shiharai hiyō
out-of-pocket expenses 488
genkin shiharai yosan
cash payments budget 378
genkin shiharaichō
cash payments book 378;
cash payments journal 378;
paid-cash book 408
genkin shijō
cash market 167, 207
genkin shikin
cash fund 378
genkin shisan
cash assets 377
genkin shishutsu hiyō
out-of-pocket expenses 407
genkin shiwakechō
cash journal 378
genkin shōkan
cash redemption 207
genkin shōmi rieki
net profit on cash basis 403
genkin shotoku
cash income 378
genkin shugi
cash basis 377
genkin shugi kaikei
cash-basis accounting 377
genkin shūnyū
money income 70; cash
earning(s) 377
genkin shūshi ichiranhyō
cash-flow statement 378
genkin shūshi mitsumori
cash forecasts 378
genkin shūshi yosan
cash budget 15, 377; cash-flow
budget 377
genkin sōkin
cash remittance 138
genkin suitōbo
cash book 377
genkin suitōchō
cash book 377
genkin tegata
cash bill 138
genkin torihiki
cash transaction 207, 291
genkin uketori
cash receipt 378
genkin uketori shiwakechō
cash receipts book 378;
cash receipts journal 378
genkin uriagechō
cash sales book 378
genkin waribiki
cash discount 377; settlement
discount 417
genkin yokin
cash and deposits (on balance
sheet) 377; cash deposit 138
genkin yosan
cash budget 377; cash-flow
budget 377
genkin yusō
shipment of currency 160, 183

gijutsuteki daitairitsu
rate of technical substitution 91
gijutsuteki dokusen
technical monopoly 109
gijutsuteki henka
technological change 109
gijutsuteki jukuren
skill(s) 446; technical skills
109, 447
gijutsuteki nijūsei
technological dualism 109
gijutsuteki shitsugyō
technological unemployment
109
gijutsuteki yōin
technical factors 109
giketsu
vote (noun) 432
giketsu suru (— ni)
vote (on —) 432
giketsu suru shikaku no
qualified to vote 431
giketsuken
voting power 363, 438; voting
right 363, 438
giketsuken o kōshi suru
exercise the right to vote 430
giketsuken o ruiseki suru
cumulate votes 430
**jishin ni yoru giketsuken
kōshi**
vote in person 432
giketsuken kabushiki
voting stock 426
giketsuken no pūru
pooling of voting power 431
gikō
skill(s) 446; technical skills
109
gimu
responsibility (duties) 359, 466
gimu kyōiku
compulsory education 18
gin hon'isei
silver standard 184
gin hoyū
silver holdings 184
gin hoyūsha
silver holder 184
gin jigane
silver bullion 184
gin kachi
silver value 184
gin kawase
silver exchange 184
gin shōken
silver certificate [US] 184
ginka
silver coin 184
ginkai
silver bullion 184; silver ingot
184
ginkai shijō
silver bullion market 184;
silver market 184
ginkō
bank(s) 10, 133
ginkō bangō
sorting code 160; transit
number [US] 162
ginkō bumon
banking sector 136

ginkō e tanpokanō na
bankable 135
ginkō eigyō jikan
banking hours 136
ginkō eigyō shikin
bank capital 134
ginkō furikomi
bank transfer 135
ginkō gōdō
bank merger 134
ginkō gōtō
bank robbery 135
ginkō gyōkai
banking circles 136; banking
community 136; banking world
136
ginkō gyōmu
banking (business) 136
ginkō gyōmu himitsusei
banking secrecy 136
ginkō gyōmu seisaku
banking policy 136
ginkō gyōsei
banking administration 136
ginkō hatan
bank crash 9, 134; bank failure
134
ginkō hikiuke shin'yōjō
bank acceptance credit 133;
banker's acceptance credit 135
ginkō hikiuke tegata
bank acceptance 133; banker's
acceptance [US] 135
**ginkō hikiuke tegata waribiki-
ritsu**
banker's acceptance rate 135
ginkō hikiuke waribikiritsu
bank acceptance rate 133
ginkō hoshō
banker's guarantee 135
ginkō junbikin
bank reserves 135
ginkō kaikei hōkoku
bank confirmation [US] 134;
bank report 135
ginkō kaisōba
bank buying rate 134, 165
ginkō kanjō
bank account(s) 9, 133
ginkō kanjō chōseihyō
bank agreement 133; bank
reconciliation 135
ginkō kanjō hōkokusho
bank statement 135; statement
of account 161
ginkō kariirekin
bank borrowing 134, 198
ginkō karikoshi
bank overdraft 135
ginkō kashidashi
bank credit 9, 134; bank
loan(s) 10, 134, 198; bank
loans and discounts 10; bank
lending 134, 198
ginkō kashitsuke
bank loan(s) 10, 134, 198
ginkō kawase
bank money order 135
ginkō kawase tegata
bank draft [UK] 134;
banker's draft [UK] 135;
cashier's cheque [US] 138

ginkō kensa
bank examination 134;
examination 146
ginkō kensakan
bank examiner 134; examiner
146
ginkō kinri
bank rate (interest) 135
ginkō kinri seisaku
bank rate policy 135
ginkō kiroku
bank records 135
ginkō kisei
bank regulations 135
ginkō kogitte
banker's cheque 135
ginkō kōza
bank account 133
ginkō kuriin-biru
banker's clean bill 135
ginkō kyōkai
bankers' association 136
ginkō kyōkō
banking panic 136
ginkō kyūjitsu
bank holiday 134
ginkō mochikabu gaisha
bank holding company [US]
134
ginkō no ginkō
banker's bank 135
ginkō no kanri shita ni aru
in the hands of the bank (to be)
435
ginkō no shiharai kakari
paying teller 155
ginkō riritsu
bank rate (interest) 135, 199
ginkō rishi
bank interest 134
ginkō ryūdōsei
bank liquidity 134; liquidity of
bank 151
ginkō sanchakubarai
bank demand 134
ginkō sanchakubarai tegata
bank demand draft 134
ginkō seido
banking 136; banking system
136
ginkō setsuritsu menkyo
bank charter [US] 134
ginkō shiharai junbikin
bank reserves 135
ginkō shihei
bank note [UK] 135, 166;
bank bill [US] 165
ginkō shinsain
bank commissioner 134
ginkō shin'yō
bank credit 9, 134, 198;
bank lending 198
**ginkō shin'yō kyūyo gendo-
gaku**
bank line [US] 134
ginkō shin'yō shōkaisaki
bank reference 135, 199
ginkō shin'yōjō
banker's L/C 136
ginkō shogakari
banking charges 136
ginkō sōkin kawase
bank remittance 135

ginkō soshiki
banking (organization) 136
ginkō suitō kakari
bank teller 135
ginkō tegata
bank bill [UK] 134; bank paper
135
ginkō tegata waribiki
banker's discount 135;
simple discount 160
ginkō tesūryō
bank charges 134; bank
commission 134
ginkō tōnan hoken
bank burglary-robbery
insurance 316
ginkō tōnan hoken shōken
bank burglary-robbery
insurance policy 316
ginkō torihiki
bank transaction 135; banking
136
ginkō torihiki teishi
suspension of banking
transactions 437
ginkō toritsuke
run on banks 159
ginkō tsūchō
bank book 134; passbook 155
ginkō un'yō sōsa
banking operation 136
ginkō uragaki
bank endorsement 134
ginkō waribiki
bank discount 134
ginkō waribiki buai
bank discount rate 134
ginkō yokin
bank deposit(s) 9, 134; bank
account 133; deposit at bank
143
ginkō yokin hoken
deposit insurance 143
ginkō yokin zandaka
bank balance 134
ginkō yūshi
bank accommodation 133;
bank credit (finance) 9, 134;
bank lending 134, 198
ginkōbarai
payment by banker 156
ginkōdan
banking syndicate 136;
syndicate 161
ginkōgyō
banking business 136
ginkōhō
banking law 136
ginkō'igai no kin'yū kikan
non-bank financial inter-
mediaries (NBFI) 249, 251
ginkō'in
bank clerk 134; bank staff 135
ginkōka
banker 135
ginkōkan kawase torihiki
inter-bank exchange dealings
149, 177
ginkōkan shijō
inter-bank market 149
ginkōkan sōba
inter-bank rate 149

gyappu
gap 42, 228
gyappu bunseki
gap analysis 42**gyogyō**
fishing 39; fishing industry 124
gyogyō rōdō kumiai
fishery co-operatives 39
gyogyōken
fishing rights 39
gyogyōsha
fishermen 39
gyōkai
business community 13;
business observers 13;
business world 13
gyōkai no hōkoku
business report (economic
experts') 13
gyoku
account (client's) 193
gyōkyō
business outlook 339
gyōkyō chōsa
business research 13
gyōkyō shindan
business diagnosis 13
gyōmu
business 338; operation (work)
354
gyōmu hōkokusho
operating report 354
gyōmu kakuchō
business expansion 338
gyōmu kanri
business management 339;
operational control 354
gyōmu kansa
business audit 374; operating
audit 405; operation audit 406
gyōmu katsudō genka
activity cost 367
gyōmu saigai
industrial accident 322, 492;
occupational accident 492
gyōmu saigai nenkin
industrial disability pension 492
gyōmu saikō sekininsha
chief operation officer 451
gyōmu shikkō shain
managing partner 352
gyōmu soshiki
business organization (set-up)
339
gyōmu suikō sekinin
responsibility of operation 360
gyōmu tantō shain
active partner 335
gyōmu tayōka
business diversification 338;
diversification of business 344
gyōmu tayōka keikaku
business diversification
programme 338
gyōmu tokō
business travel 487
gyōmujō no jiko
job-related accident 492;
on-the-job accident 326, 493
gyōmujō no saigai
on-the-job accident 493
gyōretsu
matrix 68

gyōsei
administration 4
gyōsei kaikaku
administrative reform 4
gyōsei kanchō
administrative authorities 4
gyōsei kanri yosankyoku
Office of Management and
Budget [US] 75
gyōsei kikan
administrative organ 4
gyōsei kyōtsūhi
administrative expenses 4
gyōsei seiri
administrative reorganization 4
gyōsei shidō
administrative guidance 4
gyōsei shobun
administrative action 4
gyōsei sochi
administrative measures 4
gyōseikan
administrators 4
gyōseiken
administrative power 4
gyōseki
business performance 339;
business results 375; operating
results 354; performance 79,
356, 463
gyōseki hōkokusho
business (performance) report
339
gyōseki hyōka
performance evaluation 356
gyōseki kabu
performance stock 258
gyōseki kentō
business results analysis 339
gyōsha
businessman 339; business
person (trader) 340
gyōshakan sōba
dealer market 214
gyōshōnin
commercial traveller 452;
travelling salesman 470
gyōshu
line of business 350; type of
business 362; type of industry
114
gyōshu henkō
change of line of business 340
gyōshubetsu chingin
wages classified by industries
119
gyōtai
form of business organization
41, 346

haba
margin 179; range 263
hada
character 451; temperament
469
hada ni awasenai shigoto
unsuitable work 471
hadaka nigawase tegata
documentary clean bill 144
hadaka sōba
ex-interest quotation 220;
flat quotation 225

hadaka torihiki
ex-interest transaction 220
hadō
wave 119
hādo-doru (tesūryō)
hard dollars [US] 230
hādo-rōn
hard loan 230
haenuki
'born and bred' 473
hai-pawādo-manē
high-powered money 46
haibun
allocation 6; distribution 387
haibun kōritsu
allocative efficiency 6
haibunhō
allocation 368
haifuhyō
allotment sheet 369
haigyō
winding-up of business 438
haijo
abatement 3; exclusion 35
haijo fukanōsei
non-excludability 74
haijo hiyō
abatement cost 3
haika
demonetization (abolition of a
standard) 169
haika suru
demonetize 169
haikei
background 441
haikeiteki na chishiki
background knowledge 441
haiki ginkōken
bank note unfit for circulation
166
haikibutsu
waste (matter) 119; pollutant
493
haikyū
rationing 91
haikyū busshi
rationed goods 91
haikyū gōrika
rationalization of rationing 91
haikyū kippu
rationing coupons 91
haikyū suru
ration (verb) 91
haikyū tsūchō
ration books 91
haipā-infurēshon
hyper-inflation 47
hairaku keizai
pleasure economy 80
haiseki
boycott (rejection) 11
haishi
abolition 3
haishitsu
disability 319; impairment 322,
492
haishitsu hoken
insurance against disability 322
haishitsu jōkō
disability clause 319
haishitsu kitei
disability provisions 319

haishitsu kyūfu
disability benefit 319
haishō shōken
cancelled bond 206
haita
exclusion 35
haita gensoku
exclusion principle 35
haitateki torihiki
exclusive dealing 35
haiteku kabushiki
high-tech stock 231
haiten
re-assignment 465
haitō
apportionment 370; distribution
387; dividend 219, 387
haitō o ukeru
receive a dividend 414
haitō bairitsu
dividend cover 387
haitō heikin junbikin
dividend equalization fund 387
haitō heikin tsumitatekin
dividend equalization reserve
387
haitō ininjō
proxy for dividend 412
haitō junbi tsumitatekin
dividend reserve 388; reserve
for dividends 415
haitō jutō zandaka
dividend balance 387
haitō kanjō
dividend account 387
haitō keisan
calculation of dividend 375
haitō kinyūchō
dividend register 388
haitō kōjo
dividend credit 387
haitō no happyō
declaration of dividend 385
haitō no hoshō kabu
guaranteed stock 394
haitō no shiharai
payment of dividend 409
haitō rimawari
dividend yield 219, 388
haitō seikō
pay-out ratio 408
haitō shiharai
dividend pay-out 387
haitō shiharai chōsho
payment record for dividends
409
haitō shiharaihyō
dividend list 387
haitō shiharairitsu
dividend pay-out ratio 387
haitō shotoku
dividend income 219
haitō suru
pay a dividend 408
haitō tsūchisho
dividend notice 387
haitō yūsen
dividend preference 387
haitōchō
dividend book 387
haitōfunō rieki
undistributable reserves 425

haitōkanō jōyokin
surplus available for dividends 422

haitōkanō rieki
distributable profits 387; profits available for distribution 412

haitōken
dividend check [US] 387; dividend rights 388

haitōkin
dividend 219, 387

haitōkin saitōshi shikumi
dividend re-investment plan 388

haitōkin shiharaishō
dividend warrant [UK] 388

haitōochi
dividend off 387; ex dividend 220, 389

haitōritsu
dividend rate 387; rate of dividend 413

haitōtsuki
cum dividend 213; dividend on 387

haizoku sareru (— ni)
assigned (to —) 450

hajimete no kainushi
first-time buyer 295

hakabu
broken lot 203; fractional lot 227; fractional share 227; odd lot 252; odd-lot shares 252

hakabu chūmon
fractional order 227

hakabu no burōkā
odd-lot broker 252

hakabu seiri
broken lot consolidation 203

hakabu senmon gyōsha
odd-lot dealer 252

hakabu tesūryō
differential 217; odd-lot differential 252

hakabu torihiki
odd-lot trading 253; odd-lot transaction 253

hakabu torihikisha
odd-lotter 253

hakabu tōshi
odd-lot investment 252

hakabu tōshika
odd-lot investor 252

hakaiteki kyōsō
destructive competition 25

hakasegō
Doctorate (PhD) 442

haken
hegemony 46

hakkai
first session of the month 224

hakken ginkō
bank of issue 166

hakken suru
put in circulation 183

hakkō
flotation 226; issue (of L/C, of securities) 150, 177, 238, 397

hakkō gaisha
issue house 238; issuing company 398

hakkō gendo
issue limit 238

hakkō ginkō
issuing bank 150; originating bank 154

hakkō ginkōken
bank notes issued 166

hakkō hōjin
issuing corporation 398

hakkō hoshō
reserve for note issue 183

hakkō irainin
L/C applicant 150

hakkō jimu
issue business 238

hakkō jōken
conditions of issue 380; issue terms 239, 397

hakkō kabushikisū
number of outstanding shares 404

hakkō kaheiryō
currency issued 169

hakkō kakaku
issue price 239, 397; issue value 398

hakkō kijitsu
effective date 220

hakkō shijō
financing market 224; investment market 238; issue market (shares) 239; new issue market 250; primary market 260

hakkō shōsha
issuer 239; issuing house [UK] 239; securities house 270

hakkō suru
float (verb) 225; issue (verb) 150, 177, 238, 397

hakkō tetsuzuki
issue procedure 397

hakkō todokeidesho
registration statement 265

hakkō yoryoku
issue margin 238

hakkō yotei
pipeline (securities) 259

hakkō zandaka
outstanding issue 407

hakkōbi
issue date 238, 397

hakkōbi torihiki
'when issued' transaction 286

hakkōbi torihiki kashitsuke
'when issued' transaction loan 286

hakkōbun
tranche 282

hakkōdan
issue syndicate 239, 397

hakkōgyōsha
issuer 239

hakkōji waribiki
original issue discount 255

hakkōsha
issuer 239, 398

hakkōsha rimawari
issuer's cost 239, 398

hakkōzumi kabushiki
issued shares 239, 398; issued stock 239; outstanding shares 407; outstanding stock 407; shares outstanding 418

hakkōzumi kabushiki shihonkin
allotted share capital 369; issued capital 398; issued capital stock 398

hakkōzumi kabushikisū
number of shares issued 404

hakkōzumi shihon
outstanding capital 407

hakkyū no
underpaid 485

hakō hon'isei
limping standard 178

hakō kin hon'isei
limping Gold Standard 178

hakō sōba
irregular market 238

hakuri
narrow margin (small profits) 249

hakuritabai
quick sales at small profits 412

hakushi
carte-blanche 451

hakushi ininjō
blank power of attorney 337

hakushigō
Doctorate (PhD) 442

hakusho
white paper 120

hakyū kōka
spread effects 102

han bā
half a bar (half £M) 176

hanagata kabu
leading stock 240; popular stock 259

hanbai
sales (sales and marketing) 416

hanbai buchō
marketing manager 460

hanbai genka kaikei
marketing cost accounting 401

hanbai keihi
sales expenses 416

hanbai sokushinhi
sales promotion expenses 416

hanbai tantō jūyaku
chief sales executive 451

hanbai tesūryō
selling commission 271

hanbai yosan
sales budget 416

hanbaibu
marketing department 460; sales and marketing department 466; sales department 466

hanbaidaka
sales 97

hanbaidan
selling group 271

hanbaigakari
salesman 466

hanbaihi
distribution expenses [US] 387; marketing cost 401; sales expenses 416

hanbairyō kyokudaika kasetsu
sales maximization hypothesis 97

hanbaiyō fudōsan
real estate under offer 306

hanbaiyō tochi
land for sale 299

hanbōkan
difficulty in raising money 217

han'ei
prosperity (affluence) 88

han'ei no
prosperous (affluent) 88

hangarii
Hungary 189

hanhendō hiyō
semi-variable costs 99

han'i no keizai
economies of scope 31

hanjukuren rōdō
semi-skilled labour 467; semi-skilled work 467

hanjukuren rōdōryoku
semi-skilled labour force 467; semi-skilled workforce 467

hanjukuren rōdōsha
semi-skilled labour 99; semi-skilled worker(s) 99, 467

hanjukurenkō
semi-skilled labour 99; semi-skilled worker 467

hanjunkanteki na
countercyclical 21

hanketsu saiken
judgement credit 435

hanketsu saikensha
judgement creditor 435

hanketsu saimu
judgement debt 435

hanketsu saimusha
judgement debtor 435

hanki
half-year 46

hanki haitō
semi-annual dividend 417

hanki kessan
half yearly settlement of accounts 394

hankōkyō kigyō
semi-public corporation 360

hankyō
repercussion 94

hankyū
half pay 478

hannichi
half-time 456

hannichi rōdōsha
half-timer 456

hannō
reaction (of market) 263

hanpatsu
rebound 263; recovery (rally) 264

hanpatsu suru
rally (verb) 263; recover 263

hanraku
reaction (of market) 263

hanseihin
semi-finished goods 99; semi-finished products 99

hantai
objection 431

hantai baibai
closed trade 208

hantai tōhyō
dissenting vote 430

higyōsha
strikers 105, 502
higyōyaburi
black leg 499; fink 499; strike breaker 502; strike breaking 502
hihakari akinai
in and out trade 232
hihōjin gaisha
unincorporated company 363
hihōjin kigyō
unincorporated business 363
hihōjin no
unincorporated 363
hihoken bukken
insurable property 322
hihokenbutsu
insured articles 324; insured property 324
hihokenbutsu shozaichi
location of property insured 324
hihokensha
assured, the 316; insured, the 324; person insured 327
hihoshōnin
guarantee (person) 148, 229
hijihatsuteki shitsugyō
involuntary unemployment 55, 500
hijō daisaigai hoken
catastrophe insurance 317
hijō deguchi
emergency exit 491; get-away exit 492
hijō jitai sengen
proclamation of a state of emergency 85
hijō kaidan
emergency stairs 491; fire escape 491
hijō kiken
catastrophe risks 317
hijō shikin
emergency fund 388
hijōjitai
state of emergency 104
hijōjō gaisha
unlisted company 284; unquoted company 284
hijōjō kabu(shiki)
outside stock 255; unlisted shares 284; unlisted stock 284
hijōjō no
unlisted 284
hijōjō shōken
unlisted securities 284
hijōkin jūyaku
absentee director 335; part-time director 355, 463
hijōkin kinmusha
part-time employee 463
hijōkin no
part time 463
hijōkin rōdōsha
part-time worker 463
hika
parity 182
hikae bubun
counterfoil 141; stub 161
hikaheiteki
non-monetary 181

hikaheiyō kin
gold for non-monetary use 175; non-monetary gold 181
hikaku
comparison 17
hikaku bunseki
comparative analysis 17
hikaku chingin
relativities 94
hikaku dōgaku
comparative dynamics 17
hikaku genka
comparative cost 17
hikaku kanōsei
comparability 17
hikaku keisansho
comparative statement 380
hikaku kōgyō
leather industry 125
hikaku seigaku
comparative statics 17
hikaku seihin kōgyō
leather-products industry 125
hikaku seisanhisetsu
theory of comparative costs 110
hikaku son'eki keisansho
comparative income statement 380; comparative profit and loss statement 380
hikaku taishaku taishōhyō
comparative balance sheet 380
hikaku yūi
comparative advantage 17
hikaku yūi no hōsoku
law of comparative advantage 61
hikamei ginkō
non-member bank 153
hikan
pessimism 80
hikanzei bōeki yugami
non-tariff trade distortions 74
hikanzei shōheki
non-tariff barrier (NTB) [US] 74, 75
hikari sangyō
optical industry 125
hikazei hōjin
exempted corporation 346; tax-free corporation 423
hikazei kigyō
tax-free business 423
hikazei no
tax-exempt 108; tax-free 108
hikazei no shūyōkōkanchi
non-taxable exchange of property 303
hikazei rishi shotoku
non-taxable interest income 252
hikazei shotoku
non-taxable income 75
hike
closing 208; closing of session 208; last session 240
hikeaji
closing tone 208
hikeato kehai
quotation after the close 262
hikedaka
higher quotation at the close 231

hikego sōba
street price 279
hikene
closing price 208; closing quote 208; last quotation 240
hikene de
at the close 197
hikene de kau
buy on close 205
hikenegai
buying on close 205
hikeshi
fire extinguisher 491
hikeyasu
lower closing quotation 244
hikiage kahei
coin withdrawn from circulation 167
hikiage shihei
note withdrawn from circulation 181
hikiage tsūka
money withdrawn from circulation 180
hikiate mihakkō kabu
reserve for unissued stock 415
hikiatekin
allowance (provision) 369; reserve 415
hikiatekin kansa
allowance audit 369
hikiateru
back (= to cover payment) 133
hikidashi
withdrawal 163; drawing (withdrawing) 145
hikidashikin kanjō
drawing account 145
hikidasu
make a withdrawal 151; withdraw 163
hikimodoshi
setback (market) (pull-back quotations) 272
hikinsenteki mokuhyō
non-pecuniary goals 74
hikinuki
'plucking' 448
hikin'yū chūkaika
disintermediation 218
hikin'yū shisan
non-financial assets 403
hikishimari
hardening 230
hikishime
restraint 95, 267; restrictions 95
hikishime no kaijo
removal of restrictions 94
hikishime seisaku kaijo
relaxation of monetary restraint 94
hikishime seisaku kyōka
tightening of monetary restraint 281
hikishime sochi
restraint measures 95
hikishimeki
period of restraint 79
hikitsugi shasai
assumed bond 197

hikiuke
acceptance 193; underwriting 284
hikiuke gaisha
underwriting company 284, 425
hikiuke ginkō
acceptance bank 131; accepting bank 131
hikiuke gyōmu
underwriting business 284
hikiuke gyōsha
underwriter(s) 284, 425
hikiuke jōkentsuki shin'yō
acceptance credit 131
hikiuke kanji
managing underwriter 245
hikiuke kanjidan
management group 245
hikiuke keiyaku
underwriting agreement 284, 425; underwriting contract 284, 425
hikiuke kyohi
dishonour (noun) 144
hikiuke kyozetsu
dishonour 144; non-acceptance 153
hikiuke kyozetsu shōsho
protest for non-acceptance 157
hikiuke kyozetsu shōsho sakusei menjo
protest waived 157
hikiuke kyozetsu shōsho sakusei tesūryō
protest charges 157
hikiuke kyozetsu tegata
protested bill 157
hikiuke seikyū tegata
bill for acceptance 137
hikiuke sekinin
acceptance liability 131
hikiuke shijō
acceptance market 193
hikiuke shinjikēto
acceptance syndicate 193
hikiuke tegata
acceptance [UK] 131; accepted bill 131; accepted draft 131; bill accepted 136
hikiuke teiji
presentation for acceptance 157
hikiuke tesūryō
acceptance charge 131, 193; acceptance commission 131, 193; underwriting commission 284, 425
hikiuke tsūchi
notice of acceptance 153
hikiuke uridashi
sale of securities on an underwriting basis 268
hikiuke watashi
documents against acceptance (DA) 142, 144
hikiuke watashi tegata
documents-against-acceptance bill 144
hikiukebarai
payment against acceptance 155; payment by acceptance 156

hiuragakinin
endorsee 145

hiwariatesha
allottee 195, 369

hiyameshikui
'cold-rice eaters' 473

hiyatoi rōdō
casual labour 451; casual work 451

hiyatoi rōdōsha
casual labourer 451; casual worker 451; day labourer 452; day worker 452

hiyō
cost 20, 382; expenses (general) 389, 487; outlay 407

hiyō o kiritsumeru
cut costs (verb) 384

hiyō-ben'eki bunseki
cost/benefit analysis 21, 382

hiyō-ben'eki hiritsu
benefit/cost ratio 372; cost/benefit ratio 21, 382

hiyō bunseki
expense analysis 390

hiyō chōka shūekiritsu
rate of return over cost 413

hiyō fuhen kyōkyū
constant-cost supply 19

hiyō haibun
allocation of costs 6

hiyō kansū
cost function 21

hiyō keisan
cost finding 382

hiyō kyokusen
cost curve 21

hiyō kyokushōka
cost minimization 21, 383; minization of cost 401

hiyō-seisanryoku hiritsu
cost/productivity ratio 21

hiyō teigen
decreasing cost(s) 23, 385

hiyō teigen sangyō
decreasing-cost industry 24

hiyō teizō
increasing cost(s) 51

hiyō teizō kyōkyū
increasing-cost supply 51

hiyō yūkōdo
cost-effectiveness 21, 382

hiyō-yūkōdo bunseki
cost-effectiveness analysis 21, 382

hiyō yūkōdo no
cost-effective 382

hiyoke
protection from fire 493

hiyorimi shugi
opportunism 76

hiyūin
disincentive 27

hizukego
after-date 132

hizukego tegata
after-date bill 132

hizukegobarai
payable after date 155

hizumi
distortions 27

hoan keibi sangyō
security industry 126

hōbutsusen
parabola 78

hōfu
abundance 3

hōfuku
retaliation 96

hōfuku kanzei
retaliatory tariffs 96

hōfuku suru
retaliate 96

hōgai na nedan
exorbitant prices 295

hōgin kaigaiten
overseas branch of Japanese bank 155

hogo
conservation 18; protection 88

hogo azukari
custody 142; deposit for safe custody 143; safe custody 159; safe deposit 159; safe-keeping 159; safe-keeping deposit 159

hogo azukari gaisha
safe deposit corporation 159

hogo azukari kinko
safe [UK] 159; safe-deposit box [US] 159; strong box 161

hogo azukari shōken
deposited securities (for safe-keeping) 143

hogo azukariryō
safe custody fee 159

hogo bōeki
protected trade 88; protective trade 88; sheltered trade 100

hogo bōeki ronsha
protectionist 88

hogo bōeki seisaku
protectionist policy 88; protective trade policy 88

hogo bōeki seisaku sochi
protectionist measures 88

hogo bōeki shugi
protectionism 88

hogo bōekihō
protectionist legislation 88

hogo hiyō
costs of protection 21

hogo kanzei
protective duties 88; protective tariffs 88

hogo koyō
sheltered employment 99

hogo sangyō
protected industry 88; sheltered industry 99

hogo seisaku
conservation policy 18

hogo shugisha
conservationist 18

hōhōron
methodology 68

ho'ikuen
day-care centre 476

ho'ikujo
day-care centre 476

hōjin
body corporate 337; corporate body 342; corporate person 343; corporation 343; juridical person 350; legal person 350

hōjin toshite setsuritsu sareta
incorporated 348

hōjin chochiku
corporate saving(s) 20, 141, 382

hōjin dantai
corporate body 342

hōjin gaisha
incorporated company 348; registered company 358

hōjin kabunushi
corporate shareholder 211, 382

hōjin kai'in
corporate member 342

hōjin kaikeishi
incorporated accountant 395

hōjin keitai
corporate form 342

hōjin kigyō
corporate business 342; corporate enterprise 342; incorporated business 348

hōjin kigyō bumon
corporate business sector 342

hōjin meigi
corporate name (legal person) 343

hōjin no ekikin
gross income (for tax declaration) 394

hōjin riji
corporate directors 342

hōjin rijunzei
corporate profit tax 381

hōjin ritokuzei
corporation profit tax 382

hōjin ryūho
corporate retained earnings 382

hōjin saiken
corporate bond 381

hōjin setsuritsu ninkashō
certificate of incorporation [US] 340

hōjin setsuritsusha
incorporator 348

hōjin shintaku
corporate trust [US] 382

hōjin shisan
corporate assets 381

hōjin shōken
corporate securities 382

hōjin shotoku
corporate income 381; income 395

hōjin shotokuzei
corporate income tax 20, 381

hōjin soshiki
corporate organization (legal person) 343

hōjin soshiki ni suru
incorporate 348

hōjin soshiki no
corporate 342; incorporated 348

hōjin soshiki no setsuritsu
incorporation 348

hōjin torihikisaki
corporate customers 141

hōjin yokin
corporate deposit 141

hōjin zaisan
corporate estate 292, 381; corporate property 292, 381

hōjin zeibiki hikiatekin
reserve for corporate tax 415

hōjin zeikōjo
corporation tax credit 382

hōjin zeikōjōzen rieki
net profit before tax 402

hōjinken
corporate rights 343

hōjinzei
corporate tax 20, 382; corporation tax 382

hōjinzei oyobi jūminzei
income taxes (on balance sheet) 395

hojo gaisha
subsidized company (-ies) 105, 422

hojo kahei
subsidiary coin 105

hojo kanjō
subsidiary accounts 422

hojo kinyūchō
subsidiary journal 422

hojo motochō
auxiliary ledger 371, 422

hojo sangyō
subsidiary industry 105

hojo seisaku
subsidizing policy 105

hojo shihon
auxiliary capital 371

hojokin
bounties (subsidies) [UK] 11; grant(s) 44, 296; subsidies 105

hojokin o ataeru
subsidize 105

hojokin zōka
increase in subsidies 51

hojokintsuki shijō
subsidized market 105

hojoteki hiyō
supplementary cost 422

hojoteki shitsugyō kyūfu
supplementary unemployment benefits 502

hojū
recruitment 446

hojū hōhō
recruitment method 446

hojū no tekunikku
recruitment technique 446

hojū puroguramu
recruitment programme 446

hojū suru
recruit (fill a vacancy, replace) 446

hōka
arson 316

hōka
legal tender 62, 178

hōka
domestic currency 170; national currency 181; Japanese currency, the [J] 177

hōka kawase tegata
bill in the Japanese currency 137

hoka no fusai
other liabilities 407

hoka no shisan
other assets 407

hōkai
crash (distintegration) 21; collapse 208, 212

hokan
custody (trust) 142

hokan kikan
custodian (institution) 142

hokan tsunagi
against the box 194

hokannin
depositary (trustee) 143; trustee (custodian, keeper) 162, 283

hokanryō
charge for custody 139; custody fee 142

hokansho
depository 143

hokanteki bōeki
complementary trade 18

hokanzai
complementary goods 18; complements 18

hōkatsu hoken keiyaku
floater 320

hōkatsu hoken shōken
floating policy 320

hōkatsu keiyaku
umbrella cover 330

hōkatsu yotei hoken keiyaku
open cover 326

hōkatsu yotei hoken shōken
open policy 326

hōkatsuteki ininjō
general proxy 430

hoken
assurance 316; insurance 55, 322, 479

hoken ni ireru
insure (take out an insurance) 323

hoken no kakete nai
not insured 326

hoken o hikiukeru
underwrite (insurance) 330

hoken o kakeru
covered against/for (—) 318

hoken o tsukeru
take out an insurance 329; cover against/for (—) 318

hoken burōkā
insurance broker 323

hoken chūkainin
insurance broker 323

hoken dairinin
insurance agent (person) 323

hoken dairiten
insurance agent (agency) 323

hoken eisei
public health 89

hoken eisei taisakuhi
public health service expenses 89

hoken funō na
uninsurable 330

hoken funōtai
uninsurability 330

hoken gaisha
assurance company 316; insurance company 323

hoken genka
insurance cost 323; cost of insurance 383

hoken gyōsha
assurer 316; insurance underwriter 323; underwriter(s) 330

hoken hikiuke
underwriting 330

hoken hikiukeshō
insurance certificate 323

hoken hyōkagaku
agreed-value policy 315; insurance policy valuation 323

hoken jiko
insurable risk 322

hoken jōken
terms of insurance 330

hoken jōkō
insurance clauses 323

hoken kagaku
insurable interest 322; insurable value 322; insurance value 323; insured value 324; policy value 327

hoken kagaku kadai no
overinsured 326

hoken kagaku kashō no
under-insured 330

hoken kaikei
insurance accounting 322

hoken kakekin
insurance premium 323

hoken kanjō
insurance account 322

hoken kanōtai
insurability 322

hoken kanteinin
appraiser 315; insurance appraiser 323

hoken karikeiyakusho
insurance binder 323

hoken keirinin
actuary 315

hoken keiyaku
insurance contract 323; policy contract 327

hoken keiyaku o kaijo suru
surrender an insurance policy 329

hoken keiyaku kikan
duration of policy 319

hoken keiyaku no iten
transfer of policy 330

hoken keiyakusha
insurance contractor 323; policy holder 327

hoken kensanin
insurance surveyor 323

hoken kikan
period of coverage 327; term insured 330

hoken kingaku
amount covered 315; amount insured 315; insurance amount 323; insured amount 324; sum insured 329

hoken komon
insurance adviser 322

hoken mōshikomisha
applicant (insurance) 315

hoken mōshikomisho
application for insurance 315

hoken mōshikomisho no ninka
acceptance 315

hoken no mokuteki
subject matter of insurance 329

hoken sagi
insurance fraud 323

hoken seikyū
claim 317

hoken seisannin
insurance adjuster 322

hoken shijō
insurance market 323

hoken shōken
insurance policy 323; policy 327

hoken shōken tanpo kashitsuke
loan on insurance policy 242

hoken shōmeisho
certificate of insurance 317; insurance certificate 323

hoken shorui
insurance documents 323

hoken sūrishi
actuary 315

hoken sūriteki hiyō keisanhō
actuarial cost method 315

hoken sūriteki kachi
actuarial value 315

hoken suru
insure (someone) 323

hoken tanpo
coverage 318; insurance cover(age) 323

hoken tsumitatekin
insurance fund 323

hoken yakkan
insurance clauses 323; policy clause 327; policy conditions 327; terms of policy 330

hokengyō
insurance business 323; insurance industry 124

hokengyōsha
insurance carrier 323; insurer 324

hokenkanō na
insurable 322

hokenkanō zaisan
insurable property 322

hokenkin
insurance benefits 323; insurance money 323

hokenkin ichijibarai
lump-sum settlement 325

hokenkin seikyū
claim 317; insurance claim 323

hokenkin shiharai
payment of claim 327

hokenkin uketorinin
assured, the 316; beneficiary 316

hokenkin uketorinin no shitei
nomination of beneficiary 326

hokenkin uketorinin no shitei henkō
change of beneficiary 317

hokenryō
insurance premium 323; premium 327

hokenryō haraikomi
payment of premium 327

hokenryō haraikomizumi keiyaku
fully paid policy 321

hokenryō haraimodoshi
return premium 328; surrender value 329

hokenryō kōjo
insurance premium reduction 323

hokenryō ruika hoken
increasing premium plan 322

hokenryō shūnyū
premium income 327

hokenryō suijun
premium level 327

hokenryō waribiki
premium discount 327

hokenryōritsu
insurance premium rate 323; insurance rate 323; premium rate 327

hokensha
insurer 324; insurance underwriter 323

hōkibu
legal department 459; litigation department 459

hokkinin
founder 347; promoter 357

hokkinin kabu
founder's shares 392; promoter's shares 412

hokkinin rijun
promoter's profit 412

hōkoku(sho)
report 94, 359

hokusen
North Korea 190

hōkyū
pay (noun) (wages and salaries) 481; salary (-ies) (payroll) 97, 483

hōkyū seikatsusha
salaried people 97

hōkyūbi
pay day 481

hōkyūbukuro
pay packet 481

hokyūkin
subsidies 105

hōman kashidashi
reckless lending 263

hōman kei'ei
irresponsible management 349

hōmatsu
bubble 12

hōmatsu gaisha
bubble company (-ies) 12, 338

hōmu-bankingu
home banking 148

hōnen
bumper year 12

hongenteki shōken
primary securities 260; prime securities 260

hongoku sōkan
repatriation (investment) 266

hongyō
main business 351

hon'i
standard (noun) (basis) 185

hon'i kahei
standard coin 185; standard money 185

hon'i kin
standard gold 185

hon'i kinzoku
standard metal 185

hon'i seido
standard system 185

hon'isei
standard (noun) 185; standard system 185

honkon
Hong Kong 189

honkyū
regular salary 483

honnin
principal (person) 157, 260

honnin shinpitsu shomei
genuine signature 148

honpō shihon
Japanese capital invested abroad 239

honpō shōken
domestic securities [J] 219

honsaiyō
full employment (once the probation period is over) 456; official employment 462

honsha
head-office 348

honsha jimusho
registered office 358

honshōkokin
ordinary warrant 255, 406

honten
head-office 348

horanda
Netherlands 190

hōrei zensho
statutory books 361

hōritsu no kitei
statutory provisions 361

hōritsu no shudan
statutory instrument 361

hōritsu shorui
legal documents 350

hōritsujō kyōsei dekiru saimu
legally enforceable debts 436

hōritsujō no tsūchi
legal notice 430

horyū haitō
passed dividend 408

hōsaku
bumper crop 12

hosei yosan
supplementary budget 106

hōsekigyō
precious stone industry 126

hōshin
plan (course, line) 80; policy (line of policy) 80

hoshō
compensation 491

hoshō
guarantee [UK] 148, 229; guaranty [US] 148, 230; security 270

hoshō chingin
guaranteed wage(s) 45, 478

hoshō genri
compensation principle 17

hoshō hoken
compensation insurance 318

hoshō ichijikin
lump-sum compensation 492

hoshō junbi hakkō
issue against securities 238

hoshō kabu
guaranteed stock 394

hoshō kashitsuke
loan on guarantee 242; loan with third-party guarantee 243

hoshō kogitte
certified cheque 139

hoshō nenkan chingin
guaranteed annual wage 478

hoshō saiken
guaranteed bond 230

hoshō sashiire yūka shōken
securities deposited as guarantee 270

hōshō seido
bounty system 11

hoshō sekinin
liability limited by guarantee 350

hoshō sekinin gaisha
company limited by guarantee 341

hoshō shiharai
claim settlement 317; settlement of claim 329, 493

hoshō shūnyū
guaranteed income 45

hoshō suru
guarantee (verb) 148; guaranty (verb) 230

hoshō tanpo
guaranteed mortgage 230

hoshō tegata
guaranteed bill 148

hoshō yokin
compensating balance [US] 141

hoshō yūshi
compensatory finance 17

hoshōkin
compensation money 491

hoshōkin ichijibarai
lump-sum settlement 492

hoshōnin
guarantor 148, 230

hoshōryō
guarantee fee 230

hoshōsai
guaranteed bond 230

hoshōsho
guaranty bond 230

hoshōtsuki shōken
guaranteed securities 230

hōshū
allowance (compensation, reward, perk) 369, 475; remuneration (honorarium) 94, 483

hōshū oyobi kyūyo
emoluments, salaries and allowances 388; salaries and allowances 416

hoshu shūzenhi
repairs and maintenance expenses 415

hōsō sangyō
broadcasting industry 123

hōsō sangyō
packaging industry 125

hosoku nenkin seido
supplementary pension plan 329

hosokuteki hiyō
supplementary costs 106

hossoku
inauguration 348

hossoku suru
inaugurate 348

hōtei chingin
legal minimum wage 62; minimum wage (legal) 68

hōtei dairinin
legal representative 350

hōtei heika
fixed par of exchange 173; mint par (of exchange) 179; mint parity 179

hōtei hika
mint rate 179

hōtei jōto
legal transfer 240

hōtei junbi
legal reserve 178; required reserves [US] 158

hōtei junbi shoyōgaku
legal requirement 178

hōtei junbikin
required reserves [US] 158

hōtei junbiritsu
required reserve ratio [US] 158

hōtei kabunushi sōkai
statutory meeting 432

hōtei kahei
legal money 178

hōtei kansa
statutory audit 420

hōtei kansanin
authorized auditor 371

hōtei kinjunbiritsu
minimum gold reserve ratio 179

hōtei riritsu
legal rate of interest 240

hōtei satei chingin
legal minimum wage 479

hōtei sekinin hoken
legal liability insurance 324

hōtei shiharai shoyō junbiritsu
legal reserve requirement 150, 178

hōtei shihei
Treasury note [UK] 186

hōtei shihon
legal capital 399

hōtei teisokusū
statutory quorum 432

hōtei tōshi
legal investment 240

hōtei tōshi risuto
legal list [US] 240

hōtei tsūka
legal tender 62, 178

hōteki kenryoku
legal power 350

hōteki seikaku (kigyō no)
legal status (of company) 350

hoteru shūyō
hotel accommodation 487

hotto-mane
hot money 231

hōwa
saturation 97

howaito-karā rōdōsha
white-collar workers 120

howaitoan
White Plan [US] 120

hoyū
tenure 310

hoyū kikan
holding period 231

hoyū shoken
conditions of tenure 292

hoyū shōken
securities holding 270

hoyūdaka
holdings 176, 231

hoyūken
right of tenure 308; tenure 310

hozō seikō
propensity to hoard 88

hozon
conservation (preservation) 18

hyakubun taishaku taishōhyō
percentage balance sheet 409

hyakubunritsu zaimu shohyō
percentage statement 409

hyō
schedule 98

hyōban
reputation (fame) 359

hyōgai hoken
hail storm insurance 321

hyōgenteki shain
nominal partner 353

hyōhon
sample 97

hyōhon chōsa
sampling survey 97

hyōhon chūshutsu
sampling 97

hyōji fusai
stated liabilities 419

hyōji genka
scheduled cost 416

hyōjun
standard(s) (criterion, norm) 103, 185

hyōjun chingin
standard wage(s) 103, 484

hyōjun chinginritsu
standard rate of pay 103, 484; standard wage rate 484

hyōjun genka
standard cost (prime cost) 419

hyōjun genka keisan
standard cost accounting 419; standard costing 419

hyōjun genka keisan seido
standard cost system 419

hyōjun genkahō
standard cost method 419

hyōjun genkahyō
standard cost sheet 419

hyōjun ginjigane
standard silver bullion 185

ikichi kyōtei
threshold agreement [UK] 110
ikigai kyōtsū kanzei
Common External Tariff 17
ikinai bōeki
intra-trade 57
ikizumari
deadlock 499
ikkan no nai tōkeiryō
inconsistent statistics 50
ikkatsu baikyaku no tairyō kabushiki
block 201
ikkatsu hoken
general cover 321
ikkatsu no giketsu
unanimous vote 432
ikkatsu shite sansei suru
agree unanimously 429
ikkatsu tōroku (SEC ni taisuru shōken hakkō no)
shelf registration [US] 273
ikkatsubarai shin'yō
non-instalment credit 251
ikkodate jūtaku
housing units 297
ikō
shifting 100
ikōjō
letter of intent 241, 399
imin
emigrant 33
imin rōdōryoku
immigrant labour 48
imin rōdōsha
immigrant worker(s) 48, 457; migrant worker 461
imin seisaku
immigration policy 48
inakaya
cottage 293
indekkushingu
indexing 233
indekkusu-fando
index fund 232
indekkusu-opushon
index options 233
indo
India 189
indonesia
Indonesia 189
infōmaru bumon
informal sector 54
infurasutorakucha
infrastructure 54
infure
inflation 54
infure akujunkan
inflationary spiral 54
infure atsuryoku
inflationary pressure 54
infure bōei no
index-linked [UK] 232
infure bōei sochi
index-linking [UK] 233; indexation [UK] 51, 233; inflation-proofing [US] 54, 233
infure fukyō
inflationary recession 54
infure gekka
surge in inflation 106

infure-gyappu
inflationary gap 54
infure hojokin
inflation subsidy 54
infure keikō
inflationary trend 54
infure keikō no
inflationary 54
infure kokufuku
beating inflation 10
infure mondai
inflation problem 54
infure nenritsu
annual rate of inflation 7
infure no
inflationary 54
infure no yokusei
inflation control 54
infure seisaku
inflation policy 54
infure shugisha
inflationist 54
infure shūsei kaikei
inflation accounting 54
infure shūsoku
solution to inflation 102
infure taisaku
anti-inflation measures 7; anti-inflation policy 7
infure to no tatakai
battle against inflation 10
infure yokusei
control of inflation 20
infuremiai no chin'age
inflation-compensating pay rise(s) 54, 479
infuremiai no saitei chingin
index-linked minimum wage 51, 479
infurenaki kaifuku
inflation-free recovery 54
infurenaki seichō
inflation-free growth 54
infureritsu
inflation rate 54
infurēshon
inflation 54
infurēshon no
inflationary 54
infurēshon no kasoku
accelerating inflation 3
infureteki na
inflationary 54
inin
authority 133; authorization (delegation, commission) 133; proxy 431
ininjō
letter of proxy 241, 350; power of attorney 356; proxy form 431
ininjō o kakunin suru
acknowledge a proxy 429
ininjō o ninshō suru
attest a proxy 429
ininjō kan'yū
solicitation of proxy 431
ininjō kyohi
rejection of proxy 431
ininjō torikeshi
revocation of proxy 431

ininken
power of attorney 356
ininken no shūryō
expiration of power of attorney 346
inkan
seal 160, 164 (note 7)
inkan shōmei
common seal [UK] 341; company seal 141, 164 (note 4), 341; corporation seal 164, 343; Seal 360
inkansū
implicit function 49
inpakuto
impact 48
inpakuto-rōn
impact loan [J] 232, 287 (note 15)
inpei danpingu
concealed dumping 18
inryō sangyō
beverage industry 123
insaidā
insider 233, 396
insaidā no torihiki
insider dealing [UK] 233; insider trading [US] 233
insaido-ragu
inside lag 55
insatsu-shuppan sangyō
printing and publishing industry 126
insatsugyō
printing industry 126
inshizei
stamp duty [UK] 103
insutanto shokuhin kōgyō
fast-food industry 124
intoku
cache 13
intoku shisan
hidden assets 394
intoku tsumitatekin
hidden reserve 394
inyū
immigration 48
inyūmin wariatesei
immigration quotas 48
ippan baishō sekinin hoken
public liability insurance 328
ippan boki
general book-keeping 393
ippan bukka shisū
general price index 43
ippan chingin
prevailing wages 83, 482
ippan eigyō shikin
general operating funds 394
ippan eigyōhi
general operating expenses 394
ippan genka
general cost 393
ippan giketsu
general vote 430
ippan hōjin
corporation aggregate 343
ippan jōken
general terms and conditions 321

ippan jūgyōin
rank and file 465
ippan kabushiki ōbosha
outside applicant (shares) 255, 407
ippan kaikei
general accounting 393; general account(s) 42, 393
ippan kaikei gensoku
general accounting principles 393
ippan kanrihi
general administrative costs 393; general administrative expenses 393
ippan kanrihi yosan
general administrative expenses budget 393
ippan kansa
general audit 393
ippan kansetsuhi
general overheads 394
ippan keihi
general expenses 393; indirect expenses 51
ippan keihiritsu
general expenses/current income ratio 393
ippan keizai
general economy 43
ippan keizai jōsei
general economic conditions 43
ippan kinkō
general equilibrium 43
ippan kinkō bunseki
general equilibrium analysis 43
ippan kinkō riron
general equilibrium theory 43
ippan kumiai
general union 456
ippan ryūdōsei kōka
general liquidity effect 43
ippan shikin
general fund 393
ippan shiwakechō
general journal 393
ippan taishaku taishōhyō
general balance sheet 393
ippan tanpotsuki shasai
general mortgage bond 228
ippan yakkan
general clause 321
ippan zaisei shikin
general funds (government's) 43
ippanteki chishiki
general knowledge 442
ippanteki kunren
general training 456
ippanteki nōryoku
general capabilities 442
iraku
Iraq 189
iran
Iran 189
irekae
reversal 267; swap (securities) 280
irekae torihiki
swap transaction 280
iryō
medical care 480

jigyōbukan tenkin
  inter-company transfer 458
jigyōhi
  business expenses (operating
  expenses) 374; working
  expenses 427
jigyōka
  entrepreneur (business person)
  33, 345
jigyōnushi
  business proprietor 339;
  owner of business 355
jigyōnushi hōshū
  owner's salary 408
jigyōnushi mochibun
  owner's equity 408; owner's
  interest 408; ownership interest
  408
jigyōsai
  industrial bond 233; industrial
  loan 233
jigyōsho
  business establishment 338;
  place of business 356
jigyōsho heisa
  closure 499; lock-out(s) (place
  of work) 64, 501
jigyōzei
  business tax 375
jihatsu jinin
  voluntary resignation 496
jihatsu taishoku
  voluntary resignation [J] 496,
  497 (note 45)
jihatsuteki chochiku
  voluntary saving 117
jihatsuteki hasan
  voluntary bankruptcy 437
jihatsuteki hasansha
  voluntary bankrupt 437
jihatsuteki mōshitate
  voluntary petition 438
jihatsuteki shihon idō
  autonomous capital movements
  8
jihatsuteki shitsugyō
  voluntary unemployment 118,
  503
jihyō
  formal resignation 495; letter of
  resignation 495
jijo doryoku
  self-help 99
jika
  current value 214
jika
  home (one's own home) 296;
  owner-occupied home 303
jika hakkō
  issue at market price 238
jika nōgyō
  family-unit agriculture 38
jika shoyūsha
  home owner 296; individual
  house owner 298
jika sōgaku
  market capitalization 245
jika tenkankanō
  convertible at market price 211
jikaku hakkō
  issue at market price 238
jikan atari chingin
  hourly wage(s) 478

jikan atari junshūnyū
  net hourly earnings 480
jikan atari kyūyo
  hourly wage(s) 478
jikan atari shūnyū
  hourly earnings 478
jikan atari sōshūnyū
  gross hourly earnings 477
jikan chingin
  time wage(s) 485
jikan chinginritsu
  time wage rate 485
jikan o hakaru
  clock (verb) 451
jikan senkō
  time preference 111
jikan senkōritsu
  rate of time preference 91
jikan wariate
  time allocation 111
jikanbarai shigoto
  time work 469
jikangai chingin
  overtime pay 481
jikangai kinmu teate
  overtime allowance 481
jikangai rōdō
  extra work 455; overtime work
  (out-of-hours work) 463
jikangai rōdō jikan
  overtime hours worked 481
jikangai teate shikyūritsu
  overtime premium rate 481
jikangai torihiki
  after-hours trading 194
jikankyū
  hourly wage(s) 478; time
  wage(s) 485
jikankyū rōdō
  time work 469
jikankyū rōdōsha
  time worker 469
jikanshū
  hourly earnings 478
jikanteki kachi
  time value 281
jikeiretsu
  time series 111
jiki
  next term 403
jiki e no kurikoshi
  carry forward to the next term
  377
jiki e no kurikoshidaka
  amount carried forward 369;
  amount carried over 369
jiki kessan
  next closing of account 403
jiki kurikoshi kessonkin
  deficit carried forward 385
jiki seihin seizōgyō
  porcelain industry 126
jikimono
  spot 184; spot commodity 276
jikimono kawase
  spot exchange 184
jikimono kawase sōba
  spot exchange rate 184
jikimono kawase torihiki
  spot exchange transaction 184
jikimono mochidaka
  spot position 184

jikimono sōba
  spot rate 184
jikimono torihiki
  spot operation 184; spot
  transaction 184
jikiwatashi
  immediate delivery 177, 231
jikkō kakaku
  effective price 32
jikkō kawase sōba
  effective exchange rate 170
jikkō kinri
  effective (interest) rate 220
jikkō kyōsō
  workable competition 121
jikkō rimawari
  effective yield 220
jikkō yosan
  operational budget 406;
  working budget 427
jiko
  accident 315, 491
jiko hasan
  voluntary bankruptcy 437;
  voluntary petition and
  proceedings 438
jiko kin'yū
  self-financing 417
jiko kisei dantai
  self-regulating organizations 99
jiko koyō
  self-employment 99, 466
jiko shihon
  capital 375; equity capital 389;
  net worth 403; own capital
  408; owner's capital 408;
  shareholder's equity 418
jiko shihon hiritsu
  net worth ratio 403; net worth/
  total capital ratio 403; own
  capital ratio 408
jiko shihon riekiritsu
  profits/net worth ratio 412
jiko shikin
  own funds 408
jiko shuchō kunren
  assertiveness training 450
jiko taishoku
  voluntary resignation [J] 496,
  497 (note 45)
jikyūjisoku
  autarchy (autarky) 8;
  self-sufficiency 99
jikyūjisoku keizai
  self-sufficient economy 99
jikyūjisokukoku
  self-sufficient countries 99
jimu
  clerical work 451; office duties
  462; office work 462
jimu kaizen
  improvement of business
  operations 348
jimu kanri
  management of affairs 351;
  office management 354, 462
jimu kanrihi
  office management expenses
  405
jimu keitō
  office worker 462
jimu kitei
  office manual 354

jimu kyokuchō
  executive secretary 455;
  managing executive 352
jimu shokuin
  clerical staff 451; office
  personnel 462
jimu yōhinhi
  office supplies expenses 405
jimuchō
  chief clerk 451; office manager
  462
jimuhi
  office expenses 405
jimuin
  clerk 451; office clerk 462;
  office worker 462
jimuryō
  work volume 471
jimusho
  office (place of business, place
  of work) 353, 462; premises
  356
jimusho chingariryō
  office rental 405
jimusho zenshokuin
  office force 462
jin'i sōba
  artificial market 196; artificial
  price 196; forced market 226;
  forced quotation 226;
  manipulated quotation 245
jin'i sōsa
  manipulation 245
jinin
  resignation 496
jin'in
  personnel 356, 464; staff 468
jin'in fusoku no
  undermanned 470
jin'in hojū
  personnel recruitment 445
jin'in kōsei
  personnel composition 464
jin'in sakugen
  cutbacks 499; personnel cuts
  464, 501; personnel reduction
  464, 501
jin'in seiri
  cutbacks 499; labour cuts 500;
  personnel cuts 464; personnel
  reduction 464, 501;
  rationalization 91, 465, 501
jinin suru
  resign 496
jinji
  personnel affairs 464
jinji hyōka
  personnel evaluation 464
jinji idō
  job rotation 458; personnel
  reshuffle 464; reshuffle 466;
  staff re-assignment 468; staff
  resshuffle 468
jinji kanri
  personnel administration 464;
  personnel management 464
jinji kanrisha
  personnel manager 464
jinji kiroku
  personnel records 464
jinji kōka
  merit rating 461; personnel
  rating 464; personnel review
  464

jitsubutsu shōko
real terms 92
jitsubutsu torihiki
spot transaction 276
jitsubutsu tōshi
real investment 263
jitsudō jikan
hours worked 478
jitsugen genka shōkyaku
realized depreciation 414
jitsugen rieki
realized profit 263, 414
jitsugen shita tōshi
realized investment 263
jitsugen shūeki
earned revenue 388
jitsugen sonshitsu
realized loss 263
jitsugen zōkagaku
realized appreciation 414
jitsugyō
business (industry) 12, 338
jitsugyō dantai
business group 339; business
organization 339
jitsugyō gakkō
technical school 447
jitsugyō kyōiku
business training 441;
technical education 447
jitsugyōka
business people 13; business
person 339; businessman
(-men) 13, 340; industrialist(s)
53
jitsugyōkai
business circles 338; business
community 13; business world
(industry, trade) 13, 340
jitsuhi
actual cost 4
jitsuju
actual demand 4
jitsujugai
commercial buying 209
jitsujusuji
commercial buyers 209
jitsukabu
real share 263; real stock 263;
spot share 276
jitsukabu suji
spot dealers 276
jitsumu gakkō
business college 441
jitsumu kyōiku
business education 441
jitsuyōhin
utilities (goods) 116
jitsuyōsei
practical utility 445
jittai keizai
real economy 91
jittai shihei
full-bodied money 174
jiyū bōeki
free trade 41
jiyū bōeki chi'iki
free-trade area 41
jiyū bōekiha dantai
free-trade organization 41
jiyū chūzō
free coinage 174

jiyū hoyūken
freehold 295
jiyū junbi
free reserves 147, 174
jiyū kawase shijō
free exchange market 174
jiyū kawase sōba
free exchange rate 174
jiyū kawase sōbasei
free exchange rate system 174
jiyū keiyakusha
freelancer 456
jiyū keizai
free economy 41
jiyū kigyō
free enterprise 41
jiyū kigyō keizai
free-enterprise economy 41
jiyū kin shijō
free gold market 174; private
gold market (free) 182
jiyū kyōsō
free competition 41
jiyū kyōsō shugi
laissez-faire 61
jiyū rōdō
casual labour 451; casual work
(free) 451
jiyū rōdōsha
casual labourer 451; casual
worker 451; free labourer 456
jiyū sekai
free world 41
jiyū sekai bōeki
free world trade 41
jiyū shijō
free and open market 227;
free market 41
jiyū shijō keizai
free-market economy 41
jiyū shijō shugisha
free marketeers 41
jiyū shisan
available assets 371
jiyū shokoku no keizai
free economies 41
jiyū shugi
liberalism 62
jiyū shugiteki keizai seisaku
liberal economic policy 62
jiyū tsūka
free currency 174
jiyū zaikohin
free stocks (commodity market)
227
jiyūdo
degrees of freedom 24
jiyūgyō
freelance work 456; liberal
profession 459
jiyūgyōsha
freelancer 456
jiyūka
liberalization 62, 241
jiyūka sochi
liberalization measures 63
jiyūzai
free goods 41
jizen hizuke
antedate (noun) 132
jizen hizuke o tsukeru
antedate (verb) 132

jizen hizuke kogitte
antedated cheque 132
jizen hizuke tegata
antedated bill 132
jizen jigyō
charitable enterprise 340
jizen kansa
administrative audit 368
jizen karikae (kōsai no)
advance refunding 194
jizen kikan
charitable organization 340
jizen kyōkai
benevolent institution 337
jizen no riron
second best (theory of) 99;
theory of second best 110
jizen tsūkoku
advance notice 429
jizenteki
ex-ante 34
jizenteki jōhō
advance information 194
jizokuteki seichō
sustainable growth 106
jobu-kurasuta
job cluster 58
jobu-shoppingu
job shopping 59, 444
jogai
exclusion 320
jōgai
curb 214; kerb 239; off-board
[US] 253
jōgai de
on the curb 254
jogai jōkō
exclusion clause 320
jōgai kabu nakagainin
curb broker 214; kerb broker
240
jōgai nakagainin
outside broker 255
jōgai shijō
curb 214; curb market 214;
kurb 239; kerb market 240;
off-board market 253; outside
market 255
jōgai shōken
outside securities 255
jōgai torihiki
curb dealing 214; curb trading
214; kerb dealing 240; kerb
trading 240; off-mart dealing
253; on-the-curb dealing 254;
outside dealing 255
jōgai torihiki kabu
curb stock 214; kerb stock 240
jōhi
superfluous expenses 422
jōho
concessions 18, 499
jōhō
tip (information) 281
jōhō gijutsu
information technology (IT) 54,
58
jōhō sangyō
information industry 124
jōhō tesūryō
info rate 177
jōi no kabushiki
senior issue 417

jōi no saiken hakkō
senior issue 271
jōji jūgyōsha
regular employee 466
jōjō
listing 241
jōjō sarete iru
listed 241; quoted 262
jōjō sarete nai
not quoted 252
jōjō gaisha
listed company 241; quoted
company 262
jōjō haishi
delisting 216
jōjō kabu
listed shares 241; listed stock
241
**jōjō kabushiki tanpo
kashitsuke**
loan on listed stock 242
jōjō kijun
listing standard 242, 399
jōjō meigara
listed issue 241; listed stock
issue 241
jōjō opushon
listed option 241
jōjō shinsa kijun
listing requirements 242, 399
jōjō shōken
listed securities 241
jōkan
clause (stipulation) 340
jōken
conditions 210
jōkentsuki hoken shōken
claused insurance policy 317
jōkentsuki saiken
conditional bond 209
jōkentsuki uragaki
conditional endorsement 141
jōkentsuki yūshi
conditional loan 210
jōkin koyō
full-time employment 456
jōkin no
full-time 456
jōkō
clause (article) 317, 340
jōkō keikō
bullish tendency 205
jōkyaku hoken
passenger insurance 327
jōkyaku shōgai sekinin hoken
passenger liability insurance
327
jōkyū kanrisha
senior executive 467
jōkyū kei'eisha
senior executive 360
jōkyū kei'eisō
senior management 360, 467
jōmu i'inkai
managing committee 352
jōmu torishimariyaku
executive director 345, 455;
managing director [J] 352, 460
jōmukai
board of managing directors
337; executive board 345;
managing directors' meeting [J]
430

junbi
reserve(s) (of money) 158, 183
junbi bēsu
reserve base 95
junbi ginkō
reserve bank [US] 159
junbi shikin
reserve funds 415
junbi shisan
reserve assets 95, 158, 415
junbi shisanritsu
reserve assets ratio 95, 158
junbi tsūka
reserve currency 95, 183
junbi yokin
reserve deposit 159
junbi yokin fusoku
reserve deficiencies 159
junbikin
allowance (provision) 369;
reserve(s) 158, 183, 415;
reserve supply of money 183
junbikin kanjō
reserve account 415
junbiritsu
reserve ratio 95, 159; reserve
requirement [US] 159, 183
junbun
fineness 173
junchidai
quasi-rent 90
junchō bōeki sagaku
positive balance of trade 82
junchōbo kagaku
carrying amount 377; net book
value 402
junchochiku
net savings 73
jun'eigyō rieki
net operating profit 402
jun'eki
clear profit 378
jun'ekiritsu
net profit ratio 403; profit
margin 87
junfusai
net liabilities 402
jungenka
net cost 402
jungenzai kachi
net present value (NPV) 73,
75, 250, 252
jūnin
inhabitant(s) (dwellers) 298;
resident (occupant of house)
308
junjōyokin
net surplus 73, 403
junjozuke
ranking 465
junjunbi
net reserve 403
junjuyō
net demand 73
junkan
cycle 23
junkan kabu
cyclical stock 214
junkanteki
cyclical 23
junkanteki seichō
cyclical growth 23

junkanteki shitsugyō
cyclical unemployment 23
junkawase
exchange bill payable 146
junkei yosan
net budget 73
junkigyō chochiku
net business saving 402
junkin
fine gold 173; pure gold 183
junkin'yū shisan
net financial assets 402
junkōkyōzai
impure public good 49
junkyohō
applicable law 336
junmochidaka
net position 250
junnōsei shihon
malleable capital 65
jūnō shugisha
physiocrats 80
junpō senjutsu
work to rule 121; work-to-rule
tactics 504
junpō tōsō
go-slow campaign 500;
work-to-rule campaign 504
junrieki
net income (profits) 402; net
profit(s) 402; pure profit 90
junrijun
pure profit 90
junrimawari
net yield 250
junrisoku
net interest (from account) 250
junsaimukoku
net debtor countries 73
junsanshutsuryō
net output 73
junseisandaka
net production 73
junshain
junior employee 458
junshihon
net capital 402
junshin kin hon'isei
pure gold standard 183
junshisan
net assets 402; total equity
424
junshōhi
net consumption 73
junshōhin kōeki jōken
net barter terms of trade 73
junshotoku
net income 73, 402, 480
junshūeki hiritsu
total expenses/total revenue
ratio 424
junshūnyū
net earnings 402, 480
junson'eki keisan
net profit and loss account 402
junsonshitsu
net loss 402; net operating loss
402
junsui dokusen
pure monopoly 90
junsui kyōsō
pure competition 90

junsui rishi
pure interest 90
juntōshi
net investment 73, 250
juntsūka
near money 73
jun'unten shihon
net working capital 403
jun'yushutsu
net exports 73
jūrōdō
heavy work [formal] 457
juryō yōnin tsūka
acceptable currency 165
jūryōzei
specific tax 102
jushi
credit demand 22; financing
requirements 224
jūsho
domicile 293; habitat 296;
habitation 296; home 296;
home address 296; residence
307
jūsho henkō todoke
notification of change of
address 353
jūshō shugi
mercantilism 68
jūshō shugisha
mercantilist 68
jūshō shugiteki seisaku
mercantilist economic policies
68
jusshinhō
decimalization 169
jusshinhō kaheisei
decimal coinage 169
jusshinhō tsūka
decimal currency 169
jūtaku
accommodation 289; dwelling
294; habitation 296; home
296; house 296; housing 47,
297; residence, a 307
jūtaku chi'iki
residential area 308
jūtaku fusoku
housing shortage 47
jutaku gyōmu
automated customer services
133
jūtaku jōhō
accommodation information (in
newspaper) 289
jūtaku juyō
housing demand 47
jūtaku kaihatsu
housing development 297
jūtaku kashitsuke
home loan 231, 296; home
purchase loan 231, 296;
housing loan 297; mortgage
152, 248, 302; mortgage loan
249, 302
jūtaku keikaku
housing programme 47
jūtaku kensetsu
housing construction
297; residential construction
308

jūtaku kin'yū
housing credit 47, 231; housing
finance 47; mortgage 152,
248; mortgage credit 248, 302
jūtaku kin'yū gaisha
mortgage bank 152, 248;
mortgage company 248, 302
jūtaku kin'yū kikan
building society [UK] 138, 204,
291
jūtaku kin'yū kōko
Housing Loan Corporation [J]
231, 297
jūtaku kin'yūgyō
mortgage banking 152, 248;
mortgage business 248, 302
jūtaku kōdan
housing corporations 47
jūtaku ku'iki
residential area (district) 308
jūtaku kumiai
building association [US] 291
jūtaku mondai
housing problems 47
jūtaku no shitsu
quality housing 305
jūtaku saiken
housing bond 231
jūtaku sangyō
housing industry 124
jūtaku seisaku
housing policy 47
jūtaku shijō
housing market 47, 297
jūtaku shikin hoken
mortgage repayment insurance
325
jūtaku shikin kashitsuke
mortgage 152, 248; mortgage
loan 249, 302
jūtaku shishutsu
housing expenditure 47
jūtaku shoyūsha hoken
homeowner's insurance 321
jūtaku shoyūsha hoken shōken
homeowner's insurance policy
321
jūtaku shūri kindaika
repair and modernization 307
jūtaku sōgō hoken
householder's comprehensive
insurance 322
jūtaku sōgō hoken shōken
home contents package policy
321; householder's comprehensive insurance policy 322
jūtaku teate
housing allowance 478
jūtaku teitō kashitsuke
home mortgage loan 231
jūtaku tōshi
housing investment 47
jūtaku yūshi hoken
housing loan insurance 322
jūtakunan
housing shortage 47, 297
jutakusha
trustee 162, 283
jūten
priority (preference) 84
jūten sangyō
priority industries 84

kabushiki kaitenritsu
stock turnover 278

kabushiki kaitori kōkai mōshikomi
bid for company's stock 200, 372

kabushiki kaitori seikyūken
appraisal rights 370

kabushiki kaitori sentakuken
stock option 278

kabushiki kaitoriken shasai
warrant bond 286

kabushiki kaitoriken shōsho
warrant (subscription right) 286, 427

kabushiki kaitorikentsuki shasai
stock with equity option 421

kabushiki kakikae
share transfer 272, 417

kabushiki kanjō
share account 272; shareholder's account 272, 418; stock account 277

kabushiki kōbo gaisha
public company (-ies) (public subscription) [UK] 89, 357

kabushiki kōkai
flotation (going public) 226

kabushiki kōkai gaisha
open corporation 354; publicly held company 358

kabushiki kōkai kaitsuke
take-over bid 107, 280, 362, 403; tender 281; tender offer [US] 281

kabushiki kōkai suru
go public 228, 394

kabushiki kōkaitsuki seido
offer by tender 404

kabushiki kyōkō
Stock Exchange panic 277

kabushiki meigi kakikae
stock transfer 278, 420

kabushiki meigi kakikae kinyūbo
stock transfer book 420; stock transfer register 278, 420

kabushiki meigi kakikae teishi
closing of transfer book 208

kabushiki meigi kakikae teishibi
stock record date 278

kabushiki meigi kakikae yōshi
stock transfer form 278, 420

kabushiki mihakkōgaku
capital stock unissued 376

kabushiki mizumashi
stock watering 421

kabushiki mizuwari
stock watering 421

kabushiki mochibun kakaku
stock equity 420

kabushiki mokuromisho
share prospectus 272, 417

kabushiki mōshikomi
application for shares 196, 370; share application 272, 417; stock subscription 278, 420; subscription 421

kabushiki mōshikomi ichiranhyō
subscription list 279, 421

kabushiki mōshikomi kigen
time limit for share applications 423

kabushiki mōshikomi yōshi
share application form 272, 417

kabushiki mōshikomiken
subscription right 421

kabushiki mōshikomisha
applicant (for shares) 195, 370; subscriber 279, 421

kabushiki motochō
share ledger 417; stock ledger 420

kabushiki mukimei kakikae
blank transfer of shares 201, 372

kabushiki nakagaigyō
sharebroking 272; stockbroking 278

kabushiki nakagaigyōsha
brokerage firm 204

kabushiki nakagainin
exchange dealer 221; share-broker 272; stockbroker [UK] 278

kabushiki nakagaiten
commission house 209

kabushiki ni yoru hyōketsu
vote by share 432

kabushiki no bosshū
forfeiture of shares 392; surrender of shares 280, 423

kabushiki no haraikomi
payment for shares 409

kabushiki no heigō
reverse split 267

kabushiki no jika hakkō
issue of shares at the current price 239, 397

kabushiki no kakuzuke
stock rating 278

kabushiki no kōbo
public issue of shares 412

kabushiki no kyōyū
co-ownership of shares 381

kabushiki no saihakkō
re-issue of shares 265, 415

kabushiki no shikken
forfeiture of shares 392; surrender of shares 280, 423

kabushiki no tōgō
consolidation of share capital, 380; consolidation of stock 380

kabushiki ōbo
application for shares 196, 370; stock subscription 278, 420; subscription 421

kabushiki ōboken
subscription right 421

kabushiki ōbosha
applicant (for shares) 195, 370; subscriber 279, 421

kabushiki rimawari
stock yield 278

kabushiki saishō ōbogaku
minimum subscription 247, 401

kabushiki saitei torihiki
stock arbitrage 277

kabushiki seisan
stock clearing 277

kabushiki seisanjo
Stock Exchange clearing house 277

kabushiki sekinin
liability limited by shares 350

kabushiki shiharai funō
non-payment of calls 404

kabushiki shihon
capital stock 376; share capital 417

kabushiki shijō
share market 272; stock market 278

kabushiki shijō no hōkai
stock market crash 278

kabushiki shikaku
share qualification 417

kabushiki shōkan
stock redemption 278

kabushiki shoyū
stock ownership 278

kabushiki shoyūsha
stock owner 278

kabushiki shutoku
acquisition of shares 194, 367; stock acquisition 277

kabushiki sōba
share quotation 272; stock market quotations 278; stock quotation 278

kabushiki sōba hyōjiki
ticker 281

kabushiki sōba hyōtēpu
ticker tape 281

kabushiki sōbahyō
share list 272; stock list 277

kabushiki sōsa
stock manipulation 277

kabushiki tenkan seikyūken
equity kicker 220

kabushiki tōki
speculation on the stock market 275

kabushiki torihikidaka
stock dealings 277; trading volume 282

kabushiki torihiki'in
agent (commission broker, middleman) 194; share dealer 272; share jobber 272

kabushiki torihikijo
Stock Exchange (shares) 277

kabushiki torihikijo de no torihiki
operation on the Stock Exchange 254

kabushiki torihikijo kai'in
Stock Exchange member 277

kabushiki torihikijo kijun
Stock Exchange listing requirements 277

kabushiki torihikijo kisoku
Stock Exchange regulations 277

kabushiki torihikijo kōhō
daily official list 214; official list [UK] 253; Stock Exchange Daily Official List [UK] 277

kabushiki torihikijo kōkai
Stock Exchange placement [US] 277, 420; Stock Exchange placing [UK] 277, 420

kabushiki torihikijo kyūjitsu
Stock Exchange holiday 277

kabushiki torihikijo no hyaku meigara no kabushiki shisū
One Hundred Share Index [UK] 254

kabushiki tōshi
equity investment 220; investment in shares 237; investment in stock 237; stock investment 277

kabushiki tōshi shintaku
stock investment trust [J] 277

kabushiki wariate
allotment 368; allotment of shares 195, 368; share allotment 272, 417

kabushiki wariate shōsho
allocation certificate 368

kabushiki wariate tsūchi(sho)
allotment letter 195, 368; share allotment letter 272, 417

kabushiki waribiki
stock discount 277

kabushikisū
number of shares 404

kabushu
classes of shares 378

kabuya
stock jobber [UK] 277

kachi
merit 461; value 117; worth 121, 472

kachi handan
valuation [UK] 311; value judgement 117

kachi hozō
store of value 105

kachi no nai kabu
valueless stock 285

kachi shakudozai
standard commodity 103

kachiku hoken
livestock insurance 324

kachiku hoken shōken
livestock insurance policy 324

kachiron
theory of value 110

kachō
manager 460; section chief 466

kachō dairi
acting manager 449

kadai hakkō
overissue 256, 407

kadai hyōka
overestimation 326; overvaluation 182, 303, 326

kadai hyōka no
overvalued 303, 326

kadai hyōka no kabu
overvalued stock 256

kadai hyōka suru
overvalue 303, 326

kadai hyōka tsūka
overvalued currency 182

kadai shihon
overcapitalization 407

kadai shihon no
overcapitalized 407

kadai zōshi
capital padding 376; capital watering 377; stock watering 421

kaigi ni shusseki suru
attend a meeting 429
kaigyōhi
initial cost of business 395
kaigyoku
bull account 204; long account 243
kaigyōshiki
inauguration (opening of business) 348
kaihatsu
development 26, 293; exploitation 36
kaihatsu chi'iki
development area(s) 26, 293
kaihatsu enjo
development aid 26
kaihatsu gyōsha
developer 293
kaihatsu kakusa
development gap 26
kaihatsu keikaku
development planning 26; development programme 26; development project 293
kaihatsu kin'yū
development finance 26, 217
kaihatsu senryaku
development strategy 26
kaihatsu suru
develop 25, 293
kaihatsu tojōkoku
developing countries 26
kaihatsu yūshi
development loan 217
kaihatsushitsu
development office 453
kaihejji
buy hedge 205; long hedge 243
kaihifunō genka
unavoidable costs 371, 425
kaihikanō genka
avoidable costs 371
kaihō bōeki seisaku
open trade policy 76
kaihō keizai
open economy 76
kaihō sekai bōeki
open world trade 76
kaihō shijō
open-market place 76
kaihō shijō seisaku
open market policy 76
kaihō shitsugyō
open unemployment 76
kaihōgata infurēshon
open inflation 76
kaihōgata tanpo
open-end mortgage 254
kaihōgata tanpotsuki shasai
open-end mortgage bond 254
kai'in
members 431
kai'in gaisha
member company 352
kai'in meibo
list of members 350
kai'in no hasan kokuchi (rondon kabushiki torihikijo)
hammering [UK] 230

kai'inken
seat 269
kaiire gaikoku kawase
foreign bills bought 147
kaiire gurūpu
purchase group 262
kaiire kakaku
purchase price 262; purchase price of shares 413
kaiire shōkan
purchasing redemption 262; redemption by purchase 264
kaijō hoken
marine insurance 325
kaijō hoken keiyaku
marine insurance contract 325
kaijō hoken shōken
marine insurance policy 325
kaikakekin
accounts payable 366; book debt 373
kaikakekin motochō
accounts payable ledger 366
kaikaku
reform (reorganization) 93
kaikata
bull 204; buyers 205
kaikata kata
buyers over 205
kaikata no
bullish 204
kaikata no kaisusumi
bull attack 204
kaikata rengō
bull pool 204
kaikawase
exchange bought 171; exchange buying 171
kaikawase sōba
buying quotation 166
kaikei
accounting 365; accounts 366
kaikei buchō
accounts manager 449
kaikei chōbo
accounting books 365
kaikei gaisha
accounting firm 365
kaikei gensoku
accounting principles 366
kaikei hōkoku(sho)
accountant's report 365; accounting report 366; financial report 391
kaikei hōshiki
accounting method 365; accounting technique 366
kaikei jitsumu
accounting practice 366
kaikei jittai
accounting entity 365
kaikei jōhō shisutemu
accounting information system 365
kaikei kamoku
accounting subject 366
kaikei kansa
audit (noun) 371; independent audit 395
kaikei kansa gaisha
audit company 371

kaikei kansanin
auditor (independent) 371; independent auditor 395
kaikei kansanin no ikensho
independent auditor's opinion 395
kaikei kensakan
auditor (government) 371
kaikei kessan
accounting (settlement of accounts) 365
kaikei kijun
accounting bases 365; accounting standard 366
kaikei kikan
accounting period 366; period of account 409
kaikei kiroku
accounting records 366
kaikei kisoku
accounting regulations 366
kaikei nendo
accounting period (tax year) 366; accounting year 366; business year 374; financial year [UK] 39, 391; fiscal year [US] 39, 391 [UK government] 39
kaikei nendo no kaikei
accounts for financial year 366
kaikei sagyō
accounting operations 366
kaikei seido
accounting system 366
kaikei shori
accounting processing 366; accounts processing 366; processing of accounts 411
kaikei shori hōshin
accounting policy 366
kaikei shutai
accounting entity 365
kaikei tan'i
accounting entity 365; accounting unit 366
kaikei tetsuzuki
accounting procedure 366
kaikei tsūsoku
accounting rules 366
kaikei yōgo
accounting terminology 366
kaikei yōgo no kigo seido
accounts coding system 366
kaikeibi
accounting date 365
kaikeibo
account books 365; books 373
kaikeibu
accounting department 449
kaikeigakari
accountant 365, 449
kaikeigakari no sekinin
accountant's liability 365
kaikeihō
accounting method 365; accounting system 366
kaikeishi
accountant (certified public accountant) 365, 449
kaikeishi e no shirei
instructions to accountant 396
kaikeiteki hyōka
accounting valuation 366

kaiki
buying disposition 205; buying interest 205; bullish sentiment 205; bullish support 205; bullish tone 205
kaiki
regression 94
kaiki bunseki
regression analysis 94
kaiki ōsei
aggressive buying 195
kaikin
lifting of embargo 63
kaiko
dismissal 499; termination 503
kaiko no konkyo
grounds for dismissal 500
kaiko no riyū
grounds for dismissal 500
kaiko suru
discharge 499; dismiss 499
kaiko tsūchisho
dismissal notice 499; notice of dismissal 501
kaikoken
right of dismissal 502
kaikoken ran'yō
right-of-dismissal abuse 502
kaikokin
severance pay 483, 502
kaikoritsu
discharges (employment) 26
kaikyū
rank 465
kaimochi
long position 178, 243; overbought position 256
kaimodoshi
bear covering 199; buy back 205; cover 211; covering 211; repurchase 266; share covering 272
kaimodoshi keiyaku
covering contract 212; repo 266; repurchase agreement 266
kaimodoshi nedan
call price 206; repurchase price 266
kaimodoshi sōsa
buy-back transaction 205
kaimodoshi yowakisuji
covered bear 211; protected bear 261
kaimodoshikanō shōken
redeemable security 264
kaimodoshiken
repurchase right 267
kaimodoshinin
repurchaser 267
kaimodosu
repurchase (verb) 266
kaimōshikomi
buying offer 205, 291; offer to buy 303
kaine
buying price 291; purchase price 305
kaininjō
revocation of power of attorney 360
kaininki
speculative interest 275

kaite shijō
buyer's market 205

kaitei
revision 96

kaitei keisū
revised figures 96

kaitekisa
amenities 289

kaiten kurejitto-rain
revolving line of credit [US] 159

kaiten shin'yō
revolving credit 159, 267

kaiten shin'yōjō
revolving L/C 159

kaitenritsu
turnover ratio 424

kaitonae
bid 200

kaitori
acquisition (of a company) 367;
buy-out(s) 13; purchase 335;
purchase of a company 358;
purchase of a company's equity
413; take-over 280, 362

kaitori ginkō
negotiating bank 152

kaitori tegata
bill bought 136

kaitori tesūryō
negotiation charge 152

kaitori yushutsu kawase
bill bought 136

kaitoru
acquire (a business, a
company) 335; take over
280, 362

kaitsuke sashine
buying limit 205

kaitsuke sentakuken
call option 206

kaitsuke tesūryō
buying commission 166

kaitsukeken
buyer's option 166, 205

kaitsunagi
buy hedge 205; hedge buying
230; long hedge 243

kaiuke saishūteki yakusoku
firm commitment 224

kaiume
short covering [US] 273

kaiungyō
shipping industry 126

kaiyaku
partial redemption 326
**kaiyaku made yūkō na
chūmon**
good-till-cancelled order 228;
open order 254

kaiyakusho
purchase note 262

kaiyō osen
sea pollution 98

kaiyō sangyō
ocean industry 125

kaiyobine
bid (buying price) 200

kaizairyō
bullish factor 204

kaizen
improvement (reformation) 49

kaji
fire 491

kaji kiken
fire hazard 491

kajino keizai
casino economy 15

kajino shakai
casino society 15

kajō
excess 35; surplus (over-
abundance) 106

kajō junbi
excess reserves [US] 146, 171

kajō juyō
excess demand 35

kajō koyō
overemployment 77

kajō koyō rōdōsha
overemployed workers 77

kajō nōryoku
excess capacity 35

kajō rōdō
surplus labour (over-
employment) 106

kajō rōdōryoku
surplus workforce 468

kajō ryūdōsei
excess liquidity 146

kajō seisan
overproduction 78

kajō setsubi
excess capacity (plant and
equipment) 35; surplus
capacity 106

kajō shikibetsu
overidentification 78

kajō shōhin
surplus commodities 106;
surplus goods 106

kajō tōshi
overinvestment 256

kajō yushutsu
excessive exports 35

kajō zaiko
surplus stocks 106

kajū heikin
weighted average 119;
weighted mean 120

kajū kaiki
weighted regression 120

kajū rōdō
overwork (noun) 463

kakaku
price(s) (cost) 83, 304; value
117

kakaku antei sōsa
market stabilization 246

kakaku atsuryoku infurēshon
price-push inflation 83

kakaku bakuhatsu
price explosion 83

kakaku bunseki
price analysis 83

kakaku danryokusei
price elasticity 83

kakaku hendō
price movement 83

kakaku hendō jōkō
price-fluctuation clause 83

kakaku hendōritsu
volatility 285

kakaku hikiage
price increase 304

kakaku hikisage
lowering of price 301

kakaku hyōjunka
price standardization 84

kakaku iji
price maintenance 83

kakaku jōshō
price rise 84

kakaku juyōsha
price taker 84

kakaku kakumei
price revolution 84

kakaku karuteru
price cartel 83

kakaku keisei
pricing 84

kakaku kettei
price-determining 83

kakaku ketteiteki
price-determined 83

kakaku kikō
price mechanism 83

kakaku kirisage
price cut 304; price-cutting 83

kakaku kōka
price effect 83

kakaku kotei
price-fixing 83

kakaku kōzō
price structure 84

kakaku kyōsō
price competition 83

kakaku kyōsōryoku
price competitiveness 83

kakaku kyōtei
price-fixing agreement 83

kakaku no jōken kettei
fixing 225

kakaku no ugokanai shijō
flat market 225

kakaku sabetsu
price discrimination 83

kakaku saikō gendo
price ceiling 83

kakaku sendōsei
price leadership 83

kakaku settei
price-setting 84

kakaku setteisha
price setter 84

kakaku shiji
price support 84

kakaku shijisaku
price-support scheme 84

kakaku-shōhi kyokusen
price-consumption curve 83

kakaku taikei
price system 84

kakaku to shotoku seisaku
prices and incomes policy 84

kakaku tōsei
price control 83

kakaku tōsei kaijo
price decontrol 83

kakakugai kyōsō
non-price competition 74

kakakuron
price theory 84

kakari
person in charge 463

kakarichō
chief clerk 451; group chief
456

kake
credit (charge) 212

kake kanjō
credit account [UK] 212

kakehiki kanzei
bargaining tariff 10

kakei
household economy 47

kakei chōsa
household economy survey 47

kakei shishutsu chōsa
Family Expenditure Survey [UK]
38

kakei shōhi
household consumption 47

kakei shotoku
family income 38

kakeihi
household expenses 47, 297

kakene
overbid (noun) 256
kakene o suru
overbid (verb) 256

kaketsu
adoption 429; approval 429

kaketsunagi
hedge (noun) 230; hedging
46, 230

kaketsunagi keiyaku
hedging contract 230

kaketsunagi sōsa
hedging operation 230

kaketsunagi torihiki
hedging transaction 230

kaketsunagikai
hedge buying 230

kaketsunagiuri
hedge selling 230

kakeuri
on account 254; open account
254

kakeuri jōken
credit terms 213

kakeuri tokuisaki
credit customer 212

kakeurikin
book credit 373

kaki kyūka
summer holiday 484

kakikae
renewal (rewriting) 266;
transfer 282

kakikaeru
renew 266

kakikomu (yōshi o)
fill in (a form) 146

kakkyō
activity (boom) 3; brisk
business 203; buoyancy
(prosperity) 12

kakkyō no
buoyant 12

kakkyō sangyō
expanding industry 35

kakō
decline 23; downswing 28;
downturn 28

kakō keikō
bearish tendency 200;
downtrend 28

kankinka
realization 414

kankinkanō shisan
realizable assets 413

kankōgyō
tourist industry 127

kankyō
environment 33

kankyō akka
deterioration of the environment 25

kankyō chōsa
environmental research 33

kankyō hakai
destruction of the environment 25

kankyō hogo
protection of the environment 89

kankyō hozen
preservation of the environment 82

kankyō hyōka
environmental impact analysis 33

kankyō jōka
environmental clean-up 33

kankyō jōken
environmental conditions 33

kankyō kaikaku
environmental reform 33

kankyō kaizen
improvement of the environment 49

kankyō ketteiron
environmental determinism 33

kankyō kiki
environmental crisis 33

kankyō kosuto
environmental pollution cost 33

kankyō mondai
environmental issues 33

kankyō no shitsu
quality of environment 90, 305

kankyō osen
environmental pollution 33; pollution of the environment 81

kankyō ran'yō
environmental abuse 33

kankyō saigai
environmental disaster 33

kankyō seisaku
environmental policy 33

kankyō shugisha
environmentalist 33

kankyō teika
degradation of the environment 24

kanman na
slack (slow moving) 101

kanman na shikyō
slack market 274

kannenron
ideology 48

kannō bunseki
sensitivity analysis 99

kanōsei
opportunity (possibility) 445

kanōsei no kentō
feasibility study 38

kanpō
Gazette, the 347

kanren
relation 94

kanren gaisha
affiliate [US] 335; affiliated company 336; affiliated enterprize 336; associated company [UK] 337; related company 359

kanri
administration 335, 449; control 342; management 65, 351, 460; supervision 468

kanri bumon
administration department 449

kanri furōto
managed float 178

kanri gijutsu
management technique 352

kanri hiyō
management expenses 400

kanri hyōjun
management standards 351; managerial standards 352

kanri i'inkai
administration committee 335

kanri kaikei
administrative accounting 368; accing for management 365; management accounting 400

kanri kakaku
administered prices 4

kanri keizai
governed economy 44; managed economy 65

kanri kikan
control period 381

kanri nōryoku
administrative ability 335, 449

kanri sareta hendō kawase
managed floating exchange 179

kanri sareta hendō kawase sōba
managed floating exchange rate 179

kanri sareta hendō kawase sōbasei
managed floating exchange rate system 179

kanri sareta hyōka no kokizami chōsei
managed crawling peg 178

kanri sareta kinhon'isei
managed gold standard 179

kanri sekinin
executive responsibility 345

kanri shokui
executive position 455

kanri shokuin
administrative staff 449; executive personnel 455; supervisory staff 468

kanri shokumu
executive job 455

kanri suru
manage (control) 351

kanri tesūryō
management fee 245

kanri torishimariyakukai
managing Board of Directors 352

kanri tsūka
controlled currency 167; managed currency 178

kanri tsūka seido
managed currency system 178

kanri yosan
administrative budget 368

kanri yunittogata tōshi shintaku
managed unit trust [UK] 245

kanribu
administration department 449

kanrihi
administration cost 368; administrative expenses 368; maintenance fee 244

kanrikanōhi
controllable cost 381

kanrinin
administrator (manager, supervisor) 449

kanrinin no shokumu
managerial function 352

kanrisha
management (administrators) 460; manager 460

kanrisha keihatsu
management development 351

kanrisha keihatsu keikaku
management development programme 351

kanrisha kunren keikaku
management training programme 352, 460

kanrishoku
executive job 455; managerial position 460

kanrishokui
executive position 455

kanrishokuin
executive personnel 455; managerial staff 460

kanrisō
management (level of management, strata) 351

kanryō(sei)
bureaucracy 12

kanryōteki keishiki shugi
red tape 93

kanryū
recycling (of capital) 92, 264

kanryū suru
recycle (capital) 92, 264

kansa
audit (noun) 371; auditing 371

kansa gensoku
auditing rules 371

kansa gijutsu
audit techniques 371

kansa han'i
scope of audit 416

kansa hōkokusho
accountant's certificate 365; audit opinion 371; audit report 371; auditor's report 371

kansa ippan kijun
general auditing standard 393

kansa kijun
audit standard 371; auditing standard 371

kansa kikan
audit period 371

kansa nendo
audit year 371

kansa sashizusho
audit instruction 371

kansa shisutemu
auditing system 371

kansa shōmeisho
audit certificate 371

kansa shōseki
audit trail 197, 371

kansa shūsei
audit adjustment 371

kansa suru
audit (verb) 371

kansa tetsuzuki
audit procedure 371

kansa yakuin
audit staff (of a company) 371

kansabu
auditing department 450

kansan
conversion (change) 167

kansan na shijō
inactive market 232; narrow market 249

kansan na shikyō
inactive market 232; quiet market 262; thin market 281

kansanin no iken
auditor's opinion 371

kansanritsu
conversion rate 167

kansaryō
audit fee 371

kansayaku
auditing officer 371; auditor 371, 450; company's auditors 379; controller 381

kansayaku shōmeisho
auditor's certificate 371

kansazumi zaimu shohyō
certified financial statement 378

kansei suru
execute (complete) 294

kansetsu bōeki
indirect trade 51

kansetsu fusai
indirect debt 233

kansetsu hakkō
offer for sale [UK] (direct issue) 253, 404

kansetsu kawase
indirect exchange 149, 177

kansetsu kawase tegata
indirect exchange bill 149

kansetsu keihi
indirect expenses 51

kansetsu kin'yū
indirect financing 233

kansetsu kōyō kansū
indirect utility function 51

kansetsu rōdō
indirect labour 51

kansetsu seisan
indirect production 51

kansetsu shimekirihō
journal transfer method 398

kansetsu shōkyaku
indirect depreciation 395

kansetsu songai
consequential damage 318; consequential loss 318

kansetsu songai hoken
consequential damage insurance 318

kariirekin kanjō
loan account 242

kariirekin kinri
interest on borrowing 234

kariirekin rishi
interest payable 235

kariirekoku
borrower country (-ies) 11, 203; borrowers (countries) 11

karijimusho
temporary business office 362

karikabu
borrowed stock 203

karikabuken
certificate (share) 378; scrip 269, 417; scrip certificate 417

karikae
conversion 210; reborrowing 263; refinancing 264; refunding 264; renewal 266

karikae hakkō
conversion issue 210

karikae saiken
refunding bond 264; renewal bond 266

karikanjō
suspense account 161, 423

karikata
debit (vs. credit) 142; debit side 142, 385

karikata ni kinyū suru
charge (verb) 139; debit (verb) 142

karikata kinyū
debit entry 142, 385

karikata zandaka
debit balance 142, 385

karikatahyō
debit note 142; debit slip 142

karikatahyō shiharai denpyō
debit voucher 142

karikoshi
overdraft [UK] 154

karikoshi kanjō
overdrawn account 154

karikoshi zandaka
outstanding overdraft 154

karima
rented room 307

karimokuromisho
preliminary prospectus 259, 410; red herring (prospectus) [US] 264, 414

karinushi
lessee (tenant) 301; tenant (vs. landlord) 310

kariru
borrow 203; rent (verb) 306

kado ni kariru
overborrow 256

karisashiosae
provisional attachment 437

kariseisannin
provisional liquidator 437

karishōken
scrip 269

karitaishaku taishōhyō
tentative balance sheet 423

karite
borrower (debtor) 203

kariya
hired house 296

karuteru
cartel 15

karuteruka
cartelization 15

karuteruka sangyō
cartelized industries 15

kasai
fire 320, 491

kasai hoken
fire insurance 320; insurance against fire 322

kasai keihō
fire alarm 491

kasai kiken
fire hazard(s) 320, 491

kasai ni yoru songai
damage by fire 319

kasaiyō hinan hashigo
fire escape (ladder) 491

kaseigaku
home economics 46

kasen
oligopoly 76

kasen gyogyō
river fishing 126

kasen keizai
oligopolistic economy 76

kasensha
oligopolist 76

kasenteki kōi
oligopolistic behaviour 76

kasenteki kyōsō
oligopolistic competition 76

kasetsu
assumption (supposition) 8; hypothesis 47

kasetsu kentei
hypothesis testing 47

kasetsuhi
installation cost 396

kashichi
land for rent 299; land to let 300

kashichinin
lessor (land lessor) 301

kashidaore
bad debt(s) 198, 371

kashidaore hikiatekin
allowance for bad debts 369; allowance for doubtful accounts [UK] 369; bad debt provision 371; bad debt reserve 372; provision for doubtful debts [US] 412; reserve for bad debts 415

kashidaore hoken
bad debt insurance 316

kashidaore junbikin
allowance for bad debts 369; allowance for doubtful accounts [UK] 369; bad debt provision, 371; bad debt reserve 372; provision for doubtful debts [US] 412; reserve for bad debts 415

kashidaore(kin) shōkyaku
bad debts written off 372; writing-off of bad debts 428

kashidaore sonshitsu
bad debt loss 371; loss from bad debts 400

kashidashi
lending 240; loan 151, 242

kashidashi o hensai suru
repay a loan 266

kashidashi bumon (ginkō no)
loan department (of a bank) 151

kashidashi gendogaku
credit ceiling 212; credit limit 212; credit line 212; line of credit [US] 151

kashidashi gendogaku seido
credit ceiling system 212

kashidashi hensai
repayment of loan 266

kashidashi hōhō
type of loan 283

kashidashi kijun kinri
basic lending rate 199

kashidashi kikan
lending period 240

kashidashi kinri
interest on loan 235; lending rate 240; loan rate 242

kashidashi kyōsō
lending race 240

kashidashi no kaishū
collection (of debt) 209; debt collection 215

kashidashi no karikae keizoku
renewal of loan 266

kashidashi riritsu
lending rate 240; loan rate 242

kashidashi risuku
exposure 221

kashidashi seisaku
lending policy 240

kashidashi shijō
lending market 240

kashidashi shinsa
examination of loan application 220

kashidashi shinsei
application for a loan 196

kashidashi shinsei o suru
apply for a loan 196

kashidashi yokusei seisaku
restrictive lending policy 267

kashidashi yokusei taido
restrictive lending attitude 267

kashidashi yoyaku
loan commitment 242

kashidashi zōkagaku kisei
regulatory control on bank lendings 265

kashidashidaka
amount of loan 195; lendings 241

kashidashigaku
loan value 243

kashidasu
lend 240

kashikabu
lending stock 241; stock loan 277

kashikabu shijō
stock loan market 277

kashikata
credit (vs. debit) 141; credit side 141, 383

kashikata kinyū
credit entry 141, 383

kashikata zandaka
credit balance 141, 383

kashikin
debt (advance, loan) 142, 215; money lent 248

kashikin o toritateru
collect a debt 209

kashikin no chōshū
recall of loan 263

kashikin toritatenin
debt collector 215

kashikinko
safe [UK] 159; safe-deposit box [US] 159

kashikinko chingariryō
rental fee (of safe deposit box) 158

kashikinko gaisha
safe deposit corporation 159

kashikinko hoyūsha
safe-deposit box holder 159

kashikoshi
overdraft [UK] 154; overdraft facilities 154

kashikoshi gendo
maximum limit of overdraft 151; overdraft limit 154

kashikoshi keiyaku
overdraft agreement 154

kashikoshi kyokudogaku
maximum limit of overdraft 247

kashima
room to let 308

kashima o kasu
let a room 301

kashima fuda
room-to-let sign 308

kashinushi
creditor (lender) 213; landlady (of rented property) 300; landlord (of rented property) 300; lessor 301

kashiragaki
letterhead 350

kashishōken
lending securities 241

kashite
lender(s) 62, 240

kashite no kiken
lender's risk 240

kashitsu
fire box 491

kashitsu
negligence 492

kashitsu sekinin hoken
negligence liability insurance 326

kashitsuke
loan 151, 242

kashitsuke jōken
terms and conditions of loan 281

kashitsuke kagaku
loan value 243

kashitsuke kanjō
loan account 242

kashitsuke kikan
loan period 242

kashitsuke kinyūchō
loan book 399

kashitsuke kyōsō
loan race 242

kashitsuke mōshikomi
  loan application 242
kashitsuke motochō
  loan ledger 400
kashitsuke seido
  lending facility 240
kashitsuke seisaku
  loan policy 242
kashitsuke shihon
  loan capital 242, 399
kashitsuke shijō
  lending market 240
kashitsuke shirei
  lending guidelines 240
kashitsuke shōnin
  loan approval 242
kashitsuke yūka shōken
  securities loaned 270
kashitsuke zandaka
  outstanding credit 255
kashitsukekin
  loan 242
kashitsukekin risoku
  interest on loan 149
kashitsukeru
  lend 240
kashiya
  house for rent 297; house to let
  297
  kashiya o sagasu
    look for a house to rent 301
kashiya fuda
  for-rent sign 295
kashiya kumiai
  house owners' association
  297; landlords' association 300
kashiya sagashi
  house-hunting 297
kashiya shūsengyō
  estate agent [UK] (houses-for-
  rent finding agency) 294
kashiyanin
  lessor (house lessor) 301
kashiyazumai
  living in rented accommodation
  301
kashō boshū
  undersubscription 283, 425
kashō hyōka
  undervaluation 186, 311, 330
kashō hyōka no
  undervalued 311, 330
kashō hyōka suru
  undervalue 311, 330
kashō hyōka tsūka
  undervalued currency 186
kashō koyō
  underemployment 114
kashō mōshikomi
  undersubscription 283, 425
kashō ryūdōsei
  insufficient liquidity 396
kashō seisan
  underproduction 114
kashō setsubi
  undercapacity 114
kashō shusshi
  undercapitalization 425
kashō shusshi no
  undercapitalized 425
kashō tōshi
  underinvestment 114, 283

kashobun shotoku
  disposable income 27
kaso chi'iki
  underpopulated areas 114
kasō kaikyū
  lower rank 460
kasoku(do)
  acceleration 3
kasoku genka shōkyaku
  accelerated depreciation 365
kasoku shōkyaku
  accelerated amortization 365;
  accelerated depreciation 3,
  365
kasokudo genri
  accelerator principle 3
kasokudo inshi
  accelerator 3
kasokudo keisū
  accelerator coefficient 3
kasokudo riron
  accelerator theory (of
  investment) 3
kasshu-furō
  cash flow 15, 377
kasu
  lend 240
  ie o kasu
    let a house 301
katabōeki
  one-sided foreign trade 75
katagaki
  title 469
katagawari
  novation (replacement of party
  to a contract by another party.)
  252
katai hasan
  negligent bankruptcy 436
kataku
  property (premises, domicile)
  305
kataku shingai
  trespassing 310
kataku shingaisha
  trespasser 310
kataku shinnyū
  trespassing 310
katei
  assumption 8; hypothesis 47
katei
  process (course, progress) 85
katei
  home 296; household(s) 47,
  297
katei hoken
  household insurance 322
katei keizai
  household economy 47
katei yōgu
  household appliances 297
katei yōhin
  house furnishings 297
katō kyōsō
  excessive competition 35
katō tōki
  overspeculation 256
katoki
  transition (transitory stage)
  113; transitional period 113
katoku
  family estate 295

katoku sōzoku
  inheritance of family estate 298
katsudō
  activity (liveliness) 3, 194
katsudō bunseki
  activity analysis 3
katsudō kaikei
  activity accounting 367
katsudō kanjō
  active account 131, 194
katsudō shihon
  active capital 367
katsudō shisan
  active assets 367
katsudō zandaka
  active balance 3
katsudōteki
  active (lively, brisk) 3
katsuryoku
  vitality 117
kau
  buy 205, 291
kawase (= gaikoku kawase)
  exchange (= foreign exchange)
  35, 146, 171
kawase antei
  exchange stability 172
kawase antei shikin
  Exchange Stabilization Fund
  [US] 172
kawase anteika
  exchange stabilization 172
kawase baibai sōba hiraki
  exchange margin 172
kawase burōkā
  currency broker 168; exchange
  broker 171
kawase danpingu
  exchange dumping 171
kawase deai
  cover 168; exchange cover
  171
kawase deai tegata
  exchange cover bill 146
kawase diirā
  exchange dealer 171
kawase furidashinin
  drawer 170; sender 183
kawase ginkō
  exchange bank 146, 171
kawase gyōmu
  exchange business 171
kawase hanbaigyō
  retail dealing 183
kawase heika
  exchange parity 172; par value
  of currency 182; par value of
  exchange 182
kawase heikō kanjō
  Exchange Equalization Account
  [UK] 171
kawase heikō sōsa
  exchange equalization
  operation 171
kawase hendō
  exchange fluctuation 171;
  exchange rate fluctuation 172
kawase hendō junbi
tsumitatekin
  reserve for foreign exchange
  fluctuations 415

kawase hon'isei
  exchange standard 172
kawase hoyū seigen
  exchange holdings restrictions
  171
kawase hoyūdaka
  exchange holdings 171
kawase junbi seido
  exchange reserve system 172
kawase kabā
  cover 168
kawase kachi
  exchange value 172
kawase kanri
  exchange control 171
kawase kanrihō
  exchange control law 171
kawase kansan
  exchange conversion 171
kawase kansanhyō
  conversion table 167;
  exchange conversion table
  171; exchange table 172
kawase kansanritsu
  exchange conversion rate 171
kawase kanshō
  exchange intervention 172
kawase kyoka
  exchange permit 172
kawase mochidaka
  exchange holdings 171;
  exchange position 172
kawase nakagainin
  currency broker 168;
  exchange broker 171;
  exchange dealer 171
kawase no jiyūka
  liberalization of exchange
  control 178
kawase no suwappu torihiki
  currency swap 169
kawase risuku
  exchange risk 172
kawase saeki
  exchange gain 171;
  exchange profit 172
kawase saitei
  arbitrage 165; exchange
  arbitrage 171
kawase saitei torihiki
  arbitrage operation 165
kawase sakimono
  exchange futures 171
kawase sason
  exchange loss 172
kawase sayatori gyōsha
  arbitrageur 165
kawase seigen
  exchange restrictions 172
kawase seisan
  exchange clearing 171
kawase seisan kyōtei
  clearing agreement 140
kawase seisansei
  exchange clearing system 171
kawase shiharai
  exchange payment 172
kawase shijō
  exchange market 172

kawase sōba
exchange quotation 172;
exchange rate 172; parity
(exchange rate) 182; rate of
exchange 183

kawase sōba kugitsuke
exchange pegging 172

kawase sōba kugitsuke seido
exchange pegging system 172

kawase sōba kugitsuke seisaku
exchange pegging policy 172

kawase sōba no antei
stabilization of exchange rate
185

kawase sōba no hendō
exchange rate movements 172

kawase sōba no hiraki
exchange difference 171

kawase sōba seisaku
exchange rate policy 172

kawase sōbahyō
exchange quotation table 172;
table of foreign exchange rates
186

kawase sōkin
remittance by draft 158

kawase sōsa
exchange operation 172

kawase tegata
bill of exchange 137; draft 145;
exchange bill 146, 171

kawase sōkin
remittance by draft 158

kawase tegata sōkin
remittance by draft 158

kawase tegatabarai
payment by draft 156

kawase tesūryō
charge for remittance 139

kawase tōki
exchange speculation 172;
foreign currency speculation
173

kawase tōkisuji
exchange speculator 172

kawase torihiki
exchange dealing 171;
exchange transaction 172

kawase torihiki'in
currency trader 169

kawase waribiki
exchange discount 171

kawase yoyaku
exchange contract 171

kawase yoyaku kōshin
renewal of exchange contract
183

kazai
household effects 297

kazai hōkatsu hoken
home contents floater 321

kazai hoken
household goods insurance
322

kazei
taxation (imposition of taxes)
109

kazei kijun
tax assessment basis 484; tax
base 107, 484

kazei kōjo
tax deductions 108, 484

kazei mitsumori kakaku
rateable value 305

kazei saitei shotoku
minimum taxable income 68

kazei satei
tax assessment 484

kazei shotoku
taxable income 109, 281, 485

kazei zaisan
taxable property 310

kazeihin
taxable goods 109

kazeiritsu
tax rate 108, 484

kazoku
household 297

kazoku hoshō hoken
family protection insurance 320

kazoku rōdōsha
family worker 455

kazoku shugi
paternalism 463

kazoku shugiteki na
paternalistic 463

kazoku teate
family allowance [J] 477

kega
injury 492

kehai
market tone 246; mood
(market) 248; tone (of market)
282

kehai no shihyō
sentiment indicators 271

kehaijō
stock list (securities) 277

keidanren (keizai dantai rengō kai)
Federation of Economic
Organizations [J] 38

keido infurēshon
moderate inflation 69

kei'ei
administration 335, 449;
management 65, 351, 460;
operation (running) 354

kei'ei o hikitsugu
take over the management 362

kei'ei bunseki
activity analysis 335; business
analysis 338

kei'ei gijutsu
entrepreneurial skill 345;
management technique 352;
managerial know-how 352

kei'ei gimu
executive duties 345

kei'ei gōrika
rationalization of business 358;
rationalization of management
358

kei'ei gyōseki
management performance 351

kei'ei hatan
business failure 433

kei'ei hōshin
business policy 339;
management policy 351

kei'ei jimu
office routine 354

kei'ei jisseki
management performance 351

kei'ei jissen
business practice
(management) 339

kei'ei jogen
management advisory service
351

kei'ei jōhō kanri seido
management information
system 351

kei'ei kaisō
hierarchy 457; management
hierarchy 351

kei'ei kaizen
administrative improvement
335

kei'ei kanbu
executive (leading executive)
454; executive management
345; executive staff 346, 455

kei'ei kanri
business management 339

kei'ei kanri soshiki
management organization 351

kei'ei kanrishi
business consultant 338

kei'ei kansa
management audit 400;
management review 351

kei'ei keikaku
business planning 339;
management planning 351

kei'ei keiken
experience in management
346

kei'ei keizaigaku
business economics 13

kei'ei kibo
size of business 361

kei'ei komon
business consultant 338

kei'ei kōritsu
efficiency of management 345;
management efficiency 351

kei'ei kyōiku
management education 351

kei'ei mokuteki
business objectives 339

kei'ei no keizai
managerial economies 65

kei'ei no kigyōtai riron
managerial theories of the firm
65

kei'ei nōryoku
executive ability 345, 455

kei'ei saikō sekininsha
chief executive officer (CEO)
340, 451

kei'ei sanka
participation in management
355

kei'ei seiseki
results of operations 360

kei'ei sekinin
accountability 449; management responsibilities 351

kei'ei senryaku
business strategy 339;
management strategy 351

kei'ei shihon riekiritsu
profit ratio of operating capital
412

kei'ei shindan
business diagnosis 338;
management consulting 351

kei'ei shokumu
executive duties 455

kei'ei shuwan
administrative ability 335, 449

kei'ei soshiki
administrative structure 335;
management structure 351;
management system 351

kei'ei suru
manage (run) 351

kei'ei taishaku taishōhyō
administrative balance sheet
368

kei'ei tetsugaku
operating philosophy 354

kei'ei to bunri shita shoyūken
ownership separated from
capital 408

kei'eigai ritoku
non-recurring gain 404

kei'eigai sonshitsu
non-recurring loss 404

kei'eigaku
business administration (study
of) 441; business management
studies 441; management
science 65, 444

kei'eigaku shūshi
Master's Degree in Business
Administration (MBA) 444

kei'eihi
administrative expenses 368;
expense(s) 389; managing
expenses 400; working
expenses 427

kei'eiken
management rights 351

kei'eiryoku
managerial power 65

kei'eisha
administrator 449; corporate
manager 342; employer (the
management) 454; executive
345, 454; management 351,
460; operator 354

kei'eisha baishū
management buy-out 400

kei'eisha hoken
key-man insurance 324

kei'eisha kakumei
management revolution 351;
managerial revolution 65

kei'eisha no renmei
employers' associations [UK]
32; employers' federations 32

kei'eisha no sairyōteki kōdō
managerial discretion 65

kei'eisha shihai
management control 351

kei'eisha shihon shugi
managerial capitalism 65

kei'eishasoku
management (vs. employees)
460

kei'eishi
management consultant 351

kei'eisō
management (level of
management, strata) 351

kei'eiteki tōsei
managerial control 352

keisen
chart 208
keisen bunseki senmonka
chartist 208
keisen'ya
technician 281
keishō
take-over (succession) 362
keishō suru
take over (succeed to) 362
keisū
coefficient 16; parameter 78
keitō kikan
affiliated organization 336
keiyaku
agreement 289; contract 210,
292, 318, 452
keiyaku chingin
contracted wage 476;
contractual wages 476
keiyaku enchō
extension of contract 295
keiyaku furikō
non-fulfilment of contract 303
keiyaku hizuke
contract date 292
keiyaku hōki
cancellation of contract 291
keiyaku ihan
breach of contract 290
keiyaku imin rōdō
contract immigrant labour 20,
452
keiyaku jōken
terms and conditions of a
contract 330
keiyaku jōkō
covenant 293
keiyaku keizoku
renewal of policy 328
keiyaku kigen
contract period 292; period of
contract 303
keiyaku kōshin
renewal of contract 306
keiyaku kyokusen
contract curve 20
keiyaku manki
expiration of a contract 295
keiyaku mankibi
date of expiry 319
keiyaku rōdō
contract labour 452
keiyaku rōdōsha
contracted labourer 452
keiyaku sekinin hoken
contractual liability insurance
318
keiyaku shūketsu
termination of contract 469
keiyaku suru
contract (verb) 292
keiyaku tōjisha
contracting parties 292; parties
to a contract 303
keizai
economy 31
keizai antei
economic stabilization 31
keizai bumon
economic sector 31

keizai burokku
economic block 29
keizai chidai
economic rent 31
keizai chitsujo
economic order 30
keizai chōsa
economic survey 31
keizai dōgaku
economic dynamics 29
keizai dōkō
economic trend 31
keizai dōkō bunseki
economic analysis 29
keizai dōmei
economic union 31
keizai enjo
economic support 31
keizai fukushi
economic welfare (economic
well-being) 31
keizai fūsa
economic blockade 29
keizai gakuha
school of economics 98
keizai gensoku
economic principle 30
keizai hakusho
economic white paper 31
keizai hatten
economic development
(expansion) 29
keizai hendō
economic fluctuations 30;
economic volatility 31
keizai hōkokusho
economic report 31
keizai jijō
economic affairs 29
keizai jōkyō
economic conditions 29
keizai jōsei
economic climate 29;
economic conditions 29;
economic scene 31
keizai junkan
economic cycle 29
keizai kachi
economic worth 31
keizai kaifuku
economic recovery 31
keizai kaihatsu
economic development
(exploitation) 29
keizai kaikaku
economic improvements 30;
economic reform 31
keizai kansoku
economic forecast (observation) 30
keizai kansoku shihyō
economic barometer 29
keizai katsudō
business activity 13; economic
activity 29
keizai katsudō no chūshin
economic centre 29
keizai katsuryoku
economic force 30
keizai keikaku
economic planning 30

keizai kenkyū
economic research 31
keizai kenkyūjo
economic research institute 31
keizai kiban
economic base 29
keizai kiban jōsū
economic base multiplier 29
keizai kiki
economic crisis (critical
moment) 29
keizai kiso kiban
economic infrastructure 30
keizai komon
economic adviser 29
keizai kōritsu
economic efficiency 29
keizai kōsei
economic welfare (social
welfare) 31
keizai kyōkō
economic crisis (panic, scare)
29
keizai kyōryoku
economic co-operation 29
keizai kyōryoku kaihatsu kikō
Organization for Economic Co-
operation and Development
(OECD) 75, 77
keizai kyōsō
economic competition 29
keizai mitōshi
economic outlook 30;
economic prospects 30
keizai moderu
economic model 30
keizai mondai
economic problem(s) 30;
economic question 30
keizai no jittai
economic realities 30
keizai no jittaimen
real phase (of the economy) 92
keizai no kadai
economic tasks 31
keizai no manbyō
economic ailments 29
keizai riron
economic theory 31
keizai seichō
economic growth 30
keizai seichōritsu
economic growth rate 30
keizai seisaku
economic policy 30
keizai seisaku chōsei
economic policy co-ordination
30
keizai sensō
economic warfare 31
keizai shakai rijikai
Economic and Social Council
(ECOSOC) 29, 31
keizai shihyō
economic barometer 29;
economic indicators 30
keizai shinpo
economic progress 30
keizai shisetsudan
economic mission 30
keizai shisō
economic thought 31

keizai shunō kaigi
economic summit 31
keizai sochi
economic measures 30
keizai soshiki
economic organization 30
keizai taikoku
economic superpower 31
keizai taisei
economic system 31
keizai tan'i
economic unit 31
keizai tōgō
economic integration 30
keizai tōitsu
economic unity 31
keizai tōkei
economic statistics 31
keizai tsūka dōmei
Economic and Monetary Union
29
keizai un'ei
economic management 30
keizai yosoku
economic forecast (prediction)
30
keizai zasshi
economic magazine 30
keizai zentai
overall economy 77
keizaigaku
economics 31
keizaigakusha
economist 31
keizaijin
economic man 30
keizaikai
economic community 29;
economic world 31
keizairan
financial column 222
keizairyoku
economic power 30; economic
strength 31
keizaishi
economic history 30
keizaiteki atsuryoku
economic pressure 30
keizaiteki fuanteisei
economic instability 30
keizaiteki fukōsei
economic injustices 30
keizaiteki genjitsu
economic reality 30
keizaiteki jikyūjisoku
autarchy (autarky) 8
keizaiteki jiyū
economic freedom 30
keizaiteki jiyū shugi
economic liberalism 30
keizaiteki kiseichū
economic parasites 30
keizaiteki kokumin shugi
economic nationalism 30
keizaiteki kokusai shugi
economic internationalism 30
keizaiteki kunan
economic hardship 30
keizaiteki seisai
economic sanctions 31
keizaiteki shinkaichi
economic frontiers 30

kessan
accounting (settlement of accounts) 365; closing of accounts 379; closing of the books 379; settlement of accounts 417

kessan kaisha gyōseki
corporate business results 381

kessan kansa
closing audit 379

kessan kinyū
closing entry 379

kessan seiri
closing adjustment 379

kessan shiwake
closing entry 379

kessan tetsuzuki
closing procedure 379

kessan zandaka
closing balance 379

kessanbi
closing day 379

kessanhyō
settlement sheet 417

kessanki
settlement period 417

kesson tsumitatekin
reserve for losses 415

kessongaku
deficit (amount of loss) 385

kessonkin
deficit (amount of loss) 385

kessonkin no kurikoshi
carry-over of losses 377

kessonkin no kurimodoshi
carry-back of losses 377

keta
column 379

ketsugi
resolution 431
ketsugi o suru
pass a resolution 431
ketsugi ni hantai tōhyō suru
vote against a resolution 432
ketsugi tsūchi o kōkoku suru
advertise notice of a resolution 429

ketsugō hiyō
joint costs 59

ketsugō juyō
joint demand 59

ketsugō kyōkyū
joint supply 59

ketsugō rijun no kyokudaika
joint profit maximization 59

ketsugō seisan
joint production 59

ketsugō seisanbutsu
joint products 59

ketsugō taishaku taishōhyō
combined balance sheet 379

ketsugō zaimuhyō
combined financial statement 379

ketsui
resolution 431
ketsui o tsūka suru
carry a resolution 429

ketsuin
job vacancy 444; situation vacant 446; vacancy 447; vacant position 447
ketsuin o hojū suru
fill a vacancy 442

ketsuin fuhojū
leaving vacancies unfilled 444

kettei
decision 23, 344

kettei gensoku
decision rule 23

kettei kansū
decision function 23

kettei no ragu
decision lag 23

kettei yōin
determinant 25

ketteihyō
casting a vote 429

kezaru (gatemara)
quetzal (Guatemala) 189

kibō baikyaku kakaku
asking price 290

kibo ni kansuru shūkaku
returns to scale 96

kibo ni kansuru shūkaku hōsoku
law of returns to scale 62

kibo ni kansuru shūkaku teigen
decreasing returns to scale 24

kibo ni taisuru shūeki fuhen
constant returns to scale 19

kibo no fukeizai
diseconomies of scale 27

kibo no keizai
economies of scale 31

kibo no rieki
increasing returns to scale 51

kibō taishoku
voluntary retirement 496, 497 (note 46)

kichō suru
post up accounts 410

kichū hishōkan kōshasai
non-callable public and corporate bonds 251

kifu
contribution (gift of money, subscription) 210; donation 219

kifukin
contribution (gift of money) 210; donation 219

kiga
hunger 47

kiga chingin
starvation wage(s) 103, 484

kiga kōshin
hunger march 47

kiga yushutsu
hunger export 47

kigen
term (time limit, repayment period) 281

kigen henkin
repayment at maturity 266

kigen keika hoken shōken
lapsed policy 324

kigen keika kanjō
overdue account 407

kigen keika kashitsuke
overdue loan 256

kigen keika kogitte
overdue cheque 154; past-due cheque 155

kigen keika no
overdue 256

kigen keika tegata
overdue bill 154; past-due bill 155

kigen keika yakusoku tegata
overdue note 256

kigentsuki kashidashi
term loan 281

kigentsuki kawase sōba
usance rate 163

kigentsuki kawase tegata
usance bill 163

kigentsuki kawase tegata sōba
usance bill rate 163

kigentsuki tegata
draft at a tenor 145; time bill 162; usance bill 163

kigentsuki tegata kaisōba
long rate 151

kigentsuki tegata sōba
usance bill rate 163

kigentsuki yunyū tegata
import usance bill 148

kigentsuki yushutsu tegata
export usance bill 146

kigu
appliances (utensils) 289

kigu-bihin
furniture and fittings (on balance sheet) 393

kigyō
business(es) 13, 338; business enterprise 338; company 341; concern 342; corporation(s) 20, 343; enterprise 33, 345; firm(s) 39, 346; undertaking 363
kigyō o hikitoru
take over a business 362
kigyō o hikitsugu
take over a business 362
kigyō o kaitoru
acquire a business 335, 367
kigyō o keishō suru
take over a business 362

kigyō bunka
enterprise culture 33

kigyō bunrui
classification of companies 340

kigyō chochiku seido
saving scheme [J] 483

kigyō genzei
tax cuts for businesses 423

kigyō gōdō
business combination 338; combine (noun) 341

kigyō gōrika
business modernization 339; business rationalization 339; rationalization of enterprise 358

kigyō gyōseki
business performance 13, 339; corporate performance 381

kigyō heisa
winding-up (business closure) 438

kigyō hiyō
business costs 374

kigyō hōkokusho
corporate report 381

kigyō imēji
corporate image 342

kigyō kachi
value of business 426

kigyō kaigai tōshi
corporate investment overseas 211, 381

kigyō kaikei
business accounting 374; corporate accounting 381

kigyō kaikei gensoku
business accounting principles 374; corporate accounting principles 381

kigyō kaishō
change of business name 340

kigyō kanbu hoken
key-man insurance 324

kigyō kariire
business borrowing 205, 374; corporate borrowing 211, 381

kigyō kashidashi
business lending 205

kigyō kashitsuke
business loan 205, 374

kigyō kazei
tax on business 423

kigyō kei'ei
business administration 338; business management 339

kigyō keikaku
business plan 339

kigyō keitai
form of business organization 346; form of enterprise 346; type of enterprise 363

kigyō kibo
size of firm 361

kigyō kin'yū
business finance 205; corporate credit 211; corporate financing 211, 381

kigyō kōdō no riron
behavioural theories of the firm 10

kigyō kokka
corporate state 20

kigyō komon bengoshi
corporate lawyer 342; corporation lawyer 343

kigyō kōzō
business structure 339

kigyō kyōyūsha
part-owner 355

kigyō naiyō kaiji
disclosure 218, 386

kigyō nenkin
corporate pension 495

kigyō nenkin seido
pension scheme (corporate) 495

kigyō no byōjō
business ailments 338

kigyō no kanren gurūpu
affiliated group 336

kigyō no kibo bunpai
size distribution of firms 100

kigyō no mochibun
business equity 374

kinshuku
austerity (contraction) 8;
retrenchment 96

kinshuku seisaku
austerity policy 8; retrenchment
policy 96

kinshuku seisaku sochi
austerity measures 8

kinshuku yosan
austerity budget 8; restrained
budget 95

kinshuku zaisan yosan
retrenchment budget 96

kintanpo shakkan
gold-collateral loan 228

kinyū
entry 145, 389

kin'yū
credit 21, 212; finance 222

kin'yū chōsetsu madoguchi
discount window 218

kin'yū chōtatsu
financing 224

kin'yū chōtatsu sōsa
financing operations 39, 224

kin'yū chūkai
financial intermediation 223

kin'yū chūkai kikan
financial intermediaries 223

kin'yū chūshinchi
banking centre 136; financial
centre 222

kin'yū enjo
financial aid 222; financial
assistance 222; financial help
222; financial support 223

kin'yū fusai
financial liabilities 391

kin'yū futan
financial burden 222

kin'yū gaisha
banking house 136; credit
company 212; finance
company [US] 222; financial
company 222; finance house
[UK] 222

kin'yū gaisha kijun kinri
finance house base rate [UK]
222

kin'yū ginkō
credit bank (financing) 141,
212

kin'yū gyōsha
City man [UK] 208; financier
224; money broker 247;
money lender 248

kin'yū hikishime
credit restraint 213; credit
squeeze 22, 213; monetary
restraint 70; squeeze 276;
tight money 111, 281

kin'yū hikishime seisaku
credit squeeze policy 213;
tight-money policy 111, 281

kin'yū hikishime seisaku kyōka
tightening of monetary restraint
111

kin'yū hikishime sochi
credit squeeze measures 213

kin'yū hippaku
monetary stringency 70

kin'yū jijō
monetary situation 70

kin'yū jiyūka
financial liberalization 39, 223

kin'yū jōsei
financial climate 222

kin'yū jōtai
credit conditions 212

kin'yū kakudai
monetary expansion 69

kin'yū kakumei
financial revolution 39, 223

kin'yū kanwa
credit relaxation 22, 213;
easing of money market 219;
financial deregulation 39, 222;
monetary relaxation 70

kin'yū kanwa seisaku
easy-money policy 29, 219

kin'yū kanwaki
easy-money times 29

kin'yū katsudō
banking activities 136; financial
activity 39, 222; financing
activity 224

kin'yū keizai
monetary economy 69

kin'yū kikan
banking establishment 136;
banking facilities 136; credit
institution 213; financial
institution 223

kin'yū kikō
financial machinery 39

kin'yū kisei
financial regulation 39, 223

kin'yū kōzō
financial structure 39

kin'yū kyōkō
financial crisis 222; financial
panic 223

kin'yū kyōtei
financial agreement 222

kin'yū moderu
financial model 39

kin'yū saihensei
financial reorganization 391

kin'yū saiken
financial claim 222

kin'yū saimu
financial obligation 223

kin'yū sakimono
financial futures 222

kin'yū seisaku
credit policy 22, 141, 213;
financial policy 223; monetary
policy (finance) 69

kin'yū seisaku no ragu
administrative lag (financial
policy) 4

kin'yū seisaku shudan
instrument of monetary policy
55

kin'yū senmonka
financial expert 222

kin'yū sensō
financial war 224

kin'yū setsudo
monetary discipline 69

kin'yū shigen
financial resources 223

kin'yū shijō
credit markets 22, 213;
financial markets 39, 223;
money market 70, 248

kin'yū shijō e no kainyū
money market intervention 248

kin'yū shijō no kaihō
opening of financial markets
76, 254

kin'yū shijō no un'ei
money market management
248

kin'yū shijō shōken
money market instrument 248;
money market securities 248

kin'yū shisan
financial assets 222, 391;
financial portfolio 223;
financial wealth 224

kin'yu shōhin
embargo goods 32

kin'yū shōhin
financial commodities 222

kin'yū shudan
financial instrument 223

kin'yū sōsa
financial operation(s) 39, 223

kin'yū taikei
financial system 39, 223

kin'yū tegata
finance bill 222; finance paper
222

kin'yū torihiki
financial transaction 224

kin'yūdan
financial syndicate 223

kin'yūgyō
banking industry 123

kin'yuhin
embargo goods 32

kin'yūjō no rieki
financial profits 223

kin'yūjō no sonshitsu
financial loss 223

kin'yūjō no yūgū sochi
financial inducements 39, 223

kin'yūkai
financial circles 222; financial
world 224

kin'yūsai
bank bond 134, 198; bank
debenture 134, 198

kin'yūteki hoshō
financial guarantee 222

kin'yūteki junbi
financial provisions 223

kinzoku hon'isei
metallic standard 179

kinzoku kahei
metallic money 179

kinzoku kahei kachi
metallic value 179

kinzoku kōgyō
metal mining 125; metal-
working industry 125

kinzoku nensū
continuous service 452

kinzoku shugi
metallism 179

kinzoku teate
seniority allowance 483

kinzu keizaigaku
Keynesian economics 59

kinzu no rishiron
Keynesian theory of interest 59

kinzu no seichōron
Keynesian growth theory 59

kinzu no zaisei seisaku
Keynesian monetary policy 59

kinzuan
Keynes plan, the 59

kiō kashidashi
outstanding loan 255

kiōshō
past medical history 327

kipurosu
Cyprus 189

kirei na hendō sōbasei
clean float 167

kiremono
sharp person 467

kireru
expire 295

kirikae
renewal 158

kirikae tegata
renewal bill 158

kirikae tesūryō
renewal commission 158

kirikae yakusoku tegata
renewed promissory note 266

kirisageru
devalue 170

kiritsume
cutbacks (economizing) 384

kiroku
registration (record, document)
265

kiroku shinsei(sho)
application for registration
(company) 336

kirokubo
register 265

kirokuteki suijun
record level 92

kisai
bond flotation 201; bond issue
202; flotation 226; flotation of
loan 226; issue 238; issue of
bond(s) 239; loan flotation 242

kisai shijō
bond flotation market 201;
bond-issue market 202;
bond market 202; issue
market (bonds, loans) 239

kisai suru
float (verb) (float loans, issue
bonds) 225

kisaigaku
amount issued (bond, loan)
195; issue amount 238

kisei
regulation (control) 265

kisei o teppai suru
deregulate 25, 217

kisei kanwa
easing of restrictions 28

kisei kinri
regulated interest rate 265

kisei teppai
deregulation 25, 217

kisei teppai seisaku
deregulation policy 25, 217

kisetsu chōsei
seasonal adjustment 98

kisetsu chōseizumi
seasonally adjusted 98

kisetsu chōseizumi sūji
seasonally adjusted figures 98

kōen
backing (assistance, help, patronage) 198; sponsorship(s) 102, 276, 419; support 280

kōen suru
back (assist, help, patronize) 198

kōensha
backer (patron) 198; sponsor 276

kōfukin
grants 44; subsidies 105

kogai
'raising a pet animal' 473

kōgai
suburbs 309

kōgai
pollution (environmental) 81

kōgai bōshi
pollution control (prevention) 81

kōgai hannin
polluter 81

kōgai hasseisha
polluter 81

kōgai jūtakuchi
residential suburbs 308

kōgai kosuto
pollution cost 81

kōgai kyojūsha
suburbanite 309

kōgai no
suburban 309

kōgai no saiteki suijun
optimal level of pollution 77

kōgai sangyō
industrial polluter 53

kōgai yushutsu
pollution export 81

kōgaiken
pollution rights 81

kogaisha
affiliate [US] 335; affiliated company [US] 336; associated company [UK] 337; offshoot 354; subsidiary 361

kogaisha ginkō
subsidiary bank 161

kogaisha no baikyaku
divestiture 344

kogaisha shusshikin
investments in subsidiaries 397

kogaku genkin
petty cash 409

kōgaku iryōhi hoken
major medical expense insurance 325

kōgaku shotoku
high income 478

kōgakumen
large denomination 150, 178

kogata kabu
small capital stock 418; small stock 274

kogata no risesshon
mini-recession 69

kōge
ups and downs 116

kogetsuki kanjō
frozen account 227

kogetsuki shihon
locked-up capital 243

kogetsuki yūshi
dead loan 214; frozen credit 227; uncollectible loan 283

kogetsukigashi
doubtful loan 219; frozen loan 227

kōgi no manē-sapurai
broad money 12

kogitte
check [US] 139; cheque [UK] 139

kogitte o furidasu
draw a cheque 145

kogitte furidashinin
drawer (of a cheque) 145

kogitte hoshō kādo
cheque card [UK] 139

kogitte kahei
cheque-book money 139

kogitte naatenin
drawee (of a cheque) 145

kogitte no kessai
cheque clearance 139

kogitte no shiharai o teishi suru
stop the payment of a cheque 161

kogitte yokin
cheque deposit 139

kogittebarai
payment by cheque 156

kogittechō
cheque book 139

kogittechō hikae
cheque-book stub 139

kōgu
tools (on balance sheet) 423

koguchi genkin
petty cash 409, 488

koguchi genkin denpyō
petty cash slip 410, 488

koguchi genkin kanjō
petty cash account 409, 488

koguchi genkin seido
petty cash system 410

koguchi genkin shiharai
petty cash payments 409, 488

koguchi genkin shikin
petty cash funds 409

koguchi genkin suitōbo
petty cash-book 409, 488

kōguchi kashidashi
petty loan 259

koguchi kin'yū
consumer banking 141; retail banking 159

koguchi kin'yū gaisha
small loan company [US] 274

koguchi kin'yū kikan
retail bank 159

koguchi tōshika
small investor 274

koguchi yochokin
petty savings 156; small savings 160

koguchi yokin
small deposits 160

koguchi yūshi
small loan 274

koguchisuji
small-lot traders 274

koguchiuri
small-lot sale 274

kōgyō
mining industry 125

kōgyō
industry (manufacturing) 53

kōgyō chi'iki
industrial area(s) 52, 298

kōgyō chitai
industrial district 298; industrial zone 53, 298

kōgyō chūshinchi
industrial centre 52

kōgyō danchi
industrial complex 52, 298

kōgyō danchi bunseki
industrial complex analysis 52

kōgyō gaisha
industrial concern 349

kōgyō gakkō
industrial technical school 443

kōgyō genryō
industrial materials 53

kōgyō gijutsu
industrial technology 53; technology 109

kōgyō ginkō
industrial bank(s) 52, [UK] 149

kōgyō jiritsu
industrial independence 52

kōgyō jūgyōin hoken
industrial insurance (for industrial personnel) 322

kōgyō kabu
industrial shares 233; industrials 233

kōgyō kabuka shisū
Industrial Ordinary Shares Index [US] 233

kōgyō kyōiku
industrial technical training 443

kōgyō kyōkō
industrial crisis (manufacturing industry) 52

kōgyō ritchi
industrial location 53

kōgyō ritchi seisaku
industrial location policy 53

kōgyō saihaichi
relocation of industry 94

kōgyō seihin
industrial goods (manufactured goods) 52

kōgyō seihin juyō
industrial demand 52

kōgyō seihin kakaku
industrial prices 52

kōgyō seihin seisansha bukka shisū
producer price index for manufactured goods 85

kōgyō seisaku
industrial policy 53

kōgyō seisan
industrial output 53; industrial production 53

kōgyō seisan no kakudai
industrial expansion 52

kōgyō seisan no seichō
industrial growth 52

kōgyō shōken
industrial securities 233

kōgyō shoyūken
industrial property 349; industrial rights 349

kōgyō shūdan
industrial group 349

kōgyō tegata
industrial bill 149

kōgyō tōsei
industrial statistics 53

kōgyō toshi
industrial towns 53

kōgyōhin yunyū
manufactured imports 66

kōgyōka
industrialization 53

kōgyōkai
industrial circles 52; industrial world (manufacturing) 53

kōgyōkai
manufacturers' associations 66

kōgyōkoku
industrial countries 52; industrial nations 53; industrialized countries 53

kōha no tejimai
liquidation of bulls 241; liquidation of longs 241

kōhai
junior 458

kōhai
devastation 319; dilapidation (run-down state) 293

kōhai kabu
deferred shares [UK] 385; deferred stock [US] 385

kōhai sareta
rundown 308

kōhaichi
devastated area 319

kōhatsu kigyō
latecomer 350; newcomer 353

kōhei
equity (concept of justice) 34

kōhii-burēki
coffee break 452

kōhō jimu bumon
back office 198; backroom 198

kōhō senden
public information and propaganda 89

kōhō tōgō
backward integration 9

kōhōbu
public relations department 465

kōhosha
applicant 441; candidate 429, 441

kōhōshitsu
public affairs department 465

kōhyō
good reputation 347

kōin
factory worker [general] 455; operative 463; workman 472

kōishō
after-effects 4

kojikkari shōjō
slight steadying of the market 274

kojin
individuals 52

kojin bumon
    private sector (individual) 85
kojin chintairyō shotoku
    personal rental income 304
kojin chochiku
    individual savings 149;
    personal saving(s) 80, 156
kojin chochikuka
    individual saver 149
kojin dōsanzei
    personal property tax 304
kojin fudōsan shotoku
    personal income from property
    304
kojin gaisha
    sole proprietorship 361
kojin ginkō
    private bank [US] 157
kojin haitō shotoku
    personal dividend income 258
kojin hoken
    personal insurance 327
kojin hoshō kashidashi
    personal-guarantee loan 258
kojin iryō
    personal health care 327
kojin jigyōnushi
    sole proprietor 361
kojin jūyaku
    sole director 361
kojin kabunushi
    individual shareholder 233,
    395; sole shareholder 418
kojin kashikinko
    personal safe deposit box 156;
    private safe-deposit box 157
kojin kashitsuke
    personal loan 258
kojin kashobun shotoku
    personal disposable income
    (PDI) 79, 80
kojin kei'ei no
    owner-managed 355
kojin kigyō
    individual enterprise 348;
    private concern 357;
    proprietorship 357
kojin kogitte
    personal cheque 156
kojin kōshō
    individual bargaining 51, 479
kojin mochiie kashitsuke
    loan for home-owner 242
kojin nenkin keiyaku hōshiki
    individual annuity policy plan
    322; personal annuity scheme
    327
kojin nenkin seido
    personal pension 327
kojin no tanpotsukinai
kashitsuke
    personal loan [UK] 258
kojin rishi shotoku
    personal interest income 258
kojin sekinin hoken
    personal liability insurance 327
kojin shikibetsu bangō (= PIN
bangō)
    personal identification number
    (= PIN number) 156
kojin shin'yō
    personal credit 258

kojin shisan
    individual wealth 52
kojin shishutsu
    individual expenditure 52
kojin shōgai hoken
    individual accident insurance
    322; personal accident
    insurance 327
kojin shōhi
    individual consumption 51;
    personal consumption 80;
    private consumption 85
kojin shōhi shishutsu
    private consumption
    expenditure 85
kojin shōhisha bumon
    private consumer sector 85
kojin shōnin
    sole trader 361
kojin shotoku
    personal income 80
kojin shotokuzei
    individual income tax 52, 479;
    personal income tax 482
kojin shotokuzei menjo
    personal income tax exemption
    482
kojin tegata
    individual bill 149; personal bill
    156; private bill 157
kojin torihikisaki
    individual customers 149
kojin tōshi
    individual investment 233
kojin tōshika
    individual investor 233;
    retail investor 267
kojin tōshizei kōjo keikaku
    Personal Equity Plan (PEP)
    [UK] 258
kojin tōza yokin
    personal checking account 156
kojin yokin
    individual deposit 149;
    personal deposit 156;
    private deposit 157
kojin zaimu keikaku
    personal financing planning
    258
kojin zaisan
    individual property 298;
    personal property 304
kojinmei
    individual name 348
kojinteki fusai
    personal liability 258
kojinteki na tsunagari
    personal connections 445
kojinteki nenkin
    individual pension 495
kojinteki nenkin seido
    pension scheme (individual)
    495
kojinushi
    small landowner 309
kojin'yō no ofisu
    private office 464
kojiteki shōhi
    conspicuous consumption 18;
    ostentatious consumption 77
kōjo
    deductions (from salaries) 24,
    385

kōjō
    factory 346
kōjō heisa
    closure (s) (factory) 16, 499;
    lock-out(s) (factory) 64, 501;
    plant closure 356; shutdown(s)
    100, 493
kōjō jōtai moderu
    steady-state models 104
kōjō jūgyōin
    factory worker (employee) 455
kōjō kantoku
    factory manager 455
kōjō kensetsuyōchi
    factory site (land for industrial
    development) 295; industrial
    site 298
kōjō kōshō
    plant bargaining 80
kōjō kyōgikai
    work council(s) (factories) 120,
    471
kōjō ritchi
    plant location 356; plant site
    304
kōjō rōdōsha
    factory worker 455
kōjō setsubi nōryoku
    plant capacity 356
kōjō shikichi
    factory site (industrial area)
    295; industrial site 298
kōjō shisetsu
    plant 356
kōjō shōhi
    permanent consumption 80
kōjō shotoku
    permanent income 80
kōjō shotoku kasetsu
    permanent income hypothesis
    80
kōjōchō
    factory manager 455; plant
    manager 464
kōjogaku
    amount deducted (from salary)
    475
kōjōnushi
    factory owner 346
kōjōteki seichō
    steady growth 104; steady-
    state growth 104
kōjōteki seichō keiro
    steady-state growth path 104
kōjun'i saiken
    junior bond 239
kōjun'i saiken hakkō
    junior issue 239
kōjun'i shōken
    junior securities 239
kōjun'i tanpotsuki shasai
    junior mortgage bond 239
kōjun'i teitō
    junior mortgage 239, 298
kōjunkan
    virtuous circles 117
kōka
    effect (effectiveness) 32
kōka
    performance rating 463
kōka
    coin 140, 167; hard currency
    176; metallic currency 179

kōka keisūki
    coin counting machine 140
kōka mametsu
    abrasion of coin 165
kōka no kaishū
    withdrawal of a coin 187
kokabu
    new shares 250; new stock
    251
kokabunushi
    small shareholder 274, 418;
    small stockholder 274, 418
kokabutsuki
    cum new 213, 383
kōkai
    disclosure 143, 344;
    introduction [UK] 236; offer for
    public subscription 404; offer
    for sale [UK] 253, 404; public
    offering [US] 262; public
    placement [US] 262, 413;
    public placing [UK] 262, 413
kōkai
    international waters 57
kōkai kabu
    introduced stock 236; newly
    introduced shares 251, 403;
    publicly held stock 262, 413
kōkai kakaku keisei
    open pricing 76
kōkai kakaku seido
    open-price system 76
kōkai kōbo
    initial public offering (IPO) 233,
    238, 395
kōkai kumiai
    open union 463
kōkai kyōsō
    open competition 76
kōkai nyūsatsu
    bidding (public) 200
kōkai shijō
    open market (market overt) 76,
    254
kōkai shijō sōsa
    open-market operations 76,
    254
kōkai shijō sōsa no sōba
    open-market quotation 254
kōkai yūgen sekinin gaisha
    public limited company (plc)
    [UK] 356, 358
kōkaken
    hard currency area 176
kōkan
    conversion (exchangeability,
    transferability) 167
kōkan (kinri no)
    swap (interest rate) 280
kōkan bukken
    clearing items 140
kōkan kyōtei
    swap (central bank line of
    credit) 186; swap agreement
    186
kōkan saiken
    interchangeable bonds 234
kōkan shudan
    medium of exchange 68, 179
kōkan torihiki
    swap transaction 280
kōkandaka
    amount to clear 132

kōkanfunō tsūka
soft currency (non-exchangeable) 184

kōkanjiri furikae tegata
clearing house due bill 140

kōkanjo keisansho
clearing house statement 140

kōkanjo seisanhyō
clearing house settlement sheet 140

kōkanjo shōken
clearing house certificate 140

kōkankanō tsūka
convertible currency 167; hard currency (exchangeable currency) 176

kōkankanō'en
convertible yen 168

kōkansei
convertibility (exchangeability, transferability) 20, 167

kōkeiki
activity (good economic times) 3; prosperity 88

kōkeiki jidai
period of prosperity 79

kōkendo
contribution 452; dedication 452

shigoto ni taisuru kōkendo ga aru
dedicated to one's work 452

kōki
second half of the year 417

kōki kessan
closing of accounts for the second half of the year 379; settlement of accounts for the latter half of the year 417

kōkigyōsai
public utility bond 262

kōkin
public funds 89; public money 89

kōkin yokin
public deposits 89

kōkinri
high interest rate(s) 46, 231

kōkinri jūtaku kashitsuke
high mortgage rates 296

kōkinri seisaku
dear-money policy 23, 215; high-interest rate(s) policy 46, 231

kōkinri shikin
dear money 23, 215; high-interest credit 231

kokka hasan
state bankruptcy 103

kokka keikaku
national planning 72; state planning 104

kokka keikaku keizai
state-planned economy 104

kokka kigyō kōsha
National Enterprise Board (NEB) [UK] 72, 73

kokka saimu
national debt 71, 249

kokka saimu rishi
national debt interest 72, 249

kokka shigen
national resources 72

kokka shihon shugi
state capitalism 103

kokka shin'yō
national credit 249

kokka tōsei
statism 104

kokka zaisei
state finance 103

kokko
Exchequer, the [UK] 35; Treasury, the (national treasury, state coffers) 113, 186

kokko hojo
government subsidies 44; state aid 103

kokko keisan
Treasury accounts 113

kokko keisan kamoku
Treasury accounts items 113

kokko saiken
Exchequer bonds [UK] 221; Treasury bond [US] 283

kokko shishutsu
Treasury payments 113

kokko shūnyū
Treasury receipts 113

kokko sōkin
Treasury remittances 113

kokko yokin
Treasury deposit 113, 186

kokko yoyūkin
Treasury surplus 113

kokkokin
Treasury funds 113

kōkō
high school 443

kōkōgyō seihin
industrial products 53

kōkōgyō seisan shisū
industrial production index 53

kōkoku
advertisement (ad) 441

kōkoku buchō
advertising manager 449

kōkoku yosan
advertising budget 368

kōkokubu
advertising department 449

kōkokuhi
advertising expenses 368

kōkoyō
high employment 46

kōkū jigyō
transportation business 123

kokubō
national defence 72

kokubō shishutsu
national defence expenses 72

kokubō yosan
national defence budget 72

kokuchi
disclosure 319

kokuchi gimu
obligation to disclose 326

kokuei bōeki
state trading 104

kokuei kigyō
nationalized company 353; state enterprise 361; state-run business 104, 361

kokuei no
state-run 104

kokuei sangyō
state-run industries 104

kokufu
national wealth 72

kokugai zaijūsha
expatriates (residents abroad) 35

kōkūki kōgyō
aircraft industry 123

kokumin
nation, the 71; public, the 88

kokumin bunpaibun
national dividend 72

kokumin chochiku
national savings 72, 152

kokumin chochikuritsu
national savings rate 72

kokumin hoken
National Insurance [UK] 72

kokumin hoken futan
National Insurance contributions [UK] 72, 480

kokumin hoken kikin
National Insurance Fund [UK] 72

kokumin hoken no taishoku nenkin seido
State-Earnings Related Pensions Scheme (SERPS) [UK] 99, 103

kokumin hoken sābisu
National Health Service (NHS) [UK] 72, 74

kokumin hokenryō
National Insurance deduction [UK] 480

kokumin junseisan
net national product (NNP) 73, 74

kokumin junshotoku
net domestic income 73; net national income 73

kokumin keikaku
national planning 72

kokumin keizai
national economy 72

kokumin keizai hatten shingikai
Economic Development Committee [UK] 29; National Economic Development Council (Neddy, NEDC) [UK] 72, 73

kokumin keizai hattenkyoku
National Economic Development Office (NEDO) [UK] 72, 73

kokumin keizai keisan
national accounts 71; social accounting 101

kokumin keizai kenkyūjo
National Bureau for Economic Research (NBER) [US] 71, 73

kokumin keizai shakai kenkyūjo
NIESR (National Institute of Economics and Social Research) [UK] 72, 74

kokumin kenkō hoken
national health insurance 72

kokumin nenkin seido
pension scheme (national pension for the self-employed) [J] 495

kokumin seisanbutsu
national product 72

kokumin shihon
national capital 71

kokumin shihon kanjō
national capital account 71

kokumin shishutsu
national expenditure 72

kokumin shotoku
national income 72

kokumin shotoku bunseki
national income analysis 72

kokumin shotoku keisan
national income accounting 72

kokumin shotoku tōkei
national income statistics 72

kokumin sōjuyō
gross national demand (GND) 43, 45

kokumin sōkyōkyū
gross national supply 45

kokumin sōseisan
gross national product (GNP) 43, 45

kokumin sōseisan defurētā
gross national product deflator 45

kokumin sōseisanryō
gross national output 45

kokumin sōshisan
gross national wealth 45

kokumin sōshishutsu
gross national expenditure (GNE) 43, 45

kokumin sōshotoku
gross national income (GNI) 43, 45

kokumin taishaku taishōhyō
national balance sheet 71

kokuminteki gōi
national consensus 71

kokumotsu torihikijo
grain exchange 229

kokunai bōeki
internal trade 56

kokunai juyō
domestic demand 27

kokunai keiki
national economic activity 72

kokunai keikyō
domestic business picture 27

kokunai keizai
domestic economy 27

kokunai kigyō
national company 353

kokunai kinkō
internal balance 55; internal equilibrium 56

kokunai kyōsō
domestic competition 27

kokunai sangyō
domestic industry 27

kokunai seisaku
domestic policy 27

kokunai seisan
domestic production 27

kokunai seisanryō
national output 27

kokunai shihon keisei
domestic capital formation 27

kokunai shijō
domestic market 27

kokusai tōshi
international investment 236
kokusai tōshi ginkō
international investment bank 150, 236
kokusai tōshi shintaku
international investment trust 236
kokusai tōshin
international investment trust 236
kokusai tsūka chōsei
international realignment of currencies 177
kokusai tsūka junbi
international currency reserve 177
kokusai tsūka kaigi
international monetary conference (IMC) 177
kokusai tsūka kikin
International Monetary Fund (IMF) 48, 56, 177
kokusai tsūka kikō
international monetary organization 56, 177
kokusai tsūka kyōryoku
international monetary co-operation 177
kokusai tsūka seido
international monetary system 57, 177
kokusai tsūka seido kaikaku
international monetary reform 57, 177
kokusai tsūka shugi
international monetarism 56, 177
kokusai tsūshō
international commerce 56; international trade 57
kokusai waribikiryō
discount of government securities 218
kokusaihi
national debt expenses 72
kokusaika
globalization 43; internationalization 57
kokusaiteki na seika
international reputation 349
kokusaiteki saiken hakkō
international bond issue 235
kokusaiteki seisai
international sanctions 57
kokusaku kōsha
statutory company 361
kokusanpin
domestic products 27
kokusei chōsa
census (national) 15
kokusei chōsa hōkokusho
census form 15
kokuseki
nationality 353, 444
kokuteizeiritsu
autonomous tariff 8
kokuyū
government ownership 44, 348; state control 361
kokuyū ginkō
state-owned bank 161

kokuyū kigyō
nationally owned firm 353; state-owned enterprise 361
kokuyū no
state-owned 104
kokuyū sangyō
nationalized industry 72; state industry 103; state-owned industry 104
kokuyū zaisan
national assets 71; national property 303; state-owned property 309
kokuyūka
nationalization 72, 353
kokuyūka ginkō
nationalized bank 152
kokuyūka suru
nationalize 353
kokyaku
client 140, 208, 292, 317; customer 142
kokyaku sābisu
customer services 142
kokyaku shijō
negotiated market 250
kokyaku sōdan
customer advice service 142
kōkyō
boom (period of prosperity) 11; prosperity 88
kōkyō bumon
public sector 89
kōkyō bumon kaiire juyō
public sector borrowing requirements 89
kōkyō bumon kanjō akaji
public sector financial deficit 89
kōkyō bumon kariire juyō
public sector borrowing requirements 262
kōkyō dantai
public body 357; public entity (-ies) 89, 357; public group(s) 89, 357; public organization(s) 89, 358
kōkyō fukushi
public welfare 89
kōkyō hōjin
non-taxable corporation 353
kōkyō jigyō
public services 89; public utilities 89; public works 90; utilities 116
kōkyō jigyō dantai
public utility company 358
kōkyō jigyō kankeihi
public works expenses 90
kōkyō jūtaku kikan
housing authorities 47
kōkyō keizai seisaku
public economic policy 89
kōkyō kigyō
public companies 89; public corporation [US] 357; public enterprise 357; public utility company 89
kōkyō koyō keikaku
public employment programme 89
kōkyō seisaku
public policy 89

kōkyō shijō
active market 194; broad market 203
kōkyō shisetsu
public utilities (facilities) 89
kōkyō shishutsu
public expenditure 89
kōkyō shishutsu chōsa i'inkai
Public Expenditure Survey Committee [UK] 89
kōkyō shōhi
public consumption 89
kōkyō shoyūchi
publicly-owned land 305
kōkyō tōshi
investment in public utilities 237; public investment 89, 261
kōkyō yōeki
public services 89
kōkyō zaisan
public property 89, 305
kōkyōki
boom period 11
kōkyōzai
public goods 89
kōkyū
high salary 478
kōkyūbi
public holiday 482
kōkyūhin seizōgyō
luxury goods industry 125
komekon
Council for Mutual Economic Aid (COMECON) 17, 21
kōmitsudo chi'iki
high-density area 296
komodoshi
slight recovery of the market 274
kōmoku
item 398
kōmokubetsu kanjōsho
itemized bill 298, 398, 487
kōmu
public affairs 88
kōmuin
civil servant 451; government employee 456; public employee 465
kongo
Congo 189
kongō hoken
mixed insurance 325
kongō hoken shōken
mixed policy (insurance) 325
kongō keizai
mixed economy 69; mixed-market economy 69
kongōzai
mixed goods 69
kōnin
authority (approval) 133; authorization 133
kōnin
successor 468
kōnin kaikeishi
certified public accountant (CPA) [US] 378, 383
kōnin kanzainin
official receiver 436
kōnin kanzainin no hōkokusho
official receiver's report 436

kon'in no jōkyō
marital status 444
kōnin tokkyo
registered patent 358
kōninsha
successor 468
konjō
tenacity 469
konjō ga aru
tenacious 469
konnan na jiki
difficult times 26
konpyūta sangyō
computer industry 123
konpyūtagata baibai
program trading 261
konpyūtagata baibai torihiki
computer trading 209
konpyūtagata uri
sell program 271
konran
turmoil (confusion, chaos) 186
konsarutanto
consultant 452
konsoru kōsai
consolidated stock [UK] 210; consols [UK] 210
konsoru shijō
consols market [UK] 210
konsōshiamu
consortium 342
kōporēto-sutaffu
corporate staff 343
kōransha
raider 262
kōri
usurious interest 285; usury 285
kōri no kashitsuke
usurious loan 285
kōri shugi
utilitarianism 116
kōri shugi keizai riron
utilitarian economic theory 116
kōrigashi
loan shark 243; usurer 285
kōrijun no shōsha
profitable business concern 357
kōrimawari
attractive yield 197
kōriritsu
usurious rate of interest 285
kōritsu
efficiency 453
kōritsu haitō
high dividend 394
koritsu keizai
isolated economy 58
kōritsu na
efficient 453
kōritsu waribikisai
deep discount bond 216
kōritsuki shasai
high-interest-bearing debenture 230
kōritsuki shōken
high-interest-bearing securities 230
kōritsuki yokin kōza
high-interest bearing account 148

kotei kawase
pegged exchange 182

kōtei kawase sōba
fixed exchange rate 173; official exchange rate 181; pegged exchange rate 182

kotei kawase sōbasei
fixed exchange rate system 173; pegged exchange rate system 182

kotei kinri kashidashi
fixed-rate loan 225

kotei kinrigata jūtaku kashitsuke
fixed-rate mortgage loan 225, 295

kotei rōdō kosuto
fixed labour costs 40

kotei shihon
fixed capital 40, 392

kotei shihon tōshi
fixed capital investment 392

kotei shisan
capital assets [UK] 375; fixed assets [US] 392

kotei shisan baikyakueki
gains from sale of fixed assets 393; profits on the sale of fixed assets 412

kotei shisan baikyakuson
loss on sale of fixed assets 400

kotei shisan-chōki shihon hiritsu
fixed assets/long-term capital ratio 392

kotei shisan daichō
fixed assets ledger 392

kotei shisan-fusai hiritsu
fixed assets/debt ratio 392

kotei shisan hiritsu
fixed assets ratio 392

kotei shisan hyōkaeki
gains from revaluation of fixed assets 393

kotei shisan hyōkason
loss on revaluation of fixed assets 400

kotei shisan kaitenritsu
fixed assets turnover ratio 392

kotei shisan-seika hiritsu
fixed assets/net worth ratio 392

kotei shishutsu yosan
capital budget 14

kotei shūnyū
fixed income 40

kōtei sōba
official quotation 253

kotei sōbasei
fixed exchange rate system 173

kotei tōshi
fixed investment 225

kotei tōshi shintaku
fixed-investment trust 225

kotei yōin
fixed factors 40

kotei yosan
fixed budget 392; period budget 409

koteihi
constant cost(s) 380; constant expenses 380; fixed charges 392; fixed costs 40, 392; fixed expenses 392; fixed overheads 392; standing cost 419

koteikyū
fixed salary 477; fixed wage 477

kōteki doru junbi
official dollar reserve(s) 181

kōteki fujo
public assistance 88

kōteki kainyū
official intervention 182

kōteki kessai bēsu
official settlement basis 75

kōteki kin
official gold 181

kōteki kinjunbi
official gold reserve 182

kōteki nenkin
public pension 496

kōteki nenkin seido
pension scheme (state pension, public pension) 495

kōteki seisaku
public policy 89

kōteki seisaku kettei
public policy-making 89

kōten
improvement (turn for the better) 49

kōten yōin
favourable factors 38

kotenha keizaigaku
classical economics 16

kōtō
demotion 452

kōtō
sharp rise 99

kōtō keiyaku
verbal agreement 312

kōtō kyōiku
higher education 46, 443

kōtō shikyō
soaring market 274

kōtōshiki
identity (equation) 48

kōtsūhi
transportation expenses 488

kouri
retail 95

kouri bukka shisū
index of retail prices 51; retail price index (RPI) [UK] 95, 97

kouri ginkō
retail bank 159

kouri ginkōgyō
retail banking 159

kouri kaikei
retail accounting 415

kouri kakaku
retail prices 95

kouri kakaku chōsa
retail price survey 95

kouri shijō
retail market 95

kouri shōhin
retail goods 95

kourigyō
retail industry 126; retail trade 95

kourigyōsha
retailers 95

kourishō
retailers 95

koyō
employment 32, 442, 454

kōyō
utility 116

koyō antei
job security 59; stability of employment 468; stabilization of employment 103

koyō anteisei
stability of employment 102

koyō chōsei
employment adjustment 32

koyō futekikakusha
unemployable person 503; unemployables, the 114

koyō hojokin
employment subsidies 33

koyō hoshō
guarantee of employment 456

koyō hoshō seido
guaranteed employment plan 456

koyō hyōjun
hiring standards 46, 443

koyō imin
employment migration 33

koyō jōken
conditions of employment 442, 452; employment conditions 454; terms of employment 447, 469

koyō jōsei
employment situation 33

koyō jōsū
employment multiplier 33

koyō jūyaku
employed director 345, 453

koyō kankō
employment practices 33, 454

kōyō kansū
utility function 116

kōyō kei'eisha
employed executive 345

koyō keitai
employment system 454

koyō keiyaku
employment contract 454

koyō kikai
employment opportunity (-ies) 33, 442; job opportunity 444

koyō kikai kintō
equal employment opportunity 34, 442

koyō kikai kintō i'inkai
Equal Employment Opportunity Commission [US] 34

koyō kikai kintōhō
Equal Employment Opportunity Act [US] 34

koyō kikan
duration of employment 453; period of employment 463

kōyō kyokusen
utility curve 116

koyō mitōshi
employment prospects 442

kōyō no kojinkan hikaku
interpersonal comparisons of utility 57

koyō riron
theory of employment 110

koyō rōdōsha
employed labourer 453; employed worker 454

koyō seisaku
employment policy 33, 442, 454

koyō shisū
employment index 33

koyō shūkan
employment practices 454

koyō sokushin
job development 58

koyō sokushinsaku
employment-generating measures 32

koyō sōshutsu
job creation 58, 443

koyō suru
employ (verb) 453

kōyō teigen no hōsoku
law of diminishing utility 62

koyō tōkei
employment statistics 33

koyōfunōsha
unemployable person 503; unemployables, the 114

koyōhō
Employment Act 32

koyōritsu
employment rate 33; hiring rate 46

koyōsha
employer(s) [formal, statistical] 33, 454

koyōsha sekinin
employer's liability 491

koyōsha sekinin hoken
employer's liability insurance 319

koyōsha tai jūgyōin no kankei
employer and employee relations 454

kōyū
public ownership 89

kōyū gaisha
government-owned corporation 348

kōyūchi
public land 305

kōza
account (A/C) 131

kōza bangō
account number 131

kōzairyō
favourable factor 221

kōzan shiyōryō
royalties (from mineral resources) 97

kōzangyō
mining industry 125

kozaya
narrow margin 249

kozaya torihiki
scalping 269

kozayatori
day trader 214; scalper [US] 269

kōzō
structure (construction, framework) 105

kōzō henka
structural changes 105

kūsōteki shakai shugi
utopian socialism 116

kussetsu juyō kyokusen
kinked demand curve 59

kusshin kawase sōba
flexible exchange rate 173

kusshin kawase sōba seido
flexible exchange rate system 173

kuuēto
Kuwait 190

kyaria
career 441, 451

kyaria ni taisuru yashin
career ambition 451

kyaria no kōjō
career improvement 451

kyaria-puran
career plan 441

kyasshu-kādo
cash card 138

kyasshu-kurejitto
cash L/C 138

kyasshu-pojishon
cash position 138

kyōbai
auction 197, 290; auction sale 290; sale by auction 308

kyōbai ni dasu
auction (verb) 290

kyōbai ni suru
auction (verb) 290

kyōbai kakaku
auction price 290

kyōbai nakadachinin
auction broker 197

kyōbai shobun
forced sale 226

kyōbai suru
auctioneer (verb) 290

kyōbai tesūryō
auctioneer's commission 290

kyōbai tetsuzuki
auction procedure 290

kyōbai tsūchi
auction notice 290

kyōbaijō
auction house 290; auction room 290

kyōbainin
auction broker 197, 290; auctioneer 290

kyōbō
collusion 16

kyōchō
concertation 18

kyōchō kōdō
concerted action 18

kyōchō yūshi
co-financing 208; joint financing 239; participation loan 257; syndicated credit 280

kyōchō yūshidan
syndicate (financing group) 280

kyodai kigyō
business giant 339; giant firm 347

kyodaikoku
super-power 106

kyōdō
co-operation 20

kyōdō chochiku kanjō
joint savings account 150

kyōdō chōsa
joint survey 59

kyōdō furōto
joint (currency) float 177

kyōdō hiyō
common expenses 292

kyōdō hoken
co-insurance 317

kyōdō hokenkin
co-insurance money 317

kyōdō hokensha
co-insurer 317

kyōdō jigyō
joint undertaking 349; joint venture (= joint project) 59

kyōdō kaison
general average 321

kyōdō kanjō
joint account 150

kyōdō kanri
joint control 349

kyōdō kansa
joint audit 398

kyōdō kei'ei
joint management 349; joint operation 349

kyōdō kei'eisha
partner (joint business operators) 355

kyōdō kenkyū
joint research 59

kyōdō kigyō
joint enterprise 349

kyōdō kōnyū
joint purchase 298

kyōdō kōza
joint account 150

kyōdō kumiai
association 337; co-operative 20; co-partnership 342

kyōdō kumiai'in
co-partner 342

kyōdō nenkin
joint annuity 324

kyōdō sekinin
corporate responsibility 343; joint responsibility 349

kyōdō shakuchi
tenancy of land in common 310

kyōdō shasaiken
joint corporate bond 239

kyōdō shihai
joint control 349

kyōdō shihon
joint capital 398; joint stock 398

kyōdō shijō
Common Market, the 17

kyōdō shōgai nenkin
joint life annuity 324

kyōdō shoyū(ken)
collective ownership 292; co-ownership 292, 342

kyōdō shoyūsha
co-owner 292, 342

kyōdō shusshi
joint financing 398; pool of financing 259

kyōdō shusshisha
partner (joint capital investor) 355

kyōdō sōzokunin
joint heirs 298

kyōdō tanpo
joint mortgage 298

kyōdō tōshi
joint investment 239

kyōdō yokin kanjō
joint deposit account 150

kyōdō yokinsha
joint depositors 150

kyōdō yūshi
co-financing 208; participation loan 257

kyōdōsha
co-partner 342

kyōdōtai
community 17, 292

kyōdōzai
collective goods 16

kyōfu sōba
near-panic market 250

kyōhaku
threat (intimidation) 110

kyōhaku kōka
threat effect 110

kyōhakusha
racketeer (intimidator) 358

kyōhi
rejection 158

kyōi
threat (danger, menace) 110

kyōiku
education 31, 442; training (educating young recruits) 469

kyōiku ga aru jinteki shigen
educated manpower 453

kyōikuhi
education expenditure 32

kyojū
occupancy (habitation) 303; residence, a (place of residence) 307

kyojū shoyūsha
resident owner 308

kyojū suijun
housing standards 297

kyojū suru
occupy (reside) 303

kyojūsha
occupier 303; resident 308

kyojūsha gaika yokin kanjō
resident foreign-currency deposit account 159

kyojūsha kanjō
resident account 159

kyojūsha shoyū
resident ownership 308

kyoka
licence (permit, permission) 350

kyōkai
association 337; foundation 347; institute 349; organization 77, 354

kyokaku shijō
negotiated market 250

kyōkō
crisis (scare, alarm) 22; panic 256

kyōkō kakaku
panic price 257

kyōkō sōba
panic market 257; panic quotations 257

kyokudaichi
maximum (value of a function) 68

kyokudaika
maximization 68

kyokudo no ken'yaku
parsimony 78

kyokumen
curve 22; phase 80

kyokushōchi
minimum (value of a function) 68

kyōkyū
supply 106

kyōkyū kajō
excess supply 35; glut 43; oversupply 78

kyōkyū kakaku
supply price 106

kyōkyū kansū
supply function 106

kyōkyū kyokusen
supply curve 106

kyōkyū no danryokusei
elasticity of supply 32

kyōkyū nōryoku
supply capacity 106

kyōkyū sābisu
supply services 106

kyōkyū yoryoku
excess supply capacity 35

kyōkyūbusoku
short supply 100

kyōkyūgawa keizai
supply-side economics 106

kyōkyūhaku
short supply 100

kyōkyūjō no seiyaku
supply constraint 106

kyōkyūsha
suppliers 106

kyōnen
bad year 9

kyōraku
bid at auction 290

kyōrakunin
bidder at auction 290

kyōran bukka
wild price rises 120

kyōran infurēshon
rampant inflation 90

kyōryoku
co-operation 20

kyōryokuteki sekai bōeki
co-operative world trade 20

kyōsaku
bad crop 9

kyōsan shugi
communism 17

kyōsan shugi keizai
communist economy 17

kyōsan shugi shakai
communist society 17

kyōsan shugi taisei
communist system 17

kyūshoku suru
look for a job 444
kyūshokubairitsu
job-application/job-opening ratio
58
kyūshokugakari
interviewer 443
kyūshokusha
employment seeker 442;
job applicant 443; job hunter
443; job seeker(s) 59, 444
kyūshū
absorption 335; acquisition (of
a company) 335, 367
kyūshū gappei
absorption 335; acquisition
335; merger (merger and
acquisition) 352
kyūshū kaikei
acquisition accounting 367
kyūsui
water supply 312
kyūsuiryō
water rates 312; water supply
(amount supplied) 312
kyūsuitō
water tank 312
kyūtan
coal supply 292
kyūtō
sharp advance 273;
sharp improvement 273;
sky-rocketing 274
kyūtō suru
sky-rocket 274
kyūyo
compensation 476; pay 481;
remuneration 483; salary (-ies)
97, 416, 483
kyūyo kiroku
payroll records 409
kyūyo no chōsa
salary study 97, 483
kyūyo shiharai sōgaku
payroll (total amount of salaries
paid) 409, 482
kyūyo suijun
pay level 79, 481
kyūyo taikei
salary scale 483
kyūyozei
payroll tax 409

madoguchi
counter 141; window 163, 286
madoguchi genkin
till money [UK] 162
madoguchi shidō
window guidance [J] 286, 287
(note 19)
maebarai
advance 368
maebarai hiyō
prepaid expenses 410
maebarai waribikiritsu
anticipation rate 195
maebarai yachin
rent in advance 307
maebaraikin
prepayments (on balance
sheet) 410
maebike
closing of morning session 208

maegari
advance on loan 194
maegashi tegata
advance bill 131
maeuke shūekikin
unearned income (on balance
sheet) 425
maeukekin
advances received 368
magari
renting a room 307
magarinin
lodger (room tenant) 301
maibotsu genka
sunk costs 105
maigetsu no shisū
monthly index 71
mainasu no kinri
negative interest 152
mainasu no seichōritsu
negative growth rate 73
mājin
margin 179
makanaitsuki apāto
service flat 308
makuro keizai moderu
macro-economic model 65
makuro keizai seisaku
macro-economic policy 65
makuro keizaigaku
macro-economics 65
manē-sapurai
money supply 70, 180
manē-sapurai bunseki
money supply analysis 70
manē-sentā shozai ginkō
money center bank [US] 152
manki
expiration of term 320; maturity
247
manki ni naru
fall due 221; mature 151
manki keiyaku
expired contract 295
manki rimawari
yield to maturity 286
manki saiken
matured bond 247
manki shōkan
redemption at maturity 264
manki tegata
bill at maturity 136; matured bill
151
mankibarai
payment at maturity 155, 258
mankibarai modoshikin
maturity repayment 247
mankijitsu
due date 145, 219; expiration
date 295; maturity date 247
mankizen shōkan
prior redemption 260;
redemption before maturity 264
mankizen shōkan opushon
put option (bond redemption)
262
mankizen urimodoshi
resale before maturity 267
mannō taishaku taishōhyō
all-purpose balance sheet 268
manseiteki fukyō
chronic depression 16

manseiteki infurēshon
chronic inflation 16
manseiteki shitsugyō
chronic unemployment 16
manseiteki shitsugyōsha
hard-core unemployed 46
manzoku
contentment 452; satisfaction
466
manzoku ga aru
satisfied 466
marēsha
Malaysia 190
maruku (doitsu, finrando)
mark (Germany, Finland) 189
marukusu bunpairon
Marxian theory of distribution
67
marukusu keizaigaku
Marxian economics 67
marusasu jinkōron
Malthusianism 65
marusasu shugi
Malthusianism 65
marusasuteki jinkōron
Malthusian theory of population
65
maruta
Malta 190
masatsuteki shitsugyō
frictional unemployment 42
mashi tanpo
additional collateral 194
mason
wear and tear 312, 331
masonhi
wear-and-tear expenses 312
masshō kogitte
cancelled cheque (voided,
crossed out) 138
matagari
subtenancy 309
matagarinin
sublessee 309; subtenant 309
matagashi
sublease 309; sublet 309;
subletting 309
matagashinin
sublessor 309
matorikkusu
matrix 68
mawashigyoku
cross order 213
meibo
register (name register) 358
meigara
issue (an issue, title,
description) 238, 397
meigi kakikae
transfer (name transfer) 282,
424
meigi kakikae daichō
transfer book 282; transfer
register 424; Transfer Register
[UK] 362
meigi kakikae dairinin
registrar [UK] 265, 415;
transfer agent [US] 282, 424
meigi kakikae kaishi
transfer book open 282
meigi kakikae teishi
transfer book closed 282

meigi kakikaebi
transfer day 282
meigi kakikaehyō
transfer receipt 424
meigi kakikaeryō
transfer fee 282
meigi torishimariyaku
dummy director 345
meiginin
nominee 251
meikaku na mokuhyō
fixed targets 40
meimoku
money terms 70; nominal
terms 74
meimoku chingin
nominal wages 74, 480
meimoku genkin zandaka
nominal balances 74
meimoku kahei
nominal money 181; token
money 111, 186
meimoku kanjō
nominal account 403
meimoku kawase sōba
nominal exchange rate 181
meimoku kokumin sōseisan
nominal GNP 74
meimoku rieki
nominal profit 403
meimoku rimawari
nominal yield 251
meimoku shihei
fiat money 172
meimoku shihon
nominal capital 403
meimoku shisan
nominal assets 403
meimoku shotoku
nominal income 74
meimoku shūnyū
nominal income 403, 480
meimoku sōba
nominal quotation 251
meirei
order (from the court) 436
meisai
itemization (details) 398
meisai kanjō
itemized account 398
meisai seisansho
itemized accounts 398
meishi
business card 450
meiyo kisonnin hoken
libel insurance 324
mekishiko
Mexico 190
mengyō
cotton industry 123
menjo shōken
exempt securities 221
menkyo
licence (permission) 350
menkyoryō
licence fee 350
menkyosei
licencing 350
menseki jōkō
escape clause 34; market-out
clause 246

mishobun rieki jōyokin
unappropriated earned surplus
424; unappropriated profits 424

mishobun riekikin
unappropriated retained
earnings 425

mishobun ryūho riekikin
unappropriated retained income
425

mishobun sonshitsukin
unappropriated deficit 424

mishōka shōken
undigested securities 284

mishōkan fusai
outstanding liabilities 407

mishōkan kōsai
outstanding public loan 255

mishōkan saiken
outstanding bond 255

mishōkan shōken
outstanding securities 255

mishōkyaku genka
unamortized cost 424

mishōkyaku no
unamortized 424

mishōkyaku shinkabu hakkōhi
unamortized share-issuing
expenses 424

mishū haitōkin
dividend receivable 387

mishū hokenkin
insurance claims 323

mishū kachin
accrued rent 289

mishū rishi
accrued interest receivable 193

mishū risoku
accrued interest receivable 193

mishū shūeki
accrued income 366; accrued
revenue 367

mishūshi kanjō
accrual 366

misoshiki rōdōryoku
unorganized labour force 470

misoshiki rōdōsha
unorganized labour 115;
unorganized workers 115, 470

mitomeru
authorize 133

mitōshi
outlook 77; perspective 80;
projection 88; prospects 88

mitōshi chōsa
anticipation survey 7

mitsumori
estimate 294; valuation [UK]
(evaluation) 311

mitsumori genka
estimated cost 389

mitsumori genka keisan
estimated cost accounting 389

mitsumori kaikei hōkoku
pro-forma accounting report
411

mitsumori kawase tegata
pro-forma bill 157

mitsumori okurijō
pro-forma invoice 411

mitsumori rieki
estimated profit 389

mitsumori saiken
estimated claims 434

mitsumori shikinhyō
estimated funds statement
389; projected funds statement
412

mitsumori son'eki
estimated profit and loss 389

mitsumori son'eki keisansho
estimated profit and loss
statement 389; projected
income statement 412

mitsumori sonshitsugaku
estimated loss 389

mitsumori taishaku taishōhyō
budgeted balance sheet 374;
estimated balance sheet 389;
pro-forma balance sheet 411;
projected balance sheet 412

mitsumori zaimu shohyō
estimated financial statement
389; pro-forma financial statement 411; projected financial
statement 412

mitsumorisho
written estimate 312

mitsuyu bōeki
contraband trade 20

miuragaki tegata
original bill 154

miyako ochi
'leaving the capital' 473

mizu
water 312

mizumashi
watering 427

mizumashi kabu
watered stock 427

mizumashi koyō
featherbedding 38

mizumashi shisan
watered assets 427

mizuwari kabu
watered stock 427

mizuwari shihon
watered capital 427

mizuwari shisan
watered assets 427

mochiai
no change 251

mochibun
action (= equity stake) 367;
equity (holding interest) 389

mochibun hoyūken
equity ownership 389

mochibun hoyūsha
equity shareholder 389

mochibun kaikei
equity accounting 389

mochibun rieki
return on equity 415

mochibun shihon chōtatsu
equity financing 389; equity
funding 389

mochibun shutoku
acquisition of proprietary
interest 367

mochidaka
holdings 176; position 182,
259

mochidaka gendo
trading limit 282

mochidashi ginkō
presenting bank 157

mochiie
own house 303; owner-
occupied home 303

mochikabu
holdings (stock) 231;
shareholding 273, 418

mochikabu gaisha
holding company 348

mochikabu hiritsu no teika
equity dilution 389

mochikabu seigen
restrictions on stockholdings
267

mochikabusū
holdings (stock) 231, 394;
number of shares held 404

mochikoshi hiyō
carrying cost 377; stockholding
cost 421

mochinushi
owner (proprietor) 303

moderu
model 69

moderu-apāto
model apartment 302

moderu-biru
model building 302

modori kogitte
returned cheque 159

modori takane
recovery high 264

modoriuri
selling on recovery 271

modoshi
recouping a loss 263

modoshizei
tax refund 108, 485

moenikui
non-inflammable 492

mōgejji
mortgage (noun) 152, 248, 302

mōgejji gaisha
mortgage company 302

mōgeji kashitsuke
mortgage loan 249, 302

mōgejji kashitsuke hensai
mortgage repayment 249, 302

mōgejji kashitsuke hensai kanri
mortgage servicing 249

mōgejji kashitsuke kinri
mortgage rate 249, 302

mōgejji keiyaku
mortgage agreement 302

mōkaru shōbai
profitable business concern
357

mōkete uru
sell at a profit 271

mokkōgyō
wood-working industry 127

mokuhyō
objective 75; targets 107

mokuhyō sangyō
target industries 107

mokuhyō sōbaken
target zones 186

mokuromisho
prospectus 261, 357

mokuteki
objective(s) 75, 353

mokuteki kansū
objective function 75

mokuyaku
implicit contracts 49

mokuzai kōgyō
lumber industry 125

mokuzai sangyō
timber industry 127

monako
Monaco 190

monkirigata
stereotypes (set patterns) 104

morikaesu
rally (make a comeback, be
revived) 263

morokko
Morocco 190

mosaku
tâtonnement 107

mōshikomi
application (trying one's luck
with employers) 441;
subscription 279

mōshikomi chōka
oversubscription 256, 408

mōshikomi chōka no
oversubscribed 256, 408

mōshikomi kashō no
undersubscribed 283, 425

mōshikomi sarenakatta kabu
non-subscribed shares 404

mōshikomi shōkokin
application money 370

mōshikomi shōkokin kanjō
application account 370

mōshikomi tetsuzuki
application procedure 196, 370

mōshikomi-wariatechō
application and allotment book
370

mōshikomi yōshi
application form 196, 370, 441;
subscription form 279, 421

mōshikomiken
application rights 196, 370

mōshikomikin
application money 196, 370;
subscription money 279, 421

mōshikomisha
applicant (shares) 195, 370;
subscriber 279

mōshikomisho
application letter 196, 370;
letter of application 241, 399

mōshikomu
apply 441

kabushiki o mōshikomu
apply for shares 196, 370;
subscribe (for share) 279, 421

mōshitate o suru
file (an application) 346; file
(verb) 435

moteru mono to motazaru mono
haves and have-nots 46

motochō
ledger 398

motochō ni tenki suru
post into the ledger 410

motochō furikae
ledger transfer 398

motochō kakari
ledger keeper 398

mushōkan shasai
irredeemable debenture 238
mushōkan shōken
irredeemable securities 238
mushōsho saimu
debt of honour 216
mushōsho shakkin
debt of honour 216
mutanpo kariire
clean loan 208
mutanpo kashidashi
unsecured loan 285
mutanpo kashitsuke
unsecured advance 284;
unsecured loan 285
mutanpo kōsai
unsecured bond (public) 285
mutanpo no
unsecured 284
mutanpo saiken
plain bond 259; unsecured
bond (general) 285
mutanpo saikensha
unsecured creditor 285
mutanpo shasai
naked debenture 249; simple
debenture 274; unsecured
bond (corporate) 285;
unsecured debenture 285
mutanpo shasaiken
unsecured note 285
mutanpo shin'yōjō
clean credit 208; clean L/C
140
mutanpo waribiki tegata
unsecured discount bill 285
mutanpogashi
unsecured loan 285
mutodoke kekkin
absence without permission
449; unexcused absence 470
muyuigon zaisan
intestate estate 298

naatenin
drawee 145
nagemono
spilling stock 276
nageuri
distress selling 218; dumping
219; shake-out 272
naibu bunseki
internal analysis 396
naibu bunseki hōkokusho
internal audit report 396
naibu chingin kakusa
internal wage differentials 56
naibu fukeizai
internal diseconomies 56
naibu fusai
internal debt 235
naibu hojo
cross-subsidy 22
naibu hōkoku kaikei
accounting for internal reporting
365
naibu jōhō
inside information 233, 396
naibu kahei
inside money 55
naibu kansa
internal audit 396; internal
auditing 396

naibu kansa kijun
internal audit standard 396
naibu kansa seido
internal audit system 396
naibu kansabu
internal auditing department
396
naibu kansanin
internal auditor 396
naibu kei'ei bunseki
internal business analysis 396
naibu keizai
internal economies 56
naibu kiken tanpo hoken
inherent hazards insurance
322
naibu kiken tanpo hoken shōken
inherent hazards insurance
policy 322
naibu kin'yū
internal financing 396
naibu no shinryōjo
in-house infirmary 478
naibu ryūho
retained profit (internal reserve)
415; undivided profits (retained
profit) 425
naibu shūekiritsu
internal rate of return (IRR) 56,
235, 238
naibu tenkin
inter-company transfer 458
naibu zaimu kanri
internal financial management
396
naibusha
insider 233, 396
naibusha no jōhō
insider information 233
naibusha no torihiki
insider dealing [UK] 233;
insider trading [US] 233
naifu no ha
knife edge 59
naigai kinrisa
difference between domestic
and foreign interest rates 26
naigaiju
domestic and foreign demand
27
naijiria
Nigeria 190
naiju
domestic demand 27
naikinshokuin
back-office kakusa 450
naikoku bōeki
domestic trade 27; inland trade
54
naikoku gaisha
domestic company 344
naikoku hōjin
domestic corporation 344
naikoku kawase
domestic money order 144,
naikoku kawase tegata
domestic bill of exchange 144;
inland bill 149
naikoku kigyō
domestic business 344
naikoku sainyūchō
Internal Revenue Service (IRS)
[US] 56, 58

naikoku shūzeikyoku
Inland Revenue [UK] 54
naikoku sōkin
domestic money order
(remittance) 144
naikoku tegata
domestic bill 144
naikokusai
domestic bond 219; domestic
loan 219; national loan 249
naikokuzei
internal tax 56
naira (naijiria)
naira (Nigeria) 190
naisai
domestic bond 219; domestic
loan 219; internal debt 56,
235; national loan 249
naiseiri
liquidation without court
involvement 436
naishoku
manual piecework 460, 472
(note 33); sideline 467, 472
(note 33)
nakadachigyō
broking 204
nakagai kanjō
brokerage account 204
nakagai tesūryō
broker's commission 204;
broker's fees 204; brokerage
204
nakagaigyō
brokerage business 204;
broking 204
nakagainin
broker (commission agent ,
middleman) 203; commission
broker [US] 209
nakagainin kariirekin
broker's loan 204
nakagaiten
brokerage house [US] 204
namakemono
lazy person 459
nami tegata
ordinary bill 154
nanchō
weak tone 286
nanchō shikyō
soft market 274; stagnant
market 276
nandemoya
jack-of-all-trades 458
nanjaku shikyō
heavy market 230; sluggish
market 274
nanka
soft currency 184; soft money
184
nanka keikō
weakening tendency 187
nankaken
soft currency area 184
nanpa
bears 200
nanpa no tejimai
liquidation of bears 241;
liquidation of shorts 241
nanpashite
bear operator 199

nanpin
averaging 198
nanpin de kaisagaru
average down 197
nanpin de urisagaru
average up 197
nanpingai
averaging down 198
nanpin'uri
averaging up 198
nansen
South Korea 190
nanshiki teinensei
flexible retirement scheme 320
nareai baibai
crossed sale 213; crossed
trade 213; wash sale [US] 286
nareai baibai chūmon
matched orders 247
nareai tegata
kite 150
nareai torihiki
wash 286
narikin
nouveaux riches 75
nariyuki chūmon
at best 197; no-limit order 251;
market order [US] 246
nariyuki de
at the market 197
natsuin
sealing of a document 360
natsuin shōsho
deed 293
natsuin shōsho keiyaku
covenant 293
nazudakku
NASDAQ system (National
Association of Securities
Dealers Automated Quotations
System) [US] 249
nebiraki
price spread 260; spread
(difference between prices)
276
nedan
price(s) (a figure) 83, 304
mottomo yūri na nedan de
at best 197
negasa kabu
fancy stock 221; high-price
stock 231
nehaba
price range 260; spread (price
fluctuations) 276
nehaba seigen
fluctuation limit 226
nēkiddo-opushon
naked option 249
nēkiddo-pojishon
naked position 249
nekkyō sōba
feverish market 221
nēmupurēto
nameplate 461
nenbarai hokenryō
annual premium 315
nendo chōbo shimekiri
annual closing of books 369
nendo hajime
beginning of fiscal year 372

nijūsei
duality 28

nikkei dau
Nikkei Dow Jones Average [J] 251

nikkei kabushiki shisū
Nikkei Stock Average [J] 251

nikkyū
daily wage 476

nikokukan enjo
bilateral assistance 11

nikokukan kyōtei
bilateral agreement 11

nikōtaisei
two shifts 470

niku seihin kōgyō
meat products manufacturing industry 125

nikutai rōdō
manual labour 66, 460; manual work 460; physical work 464

nikutai rōdōsha
blue-collar worker(s) 11, 450; manual worker(s) 66, 460

ninchi
post (place of appointment) 445, 464

ninchi sareta kiken soshō
assumed risk 316

ningen hyōka
human valuation 457

ningen kankei
human relations 457

ningen kankei kanri
human relations management 457

ningen kōgaku
ergonomics 34

ningen no genka shōkyakuhi
human depreciation 47, 457

ningen rōdō
human labour 47

nin'i hasan
voluntary bankruptcy 437; voluntary winding-up 438

nin'i hoken
optional insurance 326; voluntary insurance 331

nin'i hoken seido
optional insurance plan 326

nin'i kaisan
voluntary winding-up 438

nin'i kenkō hoken seido
voluntary health insurance 331

nin'i saihoken
facultative reinsurance 320; voluntary reinsurance 331

nin'i seisan
voluntary liquidation 437

nin'i shiharai funō
voluntary insolvency 437

nin'i shōkan
optional redemption 255

nin'i taishoku
optional retirement 495; voluntary retirement 496

nin'i toriage
voluntary repossession 312

ninka
approval 315; authority (permission) 133

ninka suru
approve 316

ninkazumi hikiwatashi shisetsu
approved delivery facility 196

ninki ga aru kabu
hot stock (popular) 231

ninki ga aru shinpatsu shōken
hot issue 231

ninki ga nakunakatta kabu
wallflower 285

ninki kabu
popular issue 259; popular stock 259

ninki kabushiki
active stock 194

ninki no aru gojū meigara no kabushiki
nifty fifty [US] 251

ninkyo kaikeishi
certified accountant [UK] 378

ninmei
appointment (to a post) 336, 450

ninmei sareru
appointed (to be) 450

ninmei suru
appoint 336, 450

ninmu
assignment 450; duties 345, 453; functions 347, 456; responsibilities 359, 466; task 469

ninshiki no ragu
recognition lag 92

ninshō hon'yaku
certified translation 340

ninshō tōhon
certified copy 340

nippon ginkō
Bank of Japan 135

nippon ginkōken
Bank of Japan bank note 135, 166

nisegane
counterfeit money 168

niseganetsukuri
counterfeiter 168; forger 174

nitchū nehaba seigen
daily trading limit 214

nitchū takahikune
intraday 236

nittō
daily allowance 476; daily wage (daily pay, payment per diem) 476

niwa
garden 296

niwakageiki
temporary boom 110

nobebarai
deferred payment 216, 385

nobebō
bar (gold) 166

nobewatashi
deferred deliveries 216

noboru (— o)
promoted (to —) 465

nōchi
agricultural land 5, 289; farming land 295

nōchi kaikaku
agricultural land reform 5

nōchi zōsei
land reclamation (farm land) 299

nōdōteki kōsai
active debt (public debt) 194

nōdōteki tōshi
active investment 194

nōgaku
agronomy (study) 6

nōgyō
agriculture 6, 123

nōgyō bumon
agricultural sector 6

nōgyō chingin
agricultural wages 6, 475

nōgyō chingin i'inkai
Agricultural Wages Board [UK] 6

nōgyō chingin rōdōsha
hired agricultural worker 457

nōgyō dōtai chōsa
agricultural census 5

nōgyō enjo keikaku
farm aid programmes 38

nōgyō fukakin
agricultural levies 5

nōgyō gijutsu
agricultural technology 6

nōgyō haikibutsu
agricultural waste 6

nōgyō hojokin
agricultural subsidies 6

nōgyō hoken
agricultural insurance 315

nōgyō jinkō
agricultural population 6; farming population 38

nōgyō kaikaku
agricultural reform 6

nōgyō kakumei
Agrarian Revolution 5

nōgyō kanren sangyō
agribusiness 5, 123

nōgyō kei'ei(gaku)
agronomics 6

nōgyō keizai
agricultural economy 5; agronomy (economics) 6; rural economy 97

nōgyō kikaika
agricultural mechanization 5; farm mechanization 38

nōgyō kindaika
agricultural modernization 5

nōgyō kin'yū
agricultural credit 5; agricultural financing 5

nōgyō kōzō
agricultural structure 6

nōgyō kyōdō kumiai
agricultural co-operatives 5

nōgyō kyōkō
agricultural crisis 5

nōgyō mondai
agricultural problems 6

nōgyō osen
agricultural pollution 6

nōgyō pariti shisū
agricultural parity index 5

nōgyō rōdō
agricultural labour 5; farm work 455

nōgyō rōdōsha
agricultural worker(s) 6, 449; farm worker (s) 38, 455

nōgyō saigai
agricultural disaster 5

nōgyō saigai hoshō
agricultural disaster indemnity 5

nōgyō seihin
agricultural commodities 5

nōgyō seisaku
agricultural policy 5

nōgyō seisaku no ragu
agricultural lag 5

nōgyō seisan
agricultural output 5; agricultural production 6

nōgyō seisanryoku
agricultural productivity 6

nōgyō sensasu
agricultural census 5

nōgyō shakai
agricultural society 6

nōgyō shigen
agricultural resources 6

nōgyō shotoku
agricultural earnings 5; agricultural income 5

nōgyō shūnyū
farming income 38

nōgyō tōkei
agricultural statistics 6

nōgyōkoku
agricultural country 5

nōka
farm households 38

nōka keizai
farm economy 38

nōka keizai chōsa
farm household economic survey 38

nōka kyōdō kumiai
farmers' co-operatives 38

nōkai
closing session 208

nokidate no ie
one-family house 303

nokitsuzuki no ie
semi-detached house 308

nōmin
farmers 38

nōmin mondai
rural issues 97

nōmin rison
rural exodus 97

nomiya
bucket shop 204; bucket-shop operator 204; bucketeer 204

nōnyū kokuchisho
notice of payment 153

noriai
association 337; joint enterprise 349

nōritsu
capability 450; efficiency 32

nōritsu chingin
efficiency wages 32, 476

nōritsu shotoku
efficiency earnings 32

nōritsu tan'i
efficiency units 32

nōritsu zōshin
increase in efficiency 457

nōritsukyū
payment by results 79, 482

noronoro senjutsu
work-to-rule tactics 504

noruē
Norway 190

nōryoku
ability 449; capability 450;
capacity 14

nōryoku chidai
rent of ability 94

nōryokukyū
pay according to ability 481

nōsanbutsu
agricultural goods 5;
agricultural produce 6;
agricultural products 6

nōsanbutsu kakaku
agricultural prices 6; farm
prices 38

nōsanbutsu kakaku shiji hojokin
farm subsidies 38

nōsanbutsu kakaku shiji seido
farm price support policy 38

nōsanbutsu kakaku shiji seisaku
agricultural price support policy
6

nōsanbutsu yunyū
agricultural imports 5

nōsanbutsu yushutsu
agricultural exports 5

nōson jinkō
rural population 97

nōson kaihatsu
rural development 97

nōson keikaku
rural planning 97

nōson kyōdōtai
rural community 97

nōson seisaku
rural policy 97

nōson shakai
rural society 97

nottori
acquisition (of a company) 335;
hijacking 321; take-over(s)
107, 280, 362

nottoru
take over (verb) 280, 362

nouhau
know-how 60

NOW kanjō
NOW account [US] 153

nōzei
levies 62; tax payment 108,
484

nōzei gimu
tax liability 108

nōzei kaihi
tax avoidance 107; tax evasion
108

nōzei kijitsu
tax payment date 484

nōzei shinkoku
tax declaration 484

nōzei shinkokusho
tax return [general] 108, 485

nōzei tsūchisho
tax payment notice 484

nōzeiki
tax-gathering season 108

nōzeisha
tax payers 108

nozonashiku nai gyōseki
bad performance 337

nukeana
loopholes 64

nurumayu
'tepid water' 473

nyūchō
excessive imports 35; trade
deficit 112

nyūchōkoku
deficit country (with excess of
imports) 24

nyūin hiyō hoken
hospitalization insurance 322

nyūin hiyō hoken shōken
hospitalization insurance policy
322

nyūin kikan
hospitalization 321

nyūinhi
hospital expenses 321

nyūjiirando
New Zealand 190

nyūkin suru
pay in 155

nyūkinhyō
credit slip 141; paying-in slip
155

nyūkinzumi tsūchisho
credit advice 141

nyūsatsu
tender (bid) 281

nyūsha shiken
corporate entrance exam 442

nyūsha suru
join a company 458

nyūshokuritsu
accession rate 3; engagements
(= new hires) 33; hiring rate 46

nyūyōku kabushiki torihikijo
Big Board [NYSE – US] 200;
New York Stock Exchange
(NYSE) 251, 252

nyūyōku shōhin torihikijo
Commodity Exchange of New
York (COMEX) 209

o-cha o nomu
'to drink tea' 489

ōakinai
heavy trading 230

ōbāōru-pojishon
overall position 182

ōbeya
open-plan office 462

ōbii
old boys' network 445

ōbike
closing 208

ōbike de kau
buy on close 205

ōbo
application (in response to an
advertisement) 441;
subscription 279

ōbo chōka
oversubscription 256, 408

ōbo chōka no
oversubscribed 256, 408

ōbo kakaku
subscription price 279, 421

ōbo kingaku
amount subscribed 369

ōbo shikin
subscribed capital 421

ōbo sōgaku
total amount subscribed 424

ōbo suru
apply 441

kabushiki o ōbo suru
subscribe (for shares) 279, 421

ōbo yōshi
application form 441

ōbogaku
amount subscribed 369

ōboken
application rights 196, 370

ōbosha
applicant (entrant) 441;
applicant (for shares) 195, 370;
subscriber 279

ōbosha rimawari
subscriber's yield 421;
yield to subscribers 286, 428

ochitsuki shikyō
moderate trading 247

ōdanmen
cross-section 22

ōdanmen bunseki
cross-section analysis 22

ōdanmmen shōhi kansū
cross-section consumption
function 22

ōfuku torihiki
round-trip trade 268;
round-tripping 268

ofushoa-fando
offshore funds 253

ofushoa ginkō
offshore banking units 253

ofushoa ginkō gyōmu
offshore banking 253

ofushoa-sentā
offshore centre 253

ofushoa tōshi sentā
offshore financial centres 253

ofushoa tōshi shintaku
offshore investment trust 253

ōgata gappei
big merger 337; giant merger
347; large-scale merger 350

ōgata kabu
large capital stock 398

oginau
compensate 491

ōgonritsu
golden rule 43

ōguchi
large-lot 240

ōguchi kashidashisaki
prime borrower 260

ōguchi kin'yū
wholesale banking 163

ōguchi tegata
large bill (of exchange) 150

ōguchi yokin
large deposit 150; wholesale
deposits 163

ōhaba bōeki akaji
massive trade deficit 67

oitaru kōgyōkoku
old industrial countries 76

oitate
eviction 294

oitateru
evict 294

ōkega
serious injury 493

ōki dōyō
major disturbances 65

ōkii idō
major staff reshuffle 460

okiai gyogyō
offshore fishing 125

okikae tōshi
replacement investment
(substitution) 94

ōkura daijin
Chancellor of the Exchequer
[UK] 16

ōkurashō
Treasury, the (Finance Ministry,
Department of the Treasury
[US], the Exchequer [UK]) 113,
186

ōkurashō shōken
Exchequer bills [UK] 221;
Treasury bill [UK] 283

ōkurashō shōken hakkōdaka
Treasury bills issued 283

ōkurashō shōken kinri
Treasury bill rate 283

okure
lag 61

okurijō
bill 372, 487; invoice 397, 487

okurijō bangō
invoice number 397

okurijō kingaku
invoice amount 397, 487

okurijō kinyūchō
invoice register 397

okurijō shiirechō
invoice book 397

okurijō shikirichō
invoice book 397

ōkyū teate
first aid 492

oman
Oman 190

omoteguchi kin'yū
front-door financing 227

omoteguchi sōsa
front-door operation 227

omowaku
speculation 275

omowaku o suru
speculate 275

omowaku kibun
speculative mood 275

omowaku shikyō
speculative market 275

omowaku torihiki
speculative operation 275;
speculative trading 275;
speculative transaction 275

omowaku tōshi
speculative investment 275

omowakugai
going long 228; speculative
buying 275; speculative
purchase 275

omowakugai ninki
speculative interest 275

omowakugaisuji
speculative buyers 275

omowakushi
speculator(s) 275
omowakusujii
speculative interests 275;
speculator(s) 275
omowaku'uri
going short 228; speculative
sale 275; speculative selling
275
on-rain-bankingu-shisutemu
on-line banking system 154
ongaku sangyō
music industry 125
onjō shugi
paternalism 463
onjō shugiteki na
paternalistic 463
onkyū
retirement (government
employees) 496
onkyū juryōsha
pensioners (government
employees) 79, 496
onkyū kankeihi
pensions-related expenses 79
onkyū kikin
pension fund (government
employees) 79
onkyū seido
pension scheme (govern-ment
employees) [J] 79, 495
onkyū tanpo kashitsuke
loan secured by government
pension 242
opekku
Organization of Petroleum
Exporting Countries (OPEC)
76, 77
operēshonaru-akauntingu
operational accounting 406
ōpun-pojishon
open position 182
ōpungata shin'yō
open-end credit [US] 154
ōpungata tōshi shintaku
open-end investment trust 254;
open-ended fund 254
ōpungata tōshi shintaku gaisha
open-end management
company 254
opushon
option 255
opushon keiyaku
option 182
opushon kijitsu
option date 182
opushon no hongenteki kachi
intrinsic value 236
opushon no urite
option writer 255
opushon torihiki
traded options 186
opushonryō
option premium 255; premium
(option charge) 260
orientēshon
orientation 463
orimono kōgyō
textile industry 127
oroshiuri
wholesale 120
oroshiuri bukka
wholesale prices 120

oroshiuri bukka shisū
wholesale price index (WPI)
120, 121
oroshiuri gyōsha
wholesalers 120
oroshiuri kaikei
wholesale accounting 427
oroshiuri kakaku
wholesale prices 120
oroshiuri shijō
wholesale market 120
oroshiurigyō
wholesale industry 127;
wholesale trade 120
ōryō
embezzlement 388
ōryō hannin
embezzler 388
ōryō suru
embezzle 388
osaeru
peg (verb) 258
osen
pollution (contamination) 81
osen chi'iki
polluted areas 81
osen kabuken
soiled share certificate 418
osen kisei
pollution control (regulation) 81
ōsen kogitte
crossed cheque 142
ōsen shōken
soiled certificate 274
osenbutsu
pollutants 81
osenken
pollution rights 81
osensha
polluter 81
osensha futan no gensoku
polluter-pays principle 81
oshiage chingin
push-up wages 90
oshime
dip 217
oshimegai
buying on a falling market 205;
buying on decline 205; buying
on reaction 206
ōshū chi'iki kaihatsu kikin
European Regional
Development Fund (ERDF) 34
ōshū i'inkai
European Commission 34
ōshū jiyū bōeki chi'iki
European Free Trade Area 34
ōshū jiyū bōeki rengō
European Free Trade
Association (EFTA) 32, 34
ōshū kaihatsu kikin
European Development Fund
34
ōshū keizai i'inkai
Economic Commission for
Europe (ECE) (= United
Nations Economic Commission
for Europe) 29
ōshū keizai kyōdōtai
European Economic
Community (EEC) 32, 34

ōshū keizai kyōryoku kikō
Organization for European
Economic Co-operation
(OEEC) 75, 77
ōshū keizai tsūka dōmei
Economic and Monetary Union
29
ōshū kikin
European Fund 34
ōshū kyōdōtai
European Community (EC) 29;
34
ōshū sekitan tekkō kyōdōtai
European Coal and Steel
Community (ECSC) 31, 34
ōshū tōshi ginkō
European Investment Bank
(EIB) [EC] 32, 34
ōshū tsūka
Euro-currency 170
ōshū tsūka dōmei
European Monetary Union
(EMU) 33, 34, 170, 171
ōshū tsūka kyōtei
European Monetary Agreement
(EMA) 32, 34, 170
ōshū tsūka seido
European Monetary System
(EMS) 33, 34, 170
ōshū tsūka tan'i
European Currency Unit (ECU)
170
osu
affix (seal) [J] 132
ōsutoraria
Australia 189
ōsutoria
Austria 189
ōtesuji
big traders 200; leading
speculators 240
otosu (tegata o)
honour (a bill) 148
owarine
closing price 208; closing
quote 208; last quotation 240
oya ginkō
parent bank 155
oya kādo
master card 246
oya shin'yōjō
master credit 247
oyagaisha
controlling company 342;
parent company 355; senior
company 360
oyakabu
old shares 253, 405; old stock
253
oyako rōn
two-generation loan 283
ōyō gijutsu
applied technology 7
ōyō keizaigaku
applied economics 7
ōyō kenkyū
applied research 7
ōzaya
wide margin 286
ōzoko
rock bottom 268
ōzuru (saiken ni)
subscribe (for a loan) 279

pakisutan
Pakistan 190
panama
Panama 190
paneru chōsa
panel research 78
paneru-dēta
panel data 78
paramētā
parameter 78
parēto no hōsoku
Pareto's law 78
parētoteki saiteki jōken
Pareto conditions 78
parupu sangyō
pulp and paper industry 126
pāsento no giketsukentsuki kabushiki
percentage of voting shares
431
pasu-surū shōken
pass-through security 257
pāto-taimā
part-timer 463
pāto-taimu
part time 463
pāto-taimu-wāku
part time work 445, 463
pātotaimugyō
part-time business 355
penanto
pennant 258
penii kabu
penny shares [UK] 258;
penny stock [US] 258
pēpā-gōrudo
paper gold 182
perū
Peru 190
peseta (supein)
peseta (Spain) 190
peso
**(arujenchin, boribia, chire,
firippin, koronbia, kyūba,
mekishiko)**
peso (Argentine, Bolivia, Chile,
Philippines, Colombia, Cuba,
Mexico) 189, 190
piiāru
public relations (PR) 464, 465
pike
picket 501
piketto-rain
picket line 501
PIN bangō
PIN number 156
pinku-bukku
Pink Book [UK] 80
piramiddogata kanri
pyramiding 90
pojishon
position 182
pondo
(eikoku)
pound 191; pound sterling
184; sterling 184 (United
Kingdom)
**(eirurando, ejiputo, kipurosu,
maruta, rebanon, shirai,
sūdan)**
pound (Ireland, Egypt, Cyprus,
Malta. Lebanon, Syria, Sudan)
189, 190, 191

pondo chi'iki
sterling area 185
pondo kawase
sterling exchange 185
pondo sōba
sterling rate 185
pondobarai tegata
sterling bill 161
pondodaka
strong pound 185
pondodate kawase
exchange in pounds 171
pondoyasu
weak pound 187; declining
pound 169
pōrando
Poland 190
porutogaru
Portugal 190
posuto
post 445, 464
pōtoforio
portfolio 259
puraimu-rēto
base rate [UK] 199; prime rate
[US] 84, 157, 260
purehabu jūtaku
prefabricated house 304
puro konjō
professionalism 465
purodakutibiti-bāgeningu
productivity bargaining 87, 482

ragu
lag 61
raifu-saikuru kasetsu
life-cycle hypothesis 63
rainendo no yosan
budget for the coming year 374
rakkan
optimism 77
rakuchō
declining market 216; sagging
268; weakening market 286
rakuchō shijō
sagging market 268
rakunōgyō
dairy-farming 123
rakutan
frustration 456
rando
research and development
(R & D) 90, 95
rando (minami afurika)
rand (South Africa) 190
rankōge
wild fluctuation (market) 286
rankōge shikyō
erratic market 220
ranningu-kosuto
running cost 416
rebanon
Lebanon 190
rebarejjido
leverage [US] 399
rebarejjido-baiauto
leveraged buy-out 399
rebarejjido gaisha
leveraged company 399
rebarejjido kabu
leveraged stock 241

rebarejjido tōshi gaisha
leveraged investment company
241
rebu (burugaria)
lev (Bulgaria) 189
rēdā
raider 262
reddo-kurōzutsuki shin'yōjō
red clause L/C 157
rēganomikkusu
Reaganomics 91
reibō sōchi
air conditioning 289
reibō sōchi no
air-conditioned 289
reijō
summons 437
reikyaku kikan
cooling-off period 499
reiofu
lay-off(s) 62, 501
reiofu sareru
laid off (to be) 500
reiofu suru
lay off (verb) 501
reisai chokin
small deposits 160; small
savings 160
reisai yochokin
petty savings 156
reisei na shinkei
composure (cool nerves) 442
reitōki hoken
freezer insurance 320
reja sangyō
leisure industry 125
rekishi shugi
historicism 46
rekishiteki moderu
historical models 46
rekka
raging fire 493
renka
moderate price (low) 302
renketsu
consolidation (accounts) 380
renketsu jōyokin
consolidated surplus 380
renketsu kogaisha
consolidated subsidiary 342
renketsu motochō
consolidation ledger 380
renketsu seisanhyō
consolidated work sheet 380
renketsu shūdan
consolidation group 342
renketsu son'eki keisansho
consolidated income and
expenditure account 380;
consolidated income statement
380; consolidated profit and
loss account 380
renketsu taishaku taishōhyō
consolidated balance sheet
380
renketsu unten shikin
consolidated working fund 380
renketsu zaimu shohyō
consolidated financial
statements 380
renketsumae rieki
profit prior to consolidation 412

renkyū
holiday-studded period 478
renpō chochiku kashitsuke
hoken gaisha
Federal Savings and Loan
Insurance Corporation [US]
146
renpō junbi ginkō
Federal Reserve Bank (FRB)
[US] 146, 147
renpō junbi seido
Federal Reserve System (Fed)
[US] 146
renpō shikin kinri
Federal funds rate [US] 221
renpō yokin hoken gaisha
Federal Deposit Insurance
Corporation (FDIC) [US] 146
rensa ginkōsei
chain banking 139
rensa tōsan
chain-reaction bankruptcy 434
rensaten
chain (store) 340
rensho
counter-signature (joint
signature) 141, 343
rensho suru
counter-sign (sign jointly) 141,
343
renshonin
co-signatory 343
renshonin no kengen
co-signatory powers 343
renshū
training (study and training)
469
rentai hoken
joint insurance 324
rentai hoken shōken
joint insurance policy 324
rentai hoshō
joint and several guarantee
239; joint guarantee 239
rentai saimu
joint and several obligation
239; joint debt 239
rentai saimusha
joint debtor 239, 435
rentai seimei hoken
joint life insurance 324
rentai sekinin
joint and several liability 349;
joint liability 349; several
responsibility 360
rentai yakusoku tegata
joint promissory note 239
renzoku motochō
progressive ledger 412
renzoku shōkan hakkō
serial issue 271
renzoku shōkan saiken
serial bonds 271
renzokugata hensū
continuous variable 20
reshiito
receipt 488
resshin
violent earthquake 493
retsugo saimu
subordinated debt 279
retsugo shasai
subordinated bond 279

retsugo shōken
junior securities 239
riage
increase in interest rates 232
riaru
(iran, oman)
rial (Iran, Oman) 189, 190
ribarai
debt service 216; debt
servicing 216; interest payment
235; servicing 160, 271
ribarai teishi
suspension of interest payment
280
ribia
Libya 190
rieki
benefits 372; earnings 388;
gain(s) 228, 393; income 395;
interest 55, 234; profit(s) 87,
261, 411; return 267; revenue
416
rieki o motorasu
pay off (int. verb) 257
rieki bunpai
profit sharing 412, 482
rieki bunpai kikō
profit-sharing scheme 482
rieki bunpai seido
profit-sharing scheme 482
rieki bunpairitsu
profit-sharing ratio 412
rieki gensoku
benefit principle 11
rieki haba
profit margin 411
rieki haitō
bonus (dividend) 373;
distribution of profits 387
rieki haitō kabu
participating stock 408
rieki haitō yūsen kabu
participating preference shares
[UK] 257, 408; participating
preferred stock [US] 257, 408
rieki haitōkin
dividend(s) (on balance sheet)
387
rieki jōyokin
accumulated profits 367;
accumulation 367; earned
surplus [US] 388; reinvested
profit 415
rieki junbikin
earned legal reserves (on
balance sheet) 388; earned
surplus reserves 388; legal
earned reserves 399; profit
reserve 412; revenue reserve
416; surplus reserves (on
balance sheet) 423
rieki kintensei chingin
profit-sharing wage plan 482
rieki kintō
equal advantage 33
rieki kurinobekin
deferred profits 385
rieki ryūhokin
accumulated earnings [US]
367; accumulated reserves
[UK] 367
rieki sanka shasai
participating bond 257;
profit-sharing bond 412

rieki shobun
  distribution of net profits 387; profit appropriation 411
rieki yōso
  profit factor 261
rieki yosoku
  profit forecasting 411; profit projection 412
riekikin bunpai kikō
  profit-sharing scheme 482
riekikin bunpai seido
  profit-sharing scheme 482
riekikin-haitō hiritsu
  earnings/dividends ratio 388
riekiritsu
  profit ratio 412; rate of return 91, 263
rifurēshon
  reflation 93
rigai no fuitchi
  conflict of interests 210
rigui
  profit-taking 261
riiku
  tip (leak) 281
riisu
  leasing 62
riisu sangyō
  leasing industry 125
riisugyō
  leasing industry 125
rijichō
  chief director 340
rijikai
  governing board 347
rijun
  gains (returns) 228, 393; profit(s) (return) 87, 261, 411
rijun asshuku
  profit squeeze 87
rijun atsuryoku infurēshon
  profits-push inflation 87
rijun bunpai
  profit sharing 412
rijun bunpai kabu
  profit-sharing stock 412
rijun dōki
  profit motive 87
rijun kakutoku
  profit-taking 412
rijun kansū
  profit function 87
rijun kinten
  participation in profits 408
rijun kyokudaika
  maximization of profits 401; profit maximization 87, 411
rijun shōken
  profit-sharing securities 412
rijunritsu
  profit ratio 412; rate of profit 413
riken
  interest (rights) 396
rikō
  implementation (execution, performance) 49
rikōfunō pojishon
  fail position 221
rimawari
  interest yield 235; return 267; yield (financial return) 121, 286, 428

rimawari kakusa
  yield gap 286; yield spread 286
rimawari kyokusen
  yield curve 121
rimawari no kaizen
  pick-up 259
rimawariritsu
  rate of yield 263; yield rate 286
ringyō
  forestry 124
rinji jūgyōin
  temporary employee (temp) 469
rinji ketsugi
  extraordinary resolution [UK] 430
rinji kōmoku
  extraordinary item 390
rinji koyō
  casual employment 15, 451
rinji no sochi
  expedient 35
rinji rieki
  non-recurring profit 404
rinji shigoto
  odd job 462; temporary job 469
rinji shishutsu
  extraordinary expenditure 390; non-recurring expense 404
rinji shitsugyō
  lay-off (temporary unemployment) 501
rinji shitsugyōsha
  lay-offs 62; laid-off worker 501
rinji shotoku
  extraordinary income 390
rinji shūnyū
  extraordinary revenue 390; non-recurring income 404
rinji sōkai
  extraordinary general meeting 430; extraordinary meeting 430
rinji teate
  perquisites 482
rinji yakan kinmu
  moonlighting 461
rinji yatoi
  temporary employment (temping) 469
rinji yosan
  extraordinary budget 37, 390
rinjihi
  extra expenditure 390; incidental expenses 395
rinjikai
  extra session 430
rinjiyatoi
  odd hand 462
rinose
  pyramiding 413
riochi
  ex interest 220
riochi saiken
  ex-interest bond 220
rira
  (itaria, toruko)
  lira (Italy, Turkey) 189, 191

rirekisho
  curriculum vitae (CV) [UK] 442; personal history 445; resume [US] 446
ririku
  take-off (noun) 107
riritsu
  interest rate (on loans or deposits) 149, 235; rate of interest 157, 263
riron
  theory 110
riron seikatsuhi
  theoretical cost of living 110
risatsu
  coupon 211
risatsu bangō
  coupon number 211
risatsuochi
  coupon off 211; ex coupon 220
risatsutsuki
  coupon on 211; cum coupon 213
risatsutsuki saiken
  coupon bond 211
risatsutsukisai
  coupon issue [US] 211; coupon security [US] 211
risesshon
  recession 92
rishi
  interest (interest on loans and deposits) 55, 149, 234
rishi futan
  interest burden 234
rishi hayamihyō
  interest table 149, 235
rishi heikōzei
  Interest Equalization Tax [US] 234
rishi hokyū
  interest subsidies 55
rishi kanjō
  interest account 149
rishi no kashitsuke shikin jukyūsetsu
  loanable funds theory of interest 63
rishi saitei
  interest arbitrage 234
rishi shiharai
  interest payment 235
rishi shiharai kijitsu
  interest payment date 235
rishi shiharai sashizusho
  interest warrant 235
rishi shotoku
  income from interest 232; interest income 234
rishiritsu
  interest rate (interest on loan or deposits) 149, 235; rate of interest 157, 263
rishiritsu kōzō
  interest-rate structure 55
rishitsuki shihon
  interest-bearing capital 234
rishizei
  interest tax 235
rishoku suru
  lose one's job 501

rishokuritsu
  employee turnover 454; quit rate 90
rishokusha
  quits 90
risō
  ideal 48
risoku
  interest (interest on loans and deposits) 55, 149, 234
risoku no shiharai
  payment of interest 258
risoku shūnyū
  interest revenue 235
risuku bunsangata pōtoforio
  diversified portfolio 218
ritchi jōken ni kōsoku sarenai sangyō
  footloose industries 40
ritchiron
  location theory 64
ritoku
  gain(s) (benefit, returns) 228, 393; profits (earnings, return) 87
ritokuzei
  profits tax 412; tax on profits 423
ritsu
  rate (per cent) 263
ritsuki kanjō
  interest-bearing account 149
ritsuki kashitsuke
  active debt 194
ritsuki kokusai
  fixed-rate government bond 225
ritsuki kōsai
  active bond 194; interest-bearing public bond 234
ritsuki saiken
  interest-bearing bond 234
ritsuki shōken
  interest-bearing securities 234
ritsuki tōza kanjō
  interest-bearing checking account 149
ritsuki yokin
  interest-bearing deposit 149
ritsuki yokin kanjō
  interest-bearing deposit account 149
riyāru (saujiarabia)
  riyal (Saudi Arabia) 190
riyō
  utilization (use) 116
riyōkanō shigen
  available resources 8
riyū (rūmania)
  leu (Romania) 190
rizaya
  interest margin 234; interest spread 235; jobber's turn 239; margin 245; profit margin 261; spread (interest margin) 276
rōbai
  nervousness 250
rōbai uri
  panic selling 257
robii
  lobby 63
robiisuto
  lobbyist 63

rōmubu
labour relations department
459

rōmuhi
labour cost 60, 398

rondon ginkōkan torihiki kinri
London inter-bank offered rate
(LIBOR) 151, 241, 243

rondon kabushiki torihikijo
House, the [UK] 231; London
Stock Exchange [UK] 243

**rondon kabushiki torihikijo
kai'in no hasan kokuchi**
hammering [UK] 230

**rondon kabushiki torihikijo no
tōsei kaijo**
Big Bang [UK] 200

rondon kin shijō
London Bullion Market 178;
London Gold Market 178

rondon kinzoku torihikijo
London Metal Exchange (LME)
242, 243

rondon no shitii (kin'yū machi)
City, the [UK] 16

rondon tegata kōkanjo
London Bankers' Clearing
House 151; London Clearing
151

rōnin
'a samurai without a master'
448

rōrei nenkin jukyūsha
old-age pensioner (OAP) [UK]
75, 76

rōrei nenkin kyūfukin
old-age benefits 76

rōreika suru rōdōryoku
aging workforce 5, 495

rōsai hoken
workers' accident insurance
331

rōshi
labour capital 60

rōshi
labour-management 459

rōshi kankei
industrial relations 53, 457;
labour-management relations
459

rōshi kankei kanri
industrial relations management 457

rōshi kyōgi
labour-management talk 459,
500

rōshi kyōgikai
work council(s) (employers and
employees) 120, 471

rōshi kyōgisei
labour-management conference
system 459

rōshi sōgi
industrial dispute(s) 52, 500

rōshi tōsō
industrial conflict(s) 52, 500

roshia
Russia 190

rōshikan no tōsō
conflict between labour and
management 499

rōshitairitsu
labour-management
confrontation 500

rōshutsu
leakage 492

rōso no orugu
organizer 501

rūburu
(roshia, sorenpō)
rouble (Russia, Union of Soviet
Socialist Republics [obsolete])
190, 191

ruigenzei
degressive tax 24

ruiseki
accumulation 193

ruiseki chochiku
accumulated savings 131

ruiseki haitō
accumulated dividend 367;
cumulative dividend 383

ruiseki haitō kabu
accumulative stock 193

ruiseki haitōkin
accumulated dividend 367

ruiseki rieki
accumulated income 193, 367

ruiseki rishi
accumulated interest 131, 193

ruiseki suru
accumulate 367

ruiseki tōhyō
cumulative voting 430

ruiseki tōshi
accumulative investment 193

ruiseki tōshi hōshiki
accumulation plan 193

ruiseki tōshi shintaku
accumulation trust 193

ruiseki yūsen kabu
cumulative preference shares
[UK] 214, 383; cumulative
preferred stock [US] 214, 383

ruisekiteki kashitsuke
cumulative lending 214

ruisekiteki keisan
cumulative accounting 383

ruisekiteki na
cumulative 214, 383

ruisekiteki son'eki keisansho
cumulative income statement
383; cumulative profit and loss
statement 383

ruisekiteki yūsen kabu
cumulative stock 384

ruishin kazei
progressive tax 87

ruishinzei
progressive tax 87

rukusenburugu
Luxembourg 190

rūmania
Romania 190

rupia (indonesia)
rupiah (Indonesia) 189

rupii
(indo, pakistan), seiron)
rupee (India, Pakistan, Sri
Lanka) 189, 190

ryō
dormitory 476

ryōdate
double option 219; spread
276; straddle 279

ryōgae
change (exchange) 167;
currency exchange 168;
exchange (= changing) 171

ryōgae suru
change (verb) 139, 167;
exchange (verb) 171

ryōgaeryō
charge for changing money
139, 167; exchange
commission 171

ryōgaeshō
money changer (exchange
bureau) 180

ryōgaeya
money changer (exchange
bureau) 180

ryōhi
dormitory fee deduction [J] 476

ryōkai
territorial waters 110

ryōkin
charge (rate) 139; fee 146

ryōkin chōsetsu
premium adjustment 327

ryokō(sha) kogitte
traveller's cheques 186

ryokōsha shōgai hoken
travel insurance 330

ryokōsha shōgai hoken shōken
travel insurance policy 330

ryokuchitai
green belt 296

ryōsan
volume production 117

ryōshitsu no
high-quality (staff) 457

ryōshitsu no rōdōryoku
high-quality labour 46

ryōshūsho
receipt (for expenses incurred)
414, 488

ryotei
itinerary 487

ryūdō fusai
current liabilities 384; floating
debt 40, 225; floating liabilities
392

ryūdō fusai hiritsu
current liabilities/net worth ratio
384

ryūdō hiritsu
current ratio 384; liquid ratio
399

ryūdō junbikin
liquid reserve 399

ryūdō kabu
floating shares 225; floating
stock 225

ryūdō kōsai
floating public bond 225;
unfunded public debt 284

ryūdō shihon
circulating capital 16, 378;
floating capital 392; liquid
capital 399; variable capital
117, 426

ryūdō shihonzai
liquid capital goods 63

ryūdō shikin
floating fund 392; liquid funds
399

ryūdō shisan
circulating assets 378; current
assets 384; floating assets
392; liquid assets 399; near
money 250

ryūdō shisan hiritsu
current assets/total deposits
ratio 384

ryūdō shisan kasetsu
liquid assets hypothesis 63

ryūdō shōken
floating securities 225; liquid
securities 241

ryūdōgyoku
floating supply 225

ryūdōsei
liquidity 63, 178, 399;
marketability 246

ryūdōsei aru jōtai
liquid position 399

ryūdōsei bēsu
liquidity basis 63, 399

ryūdōsei hiritsu
liquidity ratio 151, 178, 399

ryūdōsei jōtai
liquidity position 178, 399

ryūdōsei junbikin
liquid reserve 151

ryūdōsei kiki
liquidity crisis 399

ryūdōsei mondai
liquidity problems 399

ryūdōsei no aru
marketable 246

ryūdōsei seisaku
liquidity policy 178

ryūdōsei senkō
liquidity preference 63

ryūdōsei senkōsetsu
liquidity preference theory 63

ryūdosei torappu
liquidity trap 63

ryūdōsei yokin
liquid deposit 151

ryūdōseisetsu
liquidity theory 63

ryūgaku suru
study abroad 447

ryūgakutokō
trip for study abroad 447

ryūho
retentions 96, 415

ryūho rieki
accumulated earnings [US]
367; accumulated reserves
[UK] 367; retained earnings
96, 415; retained income 415;
retained profit 415; retained
surplus 415

ryūho riekikin
accumulated profits 367;
accumulation 367

ryūho shotokuzei
tax on undistributed profits 423

ryūhoritsu
retention ratio 96

ryūshutsu
spillover 102

ryūtsū
bank float 134; circulation 167

ryūtsū bumon
distribution sector 27

saikensha e no shiharai teishi
suspension of payments to creditors 437
saikensha no motochō
creditors' ledger 383
saikensha no sōkai
creditors' meeting 434
saikensha no taishite zengaku shiharau
pay one's creditors in full 436
saikingetsu
nearest month 250
saikō chin'age
maximum wage increase 480
saikō chingin
maximum wage 68, 479
saikō gendo
ceiling 15
saikō hakkō gendo
maximum amount of issue 247
saikō hoken kingaku
maximum amount of insurance 325
saikō kakaku
ceiling price 15
saikō kei'eisha
top executive 362, 469
saikō kei'eisō
top management 362, 469
saikō kinri
highest interest rate 231
saikō kiroku
all-time high 6, 195
saikō rishiritsu
highest interest rate 231
saikō shin'yō kakuzuke
highest credit rating 231
saikō shokuin
executive officer (highest-ranking) 345, 455
saikō shūgyō jikan
maximum number of hours 460
saikōki no rōdō juyō
peak period labour demand 79
saikoku
call (noun) 206
saikōsei
reorganization (reconstitution) 359
saikoyō
recall (noun) 501; rehiring 446, 466
saikoyō suru
recall (verb) 501; rehire (verb) 446, 466
saikunren
retraining 96, 466
saikunren suru
retrain 466
saimu
burden of debt 205; debt(s) 215, 434; debt burden 215; obligation (indebtedness) 252
hōritsujō kyōsei dekiru saimu
legally enforceable debts 436
saimu o manukareru
escape one's obligations 434
saimu bakudan
debt bomb 23, 215
saimu bensai
settlement of debt 272; settlement of obligation 272

saimu chōka
overindebtedness 256, 436
saimu furikō
default (noun) 216, 434
saimu furikō ni ochiiru
default (verb) 434
saimu hensai
debt retirement 216
saimu hensai hiritsu
debt service ratio 216
saimu hensai kurinobe
rescheduling 267
saimu hensai nōryoku
debt servicing capacity 216
saimu kiki
debt crisis 23, 215
saimu kanōsei
renewability (of resources) 94
saimu menjo
release from debt 437; waiver of obligation 285
saimu no kaijo
acquittance 194
saimu no kōkai
novation (replacement of old debt by new one) 252
saimu no rikō
performance of obligation 258
saimu no sokuji hensai jōkō
acceleration clause 193
saimu rikō
fulfilment of obligation 227
saimu ruiseki
debt accumulation 215
saimu seiri shōsho
deed of arrangement [UK] 216, 434
saimu shōkan
debt redemption 216
saimu shōken
debt securities 216; evidence of debt 220
saimu shōmetsu
expiration of obligation 221
saimu shōmetsushō
acquittance 194
saimu shōmetsu hasan
discharged bankruptcy 434
saimu shōsho
certificate of indebtedness 207; debt instrument 215
saimu suwappu
debt swap 216
saimu tanaage
consolidation of debt 210
saimu tenkan
debt conversion 215
saimu zandaka
outstanding obligation 255
saimu zengaku o hensai suru
clear all debts 434
saimukoku
debtor nation(s) 23, 216
saimusha
debtor 23, 434
sainō
ability (gift, talent) 449
sainyū
annual revenue 7; revenue (government revenue) 96
sainyū kekkan
revenue shortfall 96
sairiyō
recycling (waste) 93

sairiyō suru
recycle (waste) 92
sairyō
discretion 319
sairyō no chiriteki jōken
prime geographical position 84
saisan kabu
income share 232; income stock 232
saisan ni wataru keihō
repeated warnings 502
saisan suijun
break-even level of income 12
saisei
recycling (waste) 93
saisei kanōsei
renewability (of resources) 94
saisei kōgyō
recycling industry 126
saisei riyō suru
recycle (waste) 92
saisei shigen
renewable resources 94
saisekigyō
quarrying industry 126
saishinri
review 437
saishinri o motomeru
petition for review (verb) 436
saishō hiyō seisan hōshiki
least-cost method of production 62
saishō kiken
minimum risk 247
saishō kiken pōtoforio
minimum-risk portfolio 247
saishō nijō
least squares 62
saishō nijōhō
least squares method 62
saishō songai yakkan
minimum loss clause 325
saishoku nōgyō
plantation farming 125
saishū haitō
final dividend 390
saishū juyō
final demand 38
saishū kakaku
final price 295
saishū kariiresha
end borrower 220
saishū kyōkyū
final supply 38
saishū no chōsei
final adjustments 390
saishū no kashite
lender of last resort 62, 240
saishū no manki hensaigaku
balloon 198
saishū nōkai
last trading day 240
saishū rimawari
yield to maturity 286
saishū seihin
final goods 38; final products 38
saishū seisanbutsu
final products 38
saishū seizonsha
last survivor 324

saishū seizonsha hoken
last survivor insurance 324
saishū seizonsha nenkin
last survivor annuity 324
saishū shisanhyō
final trial balance 390
saishū shōhi
final consumption 38
saishū shōhisha
final consumer 38
saishū uragakinin
last endorser 150
saishutoku
replacement 328; repurchase 266
saishutoku hoken
replacement insurance 328
saishutoku kabu
re-acquired shares 414; repurchased stock 267
saishutoku kachi
replacement value 328
saishutoku kakaku
replacement price 94; repurchase price 266
saishutoku suru
repurchase (verb) 266
saishutsu
annual expenditure 7; expenditure (in Treasury's accounts) 35
saitanpo settei
rehypothecation [US] 265
saitei chingin
minimum wage 68, 480
saitei chinginhō
minimum wage legislation 69
saitei chinginritsu
minimum wage rate 480
saitei hakkō kakaku
ground-floor price 229
saitei hika
parity rate 182
saitei hokenryō
minimum premium 325
saitei hoshō chingin
guaranteed minimum wage 478
saitei hoshō chinginritsu
minimum guaranteed rate 480
saitei junbi
minimum reserve 179
saitei junbiritsu
minimum reserve ratio 179
saitei kashidashi buai
minimum lending rate (MLR) 68, 69, 247
saitei kashidashi kinri
minimum lending rate (MLR) 247
saitei kawase
arbitrated exchange 165
saitei kawase sōba
arbitrated exchange rate 165; lowest exchange rate 178
saitei kinri
arbitrated interest rate 196; lowest interest rate 244
saitei kiroku
all-time low 6, 195
saitei rishiritsu
lowest interest rate 244; minimum rate of interest 247

sangyō kūdōka
  deindustrialization 24
sangyō kumiai
  industrial associations 52;
  industrial union 457
sangyō kunren
  industrial training 457
sangyō kyōkō
  industrial crisis (any industry)
  52
sangyō minshu shugi
  industrial democracy 52
sangyō no chi'ikiteki shūchū
  localization of industry 64
sangyō no hi'idōsei
  industrial inertia 52
sangyō ritchi
  location of industry 64
sangyō rōdōsha
  industrial worker(s) 53, 457
sangyō saihensei
  industrial reorganization 53
sangyō setsubi
  industrial facilities 52
sangyō shakai
  industrial society 53
sangyō shihon
  industrial capital 52
sangyō shikin
  industrial funds 52
sangyō shūchū
  industrial concentration 52
sangyō soshiki
  industrial organization 53
sangyō supai
  industrial spy 53
sangyō tenkan
  industrial conversion 52
sangyō tōshi
  industrial investment 52, 233
sangyō toshi chi'iki
  industrialized urban area 298
sangyō tōshika
  Investors in Industry [UK] 58
sangyō yūshi
  industrial credit 52
sangyōbetsu dankō
  industry-wide bargaining 53,
  479, 500
sangyōbetsu rōdō kumiai
  industrial unions 53
sangyōka
  industrialization 53
sangyōkai
  industrial world 53
sangyōkyōtsū mondai
  industry-wide issues 53, 500
sangyōnai bungyō
  intra-industry division of labour
  57
sangyōnin
  industrialists 53
sangyōshubetsu bunrui
  industrial classification 52
sangyōteki kiken
  industrial hazard 492
sangyōyōchi
  industrial site 53
sanjutsu heikin
  arithmetic mean 7
sanka
  participation 257, 408

sanka gaisha
  participating companies 326
sanka haitō
  participating dividend 408
sanka hikiuke
  acceptance for honour 131
sanka kashitsuke
  participation loan 257
sanka shōsho
  participation certificate 257,
  408
sankaku bōeki
  triangular trade 113
sankyū
  maternity leave 479
sannyū shōheki
  barriers to entry 10
sanpin
  product 86
sanpuringu
  sampling 97
sansei hiritsu
  acid ratio 367
sansei shiken hiritsu
  acid-test ratio 367
sansei tōhyō
  assenting vote 429
sanshutsu
  output (yield) 77; production
  (yield) 86
sanshutsukoku
  producing countries 85
sanshutsuryō
  output (volume of output) 77;
  production amount 86
sanshutsuryō no kyokudaika
  output maximization 77
santei kakaku
  estimated value 294
san'yukoku
  oil-producing countries 76
san'yukoku karuteru
  oil-producing cartel 76
sarachi
  vacant lot 311
sararii
  salary 483
sarariiman
  salary man 483
sasen
  demotion 452, 472 (note 29)
sashidashinin
  sender 160
sashine
  bid (bid price) 200; limit 241;
  limit price 241
sashine chūmon
  limit order 241; stop-limit order
  278
sashine chūmon jōhō shisutemu
  limit order information system
  241
sashine de uru
  sell at a limit 271
sashine mata wa sore yori yoi kakaku de
  at or better 197
sashine santeihō
  limit calculation 241
sashiosae
  arrestment [UK] 196;
  attachment 197, 433

sashiosae meirei
  attachment order 197
sashiosae no shinsei (ni taisuru)
  application for an attachment
  (against) 433
sashizu kinshi tegata
  non-order bill 153
sashizuninbarai
  payable to order 155
sashizuninbarai kogitte
  cheque to order 139; order
  cheque 154
sashizuninbarai saiken
  bond payable to order 202
sashizuninbarai tegata
  bill payable to order 137; bill to
  order 137
sashizushiki kogitte
  cheque to order 139
sashizushiki tegata
  order bill 154
sashizushiki yakusoku tegata
  note to order 252
sasoimizu seisaku
  pump-priming 90
satei
  assessment (investigation) 316
satei kagaku
  assessed value 316
saujiarabia
  Saudi Arabia 190
sayatori
  arbitrage 196
sayatori baibai
  arbitrage 196
sayatori nakadachinin
  arbitrage broker 196;
  arbitrageur 196
sayatori shōnin
  arbitrageur 196
sayatori suji
  arbitrageur 196
sayatori torihiki
  arbitrage business 196;
  arbitrage operation 196;
  arbitrage transaction 196
sayatoriya
  arbitrage house 196
SEC ni taisuru shōken hakkō no ikkatsu tōroku [US]
  shelf registration [US] 273
sehyō
  reputation 267
sei o riyū to shita chingin sabetsu
  wage discrimination on the
  basis of sex 486
seibō
  reputation (good) 359
seibun keiyaku
  written contract 312
seichō
  growth 45, 394
seichō bumon
  growth sector 45
seichō dankai
  stages of growth 103
seichō kabu
  growth stock 229
seichō kakusa shitsugyō
  growth-gap unemployment 45
seichō keizai
  growing economy 45

seichō kyokusen
  growth curve 45
seichō meate no tōshi shintaku
  growth fund 229
seichō no fukeizai
  diseconomies of growth 27
seichō no keizaigaku
  economies of growth 31
seichō riron
  growth theory 45
seichō rosen
  growth path 45
seichō sangyō
  growing industry 45; growth
  industry 45
seichō senzairyoku
  growth potential 45
seichō shisū
  growth index 45
seichō-shūekisei kansū
  growth-profitability function 45
seichō yokuseizai
  growth retardant 45
seichō yosan
  growth budget 45
seichō yosoku
  growth forecast 45; growth
  forecasting 394
seichōki
  growth phase 45
seichōritsu
  growth rate 45
seidoha keizaigaku
  institutional economics 55
seiengyō
  salt industry 126
seifu akaji
  government deficit 43
seifu bōeki
  government trade 44
seifu bumon
  government sector 44
seifu burōkā
  government broker 229
seifu chochiku
  government savings 44
seifu chōtatsu
  government procurement 44
seifu dokusen
  government monopoly 44
seifu hojokin
  government grants 44;
  government subsidies 44
seifu hoshō
  government guarantee 148
seifu hoshōsai
  government-guaranteed bond
  229
seifu juyō
  government demand 43
seifu kaikei
  government accounts 43
seifu kainyū
  state intervention 104
seifu kariire
  government borrowing 43, 229
seifu kashidashi
  government lending 44, 229
seifu kashitsukekin
  loan to government 243

seimitsu kansa
  detailed audit 386
seimitsu kōgyō
  precision-instrument industry
  126
seiō keizai
  Western economies 120
seirengyō
  refining industry 126; smelting
  industry 126
seiri
  adjustment (re-adjustment)
  368; consolidation 380;
  liquidation 436
seiri kikin
  consolidation fund 380
seiri kinyū
  adjusting entry 368
seiri kōsai
  consolidated bond (public) 210
seiri kōsai kikin
  consolidated fund [UK] 18
seiri kōsei
  reorganization (of the company)
  359
seiri kyūka
  menstrual leave [J] 480
seiri shasai
  adjustment bond 194;
  consolidated bond (corporate)
  210
seiri suru
  adjust (re-adjust) 368
seiri tetsuzuki
  liquidation procedure 436
seiri tōgō
  reorganization and
  consolidation 359
seirigo shikisanhyō
  adjusted trial balance 368
seiron
  Sri Lanka 190
seisabetsu
  discrimination on the basis of
  sex 442, 453; sex discrimination 467
seisai
  sanctions 97
seisaku
  policy 80
seisaku kankoku
  policy recommendation 81
seisaku kanwa
  policy relaxation 81
seisaku kettei
  policy-making 81
seisaku kettei kikan
  policy-making body 81
seisaku ketteisha
  policy makers 80
seisaku mokuhyō
  policy targets 81
seisaku mokuteki
  policy objective 81
seisaku no kanri
  policy administration 80
seisaku no ragu
  administrative lag (policy) 4,
  policy lag 80
seisaku no suikō
  policy implementation 80
seisaku shihyō
  policy indicator 80

seisaku shudan
  policy instruments 80
seisaku sochi
  policy measures 81
seisaku taido
  policy stance 81
seisaku un'ei
  policy operation 81
seisaku yūsen jun'i
  policy priority 81
seisakuhi
  output cost 407
seisakujō no iken no sōi
  disagreement on policy 26
seisakujō no ragu
  implementation lage 49
seisan
  adjustment 368; liquidation
  399, 436; settlement (closing of
  contract) 272
  seisan ni hairu
    go into liquidation 435
  seisan sarete nai
    unliquidated 426
seisan
  production 86
seisan chōsei
  production adjustment 86
seisan furontia
  production frontier 86
seisan gaisha
  company in liquidation 434;
  liquidated company 436
seisan gijutsu
  production technology 86
seisan gōrika
  rationalization of production 91
seisan gyappu
  production gap 86
seisan jōyokin
  surplus at liquidation 422
seisan kachi
  break-up value 374; liquidation
  value 399
seisan kagaku
  break-up value 374
seisan kakaku
  make-up price 244
seisan kanjō
  liquidation accounts 399
seisan kanōsei
  productive potential 86
seisan kanōsei kyokusen
  production possibility curve 86
seisan kanribu
  production control department
  464
seisan kansetsuhi
  burden [UK] 374; production
  overhead cost [US] 411
seisan kansū
  product function 86; production
  function 86
seisan katsudō
  production activity 86
seisan keikaku
  production plan 86
seisan keisū
  coefficients of production 16
seisan kokumin shotoku
  national income produced 72

seisan kōritsu
  productive efficiency 86
seisan kōtei
  process (production process)
  85; production process 86
**seisan kōtei de no gijutsu
kakushin**
  process innovation 85
seisan kotei hiritsu
  fixed proportions in production
  40
seisan no genshō
  decline in production 23;
  reduction in production 93
seisan no riron
  theory of production 110
seisan nōryoku
  production capacity 86
seisan nōryoku riyōritsu
  capacity utilization rate
  (production) 14
seisan nōryoku shisū
  production capacity index 86
seisan rōdōsha
  production workers 86
seisan seigen
  production restraint 86
seisan setsubi
  production facilities 86
seisan shain
  liquidated partnership 436
seisan shigen
  productive resources 87
seisan shihon
  productive capital 86, 261
seisan shisan
  active assets 367
seisan shisū
  production index 86
seisan shotoku
  income at liquidation 395;
  liquidation income 399
seisan shotokuzei
  liquidation tax 399
seisan sokutei
  productivity measurement 87
seisan son'eki keisansho
  liquidation profit and loss
  statement 399
seisan suru
  adjust 368; liquidate 399
  tegata o seisan suru
    clear a bill 140
seisan taishaku taishōhyō
  liquidation balance sheet 399
seisan tetsuzuki
  liquidation procedure 399
seisan wariate
  production quota 86
seisan yōshiki
  mode of production 69
seisan yōso
  factors of production 37
seisanbi
  settlement day 272
seisanbusoku
  underproduction 114
seisanbutsu
  product (general) 86
seisanbutsu no kakushin
  product innovation 86

seisanbutsu no zōshoku
  product proliferation 86
seisanbutsu sabetsuka
  product differentiation 86;
  production differentiation 86
seisandaka
  output 77, 463; production
  yield 86; yield 121
seisandaka yosan seido
  output budgeting 77
seisanhi
  cost of production 383;
  production cost(s) 86
seisanhi no hōsoku
  law of cost 61
seisanhi zenzō no hōsoku
  law of increasing costs 62
seisanhyō
  work sheet (accounting) 427
seisankoku
  producing countries 85
seisannin
  liquidator 399, 436
seisanritsu
  production rate 86
seisanryō no ragu
  output lag 77
seisanryoku
  productive power 86
seisanryoku kōka
  productivity effect 87
seisansei
  productivity 87, 465
seisansei jōkō
  productivity clause 465
seisansei kansū
  productivity function 87
seisansei kōjō undō
  productivity drive 87, 465
seisansei kyokusen
  productivity curve 87
seisansei kyōyaku
  productivity deal 87, 465
seisansei shisū
  productivity index 87
seisansei shitsugyō
  productivity unemployment 87
seisansha
  producers 85
seisansha bukka
  producers' prices 85
seisansha bukka shisū
  producers' price index 85
seisansha keikaku
  producers' planning 85
seisansha kumiai
  producers' associations 85
seisansha kyōdō kumiai
  producers' co-operatives 85
seisansha shukka
  producers' shipments 85
seisansha yojō
  producer's surplus 85
seisanteki jigyō
  productive business 357
seisanteki jūgyōin
  productive employee 465
seisanteki na
  productive 465
seisanteki rōdōryoku
  productive labour 86, 465

senkoku
  adjudication 433
senkyo
  election 430
senkyo kensanin
  election inspectors 430
senkyo tantōkan
  election officers 430
senmon
  speciality [UK] 446, 468;
  specialty [US] 446, 468
senmon gakkō
  professional school 445;
  specialized school 446
senmon gijutsu
  professional skills 445; special
  skill(s) 446
senmon kei'eisha
  expert manager 346
senmon kyōiku
  professional education
  (specialist) 445; specialized
  education 446
senmon nōryoku
  special ability 446
senmon shokugyō kyōiku
  professional training
  (specialized education) 445
**senmon shokugyō sekinin
hoken**
  professional liability insurance
  328
**senmon shokugyō sekinin
hoken shōken**
  professional liability insurance
  policy 328
senmon yōhin
  special goods 102
senmonhin
  speciality goods [UK] 102;
  specialty goods [US] 102
senmonka
  specialization (persons) 102,
  468
senmonka
  specialist 468
senmonka shokuin
  professional employee 465
senmonshoku
  professional job 465;
  professions, the 87
senmonshoku sekinin hoken
  malpractice insurance 325
senmonteki kunren
  professional training
  (specialized training) 445
senmu torishimariyaku
  executive director 455;
  executive managing director
  455; managing director [J]
  352, 460; senior executive
  director 360, 467; senior
  managing director 360, 467
senninjun
  seniority (ranking) 467
senninken
  seniority (right) 467
senpai
  senior 467
senryaku
  strategy 105
senryaku busshi
  strategic goods 105

senryaku sangyō
  strategic industries 105
senryakuteki tōshi
  strategic investment 279
sensasu
  census 15
sensei yakkan
  attestation clause 316
senshin jūkakoku
  Group of Ten 45
senshin kōgyōkoku
  leading industrial countries 62
senshinkoku
  advanced countries 4;
  developed countries 26
sensō baishō
  war reparations 119
sensō hoken
  war risks insurance 331
sensō keizai
  war economy 119
sensō kiken
  war risk 331
sentaku
  preference (choice, selection)
  82
sentaku baibai kenri kōshi
  exercise 221
sentaku baibaiken
  option (right to buy or sell) 255
sentaku haitō
  optional dividend 406
sentaku hensū
  choice variable 16
sentaku koyō
  selective employment 466
sentakuken
  option (right to buy or sell) 255
sentakuken no kakaku
  option premium price 255
sentakukentsuki torihiki kikan
  option period 255
sentakuteki shin'yō kisei
  selective credit control 270
sentakuteki shōhi
  optional consumption 77
sentakuteki tōshi
  discretionary investment 218
sentan gijutsu
  advanced technologies 4
sen'yō jūtaku chi'iki
  exclusive residential area 294
sen'yū
  occupancy (exclusive
  possession) 303; possession
  304
sen'yū suru
  occupy (have exclusive
  possession) 303
sen'yūken
  possession right 304
sen'yūsha
  occupant 303; occupier
  (resident with exclusive
  possession right) 303
senzai chingin
  shadow wage 99
senzai chinginritsu
  shadow wage rate 99
senzai(teki) infurēshon
  latent inflation 61; potential
  inflation 82

senzai juyō
  latent demand 61
senzai kakaku
  shadow price 99
senzai kyōkyū
  latent supply 61
senzai shitsugyō
  latent unemployment 61
senzairyoku
  potential (noun) 82
senzaiteki kabushiki
  residual securities 267
senzaiteki kainushi
  potential buyer 304
senzaiteki kokumin shotoku
  potential national income 82
senzaiteki seisanryō
  potential output 82
senzaiteki shitsugyō
  potential unemployment 82
senzaiteki urite
  potential seller 304
seringu-pointo
  selling point 308
seriuri
  auction 290
seriuri gaisha
  auction company 290
seriurikai
  buying in and selling out 205
seron chōsa
  public opinion poll 89
sērusuman
  salesman 466
seshū zaisan
  hereditary property 296;
  patrimony 303
sesshoku
  contact (rapport) 452
setai
  households 47
setchi suru
  establish 345; found (create,
  institute) 347
setsubi
  facilities 295; plant and
  equipment 80, 410; utilities
  311
setsubi kadōritsu
  capacity utilization rate (equipment) 14; operating rate 76
setsubi kanri
  plant management 356
**setsubi kindaika shikin
kashitsuke**
  equipment modernization loan
  220
setsubi shikin
  equipment fund 389
setsubi tōshi
  equipment investment 389;
  investment in plant and
  equipment 57, 397; plant and
  equipment investment 410
setsubi yosan
  plant and equipment budget
  410
setsubihi
  cost of equipment 383
setsugen
  cutbacks 384; reduction 93
setsumei hensū
  explanatory variable 36

setsumeikai
  'explanatory meeting' [J] 442,
  448 (note 24)
setsuretsu na kei'ei
  incompetent management 348
setsuritsu
  establishment (of a company)
  345; founding 347
saikin setsuritsu no
  recently established 348
setsuritsu nengappi
  date of establishment 343
setsuritsu shōkyakuhi
  organization expenses
  amortized 406
setsuritsu shōsho
  incorporation certificate 348
setsuritsu shuisho
  prospectus 261, 357
setsuritsu suru
  establish (form, set up) 345;
  found 347; incorporate 348
setsuritsu sareta
  established 345
setsuritsu tetsuzuki
  organization process 355
setsuritsu tōki
  registration of incorporation
  359
setsuritsuhō
  act of incorporation 335
setsuritsusha
  founder 347
setsuyaku
  conservation (saving,
  economizing) 18; frugality 42
setsuyaku no gyakusetsu
  paradox of thrift 78
setsuyaku suru
  conserve 18
settai
  entertainment 487
settaihi
  entertainment expenses 389,
  487
settaihi kanjō
  entertainment expense
  account 389, 487; expense
  account 390
shachō
  managing director [UK] 352,
  460; President [US] 357, 464
shachō dairi
  acting president 335, 449
shachō no jinin
  resignation of Chairman 359
shadan
  association 337
shadan hōjin
  corporate juridical person 342;
  corporation aggregate 343;
  incorporated association 348
shafū
  office code of conduct 462;
  office customs 462
shagai jūyaku
  dummy director 345; outside
  director 355
shagai kabushiki
  outstanding shares 407;
  outstanding stock 407
shahi
  corporate expenses 381

shasai shijō
bond market (corporate) 202

shasai shōka
absorption of corporate bonds 193

shasai shōkan
debenture redemption 215; redemption of debenture 264

shasai shōkan'eki
profit from redemption of debentures 261

shasai tanpo kashitsuke
loan secured by corporate debentures 242

shasaiken
bond certificate 201; debenture bond 215; debenture stock [UK] 215, 385; debenture stock certificate 385

shasaiken hoyūdaka
debenture holdings 215

shasaiken jōto
bond transfer 202; debenture transfer 215

shasaiken shintaku
debenture trust 215

shasaiken shojinin
debenture holder 215

shasaikensha
bond holder (corporate bond) 201; debenture holder 215

shasaiyō gensai kikin
bond sinking fund 202

shashi
luxury 65

shashihin
luxury goods 65

shashizei
luxury taxes 65

shasoku
by-laws 340; company regulations 341

shataku
company housing 476; family housing [J] 477

shataku no yachin
housing rental fee deduction [J] 478

shayō kōsai
business entertaining 487

shayō kōsaihi kanjō
expense account 487

shayō no futsū yokin
corporate account 141

shayō sangyō
declining industries 23; dying industries 28

shayō settai
business entertaining 487

shayōzoku
'the expense-account tribe' 489

shekeru (izuraeru)
shekel (Israel) 189

shibo
private offering [UK] 260, 411; private placement [US] 261, 411; private placing [UK] 261, 411

shibō hokenkin
death benefits 319

shibō hokenkin seikyū
death claim 319

shibō hoshō(kin)
compensation for death 318, 491

shibō kyūfu
death benefits 319

shibō shōmei
proof of death 328

shibōritsu
death rate 23; mortality 325; mortality rate 71

shibōsha
applicant (aspirant) 441

shibu
branch office (vs. head-office) 337

shichiire
pawning 257; pledging 259

shichiire shisan
pledged assets 259

shichiire yūka shōken
pledged securities 259

shichiken
pawning ticket 257

shichimono
pawned article 257

shichioki
pawning 257

shichiya
pawnbroker [UK] 257; pawnshop [UK] 257

shichōsonzei
municipal tax (cities, towns, villages) [J] 71, 302

shichū
open market (finance) 254

shichū ginkō
city bank [J] 139

shichū kinri
market interest rates 246; money rate 248; open-market rates (interest rates) 254

shichū sōba
open-market quotation 254

shichū waribiki buai
open-market discount rate 254

shidō
supervision (guidance) 468

shidō kijun
guidelines 45, 230

shidōin
supervisor (instructor, adviser) 468

shidōsha
leaders 62

shiei hoken
private business insurance 327

shien
backing (support) 198; sponsorship(s) 102, 276, 419

shien suru
back (verb) (support) 198

shiensha
backer (supporter) 198; sponsor 276

shifuto
shift 100

shigaichi
urban land 311

shigaichi chikaku
urban land value 311

shigaichi kakaku
city land price 292

shigaisha
private company (-ies) (= limited) [UK] 85, 357

shigeki
impetus 48; stimulus 104

shigekisaku
stimulatory measures 104

shigen
resources 95

shigen fusoku
scarcity of resources 98

shigen haibun
allocation of resources 6; resource allocation 95

shigen no kokatsu
exhaustion of resources 35

shigen saihaibun
re-allocation of resources 92

shigen setsuyaku
conservation of resources 18; resource-saving 95

shigen setsuyakuteki gijutsu
resource-saving technology 95

shigen shūyakuteki gijutsu
resource-intensive technology 95

shigen shūyakuteki sangyō
resource-intensive industries 95

shigen tekisei haibun
optimal resource allocation 77

shigoto
job(s) 59, 443, 458; task 469; work (job of work) 120, 471

atarashii shigoto o hajimeru
start a new job 468

kimari shita shigoto
routine work 466

shigoto antei
job security 458

shigoto anteisei
job stability 59, 458

shigoto kyōsōron
job competition theory 58

shigoto nakama
colleague 452; fellow worker 455

shigoto ni taisuru no fumanzokukan
job dissatisfaction 458

shigoto ni taisuru no manzokukan
job satisfaction 458

shigoto no aki
job opening [less formal] 444

shigoto no aki o umeru
fill a vacancy 442

shigoto no kankyō
working environment [less formal] 472

shigoto no katagaki
job title 458

shigoto no naiyō
job content [less formal] 458; job description [less formal] 443, 458

shigoto no suikō
performance of duties 463

shigoto no yarikata
work habits 471

shigoto-yoka moderu
work-leisure model 120

shigotoba
workplace (office, working place) 472; workshop 472

shigotobetsu chingin
wage-by-job 118, 485

shigotoreki
work experience 447

shigotoryō
work load 471; work volume 471

shihai
administration (rule) 335; control (domination) 342

shihai gaisha
controlling company 342

shihaiken
corporate control 342

shihainin
manager 460

shihaiteki riken
controlling interests 342

shihanki
quarter 90, 413

shihanki ginkō kanjō hōkokusho
quarterly statement of account 157

shihanki heikin
quarterly average 90

shihanki rishi
quarterly interest 157

shihanki seichōritsu
quarterly rate of growth 90

shiharai
disbursement 217; payment 155, 258, 409, 436; settlement 417

shiharai o teishi suru
suspend payment 437

shiharai dairinin
paying agent 258

shiharai denpyō
debit slip 142; voucher 426

shiharai enki
deferment of payment 216

shiharai funō
insolvency (inability to pay) 55, 435

shiharai funō gaisha
insolvent corporation 435

shiharai funō hanketsu
decree of insolvency 434

shiharai funō hasan
insolvent winding-up 435

shiharai funō kōi
act of insolvency 433

shiharai funō no
insolvent (adjective) 435

shiharai gaikoku kawase
foreign bills payable 147

shiharai gimu ga aru
owe money 256

shiharai ginkō
paying bank 155

shiharai hoshō
certification of payment 139

shiharai hoshō ginkō
certifying bank 139

shiharai hoshō kogitte
certified cheque 139

shiharai iyoku
willingness to pay 120

shihon-riekiritsu
capital/profit ratio 15;
net profits/capital ratio 403;
profit/capital ratio 411

shihon rijun
capital gain (capital profit) 376;
capital profit 376

shihon rishi
capital interest 207

shihon ritoku
capital gain(s) 14, 206, 376

shihon ritokuzei
capital gains tax 376

shihon-rōdō hiritsu
capital/labour ratio 14

shihon-rōdō no daitai
capital-labour substitution 14

shihon ryūnyū
capital inflow 14, 376; influx of
capital 395

shihon ryūshutsu
capital outflow 14, 376

shihon saikōsei
recapitalization 414

shihon sanka
capital participation 376;
equity participation 389

shihon-sanshutsudaka hiritsu
capital/output ratio 14

shihon seigen
capital rationing (limits) 15, 376

shihon seisansei
capital productivity 207;
productivity of capital 87, 261

shihon setsubi
capital equipment 14

shihon shijō
capital market 14, 207

shihon shisan
capital assets [UK] 375

shihon shishutsu
capital expenditure 14, 375;
capital outlay 376; capital
spending 376

shihon shishutsu satei
capital expenditure appraisal
376

shihon shishutsu yosan
capital budget 14; capital
expenditure budget 376

shihon shobun
capital appropriation 375

shihon shobun kanjō
capital appropriation account
375

shihon shōhi
capital consumption 14

shihon shōkan
capital redemption 207, 376

shihon shōkan tsumitatekin
capital redemption reserve fund
376

shihon shōmō
capital consumption 375

shihon shōmō hikiate
capital consumption allowance
375

shihon shotoku
capital income 207; income
from capital 50, 232

shihon-shotoku hiritsu
capital/income ratio 14

shihon shūchū
centralization of capital 207

shihon shūeki
return on capital 267; return on
capital employed 96

shihon shugi
capitalism 15

shihon shugi keizai
capitalist economy 15

shihon shugi shakai
capitalist society 15

shihon shugi taisei
capitalist system 15

shihon shugisha
capitalist 15

shihon shugishakoku
capitalist country 15

shihon shukanjō
shareholder's equity (on
balance sheet) 418

shihon shūsei
capital adjustment 375

shihon shussho
source of capital 419

shihon shūyakudo
capital intensity 14

shihon shūyakuteki bumon
capital-intensive sector 14

shihon shūyakuteki gijutsu
capital-intensive techniques 14

shihon shūyakuteki keizai
capital-intensive economy 14

shihon shūyakuteki na
capital-intensive 14

shihon shūyakuteki sangyō
capital-intensive industries 14

shihon shūyakuteki tōshi
capital-intensive investment
14, 207

shihon sōbiritsu
capital/equipment ratio 14

shihon sonshitsu
capital loss 14, 207, 376;
loss of capital 400

shihon sutokku
capital stock 15

shihon sutokku chōsei genri
capital stock adjustment
principle 15

shihon teikei
capital tie-up 207

shihon tōhi
capital flight 14

shihon torihiki
capital transaction 207

shihon torihiki no jiyūka
liberalization of capital
transactions 241

shihon tōshi
capital investment 207

shihon wariate
capital rationing (allocation) 15

shihon yosan
capital budget 375

shihon yunyū
capital import 14

shihon yunyūkoku
capital-importing country 14

shihon yushutsu
capital export 14, 206

shihon yushutsukoku
capital-exporting country 14

shihon zōka
capital appreciation 375

shihongaku
amount of capital 369; capital
employed 375

shihonhi(yō)
capital cost 14

shihonka
capitalization 377

shihonka suru
capitalize 377

shihonkin
capital 206, 375; capital fund
376; common stock [US] (on
balance sheet) 379

shihonkin genzaidaka
capital stock outstanding 376

shihonkin gōkei
total capital 424

shihonkin kumiire hakkō
bonus issue 373; capitalization
issue 377

shihonkingaku
amount of capital 369

shihonzai
capital goods 14

shihonzai no genshō
disinvestment 27

shihonzai sangyō
capital-goods industry 123

shihonzei
capital tax 207

shihyō
indicator 51, 233

shihyō meigara
barometer securities 199;
barometer stock 199;
bellwether bond 200;
bellwether issue 200;
benchmark issue 200

shiire
purchase (laying-in of stock)
413

shiire genka
cost of purchase 383;
purchase cost 413

shiire hiyō
purchasing expenses 413

shiire kanjō
purchase account 413

shiire motochō
bought ledger 373; purchase
ledger 413

shiire okurijō
purchase invoice 413

shiire shiwakechō
purchase journal 413

shiire waribiki
purchase discounts 413

shiire yosan
purchase budget 413

shiirechō
bought day book 373;
purchase book 413;
purchase journal 413

shiji
support (maintenance) 280;
support (of currency) 106, 185

shiji kakaku
supported price 106

shiji suijun
support level 280

shiji suru
support (verb) 185

shijiteki keikaku
indicative planning 51

shijiten
support point 185

shijō
market (market place,
exchange) 67, 245

shijō o ushinau koto
missing the market 247

shijō akusesu
market access 67

shijō anteisei
market stability 246

shijō bunrui
market classification 67

shijō bunseki
market analysis 67, 245

shijō chōsaka
market researcher 67

shijō dōkō
market trend 246

shijō dōkō bunseki senmonka
market analyst 245

shijō fukanzen
market imperfection 67

**shijō genzai kakaku kehai no
shiji**
indication 233

shijō hiyō
cost of marketing 383

shijō hyōka
market appraisal 245

shijō jōhō
market data 245; market
information 246

shijō jōhō shisutemu
market data system 245

shijō juyō kyokusen
market demand curve 67

shijō kachi
market value 246

shijō kakaku
market price 246; quoted
market value 262

shijō kakaku o shiraberu koto
checking the market 208

shijō kakaku hendō risuku
market risk 246; systematic
risk 280

shijō keiyu kabushiki
stock purchased on the market
278

shijō keizai
market economy 67

shijō kinri
market rate (interest) 246;
money market rate 248

shijō kinri rendōgata futsū yokin
money market deposit account
[US] 152

**shijō kinri rendōgata tōshi
shintaku**
money market fund [US] 248

shijō kōdō
market behaviour 245

shijō konran
market disruption 245

shijō kōzō
market structure 67

shijō kyōkyū
market supply 67

shijō mekanizumu
    market mechanism 67
shijō mitōshi
    market forecast 67, 246
shijō musabetsu no hōsoku
    law of indifference 62
shijō naibu yōin
    technical factor 281
shijō naibu yōin bunseki
    technical analysis 281
shijō ninki
    market tone (sentiment, psychology) 246
shijō no heisa
    close of the market 208
shijō no rakuchō
    declining market 216
shijō no shippai
    market failure 67
shijō no shudō kabu
    market leader 246
shijō no teisei
    correction 211
shijō rimawari
    market yield 246
shijō rishiritsu
    market rate (interest) 246
shijō saikō
    market all-time high 245
shijō sannyū no jiyū
    freedom of entry 42
shijō shakai shugi
    market socialism 67
shijō shikō
    market orientation 67
shijō shisū
    market index 67, 246
shijō sōba
    market quotation 246; market rate (interbank rate) 246
shijō sōsa
    market operation 246
shijō suitai
    market decline 245
shijō waribiki buai
    market discount rate (bills) 245; market rate (bills) 246
shijō yobine
    market quotation 246
shijō yōin
    market forces 67, 245
shijō yōin bunseki
    market research 246
shijōryoku
    market power 67
shijōsei
    marketability 246
shijōsei no aru
    marketable 246
shijōsei no nai shōken
    non-marketable securities 252
shijōsei shōken
    marketable issue 246; marketable securities 246
shijūteki kōsai
    deadweight debt 214
shika
    market price(s) 67, 246
shika hendō
    market fluctuation 245; market price fluctuations 67

shika no ashidori
    movement (of market prices) 249
shika no kugizuke
    pegging of prices 258
shika shōkan
    redemption at market value 264
shikai suru (kaigi o)
    chair (a meeting) 429
shikakarihin
    work in progress 120
shikake
    appliances (gadgets) 289
shikakehin
    work in progress [UK] 427
shikaku
    qualifications 446
    shikaku no aru
    qualified (who meets requirements) 446
shikaku kabu
    qualification shares 413
shikaku no aru kōshi
    qualified instructor 465
shikaku no nai ininjō
    unqualified proxy 432
shiken
    test (noun) 447
shiken shin'yō
    paper credit 257
shiken suru
    test (verb) 447
shiki
    morale 461
shiki chōsa
    morale survey 461
shiki shiharaibi
    quarter days 157
shikichi
    site 309, 361
shikichi kagaku
    site value 309
shikichi kaihatsu
    estate development 294
shikigyō
    private enterprise 85
shikigyō seido
    private enterprise system 85
shikikin
    deposit 293; key money [US] 298
shikin
    fund(s) (capital) 42, 147, 227, 393; money 151, 247
    shikin o chōtatsu suru
    raise funds 263, 413
shikin bunsekihyō
    assay mark 165
shikin chōtatsu
    capital-raising 207, 376; financing (= procurement) 391; funding 42, 228; fund-raising 227
shikin enjo
    backing (financial help) 198; financial backing 222
shikin fūsa
    blockage of funds 137

shikin fusoku
    financial deficit 391; fund shortage 42; lack of capital 398; shortage of funds 418
    shikin fusoku o kitasu
    short of capital (to be) 418
shikin hōshutsu
    release of funds 415
shikin idō
    transfer of funds 162
shikin jijō
    financial standing (funds situation) 223, 391
shikin junkan
    flow of funds 40; money flow 70
shikin junkan bunseki
    flow of funds analysis 40; money flow analysis 70
shikin junkan kanjō
    flow of funds accounts 40
shikin juyō
    credit demand 22; credit requirements 213; financial requirements 223, 391; financing requirements 224, 391
shikin kaikei
    fund accounting 393
shikin kosuto
    cost of funds [US] 211, 383
shikin kyōkyū
    fund supply 42
shikin no shito
    use of funds 426
shikin pojishon
    bank's fund position 135; fund position 147
shikin shito
    purpose of funds 413
shikin suru
    assay 165
shikin tōsei
    fund control 393
shikin un'yō sōsa
    operation (banking operation) 154
shikin yosan
    financial budget 391
shikingen
    financial sources 223
shikinguri
    fund management 393
shikinnan
    financial difficulties 435; short of funds 418
shikiri baibai
    transaction on dealers' basis 282
shikke
    damp 292
shikken
    forfeiture (loss of rights) 227, 392
shikken kabu
    forfeited shares 392; surrendered shares 280, 423; unclaimed share 283; unclaimed stock 283
shikken kabu no saihakkō
    re-issue of forfeited shares 265, 415

shikken kabushiki jōyokin
    surplus from forfeited shares 422
shikken tsūchisho
    notice of forfeiture 404
shikki
    damp 292
shikkō i'inkai
    executive board 345; executive committee 345
shikkō kogitte
    out-of-date cheque 154; stale cheque 161
shikkō shain
    executive officer 345, 455
shikkō shōken
    nullified bond 252; voided bond 285
shikkō tsūchisho
    expiry notice 221
shikkōkan
    executive officer 345
shikkōri
    bailiff 290
shikyō
    market (tone, position) 245; market conditions 245; market position 246; market tone 246; tone (of market) 282
shikyō hōkoku
    market report 246
shikyō kaifuku
    market rally 246; market recovery 246
shikyō kenchō
    firm market 224
shikyō no hantō
    rallying of the market 263
shikyō no sūsei
    run (of market) 268
shikyō shōhin
    market-leading commodities 246
shikyū
    pay (noun) (provision) 481
shikyū chūmon
    immediate or cancel order 232
shimai gaisha
    sister company 360
shimai ginkō
    affiliated bank 132
shimanagashi
    'banishment to an island' 473
shimedashi
    crowding-out 213
shimekiri shisanhyō
    closing trial balance 379
shimekiri zandaka
    closing balance 379
shimekiribi
    closing day 379; deadline 214
shimekirigo kinyū
    post-closing entry 410
shimekirizumi kanjō
    closed accounts 379
shimohanki
    second half of the year 99, 417
shimurēshon
    simulation 100
shimyurēshon o tsukatta kiki no jōkyō
    simulated-crisis situation 493

shinchō
prudence 261

shinchō na kanrisha junsoku
prudent-man rule 261

shingaisha
trespasser 310

shingapōru
Singapore 190

shingi
authenticity 165

shingikai
open buying 254

shingiuri
open selling 254

shinjigyō o hajimeru
start a new business 361

shinjikēto
syndicate (consortium) 280

shinjikēto keiyaku
agreement among underwriters 195; syndicate contract 280

shinjikēto-rōn
syndicated loan 280

shinjun
saturation 97

shinkabu
new share 250, 403; new stock 251

shinkabu hikiukeken
stock purchase right 278, 420; subscription right (shareholders' right to new shares) 279, 421

shinkabu hikiukeken shōsho
stock purchase warrant 278, 420; subscription warrant 279, 421

shinkabu ochi
ex allotment 220; ex new 220

shinkabutsuki
cum new 213, 383

shinki boshū
recruitment 446

shinki gakusotsu rōdōryoku
new school graduates on the labour market 444

shinki hakkō
new issue 250, 403

shinki hakkō saiken
new issues 250

shinki hakkō shasai
newly issued corporate bond 251

shinki kashidashi
new loans 250

shinki kyūjin
new job offers 444

shinki saiyō
new hiring 444

shinki shūgyōsha
newly hired worker 461

shinkijiku
innovations 54

shinkin'yū shōhin
new financial commodities 250

shinkiroku
new high (record) 250

shinkisaiyō
recruiting new employees 446

shinkō
progress (march, progression) 87

shinkō keizai
young economy 122

shinkō kōgyōkoku
newly industrialized countries (NICs) 74

shinkōkoku
young country 121

shinkotenha keizaigaku
neo-classical economics 73

shinkotenha seichō riron
neo-classical growth theory 73

shinmarusasu shugi
neo-malthusianism 73

shinnenkai
new year party 487, 488 (note 39)

shinnin sareta
accredited 335

shinnyū suru
trespass (verb) 310

shinnyūshain
incoming partner 348; new employee 461

shinnyūshain kyōiku
freshman orientation 456

shinobiyoru infurēshon
crawling inflation 21; creeping inflation 22

shinpo
progress (advancement; improvement) 87

shinpuku
amplitude of cycle 7

shinrinin
referee 437

shinsa
medical examination 325

shinsa
screening 269; scrutiny 269

shinsa buchō
credit manager 141

shinsangyō
new industry 74

shinsangyō kokka
new industrial states 74

shinsatsu
medical attention 480

shinsei
application 433

shinseihin
new products 74

shinseinin
applicant 195, 336

shinseisho o teishutsu suru
file an application 346

shinseitōha
neo-orthodoxy 73

shinsetsu gappei
consolidation 342

shinsetsu kigyō
new business 353; newly established corporation 353

shinshi kyōtei
gentlemen's agreement 43

shinshukuteki chingin seisaku
flexible wage policy 477

shinshukuteki chinginritsu
flexible wage rate 477

shinshukuteki kahei chingin
flexible money wages 477

shinshukuteki kahei chingin seisaku
flexible money wage policy 477

shinshukuteki kahei seisaku
flexible monetary policy 173

shinshukuteki rōdō jikan seido
flexi-time system 455

shinshukuteki tsūka
flexible currency 173

shinsozai
new industrial materials 74

shintai shōgai hoken
disability insurance 319

shintai shōgai sekinin hoken
bodily injury liability insurance 316

shintai ukagai
informal resignation 495, 497 (note 44)

shintakane
new high (prices) 250

shintaku
trust 162, 283, 310

shintaku bumon
trust department (of a bank) 162

shintaku chochiku ginkō
Trustee Savings Bank (TSB) [UK] 162

shintaku gaisha
trust company 362; trust corporation 362

shintaku ginkō
trust bank [J] 162, 164 (note 8)

shintaku kanjō
trust account 162, 283

shintaku keiyaku
trust agreement 283

shintaku keiyakusho
trust deed [US] 283, 311

shintaku shōsho
deed of trust 216, 293; indenture 232; trust deed [US] 283, 311

shintaku zaisan
fiduciary estate 295; trust estate 311; trust property 311

shintakugyō
trust business 283

shinteikoku shugi
neo-imperialism 73

shinten
development (evolution) 26; progress 87

shintō
penetration (capital) 79

shintsūka
new money 181

shin'yasune
new low (prices) 250

shin'yō
credit 21, 212; credit (loan) 141

shin'yō de uru
sell on margin 271

shin'yō ben'eki
credit facilities 212

shin'yō bunseki
credit analysis 212

shin'yō chōsa
credit inquiry 212

shin'yō chōsabu
credit department 141, 212

ginkō no shin'yō chōsabu
credit department of a bank 212

shin'yō chōsetsu
credit control 21

shin'yō gendo
credit ceiling 212; credit limit 212

shin'yō ginkō
credit bank 141, 212

shin'yō hakkō
fiduciary issue 172

shin'yō hikishime
credit restraint 22; credit tightening 213

shin'yō hoken
credit insurance 318

shin'yō hōkokusho
credit report 213

shin'yō hoshō
credit guarantee 212

shin'yō hoshōjō
letter of guaranty (L/G) 150, 151

shin'yō hyōka
credit evaluation 212

shin'yō infurēshon
credit inflation 22

shin'yō jōken
credit terms 213

shin'yō jōtai
credit conditions 212; credit standing 213; credit status 213

shin'yō jōtai chōsa
inquiry into financial situation 233

shin'yō junbi
fiduciary reserve 173

shin'yō kahei
fiduciary money 173

shin'yō kakuchō
easy credit 219

shin'yō kakuchō seisaku
easy-credit policy 219

shin'yō kakudai
credit expansion 212

shin'yō kakuzuke
credit rating 213

shin'yō kanri
credit management 213

shin'yō kashitsuke
fiduciary loan 222

shin'yō kinko
credit association [J] 212, 287 (note 10)

shin'yō kisei
credit regulations 213; credit restrictions 22, 213

shin'yō kumiai
credit union [J] 213, 287 (note 12); credit union [US] 213

shin'yō kyōdō kumiai
credit co-operative [J] 212, 287 (note 11)

shin'yō kyōkō
credit crisis 22, 212

shin'yō kyōyo
credit accommodation 212; granting of credit 229

shin'yō kyōyo gendo
credit line 212

shitsu
office (department, room) 462

shitsugyō
unemployment 114, 503

shitsugyō shite iru
unemployed (to be) 503

shitsugyō chōsa
unemployment census 114

shitsugyō hoken
unemployment insurance 115, 330

shitsugyō hokenryō
unemployment insurance deduction 485

shitsugyō hoshō
unemployment compensation 114, 503

shitsugyō kikan
duration of unemployment 28, 499

shitsugyō kinkō
unemployment equilibrium 115

shitsugyō kyūfu
unemployment benefits 114, 503

shitsugyō no riron
theory of unemployment 110

shitsugyō no tansaku riron
search unemployment (concept of) 98

shitsugyō no zōka
rise in unemployment 96

shitsugyō rōdōsha
unemployed worker 503

shitsugyō taisaku
unemployment measures 115

shitsugyō taisakuhi
unemployment expenses 115

shitsugyō teate
dole money 499; unemployment benefits 114, 503; unemployment compensation 503

shitsugyō teate o ukete iru
to be on the dole 27, 499

shitsugyō tōkei
jobless figures 59; unemployment statistics 115

shitsugyōchū
out of work 501

shitsugyōritsu
jobless rate 59; unemployment rate 115

shitsugyōsha
jobless, the 59; jobless person 500; unemployed, the 114; unemployed person 503

shitsugyōsha meibo
unemployment roll 115

shitsumonsho
questionnaire 90

shiwake kanjō
itemized account 398

shiwake suru
post (verb) (accounts) 410

shiwakechō
journal (accounts) 398

shiwakechō kinyū
journal entry 398

shiwakechōshiki motochō
journal-form ledger 398

shiyō hiyō
user cost 116

shiyō kikan
probation period 464; trial period 470

shiyō shihon
employed capital 388

shiyō shihongaku
capital employed 375

shiyū
private ownership 85

shiyū zaisan
private property 85, 304

shizai
private funds 411

shizei
municipal tax (city tax) 302

shizen dokusen
natural monopoly 72

shizen hokenryō
yearly renewable premium 331

shizen kakaku
natural price 72

shizen keizai
natural economy 72

shizen seichōritsu
natural rate of growth 73

shizen shitsugyōritsu
natural rate of unemployment 73

shizen tōta kasetsu
natural selection hypothesis 73

shizen zōka
accretion 193, 366

shizenhō
natural law 72

shizenteki bungyō
natural division of labour 72

shizenteki kiken
natural risk 326

shoazukarikin
deposits received (on balance sheet) 386

shōbai
business (commerce) 12, 338; trade 111

shōbai o kizuku
set up business 360

shōbai o kizukiageru
build up a business 338

shōbai o yameru
close one's business 340

shōbai o yuzuru
hand over a business 348

shōbai gataki
business competitor 338; rival business 360

shōbō enshū
fire drill 491

shōbō kunren
fire drill 491

shōbōto
fire door 491

shobun
appropriation (on balance sheet) 370; disposal (of securities) 218

shobun-seisan keisansho
statement of realization and liquidation 420

shobunkanō riekikin
available profit 371

shobun'uri
sell-out 271

shōdan
negotiation (business talks) 303

shodo kansa
initial audit 395

shōgai
barrier (obstacle) 10

shōgai
accident 315, 491; casualty 317; injury 492

shōgai hoken
accident insurance 315; casualty insurance 317

shōgai hoken shōken
accident policy 315

shōgai hokenkin
casualty insurance claim 317; casualty insurance money 317

shōgai hokenryō
casualty insurance premium 317

shōgai hoshō hoken
accident and indemnity insurance 315

shōgai shippei hoken
accident and sickness insurance 315

shogakari
overheads (various charges, expenses) 407

shōgaku
small sum 160

shōgaku kokusai
small government bond 274

shōgaku saiken
baby bond [US] 198; small bond [US] 274

shōgaku shihei
small note 184

shōgaku yokinsha
small saver 160

shōgeki
impact (shock) 48

shōgō
business name 339; corporate name 343; name of company 353; trade name 362

shōgō bangō
reference number 328

shōgō henkō
change of trade name 340

shōgō kaishō
change of name (company) 340

shōgō no fumeiryō
misleading name (of a company) 352

shōgō tōroku
registration of business name 359

shōgyō
business 338; commerce 17; commercial business 341; trade 111

shōgyō bumon
commercial sector 17

shōgyō chūshinchi
business centre 338

shōgyō gakkō
commercial school 442

shōgyō ginkō
business bank 138; commercial bank(s) 17, 140; merchant bank(s) 68, 151

shōgyō ginkōgyō
commercial banking 140

shōgyō kaigisho
Chamber of Commerce 16

shōgyō kaikei
commercial accounting 379

shōgyō kashidashi
commercial loan 209

shōgyō katsudō
commercial activity 17

shōgyō kin'yū
commercial finance 209

shōgyō kōsei
commercial offensives 17

shōgyō kōshinjo
credit agency [UK] 212; credit bureau [US] 212

shōgyō kumiai
trade association (business) 111

shōgyō sensasu
business census 338

shōgyō shin'yō
commercial credit 209

shōgyō shin'yō gaisha
commercial credit company [UK] 209

shōgyō shin'yōjō
commercial L/C 140

shōgyō shorui
commercial documents 140

shōgyō shugi
commercialism 17

shōgyō tegata
commercial bill 140; commercial paper 140, 209; trade bill 162

shōgyō tōki
company registration 341; trade register 362

shōgyō tōkibo
register of companies 358

shōgyō tōkibo tōhon
certificate of registration 340; company registration 140, 164 (note 3); company registration certificate 341

shōgyōnin meibo
commercial directory 341

shohatsu kabu
original issue stock 255, 407

shōheki
barrier (wall) 10

shōhi
consumption 19

shōhi būmu
spending boom 102

shōhi dantai
consumer groups 19

shōhi gōrika
rationalization of consumption 91

shōhi infurēshon
consumption inflation 20

shōhi kansū
consumption function 20

shōhi keizaigaku
economics of consumption 31

shōhi kyokusen
consumption curve 19

shōhi no ragu
consumption lag 20

shōken kakaku no jōshō
appreciation of securities 196

shōken kin'yū
securities financing 270

shōken kin'yū gaisha
securities finance corporation
[J] 270

shōken no bunpai
distribution (securities) 218

shōken no kokusai torihiki
international trading of
securities 236

shōken ōbo
subscription to securities 279

shōken oyobi tōshi i'inkai
Securities and Investment
Board [UK] 269

shōken rimawari
securities yield 270

shōken shijō
securities market 270

shōken shojinin
bond holder (general) 201

shōken shoyūsha
securities holder 270

shōken tanpo kashitsuke
advance against securities 194

shōken torihiki i'inkai
Securities and Exchange
Commission (SEC) [US] 269

shōken torihiki no posuto
post (securities) 259

shōken torihikihō
Financial Services Act [UK]
223; Securities and Exchange
Law [J] 269

shōken torihikijo
Stock Exchange (securities)
277

shōken torihikijo junkai'in
allied member [NYSE – US]
195

shōken torihikijo kai'in
member firm 247

shōken torihikijo no torihiki
transaction on the exchange
282

shōken tōroku
registration of securities 265

shōken tōshi
investment in securities 237;
securities investment 270

shōken tōshi shintaku
securities investment trust 270

shōken yōshi
policy form 327

shōkengyō
securities business 270

shōkengyō kyōkai
Securities Association [UK]
269; Securities Industry
Association [US] 270

shōkengyōsha
securities broker-dealer 270;
trader (securities) 282

shokenri ochi
ex all [US] 220

shokenritsuki
cum all 213

shōki
business opportunity 339

shoki shōkyaku
initial depreciation 395

shoki tōshi
initial investment 233

shōkibo kigyō
small business 361

shōkibo no dōzoku kigyō
small incorporated family firm
361

shōkibo seisan
production on a small scale 86

shōkigyō
small business 361; small
concern 361; small enterprise
361; small firm 101, 361

shōkin
gold 175; specie (cash) 184

shōkin ginkō
specie bank 184

shokku
shock 100

shokku kōka
shock effect 100

shōkō kaigisho
Chamber of Commerce and
Industry 16

shōko shorui
documentary evidence 144

shōkokin
margin (deposit money) 245;
margin money 245

shōkokin kanjō
margin account 245

shōkokin keiyakusho
margin agreement 245

shōkokin shoyōgaku
margin requirement 245

shōkokin torihiki
margin trading 245; margin
transaction 245

shōkokin yōkyū
maintenance requirement 244

shōkokin yōkyū tsūchi
maintenance call 244

shōkokinritsu
margin rate 245

shoku
jobs (employment, work) 59;
position (job, work) 445, 464

genzai no shoku o kaeru
leave one's current position
495

shoku o kaeru
change jobs [less formal] 441

shoku yokose undō
right-to-work demonstration
502

shokuba
workplace (post) 472

shokuba o ridatsu suru
walk out (verb) 504

shokuba daihyōsha
shop steward 467, 502

shokuba fukki
return to work 502

shokuba haichi tenkan
job rotation (position rotation)
458

shokuba hōki
walk-out strike 504

shokuba i'inkai
shop committee 467; work
committees 120, 471

shokuba kiritsu
disciplinary rules 453

shokuba ni okeru ningen kankei
inter-relations in the workplace
458

shokuba sōon
noise 492

shokuba taikai
workshop meeting 504

shokubagai kunren
off-the-job training 462

shokubanai kenshū
on-the-job training 462

shokubanai kunren
on-the-job training 462

shokubetsu chingin
wages classified by
occupations 119

shokuchō
foreman 455

shokudō
cafeteria 475

shokugyō
career 441, 451; job(s) 59,
443, 458; occupation 75, 462;
profession 465

iyashii shokugyō
lowly occupation 460

shokugyō bunka
occupational differentiation 75

shokugyō bunpai
occupational distribution 75

shokugyō chingin kakusa
occupational wage differentials
75

shokugyō fujin
career woman 451;
professional woman 446

shokugyō gakkō
vocational school 447

shokugyō hodō
career counselling 441

shokugyō keiken
job experience 443

shokugyō kunren
job training 59, 458; vocational
training 447

shokugyō kyōiku
professional education 445;
vocational education 447

shokugyō kyūyo kōzō
occupational wage structure 75

shokugyō saikunren
job retraining 458

shokugyō shidō
occupational guidance 445;
vocational guidance 447

shokugyō shidōka
employment bureau (of
Japanese schools) 442

shokugyō shidōsha
career counsellor 441;
vocational counsellor 447

shokugyō shōkai
job introduction 444

shokugyō shōkai tōkei
employment exchange statistics
32

shokugyō shōkaijo
employment agency 442;
employment exchange 442; job
centre(s) [UK] 58, 443; labour
exchange 444

shokugyō shūdan
occupational groups 75, 462

shokugyō sōdan
career counselling 441;
vocational counselling 447

shokugyō sōdannin
career counsellor 441;
vocational counsellor 447

shokugyō sōshutsu
job creation 58, 443

shokugyō tekisei
vocation 447; vocational
aptitude 447

shokugyō tekisei kensa
vocational test 447

shokugyō tōkei chōsa
occupation census 75

shokugyōbyō
industrial disease 492;
industrial illness 492;
occupational disease 492

shokugyōjō no kiken
occupational hazard 492;
occupational risk 493

shokugyōteki hikō hoken
malpractice insurance 325

shokuhin kakōgyō
food-processing industry 124

shokuhin kōgyō
food industry 124

shokuin
employee (member of white-
collar staff) 454; member of
staff 461; personnel 356, 464;
staff 468

shokuji teate
meal allowance 487

shokukaisei
job classification 58

shokuken
luncheon vouchers 479

shokumu
duties 345, 453; functions 347,
456; job 443, 458; office (post)
462; occupation 462; task 469

shokumu o hatasu
fulfil one's duties 347, 456

shokumu o okotaru
neglect one's duties 353, 461

shokumu bunrui
occupational classification 75,
462

shokumu bunseki
job analysis 58

shokumu chishiki
knowledge of the job 459

shokumu hyōka
job evaluation 58, 458;
job rating 458

shokumu keiken
job experience 443

shokumu kijutsusho
job description (written
description) 443, 458

shokumu no naiyō
job content [formal] 458; job
description [formal] 443, 458;
job specifications 444

shokumu no suikō
performance of duties 463

shokumu shikaku
job requirements 444, 458

shokumu yōso
job factor 59

shotoku kaisō
income bracket 50, 479;
income group 50
shotoku kansū
earnings function 28
shotoku kettei
income determination 50
shotoku kettei no riron
theory of income determination
110
shotoku kōeki jōken
income terms of trade 50
shotoku kōka
income effect 50
shotoku kōzō
income structure 50
shotoku meate no
income-oriented 232
shotoku meate no tōshi
income-oriented investment
232
shotoku no anteisei
stability of income 484
shotoku no fubyōdō
inequality of incomes 54
shotoku no genkai kōyō
marginal utility of income 66
shotoku no sashiosae
attachment of earnings [UK]
197
shotoku o umu kabushiki
income-producing stock 232
shotoku seisaku
incomes policy 50
shotoku-shishutsu moderu
income-expenditure model 50
shotoku shisū
income index 50
shotoku-shōhi kyokusen
income-consumption curve 50
shotoku suijun
income level 50, 479
shotoku sūryōsetsu
transaction theory of money
112
shotoku yokin
income deposit 149
shotoku zōshutsu kin'yū
income-creating finance 232
shotokugen
source of income 102, 483
shotokuritsu
net income ratio 402
shotokusha
income earners 50
shotokusō
income bracket 50, 479;
income group 50
shotokuzei
income tax 50, 479
shotokuzei no kiso kōjo
personal exemptions (tax) 482
shotokuzei shinkoku
income tax return 50, 479;
tax return 485
shotokuzei shinkoku shimekiri kijitsu
income tax filing deadline 50,
479; tax return filing deadline
485
shotokuzei shinkokusho
income tax return (form) 50,
479; tax return (form) 485

shotokuzeihyō
income tax schedule 50, 479
shotokuzeiritsu
income tax rate 479
shōtorihiki
commercial transaction 17
shōtotsu hoken
collision insurance 317
shōwa
harmony 457
shōyo(kin)
bonus(es) 373, 475
shōyō
business engagement 338
shoyū
possession (ownership) 304
shoyū dōsan fudōsan
real estate and properties 306
shoyū kei'eisha
owner-manager 355**shoyū to kei'ei no bunri**
separation of ownership from
control 99
shoyūbutsu
possessions 304; property 305
shoyūchi
freehold land 295; landed
property 300; property (land)
305
shoyūchi o toriagerareru
have one's property
repossessed 296
shoyūken
ownership 303, 355;
proprietary rights 305;
right of ownership 308
shoyūken iten
ownership transfer 310
shoyūken no
proprietary 305
shoyūken no toriage
expropriation 295
shoyūnushi mochibun
capital (owner's equity) 375
shoyūsha
owner 303, 355; possessor
304; proprietor 305, 357
shoyūsha kigyō
owner-controlled firm 355
shoyūsha mochibun
owner's equity 408; owner's
interest 408; ownership interest
408
shoyūsha sekinin hoken
owner's liability insurance 326
shoyūsha shihai
owner control 355
shozaichi
location (of property) 301
shozaichi henkō
change of address (company)
340
shu o riyū to shita chingin sabetsu
wage discrimination on the
basis of race 486
shūatari chingin
weekly wages 486
shūatari heikin shūnyū
average weekly earnings 475
shūatari junshūnyū
net weekly earnings 480

shūatari shūnyū
weekly earnings 486
shūatari sōshūnyū
gross weekly earnings 477
shūchū
concentration 18
shūchū gimu
surrender requirements 186
shūchū keisū
coefficient of concentration 16
shūchū tōshi
concentrated investment 209
shūchūdo
concentration ratio 18
shudan
instruments 55; measure
(means, way) 68
shūdan chūseishin
group loyalty 456
shūdan ginkōsei
group banking [US] 148
shudan hensū
instrumental variables 55
shūdan hoken
collective insurance 317
shūdan kei'ei
corporate enterprise (group)
342
shūdan kenkō hoken seido
group health insurance plan
321
shūdan kunren
group training 456
shūdan kyōyaku
collective agreement 16, 452,
476
shūdan sekinin
collective responsibility 292
shūdan shōgai hoken
collective accident insurance
317
shūdan sōgo sayō
group interaction 456
shūdanteki sentaku
collective choice 16
shudō kigyō
leading company 350; leading
firm 350
shūeki
earnings 388; gains 228, 393;
income 232, 395; profit(s) 87,
261, 411; return 267; revenue
96, 267, 416
shūeki bēsu
earnings basis 388
shūeki haitō kanjō
appropriation account 370
shūeki hōkokusho
earnings report 388
shūeki ittei
constant returns 380
shūeki jigyō
profit-making business 411
shūeki jōkyō
profits position 412
shūeki rimawari
earnings yield 388
shūeki saiken
income bond 232
shūeki shasai
income debenture 232

shūeki shisan
earning assets 388
shūekiritsu
earning rate 388
shūekiryoku
earning power 388
shūekisei
profitability 87, 261
shūekisei bunseki
profitability analysis 261
shūekisei genri
profitability principle 87
shūekizei
profits tax 412
shūgō kanjō
summarizing account 422
shūgō sekinin
collective responsibility 292
shūgō son'eki kanjō
profit and loss summary
account 411
shūgōzai
collective goods 16
shūgyō
employment (work) 442, 454
shūgyō jikan
office hours 462; working hours
472
shūgyō kisoku
office regulations 354; work
regulations 471
shūgyō nenrei
working age 121
shūgyō nissū
number of days worked 462
shūgyō shōrei
incentive to work 457; work
incentive 471
shūgyō shōrei keikaku
work incentive programme 471
shūgyō tōkei
employment figures 32
shūgyōhi
work day 471
shūgyōka
employment bureau (of
Japanese schools) 442
shuisho
letter of intent 240, 399
shūji kessan
weekly accounting 427
shujutsuhi hoken
surgical expenses insurance
329
shūkai
convocation 429
shūkaku
crop (harvest) 22
shūkaku fuhen no hōsoku
law of constant returns 61
shūkaku teigen
decreasing returns 24
shūkaku teigen no hōsoku
law of diminishing returns 62
shūkaku teizō
increasing returns 51
shūkaku teizō no hōsoku
law of increasing returns 62
shūkakudaka
crop yield 22
shūkan shisanhyō
weekly trial balance 427

shuyō na shain
principal members 357

shuyō na shōgyō ginkō
high-street bank [UK] 148

shuyō posuto
top job (key job) 469

shuyō rōmusha
key worker 459

shuyō sangyō
main industries 65; major
industries 65; staple industries
103

shuyō shijō
primary market (key, main) 84

shuyō songai
major loss 325

shuyō tsūka
leading currency 178; major
currency 178

shuyō yushutsuhin
key exports 59

shuyōkoku
major countries 65

shūyonjū jikansei
forty-hour week system 455

shuyōso
prime factor 84

shūzei
tax collection 107

shūzeinin
tax collector 107

shūzen-iji
repair and maintenance 307

shūzen-ijihi
repair and maintenance
expenses 307

shūzen junbikin
reserve for repairs 415

shūzen suru
repair (verb) (recondition) 307

shūzenhi
cost of repairs 383; repair
expenses 307

shūzenhi hikiatekin
provision for repairs 412

shūzenkō
repairman 307

sōba
market 245; market price 246;
quotation 262

sōba ni te o dasu
dabble in speculation 214

sōba kokuchiban
quotation board 262

sōba no ashidori
movement (of market prices)
249

sōba no biraku
marginal decline 245

sōba no bōraku
break 203; market slump 246

sōba no dōkō
market movements 246

sōba no fukisoku na ugoki
random walk 263

sōba no gekihen
sharp fluctuation 183;
sharp market fluctuation 273

sōba no ōatari
killing 240

sōba no ryōdate
exchange option 172

sōba no teikōsen
resistance barrier 267

sōba no uwamuki
upward tendency 285

sōba rankōge
erratic market 220

sōba shiji
support of currency 185

sōba shiji sōsa
support operation 185

sōba sōjū
manipulation 245

sōba tatene
fixing (of exchange rate) 173

sōbahyō
list of quotations 241

sōbakan
market forecast 246

sōbashi
operator (stock jobber) 255;
professional speculator 261;
speculator(s) [J] 275

sōbetsukai
farewell party 487

sochi
measure (action, step) 68

sōchi kōgyō
process industry 126

sochin suru
take to court 437

sōchochiku
gross savings 45

sōekiritsu
gross profit ratio 394

sofuto-doru (tesūryō)
soft dollars [US] 274

sofuto-rōn
soft loan 274

sofutouea sangyō
software industry 126

sogai
alienation 6

sōgai hoken
frost insurance 320

sōgaku
total amount 162, 423

sogan
appeal 433

sogannin
appellant 433

sōgenka
final cost 390; gross cost 394

sōgi
dispute 499

sōgo chochiku
mutual savings [US] 152

sōgo chochiku ginkō
mutual savings bank [US] 152

sōgo enjo
mutual aid 71

sōgo fujo kumiai
benevolent association 337

sōgo ginkō
mutual loan and savings bank
[US] 152

sōgo hoken
all-risks insurance 315;
compound insurance 318;
comprehensive insurance 318;
mutual insurance 326

sōgo hoken gaisha
mutual insurance company 326

sōgo hoken shōken
all-risks insurance policy 315;
comprehensive insurance
policy 318

sōgo ison
interdependence 55

sōgo jidōsha hoken
comprehensive motorcar
insurance 318

sōgo jidōsha hoken shōken
comprehensive motorcar
insurance policy 318

sōgo juyō
reciprocal demand 92

sōgo kanjō
overall accounts 407

sōgo nōritsu
overall efficiency 463

sōgo sayō
interaction 458

sōgo seisaku
overall policy 78; policy
package 81

sōgo shiwakechō
summary journal 422

sōgo shōsha
general trading company [J]
347

sōgo shūshi
overall balance (of payments)
77

sōgo taisaku
package of measures 78

sōgo tanpo hoken shōken
comprehensive coverage 318

sōgo un'ei
integrated management 349

sōgo yosan
overall budget 77, 407

sōgōteki ippan sekinin hoken
comprehensive general liability
insurance 318

**sōgōteki ippan sekinin hoken
shōken**
comprehensive general liability
insurance policy 318

sōgōteki jūtaku hoken
comprehensive house
insurance 318

sōgōteki jūtaku hoken shōken
comprehensive house
insurance policy 318

sōgōteki kojin sekinin hoken
comprehensive personal liability
insurance 318

**sōgōteki kojin sekinin hoken
shōken**
comprehensive personal liability
insurance policy 318

sōgōteki na nōryoku
general capabilities 442

sōgyō
operation (work) 354

sōgyō
establishment (of a company)
345; founding 347; start of
business 361

sōgyō kaishi
start of business 361

sōgyō kaishi kyokashō
certificate to commence
business 340

sōgyō menkyo
permission to deal 356

sōgyō nengappi
date of start of business 343

sōgyō suru
found (establish, start business)
347

sōgyō tanshuku
curtailment of operations 343;
short-time working 100

sōgyōhi
initial expenditure 395; initial
expenses 395; organization
cost 406; organization
expenses 406; promotion
expenses 412; setting-up cost
417; setting-up expenses 417;
start-up cost 419

sōgyōki kesson
initial loss 395

sōgyōritsu
operating rate 354; rate of
operation 358

sōgyōsha
founder 347

sōgyōsha ritoku
founder's profit 392

sōhigyō
general strike 43, 499

sōhiyō
total expenses 424

sōhiyō kyokusen
total cost curve 111

sōhō dokusen
bilateral monopoly 11

sohō genkai
extensive margin 37

sohō nōgyō
extensive farming 124

sōhoteki juyō
complementary demand 18

sōji
cleanliness 491; hygiene 492

sōjuyō
aggregate demand 5; overall
demand 77; total demand 111

sōjuyō kyokusen
aggregate demand curve 5;
total demand curve 111

sōkai
general meeting 430; meeting
430

sōkai o enki suru
adjourn a meeting 429

sōkai no basho
place of meeting 431

sōkai no ketsugi
decision of general meeting
430

sokaku
alienation 6

sōkan
correlation 20

sōkanjō motochō
general ledger 393; key ledger
398

sōkanjō motochō kanjō
general ledger account 393

sōkatsu
summarization 422

sōkatsu hoken
blanket insurance 316

sōkatsu hoken shōken
blanket insurance policy 316

sōshihon
gross capital 394; total capital 424

sōshihon riekiritsu
profit ratio of total capital 412; rate of earnings on total capital 413

soshiki
organization 77, 354, 463

soshiki kōzō
organization structure 355

soshiki nōryoku
organizational ability 355, 463

soshiki rōdōsha
organized labour 77, 463; organized worker 463

soshiki taisei
organization control 355

soshikijō no kaizen
organizational improvement 355

soshikinin
organization man 355

soshikizu
organization chart 354

sōshisan
gross assets 394

sōshisan shōkyakuritsu
rate of depreciation to total assets 413

sōshishutsu
aggregate expenditure 5; gross expenditure 45, 394; total expenditure 111, 424

sōshitsu
forfeiture 227, 392

sōshitsu suru
forfeit 227, 392

soshō
litigation 436

soshō hiyō
litigation costs 436

soshō jiken
legal case 436

soshō tetsuzuki
legal proceedings 436

soshō tōjisha
litigant 436

soshōnin
plaintiff 436

sōshotoku
aggregate income 5; gross income 394, 477; total income 111, 424, 485

sōshūeki
gross earnings 394; gross revenue 394; total earnings 424; total return 282

sōshūnyū
gross earnings 45, 394, 477; gross income 394; total receipts 424; total revenue 111, 424

sōsonshitsu
gross loss 394

sōtai chingin
relative wages 94

sōtai kakaku
relative price 94

sōtai seisan kansū
aggregate production function 5

sōtai shotoku
relative income 94

sōtai shotoku kasetsu
relative income hypothesis 94

sōtaiteki keizai bunseki
aggregate economic analysis 5

sōtaiteki keizai katsudō
aggregate economic activity 5

sōtaiteki kyūbōka
relative deprivation 94

sōtan
short-time working 100

sōtan higyō
slow-down strike 502

sōtokeai
all-out liquidation 433

sōtōshi
gross investment 45, 229

sotsugyō suru
graduate (verb) 443

sotsugyōsha
graduate (noun) 442

sotsui
legal action 435

sōunten shihon
gross working capital 394

sōuriagedaka
sales revenue [US] 416; turnover [UK] 113, 424

sōuriagezei
turnover tax 113, 424

sōyosan
general budget 43, 393

sōzaika
total goods 111

sōzaisan
gross worth 394

sozei
local tax 64; rates 306; tax(es) 107, 109; taxation 109

sozei futan
impact of taxation 48; incidence of taxation 50; tax burden 107; tax incidence 108

sozei futanritsu
tax burden ratio 107

sozei gensoku
canon of taxation 14; principle of taxation 84

sozei hikisage
tax cuts 108

sozei hinanchi
tax havens 108

sozei hiyūin
tax disincentive 108

sozei jōyaku
tax treaty 109

sozei kanpu
tax rebate 108, 484

sozei kanpukin
tax rebate 108, 484; tax refund 108, 485

sozei kanri
tax administration 107

sozei kanrisha
tax administrators 107

sozei kōjo
tax deductions 108, 484; tax offset 108

sozei kōzō
structure of taxes 105; tax structure 108

sozei kyokushōka
tax minimization 423, 484

sozei menjo
tax exemption 108

sozei no juekisha futan gensoku
benefit theory of taxation 11

sozei no nukeana
tax loophole 108

sozei no sonshitsu
tax loss 423

sozei oyobi inshi shūnyū
tax and stamp receipts 107

sozei satei
tax assessment 107

sozei shishutsu
tax expenditure 108

sozei shūnyū
tax receipts 108; tax revenue 108; tax yield 109

sozei taikei
taxation system 109

sozei tōkyoku
tax authorities 107

sozei yūin
tax incentives 108

sōzoku
inheritance 298; succession 309

sōzoku arasoi
succession dispute 309

sōzoku gaisha
inherited firm 349

sōzoku kitai
expectation of inheritance 295

sōzoku suru
inherit 298

sōzoku zaisan
inheritance property 298; inherited property 298

sōzokuken
heirship 296; right of inheritance 308

sōzokunin
heir 296

sōzokunin no nai zaisan
vacant estate 311

sōzokusha
successor 309

sōzokuzei
estate tax 294; inheritance tax [UK] 54, 298; succession tax 309

sūdan
Sudan 190

suēden
Sweden 190

sueoki fusai
deferred liabilities 385

sueoki haitōkin
deferred dividend 385

sueoki nenkin
deferred annuity 319

sueoki saiken
deferred bond 216

sueoki tanpo
fixed collateral 224

sueokibarai
deferred payment 216, 385

sueokizei
deferred tax 385

sugureta eigyō tantōin
high performer 457

suichoku bōeki
vertical trade 117

suichokuteki bungyō
vertical division of labour 117

suichokuteki gappei
vertical merger 117, 363

suichokuteki kōhei
vertical equity 117

suichokuteki tōgō
vertical integration 117, 363

suidō ryōkin
water rates 119

suidōkōatsuhi
water, lighting and heating expenses 312

suidōryō
water rates 118, 312

suidōryōkin
water charges 312

suigai
damage by water 319; flood damages 320; flood disaster 40; water damage 331

suigai hoken
water damage insurance 331

suigai taisaku
flood disaster relief 40

suihei bōeki
horizontal trade 47

suiheiteki bungyō
horizontal division of labour 47

suiheiteki gappei
horizontal merger 47, 348

suiheiteki tōgō
horizontal integration 47, 348

suijun
level 62

suikō
performance (execution) 463

suimin kōza
dormant account 144

suiryoku kōgyō
hydraulic power industry 124

suisangyō
fishing industry 124

suisen
(recommendation)
kuchi kara kuchi e no suisen
word-of-mouth recommend-ation 447

suisenjō
letter of recommendation 444

suishin
promotion 88

suishin soshiki
promotional bodies 88

suishitsu
water quality 312

suishitsu osen
water pollution 119

suishō kabu
recommended issue 263, 414

suisoku
inference (statistical) 54

suisu
Switzerland 190

suitei
estimation (assumption) 34

suitei songaigaku
estimated damage 320

suiteiryō
estimates 34

tairyōgyoku torihiki
block trading 201; block transaction 201

taisaku
counter-measure 21

taisei
structure 361

taisei
general trend 43

taisha
leaving the office 459; withdrawal from a company 363

taishaku
borrowing and lending 203

taishaku kessai
loan clearance 242

taishaku kigen
term of loan 281

taishaku taishōhyō
balance sheet 372; financial position statement (balance sheet) 391

taishaku taishōhyō bunseki
analysis of balance sheet 369; balance sheet analysis 372

taishaku taishōhyō kamoku
balance sheet item 372

taishaku taishōhyō kansa
balance sheet audit 372

taishaku taishōhyō kōmoku no bunrui
classification of balance sheet items 378

taishaku taishōhyō no hizuke
balance sheet date 372

taishaku taishōhyō sōkei
balance sheet total 372

taishoku
retirement 96, 328, 496; withdrawal from a partnership 363

taishoku ichijikin
retirement allowance (in lump sum) 496

taishoku kyūyo
retirement allowance 496

taishoku kyūyo hikiatekin
reserve for retirement allowance 415

taishoku nenkin
retirement annuity 496; retirement pension 496

taishoku nenkin hoken shōken
retirement income insurance policy 328

taishoku no aisatsu
'paying respects upon resignation' 497

taishoku shain
retiring partner 360

taishoku shōmeisho
leaving certificate 459

taishoku teate
retirement allowance 496

taishoku teinen
retirement age 496

taishokukin
retirement allowance 496; retirement benefits 96; retirement fund 415, 496

taishokuritsu
employee turnover 454

taishokusha
retiree 496; retiring employee 496

taishū baitai
mass media 67

taishū shōhi shijō
mass market 67

taishū tōshika
investing public 236; public investor 261

taishūteki hinkon
mass poverty 67

taisō
gymnastics 456, 472 (note 31)

taitō gappei
merger on equal terms 352

taiyōnetsu denryoku kōgyō
solar power industry 126

taizō
hoarding 46, 176

taizō busshi
hoarded goods 46

taizō genkin
hoarded cash 176

taizō kahei
hoarded money 176

taizō kin
hoarded gold 176

taizō tsūka
hoarded currency 176

takai kinrō iyoku
high morale 457

takai shin'yō kakuzuke
high credit rating 230

takaku bōeki
multilateral trade 71

takaku enjo
multilateral aid 71

takaku kei'ei
diversification management 344; diversification operation 344; multiple management 353

takaku kei'ei gaisha
multi-market corporation 352

takaku shugi
multilateralism 71

takaku tōshi
diversification 218; diversified investment 218

takaku uru
sell at a high price 271

takakuteki gappei
multi-merger 353

takakuteki nōgyō
multiple agriculture 125

takakuteki tsūshō kōshō
multilateral trade negotiations 71

takane
high price 231; highest price 231; record price 263

takane de uru
sell at the best price 271

takane kabu
high flyer 230

takane machi
anticipation of rising market 195

takane-yasune
highs and lows 231

takane-yasune no haba
trading range 282

takanebike
closing high 208

takayori
opening high 254

taketashiki chōbo
column book 379

taketashiki genkin suitōbo
column cash book 379

taketashiki motochō
column ledger 379

tako haitō
bogus dividend 373; unearned dividend 425

takōjō gaisha
multi-plant company 353

takokukan bōeki kōshō
multilateral trade negotiations 71

takokukan enjo
multilateral aid 71

takokukan kyōtei
multilateral agreement 71

takokukan tsūka chōsei
multinational currency alignment 181

takokuseki ginkō
multi-national bank 152

takokuseki kigyō
multinational corporations 71; multinational(s) 353

takuchi
building land 291; housing land 297; residential land 308

takuchi kaihatsu gyōsha
property developer 305

takuchi zōsei
land reclamation for housing development 299

tamokuteki zaimu shohyō
all-purpose financial statement 368

tanaoroshi
inventory (stock-taking) 396

tanaoroshi genmō sonshitsu
loss from inventory 400

tanaoroshi hyōka
inventory valuation 397

tanaoroshi kagaku
inventory value 397

tanaoroshi kansa
inventory audit 397

tanaoroshi shisan
inventory assets 396

tanaoroshi shisan hikiatekin
inventory reserve 397

tanaoroshi shisan kaikei
inventory accounting 396

tanaoroshi shisan kaitenritsu
inventory turnover 397

tanaoroshi shisan rieki
inventory profit 397

tanaoroshihyō
inventory (stock-taking list) 396

tanaoroshison
inventory loss 397

tanbunshiki hōkokusho
short-form report 418

tanbunshiki kansa hōkokusho
short-form audit report [US] 418

tanchō rōdō
monotonous work 461

tandoku ginkō
unit bank [US] 163

tandoku ginkōsei
unit banking system [US] 163

tandoku hōjin
corporation sole 343

tandoku kaison
particular average 326

tandoku kawase tegata
sola bill 160

tandoku shoyūken
sole ownership 361

tanhon'i kahei seido
monometallic standard 181; monometallism 181

tanhon'isei
monometallic standard 181; monometallism 181; single standard 184

tan'i
lot (securities) 244

tan'i kabu
round lot 268

tan'imei
denomination (unit name) 142, 169

tanin no seimei hoken keiyaku
insurance on someone's life 323

tanin shihon
borrowed capital 373; outside capital 407

tan'itsu genka keisan
unit costing 426

tan'itsu ginkō
unit bank [US] 163

tan'itsu ginkō seido
unit banking system [US] 163

tan'itsu hokenryō
single premium 329

tan'itsu kawase sōba
single rate of exchange 184

tan'itsu kigyō
single firm 360

tan'itsu no taishaku taishōhyō
single balance sheet 418

tan'itsu sekinin
single liability 329

tan'itsu tegata
single bill 160; sola bill 160

tanjun hikiuke
absolute acceptance 131; clean acceptance 140

tanjun kanjō
simple account 418

tanjun kanjōshiki
simple account form 418

tanjun rōdō
simple work 467; unskilled labour 471

tanjun sagyō
monotonous work 461

tanjun shiwakechō
simple journal 418

tanjun sōgō genka keisan
simple cost accounting 418

tanjun sōkan to kaiki
simple correlation and regression 100

tanjun tokkentsuki baibai
simple option 274

tayōka
diversification 27

teate
allowance 369, 475

tebari
trade on one's own account 282

tedori
take-home pay 484

tedori chingin
net pay 480; take-home pay (wages) 107, 484

tedori kyūryō
take-home pay (salary) 484

tegata
bill 136; bill (statement of money owed) 200; paper (bill) 155, 257

tegata o seisan suru
clear a bill 140

tegata burōkā
bill broker 200

tegata enki tsūchijō
bill advice 136

tegata furidashi annai
advice of bill 132

tegata furidashi sashizu
draft instructions 145

tegata furidashinin
drawer (of a bill) 145

tegata henkō
alteration of bill 132

tegata hikiuke
acceptance of bill 131

tegata hikiuke gyōsha
acceptance house [US] 193; accepting house [UK] 193

tegata hikiuke shorui watashi
documents against acceptance (DA) 142, 144

tegata hikiuke shōsha
acceptance house [US] 193; accepting house [UK] 193

tegata hiuragakinin
draft endorsee 145

tegata hoyūdaka
draft holdings 145

tegata kaiire tesūryō
handling charge (for a bill) 148

tegata kaitori ginkō fushitei shin'yōjō
general L/C 148; open L/C 154

tegata kaitori ginkō shitei shin'yōjō
restricted L/C 159; special L/C 161

tegata kaitori sashizusho
letter of instruction 151

tegata kanjō
bill account 136

tegata kanjō chōbo
bill book 136

tegata kashitsuke
loan on bills 242

tegata kessaibi
value date 163

tegata kikan
usance 163

tegata kingaku
amount of bill 132

tegata kōkan
bank clearing 134; bill clearing 136; clearing 140; clearing of bill 140; transit operation 162

tegata kōkan kamei ginkō
clearing bank [UK] 140

tegata kōkan kanjō
clearing account 140

tegata kōkan kessanhyō
clearing house proof 140

tegata kōkan kumiai ginkō
clearing banks 16

tegata kōkan seido
clearing system 140

tegata kōkandaka
amount cleared 132

tegata kōkanjiri
balance of clearing 133; clearing balance 140

tegata kōkanjo
Banker's Clearing House [UK] 135; clearing house 140

tegata kōkanjo kanji
clearing house inspector 140

tegata kōkanjo kumiai ginkō
member of the clearing house 151

tegata kōsen
bill brokerage 200

tegata manki made no kikan
tenor 162

tegata mochidaka
bill holdings 137

tegata naatenin
drawee (of a bill) 145

tegata nakagainin
bill broker 200

tegata no furidashi
drawing of bill 145

tegata no teiji
presentation of bill 157

tegata no tsūchi nashi
'no advice' 153

tegata operēshon
operation in bills 254

tegata saiwaribiki
bill rediscounting 137, 200

tegata shiharai basho
domicile of a bill 144

tegata shiharai hoshō
guarantee of a bill 148

tegata shiharai kigen enchō
draft extension 145

tegata shiharai kikan
usance 163

tegata shiharai shorui watashi
documents against payment (DP) 144

tegata shijō
bills market 200; commercial paper market 209

tegata shojinin
bill bearer 136; bill holder 137; draft holder 145

tegata tōjisha
parties to a bill 155

tegata toritate
bill collection 136

tegata toritatenin
bill collector 137

tegata toritateryō
charge for collection of a bill 139

tegata toritsuginin
running broker 268

tegata uragaki
draft endorsement 145

tegata uragakinin
draft endorser 145

tegata uridashi
sale of bills 268

tegata waribiki
bill discounting 137, 200; discounting of bills 144

tegata waribiki gyōsha
bill discounter 200

tegata waribiki nakagainin
discount broker (bills) 218

tegata waribiki shijō
bill discounting market 200; discount bill market 218

tegatabarai
payment by bill 156

teian
proposal 88, 431

teian suru
propose 431

teiatsu keizai
low-pressure economy 65

teichingin
low wages 65, 479; moderate wage 480

teichingin keizai
low-wage economy 65

teichingin rōdō
cheap labour 16

teichingin rōdō seisaku
cheap labour policy 16, 451

teichingin rōdōryoku
cheap labour 451

teichingin rōdōsha
low-paid worker 479

teichinginkoku
low-wage nation 65

teigaku hoken shōken
valued policy 330

teigaku rieki ruisekigata tōshin
constant dollar plan [US] 210; pound-cost averaging [UK] 259

teigakukyū jūgyōin
salaried employee 483

teigakumen kabushiki
low-value stock 244

teigakumen teigen
gradual decrease 44

teigen
gradual decrease 44

teihai kabu
low-dividend stock 244, 400

teihakujo
haven 230

tei'i kabu
low-grade stock 244

teijibarai
payment on presentation 156

teijibarai tegata
bill for presentation 137

teijō jōtai
stationary state 104

teikaihatsu
underdevelopment 114

teikaihatsu chi'iki
underdeveloped region 114

teikaihatsu no
underdeveloped 114

teikaihatsukoku
less developed countries (LDCs) 62; underdeveloped country 114

teikan
articles of association [UK] 336; articles of incorporation [US] 337; charter 340

teikan henkō
amendment of articles 336

teikan no sakusei
drawing up the Articles of Incorporation 344

teikei
affiliation (tie-up) 336

teikei no kaishō
dissolution of partnership 344

teikei suru
go into partnership 347

teikeisha
associate 337

teikeizai seichō
slow economic growth 101

teiketsu
drawing up (of a contract) 294

teiketsu suru
keiyaku o teiketsu suru
draw up (a contract) 294
to no gyōmu teikei o teiketsu suru
enter into business (with) 345

teiki
term (fixed term) 281

teiki chinshakuken
leasehold (fixed-period lease) 300

teiki fudōsankensha
termor 310

teiki hoken
term insurance 329

teiki kansa
periodic audit 409

teiki kashitsuke
fixed loan 225; time loan 281

teiki kenkō shindan
regular physical check-ups 482

teiki saiyō
annual recruitment 441; regular recruitment 446 (note 25); yearly recruitment 447

teiki seimei hoken
term life insurance 330

teiki shakuchi
leaseholding 300

teiki shasai
term bond 281

teiki shōkyū
regular pay rises 482

teiki sōkai
regular meeting 431

teiki taishaku taishōhyō
periodic balance sheet 409

teiki tanaoroshi
periodic inventory [US] 409; periodic stock-taking [UK] 409

teiki torihiki
dealing within the account 215

teiki yokin
fixed deposit 146; fixed-time deposit 146; time deposit [US] 162

tenkan kabu(shiki)
conversion stock 381; convertible stock 211

tenkan kachi
conversion value 211

tenkan kakaku
conversion price 210

tenkan kanōsei
convertibility 211, 381

tenkan puremiamu
conversion premium 210

tenkan shasai
convertible bond 211; convertible debenture 211; loan stock 243

tenkan shōken
convertible securities 211; convertibles 211

tenkan waribiki
conversion discount 210

tenkan yūsen kabu
convertible preference shares 381; convertible preferred stock 381

tenkanken
conversion rights 210, 381

tenkanki
transition (turning point) 113

tenkanten
turning point 113

tenken
inspection 322

tenken hōkoku
inspection report 322

tenki
posting (accounts) 410

tenki no ayamari
posting error 410

tenki suru
post (verb) 410

tenkibo
posting book 410

tenkin
transfer 470

tenkin no aisatsu
'paying one's respects upon transferral' 473

tenkin suru (— ni)
transferred to (—) 470

tennin
transfer 470

tennin negai
request for transfer 466; transfer request 470

tennōzan
tennōzan [J] 504

tenpo seikyūgaku no satei
assessment of insurance claim 316

tenpokin
claim payable 317

tenpu shorui
accompanying documents 131, 335; attached documents 132

tensha suru
change jobs (change companies) 441

tenshaku
subtenancy 309

tenshakunin
sublessee 309; subtenant 309

tenshoku
change of jobs 441

tenshoku suru
change jobs [formal] 441

tentō
counter 211

tentō baibai
over-the-counter trading 256

tentō kabu
counter stock 211; over-the-counter stock 256

tentō kogitte
cheque cashed over the counter 139

tentō shijō
over-the-counter market 256; unlisted securities market [US] 284

tentō torihiki
over-the-counter transaction 256

tenzen shigen
natural resources 72

tesaguri
tâtonnement 107

tesūryō
charge 139; commission 140, 167, 209; fee 146; load 242

tesūryō baibai
commission sale 292

tesūryō kanjō
commission account 379

tesuto
test (noun) 447

tesuto suru
test (verb) 447

tetsukekin
deposit 293; key money [US] 298

tetsukekin o utsu (ie ni)
leave a deposit (on a house) 300

tetsuzuki
proceedings 436

tetsuzuki o kyakka suru
dismiss proceedings 434

tetsuzuki no kaishi
initiation of procedure 435

tezume
forced liquidation 226

tezume uri
liquidation sale 399

tobasu
'to let fly', 'to send flying' 473

tochi
land 61, 298; land (on balance sheet) 398; property , a (land) 305

asonde iru tochi
idle land 297

tochi burōkā
land broker 299

tochi chingariryō
land rental revenue 299

tochi chintaiken
land lease 299

tochi daichō
land register 299

tochi fudōsan
landed estate 300

tochi fukkiken
escheat (land) 294

tochi genka
depreciation of land 293

tochi haraisage
land grant [US] 299

tochi hoyū(ken)
land tenure 61, 299

tochi hoyūsha
land tenant 299

tochi kaihatsu
exploitation of land 295; land development 299

tochi kaihatsu gyōsha
land developer 299

tochi kaikaku
land reform 61

tochi kairyō
land improvement 299

tochi kakaku
land price 299; land value 300

tochi kanri
land management 61, 299

tochi kanrinin
land agency (administrators, managers) 299

tochi kubun
land classification 61, 299

tochi kukaku seiri
land re-allocation 299

tochi no mitsumori
valuation of land 311

tochi no shoyūken
property in land 305

tochi oyobi tatemono
land and building(s) 299

tochi riyō
land use 300; land utilization 300

tochi seido
land system 299

tochi seisansei
land productivity 299

tochi setsuyakuteki
land-saving 299

tochi settei
land settlement 299

tochi shakuyō
land tenancy 299

tochi shiyōteki
land-using 300

tochi shoyū
land ownership 299; landholding 300

tochi shoyūhō
land laws 299

tochi shoyūken
domain (private) 293; land ownership 299

tochi shoyūken iten
land transfer 300

tochi shoyūsei no jinushi
freehold landlord 295; freeholder 295

tochi shoyūsha
landowner 300; landed proprietor 300; landholder 300; landlady 300; landlord 300

tochi shūeki
land revenue 299

tochi shūsengyō
land agency (commission agency) 299

tochi shūsengyōsha
land agent 299

tochi shutoku
land acquisition 299

tochi shutoku kakaku
land acquisition price 299

tochi shūyakuteki na
land-intensive 61

tochi shūyō
land expropriation 299

tochi tatemono chinshakuryō
rent of land and building(s) 307

tochi-tatemono teitō shasai
mortgage on land and buildings (company's) 302

tochi tōki
land registration 299

tochi tōkisho
land registry 299

tochi torihiki
land transaction 300

tochi zōka
land appreciation 299

tochi zōsei
land reclamation 299

todoke
notification 353

todokōri
arrear (being in arrear) 196

tōgetsu kagiri yūkō na chūmon
good-this-month order 228

tōgi
discussion 430

tōgō
consolidation (accounts) 380; integration 55, 349

tōgō kanjō
consolidated accounts 380

tōgō keizai
integrated economy 55

tōgō kigyō
partnership (combined businesses) 355

tōhi kyokusen
iso-cost curves 58; iso-outlay curve 58

tōhi kyūsū
geometric progression 43

tōhi shihon
flight capital 225; refugee capital 264

tōhō kanjō
nostro account 153

tōhon
duplicate 345

tōhyō
ballot 198, 429; ballot (draw for shares) 372; vote 432, 503

ikko no tōhyō o suru
cast one's vote 429

tōhyō o eru
obtain votes 431

tōhyō o henkō suru
change one's vote 429

tōhyō o keisan suru
count votes 430

tōhyō o kyohi suru
reject a vote 431

tōhyō gizō
vote forgery 432

tōhyō keisan
counting of votes 430

tōhyō keisan no kekka
result of the counting of votes 431

tokubetsu rigai kankeinin
affiliated person 336; control person 342

tokubetsu shikin
special fund 419

tokubetsu shōkyaku tsumitatekin
special depreciation reserve 419

tokubetsu shōyo
special bonus 484

tokubetsu son'eki
extraordinary profit and loss 390; special profits and losses 419

tokubetsu sonshitsu
extraordinary loss 390; special losses 419

tokubetsu teate
extra allowance 390; special allowance 419, 483

tokubetsu tōza yokin
special checking account [US] 161

tokubetsu uridashi
special offering [US] 275

tokubetsu waribiki
special discounts 419

tokubetsu yokin kanjō
convertible account 141

tokui
forte 442; strong point 447

tokuisaki
client 208; customer 142

tokuisaki hikiuke tegata
customer's acceptance 142

tokuisaki kanjō
customer's account 142

tokumei gaisha
dormant company 344

tokumei kumiai
anonymous association 336

tokumei kumiai'in
dormant partner (anonymous) 344

tokumei shain
dormant partner (anonymous) 344; silent partner 360; sleeping partner 361

tokurei shigaisha
exempted private company 346

tokusei riron
characteristics theory 16

tokushu kashitsuke
special loan 275

tokushu motochō
special ledger 419

tokutan bunson
particular average 326

tokutei haitōritsu
specified rate of dividend 419

tokutei hoken
special insurance 329

tokutei ininjō
special power of attorney 361

tokutei kiken
named risk 326

tokutei kiken hoken
named risk insurance 326

tokutei meigara
specified issue 275, 419

tokutei mokutekiyō zaimu shohyō
special-purpose financial statement 419

tokutei ōsen
special crossing 161

tokutei ōsen kogitte
special crossed cheque 161

tokutei shisan
special assets 419

tokuteinin waribiki shin'yōjō
straight L/C 161

tokuyaku saihoken
treaty reinsurance 330

tokuyū zaisan
separate property 308

tōkyō shōken torihikijo
Tokyo Stock Exchange 282

tōkyūzuke
grading (of commodities) 229

tomi
wealth (a fortune, riches) 119

tomi kōka
wealth effect 119

tomi no bunpai
wealth distribution 119

tomi no saibunpai
wealth redistribution 119

tomi seiyaku
wealth restraint 119

tomobataraki
working couples 121

tomokasegi katei
double-income families 28

tonae
quoting 262

tōnan ajia shokoku rengō
Association of South-East Asian Nations (ASEAN) 8

tōnan hoken
burglary insurance 317; insurance against theft 323; robbery insurance 329

tōnan kabu
hot stock (stolen) 231

tōnan kogittechō
stolen cheque book 161

tōnan tegata
stolen bill 161

tōnan yobo keihōki
burglar alarm system 317

tōnen
current year 384

ton'yagyō
commission agency business 341

tōnyū
input 54

tōnyū-sanshutsu bunseki
input-output analysis 54

tōnyū-sanshutsu hiritsu
input/output ratio 55

tōnyūdaka
input amount 54

tōō keizai sōgo enjo kaigi
Council for Mutual Economic Aid (COMECON) 17, 21

tōrakusen
advance-decline line 194

torēdo-ofu
trade-off 112

toriage
expropriation 295; repossession 307

toriage kaoku
repossessed property 307

toriage tetsuzuki
repossession proceedings (legal proceedings for vacation of property) 307

toriageru
repossess 307

toriatsukai
handling 148

toriatsukai tesūryō
handling charge 148

toriatsukau
handle (verb) 456

torihiki
business 338; deal 214; negotiation (transaction) 250; trade 111; trading 282; transaction 162, 186, 282

torihiki bun'ya
area of operation 336

torihiki dōki
transactions motive 113

torihiki ginkō
bankers (a company's) 136; company's bankers 140, 379

torihiki hiyō
transactions costs 112

torihiki kaishi
opening of account 154

torihiki kaishibi
date account opened 142

torihiki kankei
business connections 338

torihiki nashi
'no account' 153

torihiki o sosei suru hito
originator 154

torihiki ryūdō sokudo
transactions velocity of circulation 113

torihiki seigen kankō
restrictive trade practices 95

torihiki seigen kankōhō
Restrictive Trade Practices Act [UK] 95

torihiki seigen saibansho
Restrictive Practices Court [UK] 95

torihiki shikkō
execution 221

torihiki suru
do business 344; negotiate (carry out a transaction) 250; trade (verb) 111

(— to) torihiki suru
bank with (—) 135

torihiki tan'i
round lot 268; trading unit 282

torihiki tantōsha
account executive 193

torihiki teishi
suspension of transactions 161, 280

torihiki teishibi
date account closed 142

torihiki tesūryō
transaction fee 282

torihiki zandaka
transactions balances 112

torihikibi
trading day 282

torihikidaka
trade turnovers 112; volume (of trading) 285

torihiki'in
authorized dealer 197; broker 203

torihikijo
exchange (place of trading) 35, 221

torihikijo bunbai
exchange distribution 221

torihikijo kai'in
exchange members 221

torihikijo kai'in sōba
members' rate 247

torihikijo nakagainin
exchange broker 221

torihikijo no jidōteki sōba seido
Stock Exchange Automated Quotation System (SEAQ) [UK] 269, 277

torihikijo owarine no insatsu
run-off 268

torihikisaki
client 140; customer (accounts) 142

torikae
replacement 328

torikae genka
replacement cost 94, 415

torikae hiyō
replacement cost 328

torikae hoken
replacement insurance 328

torikae kachi
replacement value 328

torikaehi hoken
depreciation insurance 319

torikeshifunō ininjō
irrevocable proxy 430

torikeshifunō shin'yōjō
irrevocable L/C 150

torikeshikanō shin'yōjō
revocable L/C 159

torikowasu
knock down 298

torikumi
open interest 254

torishimariyaku
administrator 335; director 344, 453

torishimariyaku kaichō
Chairman of the Board of Directors 340, 451

torishimariyaku no hōkoku
director's report 344

torishimariyaku no ketsugi
directors' vote 430

torishimariyaku no ninmei
appointment of directors 336

torishimariyaku oyobi kanji meibo
Register of Directors and Secretaries 358

torishimariyaku shōshū
directors' meeting 430

torishimariyakukai
board meeting 429; Board of Directors 337

tōshi shūeki
return on investment 267

tōshi sōdan
investment advice 237

tōshi sōdannin
investment adviser 150

tōshi suru
invest 236

tōshi taishō
investment outlet(s) 57, 238

tōshi tekikaku
investment grade 237

tōshi tekikaku no ichiranhyō
approved list (securities) 196

tōshi tsūka
investment currency 237

tōshi yosan
investment budget 237, 397

tōshi yūin
investment incentives 57, 237

tōshi yūka shōken
investment securities 238

tōshi yūka shōken baikyaku'eki
profits on the sale of investment
securities 412

tōshi zeikōjo
investment credit [US] 237;
investment tax credit [US] 238

tōshigai
investment buying 237

toshika
urbanization 116, 311

tōshika
investor 238

tōshika bēsu
investor base 238

tōshikanō shikin
investible funds 236, 397

tōshikoku
investing country 236

tōshikyaku
investing client 236

tōshitō
investments and advances (on
balance sheet) 397

tōshizai
investment commodity 237

tōshizai sangyō
investment goods industry 124

tōshō kabuka heikin shisū
Tokyo Stock Exchange stock
price average 282

tōshō rimawari
initial yield 233

tōshō shishutsu
initial outlay 395

tōshō shōkokin
initial margin 233

tōshō tōnyū shikin
seed money 270

tōshō tōshi
initial investment 233

tōshō tōshigaku
original investment 255

tōshō yosan
initial budget 395; original
budget 77, 406

tōshū kagiri yūkō na chūmon
good-this-week order 228

tōshūnyū kyokusen
iso-revenue curve 58

tōsō
dispute 499; labour offensive
500

tōsō shikin
strike fund 502

tōsū ni yoru hyōketsu
vote by the head 432

totei
apprentice 450

totei kikan
apprenticeship period 450

totei yōsei
apprenticeship training 450

toteisei
apprenticeship 450

tōza furikomi
credit to current account 142

tōza hiritsu
quick ratio 413

tōza kanjō
checking account [US] 139;
current account [UK] 142

tōza karikoshi
current loans payable 384

tōza karikoshi o mitomeru
grant an overdraft 148

tōza kashikoshi
current loans receivable 384

tōza kashikoshi risoku
interest on overdraft 149;
rate on overdraft 157

tōza shihon
quick capital 413

tōza shisan
quick assets 413

tōza yokin
cash at bank 377; cash in bank
138; checking account [US]
139; current account [UK] 142;
current deposits 22, 142;
deposit into current account
143

tozama
'outsider' 473

tsu
unit for counting companies [J]
363

tsūchi
advice 131; notice 153, 353;
notification 153, 431; written
notice 363

tsūchi o ataeru
notify 353

tsūchi o hassuru
issue notice 430; notify 431

tsūchi ginkō
advising bank 132; notifying
bank 153

tsūchi no de
as per advice 132

tsūchi tesūryō
advising charge 132

tsūchi yokin
deposit with notice 143; time
account 162

tsūchibarai
advice and pay (A/P) 131

tsuchijō
advice note 132; letter of
advice 150; notification 353

tsugu
inherit 298

tsugunau
compensate 491; indemnify
322

tsuika hoken
additional insurance 315

tsuika kentsuki baibai
put of more 262

tsuika shin'yō
additional credit 194

tsuika shōkokin
additional margin 194; margin
call 245; remargin 266

tsuika yosan
additional budget 4;
supplementary budget 422

tsuishō
remargin 266

tsūjō haitō
regular dividend 415

tsūjō kessan
general closing 393

tsūjō ketsugi
ordinary resolution 431

tsūjō kinri
ordinary interest rate 255

tsūjō kumiai
general partnership 347

tsūjō risoku
ordinary interest 255

tsūjō teikan
articles of company 336

tsūjō ukewatashi
regular-way delivery 265;
regular-way settlement 265

tsūjōgata fudōsan kashidashi
conventional mortgage loan
292

tsūka
currency 22, 168

tsūka aberabititii
currency availability 168

tsūka antei(ka)
currency stabilization 169;
monetary stabilization 70, 180

tsūka anteisei
currency stability 169;
monetary stability 70, 180

tsūka basuketto
currency basket 168

tsūka basuketto hōshiki
currency basket system 168

tsūka bōchō
currency inflation 169

tsūka burokku
currency block 168

tsūka chitsujo
monetary order 180

tsūka chōsei
currency alignment 168

tsūka chōsetsu
currency regulation 169

tsūka fuan
currency instability 169;
monetary instability 69, 179;
monetary uncertainty 180;
monetary unrest 70, 180

tsūka genka
depreciation 169

tsūka haishi
demonetization (withdrawal of a
certain currency) 169

tsūka infurēshon
currency inflation 169

tsūka junbi
monetary reserve(s) 70, 180

tsūka kachi
currency value 169; monetary
value (currency) 180; value of
currency 117, 187

tsūka kachi geraku
depreciation (currency) 25;
currency depreciation 168

tsūka kachi no iji
maintenance of the value of a
currency 178

tsūka kachi no teiraku
depreciation 169

tsūka kachi no tōki
currency appreciation 168

tsūka kaikaku
monetary reform 69, 180

tsūka kanri
currency control 168; monetary
management 69

tsūka kantokukan
Comptroller of the Currency
[US] 167

tsūka kiki
monetary crisis 69, 179

tsūka kirikae
currency conversion 168

tsūka kirisage
currency devaluation 168

tsūka kōkansei
currency convertibility 168

tsūka kyōkyū nobiritsu
monetary growth 69, 179

tsūka kyōkyūryō
money supply 70, 180

tsūka kyōtei
monetary agreement 69, 179

tsūka no
monetary 179

tsūka no antei
stabilization of currency 185

tsūka no hakkō junbi
legal backing 178

tsūka no kachi o sageru
depreciate 169

tsūka no kaishū
withdrawal of a currency 187

tsūka no ryōgae tesūryō
agio (charge for changing
money) 165

tsūka no ryūtsū sokudo
velocity of circulation 117

tsūka ryūryō
currency flow 22, 168

tsūka ryūtsūdaka
currency in circulation 168

tsūka saibōchō
reflation 93

tsūka saichōsei
currency re-alignment 169

tsūka sakimono torihiki
currency futures 168, 214

tsūka seido
currency system 169;
monetary system 70, 180

tsūka seisaku
monetary policy (currency) 69,
180

unsōchū no genkin
cash in transit 138

unten hiyō
operating costs 405; operating expenses 405

unten shihon
operating capital 405; working capital 121, 427

unten shihon hiritsu
working capital ratio 121, 427

unten shihon jōtai
current position 384

unten shikin
operating funds 405; operation funds 406; working funds 427

untenhi
operating costs 405; operating expenses 405; operation cost 406; operational costs 406; running expenses 416

un'yō
investment (use of capital) 237, 397

un'yō rimawari
investment yield 238; yield on investment 286

un'yō shisan
operating assets 405; working assets 427

un'yō zandaka
working balances 427

un'yugyō
transport industry 127

uragaki
endorsement 145

uragaki kinshi tegata
non-negotiable endorsement 153

uragaki suru
endorse 145

uragaki tegata
endorsed bill 145; made bill 151

uragakinin
endorser 145

uraguchi kin'yū
back-door financing 198

uraguchi sōsa
back-door operation 198

urenokori
undigested stock 284

uri
sale 183; selling 183

uri ni dasu
offer for sale (verb) 303

uri ope
open-market selling operation 254; selling operation 271

uri yobine
asked price [US] 196

uriage
sales 416

uriage bunseki
sales analysis 416

uriage genka
cost of sales 383; sales cost 416

uriage hanbai kaikei
sales accounting 416

uriage junrieki
net profit on sales 403

uriage junriekiritsu
net profit margin 403

uriage junsonshitsu
net loss on sales 402

uriage kanjō
sales account 416

uriage kingaku
proceeds from sale 304

uriage motochō
sales ledger 416

uriage okurijō
sales invoice 416

uriage rieki
sales profit 416

uriage shiwakechō
sales journal 416

uriage shūeki
sales revenue [US] 416

uriage sōrieki
gross profit on sales 394

uriage waribiki
sales discounts 416

uriage waribiki hikiatekin
allowance for sales discounts [UK] 369

uriage waribiki junbikin
provision for discounts allowable [US] 412

uriagechō
sales book 416

uriagedaka
sales amount 416

uriagedaka-eigyōhi hiritsu
operating expenses/sales ratio 405

uriagedaka-junriekiritsu
net profits/sales ratio 403

uriagedaka yosoku
sales forecasting 416

uriagezei
sales tax [US] (= turnover tax [UK]) 97

urichūmon
selling order 271

uridashi
primary offering 260; sale (bonds) 268

uridashi kabu
publicly offered shares 262, 413

uridashi kakaku
offering price (selling price) 253

urigata rengō
bear pool 199

urigyoku
bear account 199

urihejji
short hedge 273

uriichijun
sold-out 274

urikake(kin) kanjō
charge account 207; credit account [UK] 212

urikakekin
accounts receivable 366; book credit 202

urikakekin motochō
accounts receivable ledger 366

urikata
bear (seller) 199

urikata kata
bears over 200; sellers over 271

urikata no
bearish 200

urikatazeme
bear squeeze 199

urikawase
exchange selling 172; selling exchange 183

urikawase sōba
selling quotation 183

urikomi
heavy selling 230

urikuzushi
banging the market 198; bear raid 199; raiding the market 262; sell-off 271; selling-off 271

urimochi
oversold position 256; short position 184, 273

urimodoshi
long liquidation 243; resale 267

urimōshikomi ukesha
offeree 253

urimōshikomisha
offerer 253

urimukai
bear drive 199

urine
offer (asked price) 253; offer price [UK] 253; offering price 253; opening price 254; selling price 271

urininki
bearish tone 200

urinushi
vendor 312

uriopushon
put option (selling option) 262

urisabaku
bang 198

urisashine
selling limit 271

urisōba
exchange selling rate 172; bear market 199; seller's rate 271; selling rate 183

urisugi
overselling 256

urisugi no sōba
oversold market 256

urisugiru
oversell 256

uritataki
hammering the market [US] 230

uritataku
bear the market 199; hammer the market [US] 230

urite
seller 271, 308; vendor 312

urite sentaku
seller's option 271

urite shijō
seller's market 271

uritsuki sentakuken
put option (selling option) 262

uritsunagi
hedge selling 230; selling hedge 271; short hedge 273

uriwatashi gaikoku kawase
foreign bills sold 147

uriya
house for sale 297

uriya fuda
for-sale sign 295

uriyobine
asked price [US] 196; offer 253; offer price [UK] 253; offering price 253

urizairyō
bearish factor 200

uru
sell 308

usuakinai
light trading 241

uwabanare
break-out 203

uwamuki
improvement 232; upswing 116; upward trend 116

wadai
subject for discussion 432

wagi tetsuzuki
composition procedures 434

waidā-bando
wider band 187

wan
(hokusen - chōsen minshushugi jinmin kyō wakoku)
(nansen - daikan minkoku)
wan (North Korea – Democratic People's Republic of Korea) (South Korea – Republic of Korea) 190

wanryoku sōba
forced market 226; forced quotation 226

warantotsuki shasai
bond with warrant 202

wariate
allocation (assignment) 6; apportionment 370; quota 90

wariate kijun
basis of apportionment 372

wariate kiken buntan
assigned risk 316

wariate suru
allot 195, 368

wariate tsūchisho
allotment letter 195

wariategaku
allotment value 369; quota 90

wariatesei
quota system 90

wariatesū
quota (human quota) 90

waribiki
discount (noun) 143, 218; discounting 26, 144, 218

waribiki buai
Bank Rate 135, 199; discount rate 143, 218

waribiki buai seisaku
discount rate policy 26

waribiki gaisha
discount company 218

waribiki ginkō
discount bank 143; discounting bank 144

waribiki gyōsha
discount house [UK] 218

yōchi sangyō hogoron
infant industry argument for protection 54

yochokin
bank deposits and savings 134; savings and deposits 98

yochokin no hikidashi
drawing of money 145

yochokin o hikidasu
draw money 145

yogashiritsu
loan/deposit ratio 242

yōgyō
ceramic industry 123; pottery industry 126

yōgyō-doseki seihin kōgyō
ceramic, stone and clay products industry 123

yōgyogyō
fish-farming 124

yōhō
bee-keeping 123

yōhōgyō
apiculture 123

yoi kyūyo
good pay 477

yōin
factor (primary factor) 37

yōin bunseki
factor analysis 37

yōji ga aru
busy ('have things to do') 450

yōji rōdō
child labour 16

yojō
overhang 256; redundant 502; surplus 106

yojō jin'in
surplus staff 468; surplus workers 503; unneeded workers 470

yojō rōdōryoku
redundant labour force 93, 502; surplus labour 106

yojō rōdōsha
extra worker 455; redundancy (-ies) 93, 501; redundant worker 502

yojō rōdōsha hoshō
redundancy indemnity 501

yojō rōdōsha hoshōkin
redundancy payment(s) 93, 414, 502

yojō shikin
surplus funds 106

yojō shisan
surplus assets 422

yojō shokuryō
surplus food 106

yojō zaiko
overstock 77

yoka
leisure 62

yoka juyō
demand for leisure 24

yōkansū
explicit function 36

yōkeigyō
poultry-farming 126

yōkeikai meigara
watch list 286

yōken
business matter 339

yoki na
cheerful 451

yokin
deposit 142; deposited money 143; depositing 143; funds 147; money deposited 152; money on deposit 152

yokin o orosu
withdraw 163

yokin fusoku
insufficient funds 149; 'no funds' 153; 'not sufficient funds' 153; shortage of funds (in account) 160

yokin fusoku kogitte
insufficient funds cheque 149; short cheque 160

yokin ginkō
bank of deposit 135; deposit bank 143

yokin jutaku kikan
deposit-taking institution 143

yokin kanjō
deposit account [UK] 143

yokin-kashitsuke hiritsu
deposit/loan ratio 25

yokin kinri
interest on deposit 149

yokin nyūkinchō
paying-in book 155

yokin riritsu
deposit rate (Bank of Japan) 143

yokin rishi
interest on deposit 149

yokin rishi kazei
tax on deposit interest 161

yokin shiharai junbiritsu
bank reserve ratio 135

yokin shōsho
certificate of deposit (CD) 138, 139, 207; deposit receipt 143; deposit slip 143

yokin suru
deposit (verb) (money) 142

yokin tanpo kashitsuke
loan on deposits 242

yokin tsūchō
bank deposit passbook 134; deposit book 143; passbook 155

yokin tsūchō kōza
passbook account 155

yokin tsūka
bank money 10, 135; deposit currency 143

yokin ukeireshō
deposit receipt 143

yokin zandaka
balance of account 133

yokin zandaka fusoku
short balance 160; short deposit balance 160

yokin zōka
increase in deposit 149

yokin zōkaritsu kisei
corset [UK] 141

yokindaka
amount deposited 132

yokinsha
depositor 143

yokinsha hogo
protection of depositors 157

yokinsha no kimitsusei
confidentiality of depositor 141

yokobai
levelling-out 62

yokobai suru
level out 62

yokodori suru
intercept 55

yokomeshi
business lunch or dinner with foreign visitors 487, 488 (note 37)

yokuatsugata infurēshon
repressed inflation 94

yokubō sōshutsu
want creation 119

yokujitsu mono
day-to-day money 214; overnight securities 256

yokujitsu mono no repo
overnight repo 256

yokujitsu watashi
overnight delivery 256

yokujitsubarai kashitsuke
overnight call loan 256; overnight loan 256

yokujitsubarai shikin
overnight money 256

yokuyokujitsu kessai
skip-day [US] 274

yōkyū
need 73

yōkyūbarai
on demand 154; payable at call 257; payable on demand 155, 257

yōkyūbarai o suru
pay on demand 155

yōkyūbarai kashitsuke
demand loan 217

yōkyūbarai tegata
bills on demand 137; demand draft 142; draft on demand 145

yōkyūbarai yokin
demand deposit [US] 142; sight deposit [UK] 160

yōmōgyō
wool industry 127

yoritsuki
opening 254; opening session 254

yoritsuki de
at the opening 197

yoritsuki de kau
buy on opening 205

yoritsuki kehai
opening tone 254

yoritsuki nedan
opening price (opening quotation) 254

yoritsuki sōba
opening quotation 254

yoritsukigai
buying on opening 206

yoritsukine
opening price (opening quotation) 254

yoritsukine de kau
buy on opening 205

yoriyobine
opening call 254

yōrō hoken
endowment 319; endowment assurance 320

yōrō hoken shōken
endowment policy 320

yōrō nenkin
endowment annuity 319; old-age pension 76

yōrō nenkin tokuyaku hoken
endowment assurance 320

yōrō seimei hoken
endowment annuity insurance 319

yōrō shikin
endowment 319

yorudan
Jordan 189

yosan
budget 12, 374

yōsan
sericulture 126

yosan akaji
budget deficit 12

yosan chōka
budget overrun 12

yosan fuseiritsu
rejection of budget proposal 94

yosan gen'an
draft budget 28

yosan genka
budgeted cost 374

yosan genka hikiatekin
budget cost allowance 374

yosan hensei
budget compilation 12; budgeting 374

yosan hōkokusho
budget report 374

yosan i'inkai
appropriation committee 7; budget committee 12

yosan jōyo
budget surplus 12, 374

yosan kaikaku
budget reform 12

yosan kanjō
budget account 374

yosan kanri
budgetary control 374

yosan keikaku
budget planning 374

yosan kikan
budget period 374

yosan kōmoku
budget items 12, 374

yosan mitsumori(sho)
budget forecast (estimation) 12

yosan no shikkō
budget implementation 12

yosan sakugen ronsha
budget cutters 12

yosan sakusei
budget drafting 12

yosan seido
budgeting system 374

yūka shōken kinyūchō
securities register 270

yūka shōken meisaisho
portfolio 259; stock portfolio
278

yūka shōken motochō
investment ledger 397;
securities ledger 417

yūka shōken nakagainin
securities broker 270

yūka shōken no hyōkason
loss from securities revaluation
244

yūka shōken no jōto
transfer of securities 282

yūka shōken shintaku
securities trust 270

yūka shōken tanpo kashitsuke
loan secured by stocks and
bonds 242

yūka shōken tanpo sashiire
hypothecation [US] (pledging of
securities) 231

yūka shōken todokeidesho
registration statement 265;
securities registration statement
270

yūka shōken torihiki
securities transaction 270

yūka shōken torihikizei
securities transaction tax 270

yūkei bōeki
visible trade 117

yūkei shisan
material assets 401; tangible
assets 423; visible assets 426

yūkei shōmi shisan
tangible net worth 423

yūkei yunyū
visible imports 117

yūkei yushutsu
visible exports 117

yūkei zaisan
material property 301

yūki shasai
redeemable debenture 264

yūkin
idle money 48, 231

yūkō
validity 432

yūkō juyō
effective demand 32

yūkō kyōsō
effective competition 32;
workable competition 121

yūkō no
valid 432

yūkō no pōtoforio
efficient portfolio 220

yūkō seisanritsu
effective rate of production 32

yūkōteki na baishūsha
friendly buyer 347; white knight
363

yūkōteki na nottori
friendly take-over 347

yūkyū
with pay 486

yūkyū byōki kyūka
paid sick leave 481; sick leave
with pay 483

yūkyū jūgyōin
paid employee 481

yūkyū jūtaku
idle properties 297

yūkyū kyūka
annual paid holidays 475;
holiday with pay 478; paid
holidays 481; paid leave 481;
paid vacation 481

yūkyū rōdō
paid labour 481

yūkyū rōdōsha
paid labourer 481; paid worker
481

yūkyū seisan nōryoku
idle capacity (production) 48

yūkyū setsubi
idle capacity (equipment) 48

yūkyū shigen
idle resources 48

yūkyū shihon
idle capital 48, 231;
unemployed capital 114, 284,
425

yūkyū shikin
idle money 48, 231

yūkyū tatemono
unused building 311

yūkyū tochi
unused land 311

yūkyū zandaka
idle balances 48

yunaiteddo-arabu-emirētsu
United Arab Emirates 191

yunidō
United Nations Industrial
Development Organization
(UNIDO) 115

yunidō no gaidorain
UNIDO guidelines 115

yunion-shoppu
union shop 115, 470

yuniraterarizumu
unilateralism 115

yunittogata seimei hoken
unit-linked life assurance [UK]
330

yunittogata tōshi shintaku
unit trust [UK] 284

yunō na
able 449; capable 450

yunyū
import (noun) 49

yunyū bōeki
import trade 49

yunyū bōeki tegata
import trade bill 148

yunyū buchō
import manager 457

yunyū bukka shisū
import price index 49

yunyū chōka
adverse balance of trade 4;
excessive imports 35

yunyū daitai
import substitution 49

yunyū daitaizai
import substitutes 49

yunyū gendo
ceiling on imports 15

yunyū genka
cost of import 21

yunyū genzairyō
imported raw materials 49

yunyū gijutsu
imported technology 49

yunyū gyōsha
importers (individual firms) 49

yunyū infure
imported inflation 49

yunyū izon
dependence on imports 25

yunyū kanzei
import duties 49

yunyū kawase tegata
import draft 148

yunyū kessai
import settlement 148

yunyū kessai tegata
import settlement bill 148

yunyū kinshi
ban on imports 9

yunyū kisei
import controls 49

yunyū kisoku
import regulations 49

yunyū maegashi tegata
import advance bill 148

yunyū nigawase tegata
documentary import bill 144

yunyū no chōryū
tide of imports 110

yunyū seigen
import restrictions 49; limitation
on imports 63; restrictions on
import 95

yunyū seikō
propensity to import 88

yunyū shikin kin'yū
import-financing credit 49

yunyū shin'yōjō
import L/C 148

yunyū shōheki
barriers to imports 10; import
barriers 49

yunyū shōreikin
import bounties 49

yunyū suru
import (verb) 49

yunyū tanpo nimotsu hokanshō
trust letter 162; trust receipt
162

yunyū tegata
import bill 148

yunyū tegata kessai sōba
acceptance rate 131

yunyū tōsei
import controls 49

yunyū wariate
import quota 49

yunyū wariate seido
import quota system 49

yunyū wariate seigen
import quota restriction 49

yunyū yotakukin
import deposits 49

yunyū yūsen jun'i
import priority 49

yunyū zeiritsu
import tariffs 49

yunyūbu
import department 457

yunyūhin
imported goods 49; imports 49

yunyūkoku
importers (countries) 49

yunyūryō
import volume 49

yunyūsha kigentsuki tegata
refinance bill 158

yūrei gaisha
bogus company 337

yūrei kabu
bogus stock 201

yūri na jigyō
lucrative business 351; profitable business concern 357

yūri na tōshi
profitable investment 261

yūrō-darā
Euro-dollar 170

yūrō-darā shijō
Euro-dollar market 170

yūrō kin'yū shijō
Euro-market 220

yūrō shijō kisai
Euro-issue 220

yūrō shin'yō
Euro-credit 220

yūrō tsūka
Euro-currency 170

yūrō tsūka shijō
Euro-currency market 170

yūrōginkō
Euro-bank 146

yūrōsai
Euro-bond 220; Euro-loan 220

yūrōsai shijō
Euro-bond market 220

yuruyaka na shōkyū
moderate raise 480

yūryō bukken waribiki
premium discount for good risk
327

yūryō gaisha
blue-chip company 337

yūryō kabu
blue-chip stock 201; gilt-edged
stock [UK] 228

yūryō karite
blue-chip borrower 201

yūryō kigyō
prime business 357

yūryō kiken
good risk 321

yūryō shasai
high-grade corporate bond 230

yūryō shisan jōtai
good financial standing 228,
394

yūryō tegata
fine bill 146; prime bill 157,
260

yūryō tegata waribiki buai
fine rate 224

yūryō torihikisaki
prime customer 260

yūryō tōshi
good investment 228

yūryoku suji
leading operators 240

yūryōzai
superior goods 106

yūsen
preference 82; priority
(emphasis) 84

yūsen bensai saimu
senior debt 437

zaikai no antei
financial stability (financial world) 223

zaikai no fuan
financial unrest 224

zaikai no ōdatemono
financial magnate 223

zaiko
inventory (-ies) 57, 396; stock 104

zaiko bunseki
inventory analysis 57

zaiko chikuseki
stockpiling 104

zaiko junkan
inventory cycle 57; stock cycle 104

zaiko kachi tōki
stock appreciation 104

zaiko kanri
stock control 104

zaiko kin'yū
inventory financing 236

zaiko shisū
inventory index 57

zaiko tōshi
inventory investment 57

zaiko tōshi junkan
inventory cycle 57; inventory investment cycle 57

zaiko tsumimashi
stock building 104

zaiko-uriage hiritsu
inventory/sales ratio 397

zaikohin
stock (goods) 420

zaikohin hyōka
stock valuation 421

zaikohin kaitenritsu
stock turnover 420

zaikohin motochō
stock ledger (goods) 420

zaikoritsu
stocks/sales ratio 105

zaimu
finance 222; financial affairs 39, 222, 391

zaimu buchō
treasurer 424, 470

zaimu bumon
financial department 391

zaimu bunseki
financial analysis 222, 391

zaimu bunsekika
financial analyst 222

zaimu dairinin
fiscal agent 224

zaimu funō
financial insolvency 391

zaimu hiritsu
financial ratio 391

zaimu i'inkai
finance committee 390

zaimu jōtai
financial position 391; financial situation 391; financial standing 391; state of the company's affairs 419; status 420

zaimu kaikei
financial accounting 390

zaimu kanjō
financial accounts 390

zaimu kanri
financial control 391; financial management 223, 391

zaimu kanrisha
financial director 455

zaimu kansa
financial audit 391

zaimu keikaku
financial planning 223, 391

zaimu keisū
financial figures 391

zaimu komon
financial adviser 146, 222, 390

zaimu konnan
financial difficulty 391; financial straits 391

zaimu kōsei
financial structure 391

zaimu ryūdōsei
financial solvency 391

zaimu satei
financial appraisal 222

zaimu shohyō
financial statement 391; statement 420

zaimu shohyō bunseki
analysis of financial statement 369; financial statement analysis 391; statement analysis 420

zaimu shohyō fuzoku meisaihyō
schedule of financial statement 371, 416

zaimu shohyō kansa
audit of financial statement 371; examination of financial statement 389; financial statement audit 391

zaimu shūeki
financial income 223

zaimu yūin
financial incentives 223

zaimubu
finance department 455

zaimushō
Treasury, the [US] 113, 186

zaimushō shōken
T-bill [US] 280; Treasury bill [US] 283

zaimuteki kekka
financial results 391

zairyō
factor (impetus) 221

zairyō
materials 67, 401

zairyō kaikei
materials accounting 401

zairyō oyobi chozōhin kanjō
materials and supplies account 401

zairyōhi
materials cost 401

zairyōhi bunseki
materials cost analysis 401

zairyōhi yosan
materials cost budget 401

zairyōhihō
materials cost basis 401

zairyoku
financial ability 222; financial power 223; means 247

zaisan
means 302; possessions 304; property (estate, fortune) 305

zaisan o shobun suru
dispose of one's possessions 293

zaisan baikyakueki
profit on sale of property 305

zaisan baikyakuson
loss on sale of property 301

zaisan bukken no junsui kakaku
equity (in mortgage or hire-purchase contract) 220

zaisan bunri
separation of property 308

zaisan daichō
property ledger 412

zaisan hyōka
property valuation 305; valuation of property (estate, fortune) 311

zaisan jōto
conveyance 292; conveyance of estate 292

zaisan kanri
property management 305

zaisan kanrinin
administrator of property 289

zaisan mokuroku
inventory 298; property inventory 305

zaisan no jōto
alienation of property 289

zaisan no sashiosae
attachment of property 290

zaisan no shutoku
acquisition of property 289

zaisan senshuken
prior lien on property 304

zaisan shotoku
income from property 232, 297

zaisan songai
damage to property 319; property damage 328

zaisan sōzoku
inheritance of property 298

zaisan sōzokunin
heir to property 296

zaisanka
property man 305

zaisanken
property rights 305; title to a property 310

zaisanken iten
transfer of title to a property 310

zaisanzei
property tax 305

zaisei
finance (financial affairs of the State) 222; public finance 89

zaisei akaji
budget deficit 12

zaisei antei
financial stability (financial affairs) 223

zaisei enjo
financial aid 222; financial assistance 222; financial support 223

zaisei futan
fiscal burden 39

zaisei jōsū
fiscal multiplier 39

zaisei jōtai
financial status 223

zaisei keikaku
financial programme 223; financial scheme 223

zaisei kiki
financial crisis 39

zaisei-kin'yū seisaku
fiscal and monetary policy 39

zaisei komon
financial adviser 39

zaisei kuroji
budget surplus 12

zaisei seisaku
financial policy 223; fiscal policy 39

zaisei shikin
fiscal funds 39

zaisei shishutsu
fiscal expenditure 39; government spending 44

zaisei shūnyū
fiscal revenue 39

zaisei shūshi
fiscal revenue and expenditure 39

zaisei tatenaoshi
financial reconstruction 39

zaisei tōyūshi
fiscal investments and loans 39

zaisei yosan
fiscal budget 39

zaiseika
financier 224

zaiseiteki hadome
fiscal drag 39

zaishoku shōmei
certicate of employment 139, 164 (note 2), 451

zandaka
balance (remaining sum) 133, 372

zandaka fusoku
'no funds' 153; 'not sufficient funds' 153

zandaka shōkai
balance enquiry 133

zandakachō
balance book 372

zangyō
overtime 77; overtime work 463

zangyō teate
overtime allowance 481

zankabu shōmeisho
balance certificate 198

zanson ganpon
outstanding principal 255

zantei sūji
preliminary figures 82; provisional figures 88

zantei yosan
interim budget 55; provisional budget 88

zan'yo
residual, a 95

zan'yo kachi
residual value 95

zan'yo shitsugyō
residual unemployment 95

zettai yūi
absolute advantage 3

zettaichi
absolute value 3

zettaiteki hinkon
absolute poverty 3

zettaiteki hiyō no rieki
absolute cost advantage 3

zettaiteki kishō
absolute scarcity 3

zōchi hoken
increased value insurance 322

zōchi kagaku
increased value 322

zōdai
increase (augmentation) 51

zōeki
increased profits 395; profit increase 411

zōgaku keizoku
increased renewal of loan 232

zōge kaigan
Ivory Coast 189

zōhai
dividend increase 387

zōhei
coinage 167; mintage 179; minting 179

zōheikyoku
Bureau of the Mint [US] 166; mint (the Mint) 179

zōka
increase (addition, rise) 51; increment 315

zōka
appreciation 7, 196, 289; appreciation in value 315; increase in value 297

zōka haraikomi shihonkin
additional paid-in capital 367

zōka hiyō
increased costs 395

zōka kachi
increased value 298

zōka sekinin junbikin
additional reserve 368

zōka shihon
additional capital 367

zōka suru
appreciate (increase in value) 196, 289

zōka unten shihon
additional working capital 368

zōka unten shikin
additional working funds 368

zōsakutsuki kashiya
furnished house to let 295

zōsan
increase in production 51

zōsengyō
ship-building industry 126

zōshi
capital increase 376; increase of capital 395

zōshi haraikomikin
subscription to the increased capital 421

zōsō
finance minister 39

zōyo
donation (present) 219

zōyo kabushiki
donated stock 219

zōyosha
donator 219

zōyozei
donation tax 219

zōzei
tax increases 108

zubora na
negligent 461

zuiji shōkan kōsai
redeemable bond (public) 264

zuiji shōkan saiken
redeemable bond (general) 264

zunō na
intelligent 458

zunō rōdō
non-manual labour 74; non-manual work 461

zunō rōdōsha
non-manual worker(s) 74, 461; white-collar worker 471

zunō ryūshutsu
brain drain 12